Clinical Hypnosis:
Principles and Applications
Second Edition

Clinical Hypnosis: Principles and Applications
Second Edition

Harold B. Crasilneck, Ph.D.

Clinical Professor of Psychiatry
Clinical Professor of Anesthesiology

James A. Hall, M.D.

Clinical Associate Professor of Psychiatry

University of Texas Health Science Center
Southwestern Medical School
Dallas, Texas

Allyn and Bacon
Boston · London · Toronto · Sydney · Tokyo · Singapore

Library of Congress Cataloging in Publication Data

Crasilneck, Harold B., 1921–
  Clinical hypnosis.

  Includes bibliographies and index.
  1. Hypnotism—Therapeutic use. I. Hall, James A.
(James Albert). 1934– . II] Title. [DNLM: 1. Hypnosis. WM 415 C894c]
  RC495.C73   1985   615.8'512   84-19181

ISBN 0-205-10082-1

Printed in the United States of America

98 97 96 95 94 93 92   10 9 8 7 6 5 4 3 2

To my wife Sherry, whose love, devotion, encouragement, advice, and motivation have given me the psychic strength required in the preparation of this book.

Harold B. Crasilneck

To Suzi, loving wife, helper, friend, understanding and forgiving companion.

James A. Hall

Contents

Foreword

The virtue of this volume is that it fills a long-empty gap in the field of hypnosis: a handbook of clinical applications. To the therapist floundering about for modes of managing the many syndromes confronting him in his practice, the book will act as a methodological beacon. It summarizes the rich explorations of the authors who have worked diligently with hypnosis over many years. Since all therapies are blends of techniques with unique, highly individual styles of application, continued experimentation with the suggested applications will determine how these can best blend with the therapist's personality, theoretical biases, skills, and preferred modes of operation.

There is an advantage in knowing broad-spectrum approaches such as are detailed in the chapters on therapy. The learning patterns of patients are so finely attuned to specific stimuli that their response may be enthusiastic to one set of maneuvers and not at all to others, no matter how expertly these are implemented. This differential selection is one of the greatest arguments for eclecticism in method—the acquaintance with the expertise in a variety of techniques that can coordinate with the patient's learning potentials. A well-trained professional with a wide range of skills is capable both of sensitizing himself to the reactions of the patient to his interventions and of modifying his tactics should his methods fail to promote improvement. Obviously not all of us execute every modality that is available today, and one of the tasks of an effective therapist is convincing the patient through relationship and education of the validity of those interventions in which the therapist invests his faith. The ineffective operator attempts to manipulate, argue, cajole, and persist in applying his procedures to his patients, no matter how reluctant they are to accept his premises, without ever offering them proper instruction regarding the merits of what he is trying to do.

Fortunately hypnosis by itself is uniquely suited to stimulate nonspecific elements which are parcels of all helping processes and serve in themselves to bring relief. During the induction phase, most patients assume that they will undergo some kind of manipulation, hopefully for the good. This enhances the placebo effect which in itself can markedly reduce tension. Of all therapies, hypnosis is probably the most effective instrument in promoting acceptance of suggestions, direct or indirect. Through this instrumentality alone many patients are enabled to alleviate their symptoms and to restore themselves to a functional equilibrium. Since effective learning can proceed best in a medium of a good interpersonal relationship, hypnosis, by its extraordinary impact on rapport and by inspiring in the trance state the soothing support of an idealized parental figure in the body of the therapist, may catalyze the therapeutic process whether this be oriented toward symptom removal, education, or exploration. Moreover, communication is enhanced, both during the trance when emotional catharsis becomes more facile as well as posthypnotically by helping the patient to integrate the interpretations and suggestions of the operator.

These effects, while beneficial in themselves, merely supplement the impact scored by the special techniques of the psychotherapist. Over the years these techniques have accumulated so that we have available for our eclectic choice a large number of assorted maneuvers, some of which have been included in this volume. The question that concerns us as practitioners is whether we can select techniques of proven merit and whether we as scientists can differentiate through experimental means those that are grounded in verifiable assumptions from those that have a less substantial base—and hence utility.

The answer would seem to be in adequately controlled studies. In this reference Percival Bailey, in an unmerciful attack on psychiatric therapies, has depreciated "The Great Psychiatric Revolution" and enjoined psychiatrists to abandon their theoretical premises and to return "into the asylums and laboratories which they are so proud to have left behind them and prove, by established criteria, that their concepts have scientific validity." This evaluative task is more easily said than done; indeed research in psychotherapy at our present stage of sophistication seems to be more a job for a magician than for a scientist.

The problems that confront us as researchers are formidable. For example, Dr. Thomas Jones is a psychiatrist who, after completion of his residency, has had several postgraduate courses of a broadly eclectic nature, including hypnotherapy. As a result of five years' practice, he has evolved a technique of doing psychotherapy that scores greater successes for him than any of the others with which he has been experimenting. The patient removes himself for one week from his family or accustomed surroundings and takes up residence in a small, quiet hotel near Dr. Jones's office. During this time there are daily visits with Dr. Jones, the first part of which consists of exposure to hypnosis and challenging posthypnotic confrontations followed by evening group sessions and writing assignments on self-analysis of the day's events and personal reactions. After the first week, the patient returns to his usual environment and reports five more times on a weekly basis for individual sessions conducted along behavioral lines, employing hypnosis, and to top things off, an evening encounter group. Dr. Jones reports an 80–90 percent improvement rate with his technique.

Can we reasonably assume that Dr. Jones's results can be replicated by other therapists? Our answer would probably be "yes" if the therapists had training of at least as great amplitude as that of Dr. Jones, if they were as intelligent and could arrive at the same judgments, if they had the same ways of looking at pathology and behavioral styles, if they were as dedicated to what they were doing and applied themselves with the same enthusiasm and conviction, and if their patient populations were similar to those who came to Dr. Jones. These are complicated "ifs" and it is scarcely possible that we could fulfill any of them. Patients and therapists are highly distinctive in historical background, education, value systems, and personality structure. Moreover, the interactions between individual therapists and individual patients are unique and cannot be readily duplicated. The complexity of variables is so great that only by testing himself with a set system of interventions can a therapist decide whether they work for him. And even if they do appear to bring preferred results, we cannot say that they will always do so.

Another example: Dr. John White has taken a postgraduate course in hypnotherapy and is greatly elated at his ability to induce trance states among his patients who seem to respond rapidly and sometimes miraculously to his suggestive exhortations. Several months after he has established himself as an expert on hypnosis, Dr. White encounters several patients who insist that they have not been hypnotized even though to all outward appearances they have succumbed to a trance. Shortly thereafter he notices that a number of his patients fail to follow hypnotic suggestions. His confidence in the powers of hypnosis somewhat shaken, Dr. White applies himself to trance induction less sure of himself, and his waning conviction in the utility of hypnosis carries over into his intonations, his firmness of expression, and his confidence in what he is doing. This has a negative effect on his results. Can we then say that it is the technique that is at fault, or is it the less than enthusiastic way Dr. White is managing the technique?

The fact that faith in a therapist's procedures on the part of both patient and practitioner is an important ingredient in cure makes it difficult to substantiate the other variables that enter into the treatment process. This is only one of the many obstructions that impose themselves on attempts to establish empirical platforms for psychotherapy.

Behavior, unlike sugar and cholesterol, cannot be adequately measured. The linguistic base around which the data language is organized is demonstrably inadequate. Fundamental behavior laws are assumed and generalized on the basis of no experimental evidence whatsoever. The independent, intervening, and dependent variables are loosely defined and handled inadequately in formulation of the postulates. Construct-interrelationships are more or less indeterminate. Standards of explicitness of axiomatization are low. The units for quantification can scarcely be defined let alone manipulated.

Statistics emanating from research in hypnosis do not mean too much, because there may be something wrong with both the statistics and the research. Indeed, a good deal of the ongoing research in the field is anything but impressive in both design as well as results. Probably the reason for this is that we are dealing with a bewildering number of variables which shift their dimensions faster than we can unravel them. But part of the problem lies in the researcher himself, who may not be immune to boosting his ego through deliberate or unconscious presentation of fraudulent data or by overlooking certain facts and exaggerating others (experimenter bias). There may be a misuse of statistics; for example, correlation coefficients, while important as measures of relationships among variables, may in error be considered synonymous with causation. There may be a false selection of experimental and control groups, weighting them with individuals from special classes not commonly encountered. There may be insufficient numbers of subjects to test adequately for factors that do not occur too frequently. There often is a tendency to generalize beyond the data toward universal conclusions. There is usually no consideration of the special predilections of the patient for hypnosis, his readiness for change, and his singular learning potentials which synchronize better with certain kinds of methods than with others.

Many practitioners, discouraged by present-day handicaps enveloping empirical studies, have drifted into a self-defeating attitude and insist that hypnotherapy is more art than science. There is certainly a good deal of validity to artistry in working with hypnosis; but this does not necessarily preclude a scientific posture. One may, in his artistry, be scientifically oriented. I remember a conversation with a psychiatrist, a member of both leading organizations of hypnosis, who was firm in his belief that the sooner we dissociate ourselves from trying to make hypnosis, or for that matter all of psychotherapy, into a science, the more attention we could pay to the art of working with people. I asked him what he felt he did when he practiced hypnoanalysis. "First," he declared, "I diagnose what I'm up against. I note from the case history, from the patient's productions and reactions toward me, those aspects I consider important. I want to know what I'm dealing with. Second, I come to certain ideas about the origin, the nature, and the consequences of the patient's patterns. Third, I formulate plans of approaching the patient in terms of the problems he presents. I develop a plan of action based on what I feel he will best respond to. Finally, I determine how the plan works and watch the patient's responses, modifying my ideas of his illness as we go along." What my colleague did not seem to be aware of was that he was in his artistry practicing scientific method. From data of observation he developed hypotheses about the patient's illness. He then planned a method of approach and subjected this to testing. On the basis of the patient's reactions, he either verified his hypotheses or failed to do so, in which case he altered his tactics and started all over again.

In spite of the existing obstacles, a number of recent attempts have been made with some success to investigate the effective mechanisms that are operative in certain therapeutic maneuvers. Research publications, particularly in behavior therapy and conditioning, have expanded exponentially, and some of these appear to have important implications for practice. However, we are still far from the day when we can say our research designs are sufficiently refined to make our conclusions universally applicable or that they permit us to replicate our findings with any precision. Recognition of these impediments to the establishment of a strong empirical base for hypnosis should, in some ways, help to reduce the dogmatism that has for years blighted the hypnotherapeutic arena. There are signs that we are approaching problems with a more open acknowledgement of the difficulties in our path while striving for greater discipline in systematic research.

In the meantime, we may have to adapt a pragmatic stance of applying ourselves to the testing of the various techniques with different patients and varying syndromes to determine those that are attuned to our personal craftsmanship and tastes. Many of us are victims of a pseudotechnological ethos which purports that all we have to do to alter disturbed behavior is to execute a set of ritualized interventions. Because these have scored successes with some (or most) of our patients, we may assume that our techniques are specific, inviolable, and universal.

It is to be expected that implementation of the different methods advocated in this volume will bring forth singular reactions in different patients. Not only will a patient respond to cues, explicit and implicit, of what he believes is expected of him and of what he expects of himself, but he will also incorporate in his behavioral patterns some of his intrapsychic machinations, particularly resistance toward yielding symptoms and defenses that have a special meaning for him. Transference manifestations are particularly insidious and may never be openly acknowledged by the patient, revealing themselves solely by negative therapeutic reactions and by acting out. The therapist with a dynamic outlook will have an advantage over his nondynamic colleagues, since he will alert himself to obstructions in progress by studying the patient's dreams, fantasies, associations, and nonverbal behavior. It is quite remarkable how readily one may cut through resistance by properly timed interpretations of behavior and fantasies that the patient unwittingly seeks to conceal from the therapist and from himself. By the same token, a dynamically oriented therapist who utilizes broad-spectrum therapies will constantly examine his own irrational thinking and feeling patterns (countertransference) in relation to his patients. Obviously these will vary with different personalities and situations. Countertransferential contaminants account for abundant failures in hypnotherapy: some therapists who otherwise function objectively are not able to control their own neurotic reactions after they succeed in putting their patients into a trance.

Another dimension of importance in helping our patients maximally utilize the benefits that our techniques bestow upon them involves the milieu in which the patient lives and will continue to function after he has terminated therapy. I have seen in consultation innumerable patients who, having rapidly been brought to homeostasis with hypnotherapy, relapse when they attempt to adapt themselves to an inimical environment. For some reason, certain therapists are so concerned with the resolution of symptoms and the pursuit of inner conflicts that they lose sight of the fact that the patient will need to operate in an environment that may contain emotional pollutants which inspire pathology, indeed even make symptoms essential to survival. The fact that a therapist does hypnosis combined with a host of valuable interventions should not preclude a careful study of the atmosphere enveloping the patient nor helping him alter or remove himself from elements that can potentially bring about a recurrence of illness.

In summary, there are infinite numbers of ways through which emotional problems may be helped. But for some persons and certain problems, special methods like hypnosis have proven to be more effective than other methods. The establishment of an empirical base for hypnosis implies a refinement of operations that is still a distant aspiration. Progress in delineating which problems in which patients respond best to identifiable hypnotic techniques with selected therapists has been painfully slow. We still do not know whether it is the special technique which is the most significant variable, the skill with which it is applied, or the personality properties and empathic abilities in the therapist. There are some who feel that a therapist with the proper kind of "therapeutic personality" can utilize almost any type of technique including hypnosis as a communication medium and get the same results. Other authorities are not convinced that technical choices are so general. Personally, I am convinced that different patients have an affinity for certain kinds of techniques which are apparently in greater harmony with their special learning needs and capacities.

Frozen operational concepts have no place in modern psychotherapy. Since there is no optimal therapy for all patients, it would seem appropriate for the therapist to study the learning patterns of his patients and to attempt to apply those techniques that satisfy their specific learning needs. This requires, in addition to diagnostic skills, acquaintance with a diversity of methods. It is here that the present volume can make a significant contribution; for in opening up broad technical vistas, it encourages hypothetical formulations which, on testing, may help to resolve in the future the questions about process that burden us today.

Lewis R. Wolberg, M.D.

Preface to Second Edition

Since the first edition of *Clinical Hypnosis* we have been gratified at the increased availability of courses in teaching hypnotherapy techniques for medical, psychological, and dental training throughout the United States and abroad. The scholarly organizations devoted to the study and application of hypnosis have matured, thrived, cooperated with one another, increased in membership and influence, and are a source of professional pride to ourselves and our colleagues. At the same time, there is a growing debate as to the necessary qualifications to responsibly utilize hypnotherapy. Our own judgment remains clear: hypnotic techniques should be used only by well-trained and licensed professionals who are capable of treating the same problems without the use of hypnosis. Hypnosis is a specialized area of knowledge and treatment, not a substitute for good clinical training.

We are pleased to find an increased acceptance of our own early emphasis on the need for investigation of neurophysiological substrates of hypnosis, together with the need of quantitative studies that do not obscure the subtle nature of the hypnotic trance as a clinical reality.

There have been some surprising developments, such as the increasing controversy about forensic uses of hypnosis, and disagreements about the stature of well-accepted tests of hypnotizability. These are passing problems; the field of hypnotherapy itself is more vital and growing than in 1975. The future applications, both in theoretical understanding and practical clinical application, are, perhaps, more widespread than can ever be imagined today.

Our particular and deepest gratitude are acknowledged to Sherry Gold Knopf, whose advice and aid have been, again, invaluable in the preparation and editing of this volume. Suzanne Hall has once more provided valuable encouragement and advice.

Preface to First Edition

Hypnosis is a therapeutic procedure so interesting to both professionals and laymen that people are intensely curious about its real effects and the exaggerated and erroneous misrepresentations. It has often been difficult to sort truth from fiction regarding hypnosis, although the field is becoming more scientifically grounded year by year.

We both learned hypnotic techniques as part of our formal training in clinical psychology and medicine. We were fortunate, for few schools offered training in hypnosis to their students. Today such training in hypnotherapy is becoming both more recognized and more available in graduate professional schools.

In the years that we have worked together we have seen hypnosis change from a topic that induced ridicule and incredulity to a serious and valuable aspect of comprehensive treatment in medical specialties, psychology, and dentistry. We have ourselves been privileged to contribute some unique treatment modalities and concepts to this growing stature of hypnosis. It has been especially gratifying to see our students, here and abroad, successfully apply and teach hypnotherapy to others.

No book is produced alone. We wish to acknowledge the important contribution of our mentors and colleagues, who have influenced our use of hypnosis both by their writings and by personal communication and teaching.

Although it is impossible to mention everyone (they know who they are), we would like to single out for special thanks the following teachers: Lewis Wolberg, M.D., Clinical Professor of Psychiatry at New York University Medical School, and the late James L. McCary, Ph.D., Professor of Psychology, University of Houston.

Over the years, tremendous strides in research were made with many great clinicians: James L. McCranie, M.D., Professor and Chairman, Department of Psychiatry, Medical College of Georgia; Don P. Morris, M.D., Clinical Professor of Psychiatry, University of Texas Health Science Center at Dallas, Southwestern Medical School; Carmen Miller Michael, Ph.D., Professor of Psychology, University of Texas Health Science Center at Dallas, Southwestern Medical School; M. T. Jenkins, M.D., Margaret Milam McDermott Professor and Chairman, Department of Anesthesiology, University of Texas Health

Science Center at Dallas, Southwestern Medical School; Karl Erwin, M.D., Clinical Assistant Professor of Pharmacology, University of Texas Health Science Center at Dallas, Southwestern Medical School; William Mengert, M.D., formerly Professor and Chairman, Department of Obstetrics, Southwestern Medical School; Ben J. Wilson, M.D., formerly Chairman, Department of Surgery, Southwestern Medical School; Morris J. Fogelman, M.D., Clinical Professor of Surgery, University of Texas Health Science Center at Dallas, Southwestern Medical School; Kemp Clark, M.D., Professor and Chairman, Department of Neurosurgery, University of Texas Health Science Center at Dallas, Southwestern Medical School; Jerry Stirman, M.D., formerly of the Department of Surgery, University of Texas Health Science Center at Dallas, Southwestern Medical School; C. W. Browning, M.D., Clinical Professor of Ophthalmology, and Lester Quinn, M.D., Clinical Professor of Ophthalmology, University of Texas, Health Science Center at Dallas, Southwestern Medical School.

There are thousands of students whom we have taught in their medical schools, dental schools, postgraduate medical and dental assemblies, graduate and postgraduate psychological seminars, nationally and internationally, and workshops for both the Society for Clinical and Experimental Hypnosis and the American Society for Clinical Hypnosis. Their interest and stimulation have been a recurrent inspiration in preparation of this book. We feel it will meet their repeated requests for a basic text in clinical applications of hypnotherapy.

Recognition and thanks are due to physicians, psychologists, and dentists who over many years have trusted us to help in the care of thousands of patients whose treatment forms the basic material presented in the text.

The two writers have known each other as close friends for over twenty years, originally as Crasilneck, the teacher, and Hall, the student; then, since 1958, as colleagues and collaborators. When writing papers throughout the years, we always hoped some day to consolidate our experience of hypnotherapy into a book such as the present volume. Over the past five years we have taken time from busy practice and teaching schedules to prepare this book. It has been a gratifying experience, both as a mutual personal endeavor and as our contribution to the important field of hypnotherapy with its complexities, mysteries, and potentials for health.

Special thanks go to our two research associates—Sherry Gold Knopf and Suzanne McKean Hall—who have spent countless months aiding us in statistical evaluations, bibliographic research, and the actual preparation and proofing of the manuscript.

Clinical Hypnosis:
Principles and Applications
Second Edition

Introduction

Hypnosis is an altered state of consciousness. It is characterized by an increased ability to produce desirable changes in habit patterns, motivations, self-image and life-style. Alterations may be produced in physiological functions, such as pain, that are usually inaccessible to psychological influence.

We do not know the earliest origin of hypnosis. It is perhaps as old as the ancient rites of healing known as "temple sleep," which may have utilized many principles of influence that underlie the modern practice of hypnotherapy.

In spite of its great utility, hypnosis in the past has been a stepchild, rejected by many as "unscientific." Others endorsed hypnosis in an over-enthusiastic manner, advocating it as virtually a panacea. The voice of moderation and reason has been rare. Even in the most recent past those practitioners who chose to use hypnosis were often ostracized, risked discharge from academic positions, or were ridiculed. This frequently occurred in spite of their high reputations in other fields of science.

The suggested use of therapeutic hypnosis with certain problems was often met with severe rejections and hostility. For example, as recently as the 1950s, at a medical grand rounds in one of the nation's leading schools, hypnosis was recommended for appetite control and weight reduction in the case of a patient who weighed more than 500 pounds. The patient suffered both from circulatory inadequacy and from the Pickwickian syndrome, which is a severe difficulty in breath-

1

ing caused by the massive weight of flesh that had to be moved with each inspiration. When hypnosis was suggested, one well-trained and respected clinician objected violently on the grounds that removal of the patient's excessive appetite might cause him to become psychotic. No amount of careful explanation seemed to convince the critic that symptom removal was not the only use of hypnosis and that adequate attention would also be given to psychodynamic factors involved in the obesity.

The critic's argument prevailed, however, and hypnotherapy was rejected. In spite of excellent conservative medical management, the patient's condition worsened. Even if hypnosis had been employed to help him lose weight, he might not have lived, but this doctrinaire rejection was all too often typical of the thinking of those days.

This case history probably typified how much of the most common disagreement about hypnosis was originated in a simple error—equating any use of hypnosis only with the direct removal of symptoms. Although direct symptom removal was the technique of such pioneers as Franz Mesmer and Jean Charcot, in current clinical practice the goal is always treatment of the entire patient, and the suppression of symptoms must be seen and managed as part of the overall psychodynamic picture.

Another case from the same time period illustrates the old attitude toward hypnosis, now outgrown. A 50-year-old man with severe emphysema called and asked for hypnotherapy to help him quit a severe tobacco addiction, which was continuously worsening his pulmonary condition. The patient was told that he must have a referral from his internist, who was treating the emphysema; the internist would not give approval, however, saying "If you remove one symptom with hypnosis, a worse symptom will appear!" This rigid attitude toward the "dangers" of hypnosis was not uncommon 30 years ago, whereas today it is common practice to use hypnosis in the treatment of tobacco addiction (Crasilneck and Hall, 1968; Hall and Crasilneck, 1970).

In the early 1950s, there were professionals who hesitated to report their findings concerning hypnosis or to attend national meetings dealing with it for fear of rejection by those in power and in their academic institutions. During this era there was little support for hypnosis research by federal grants. In spite of a growing number of reliable and careful reports, the occasional sensational, undocumented paper kept controversy alive. Until recently, therefore, the modern story of hypnosis in some ways paralleled previous history. Periods of sensational and widespread interest were followed by times of rejection. Only gradually has the accumulated weight of evidence tipped in favor of scientific recognition.

The last 3 decades have seen more advancement in the utilization of professional hypnotherapy than any comparable time in the past. A 1978 survey revealed that one third of American medical and dental schools were offering courses in hypnosis, twice as many as in a similar survey in 1974. It is estimated that more than 10,000 physicians, psychologists, and dentists in North America are trained in the use of hypnotherapy as an adjunct to traditional forms of medical and dental treatment (Sachs, 1982). There are now more than 4700 full members of the American Society of Clinical Hypnosis, all of whom hold an MD, DDS, DMD, DO, PhD, or the equivalent (Chiasson SW, quoted in Medical News, 1983). The Society for Clinical and Experimental Hypnosis has equally high professional qualifications for membership. The International Society of Hypnosis, of which both the ASCH and the SCEH are component societies, has done much to establish a scientific use of hypnosis throughout the world.

Those of us who were active in the field of this early modern era realized that the potential helpfulness of hypnosis was vastly underrated, that there was then little appreciation of its benefits by the general medical, psychological, and dental professions. We would often get referrals for hypnosis only as a last resort, when other treatment methods had proved inadequate.

We have ourselves been privileged to participate in the growth and gradual acceptance of hypnosis, both as a clinical tool and as a recognized area of research. Today the field has stabilized. Hypnosis is accepted as the initial treatment of choice in some conditions—smoking, control of food intake, recovery or memory in traumatic neuroses—for certain pain problems, and in many psychosomatic and dermatologic cases. Hypnosis has been used in the rehabilitation of complicated vascular and posttraumatic neurological patients (Crasilneck and Hall, 1970). Hypnosis has been demonstrated to be effective in such difficult areas as the control of bleeding in hemophiliacs (Cooper, 1983; LaBaw, 1975).

After 30 years of practice in the clinical applications of hypnosis, we have felt a need to make available in one volume our own experiences and theories. Though trained in different disciplines—clinical psychology and psychiatry—we both follow an eclectic, empirical approach with maximum patient benefit a constant goal. This had led us to develop techniques of using hypnosis, at times, in cases where its full potential had not been appreciated.

Like an antibiotic drug, hypnosis is a useful tool that can be life saving in proper cases. There are some limitations. Any effective treatment has a certain incidence of failures and of occasional side effects that do not detract from the advantages, though they demand that it be used with caution and with knowledge.

This book is intended for those serious students or practitioners in medicine, clinical psychology, and dentistry who desire a fundamental knowledge of the principles and applications of hypnosis. Fortunately, in more recent years the gap between what we see as the possible therapeutic applications of hypnosis and its actual delivery to patients has narrowed. This is partly the result of elimination of past prejudices, which until recently prevented hypnosis from being taught as an ordinary part of the education of the medical, psychological, or dental specialist.

An almost complete reversal of attitude has occurred. Hypnosis is now widely taught in a majority of professional schools of medicine, psychology, and dentistry. At present, hypnosis and hypnotherapy are widely employed in the treatment of a variety of physical and psychological problems (Hall and Crasilneck, 1978). Hypnotherapy is used in military medicine in all service branches (Garver, 1979).

Our text reviews the therapeutic uses of hypnosis in a concise form, brief enough for it to be an introductory textbook in medicine, anesthesiology, psychiatry, and other specialties, yet sufficiently comprehensive for the reader to feel confident that he or she is aware of the wide spectrum of cases in which hypnosis might be of value to his or her patients.

We feel that the techniques of hypnosis are a specialized part of medical, clinical psychological, and dental knowledge. They are best and most safely learned under the direct guidance of an experienced teacher.

Unfortunately, there still are few state laws that restrict the use of hypnotherapy to professionals who are qualified to diagnose and treat serious medical, psychological, and dental problems. The use of hypnosis, therefore, is often advertised by persons who are not professionally trained. Like any powerful tool, hypnotherapy should be used only as part of a more complete treatment plan, since hypnosis is a technique and not a comprehensive model of psychophysiological functioning. In our opinion, hypnotherapy should be used only by licensed professionals who are able to treat the same problems without hypnosis. There is no place for a "profession" of hypnosis as a freestanding practice. In the present state of confusion, a lay person is advised to seek the advice of his physician, psychologist, psychiatrist, or dentist about those persons in the community qualified to practice hypnotherapy. Alternatively, a county medical or dental society or the equivalent organization of licensed psychologists can direct the enquirer to a qualified practitioner of hypnotherapy or hypnoanalysis. It is also possible to contact directly the American Society of Clinical Hypnosis (2250 East Devon, Suite 336, Des Plaines, IL 60018) or the Society for Clinical and Experimental Hypnosis (129-A Kings Park Drive, Liverpool, NY 13088) for lists of professionals who utilize hypnotherapy. These two societies held a joint meeting with the International Society of Hypnosis in Toronto in 1985, with Allan Banack and Cyril Marks as Chairpersons of local arrangements and workshops respectively. This may indicate increasing cooperation between these major societies devoted to the scientific investigation of hypnosis. Kenneth Bowers chaired the scientific program and George Matheson was the Congress chairperson.

Hypnosis, like surgery, is not to be learned from textbooks, though textbooks are an important part of its study. In our opinion the best way to teach hypnosis is through empirical learning in a one-to-one relationship with a qualified teacher; however, specific techniques can be taught in a book such as the present text.

Our approach to the therapeutic uses of hypnosis is based on our own experience and success with thousands of acute and chronic patients. Statements in this book may be somewhat at variance with other responsible authors. Such variation is inevitable in any clinical art. We have found our particular approach best suited to the type of patient we usually treat; however, techniques must be individually modified to meet the particular needs of the therapist and patient. Generally, our patients are medicaly referred and well-motivated. Many have organic problems or organic problems with psychological complications. Except in emergency conditions, all are assessed for general personality stability before hypnosis is begun (Crasilneck, 1980).

For the professional unacquainted with hypnosis, the book is best read straight through. The specialist approaching a particular clinical problem might wish to refer first to the index, where he or she will quickly find reference to the possible aid one might expect from hypnosis. A section is included on our own theoretical views. Practicing clinicians who are already using hypnosis and wish to glean specific technical suggestions can find them grouped in the chapter on techniques, though precise descriptions of wording are often interspersed in the clinical chapters. In most instances we have included the exact wording of our induction techniques.

This book is not, however, a summary of the important field of research in hypnosis, nor is it specifically an introduction to hypnoanalysis, the blending of hypnosis with more classic psychoanalytic tools. Although theoretical concepts can be learned from this book, no one should attempt the practice of hypnosis until their formal training in medicine, clinical psychology, or dentistry is completed, including a thorough understanding of psychopathology. The choice about the use of hypnosis is a professional decision, and the administration of hypnosis should always be done by a qualified professional working in an clinical setting.

REFERENCES

Cooper L: Hypnotherapy for hemophilia. Paper presented at the International Congress of the Israel Society of Hypnosis in Psychotherapy and Psychosomatic Medicine. Haifa, Israel, August 28–September 2, 1983

Crasilneck HB: Clinical assessment and preparation of the patient, in Burrow GD, Dennerstein L (eds): Handbook of Hypnosis and Psychosomatic Medicine. Amsterdam, Elsevier/North-Holland Biomedical Press, 1980, pp 105–118

Crasilneck HB, Hall JA: The use of hypnosis in controlling cigarette smoking. J Southern Med Assoc 61:999–1002, 1968

Crasilneck HB, Hall JA: The use of hypnosis in the rehabilitation of complicated vascular and posttraumatic neurological patients. Int J Clin Exp Hypn 18:149–159, 1970

Garver RB: The genesis of development of a new hypnotherapy clinic. Address presented at the 8th International Congress of Hypnosis and Psychosomatic Medicine. Melbourne, Australia, 1979

Hall JA, Crasilneck HB: Development of a hypnotic technique for treating chronic cigarette smoking. Int J Clin Exp Hypn 18:283–289, 1970

Hall JA, Crasilneck HB: Hypnosis, JAMA 239:760–761, 1978

LaBaw WL: Auto-hyponosis in haemophilia. Haemotologia 9:103–110, 1975.

Medical News: JAMA 249:319–323, 1983

Sachs BC: Hypnosis in psychiatry and psychosomatic medicine. Psychosomatics 23:523–525, 1982

1
History

Although the history of hypnosis is often begun with Franz Mesmer (1734–1815), an eighteenth-century Viennese physician who practiced in Paris, the use of hypnosis under other names may be almost as old as man's earliest efforts at healing. Glasner (1955) writes that "although it is impossible to state with any definiteness that hypnosis is referred to in the Bible (Old and New Testament) and in the Talmud, there would seem to be considerable evidence that the authors of these works were indeed familiar with the phenomena which we today should call hypnotic or which we should explain in terms of suggestion."

Wolberg (1972) suggests that the earliest description of hypnosis may be in Genesis 2:21–22:

> And the Lord God caused a deep sleep to fall upon Adam, and he slept; and he took one of his ribs, and closed up the flesh instead thereof; And the rib, which the Lord God had taken from man, made he a woman, and brought her unto the man.

Musès (1972) has found the earliest hypnotic sessions recorded on a stone stele from Egypt in the reign of Ramses XII of the Twentieth Dynasty, some 3000 years ago. More specific descriptions of what must have been a self-hypnotic technique, using a lighted lamp, are found in the so-called Demotic Magical Papyrus of London and Leiden (British Museum Manuscript 10070 and Leiden Museum Manuscript 1.383).

Among others mentioned as predecessors of Mesmer, Ludwig (1964) included the alchemist Fludd (1574–1637) and Apollonius of Tyana in the third century AD. However, as already noted, it is Franz

7

Mesmer who is most universally considered the "father" of modern hypnosis.

Several authors link hypnosis to the temple sleep of the Asclepian healing cult in ancient Greece (Machovec 1979), although that is somewhat disputed by others (Stam and Spanos, 1982). The "evil eye," which can be traced back to as early as 3000 BC, may have involved aspects of what is now called hypnosis (Machovec, 1976). Over a century before Mesmer, Shakespeare described altered states of consciousness resembling hypnosis (Machovec, 1975b, 1981).

MESMERISM

Mesmer believed that hypnotic effects were caused by "animal magnetism," a force assumed to be analogous to physical magnetism. This "magnetism" was thought to arise from living bodies—from the hypnotist himself—and to pass to patients as an invisible magnetic fluid. Mesmer also thought that the "fluid" could be transmitted to inanimate objects, to the *bacquet* (a large tub filled with water and iron filings), or even to certain trees, from which the patients could draw the "magnetism." He often used a metal "magnetic" wand to "equalize" the supposed energy. Mesmer's history has been clearly traced by Conn (1957) and Rosen (1959) and has also been presented in a dramatized form by Jensen and Watkins (1967). The practice of animal magnetism was also called *mesmerism*.

Although Mesmer had many spectacular cures with his hypnosis, including a case of apparent hysterical blindness, he fell into disfavor in 1784 after a negative report from a special commission of the French Academy. Among the commission members were Benjamin Franklin, then the American ambassador to France, Dr. Guillotine, who invented the "merciful" machine of execution, and Lavoisier, a noted chemist. Disgraced, Mesmer left France. He died at Meersburg in 1815 at the age of 81. Only 10 years later, in 1825, the French Academy of Medicine issued a report favorable to animal magnetism, while a third commission (1837) again doubted its existence.

By the second half of the nineteenth century, the attitude toward mesmerism was more stable. Many British and American reports began to appear in the hypnosis literature. An American physician, Morton Prince (1854–1919), became noted for the use of hypnosis in cases of multiple personality. An active Société du Magnetism flourished in New Orleans from 1845 until the Civil War (Tomlinson and Perret, 1974).

Unlike Benjamin Franklin and his colleagues on the 1784 French commission, Benjamin Rush, the father of American psychiatry, incorporated hypnotherapy and imagination into his practice, while still not accepting Mesmer's theories of animal magnetism (Schneck, 1978). Mesmer has been considered the founder of psychotherapy (Watkins, 1976). There are signs of a new interest in an historical analysis of the events of Mesmer's life (MacHovec, 1975a). Some studies cast doubt on former versions of events, such as Mesmer's supposed attendance at a concert by a former patient, Miss Paradis, which may have been a later fictional elaboration (Pattie, 1979).

The Marquis de Puységur (1751–1828) was the first to suggest a similarity between the hypnotic state and sleep, defining the deep state of trance as artificial somnambulism. Puységur found that trance could be induced without the "crisis" that Mesmer had considered essential. He also felt that hypnosis was associated with clairvoyance, a speculation that served to maintain popular interest in the phenomena.

John Elliotson (1791–1868), Professor of Theology and Practice of Medicine at London University, undertook experimentation with mesmerism, accepting Mesmer's own theories of a physical force that could be transmitted from the living operator or from objects previously charged. A distinguished physician, an outstanding leader, and a specialist in medicine who introduced the stethoscope into England, Elliotson was publicly castigated for his writings and therapeutic use of hypnosis. Although he received notice in *Lancet*, an influential medical publication, Elliotson was severely criticized by its editor (Marmer, 1959). He was particularly ridiculed when the substitution of lead for nickel, which Elliotson believed was particularly suited to holding magnetism, did not alter the effectiveness of the treatments. In 1846 he was asked to resign his post for choosing magnetism as the topic for his Harveian Lecture before the Royal College of Physicians, Elliotson was instrumental in publishing the *Zoist*, a "journal of cerebral physiology and mesmerism and their application to human welfare," began in 1843 and continued for 13 volumes. To his death, Elliotson continued to affirm a physical, magnetic theory of mesmerism. Pulos (1980) has suggested a reconsideration of Mesmer's magnetism theory in light of modern knowledge of body electrical fields.

MODERN HYPNOSIS

James Braid (1785–1860), a contemporary of Elliotson, first coined the word *hypnosis*, which is derived from the Greek *hypnos* (sleep). Braid rejected the magnetic theory and instead emphasized suggestion and "monoideism." His book *Satanic Agency and Mesmerism Reviewed*, which details his theory, has recently been reprinted by Tinterow (1970) in his history of hypnosis.

During the same period that Braid conducted his work with hypnosis, James Esdaile (1808–1859) in India performed a number of operations, many on major cases, using only hypnotic anesthesia. A commission appointed by the governor of Bengal reported favorably on his work, although upon his return to Scotland his interest in mesmerism led to the same ostracism that had befallen Elliotson (James, 1975).

The great French neurologist Jean Marie Charcot (1825–1893) was very interested in hypnosis, and he actively pursued its study. The weight of his authority and reputation did much to make investigation in this field respectable. Charcot himself believed that hypnosis was similar to hysteria and that both were the product of a diseased nervous system. Many students were drawn to Paris by Charcot's clinical experiments, including Sigmund Freud in 1885.

Ambroise-Auguste Liebeault (1823–1904) and Hippolyte Bernheim (1837–1919) emphasized the role of suggestibility in hypnosis over the pathological theories of Charcot. Eventually their ideas gained wider approval. Liebeault's book *Sleep and Related States*, published in 1866, was largely ignored until Bernheim, a noted physician, called attention to it years later (Chertok, 1968). As a busy country physician in the Nancy region of rural France, Liebeault had wide experience with hypnosis, especially since he customarily did not charge for hypnotic treatment. Later Freud also spent some time at Nancy, and there became aware of the suggestibility theory and the similarities postulated between hypnosis and sleep. Weitzenhoffer (1980) has reviewed the events of Bernheim's contribution to hypnosis.

In 1880, Josef Breuer (1842–1925) initiated a profound shift of emphasis in hypnotic treatment. In the famous case of Anna O, which he reported with Freud, Breuer found that the patient did not consistently respond to the hypnotic technique of direct symptom removal; rather, she showed only limited improvement. He noted that certain of her symptoms, such as the refusal to drink water, seemed to arise from incidents of her past and were diminished when the original memory was recovered in hypnotic trance. She recalled under hypnosis, for example, that a maid had allowed her dog to drink out of the same glass as she had. She had not drunk water for 6 weeks until this previous trauma was recalled, quenching her thirst only with melons and fruit. This was the first appreciation of the value of abreacting or vigorously re-experiencing forgotten emotion, a process that can be facilitated by hypnosis. The observations of Breuer and Freud published as *Studien über Hysterie* in 1895 may be considered the first stirrings of psycho-analysis. Their method was "cathartic," for it was thought to release stored-up emotions from the unconscious, emotions that belonged to repressed memories.

Freud's Rejection of Hypnosis

In dealing with difficult cases that did not seem to respond well to hypnosis, Freud developed his technique of free association, allowing all the patient's associations to come into consciousness without discrimination or selection. Freud felt strongly that it was unwise to indiscriminately remove symptoms that still had meaning for the patient. In addition, he sensed a sexual connotation to the hypnotic situation, the patient "giving" herself emotionally to the hypnotist. A further limitation on hypnosis was the inability of all patients to achieve a hypnotic state. Finally, Freud began to feel that the system of psychoanalysis that he elaborated was superior to hypnosis.

Freud's rejection of hypnosis, after his earlier enthusiasm, has had a profound negative effect on the development of the field (Glasner, 1955). It now seems evident, however, that Freud's criticisms were not all objective. He himself felt disappointed by his failure to induce trance. And on at least one occasion he was embarassed by a female patient throwing her arms around him in a romantic way. In Freud's day hypnosis frequently was used merely for symptom suppression; Freud came to realize that symptoms often served a protective function. He even suggested that hypnosis was psychologically similar to falling in love or to giving undue influence to the leader of a group. His early denunciation of hypnosis lingered, casting a haze over investigations for many years.

Gruenewald (1982) has traced the contributions to hypnosis of the early psychoanalytic pioneers Freud, Ferenczi, and Schilder as well as the later work of Kubie and Margolin, Gill and Brenman, and Erika Fromm. Macmillan (1977) has recently reviewed the famous case of Anna O, whom Freud treated together with Breuer. Dacquino (1982) has reviewed possible reasons for Freud's rejection of hypnosis, although Freud seemed always to be fascinated by the enigma of hypnosis (Chertok, 1977). Several authors have failed to find historical support for the claim of a stage hypnotist that he had worked together with Freud (Gravitz, 1982; Schneck, 1976). An appreciation of Freud's work with hypnosis is now often noted (Strosberg 1980).

Later Freud modified this earlier rejection of hypnosis. In his 1919 paper "Turnings in the Ways of Analysis," Freud stated that in "the application of our therapy to numbers . . . hypnotic influence might find a place in it again, as it has in the war neurosis." Long after he had developed psychoanalytic technique, Freud (1959) spoke of the need to blend "the pure gold of analysis plentifully with the copper of direct suggestion," including hypnosis.

A contemporary of Freud, Pierre Janet (1859–1947), continued the investigation of hypnosis, even though the rise of Freudian psychoanalysis had brought it into relative disrepute. Janet emphasized dissociation as a primary defense of the mind rather than the repression that Freud preferred as an explanatory model.

The Decline of Investigation

Following Charcot's death in 1893, the scientific study of hypnosis declined. Interest was diverted in the surgical field to chemical anesthetics such as ether, which had first been used in surgery in the United States in 1846. In the treatment of emotional and neurotic disorders attention passed to the rising theory of psychoanalysis.

There is some evidence for a continuation of interest in hypnosis in America during the nineteenth century. A Phreno-Magnetic Society of Cincinnati flourished in 1842 (Wester, 1976). Hypnosis may have been a major component of the Emmanuel movement in Boston, a medical-religious cult (Aldrick, 1978). Gravitz (1981) has recently compiled an important bibliographic reference source for hypnosis literature in the nineteenth century.

The dormancy in the study of hypnosis lasted until World War I, when interest in the techniques were revived as a means of treating traumatic war neurosis by abreaction.

The term "hypnoanalysis" was coined during the war by J. A. Hadfield, who used the hypnotic trance to abreact emotions of traumatic battle situations. Similar techniques were used in World War II and are reported in Watkins' *Hypnotherapy of Wartime Neurosis* (1949).

Between the two world wars only a trickle of serious studies involving hypnosis continued, notably those of Clark L. Hull (1884–1952), the American psychologist, who experimentally criticized the contentions of Pavlov, the famous Russian physiologist, that both hypnosis and sleep involved selective inhibition of certain brain centers. Other significant workers in hypnosis at this time were Prince, Schilder, Young, White, and Sears. During this era the British psychologist McDougall (1926) wrote of hypnosis in terms suggestive of the dissociation hypothesis of Janet, picturing relations between various dissociated parts of the personality. Triplet (1982) has pointed out the contribution of Hull's experience with hypnosis to his later development of learning theory.

THE RISE OF SCIENTIFIC HYPNOSIS

Since World War II the intellectual climate concerning hypnosis has radically improved. The Society for Clinical and Experimental Hypnosis was founded in 1949 in the United States, and in 1959 it was expanded into an international society. A second society, The American Society of Clinical Hypnosis, was founded in 1957. Originally divergent, with strong personalities in both groups, these two societies in recent years have grown closer together, holding their first joint scientific section meeting in 1971.

Stature was added to the study of hypnosis in 1958 by a policy statement from the American Medical Association recognizing hypnosis as a legitimate treatment method in both medicine and dentistry. The British Medical Association in 1955 had passed a similar resolution. In 1969 the American Psychological Association created a section for those psychologists concerned primarily with hypnosis.

Rarely today does one find the loss of intellectual perspective that formerly occurred when hypnosis was under consideration and that saw both advocates and opponents of hypnosis taking extreme positions. Partisan statements picturing hypnosis as a virtual miraculous treatment are still heard, though less and less from trained persons. Unfortunately, popular articles may occasionally exaggerate, even though professional publications generally demand high levels of scientific observation and statements of realistic conclusions.

The authors feel that the future of hypnosis rests firmly on its being of unique value in three important areas:

1. Hypnosis offers unique opportunities to demonstrate mental mechanisms for teaching purposes. Some defense mechanisms, such as amnesia, can be dramatically demonstrated to the medical resident or student, to the graduate student in psychology, or to the dentist in training. For example, the concept of *regression* can be vivified by a demonstration of hypnotic age regression. The use of hypnosis in teaching can bring life to theoretical constructs, and in our experience it has often increased the interest and motivation of students who witnessed demonstrations of hypnotic technique.
2. Hypnosis has great potential in research, not only into the nature of the hypnotic state itself but also as a means of more controlled

emotional variables in psychological and psychosomatic research. Psychological factors involved in pain, for example, can be studied without the pharmacological effects of medication. Residents in surgery and anesthesiology may find hypnosis useful as a control in studies evaluating other forms of pain relief, since the hypnotic effects are clearly initiated by psychological means.

3. Hypnosis is of great value in medical, psychological, and dental treatment, both for psychological problems and as part of the treatment of many physical disorders or compulsive habit patterns, such as cigarette smoking by emphysema patients.

After almost two centuries of episodic popularity and abandonment, we feel that the use of hypnosis as a standard tool in psychotherapeutic, medical, and dental treatment now is assumed. Articles on hypnosis appear not only in the specialized journals devoted to the subject but also in more general scientific journals. More and more, hypnotherapy is being seen as a valuable treatment modality with certain indications and contraindications rather than as a last-resort treatment to be used only in extreme situations. The professional American societies devoted to hypnosis, as well as similar organizations in many other countries, offer continuing forums for interchange among serious workers in the field. These societies are influential bodies whose opinions are respected in the medical, dental, and psychological fields. A growing appreciation of the history of hypnosis is seen in many fine contemporary reviews, such as those of Chertok (1980), Connery (1982), and Servadio (1975).

REFERENCES

Aldrick JM: Hypnosis and the Emmanuel movement: a medical and religious repudiation. Am J Clin Hypn 20:224–234, 1978
Breuer J, Freud S: Studies in Hysteria. New York, Basic Books, 1957
Chertok L: From Liebeault to Freud. Historical note. Am J Psychother 22:96–101, 1968
Chertok L: Freud and hypnosis: An epistemological appraisal. J Nerv Ment Dis 165:99–109, 1977
Chertok L: Early theories of hypnosis, in Burrows GD, Dennerstein L (eds): Handbook of Hypnosis and Psychosomatic Medicine. Amsterdam, Elsevier/North-Holland Biomedical Press, 1980, pp 1–10
Conn JH: Historical aspects of scientific hypnosis. J Clin Exp Hypn 5:17–24, 1957
Connery DS: The Inner Source, New York, Holt, Rinehart & Winston, 1982
Dacquino G: Psychoanalysis and hypnosis in theory and clinical practice. Minerva Med 73:3207–3212, 1982
Freud, S: Turnings in the ways of psychoanalytic therapy, in Jones E (ed): Sigmund Freud: Collected Papers. New York, Basic Books, 1959, pp 392–402
Glasner S: A note on allusions to hypnosis in the Bible and Talmud. J Clin Exp Hypn 3:34–39, 1955

Gravitz MA: Bibliographic sources of nineteenth century hypnosis literature. Am J Clin Hypn 23:217–219, 1981

Gravitz MA, Gerton MI: Polgar as Freud's hypnotist? Contrary evidence. Am J Clin Hypn 24:272–276, 1982

Gruenewald D: A psychoanalytic view of hypnosis. Am J Clin Hypn 24:185–190, 1982

James CD: Mesmerism: a prelude to anaethesia. Proc Roy Soc Med 68:446–447, 1975

Jensen A, Watkins ML: Franz Anton Mesmer: Physician Extraordinaire. New York, Garret, 1967

Ludwig AM: An historical survey of the early roots of mesmerism. Int J Clin Exp Hypn 12:205–247, 1964

MacHovec FJ: Hypnosis before Mesmer. Am J Clin Hypn 17:215–220, 1975a

MacHovec FJ: Shakespeare on hypnosis: The Tempest. Am J Clin Hypn 24:73–78, 1975b

MacHovec FJ: The evil eye: Superstition or hypnotic phenomenon? Am J Clin Hypn 19:74–79, 1976

MacHovec FJ: The cult of Asklipos. Am J Clin Hypn 22:85–90, 1979

Macmillan MB: The carthartic method and the expectancies of Breuer and Anna O. Int J Clin Exp Hypn 24:106–118, 1977

Marmer MJ: Hypnosis in Anesthesiology. Springfield, Ill., Charles C Thomas, 1959

McDougall W: Outline of Abnormal Psychology. New York, Scribners, 1926

Musès C: Trance-induction techniques in ancient Egypt, in Musès C, Young AM (eds): Consciousness and Reality. New York. Outerbridge and Lazard, 1972, pp 9–17

Pattie FA: A Mesmer-Paradis myth dispelled. Am J Clin Hypn 22:29–31, 1979

Pulos L: Mesmerism Revisited: the effectiveness of Esdaile's techniques in the production of deep hypnosis and total body hypnoanesthesia. Am J Clin Hypn 22:206–11, 1980

Rosen G: History of medical hypnosis, in Schneck JM (ed): Hypnosis in Modern Medicine (ed 2). Springfield, Ill., Charles C Thomas, 1959

Schneck JM: Freud's "medical hypnotist". Am J Clin Hypn 19:80–81, 1976

Schneck JM: Benjamin Rush and animal magnetism, 1789 and 1812. Int J Clin Exp Hypn 26:8–14, 1978

Servadio E: Hypnosis in history and at present. Minerva Med 66:3811–3817, 1975

Stam HJ, Spanos NP: The Asclepian dream healings and hypnosis: A critique. Int J Clin Exp Hypn 30:9–22, 1982

Strosberg IM: Hypnosis—Living—Comfort. J Am Soc Psychosom Dent Med 27:2932, 1980

Tinterow MM: Foundations of Hypnosis from Mesmer to Freud. Springfield, Ill., Charles C Thomas, 1970

Tomlinson WK, Perret JJ: Mesmerism in New Orleans, 1845–1861. Am J Psychiatry 131:1402–1404, 1974

Triplet RG: The relationship of Clark L Hull's hypnosis research to his later learning theory: The continuity of his life's work. J Hist Behav Sci 18:22–31, 1982

Watkins JG: Hypnotherapy of War Neurosis. New York, Ronald Press, 1949

Watkins DC: Franz Anton Mesmer: Founder of psychotherapy. Nurs Mirror 142:66–67, 1976

Weitzenhoffer AM: What did he (Bernheim) say? A postscript and an addendum. Int J Clin Exp Hypn 28:252–260, 1980

Wester WC: The phreno-magnetic society of Cincinnati—1842. Am J Clin Hypn 18:277–281, 1976

Wolberg LR: Hypnosis—Is It For You? New York, Harcourt Brace Jovanovich, 1972, p 22

2
Theories

Many theories of hypnosis have been outlined succinctly by Wolberg (1962):

> For example, there are the hereditary models which conceive of hypnosis as an inherited characteristic that reflects a phylogenetic and regressive group of qualities and traits. Involved here also are the analogical linkages with animal hypnosis . . . there is a physiological model which conceives of hypnosis as a product of ordered or disordered activity in different portions of the brain, such as areas of inhibition and areas of excitation, or the action of the reticular activating system. There is an internal environmental model which deals with the exchanges and interchanges of biochemical substances in the neural system throughout the brain. There is a learning model that conceives of hypnosis as a form of learning, like conditioning. There is a cultural social model which explains hypnosis in terms of contagious suggestibility and role-playing. There is a developmental motivational model which deals with various interpersonal and intrapsychic dimensions, such as dissociation and ontogenetic regression to earlier modes of thinking, feeling and behavior, involving an anachronistic revival of the child-parent relationship and related transference phenomena.

DEFINITION OF HYPNOSIS

From the beginning of interest in hypnosis, there have been many competing theories to explain the phenomena. Chertok (1980) has reviewed some of the early theories of hypnosis. Before these theories are examined, however, it is useful to consider varied definitions of hypnosis from current experts in the field. More recently, Chertok (1983) has related psychoanalysis to hypnotic theory, with illustrative case examples.

Meares (1961) emphasizes the atavistic aspects of hypnosis, i.e., those that suggest a primitive phylogenetic response. He defines hypnosis as basically a "regression to the primitive mode of mental functioning in which ideas are accepted uncritically by the primitive process of suggestion." He adds that various psychological mechanisms may operate "on top" of this basic regression, including identification, introjection, conditioning, dissociation, role-playing, hysteric defenses, and communication by behavior rather than verbally.

Raginsky (1962) stressed that "any theory of hypnosis must of necessity be a biological one," although he indicated the importance of other conceptual models, including sociological, anthropological, and physiological models. Raginsky felt that any definition of hypnosis must consider "the way in which the hypnotized person moves in the direction of functioning which approaches the most primitive level of psychophysiological existence where an awareness of individual–environment differentiation diminishes toward infinity."

Marmer (1959) defined hypnosis as a "psychophysiological tetrad of altered consciousness" consisting of (1) heightened suggestibility, (2) narrowed awareness, (3) selective wakefulness, and (4) restricted attentiveness.

Erickson (1958) defined hypnosis as "a state of intensified attention and receptiveness and an increased responsiveness to an idea or to a set of ideas."

Schneck (1962) has written that "the hypnotic state, in terms of its basic ingredient, is that condition represented by the most primitive form of psychophysiological awareness of individual–environmental differential attainable among living organisms."

Alexander (1972) feels that "hypnosis may be defined as a state manifested by an inward turning of the mind, facilitating an enhancement of the creative imagination, favoring inductive over deductive reasoning, and reducing the need for reality testing, thus providing a mental setting in which, with appropriate suggestions, ideas can be perceived and experienced in such a vivid manner as to allow their revivification to the point of hallucinations."

Conn (1949) has described hypnosis as a multilevel, dynamic, interpersonal relationship with imagination as the essential factor. Bartlett (1968) defines hypnosis as "a control of the normal control of input (information) for the purpose of controlling output (behavior)."

Zimbardo, Maslach, and Marshall (1972) suggest that "hypnosis (a) is a state in which the effects of cognitive processes on bodily functioning are amplified; (b) enables the subject to perceive the focus of causality for mind and body control as more internally centered and volitional; (c) is often accompanied by a heightened sense of visual imagery; and (d) can lead to intensive concentration and elimination of distractions."

Orne (1972) has devoted careful attention to distinguishing those aspects that define hypnosis as distinct from normal behavior:

> The presence of hypnosis can be identified by the way in which a subject(s) responds to suggestions. Heuristically, then, hypnosis is considered to be that state or condition in which suggestions (or cues) from the hypnotist will elicit hypnotic phenomena. Hypnotic phenomena can operationally be distinguished from nonhypnotic responses only when suggestions are given that require the S to distort his perception or memory. Accordingly, the hypnotized individual can be identified only by his ability to respond to suitable suggestions by appropriately altering any or all modalities of perception and memory.

In his definition of hypnosis, West (1960) blends both psychological and physiological concepts:

> Psychophysiologically, the hypnotic trance may be defined as a controlled dissociated state. This state of altered awareness is maintained through parassociative mechanisms mediated by the ascending reticular system . . . when the subject is in the hypnotic state, alertness is maintained relative to the inhibition or exclusion from awareness of considerable amounts of incoming information that would ordinarily be consciously perceived in the process of reality-testing. Under these circumstances the information inserted into the restricted area of the subjects' awareness by the hypnotist, through his suggestions, is accepted as reality to a greater or lesser extent, depending upon the subject's dissociation of other information from awareness, moment by moment.

In discussing hypnosis as an adjunct to psychotherapy, Spiegel

(1967) presents an operational definition of hypnosis as "an altered state of intense and sensitive inter-personal relatedness between hypnotist and patient, characterized by the patient's nonrational submission and relative abandonment of executive control to a more or less regressed, dissociated state." He emphasizes that in clinical practice the hypnotist structures this regressed state to facilitate achievement of desired goals. Elsewhere, Spiegel (1974) defines hypnosis as "a response to a signal from another or to an inner signal, which activates a capacity for a shift of awareness in the subject and permits a more intensive concentration upon a designated goal direction. This shift of attention is constantly sensitive to and responsive to cues from the hypnotist or the subject himself if properly trained." This definition is somewhat unique in emphasizing the possible intrapsychic onset of hypnosis.

Gruenewald (1982) has helped to clarify the definition of hypnosis by distinguishing the hypnotic *situation* from the hypnotic *condition*. The hypnotic situation is an encompassing compliance with suggestion, role-taking, and transference; the hypnotic condition or state is characterized by alternations of perception and memory with a sense of the reality of the subjective state. In a recent review, Orne (1980) points to the subjective reality of hypnotic phenomena as an argument against volitional role-playing. He concludes that it is most useful to establish links between hypnosis and other phenomena rather than search for unique psychobiological correlates of hypnosis.

PHYSIOLOGICAL THEORIES

The varied definitions of hypnosis reflect differences of emphasis. Theories likewise show preferences for emphasizing one or another aspect of the complicated phenomena of hypnosis.

Theories of hypnosis can be divided into two categories—the physiological theories, such as Pavlov's theory that views hypnosis as a selective inhibition of certain brain centers, and the psychological theories, such as hypersuggestibility. The psychological theories are those most widely held in popular opinion, although some observations seem to require the more organic model. When hypnosis is more fully understood, both approaches will most likely be found to describe the same phenomena as seen from the psychological or from the physiological viewpoint.

Mesmer himself believed in an essentially organic theory. He called the force that brought about hypnotic effects "animal magnetism." Having done his doctoral dissertation on the influence of planets on the human body, Mesmer thought that a subtle "magnetic fluid" was generated in his own body and transmitted through elaborate passes of his hands to the patient. Mesmer seemed never to consider the psychological meaning of the phenomena.

Although Mesmer's "animal magnetism" has been discredited, there is consistent speculation about physiological correlates of hypnosis. Physiological changes associated with hypnotic trance have been reviewed several times since World War II, notably by Gorton (1949a,b), Crasilneck and Hall (1959), and Levitt and Brady (1963). Some of the older reports are confusing, since it is not possible to tell from the published sources if the reported changes are due to hypnosis itself or to emotions arising from the suggestion of altered perception. To help clarify this question, the authors (Crasilneck and Hall, 1959) introduced the term "neutral hypnosis" for the hypnotic state before suggestions are given for specific change. We later reported (1960) no statistically significant alteration in pulse rate, blood pressure, and respiratory rate with the induction of neutral hypnosis. Edmonston (1977) and others have found *neutral hypnosis* to be a useful term in the discussion of hypnotic research and its clinical application.

Subsequently, a number of authors recorded findings in neutral hypnosis as well as in the experimental state. Reid and Curtsinger (1968) studied changes in peripheral vasomotor responses, finding an increase in oral temperature in neutral hypnosis with greater increases in temperature measured in other regions of the body. Similar findings were reported by Timney and Barber (1969), who suggested that the increased temperature might be due to greater anxiety in the hypnotic situation. Peters and Stern (1973), however, found that "neutral hypnosis" does not involve changes in these measures which are appreciably different from the changes associated with relaxation. Edmonston (1968) reported that electrodermal responses in neutral hypnosis did not differ from a relaxed but not hypnotized condition. According to Jana and Pattie (1965), there is no alteration of blood glucose, calcium, or phosphorous in neutral hypnosis alone.

The role of emotions or emotionally charged images in producing physiological changes frequently has been raised. Damacer, Shor, and Orne (1963) observed that physiological changes occurred consistently in hypnotically requested emotions, but they also occurred as easily in waking control conditions by simulators. Levitt, den Breeijen, and Persky (1960) noted that hypnotically induced anxiety affected blood pressure and pulse rate but did not significantly alter plasma hydrocortisone levels.

In his research, Jana (1965) found no significant alteration in basal metabolism between the waking and hypnotic state in 14 healthy male subjects; however, natural sleep lowered the rate by 8.72 percent. Vanderhoof and Clancy (1962) noted that venous blood flow through a limb increased during recall of stressful experiences under hypnosis but not during recall of the same events during the waking state. Strosberg, Irwen, and Vics (1962) observed physiological changes in the eye during hypnosis, including a reduction of the blood supply in vascular anastomoses and engorgement of the vessels of the sclera. They speculated that changes might take place elsewhere in the body, and suggested that hypnotic trance may cause a relaxation that permits the cornea to assume a more rounded shape, thus reducing astigmatism.

A striking physiological change in response to hypnosis was reported by Chapman, Goodell, and Wolff (1959). One arm of each hypnotic subject was made resistant to injury, while it was suggested that the other become more susceptible to injury. The same area on both arms was then given a carefully measured equal amount of thermal radiation. The "sensitive arm" not only showed a marked wheal reaction, with reddening, but it was also possible to show that perfusate from that arm contained more bradykininlike substance than did the arm that had been suggested to be anesthetized. These researchers concluded that "the neural apparatus may alter the tissue subserved in such a way as to augment inflammation and to increase tissue vulnerability." Hypnosis obviously decreased such vulnerability.

Some reports on physiological functioning have emphasized more directly the role of the nervous system. Erickson (1965) has reported a case in which pupillary responses were subjected to voluntary control with hypnosis in an eight-year-old girl. Writing in *Science*, Brady and Levitt (1964b) have reported using electro-oculograms to detect the presence of optokinetic nystagmus in subjects hypnotically hallucinating a visual situation.

Several authors have speculated that hypnosis may have an effect on the central nervous system. Akstein (1965), De Moraes Passos (1967), and Raikov (1975) emphasized the reticular activating system, while Bartlett (1966) suggested that hypnosis may alter the relation of cortical and subcortical communication, particularly involving the hypothalamus, the reticular formation, and the limbic system. Arnold (1959) has suggested that the set to imagine is mediated by the hippocampal action circuit, connected with the diffuse thalamic system. According to Roberts (1960), "Hypnosis is brought about by an electrical blockage between the brain stem reticular formation and the specific-sensory, parasensory, and coordinate neuronal channels," and he proposes "the selective activity of brain rhythms of the delta frequency . . . as a possible mechanism of inhibition." Noting that strain gauge plethysmograph recordings showed greater changes in peripheral pulse and finger volume during deep hypnosis, Bigelow, Cameron, and Koroljow (1956) suggest that in hypnosis the inhibiting tendency of the cortex on the autonomic nervous system is greatly reduced. Possible central nervous system models of hypnosis have been considered by Granone (1972) and Reyher (1964). Recently, Stewart and Crasilneck (1984) have used a subject with bilaterally implanted thalmic electrodes to demonstate that electrical stimulation of that part of the brain can interrupt hypnotic trance, *if* the stimulation is sufficienctly strong. They believe that the effect is mediated through the reticular activating system.

While there have been many speculations about the role of the nervous system in hypnosis, there have been few direct observations on humans. One striking clinical observation strongly supporting the neurophysiological basis of hypnosis was reported by Crasilneck, Mc-Cranie and Jenkins (1956). A patient under both hypnosis and local chemical anesthesia of the scalp suddenly awakened during brain surgery when the neurosurgeon touched the hippocampal area. She was quickly rehypnotized, but she again abruptly terminated hypnosis when the hippocampus was touched once more. Hypnosis was again induced, and the surgery continued. It seemed obvious that the mechanical stimulus to the hippocampal region somehow abruptly interfered with the hypnotic state, strongly suggesting that the hippocampus is involved in whatever neural circuits underlie hypnosis.* When Lieberson, Smith, and Stern (1961) conducted experiments with "animal hypnosis" in guinea pigs, hippocampograms were "found useful as an indicator of the degree of internal activity of the animal." Although the relation of animal hypnosis to human hypnosis is not at all clear, we feel that future studies of brain functioning will show that there is some clear neurophysiological alteration during hypnosis. Such studies are only now becoming technically feasible and are still quite experimental.

Although Mesmer was wrong about the existence of a magnetic field, he may well have been right in his intuition that hypnosis had a physiological basis. Physiological activity is also implied in the sleep theories of hypnosis and in the conditioned reflex model elaborated by Pavlovians. A most consistent and impressive clinical observation, and one that favors a physiological theory, is that the appearance of subjects in the somnambulistic state of trance is identical the world

*This case is discussed clinically in Chapter 8. "Hypnosis in Surgery."

over, in spite of immense differences in "role" and cultural expectations. A circumoral pallor of the lip margins frequently appears in good hypnotic subjects from many different cultures, an observation that we first noted in 1954 and have had many opportunities to confirm. Other colleagues and students have been able to observe this pallor over the years.

In spite of the large number of studies on the physiology of hypnosis, Fromm (1972a) in reviewing current experimental work contends that this may be an area of decreasing emphasis:

> In my judgment, as interest in the subjective aspects of hypnosis increases—with increasing awareness that hypnosis is an altered state of consciousness and that the very essence of hypnosis is in the subject's subjective experience—the search for physiological and neuroelectric substrata of hypnosis as proof of the existence of a hypnotic state will fade into the background. Researchers will no longer feel as compelled to look intently for *objective* measures of the subjective experience.

She is perhaps indicating a preference for the psychological and psychoanalytic models.

Ericksonian Techniques

In recent years, there has appeared a devoted interest in the techniques and clinical theories of Milton Erickson, a seminal founding member of the American Society for Clinical Hypnosis. His approach has been presented notably by Erickson, Rossi, and Rossi (1976), Haley (1973), and in a large number of published papers (for example, Erickson 1977a,b). Erickson's artistry in the use of hypnotic techniques focused upon a subtle interweaving of covert hypnotic suggestions amid other verbal interaction with the subject (Erickson, 1982) and with a skill in structuring all interaction with the patient to facilitate the therapeutic purpose, not limiting the interaction to formal hypnotic induction. Rossi (1984) has recently highlighted an Ericksonian use of ultradian rhythms (more rapid than daily alterations in rest/activity cycles) to combine posthypnotic suggestions with triggering activities that are part of daily life. Also, myths about Erickson and Ericksonian hypnosis are discussed by Hammond (1983). Some other hypnotherapists who have refined and taught Erickson's methods are Barber, Goodman, and Griffin, Pearson, Rodger, Rosen, and Thompson, all of whom presented papers at the Second Ericksonian Congress in 1982.

Although Erickson himself had little interest in theory (Moore,

1982), others have used his vivid case descriptions as a mine of hypnotic understanding of social influence (Stricherz, 1982), symptom prescription, (Zeig, 1980), transforming of symptoms (DeShazer, 1979), and techniques of short-term therapy (Sanders, 1977). Erickson was a master in the use of the therapeutic double-bind, (Erickson and Rossi, 1975), and multilevel verbal communications (Erickson and Rossi, 1976).

Neurolinguistic programming is a style of clinical interaction that appears to have been strongly influenced by the Ericksonian tradition in hypnotherapy. Assumptions are made about the neurological substrate of observable behavior, such as eye movement to one lateral side indicating activation of the opposite cerebral hemisphere. At this time, such "neurolinguistic" hypnotheses have not become a significant part of the scientific discussion of hypnosis and hypnotherapy.

Gravitz and Gravitz (1977) have published a definitive bibliography of Erickson's writings on hypnosis. A tribute to Erickson was published in the *American Journal of Clinical Hypnosis* in 1977.

Hypnosis as Sleep

The similarity of sleep and hypnosis was first suggested by the Marquis de Puységur, a contemporary of Mesmer. The Abbé Faria of Portugal (1756–1819) introduced the term "lucid sleep," but he disagreed with Mesmer's theory of magnetic transmission. James Braid in the middle of the nineteenth century wrote of the phenomena as neurohypnotism, suggesting an organic neural change.

The analogy of hypnosis to sleep has persisted throughout much of the clinical literature since the days of Liebeault and Bernheim. This is perhaps more the persistence of techniques of hypnotism than of theories about its nature, for there have always been distinctions between hypnotic sleep and normal sleep.

Most modern investigators seem to have collected a weight of evidence against the identicalness of sleep and hypnosis. As early as 1939, Nygard directly observed the blood flow to cerebral vessels to be unchanged in hypnotic induction but notably altered (by increased pulsation) with the onset of natural sleep. Although studies such as those of McCranie, Crasilneck, and Tetter (1955) have shown no change in electroencephalograms in the waking state and the hypnotic state, it seemed possible when suggestions for sleep were given for the subject to pass from a state resembling the alertness of waking to one resembling normal sleep.

A number of EEG studies have been done concerning sleep and

hypnosis. Dittborn and O'Connell (1967) found that neither the tendency to develop EEG sleep patterns nor the ability of some subjects to respond while in EEG sleep was related to hypnotizability. But five subjects, all known to the highly hypnotizable, showed a type of dissociation between the EEG sleep and both behavioral and subjective sleep experiences. Similarly Lerner (1963) found that the EEG of hypnotized subjects showed neither a state of physiological sleep nor a state of ordinary conscious awareness, although in some instances there were minor similarities. Schwartz, Bickford, and Rasmussen (1955) reported that "hypnosis and wakefulness have identical EEG patterns, but typical sleep patterns can be brought about in hypnotized individuals by means of appropriate suggestions." Emphasizing the similarity of sleep and hypnosis, Horvai (1959) has noted that a description of phenomena that ordinarily takes place during falling asleep constitute a large part of the usual induction suggestions for hypnosis. It would seem that sleep and hypnosis are not the same, although they share some phenomena. Subjects may pass from the waking state toward the sleeping state during hypnosis, depending upon the set of the situation and the suggestion of the hypnotherapist.

Hypnosis as Cerebral Inhibition

The great Russian physiologist Ivan Petrovich Pavlov constructed a theory of conditioned responses involving presumed cortical areas of increased excitation and inhibition. Finding that dogs held in laboratory harnesses while presented with a monotonously repeated stimulus tended to sleep or to show rigidity in certain limbs, he suggested a similar explanation for hypnosis. Pavlov envisioned that the monotony of a low-intensity stimulus, presented to a subject whose motor functioning was inhibited, would produce in the cerebral cortex a radiating area of neural inhibition. In his view only the localization of the inhibition differed from normal sleep, which was pictured as general cortical inhibition. Reminiscent of Pavlov's theory is that of Kubie and Margolin (1944), who describe hypnosis as "partial sleep" in a regressed state.

There have been criticisms of Pavlov's theory of hypnosis. Hull (1933) considered it vague and untestable. He placed emphasis on hypersuggestibility as the primary theoretical basis of hypnosis.

Das (1959), on the other hand, has presented a theory of hypnosis based on Pavlovian theory, defining hypnosis as a "learned state of partial cortical inhibition." In an experimental study (1958) he found that the development of inhibition in the presence of monotonous sound and light stimuli improved with practice and could possibly be correlated with increasing hypnotizability. The use of hypnosis in Russia, based on Pavlovian concepts, is reviewed by Hoskovec (1967) and Volgyesi (1950). Roth (1962) and Kraines (1969) also rely on concepts of a Pavlovian nature.

It is likely that the importance of the Pavlovian concepts of areas of cortical inhibition and excitation will become more important in the thinking of Western theorists when it is technically possible to make more discrete measurements of cerebral functioning, either through refined EEG technology or through studies of implanted electrodes in the treatment of disorders of the central nervous system. The nature of such research, however, is slow and specialized, consequently, a gradual accumulation of observations is more likely than any sudden breakthrough.

Pathology

The major representatives of the position that hypnosis is the result of a pathological neural phenomenon are Charcot and his students Pere and Binet. These men worked at the Salpêtrière in Paris and taught that both hypnosis and hysteria were a product of some disease process in the central nervous system. Liebeault's school of thought at Nancy, stressing suggestibility, finally won out in acceptance over the pathological theory. Since Charcot, no one has seriously suggested that hypnosis is a phenomenon dependent on innate lability or disease of the nervous system. Rather, the focus has increasingly been on various means of inducing hypnosis in subjects previously thought to be resistant and on reformulating the hypnotic state in interactional and interpersonal terms.

Although there is no present theoretical emphasis that is equivalent to Charcot's view that hypnosis is a pathological state, there is much to be said for his position, although a more psychological view must be taken. Charcot believed that both hysteria and hypnosis arose from a disordered nervous system, placing the emphasis on the supposed neural substrate of both conditions. He may well have been right in the similarity but wrong in his explanation, since hypnosis and hysterical phenomena both may occur in persons whose central nervous systems are normal by any means of measurement now available. The similarity of hypnotic and psychoneurotic phenomena must be sought not in the nervous system but in its psychological functioning. A computer analogy will illustrate this: the nervous system (computer) is working well, but the psychological set (programming) is faulty.

Much psychoneurotic behavior can possibly be seen as analogous to hypnosis. In hypnosis a perfectly healthy man may be unable to bend his arm or to feel in a normal way an actual painful stimulus. In neurosis a perfectly healthy man may be unable to use his obvious abilities—feeling himself inferior in spite of many superior accomplishments, experiencing anxiety in the absence of any external threat, having delusional beliefs of worthlessness in the face of reassurance from family and friends that he is important and loved. In neurosis it is as if the person had been hypnotized; the psychotherapy of the neurotic is analogous to trying to awaken a hypnotic subject who wishes to remain asleep.

Some of the striking changes that can be produced at times in hypnoanalysis may owe their efficacy to the trance state engaging some of the same parts of the central nervous system (or mind) that are already utilized in the neurotic patterning. Further understanding of hypnosis may lead to a deeper appreciation of the mechanisms of neurosis and facilitate speed of treatment, as Freud seemed to foresee. And these possible future findings would vindicate the intuition if not the theoretical explanation of Charcot.

PSYCHOLOGICAL THEORIES

Those theories that are considered psychological in this work deemphasize the physiological or neural changes associated with hypnosis and stress instead psychological factors that are expressed more in a language of role definition, expectation, motivation, and the mental "mechanisms" of psychoanalytic theory.

Conditioned Response

Extrapolating from the classical model of conditioned-response theory, in which emphasis was placed on brain mechanisms, several writers have suggested that hypnosis is a "generalized conditioning." Theories based on this concept picture the stimulus words of trance induction as a conditioned stimulus, while the response of the subject is the same as if the phenomena represented by the words were also presented. This was the central idea of Hull's theory of hypersuggestibility (1933) as well as Welch's *abstract conditioning*. The concept of abstract conditioning was experimentally approached by Corn-Becker, Welch, and Fisischelli (1959), who felt that everyone while growing up repeatedly experienced that a person who said he was a dentist fixed teeth, that a person who said he was a mechanic was able to repair cars, and so on. As a result of these "proven" facts of experience the subject comes to the hypnotic situation with an already reinforced idea that what was said by an authority was usually proven to be correct by subsequent experience. He thus had a preconceived set to respond to the hypnotic state by producing the phenomena suggested. This theoretical approach has been experimentally criticized by Gladfelter and Hall (1962), whose findings did not support the concept of "abstract conditioning," Edmondston (1967) feels that a stimulus response offers the most parsimonious understanding of hypnotic behavior.

There is indeed much similarity between some hypnotic phenomena and conditioned reflexes. Without knowing if a response had been implanted by hypnosis or by classical conditioning, it might be impossible to determine by observation which technique had in fact been utilized. A strongly accepted posthypnotic suggestion behaves in a manner almost identical to a conditioned response.

Alexander (1968) has succinctly outlined the major similarities:

The compelling nature of an effective posthypnotic suggestion which becomes fully incorporated in the mental life of the patient, who accepts it as an idea of his own rather than something he learned from the therapist, is inexplicable by traditional psychodynamic concepts. It is characterized by what is best described as a compulsive triad, namely: compelling powers of the suggested idea, amnesia of the source of the idea, and confabulatory rationalization of the amnesia if challenged.

Weitzenhoffer (1972) has related the behavior modification technique of Wolpe to the earlier "reconditioning" described by Wolberg (1948). It is perhaps not surprising that the realization that is part of the paradigm of Wolpe's (1961) technique of reciprocal inhibition is quite similar to a hypnotic induction, injecting a hypnoticlike trance into the very core of behavior modification techniques. In the technique of reciprocal inhibition, Wolpe relaxes the subject, then presents gradually increasing stress images (as a situation the patient fears) until the anxiety response is diminished.

The growing body of knowledge of biofeedback and autonomic conditioning is concerned with producing physiological changes similar to those than can be elicited in some good hypnotic subjects.

Suggestion

Similar to the conditioned-response theories are those of suggest-ibility. These may be considered in terms of (1) directed, goal-oriented striving, and (2) role-playing. These variations differ only in the degree of conscious of unconscious motivation.

White (1941) made the first distinct statement of the position that goal-oriented striving occurs at a more unconscious level than "role-playing," thereby utilizing more of the unconscious abilities of the hypnotic subject. Sarbin and Coe (1972) have greatly expanded the suggestion and role-taking view of hypnosis. Weitzenhoffer, who speaks of a three-factor theory that emphasizes variables that facilitate hyper-suggestibility (1953), also has spoken to the question of the hypnotist's ability to recognize when the subject is in a "trance state" (1964):

> I have been particularly struck by the fact that while responsive-ness to suggestions is more often than not a good indicator of the presence of hypnosis, experienced hypnotists, among which I include myself, frequently conclude a person is hypnotized in spite of poor response to suggestions or no response at all, and con-versely, we often decide that an individual giving definite, even good, response to suggestions is not hypnotized, or only very lightly so. There seems to be some sort of intuitive clinical judg-ment going on which appears to be amazingly correct much of the time.

Weitzenhoffer further points out that from the observer's point of view the subject loses spontaneity and develops "trance stare" and that the subject may verbally report a lack of intrarelatedness or intraconsistency in the events that are occurring in hypnosis. He also suggests that the "artificial somnambulism" of the older hypnosis literature may be rare in today's reports, making comparisons difficult. Other variations in the reports of the current and past literature concerning hypnosis should be noted. The older hypnotherapists prob-ably took much longer to induce trance, and there may have been subtle psychological effects from some of the induction procedures, such as "passes" of the hands, which are not used today. Zikmund (1964) has observed that subjects entering hypnosis lack the undulatory eyeball movements characteristic of falling asleep.

In his usual lucid style, Orne (1971) has reviewed the problems of the simulation of hypnosis:

> . . . though it has been shown that subjects are able to simulate successfully and can deceive highly trained hypnotists, this ob-

servation does not challenge the reality of subjects' experiences nor does it question the genuineness of hypnosis. Furthermore, in most contexts, simulation does not occur spontaneously and ought not to preoccupy either the therapist or the investigator . . . it [simulation of hypnosis] indicates only that observations made in the usual clinical contexts do not hold when subjects are motivated to deceive.

Evans and Orne (1971) showed that simulating subjects behaved very differently from hypnotized subjects when they felt that the experimental task was interrupted by a supposed power failure that interfered with a tape-recorded hypnotic session. When the experimenter left the room after the "power failure," simulating subjects almost immediately ceased faking, while hypnotized subjects in the same group only slowly and with difficulty terminated hypnosis by themselves. Sheehan (1971) too has discussed differences between hypnotized and simulating subjects. Orne (1959) has found that "real" and "fake" hypnotic subjects differed mainly in the higher tolerance of the "real" subjects for logical inconsistencies. He concluded that "in the absence of objective indices of hypnosis the existence of trance may be considered a clinical diagnosis."

Role-Playing

Much of the discussion about hypnosis as role-playing has centered on the concept of "trance". Barber (1972) has attacked in particular the trance concept as unnecessary; he asserts that his studies have shown hypnosis not be a "state" intrinsically different from ordinary waking consciousness. On the other hand, Ludwig (1968) has defended the concept of trance:

Thus, the trance, as produced by traditional induction methods, seems to have become an experimental strawman which some investigators use to support their theories, others use to destroy the theories of others, and still others use to attack the validity of the very state they produce . . . it should be recognized that the hypnotic trance represents only one variety of trance. Second, trance phenomena are more widespread than generally supposed and represent a normal mental faculty. Third, trance may be produced by a variety of means and in many different contexts. With these considerations in mind, it seems more productive to raise the question concerning the function of trance for man rather than dwell on its nature. It appears that it may serve important individual and social survival purposes in man.

In a scholarly and careful clinical study Josephine Hilgard (1970) has made much the same point, that hypnosis itself is on a continuum with other states of experience. She found that some tendency for hypnotizability seems to "go along" with a history of emotional involvements in reading, drama, religion, scenery, music, imaginary experiences, and real or imagined adventures. Some positive correlation was also noted with a childhood history of severe punishment, similarity of temperment to the opposite-sex parent, and some aspects of a "normal" and "outgoing" personality. Involvement in competitive sports did not correlate with hypnotizability. Ernest Hilgard (1967) emphasizes that hypnosis is a state of heightened response to the type of suggestions given in hypnotic inductions. Similarly, Gravitz and Kramer (1967) found that although hypnoticlike behavior is fairly common in both sexes, it is apparently higher in females. Although such behavior correlated well with higher intelligence, their studies showed no difference in the sexes in this regard. Williams (1963) has suggested that some accidents on superhighways may be attributed to "highway hypnosis," which is produced by such factors as monotony and bright points of fixation. Aaronson (1968) concludes that "most mothers carry out . . . standard hypnotic procedures when they are putting their babies to sleep," using monotonous but smoothing words, rocking rhythmically, and suggesting muscular relaxation. The focusing of attention inwardly is seen as similar to some mediative states.

Since most hypnotic phenomena are subjectively experienced, it is not surprising that the role-playing theory of hypnosis has found strong advocates.

Sarbin and Lim (1963) for example, have shown that ability to take roles and hypnotizability are related. Barber (1972) makes the analogy to a spectator watching a play. If the spectator is well disposed to enjoy the vicarious emotions portrayed by the actors, the play may indeed evoke in him similar feelings, leading to cartharsis and relief of tension. If the spectator is unwilling, however, and is only attending the performance for other reasons, the drama may evoke little response.

One of the arguments against role-playing as a basic component in hypnosis is that some phenomena can be produced under hypnosis that are not ordinarily within the normal range of voluntary response. Weitzenhoffer (1953) reviews this question, concluding that involuntary and semivoluntary functions are influenced in an indirect manner, being mediated by emotional arousal, and that there is no real "super" ability shown during hypnosis. The argument is more difficult, however, when more spectacular phenomena are discussed. Thompson (1970) puts the comparison well:

> I find it difficult to conceive of any simulator calmly undergoing an abdominal operation without an anesthetic, and I am further convinced that, if he does, he is no longer simulating. Once an individual learns how to use hypnosis no one can take this learning away from him. . . . For instance, if I have two burned hands, it is unlikely that I would accept a suggestion to utilize hypnosis to increase healing only on one of the hands. . . . In both clinical and laboratory situations the sophisticated subject utilizes only enough of his "hypnotic potential" to satisfy the needs of the moment. . . . For example, patients get apprehensive about one particular tooth which for unknown reasons has more significance to them than other teeth, and consequently go far more deeply into trance for that tooth because psychologically they have been conditioning themselves in addition to the cues of the operator. Their motivation determines their depth . . . it seems to me that there is an intensity in the clinical trance that is lacking in the experimental situation.

Others have made similar observations about the apparent difference in clinical and experimental hypnotic states, casting doubt on the adequacy of role-playing as a sole explanatory model. Pearson (1970) quotes a subject who said that in demonstrations of hypnosis she had to "erect a wall around herself" because she knew what people would impose upon her—sticking pins in her, for example, to prove it was "real" hypnosis. She did not have the feeling of being walled-in in the usual clinical trance to which she was accustomed.

Ernest Hilgard (1963) instructed 12 subjects to resist under hypnosis selected suggestions that they had previously performed in earlier hypnotic sessions. Thus, the subjects were asked to play the role of not being hypnotized for these selected tasks. One was unable to resist any of the tasks, 5 resisted one of the two items, and 6 were able to resist both. It seemed to the observer that even those who successfully resisted the hypnotic suggestions did so only with marked effort.

An interesting observation bearing on role-playing is that of Brady and Levitt (1964a), who suggest that the subjects who are told that they have no sense of smell may fail to respond to ammonia fumes, but those sophisticated subjects who know that ammonia also stimulates pain fibers (even in persons who have organically lost the ability to smell) may still repond. Thus, the prior knowledge of the subject affects how he interprets the hypnotic suggestions.

Barber (1964, 1967, 1969, 1970) has leaned heavily on the role-playing theory of hypnosis, though he emphasizes antecedent variables and variations in the situation of "hypnosis," particularly stressing motivational set and relation to the experimenter.

In his theoretical formulations of the phenomena of neurosis, Pierre Janet stressed the dissociability of the mind as a basic explanatory concept. Janet (1925) wrote of *idées fixes*, similar to the emotionally toned "complex" of Jung, Riklin, and Binswanger. He also spoke of the *abaissement du niveau mental*, a lowering in the functional level of the mind. Morton Prince (1929) echoed the dissociation emphasis of Janet, particularly in the study of multiple personality and hypnosis. William McDougall (1926) used similar terms but emphasized the possibility of a functional isolation of some neuronal areas from their usual contacts.

Today the dissociative theory of hypnosis is largely absorbed into the psychoanalytic literature.

Interpersonal Theories

In a sense, all psychological theories of hypnosis are interpersonal theories, including the psychoanalytic theories that also emphasize the unconscious substrates of interpersonal interaction. Smyth (1981) has emphasized hypnotic suggestibility as a type of social learning through cues that model behavior. Hunt (1979) views hypnosis as a state in which the subject gives up autonomy and relinquishes responsibility for his actions to the hypnotist, but maintaining responsibility to the hypnotist to perform as a hypnotic subject, as that role is continually defined by the hypnotherapist.

Frankel (1976) has clearly described how demand characteristics of the hypnotic situation are a major influence in hypnotic behavior, rather than the mere presence of hypnosis per se. Using a "resistant" instructor, as well as a compliant hypnotic instructor, Levitt and Baker (1983) showed the interactional social nature of hypnotic behavior.

PSYCHOANALYTIC THEORIES

Freud studied with both Charcot and with the school at Nancy, whose chief figures were Liebeault and Bernheim. Freud's first psychological work, *Studien über Hysterie*, was published in 1895 jointly with Josef Breuer, a Viennese physician who had found that hysterical patients would often improve after hypnotic trance. Freud's observations of the utility of hypnosis in such cases led him to describe the value of abreaction of traumatic events of the past, but his pessimism at the impermanence of the cures he produced stimulated his development of psychoanalytic theory.

In psychoanalysis, hypnosis is viewed primarily as a regressive phenomena in which the subject reacts to the hypnotherapist as he might to a significant figure of his past. Ernest Jones suggested the similarity of the hypnotic situation to the Oedipal model, while Sandor Ferenczi (1873–1933) saw it as a projection onto the hypnotist of the pre-Oedipal ambivalent feelings toward a powerful parent. Freud himself later likened the hypnotic state to the process of falling in love, in which many qualities are attributed to the "loved" object that are not founded in reality.

A more recent and far more sophisticated psychoanalytic view is that of Gill and Brenman (1959), who view hypnosis as the subject's "lending" of a subsystem of his or her ego to the temporary control of the hypnotist while the subject potentially is always able to revoke the dissociation of the ego functions and resume the normal waking state. Watkins (1963) has developed an effective technique of the "affect bridge" in which an emotion that is unpleasant in the present is intensified until it can act as a memory bridge to a previous traumatic event that involved the same emotion.

The interesting atavistic theory of the Australian psychiatrist Meares (1961), previously mentioned, is very close to the regression emphasis of the psychoanalytic theories. Meares suggests that normal mechanisms, such as role/playing and identification, assume under hypnosis a more primitive form. Meares has also introduced the technique of hypnoplasty, utilizing hypnosis to facilitate clay modeling as a means of externalizing unconscious processes.

Clinical evidence for a regressive model of hypnosis is furnished by the phenomena of hypnotic age regression. It has been found, however, that subjects making the Bender-Gestalt test under four conditions (awake, awake and pretending to be 4 years old, hypnotized and pretending to be 4, and hypnotically regressed to age 4) were noted by independent judges to comply to some degree with the regression (Crasilneck and Michael, 1957). They did not, however, seem to reach the actual age level that had been suggested in hypnotic age regression.

Schneck (1953) thus discussed transference feelings that may be accentuated in hypnosis or hyponanalysis. He cited tendencies of the patient to unconsciously respond to hypnosis "as if" it were a sexual situation, a parent–child relationship, or even as symbolic death.

Solovey and Milechnin (1957) have spoken of two types of hypnosis, "positive" and "negative." The positive state is thought of as corresponding to the peculiar emotional state experienced by the infant receiving the care of his or her mother. The negative state is thought to be based on "the authoritarian attitude of the parents." They define the degree of hypnosis as "the extent of retrogression to the psychology of early childhood which accomplishes the production of the hypnotic state." They suggest that everyone has been repeatedly "hypnotized" in the process of growing up.

Hypnoanalysis refers to the use of hypnosis in connection with other psychoanalytic techniques and is seen by Granone (1962) as being in contrast to the use of hypnosis as direct suggestion for symptom suppression and its use in "rational psychotherapy" to enhance ego strength.

Spiegel (1959) compares the similarity of the hypnotic state with the state of transference, both involving regression, but the hypnotic state differs in the intentionality with which it is actively structured by the therapist. The regression involved may cause some patients to feel guilty for relying on the therapist (Levitsky, 1962), which may induce resistance. Gruenewald (1971) discusses spontaneous transference in experimental subjects. Stein (1970) has suggested other sources of resistance, including the residue of older interpersonal interactions, seeing hypnosis as penance or as an equivalent of depression and also unacknowledged reluctance to change.

Sometimes material erupting spontaneously during hypnosis reveals underlying object relations (Klemperer, 1961). Fromm (1972b) has introduced a most useful concept of ego passivity or ego activity to describe various ego states induced during hypnosis. She carefully differentiates ego passivity and activity from their external behavioral counterparts.

Fromm and Hurt (1980) have suggested that hypnotic typology can be usefully described along three major axes: (1) primary process/secondary process; (2) whether the ego mode is active, passive, or receptive; and (3) reorganization of individual cognitive structures such as attention.

CONCLUSION

At the present stage of understanding of hypnotic phenomena, it may well be true that the only test for distinguishing the truly hypnotized subject from one who is simulating a trance are differences in the experience of the internal subjective state, a criterion that is open to all the difficulties of dealing with subjectivity. The differentiation then would essentially depend on the reliability of the subjective reporting. As physiological correlates of hypnosis can be defined, the question may become clearer. Recent work in biofeedback moves in this direction, but this work reopens the danger of the measured variable omitting all phenomena of a purely subjective nature. Josephine Hilgard (1970) agrees that a complete theory of hypnois would also deal with events in the brain and nervous system, but "such a complete theory is not available, at least not in a form to gain wide acceptance."

Since we have strong expectation in the mind–body unity of experience, we feel that any durable theory of hypnosis must relate the psychological and subjective factors with other, more measurable structural factors—hence our preference for *psychostructural* to describe the direction in which we feel the growth of a comprehensive theory of hypnosis will occur. "Structural" is deliberately left unspecified in our terminology since it is our belief that the structural aspects of hypnosis will eventually be found to have a similarity of gestalt, whether expressed in terms of neurophysiology, of interpersonal relationship, of psychoanalytic concepts, or other conceptual languages.

For example, almost all hypnosis induction techniques involve a situation in which the hypnotherapist is more active than the patient, giving verbal suggestions while the patient gives primarily nonverbal ideomotor responses. This gestalt of active hypnotherapist and passive subject is reflected in the regressive and atavistic theories, such as those of Ferenczi and Meares. In the Jungian psychoanalytic terminology, the same gestalt would obtain between the ego and the self (central archetype) as the center of both the psychic organization of the mind and the somatic organization of the body. The ego is more subjective recipient and the central archetype is the more comprehensive psychosomatic organization that originated, sustains, and modifies the particular ego state. A further similar subjective gestalt would be the experiences of the dream ego within the dream, an experience that is theoretically under the control of the central archetype as well. The seemingly real experiences of the dream ego within the dream are analogous to the positive and negative hallucinations that can be induced in a somnambulistic hyponotic subject under the influence of the hypnotherapist, who stands in relation to the hypnotized ego of the subject as the central archetype as dream-maker stands to the dream ego of sleep.

Another structural aspect that seems characteristic of the hypnotic state and those states related to it is that of trust. This is often alluded to in the older literature as "rapport" and can be considered similar to

Erik Erikson's "basic trust" as the first achievement of the developing ego. We have repeatedly had the experience of being able to induce deep hypnotic trance in persons who had been resistant to previous induction attempts when they had been tried by nontrained persons, often friends inappropriately using hypnosis as a parlor game stunt or stage hypnotists misappropriating hypnosis for supposed entertainment purposes. The difference in susceptibility in the serious medical situation and in the inappropriate situation seems to be one of trust of the subject in the integrity, competence, and well meaning of the hypnotherapist. The subject, trusting the situation, allows more modification in his or her ego and his or her physiology than in a situation he or she does not trust.

Two Levels of Psychostructural Theory

The progressive development of a psychostructural form of hypnotic theory will inevitably involve two distinct and separable conceptual levels. Nevertheless, in any measurable hypnotic state, clinical or experimental, these two levels will be inseparably intertwined. The levels are (1) the structure of the neurophysiological substrate, and (2) the structure of the dynamic psychological state involved in the hypnotic experience. These are analogous to (1) the hardware of a computer, and (2) the software programming.

Relation of the Levels

The relation of *Level I* (the organic neurophysiological substrate of brain functioning) is related to the hypnotic functioning at *Level II* (the psychological "state" of hypnosis) in the following manner: Level-I functioning is a necessary but not sufficient condition for the emergence of Level II; interference with Level I can destroy the hypnotic state at Level II; Level I exerts a permissive influence on Level II, but the specific contents of the Level II hypnotic state depend for their specifity upon the psychological structure of the therapist/subject dyad; Level II can exert some influence through Level I, upon the neurophysiological substrate itself.

It will be helpful to add a few specific remarks about the connection of the interaction of Level I and Level II with the general nature of hypnotic observation.

Level-I functioning is a necessary but not a sufficient condition for the emergence of Level II hypnotic phenomena. In its most trivial form, this statement simply asserts that psychological functioning cannot be known to occur in the absence of brain functioning. It is metaphysically possible that "mind" can exist in the absence of brain, but there is at present no empirical observation that can establish the validity of such an assertion. What can be observed is that there is no evident presence of "mind" without a sufficient presence of brain functioning, although our 1962 observation shows how close to the cessation of brain functioning at death one can still elicit hypnotic responses. A more complex form of this statement is that certain neurophysiological functions must take place for there to be a psychological state of hypnosis (allowing for various levels or "penetrance" of the hypnotic state). What are these neurophysiological functions? At present, they remain largely unknown, although there are a few observations that suggest that direct stimulation of the hippocampus or the thalamus can interrupt the hypnotic state, perhaps through effects on the reticular activating system (Crasilneck, McCranie, and Jenkins, 1956; Crasilneck and Hall, 1962; Kroger, 1977; Stewart and Crasilneck, 1984). These admittedly rare observations nevertheless establish the second premise: Interference with Level I can destroy the hypnotic state at Level II.

Level I exerts a permissive influence on Level II, but the specific contents of the Level-II hypnotic state depend for their specificity upon the psychological structure of the therapist/subject dyad. The neurophysiological substrate of Level I is a necessary but not a sufficient condition for the psychological functionings of the hypnotic state, which are more finely determined by the unconscious or tacit psychological structure of the subject. Questions of psychological structure must be couched in theoretical language and are therefore open to more controversy than the neurophysiological observations of Level I, although such Level-II observations are much more readily available to direct observation in many clinical and experimental settings. Such constructions as Orne's *trance logic* as a distortion of perception of memory (Orne 1980) or the emphasis of Fromm and Hurt on an ego activity/passivity spectrum are immensely useful in hypnotic theory but rest fundamentally upon observations that are open to alternate interpretation. This vulnerability is true of much hypnotic conceptualization, including more recently the eye-roll sign of hypnotizability and the long-established Stanford scales of hypnotic susceptibility.

We do not propose at this stage of controversy to settle such deep questions of the psychological Level-II structure of hypnosis, which must wait upon extended experimentation, observation, and discussion. Still, we would strongly affirm that there will eventually emerge a consensus on the psychological structure of the basic hypnotic interaction to which clinicians of various theoretical persuasions—

Freudian, Jungian, and eclectic—can assent without compromise of their own deeply held convictions about the nature of the psyche. It is possible, however, to discern several likely directions of Level-II developments.

DIRECTIONS OF LEVEL-II CONCEPTUALIZATION

There are several directions that are likely to emerge in development of future integrations of Level II theories of hypnosis:

1. The hypnotic interaction permits de-integration of the usual ego states (or ego images) in a safe interaction guided by the therapist.
2. Such de-integration permits the emergence during hypnosis of various dissociated and repressed relational structures involving both an identity of the ego and an identity of a significant other person.
3. All hypnotic phenomena are interactive with the therapist, so that any "state" characteristics of hypnosis must be related to the interactive dyad of patient/therapist, which will become a new focus of investigation.

What is ordinarily experienced as the waking personality, the ego, is actually a composite of many different ego-other models, many of which can be seen in dream material, in hypnoanalytic revivifications of past events, or in various projective techniques. In usual waking interaction, the waking-ego must represent all of these ego states that are constellated, even though some are contradictory, leading to ambivalence. The waking-ego cannot afford to relax its integrative role, but such a role can be safely and temporarily abandoned in a hypnotic state that is defined as safe because of reliance on a trusted therapist. The therapist can then guide the hypnotic experience of ego states, which are only tacitly present in the experience and awareness of the waking-ego. Since what is actually repressed or dissociated seems to be models of relation between an ego-identity and a significant other person, the emergence of such states in hypnosis may produce unforeseen transference distortions of the therapist–patient interaction. Therefore, such hypnotic dissociation should be initiated only by therapists who are competent to treat the transference distortions that may arise, whether such distortions are positive or negative in emotional tone. The dyadic interaction of subject and therapist will eventually be studied; at present there are largely anecdotal observations, such as the therapist entering a light state of hypnosis along with the subject or the occasional and rare phenomenon of telepathy that seems to occur between patient and therapist.

We anticipate that eventually techniques of research in the central nervous system will permit an extension of psychostructural theory in terms of neurophysiology. The waking brain, with which the ordinary ego state of waking consciousness is associated, relies for consciousness on the brain-stem structures, including the thalamic connections and projections onto the cortex of the reticular-activating system. Perhaps it will eventually be possible to define with some precision a similar gestalt in terms of anatomical and functional units of the brain. In the present state of the art of hypnosis, an overelaboration of theory is not, in our opinion, a useful undertaking. The considerations implied in the schematic of *psychostructural* will provide useful orientation for clinical practice and theoretical observation.

REFERENCES

Aaronson BS: Hypnosis in experimental psychology. Am J Clin Hypn 2:12–15, 1968

Akstein D: The induction of hypnosis in the light of reflexology. Am J Clin Hypn 7:281–300, 1965

Alexander L: Conditional reflexes as related to hypnosis and hypnotic techniques. Am J Clin Hypn 10:157–159, 1968

Alexander L: Hypnotically induced hallucinations. Am J Clin Hypn 15:66, 1971

Arnold MB: Brain function in hypnosis. Int J Clin Exp Hypn 7-109–119, 1959

Barber J: The management of chronic pain. Presented at the Second Ericksonian Congress, Dallas, Texas, 1982

Barber TX: Hypnotizability, suggestibility and personality. V. A critical review of research findings. Psychol Rep 14:299–320, 1964

Barber TX: Reply to Conn and Conn's "discussion of Barber's 'hypnosis as a causal variable . . . '." Int J Clin Exp Hypn 15:111–117, 1967

Barber TX: Hypnosis: A Scientific Approach. New York, Van Nostrand Reinhold, 1969

Barber TX: Marihuana, Yoga and Hypnosis. Chicago, Aldine-Atherton, 1970

Barber TX: Suggested ("hypnotic") behavior. The trance paradigm versus an alternative paradigm, in Fromm E, Shor R (eds): Hypnosis: Research Developments and Perspectives. Chicago, Aldine-Atherton, 1972, pp 115–182

Bartlett EE: Hypnosis and communications. J Am Med Wom Assoc 21:662–665, 1966

Bartlett EE: A proposed definition of hypnosis with a theory of its mechanism of action. Am J Clin Hypn 2:69–73, 1968

Bigelow N, Cameron GH, Koroljow SA: Two cases of deep hypnotic sleep investigated by the strain gauge plethysmograph. J Clin Exp Hypn 4:160–164, 1956

Brady JP, Levitt EE: Hypnotically induced "anosmia" to ammonia. Int J Clin Exp Hypn 12:18–20, 1964a

Brady JP, Levitt EE: Nystagmus as a criterion of hypnotically induced visual hallucinations. Science 146:85–86, 1964b

Breuer J, Freud S: Studies in Hysteria. New York, Basic Books, 1957

Chapman LF, Goodell H, Wolff NG: Changes in tissue vulnerability induced during hypnotic suggestion. J. Psychosom Res 4:99, 1959

Chertok L: Early theories of hypnosis, in Burrows GD, Dennerstein L (eds): Handbook of Hypnosis and Psychosomatic Medicine. Amsterdam, Elsevier/North-Holland Biomedical Press, 1980, pp 1–11.

Chertok L: Psychoanalysis and hypnotic theory: Comments on five case histories. Am J Clin Hypn 25:209–224, 1983

Conn JA: Hypno-synthesis: Hypnosis as a unifying interpersonal experience. J Nerv Ment Dis 109:9, 1949

Corn-Becker F, Welch L, Fisischelli V: Conditioning factors underlying hypnosis. J Abnorm Soc Psychol 44:212–222, 1959

Crasilneck HB, Hall JA: Physiological changes associated with hypnosis: A review of the literature since 1948. Int J Clin Exp Hypn 7:9–50, 1959

Crasilneck HB, Hall JA: Blood pressure and pulse rates in neutral hypnosis. Int J Clin Exp Hypn 8:137–139, 1960

Crasilneck HB, Hall JA: The use of hypnosis with unconscious patients. Int J Clin Exp Hypn 10:141–144, 1962

Crasilneck HB, McCranie EJ, Jenkins MT: Special indications for hypnosis as a method of anesthesia. JAMA 162:1606–1608, 1956

Crasilneck HB, Michael C: Performance on the bender under hypnotic age regression. J Abnorm Soc Psychol 54:319, 1957

Damacer EC, Shor RE, Orne MT: Physiological effects during hypnotically requested emotions. Psychosom Med 25:334–343, 1963

Das JP: The Pavlovian theory of hypnosis: An evaluation. J Ment Sci 104:82–90, 1958

Das JP: A theory of hypnosis. Int J Clin Exp Hypn 7:69–77, 1959

De Moraes Passos AS: Reflections on hypnosis and the reticular system of the brain stem. Hypnosis and Psychosomatic Medicine. New York, Springer-Verlag, 1967, pp 228–232

DeShazer S: On transforming symptoms: An approach to an Ericksonian procedure. Am J Clin Hypn 22:17–28, 1979

Dittborn JM, O'Connell DN: Behavioral sleep, physiological sleep and hypnotizability. Int J Clin Exp Hypn 15:181–188, 1967

Edmonston WE: Stimulus-response theory of hypnosis, in Gordon JE (ed): Handbook of Clinical and Experimental Hypnosis. New York, Macmillan, 1967, pp 345–387

Edmonston WE: Hypnosis and electrodermal responses. Am J Clin Hypn 11:16–25, 1968

Edmonston WE Jr: Neutral hypnosis as relaxation. Am J Clin Hypn 20:69–75, 1977

Erickson MH: Hypnosis in painful terminal illness. Am J Clin Hypn 1:117–121, 1958

Erickson MH: Acquired control of pupillary responses. Am J Clin Hypn 3:207–208, 1965

Erickson MH: Control of physiological functions by hypnosis. Am J Clin Hypnosis 20:8–19, 1977a

Erickson MH: Hypnotic approaches to therapy. Am J Clin Hypn 20:1–7, 1977b

Erickson MH: The interspersal hypnotic technique for symptom correction and pain control, in Barber J, Adrian C (eds): Psychological Approaches to the Management of Pain. New York, Brunner/Mazel, 1982, pp 100–117

Erickson MH, Rossi EL: Varieties of double bind. Am J Clin Hypn 17:143–157, 1975

Erickson MH, Rossi EL: Two level communication and the microdynamics of trance and suggestion. Am J Clin Hypn 18:153–171, 1976

Erickson MH, Rossi EL, Rossi SI: Hypnotic Realities. New York, Irvington, 1976

Evans FJ, Orne MT: The disappearing hypnotist: The use of stimulating subjects to evaluate how subjects perceive experimental procedures. Int J Clin Exp Hypn 19:277–296, 1971

Frankel F: Hypnosis: Trance as a Coping Mechanism. New York, Plenum, 1976

Fromm E: Quo vadis hypnosis: Predictions of future trends in hypnosis research, in Fromm E, Shor RE (eds): Hypnosis: Research Developments and Perspectives. Chicago, Aldine-Atherton, 1972a, p 583

Fromm, E: Ego activity and ego passivity in hypnosis. Int J Clin Exp Hypn 20:238–251, 1972b

Fromm E, Hurt S: Ego-psychological parameters of hypnotic and other altered states of consciousness, in Burrow GD, Dennerstein L (eds): Handbook of Hypnosis and Psychosomatic Medicine. Amsterdam, Elsevier/North-Holland Biomedical Press, 1980, pp 13–27

Gill MM, Brenman M: Hypnosis and related states: Psychoanalytic studies and regression. New York, International Universities Press, 1959

Gladfelter JH, Hall JA: The relationship of hypnotic phenomena to conditioning. Tex Rep Biol Med 20:53–60, 1962

Goodman ED, Griffin AN: Erickson annotated, disentangling the yarn. Presented at the Second Ericksonian Congress, Dallas, Texas, 1982

Gorton BE: The physiology of hypnosis. I. Psychiatr Q 23:317–343, 1949a

Granone F: L'ipnotismo come fenomeno biologico, mezzo di indagine e strumento terapeutico. Torino, Italy, Boringhiere, 1962

Granone F: Tratti Di Ipnosi (Sofrologia) (Treatise of Hypnosis-Sophrology.) Torino, Boringhieri, 1972

Gravitz MA, Gravitz RF: The collected writings of Milton H. Erickson: A complete bibliography 1929–1977. Am J Clin Hypn 20:84–94, 1977

Gravitz MA, Kramer MF: A study of some factors associated with hypnotic-like experience. Am J Clin Hypn 10:48–51, 1967

Gruenewald D: Transference and countertransference in hypnosis. Int J Clin Exp Hypn 19:71–82, 1971

Gruenewald D: Some thoughts on the distinction between the hypnotic situation and the hypnotic condition. Am J Clin Hypn 25:46–51, 1982

Haley J: Uncommon Therapy: The Psychiatric Techniques of Milton H. Erickson, M.D. New York: W.W. Norton, 1973

Hammond DC: Myths about Erickson and Ericksonian hypnosis. Presented at the 26th Annual Meeting of the American Society of Clinical Hypnosis, Dallas, Texas, 1983

Hilgard ER: Ability to resist suggestions within the hypnotic state, responsiveness to conflicting communication. Psychol Rep 12:3–13, 1963

Hilgard ER: Individual diffrences in hypnotizability, in Gordon JE (ed): Handbook of Clinical and Experimental Hypnosis. New York, MacMillan, 1967

Hilgard JR: Personality and Hypnosis: A Study of Imaginative Involvement. Chicago, University of Chicago Press, 1970

Horvai I: Hypnosi v le karst vi [Hypnosis in medicine]. Praha statni zdravotnicke nakeadate-lstvi, 1959. Am J Clin Hypn 2:167–168, 1960

Hoskovec J: A review of some major works in Soviet hypnotherapy. Int J Clin Exp Hypn 15:1–10, 1967

Hull C: Hypnosis and Suggestibility. New York, Appleton-Century, 1933

Hunt, SM: Hypnosis as obedience behavior. Br J Soc Clin Psychol 18:21–27, 1979

Jana H: Energy metabolism in hypnotic trance and sleep. J Appl Physiol 20:308–310, 1965

Jana H, Pattie S: Biochemical changes in blood during hypnotic trance. Ind J Med Res 53:1000–1002, 1965

Janet P: Psychological Healing. New York, Macmillan, 1925

Klemperer E: Primary object-relationships as revealed in hypnoanalysis. Int J Clin Exp Hypn 9:3–11, 1961

Kraines SH: Hypnosis: Physiologic inhibition and excitation. Psychosomatics 10:36–41, 1969

Kroger WS: Clinical and Experimental Hypnosis (ed 2). Philadelphia, J. B. Lippincott Co., 1977, pp 146–155.

Kubie LS, Margolin S: The process of hypnotism and the nature of the hypnotic state. Am J Psychiatry 100:613–619, 1944

Lerner M: Electroencefalograma e hipnosis. Acta Hipno Latinoamericana 4:35–41, 1963.

Levitsky A: Guilt, self-criticism and hypnotic induction. Am J Clin Hypn 5:127–130, 1962

Levitt E, Baker E: The hypnotic relationship—another look at coercion, compliance, and resistance: A brief communication. Int J Clin Exp Hypn 31:125–131, 1983

Levitt EE, Brady JP: Psychophysiology of hypnosis, in Schneck JM (ed): Hypnosis in Modern Medicine (ed 3). Springfield, Ill., Charles C Thomas, 1963, pp 314–362

Levitt EE, den Breeijen A, Persky H: The induction of clinical anxiety by means of a standardized hypnotic technique. Am J Clin Hypn 2:206–214, 1960

Lieberson WT, Smith RW, Stern MA: Experimental studies of the prolonged "hypnotic withdrawal" in the guinea pig. J Neuropsychiatry 3:28–34, 1961

Ludwig AM: The trance. Compr Psychiatry 8:7–15, 1968

McCranie EJ, Crasilneck HB, Tetter HR: The electroencephalogram in hypnotic age regression. Psychiatr Q 29:85–88, 1955

McDougall W: Outline of Abnormal Psychology. New York, Scribners, 1926

Marmer MJ: Hypnosis in Anesthesiology. Springfield, Ill., Charles C Thomas, 1959, p 20

Meares A: The atavistic theory of hypnosis in relation to yoga and pseudo trance states. Proceedings of the Third World Congress of Psychiatry, Montreal, 1:712–714, 1961

Moore M: Ericksonian theories of hypnosis. Am J Clin Hypn 24:183–184, 1982

Orne MT: The nature of hypnosis: Artifact and essence. J Abnorm Soc Psychol 58:277–299, 1959

Orne MT: The simulation of hypnosis: Why, how and what it means. Int J Clin Exp Hypn 19:183–210, 1971

Orne MT: On the stimulating subject as a quasi-control group in hypnosis research: What, why and how, in Fromm E, Shor SE (eds): Hypnosis: Research, Development, and Perspectives. Chicago, Aldine-Atherton, 1972, p 400

Orne MT: On the construct of hypnosis: How its definition affects research and its clinical application, in Burrow GD, Dennerstein L (eds): Handbook of Hypnosis and Psychosomatic Medicine. Amsterdam, Elsevier/North-Holland Biomedical Press, 1980, pp 29–51

Pearson RE: Clinical and experimental trance: What's the difference? Am J Clin Hypn 13:1–2, 1970

Pearson RE: Helping people with pain. Presented at the Second Ericksonian Congress, Dallas, Texas, 1982

Peters JE, Stern RM: Peripheral skin temperature and vasomotor response during hypnotic induction. Int J Clin Exp Hypn 21:102–108, 1973

Prince M: Clinical and Experimental Studies in Personality. Cambridge, Sci-Art, 1929

Raginsky BB: Discussion, in Kline MV (ed): The Nature of Hypnosis. New York, Institute for Research in Hypnosis, 1962, pp 94–96

Raikov VL: Theoretical substantiation of deep hypnosis. Am J Clin Hypn 18:23–27, 1975

Reid A, Curtsinger G: Physiological changes associated with hypnosis: The affect of hypnosis on temperature. J Clin Exp Hypn 16:111–119, 1968

Reyher J: Brain mechanisms, intrapsychic processes in behavior: A theory of hypnosis and psychopathology. Am J Clin Hypn 7:107–119, 1964

Roberts DR: An electrophysiological theory of hypnosis. Int J Clin Exp Hypn 8:43–53, 1960

Rodger BP: Vehicle of comfort. Presented at the Second Ericksonian Congress, Dallas, Texas, 1982

Rosen S: Ericksonian hypnotherapy simplified. Presented at the Second Ericksonian Congress, Dallas, Texas, 1982

Rossi EL: Hypnosis and ultradian cycles: A new state(s) theory of hypnosis. Am J Clin Hypn 25:21–32, 1984

Roth B: Narkolepsie und Hypersommie. Berlin, Veb Verlag Volk und Gesundheit, 1962

Sanders S: An exploration of utilization techniques in short-term hypnotherapy. Am J Clin Hypn 20:76–79, 1977

Sarbin TR, Coe WC: Hypnotic Behavior: The Psychology of Influence Communication. New York, Holt, Rinehart & Winston, 1972

Sarbin TR, Lim DT: Some evidence in support of the role-taking hypothesis in hypnosis. Int J Clin Exp Hypn 11:98–103, 1963

Schneck J: Hypnosis in psychiatry, in Schneck J (ed): Hypnosis on Modern Medicine (ed 1). Springfield, Ill., Charles C Thomas, 1953, p 151

Schneck JM: Discussion of A Meares, "An atavistic theory of hypnosis," in Kline MV, Wolberg LR (eds): The Nature of Hypnosis: Contemporary Theoretical Approaches. New York, Postgraduate Center for Psychotherapy and the Institute for Research in Hypnosis, 1962, pp 97–100.

Schwartz BE, Bickford RG, Rasmussen WC: Hypnotic phenomena, including hypnotically activated seizures, studied with the electroencephalogram. J Nerv Ment Dis 122:564–574, 1955

Sheehan PW: A methodological analysis of the simulating techniques. Int J Clin Exp Hypn 19:83–99, 1971

Smyth LD: Towards a social learning theory of hypnosis: I. Hypnotic suggestibility. Am J Clin Hypn 23:147–68, 1981

Solovey G, Milechnin A: Hypnosis in everyday life. Dis Nerv Syst 28:1–7, 1957

Spiegel H: Hypnosis and transferance, a theoretical formulation. AMA Arch Gen Psychiatry 1:634–639, 1959

Spiegel H: Hypnosis: An adjunct to psychotherapy, in Freedman AM, Kaplan HI (eds): Comprehensive Textbook of Psychiatry. Baltimore, Williams & Wilkins, 1967, pp 1228–1233

Spiegel H: Eye-roll levitation method. Manual for Hypnotic Induction Profile. New York, Soni Medica, 1974

Stein C: Trance, transference and countertransference in the restrictive patient. Am J Clin Hypn 12:213–221, 1970

Stewart RM, Crasilneck HB: Neurophysiology of hypnosis interruption of the trance state following thalamic stimulation. Am J Clin Hypn, 1984, (in press)

Stricherz ME: Social influence, Ericksonian strategies and hypnotic phenomena. Am J Clin Hpyn 24:211–218, 1982

Strosberg IM, Irwen M, Vics II: Physiologic changes in the eye during hypnosis. Am J Clin Hypn 4:264–267, 1962

Thompson KF: Clinical and experimental trance: Yes, there is a diffrence. Am J Clin Hypn 13:1–5, 1970

Thompson KF: Language of hypnosis. Presented at the Second Ericksonian Congress, Dallas, Texas, 1982

Timney BN, Barber TX: Hypnotic induction and oral temperature. Int J Clin Exp Hypn 17:121–132, 1969

Tributes to Erickson. Am J Clin Hypn 20:1–7, 1977

Vanderhoof E, Clancy J: Effect of emotion on blood flow. J Appl Physiol 17:67–70, 1962

Vics II: Observable physical phenomena in the eye under hypnosis. Am J Optom
    39:362–366, 1962
Volgyesi FA: The recent neuro-psychiatric and bio-morphologic justifications of hypno-
    therapeutic empiricism. Br J Med Hypno 2:6–25, 1950
Watkins JD: Psychodynamics of hypnotic induction and termination, in Schneck JM (ed):
    Hypnosis in Modern Medicine (ed 3). Springfield, Ill., Charles C Thomas, 1963, pp
    365–389
Weitzenhoffer AM: Hypnotism: An Objective Study in Suggestibility. New York, John
    Wiley & Sons, 1953
Weitzenhoffer AM: The nature of hypnosis. Ii. Am J Clin Hypn 6:40–72, 1964
Weitzenhoffer AM: Behavior therapeutic technique and hypnotherapeutic methods. Am
    J Clin Hypn 15:71–82, 1972
West LJ: Psychophysiology of hypnosis. JAMA 172:672–675, 1960
White RW: A preface to a theory of hypnotism. J Abnorm Soc Psychol 36:477–506, 1941
Williams GW: Highway hypnosis: An hypothesis. Int J Clin Exp Hypn 11:143–151, 1963
Wolberg LR: Medical Hypnosis. The Principles of Hypnotherapy, vol 1, New York,
    Grune & Stratton, 1948, p 82
Wolberg LR: Forward, in Kline MV, Wolberg LR: The Nature of Hypnosis: Contem-
    porary Theoretical Approaches. New York, Postgraduate Center for Psychotherapy
    and the Institute for Research in Hypnosis, 1962, pp 6–8
Wolpe J: The systematic desensitization treatment of neurosis. J Nerv Ment Dis
    132:189–203, 1961
Zeig JK: Symptom prescription and Ericksonian principles of hypnosis and psycho-
    therapy. Am J Clin Hypn 23:16–22, 1980
Zikmund V: Some physiological characteristics of natural and hypnotic sleep in man.
    Physiol Bohemoslov 13:196–201, 1964
Zimbardo P, Maslach C, Marshall G: Hypnosis and the psychology of cognitive and
    behavioral control, in Fromm E, Shor RE (eds): Hypnosis: Research Developments
    and Perspectives. Chicago, Aldine-Atherton, 1972, pp 539–571

3
Screening for Hypnosis

Each of our patients who is considered for hypnosis has one psychiatric interview for "screening." This interview is primarily designed to screen out those for whom hypnosis might be contraindicated. These would include persons suffering from most psychoses, particularly paranoid types with ideas of influence, and would also include depressed patients with suicidal ideation. Some individuals may be inappropriately asking for hypnosis when other forms of treatment are indicated. The latter group might include patients whose symptoms are likely to be the result of an organic condition that requires medical or surgical treatment.

The screening interview is also used to assess the psychodynamic meaning, if any, of the symptom, so that before hypnosis is undertaken, there is some understanding of the possible symbolic meanings of the presenting complaint. Several questions are considered in the screening assessment.

Why does the patient come for treatment at this time? If the symptom has been present for several years, with no exacerbation or change, why has the patient chosen to come now? In general, if the patient comes for treatment soon after the onset of the symptom, his or her motivation is high and there is a greater chance for successful treatment. We have consistently found that those who have delayed in asking for treatment are more likely to require longer periods of therapy and may offer greater resistance to change.

Who sent the patient and did he or she decide on treatment himself or herself? Although it is our practice to see only patients sent by referral, it frequently seems that the actual desire for hypnotherapy comes from the patient himself or herself or from a relative or friend who has had successful treatment. The patient often has asked the family physician for the referral. Motivation in such cases is usually good. In some instances, however, the person coming for therapy is not well motivated and is responding only to pressure from someone else, a physician or a spouse in many cases. When the patient does not have a personal motivation, hypnotherapy is likely to be less successful.

In recent years some of the most motivated and successful candidates for hypnotherapy have been physicians, dentists, and psychologists who have seen for themselves the successful treatment of patients whom they had referred. Doubtless this observation increased their own motivation and acceptance of hypnotherapy as a treatment modality.

Is the patient sufficiently motivated to give up his or her symptom? Some symptoms are "empty habits," having no strong hidden unconscious meaning. These are more readily removed by hypnosis without high risk of substitute symptoms being formed. Cigarette smoking is a common example. It may have originally been a form of defiance against parental authority or an attempt to identify with a more "adult" image, but through the years smoking may have become a mere repetitive habit.

At times, however, the symptom may indeed have a hidden meaning. This hidden meaning may be either an unconscious and symbolic process or a more conscious but unconfessed interpersonal conflict. For example, the woman with orgasmic dysfunction may unconsciously be avoiding orgasm during intercourse to assuage guilt feelings arising from excessive superego inhibitions. Alternately, she may be using her lack of orgasmic response to express conscious anger that is being suppressed. It may be necessary in such cases to treat the meaning of the chief complaint before successful symptom removal is possible.

Is the symptom being used to manipulate others? An enuretic child who has no organic urinary problem may have fallen into the pattern of emotionally dominating the family with his or her symptom, so that all trips, all family outings, even the primary topic of conversation can be his or her bed-wetting. Many times this symptom responds rapidly when the enuresis interferes with something that the child wants more than he or she wants the attention of the family. If a manipulative symptom is discovered during screening, it may be possible to increase the patient's motivation to lose the symptomatic behavior or to shift the family balance so that the symptom no longer has such marked secondary gain.

Is the symptom organic or psychogenic? Although hypnosis may be effective for either organic or psychogenic symptoms, it is important to assess clearly whether a symptom comes from an organic pathologic condition, whether it is symbolic and psychogenic, or a combination. If there is uncertainty about organic causes, the patient may underdo further medical, dental, or psychological examination before hypnosis is utilized.

What is the patient's degree of impulsivity and what is his or her level of frustration tolerance? Hypnotherapy attempts to rapidly alter the internal checks and balances of the patient's mind, shifting conflict situations toward a more healthy resolution by enhancing healthy impulses while diminishing and minimizing those that tend toward a pathologic state. When such a dramatic and direct approach is attempted, it is important to have carefully assessed the stability of the patient in terms of impulsivity and frustration tolerance. Even if a habit is "empty," no longer carrying unconscious meanings, there is still a certain element of inertia; for example, the would-be-dieter who "finds" candy in her mouth, "but I don't remember reaching for it." If there is a past history of being able to control impulses and tolerate the resultant frustration, we feel that it is more reasonable to push for rapid and marked change. If there is a history of poor frustration tolerance and lack of impulse control, we often discuss the problem with the patient before hypnosis so that the patient is made aware of the need to also utilize some degree of conscious effort to achieve the desired change.

What is the patient's general personality and history? As in any psychiatric evaluation, an assessment is made of the patient's past history, family history, and medical history as well as a detailed mental status examination with some questions specifically chosen for hypnotic screening. During this survey we look for any indicators of instability in the patient's family life, work, and personal fantasy life. The patient's system of values is briefly explored with such questions as "Please tell me the best and the worst thing you have ever done." We also assess recent, recurrent, and childhood dreams as well as the earliest memories of childhood. During the formal mental status examination, proverb interpretations are used to check for looseness of association and the ability to think abstractly and also to gain some idea of the various points of view from which the patient understands the proverb, thus indicating some measures of his or her intelligence and ego strength.

MISCONCEPTIONS OF HYPNOSIS

The screening interview also is used to give the patient a positive set for the coming experience of hypnosis. We inquire about any past experience with hypnosis and attempt to correct any misconceptions and diminish any fears that might have been generated by improper nonclinical uses of hypnosis. Some persons are afraid that they will be asked to do ridiculous things, as they may have seen in a stage performance; they are told that there will be nothing of this sort in a serious clinical use of trance.

Patients who have not experienced hypnosis themselves, but have formed an impression of it from movies, television, or novels, are reassured that it is not a coercive Svengali-like "control" of the subject by the hypnotherapist. Rather, they are informed that it is very similar in many ways to the normal state of mind one experiences each night just before falling asleep, a state in which the body is extremely relaxed and the mind free of anxiety. Yet, hypnosis is actually different from such a presleep state because the therapist takes responsibility for focusing the patient's mind, whereas in the presleep state the mind drifts from image to image. The constant input of verbal suggestions from the therapist helps focus the patient's attention. In a sense, the therapist is the guardian who holds the situation in a steady state and allows the subject to safely regress into the unusual "trance" state of mind.

Since many misconceptions exist in the lay mind about the nature of the hypnotic experience, it is often helpful to answer most questions during the screening interview. Unspoken expectations regarding hypnosis, if at variance with the initial experience of induction, may produce unnecessary resistance to entering a trance state.

The usual questions that may be asked are (Crasilneck, 1980):

Can everyone be hypnotized?   No, but most people can enter at least a light state of hypnosis. In fact, most persons have already experienced a state of consciousness similar to hypnosis, but may not have defined it as such. Imaginal involvement in movies or novels can resemble the hypnotic state, as can the deep state of relaxation that just precedes falling asleep.

Can I be forced to do something against my will while in hypnosis? No. A person asked to do something against his or her principles will simply come out of the trance state. There is no conclusive experimental or clinical evidence that hypnosis can be used against a person's own moral principles.

Is it dangerous to be hypnotized? The use of hypnosis by qualified professionals is not dangerous and can be beneficial. The use of hypnosis by unqualified persons can produce difficulty in some cases, since untrained persons will not sufficiently understand complications that can arise.

If I do not wish to give up my symptom can I get well? A person with a psychodynamic symptom may have strongly mixed feelings. Part of the personality may wish to relinquish the symptom, while another part may cling to it. Hypnotherapy, in skilled hands, can often alter this balance in favor of the restoration of health.

Is it possible that I will not go into a deep trance? Yes. Not everyone enters deep levels of hypnotic trance. Some persons experience deep trance on the first induction, others after repeated inductions. Some subjects experience only a light trance, with feelings of relaxation and well-being but have complete memory for all that transpires. There is, however, no consistent correlation between depth of trance and clinical results for many types of problems, so that even in light trance significant improvement may take place.

Will I be sound asleep? A person in deep hypnosis will experience a sense of lapsed time just as a person who awakens from sleep. More subjects will experience lighter states of trance, at least initially. It is not unusual for a subject to pass in and out of deeper states, so that part of the hypnotic experience is remembered while other parts are not. If a subject in hypnosis feels that he or she is "going to sleep," they should let that happen since there is little subjective difference in the experience of going more deeply into hypnosis or in falling into natural sleep.

Will I know what is happening or will I be unconscious? That will depend upon the level of trance, which may fluctuate. A part of the subject's mind always knows what is happening whether it is consciously remembered or not.

Can I be hypnotized if I have had little education? There is little connection between education level or intelligence and the ability to be hypnotized. Hypnosis relies upon the ability to vividly experience the imagination.

Is it possible I will not awaken from hypnosis? No. A number of studies have shown that in such rare circumstances the hypnotized person comes out of the trance state or passes into natural sleep and then awakens.

MOTIVATING THE PATIENT TO A SUCCESSFUL RESPONSE

After misconceptions are removed, we try to consciously motivate the patient and produce an expectation of positive results. With smokers we quote the statistics about the success rate of treatment. We are careful not to promise cure reminding the patient that there is no certain way to know beforehand if he or she will fall in the successful or unsuccessful category.

Such attempts at conscious motivation and suggestion for success may produce some of the same effects as hypnosis and are often called "waking suggestion." In an experimental situation it would be important to control for such waking suggestion so that the relative effectiveness of hypnosis would be more evident. In a clinical practice, however, we feel strongly that increasing the patient's chances for success takes precedence over the isolation and study of treatment variables.

If the patient passes the screening interview, an appointment is made for the first hypnotic induction. Those few who are judged unsuitable for hypnosis are told in general terms why such a decision seemed necessary and are referred for whatever treatment is appropriate. In emergency cases, the screening process may be greatly abbreviated, and in some terminal patients it is selectively omitted.

REFERENCES

Crasilneck HB: Clinical assessment and preparation of the patient, in Burrows GD, Dennerstein L (eds): Handbook of Hypnosis and Psychosomatic Medicine. Amsterdam, Elsevier/North-Holland Biomedical Press, 1980, pp 105–113

4
Techniques of Hypnosis

MOTIVATION FOR HYPNOSIS

One of the most important factors in the success of hypnotherapy is the patient's unconscious motivation, which may be more important than "depth" of trance (von Dedenroth, 1962; Estabrooks and May, 1965). Patients themselves cannot assess this, nor can the therapist, before there is an actual trial of hypnosis. The various tests of suggestibility, such as postural sway or hand clasping, may not correlate with clinical effectiveness of the trance state.

When the patients' conscious and unconscious motivation are both high, success in hypnotherapy is most likely. A 25-year-old male stutterer with such high motivation came for his appointments in spite of inclement weather, business pressures, and his living a considerable distance from our offices. He had been seen previously by speech therapists without success. The psychiatrist who referred him had treated him for 6 months without improvement in the patient's speech. He sometimes stuttered for a full minute before being able to complete a simple sentence. He had decided never to marry, feeling that his children would have difficulty learning to speak clearly. He was, as one might expect, a good hypnotic subject, entering a somnambulistic state during the first session. After 6 months of treatment his speech impediment was greatly improved; the patient himself estimated that it was 90 percent better. During the course of treatment he gained excellent insight into his emotional problems. Sessions were then reduced to once a month, and he terminated treatment at the end of the year. His speech was normal. He has since married, is working successfully, and is the father of two children.

What the patient says or thinks before the first induction does not necessarily correlate well with the subsequent effectiveness of hypnosis. Another stutterer, a 19-year-old student, was "sent by my parents" for treatment. She did state, however, that she came willing to cooperate, but when asked about her own desire to speak more clearly, she said, "My boyfriend thinks stuttering is cute." In spite of her consciously expressed desire to cooperate, she was a poor hypnotic subject and discontinued treatment after five visits without improvement.

There are patients whose conscious resistance to hypnosis overlies a strong unconscious desire to cooperate. This is frequently seen in the case of cigarette smokers, often sent for hypnosis by their physicians when emphysema or coronary disease is diagnosed. Many of these smokers admit that they do not consciously wish to stop smoking. They enjoy cigarettes and frequently express doubt about their ability to be hypnotized. Perhaps 50 percent of the smokers whom we have seen are of this type. Such conscious ambivalence and resistance, however, has not seemed to decrease their successful response to hypnotherapy.

We have often observed clinically that unconscious motivation and hypnotic susceptibility increase with the severity of the illness or the need for relief, an observation consistent with the experimental findings of Podolnick and Field (1970). On several occasions we have seen patients who previously had been used as subjects in medical demonstrations of hypnosis. Even those who had been poor hypnotic subjects in the earlier settings were able to respond quite adequately when being seen for actual treatment for such a condition as cigarette smoking aggravating emphysema. Often patients who have been unresponsive to hypnotic attempts by nonprofessionals enter trance when they have confidence in the skill and integrity of the therapist (Blumenthal, 1959).

Motivation does not necessarily correlate with the medical severity of illness; it may be related more to the emotional meaning of the problem. One teenage boy was miserable because his hands were covered with warts. He would want to hold hands with his dates, but they often drew back at the first rough feel of the touch. In frustration he frequently tried to pick the warts off, leading to infection and bleeding. All of the usual dermatological treatments had been tried, including x-ray, but none had been successful in removing the warts permanently. Two weeks after his first and only hypnotic session, the warts vanished. During the last 6 years they have not recurred. Although not a severe medical problem, the warts were a severe psychological stress. It is possible that his strong motivation helped him achieve effective hypnosis.

In several cases of obesity in women, it was learned, during the preliminary screening interviews, that sexual promiscuity had been frequent prior to the weight problem. Although this was consciously admitted and the women considered themselves happily married and in no danger of extramarital affairs, they failed to respond to hypnotic suggestion for appetite suppression. Once their real feelings in regard to their sex habits were worked out in psychotherapy or hypnotherapy, most responded effectively to direct symptom suppression.

At times a patient will have several symptoms of one type, such as the "oral" habits of smoking, nail biting, and overeating. Interestingly, one of these symptoms will often yield to hypnosis, but not all of them. It seems as if the unconscious mind is willing to negotiate away part of its oral gratification but not all. Of course, certain developmental and dynamic factors may make one habit more overdetermined in meaning than another.

Motivation is more than persistence, greater than mere investment of time in problem solving. It is an energizing process, the momentum of which carries forward in spite of momentary reverses or discouragements. True motivation often pushes relentlessly toward its goal in spite of consciously held resistance. Motivation is the inculcation of hope.

For motivation to work maximally, the patient must believe in the suggestion being given, must accept the integrity and well-meaning of the hypnotherapist, and must (most importantly!) feel that the suggestions being given by the therapist echo in a profound way the patient's own deeper inner voice.

During one routine prehypnotic screening we attempt to assess the patient's motivation, clarify it, and increase the expectation of positive benefit. Such a screening comprises one interview in which the meaning of the patient's symptoms are assessed as well as his overall emotional stability and suitability for hypnotherapy. Most patients are referred by physicians, which is already a strong motivating factor. Additional motivation is attempted through explanation of the meaning of certain organic symptoms, discussion of any misconceptions or fears of hypnosis, and establishment of positive transference.

When motivation ceases, previously adequate response to hypnosis may vanish (Barber, 1972). If it cannot be rewakened, treatment may terminate or other forms of psychotherapeutic motivation may be substituted.

TESTS FOR SUGGESTIBILITY

Although a number of tests for hypnotizability have been published, it is difficult to tell whether a person will be a good hypnotic subject until an actual induction is attempted. Suggestibility tests that have been generally employed are postural sway, hand levitation, and hand clasping.

Postural Sway

In the postural sway tests, the therapist stands behind or in front of the subject with his or her hands on the subject's shoulders while giving suggestions that the subject is beginning to sway toward or away. A positive result is taken as evidence of suggestibility. We feel, however, that, if this test is employed at all, it is preferable to induce the swaying from side to side since the sway toward the operator can be interpreted by some hysterical patients as having veiled sexual meanings. The significance of body sway has been questioned by Garmize and Marcuse (1969), and Das (1961) found that the body sway did not distinguish "normals" from "mental defectives." In actual practice we find this test of little value in determining hypnotizability.

Hand Levitation

Some therapists employ hand levitation to assess if an individual will be a cooperative subject. Suggestions are given that the subject's hand is becoming lighter and lighter, drifting up from the chair or table, perhaps floating toward his or her forehead. A positive response is again evidence for suggestibility.

Suggestions can also be given that an arm or hand that is already held in an elevated position will become "heavier" in sensation and will move downward. This hand-drop technique utilizes, of course, the natural pull of gravity on the extended limb and may be more successful in subjects who are initially too resistant for the hand-levitation test. Kroger (1977) discusses using the "Kohnstamm test", which is not actually a test of hypnotizability but a normal neuromuscular reaction adapted to increase the positive mind-set for hypnosis. In this "test" the subject is asked to stand in a doorway with the arms at his or her sides. He or she is instructed to press one fist laterally against the door jamb for perhaps a minute before walking through the door. The subject is told that as he or she walks through the door his or her arm will feel lightened and will rise. This happens, of course, because of the normal reflexes of the muscles. We do not think it desirable to present this to a subject as evidence of hypnosis, although it might be of some use, as Kroger suggests, for increasing positive mind-set for induction procedures.

Sensory Alterations

Suggestions for alteration of sensory experience may also indicate a positive test for suggestibility. Temperature changes (warm or cold) may be tested by asking the subject to imagine a warm or hot roll or an ice-cube wrapped in a cloth held in one hand or the other. General instructions for imagining that the room temperature is rising or falling, and olfactory suggestions ("smoke," "roses," "spice," etc.) may be used.

A lively discussion recently has developed about the reliability and relevance of various rating scales to hypnotic phenomena. Virtually all the traditional rating scales have come under some attack. Hilgard (1981b, 1982) suggests that the eye-roll sign of hypnotizability may have little correlation with hypnotic responsiveness. Weitzenhoffer (1980) has challenged the venerable Stanford rating scales and was countered by Hilgard (1981a). Hilgard's critique of the eye-roll sign was itself critiqued by Frischolz et al. (1981), to which Hilgard (1981c) offered a further rebuttal. Bowers (1981a,b) has defended the usefulness of the Stanford scales of hypnotic susceptibility.

Radtke and Spanos (1982) found that subjects who were given self-rating scales of "absorption" in addition to hypnotic depth estimates tended to make fewer ratings of themselves as hypnotized. They suggest caution in the use of hypnotic depths scales, since many factors may be involved.

Despite these disputes, the hypnotic rating scales remain an important part of research in the nature of hypnosis although they are rarely used in clinical practice, largely because of the amount of time needed to administer them and their limited usefulness in the therapeutic applications of hypnotherapy. In questioning a group of experienced clinicians, composed of 45 physicians, clinical psychologists, and dentists, results indicated that "30 percent currently used scales in their clinical practice, 24 percent had abandoned them and 46 percent had never used tests of hypnotizability" Cohen (1983). There remains a need for evaluating scales of hypnotizability across cultures (Horne, De, and Powlett, 1980).

Hypnotizability is often felt to correlate with therapeutic responsiveness (Mott, 1979). We have often noted that hypnotizability may increase with the subject's need for treatment. Repeated inductions may increase susceptibility in some subjects (Reilley et al., 1980), although claims for modifiability need to be treated with caution (Perry, 1977). Also, see this issue discussed in the International Journal of Clinical and Experimental Hypnosis 55(4): 1982. Interpersonal interactional variables are certainly crucial in hypnotizability (Fourie, 1980). Some "unhypnotizable" subjects may respond to nonauthoritarian techniques (Barber, 1980). Bowers (1976) notes that the ability to become involved in imaginal experiences can indicate hypnotizability, which may involve a greater activity at right-hemisphere processing.

Hand Clasping

The third test commonly employed to determine positive response is hand clasping. The subject is instructed to clasp his or her hands tightly together, imagining them glued and firmly interlocked. The subject is told that he or she cannot unclasp his or her hands even though he or she tries vigorously to do so. If the subject is unable to unclasp the hands or parts them only with difficulty, a positive test for suggestibility is noted.

Value of Suggestibility Tests

These tests for suggestibility, though widely mentioned in the literature, seem to us of little value clinically and to involve, perhaps, even some risk. For example, the postural sway test, as mentioned, may evoke sexual fantasies that could lead to resistance to trance induction. Also, we have felt that the hand-clasp technique perhaps makes use in a veiled way of purely physiological effect since it decreases the blood supply to the hands. This may well account for the hesitancy in unclasping the hands in some subjects. Such indirect attribution of hypnotic effects to normal physiological responses can undermine the confidence of the subject in the integrity of the therapist.

Other Ways to Determine
Hypnotic Susceptibility

There is, after all, no better test for susceptibility to hypnosis than a trial induction of hypnosis itself. We feel that our standard screening interview, always done prior to the first attempt at induction, accomplishes the same purposes as the suggestibility tests and, in addition, helps to establish psychological rapport on a more conscious level. Mistaken assumptions about hypnosis often can be corrected during the screening interview. Excessive fantasy expectations can be modified so that the actual induction is approached with a calm, more confident attitude.

In experimental work, however, there is certainly justification for attempts to relate hypnotic susceptibility with other waking variables. The only reliable test for hypnotizability is a clinical attempt at induction, repeated several times. Deckert and West (1963), for example, were relatively unsuccessful in relating hypnotizability to sex, age, psychiatric diagnosis, and various personality traits.

Spiegel (1972) has described an eye-roll sign that correlates highly with hypnotic trance capacity as measured, he reports, by a hypnotic induction profile in 2000 consecutive psychotherapy cases. A positive eye-roll sign is the subject's ability to simultaneously look upward while closing the eyelids. Spiegel feels that the more completely the eye roll is performed (measured on a four-point scale of estimation) the higher the trance capacity. He reported it as a clear predictor of hypnotizability in three out of four cases.

A number of tests of hypnotic susceptibility have been developed for experimental work, though they are of limited value in clinical situations where a trial induction may yield more useful information. The *Stanford Hypnotic Susceptibility Scale*, developed by Weitzenhoffer and Hilgard (1962), has two equivalent standardized forms. A modification of the Stanford scale, the *Children's Hypnotic Susceptibility Scale* (London, 1962), has two forms, one for ages 5 to 13, another for ages 13 to 17.

Another susceptibility scale developed by Shor and Orne (1962) is the *Harvard Group Scale of Hypnotic Susceptibility*. The norms from this group scale are congruent with norms derived from an individually administered version (Shor and Orne, 1963), making it particularly useful for screening large numbers of individuals to locate the most promising hypnotic candidates for experimental work. Barber (1965) has also developed a suggestibility scale for experimental work.

INDUCTION TECHNIQUES

The techniques for hypnosis should be learned through personal supervision by an experienced clinician. The actual wording and type of suggestion varies with different hypnotherapists, many of whom have extensively described their techniques in print. Two of the most respected therapists in this regard are Wolberg, whose two-volume

Medical Hypnosis (1948) is a rich sourcebook, and Erickson (1967), whose hypnotic techniques have been collected by Haley.

While induction methods are simple, the real skill of the hypnotherapist lies in his or her knowledge and understanding of psychodynamics, including the possible complications of transference reactions. Such knowledge is usually acquired only in a formal training program for clinical psychology or psychiatry or through long supervision by a qualified hypnotherapist.

The casual application of hypnotic techniques without full understanding of psychological theories and their clinical application is as irresponsible as amateur brain surgery.

Our own induction technique involves steady, monotonous repetition of suggestions for relaxation and rest, coupled with a constant readiness to investigate, in the waking or hypnotic state, any sign of negative reaction to the hypnotic procedure. It has been shown by Dittborn, Munoz, and Artistequieta (1963) that a monotonously repeated light flash did not, in itself, produce sleep unless specific suggestions for sleep were included. Evans (1967) has demonstrated that hypnotic phenomena can often be induced, even if the subjects do not recognize that hypnosis is involved. By "teaching relaxation" he was able to produce phenomena equivalent to those achieved with a usual hypnotic induction. Hartland (1967) emphasizes using rhythm and certain stressed words and phrases ("You're *so* sleepy, *so* relaxed. . . ."). The effectiveness of pauses is mentioned by Blum (1967), who feels that in hypnosis the patient tends to think of the last thoughts presented before the pause.

It is important that the transition from waking to the trance state be as gentle as possible for the patient. Conforming the induction to his or her expectations arouses less anxiety, as does a setting of quiet relaxation, free from such interruptions as the telephone. The subject should be comfortable, usually seated in a chair with an ottoman, or reclining on a couch, with head support, or reclining on an examining table. Lighting should be adequate, but there should be no direct light in the patient's eyes. If the patient wears contact lenses they should always be removed before induction.

Rapport is the initial consideration. In the usual professional setting this is often taken for granted, being conferred by the reputation of the therapist, the recommendations of the referring physician, and the appearance of a well-ordered and appropriate office setting. A few inquiries about the patient's previous knowledge of hypnosis, fear, or expectations may allay otherwise unexpressed anxieties and will strengthen the rapport between patient and therapist.

Before induction is begun, the therapist should explain the stages of hypnosis to the patient, assuring the patient that he or she may well remember everything that is said, for he or she is unlikely in the initial session to enter the deeper stages where spontaneous amnesia might occur. The therapist informs the patient that, contrary to popular thought, hypnosis is not like anesthesia. No one will "bludgeon" him or her into unconsciousness, nor is it a case of the therapist's "stronger" mind controlling his or her "weaker" one. It is a cooperative effort in which the therapist aids the patient, by means of specialized knowledge and technique, to achieve a purpose that both have agreed upon as valid and worthwhile.

The specific purpose of the induction is reviewed—to help the patient achieve a specific goal, such as stopping smoking, controlling pain, decreasing excessive appetite, or other such goals. The value of achieving the desired result is emphasized.

Induction is then begun, using techniques with which the therapist is comfortable, tailored to the individual needs of the patient. A slow, monotonous, soft, and assuring tone is used. Patients easily detect anxiety and insecurity in the therapist, often responding by tenseness and a failed induction. The approach should be positive and direct, with suggestions such as "You *will* feel less pain." The patient's attention is gently guided to relaxing bodily sensations and away from thoughts associated with anxiety.

The method of induction is ideally based upon an understanding of the patient's personality structure. For example, a patient with a positive response to authority may find an authoritarian approach most acceptable, while a patient with authority conflicts might be resistant to such a tone. If a particular technique is not working, the therapist should be prepared to unobtrusively move toward a different approach, a shift that can often be accomplished with a mere change in the tone of the voice. Some subjects will respond to slightly indirect suggestions for induction, such as "Now tell yourself to relax your body," instead of the more authoritarian "Now relax your body."

The type of vocabulary used will depend on the patient's verbal skills. It is not wise to "talk down" to a patient, for if he or she feels that the therapist is assuming a superior attitude, he or she might respond by marked resistance. We normally use the same vocabulary as we would in a standard psychotherapeutic session.

The therapist should speak in a calm tone, enunciating the words clearly. We use a tempo of suggestions that is coordinated with the patient's breathing. If at all possible, an induction should occur in a quiet room devoid of distracting sounds or noises. We have, however, hypnotized patients in a teaching hospital under conditions where other patients were in the same room and radios blared in the outer office. In one hospital we conducted hypnotherapy in an area where sirens could be heard entering the hospital grounds virtually 24 hours a day. If the unconscious motivation of the patient is sufficient, he or she will respond by entering a hypnotic trance.

Many actual "wordings" are discussed in chapters dealing with specific clinical entities, such as obesity and pain. Here we shall emphasize the necessity for the therapist keeping his or her mind on what is being said so to avoid hesitancy or inconsistent suggestions. One must not, for example, begin a suggestion of a light floating sensation in the right arm and then, by error, speak of the left arm. Such inconsistencies arouse anxiety in the subject. One neophyte therapist reported that when attempting to treat plantar warts hypnotically he forgot on which foot they were and suggested that they would diminish on the other foot, which was actually free of warts. Although this inconsistency did not awaken the patient, when she was brought out of trance, she had a hoarseness, apparently a hysterical symptom expressing both the desire to speak, to tell the therapist of his mistake, and the inability to do so because of the need to remain in a trance state. The hoarseness soon passed, but she discontinued treatment. In rare circumstances confusing suggestions may be deliberately employed as an induction technique, but this "confusion method" is best left to expert and experienced therapists (Erickson, 1965).

In addition to suggestions being clear and accurate, they must be discretely limited to the purpose intended. For example, a patient burned over 80 percent of his body was in severe negative nitrogen balance and rapidly losing weight. He was given the posthypnotic suggestion that he would be very hungry and would eat "anything and everything" offered to him. Soon after he awakened, he rapidly consumed an entire box of 24 candy bars that a friend had brought him as a gift. He consequently developed severe diarrhea, temporarily losing all the additional weight he had acquired.

Since hypnotic suggestions may act as artificially induced compulsive ideas, it is most important that they be clearly worded. It would not be wise, for example, to remove *all* lower abdominal pain from a patient suffering from separation of the pubic symphysis since the absence of pain might prevent the detection of some other treatable condition, even cancer, which might subsequently arise. Lerner (1958) suggests that as hypnosis is achieved, the operator's image acts as if it is intrapsychic, becoming a source of security and reassurance.

At times a patient may consciously or unconsciously resist the induction of hypnosis, particularly when some emotionally charged material is involved in the treatment. There are a number of possible psychodynamics for such resistance (Cheek and LeCron, 1968; Gravitz, 1971). Motivation, as previously discussed, is a prime factor, but it should be maximized if a careful screening procedure has been conducted and if rapport has been established. Some patients seek hypnosis because of pressure from members of their families; they must be led to discover motivations in themselves before hypnotherapy can be successful. Misunderstandings about hypnosis are a frequent source of resistance, as already noted. Many people equate it to a traumatic experience previously associated with anesthesia. There may have been earlier actual experience of loss of consciousness, to which hypnosis is mistakenly assimilated in the patient's mind. Many other forms of unconscious psychodynamic resistance may exist, and these must be uncovered in difficult cases. They may include fantasies of loss of control, fear of dominance, and activation of sexual fantasies of an aggressive, submissive, or homosexual nature.

After induction, various "challenges" may be used to demonstrate to the patient that he has been hypnotized. A usual challenge is, "Your eyes are tightly closed, so tightly closed that you cannot open them even if you try; now try to open your eyes!" It is essential that such challenges not be used to excess or continued to the point that they tire the patient and interfere with the basic set of relaxation. In some of the challenge tests, such as inducing insensitivity to pain in a finger, it is necessary for the therapist to touch the patient. This should never be done without warning. The patient should never be surprised or startled by the therapist's actions.

After several successful inductions have established the trance as a pattern, the trance can then be elicited by a shorter cue, which has been presented as a posthypnotic suggestion on previous inductions (Kubie, 1961).

Since hypnosis may involve heightened transference reactions, it is even more important than in conventional psychotherapy that the therapist himself or herself be relatively free of neurotic countertransference problems and that he or she remain highly conscious of those areas of conflict that remain partially unresolved. In addition, he or she must realize that the heightened tendency of the patient to form transferance ties prohibits suggestions that might have double meanings, such as "You will become hot all over." Stein (1966) has listed a number of items that may suggest to a therapist that he or she is having an unrecognized countertransference reaction to a patient: alterations in usual fees, overlooking failures to take medications as prescribed, signs of familiarity (as first names), allowing abuses of the telephone, repeated discussions with colleagues concerning a particular patient, neglect of history taking, and others. Orne (1972) lists warning signs that might indicate to a therapist that he or she has power problems: if he or she (1) uses hypnosis for all patients, (2) enjoys inductions but is less concerned about effectiveness, (3) is overly concerned with always obtaining maximum depth of trance, (4) is afraid of patients falsifying hypnosis, (5) experiences induction as a test of wills, or (6) particularly looks forward to hypnotizing attractive patients.

At times a third person should be in the room during hypnotic induction, both as a reassurance to the patient that fantasies are not likely to be acted out and as a legal protection to the therapist. A nurse or professional secretary might act as chaperone when the patient is likely to enter deep levels and experience spontaneous amnesia, unless, of course, the purpose of the trance is to elicit cloistered material that the patient might not wish revealed to a third party. When treating women for sexual unresponsiveness, we have found it particularly helpful to ask the woman's husband to act as chaperone; this decreases the possibility of an embarrassing situation should the women experience spontaneous orgasm during trance. If she awakens with newly aroused libidinous feelings, as is hoped for in the treatment, the husband's presence allows these feelings to focus immediately on him as an appropriate person. There can also be no doubt that the feelings are due to posthypnotic suggestions rather than any impropriety during the trance state.

At the termination of trance, posthypnotic suggestions should be given for a slow gradual return to the waking state. Although it is possible to awaken the patient rapidly, this is seldom indicated.

After awakening the patient, it is often useful to inquire about whether he or she experienced any unusual images or feelings during trance. If so, the material is handled in a psychotherapeutic way.

Toward the final stages of a treatment program, we add to the posthypnotic suggestions the following statement:

"You will never allow anyone to hypnotize you who is not professionally qualified, and only then if you so desire. Should you experience hypnotic suggestions under other conditions you simply will not respond, in any sense of the word."

As one's training and experience increase, these considerations of technique become automatic and integrated into a smooth, flowing induction.

Recorded Inductions

Although some therapists use recorded suggestions for induction, we personally feel that such mechanical devices should be used only with discretion, such as when the patient cannot physically come for treatment as often as needed. Even then, recordings should be under the close supervision of the therapist, who frequently should review the course of treatment. Recorded suggestions cannot provide the careful attention of a therapist. In our experience self-hypnosis is more effective than recorded instructions. Although self-hypnosis may be useful, particularly in well-circumscribed areas of symptom suppression, it cannot be recommended without initial treatment in a conventional two-person hypnotic interaction or without periodic review and supervision by the therapist. In preference to using recorded instruction, we have at times induced hypnosis by telephone at the request of patients who live in remote areas, always requiring a member of the family of the patient to be present with the patient to assist by holding the phone to the patient's ear until the session is over. This procedure is done only with patients who have been seen by us personally in active treatment.

When taped hypnotic suggestions are recorded, it is vital to personalize the message for the particular person and particular purpose. Such words as these may be used at the beginning of the tape: "This taped message is being recorded specifically for (patient's name) and if it is played or heard by anyone else they will simply not respond to the suggestions." The tape should be for a specified purpose and this should be stated, to remind the patient not to attempt alteration of other areas of mental or physical functioning, since such attempts at alteration without professional guidance could lead to complications. Instructions such as "This recorded message is to be used only for eliminating the smoking habit" can be inserted.

The tape should include such instructions as "If while listening to this tape you should fall into a state of normal sleep, you may sleep for an appropriate period of time and upon awakening the trance will have terminated, but the post-hypnotic suggestions that have been given will remain in effect." The end of the tape might usefully include a suggestion such as "You may now turn off this machine if you wish, and either resume your normal activities in a full state of normal consciousness or, if you wish, enter a state of deep, restful, natural sleep from which you will awaken at an appropriate time with the trance terminated but with the posthypnotic suggestions still in effect."

Hypnosis By Telephone

Since hypnosis is most often a verbal interaction between therapist and patient, it is possible to induce trance by telephone suggestions as well as by recorded suggestions. The interaction by telephone, although not as controlled and sensitive as face-to-face interaction, is often worth considering, particularly when long distances (and the expense of travel) might otherwise limit the availability of appropriate treatment. Hypnosis by telephone also can be used in some emergency situations. We strongly advise that the initial induction not be by telephone, since a personal contact is vital in the establishment of a positive therapist-patient alliance.

During an ice storm in Dallas in 1960, a patient who was being treated daily by Crasilneck could not drive nor find any available transportation to the office because of the hazardous conditions. Since reinforcement to hypnotic suggestion was crucial in controlling her pain, it was decided and agreed by the patient to try "telephone therapy." By the end of the 45-minute session, the patient was free from most of her pain and very comfortable. Many patients who live out-of-state prefer telephone reinforcement rather than travel the great distance for the same results. At this time, 30-minute sessions on the telephone are sufficient.

This adjunct of reinforcement has been a source of immediate relief for those hospitalized pain patients who must have reinforcement three to five times in a 24-hour period. Crasilneck has utilized this verbal interaction safely and satisfactorily from office or home and sometimes in the middle of the night, thus avoiding exacerbation of pain.

There are some precautions to be considered: only those patients who have been previously hypnotized and who are well known to the therapist are the best candidates for telephone therapy; they should be advised that if the line of communication is disrupted, they would immediately come out of trance, and they should be assured that if they slip into a normal state of sleep, they would awaken shortly thereafter feeling refreshed and completely awake. All suggestions given during telephone therapy will be equally as effective as face-to-face therapy in the office or hospital (Crasilneck, 1965).

Telephone hypnotherapy has become a valid treatment modality in the last 15 years. Stanton (1978) and Cooperman and Schafer (1983) have also reported the use of therapy by telephone. Gravitz (1983) cites early hypnotic uses of the telephone and recordings in the nineteenth century.

Special Techniques of Induction

The literature of clinical hypnosis contains many descriptions of specialized techniques. Klemperer (1969) suggests a "lullaby" technique, the use of an intentional rhythm in whatever is said. This is similar to Pfeiffer and Pfeiffer's adaptation of Buddhist breathing techniques (1966) and to our own method of slowing the phrasing of suggestions as the subject's breathing rate decreases. Hartland (1967) discusses authoritarian suggestions and a technique of expressing suggestions more positively as the depth of trance deepens. Meares (1957) has used painting techniques: Coulton (1966) notes that writing often spontaneously produces a hypnoidal state. Tart (1967) reports deepening of trance by "mutual hypnosis," in which the hypnotherapist is hypnotized by the subject he or she has just induced. Certain dangers, including the psychedeliclike responses, restrict this technique to the experimental situation. Imagining words appearing on a blackboard or a TV screen may be used to facilitate induction (Stein, 1972). Yarnell (1972) has had subjects imagine a cave with a monster that gradually becomes smaller and friendlier.

In his many writings replete with instruction in techniques, Erickson mentions such unusual procedures as induction by pantomine (1964b) and his unique "confusion technique" (1964a), which exhausts the defenses of the resistant subject by giving him or her a quick succession of grave but actually irrelevant suggestions while never allowing the subject sufficient time to make a clear response. Isasi (1962) has described a technique for hypnotic induction of deaf mutes, and Alderete (1967) has described induction through an interpreter if the patient and therapist speak different languages. Martorano and Oestreicher (1966) have published their experiences in inducing hypnosis in 12 congenitally deaf mentally ill patients.

Success in inducing hypnosis in other groups previously thought to be resistant has been reported by Sternlicht and Wanderer (1963) for mental defectives, by McCord for the "mongoloid-type child" (1956), and by a number of investigators for psychotic and institutionalized patients (Friedman and Kleep, 1963; Gale and Herman, 1956; Green 1969; Kramer, 1966; Polak, Mountain, and Erncle (1964). Pattie and Griffith (1962) had no success in attempting to induce hypnosis in patients with Korsakoff's syndrome, but Heath, Stratas, and Davis (1962) tested patients in the geriatric and chronic wards of Dorothea Dix State Hospital, North Carolina, finding that more than half could attain light or deeper trance states. They related their failures more to lack of cooperation and increased psychomotor activity rather than to loss of contact with reality. Hartman (1965) found no correlation between diagnosis and hypnotic susceptibility. Staples (1963) emphasizes that some resistant patients may respond to hypnosis simply if extra time is allowed for induction.

Depth of Trance

The concept of depth of hypnotic trance is an analogy to "depth" of sleep, which was perhaps originally suggested by Puységur. To some researchers, it implies regression to more primitive psychological mechanisms (Solovey and Milechin, 1955). In recent years certain standardized scales to "measure" the depth of trance have been proposed, notably those of Weitzenhoffer and Hilgard (1962), Shor and Orne (1962, 1963), London (1962), and Barber (1965).These are essentially trials of hypnosis; with specified suggestions and numerical ratings for the responses. There are also several self-rating hypnotic scales; these have been reviewed by Tart (1970, 1972). The inventory scales proposed by Field (1965) consists, for example, of 300 items describing subjective experiences.

Various phenomena do occur under hypnosis or can be induced by appropriate suggestion, for example, closing of the eyes, heaviness or catalepsy (immobility) of limbs, hallucinations of the presence of objects that are not at hand (positive hallucinations), or the absence of something that is actually present (negative hallucinations). Also, anesthesia to painful stimuli can be produced as well as hand levitation. It is not always clear, however, that such phenomena can be arranged in clearly defined stages to be used as indicators of depth. Depth is a clinical judgment, and it was clinical observation itself that first suggested a correlation between phenomena and "depth."

The most reliable criterion that we have observed in our practice is that the more a patient needs the benefits of hypnosis, the more likely he is to achieve a "deep" trance state. The patient suffering from severe pain, unrelieved by the usual doses of chemical analgesia, is more likely to achieve deep and effective hypnosis than the casual participant in a psychological experiment. We also have often found that the observable depth has little correlation with the results of treatment, especially in patients with less severe problems. The smoker who claimed he was never "under" hypnosis may at times relinquish cigarettes as rapidly as the somnambulistic patient, though failures may occur with both.

A frequently noted and apparently paradoxical response is that the subject abruptly goes into a deeper state of trance when the suggestions

Table 4-1
Classification and Test for Depth of Clinical Trance

Stage	Test
Hypnoidal	Fluttering of the eyelids
	Physical relaxation
	Closing of the eyes
	Feelings of muscular lethargy
Light trance	Inability to open the eyes
	Deep and slow breathing
	Progressive deepening of lethargy
	Catalepsy
Medium trance	Glove anesthesia
	Partial amnesia
Deep trance	Hallucinations
(Somnambulism)	Ability to open the eyes without affecting the trance
	Virtually complete amnesia
	Extensive amnesia
	Posthypnotic anesthesia and analgesia
	Age regression
	Posthypnotic positive and negative hallucinations
	Lip pallor

for awakening are begun. We often employ a technique of counting backward from ten to one for awakening. Many of our patients report not hearing some of the numbers usually from seven to four. Cheek and LeCron (1968) have used a finger-signaling ideomotor technique to demonstrate the same phenomena. Quite possibly this paradoxical deepening represents a final "plunge" into the hypnotic state as the patient is able to more fully relax, realizing that the hypnotic session is almost over, only lacking the last few digits of the awakening count. Schneck (1962) has suggested that such "depth reversal" may represent (1) a wish to continue in the hypnotic state, (2) the patient's attending to unfinished material, or (3) the relinquishing of defenses that had been employed during hypnosis to avoid the surfacing of unconscious material.

The depth of clinical trance can be divided arbitrarily into many categories. In Table 4-1 we offer a practical and simple classification with a few major tests for each stage. In beginning work with hypnosis, the therapist, as part of his or her own learning experience, may wish to make several tests to establish the depth. The more experienced clinician will probably test for depth only for teaching or experimental purposes.

In the usual induction of hypnosis these stages may be seen progressively in a single subject if he or she reaches the depth of somnambulism. The hypnoidal state is similar to marked waking relaxation and may represent a certain I–Thou quality of transference relationship (Rodger, 1964). During this stage the subject develops a sense of safety and trust in the hypnotic relationship; rapport is established and deepened. Kubie (1961) has suggested that the hypnoidal state has "research possibilities—both as an object and as an investigative tool, particularly in the phenomenology of transit from one stage of phsychological organization to another." Suggestions for symptom change or for hypnoanalytic investigation are not advised in this hypnoidal state.

In light trance the subject begins to look as if he or she is in a state different from relaxation. He or she may appear almost as one asleep, except that maintenance of posture and response to suggestions demonstrate a clear awareness of the therapist's presence.

Medium trance is not readily evident unless specific tests are made to demonstrate it. Without such tests the subject may pass progressively and rapidly from light trance into a deeper or somnambulistic stage, where many of the classic signs of hypnosis are elicitable, including such psychologically rare phenomena as controlled age regression.

We know of no previously reported indicator of this somnambulistic stage that can be observed without subjecting the hypnotized person to a challenge test, such as anesthesia or opening the eyes while remaining in trance. In several thousand subjects, though, we have observed what may be a sign of somnambulism that can be seen without evoking a test challenge. This is a circumoral area of pallor about the lips for a space of approximately 1 centimeter just beyond the mucocutaneous margin. If present, this seems to appear when the somnambulistic stage is reached and persists about a minute after the subject is brought out of trance. Other clinicians have independently observed this sign. A neurologist colleague has reported that a similar phenomenon is sometimes seen in users of morphine, though we have not been able to verify his observation in the literature.

In hypnoidal, light, and medium stages of trance the subject may be aware of outside sounds and may recall all suggestions given. This does not indicate a failure of trance induction, although many who imagine hypnosis as anesthesia or as control by another may interpret awareness as failed induction. In the deeper somnambulistic stage immediate self-reflective awareness is absent, as in sleep.

Very rapid onset of hypnosis, usually induced through posthypnotic suggestion, is certainly possible and is used by some hypnotherapists, particularly in trained subjects. We feel, however, that excessively rapid induction may be experienced by the untrained subject as a psychic shock. Even when the various stages are not demonstrated by challenge tests, we prefer to take the subject gradually from the waking state into the lighter stages with suggestions of relaxation, then progressively deepen the trance.

Awakening is also achieved in a slow, controlled manner, in order to make the transition to the waking state as gentle and free of anxiety as possible. It is important at all times to keep faith with the subject's justified expectation that he or she will be treated in a dignified, helpful manner and not subjected to unnecessary dramatic or abrupt changes in the state of consciousness. There are two exceptions in which rapid movement from waking to the somnambulistic stage may be desirable: (1) training for obstetrical anesthesia so that the patient may move in and out of deep trance as uterine contractions occur, and (2) where hypnoanesthesia is used in medical or surgical emergencies.

SPECIFIC EXAMPLES OF METHODS OF INDUCTION

Numerous methods are available to the hypnotherapist for hypnotic induction. An excellent review of this topic is provided by *A Syllabus on Hypnosis and A Handbook of Therapeutic Suggestions*, published in 1973 by The American Society of Clinical Hypnosis Education and Research Foundation (Chiasson) for participants in workshops sponsored by that society.

It is most important that a therapist using hypnosis be well versed in the use of a variety of induction techniques. One must quickly decide what technique is best suited to the patient's personality or the type of problem. Quite often a trained therapist will rapidly perceive that a patient is not reacting to one method of induction, yet with a change in technique the patient quickly responds by entering a deep level of hypnotic trance. Most experienced therapists prefer a method that best suits their own personality. It is difficult to imagine, for example, that introverted therapists employing hypnosis would generally use a strong authoritarian induction approach with patients.

It is always of interest to see the effect of the preconceived set of the patient concerning the induction of hypnosis, particularly since hypnosis is so popular with laymen. Frequently, patients describe a technique and ask if you intend to use it. If the therapist sees no contraindications, it is usually beneficial to choose a technique that matches the patients' preconditioned set and attitude.

The methods of induction we employ most consistently include

1. Hand levitation
2. Eye fixation
3. Wolberg's theater technique
4. Television methods for children
5. Coin technique
6. Nonverbal communication
7. Chaisson's method
8. Relaxation technique

There are other excellent approaches, some of which we detail in the discussion about relaxation. We feel that the eight listed here best suit our personalities, the type of patients we see, and the usual problems referred to us. They are presented as suggestions only. Each therapist must utilize the technique that suits him or her best, extending these sample inductions to suit the patient and the clinical situation so as to achieve the optimal depth of trance in each case. With practice the therapist will be able to recognize when the patient is in adequate trance, even if only minimal suggestions for induction have been completed. Therapeutic suggestions should then be given since further unnecessary induction phrases may be distracting and can interfere with the depth of trance already achieved.

Hand Levitation

At the start of hand levitation the patient is asked to sit comfortably with his or her hands resting in a cupped position on the thighs. We consciously suggest that he or she spread apart the fingers of the dominant hand. The patient is then told,

"Take a deep breath and start staring at one of the knuckles on your hand. . . . Just listen to my voice. . . . Try and pay no attention to other sounds and noises. . . If you have extraneous thoughts, don't worry about it, but try to focus your thinking on what I am saying and on your hand that is cupped. . . . Notice how relaxed your breathing has become. . . . Good . . . and now begin to notice some facts about your hand. . . . It's becoming more sensitive. . . . Pay attention, for example, . . . to the texture of the material of your clothing, to the heat in your hand. . . . You can feel these things occurring and as you do, nod your head gently yes . . . good . . . and now in a moment one of the fingers will move slightly. . . . I don't know which finger, but it will move slightly. . . . Good . . . now your hand will begin to feel rather light, feathery and floaty. . . . The wrist feels like a string is around it, attached perhaps to some balloons gently pulling your arm up . . . light . . . feathery . . . floaty . . . coming up . . . up toward your forehead . . . good. Coming up and when your hand touches your forehead, you will be well relaxed, at ease and in a good state of hypnosis. . . . Now as your hand touches your forehead, . . . your eyes will close . . . your eyes are closed . . . your hand will return to your lap with normal sensation returning to your hand and you are now extremely relaxed and so drowsy, at ease, relaxed, so *very* relaxed . . . throughout your body . . . relaxed and at ease."

Eye Fixation

Ask the patient to sit comfortably in a chair or if hospitalized to be as comfortable as possible in the bed and then begin your eye fixation. "Put your right hand on your abdomen and let your left hand and arm rest comfortably to the side. . . . Uncross your legs so that you won't put prolonged pressure on them. . . . Now, if you will, please look at this coin that I am holding . . . keep your face looking forward, but I am going to hold this coin slightly above the level of your eyes so that you will strain slightly to look at the object . . . now fixate your vision on the coin, . . . good . . . your breathing is deep and relaxed. . . . You notice that as you continue staring at the coin your eyes become tired and they are beginning to blink . . . yes . . . the lids are blinking . . . Your eyes are tearing . . . watering from staring at the object and they want to close and they are now closing, closing, closed. . . . Let them remain so very heavy, relaxed, and at ease . . . breathing easily . . . free from tension, tightness, stress and strain, having now entered a good level of hypnosis and responding to my suggestions extremely well . . . relaxed and at ease . . . free from tension, tightness, stress and strain."

The therapist should take care not to hold the coin in such a strained position that his or her own arm becomes fatigued during the induction.

Theater Technique

We have frequently used Wolberg's theater method (1948), combining it with a number of variations of our own. This technique is especially good in the induction of patients with psychological problems, for it allows the patient to project his or her own conflicts and turmoil into the technique.

The patient sits comfortable in a chair with his or her feet on an ottoman, or if hospitalized, lying comfortably in bed. The dominant hand is placed on the abdomen and the other rests comfortably at the side next to the body. What follows is a typical session using the theater technique for hypnosis.

"I want you to close your eyes and begin to concentrate on the fact that you can relax your entire body . . . the muscles, the nervous system . . . just relaxed . . . your breathing . . . so relaxed . . . your entire body free from other thoughts for the moment . . . just listening to me. . . . I want you to concentrate on your right hand . . . concentrate on the breathing of your abdomen . . . the texture of the material in your clothing. . . . Your hand is becoming more sensitive to touch and sensation. . . . As you are doing this, nod your head, yes. . . . Good . . . a deeper and a sounder state . . . you are doing fine . . . normal sensation returns to your hand. . . . Now I give you the suggestion that your right leg begins to feel quite heavy . . . like it is in sand . . . so heavy that you cannot lift your leg. . . . Try, but you cannot . . . no matter how hard you try you cannot raise the leg . . . Now normal sensation returns to the leg. . . . Now you are aware of a slight irritation on the top of your right hand, like a fly walking across the hand . . . as you are aware of this, brush it away. . . . Good . . . now much deeper and relaxed and more profound state . . . Now listen very carefully to what I describe. . . . You are entering a theatre and you walk down to the first row of seats and sit down . . . front row center. . . . As you are doing this, nod your head, yes . . . good. . . . Now you envision a bright red curtain on the stage . . . fine. . . . Now you are aware of white spotlights on the red curtain . . . very good. . . . Now the curtain gently begins to rise and you can see [whatever the therapist wants to suggest]."

Should the patient be phobic of being alone, we have suggested that they are accompanied to the theater by the therapist.

Television Approach

We have generally used the television approach with children. The child is asked to rest comfortably in the chair or bed. We then usually proceed in the following manner:

"We are going to play a game if you like, and this is going to help you get well . . . but you have to cooperate and help me so that I can help you. . . . Now close your eyes and begin to see what is apparently a television set like you have at home. . . . See it? . . . Good . . . just relaxed and at ease . . . breathing easily . . . just relaxing all over . . . listening to every word I say. . . . Now the television set comes on and you can see one of your favorite programs coming on and as you do, nod your head, yes . . . good . . . Now just let the television scene fade out and you are going to become very relaxed and able to do what I tell you . . . just relaxed and at ease."

Coin Technique

The patient sits upright in a chair for the coin method. He or she is asked to extend the dominant arm forward at a level even with the shoulder. The palm is up, and a coin, usually a quarter or fifty-cent piece, is placed on the ulnar edge of the patient's hand. He or she is told,

"Breathe in a relaxing fashion concentrating your thoughts on the coin, but listening to my voice. . . . Now I am going to start counting, and as I count, your hand will begin turning. . . . do your understand? . . . good . . . and the coin will fall off. . . . When the coin falls off . . . your eyes will close and you will be relaxed . . . extremely relaxed and drowsy and at ease . . . capable of entering a very deep level of trance . . . the arm will be dramatically relaxed . . . it feels like a heavy weight, then this feeling will spread throughout your body . . . heavy . . . relaxed and at ease. . . . Do you understand? . . . good . . . now do exactly as I have instructed you to do. . . Now the coin falls and you are in a state of hypnosis."

Non-Verbal Technique

There are times when a patient cannot talk to the therapist because of illness or because he or she is no longer conscious (Crasilneck and Hall, 1968). In such instances the patient can either squeeze the therapist's hand with prearranged signals for yes and no or use ideomotor finger signals, such as lifting and lowering an index finger. Even blinking of the patient's eyelids may be used for prearranged signals for yes and no.

Chiasson's Method

Chiasson, an obstetrician, has developed a popular method of induction that relies on linking normal physiological responses with suggestions for hypnotic induction (1973). The patient is instructed to place his or her hand in front of the face, palm facing away, with the fingers held together. A distance of about a foot from the face is recommended. This position places a natural strain on the fingers, which spontaneously tend to spread apart. This natural response is linked with the suggestion that "as your fingers spread, you will fall into a hypnotic state." Suggestions are also usually given that the entire hand will approach the face and that when the hand touches the face, the subject will enter a deep state of hypnotic trance. Should there be any difficulty in the induction, it is helpful to add the suggestion that "each time that you breathe out, your hand will approach your face a little bit more." This last suggestion utilizes the normal tendency of the hand, when held in this position, to move toward the chest during expiration. We have found Chiasson's method particularly useful with persons who resist a relaxation approach.

Relaxation Technique

The patient sits comfortably in a chair with his or her feet on an ottoman and his or her legs uncrossed. If hospitalized, he or she lies comfortably in bed. These positions are most conducive for the relaxation technique. After the patient assumes a relaxed position, we start our session.

"Now just concentrate your thoughts on my voice and let your body relax as deeply as you can. . . . Take a series of breaths as deep as you like. . . . Good. . . . Your eyes, especially your eyelids, will begin to feel very very heavy, drowsy and somewhat sleepy . . . yes, they begin to blink . . . and as they do they are becoming very, very heavy. . . . It's hard to keep them open . . . Your eyes are watering . . . blinking rapidly . . . tired . . . Let them close . . . so heavy you can hardly keep them open and they are now closed. . . . The feeling that you can attain in your body is of complete and total muscular relaxation . . . you are just relaxing into a deep and relaxed state. . . . You are just listening to my voice . . . and you are drifting into a very, very pleasant state of mind and body . . . free from all tension, tightness, stress, and strain . . . listening to my voice guiding you into a complete and total state of relaxation . . . your mind . . . your body . . . the muscular system . . . the nervous system . . . limp relaxed muscles . . . your respirations are the epitome of relaxation. . . . Now your entire body will become completely and totally relaxed . . . your head, your face, neck, shoulders, back, chest, arms, hands, abdomen, buttocks, pelvis, thighs, legs, and feet . . . just completely relaxed . . . completely, totally relaxed . . . your mind and body . . . free from tension, tightness, stress, and strain."

Other Common Techniques

It is impossible even in classroom teaching to describe precisely the hypnotic suggestions a therapist must use with each type of patient. As we have previously stated, the actual wording will vary with individual patients and their own idiosyncrasies. We have attempted to illustrate various therapeutic approaches that we advocate with certain types of problems. There are, however, some generalizations that we can briefly explore. In many cases, as a part of the induction, we introduce the concept of glove anesthesia.

"You will be aware of your finger [or if appropriate, the hand] becoming numb and insensitive to feeling. . . . It now has the feeling of a thick leather glove around it . . . as you are aware of this glovelike feeling, nod your head. . . . Good. . . . Now open your eyes and notice that I am sticking your finger quite severely with a nail file, but no pain . . . and with a little more force I would break the skin . . . no pain. . . . I stop. . . . I now suggest that normal feeling return to the finger. . . . Now, I am going to stimulate the same

finger. . . . Now you are withdrawing your finger. . . . You withdrew it . . . yes
. . . with only slight pressure . . . demonstrating to you the power of your
unconscious mind over your body in the control and feeling of severe pain. . . .
The anesthetized finger felt nothing with severe stimulation, but when the finger
that was not anesthetized you felt only a minor amount of stimulation."

This approach is applicable to virtually every problem that a
therapist might see. It can be used to control pain by transferring the
glove anesthesia to another part of the body. It can be used with
constant reinforcement in the form of hypnoanesthesia for surgical
problems or in obstetrical cases. It can be used quite well in terminal
pain problems.

It also has great advantage in functional problems. For example:

"I have now demonstrated the power of your mind over your body, and
if you can block severe pain as you have just done, you can block the craving
for [tobacco, excessive food intake, alcohol]."

There are times during a therapeutic session when the therapist
must be discrete in the descriptive choice of words. If the suggestion is
too volatile or too compulsive, rigid, and authoritarian, the patient
might respond excessively.

Several years ago a physician patient was told by a neophyte
therapist that any cigarette that he smoked would have a sickening odor
of vomitus. The physician reported subsequently that any time that he
attempted to smoke he immediately became nauseated. The reaction
was so severe that it began to interfere with his work. We feel that the
strength of such hypnotic suggestions can be quite debilitating and in
our opinion are contraindicated. Less dramatic suggestions are usually
of equal effectiveness and are more in keeping with a dignified regard
for the patient's sensibilities.

There are times in an exploratory hypnoanalytic session when the
therapist is obligated to take an active part verbally in a patient's
fantasy or recall. Hypnotic age regression was used with a retrograde
amnesic female who had been attacked and beaten. She was hypnotized by a hand-levitation method. After attaining a deep level of
trance, she was told the following:

"Nothing is ever forgotten. . . . You can recall any fact or memory . . . no
matter how long ago . . . no matter how unpleasant . . . you can remember and
you will [patient begins to whimper and moves on the couch]. . . . You are
going back in time and space . . . back to this period of your life that you have
forgotten and you begin to move backward in your life span . . . back to exactly
where you were at [date and time]. . . . You can see everything happening . . .
you can feel someone breathing . . . The hair is standing up on your body as it

did then. . . . You are petrified. . . . You are back there . . . remembering
every moment."

The patient screamed, abreacting violently the entire episode as
she recalled it. In such a case the therapist must use the words,
thoughts, and description during the regression that will bring forth the
best recollection possible. Through interviewing and review of the case
history, we note significant events that may help the patient to exactly
recall the past events. Questions during hypnotic age regression are
based on this information. Following recall, the therapist will then
decide whether it is preferable that the patient (1) remember all the facts
immediately, (2) recall some of the facts, (3) slowly recall all of the
facts, or (4) allow the therapist to help recall these facts in hypnotherapy. At the conclusion of the age regression the therapist then
states (after making the above decision),

"You are now returning to the present time and place and you can rest
assured that this psychological approach has helped you to overcome your
problem."

In the course of hypnotherapy, age regression was used with a
veteran of World War II who suffered a severe anxiety neurosis,
overreacting to the sounds of machinery in the factory where he
worked. His symptoms had begun as a traumatic neurosis on the
battlefield. During the session he was told, "You can remember, feel,
respond, react exactly as you did at [location] on [date]." The abreaction was moderate to severe, but when the therapist whistled to
simulate the sound of a falling bomb, the patient had to be forceably
held down and his screaming could be heard throughout the entire
ward. Some persons might argue that such realism is not necessary. Of
course, the final decision rests with the therapist; however, the release
of this repressed material helped in the resolution of the patient's
neurosis.

Certain precautions should be taken in giving hypnotic suggestions
for the hallucinating of past traumatic events. In our opinion, once the
desired goal is achieved, it is not necessary to prolong or increase the
severity of abreaction. For example, if a patient is told he is running a
foot race and he responds by panting, with a definite increase in pulse
rate, it is not necessary to then suggest that he is "running up an incline
faster and faster."

PERSONALIZED HYPNOTIC TECHNIQUES

In addition to tailoring hypnotic suggestions to the needs of the subject, the therapist should develop induction techniques that are compatible with his or her own personality. A therapist who is emotionally uncomfortable with authoritarian techniques should not attempt to use them routinely, since they will most often prove unconvincing because the subject may be aware of the therapist's strained voice. After all, as Spiegel and Spiegel (1980) state, an induction procedure is in essence merely a ceremony through which the therapist and patient agree that the subject will have full permission to experience hypnotic phenomena to the greatest extent he or she can. The development of technique may be a gradual process, altering over time as the therapist gains experience with various hypnotic techniques. A general principle of technique is to give suggestions that follow the natural physiological changes that can be observed in the subject. As the hand is seen to levitate, for example, this is acknowledged as "Now your hand is moving." Any objective or even subjective experience of the patient may be utilized, although subjective experiences that cannot be verified by observation should be stated more tentatively, as "You may experience the weight of your legs against the couch as you relax more and more, deeper and deeper." Hunchak (1980) has even suggested using as a focus of attention such phenomena as the vague fields of gray light that can be seen in the visual field when the eyes are closed.

Another principle that may be utilized in the development of personalized hypnotic techniques is the pairing of hypnotically induced sensory or motor alterations with the target symptom to be treated. For example, two of the most useful induced hypnotic experiences are glove anesthesia and catalepsy (stiffening) of an arm. After glove anesthesia has been successfully induced (perhaps limited to one fingertip), the patient may be asked to open his or her eyes and observe while the therapist vigorously stimulates the anesthetized area with a blunt nail file or similar instrument. Even if the anesthesia is incomplete, the subject may be able to experience a marked decrease in painful sensations compared with the waking state. This analgesia may then be directly transferred to a painful area, as "The analgesia that you have experienced in your fingertip will now also occur in the painful area of your back, the discomfort becoming less and less, pain decreasing more and more." An alternate use of the glove analgesia is to facilitate the general ability of the patient to alter pathological symptoms, as "Your unconscious mind is able to decrease the pain sensitivity of your fingertip, as you have just experienced, and it can and will use this same ability to alter, diminish, and decrease your unwanted unhealthy, outgrown habit of cigarette smoking."

Some sensory and motor alterations are more analogous to the treatment of certain symptoms. Arm catalepsy, for example, may be made to symbolically suggest a cure of impotence, the stiff arm being like the stiffening of the penis. Since the unconscious seems to be associated in symbolic ways, such analogies can be quite effective most of the time.

SUMMARY

In this chapter we have presented those techniques of induction that we have found to be best suited to our personalities and to be most successful with our patients. We, in addition, have included some techniques that have proved successful for other therapists. As we have already stated, these are not a definitive list of available procedures. Each therapist must find what is most satisfactory for him or her and for his or her patients. In the ensuing chapters further suggestions are incorporated for specific types of induction and the wording to be used with the special type of problems seen in the clinical practice of hypnotherapy.

REFERENCES

Alderete JF: The induction of hypnosis through an interpreter. Am J Clin Hypn 10:138–140, 1967
Barber J: Hypnosis and the hypnotizable. Am J Clin Hypn 23:4–9, 1980
Barber TX: Measuring "hypnotic-like" suggestibility with and without "hypnotic induction." Psychol Rep 16:809–844, 1965
Barber TX: Suggested ("hypnotic") behavior: The trance paradigm versus an alternative paradigm, in Fromm E, Shor RE (eds): Hypnosis Research Developments and Perspectives. Chicago, Aldine-Atherton, 1972, p. 115–182
Blum GS: Experimental observation on the contextual nature of hypnosis. Int J Clin Exp Hypn 15:160–177, 1967
Blumenthal LS: Confidence, the keystone of the physician, patient relationship: How hypnotism is based on this confidence. Am J Clin Hypn 1:169–175, 1959
Bowers KS: Hypnosis for the Seriously Curious. New York, W. W. Norton, 1976, pp 110–125
Bowers KS: Do the Stanford scales tap the "classic suggestion effect"? Int J Clin Exp Hypn 29:42–53, 1981a
Bowers KS: Has the sun set on the Stanford scales? Am J Clin Hypn 24:79–88, 1981b
Cheek DB, LeCron LM: Clinical Hypnotherapy. New York, Grune & Stratton, 1968
Chiasson SW: A Syllabus on Hypnosis. American Society of Clinical Hypnosis Education and Research Foundation, Des Plaines, Ill., 1973, p 14

Cohen SB: Tests of susceptibility/hypnotizability, in Wester WC, Smith AH (eds): Clinical Hypnosis: A Multidisciplinary Approach. Philadelphia, J. B. Lippincott, 1983

Cooperman S, Schafer DW: Hypnotherapy over the telephone. Am J Clin Hypn 25:277–279, 1983

Coulton D: Writing techniques in hypnotherapy. Am J Clin Hypn 8:287–298, 1966

Crasilneck HB: (Panelist) The practical uses of "telephone therapy" for pain reenforcement. The Society for Clinical Experimental Hypnosis Annual Meeting, Los Angeles, 1965

Crasilneck HB, Hall JA: The use of hypnosis with unconscious patients. Int J Clin Exp Hypn 10:141–144, 1968

Crasilneck HB, Hall JA: The use of hypnosis in the rehabilitation of complicated vascular and post-traumatic neurological patients. Int J Clin Hypn 18:145–159, 1970

Das JP: Body-sway suggestibility and mental deficiency. Int J Clin Exp Hypn 9:13–15, 1961

Deckert GH, West LJ: The problem of hypnotizability: A review. Int J Clin Exp Hypn 11:205–235, 1963

Dittborn JM, Munoz L, Artistequieta A: Facilitation of suggested sleep after repeated performances of the sleep suggestibility test. Int J Clin Exp Hypn 11:236–240, 1963

Erickson MH: The confusion technique in hypnosis. Am J Clin Hypn 4:183–210, 1964a

Erickson MH: Pantomine techniques in hypnosis and the implications. Am J Clin Hypn 7:64–70, 1964b

Erickson MH: The use of symptoms as an integral part of hypnotherapy. Am J Clin Hypn 8:59–65, 1965

Erickson MH: Advanced Techniques of Hypnosis and Therapy: Selected Papers. Haley J (ed). New York, Grune & Stratton, 1967

Estabrooks GH, May JR: Hypnosis in integrative motivation. Am J Clin Hypn 7:346–352, 1965

Evans FJ: An experimental indirect technique for the induction of hypnosis without awareness. Int J Clin Exp Hypn 15:72–85, 1967

Field PB: An inventory scale of hypnotic depth. Int J Clin Exp Hypn 13:238–249, 1965

Fourie DP: Relationship aspects of hypnotic susceptibility. Percept Mot Skills 51:1032–1034, 1980

Friedman J, Kleep W: Hypnotizability of newly admitted psychotic patients. Psychosomatics 4:95–98, 1963

Frischolz Z, Spiegel H, Tryon W, Fisher S: The relationship between the Hypnotic Induction Profile and the Stanford Susceptibility Scale, Form C: revisited. Am J Clin Hypn 24:98–105, 1981

Gale C, Herman M: Hypnosis and the psychotic pain. Psychiatr Q 30:417–424, 1956

Garmize LM, Marcuse FL: Some parameters of body sway. Int J Clin Exp Hypn 17:187–194, 1969

Gravitz MA: Psychodynamics of resistance to hypnotic induction. Psychother Theory Res Practice 8:185–187, 1971

Gravitz MA: Early uses of telephone and recording in hypnosis. Am J Clin Hypn 25:280–282, 1983

Green JT: Hypnotizability of hospitalized psychotics. Int J Clin Exp Hypn 17:103–108, 1969

Hartland J: The general principles of suggestion. Am J Clin Hypn 9:211–219, 1967

Hartman BJ: Hypnotic susceptibility assessed in a group of mentally ill geriatric patients. J Am Geriatr Soc 13:460–461, 1965

Heath ES, Stratas NE, Davis DF: Hypnotizability in senile and arteriosclerotic chronic brain syndromes. Dis Herv Syst 23:23–24, 1962

Hilgard ER: Hypnotic susceptibility scales under attack. An examination of Weitzenhoffer's criticisms. Int J Clin Exp Hypn 29:24–41, 1981a

Hilgard ER: The eye roll sign and other scores of the Hypnotic Induction Profile (HIP) as related to the Stanford Hypnotic Susceptibility Scale, Form C (SHSS:C): A critical discussion of a study by Frischhoiz and others. Am J Clin Hypn 24:89–97, 1981b

Hilgard ER: Further discussion of the HIP and the Stanford Form C: A reply to a reply by Frischholz, Spiegel, Tryon, and Fisher. Am J Clin Hypn 24:106–108, 1980

Hilgard ER: Illusion that the eye-roll sign is related to hypnotizability. Arch Gen Psychiatry 39(8):963–966, 1982

Horne DJ, De L, Powlett V: Hypnotizability and rating scales, in Burrows GD, Dennerstein L (eds): Handbook of Hypnosis and Psychosomatic Medicine. Amsterdam, Elsevier/North-Holland Biomedical Press, 1980, pp 119–131

Hunchak J: Hypnotic induction by entopic phenomena. Am J Clin Hypn 22:223–224, 1980

Isasi A: Dos casos de sofrosis en sordomedos. Rev Lat Am Hypn Clin 3:92–94, 1962

Klemperer E: Techniques of hypnosis and hypnoanalysis. Int J Clin Exp Hypn 17:137–152, 1969

Kramer E: Group induction of hypnosis with institutionalized patients. Int J Clin Exp Hypn 14:243–246, 1966

Kroger WS: Clinical and Experimental Hypnosis (ed 2). Philadelphia, J. B. Lippincott Co., 1977, pp 39–44

Kubie LS: Hypnotism. Arch Gen Psychiatry 4:40–54, 1961

Lerner M: Feñomenologia de la inducion hipnotica. Bol Brasil Soc Int Hipn Clin Exp 1:540–548, 1958

London P: The Chidren's Hypnotic Susceptability Scale. Urbana, University of Illinois Press, 1962

McCord H: The hypnotizability of the mongoloid-type child. J Clin Exp Hypn 4:19–20, 1956

Martorano JT, Oestreicher C: Hypnosis of the deaf mentally ill: A clinical study. Am J Psychiatry 123:605–606, 1966

Meares A: Hypnography: A study in the therapeutic use of symbolic painting. Springfield, Ill., Charles C Thomas, 1957

Mott T Jr: The clinical importance of hypnotizability. Am J Clin Hypn 21:263–269, 1979

Orne MT: Can a hypnotized subject be compelled to carry out otherwise unacceptable behavior? Int J Clin Exp Hypn 20:101–117, 1972

Pattie FA, Griffith R: The non-hypnotizability of Korsakoff patients. Am J Clin Hypn 5:61–62, 1962

Perry C: Is hypnotizability modifiable? Int J Clin Exp Hypn 25:125–146, 1977

Pfeiffer W, Pfeiffer M: Konzentrative selbstent-spannug, die sich aus der buddhistischen Atemmedication und ares der Atemtherapie herleiten [Concentrative selfrelaxation through exercises originating from the Buddhist breathing meditation and from breathing exercises.] Z Psychother Med Psychol 16:172–181, 1966

Podolnick EE, Field PB: Emotional involvement, oral anxiety, and hypnosis. Int J Clin Exp Hypn 18:194–210, 1970

Polak PR, Mountain NE, Erncle RN: Hypnotizability and prediction of hypnotizability in hospitalized psychotic patients. Int J Clin Exp Hypn 12:252–257, 1964

Radtke HL, Spanos NP: The effect of rating scale descriptors on hypnotic depth reports. J Psychol 111:235–245, 1982

Reilly R, Parisher D, Carona A, Dobrovsky N: Modifying hypnotic susceptibility by practice and instruction. Int J Clin Exp Hypn 28:39–45, 1980

Rodger BP: Recognition and use of hypnoidal behavior in the surgical patient. Am J Clin Hypn 6:355–360, 1964

Schneck JM: Hypnoanalysis. Int J Clin Exp Hypn 10:1–12, 1962

Shor RE, Orne EC: The Harvard Group Scale of Hypnotic Susceptibility, Form A. Palo Alto, Calif., Consulting Psychologists Press, 1962

Shor RE, Orne EC: Norms on the Harvard group scale of hypnotic susceptibility, form A. Int J Clin Exp Hypn 11:39–47, 1963

Solovey D, Milechin H: Concerning the concept of hypnotic depth. J Clin Exp Hypn 3:243–252, 1955

Spiegel H: An eye-roll test for hypnotizability. Am J Clin Hypn 15:25–28, 1972

Spiegel H, Spiegel D: Induction techniques, in Burrows GD, Dennerstein L (eds): Handbook of Hypnosis and Psychosomatic Medicine. Amsterdam, Elsevier/North-Holland Biomedical Press, 1980, pp 131–145

Stanton EE: Hypnotherapy at a distance through the use of the telephone. Am J Clin Hypn 20:278–281, 1978

Staples LM: Time and patience: important factors in successful hypnotic induction and response. Am J Clin Hypn 5:200–204, 1963

Stein C: Some old-fashioned uncovering techniques in psychotherapy. Am J Clin Hypn 9:140–145, 1966

Stein C: Hypnotic projection in brief psychotherapy. Am J Clin Hypn 14:143–155, 1972

Sternlicht M, Wanderer ZW: Hypnotic susceptibility and mental deficiency. Int J Clin Exp Hypn 11:104–111, 1963

Tart CT: Psychedelic experiences associated with a novel hypnotic procedure, mutual hypnosis. Am J Clin Hypn 10:65–78, 1967

Tart CT: Self-report scales of hypnotic depth. Int J Clin Exp Hypn 18:105–151, 1970

Tart CT: Measuring the depth of an altered state of consciousness, with particular reference to self-report scales of hypnotic depth, in Fromm E, Shor RE (eds): Hypnosis: Research Developments and Perspectives. Chicago, Aldine-Atherton, 1972

von Dedenroth TEA: Trance depths: An independent variable in therapeutic results. Am J Clin Hypn 4:174–175, 1962

Weitzenhoffer AM, Hilgard ER: Stanford Hypnotic Susceptibility Scale, Forms A and B. Palo Alto, Calif., Consulting Psychologists Press, 1962

Weitzenhoffer A: Hypnotic susceptibility revisited. Am J Clin Hypn 22:130–146, 1980

Wolberg LR: Medical Hypnosis, vols. 1 and 2. New York, Grune & Stratton, 1948

Yarnell T: Symbolic assertive training through guided affective imagery in hypnosis. Am J Clin Hypn 14:194–195, 1972

5
Symptom Alteration with Hypnosis

One of the oldest arguments against symptom removal with hypnosis goes back to Freud, who initially was enthusiastic about hypnosis but largely abandoned it after his development of psychoanalysis. There are two apparent reasons for Freud's attitude. First, he apparently was not a successful hypnotherapist, and second, he considered hypnotic cures "superficial." Freud's failures must have caused him much consternation, for he later wrote that he gave up the "suggestion technique" and hypnosis, early in practice, because he despaired of making hypnotic suggestions "powerful and enduring enough" to effect his goal of permanent cure.

In Freud's developing psychoanalytic theory, symptoms were looked upon as a defense against underlying anxiety. Many of Freud's major disciples continued to share his deprecation of hypnosis, identifying it with a mere "cathartic treatment" or abreaction of repressed emotion. There has been a general feeling among psychoanalytically oriented therapists that the removal of a symptom with hypnosis would lead to the formation of a substitute symptom to express the same unresolved, unconscious conflict (Meldman, 1960).

In classic psychoanalytic therapy the making conscious of repressed memories and affects was viewed as the method of cure itself. More recently emphasis has been placed on the development and analysis of the so-called "transference neurosis," a presumed reawakening of the "original" infantile neurosis with the analyst being seen, in a distorted fashion, as the important parent figure.

Our clinical experience has not supported the traditional view that "insight" first occurs, followed by improvement in the presenting symptoms. In both psychotherapy and hypnotherapy patients have repeatedly shown an initial improvement in their presenting symptoms; *then* they have begun to see the origins of the symptoms in the unresolved psychological conflicts.

In the reality of the psychotherapeutic situation, the doctor is an authority figure and the patient actually does come to him for expert and technical treatment. This is like a parent–child relationship only in some ways, but it more resembles many situations of everyday life in which the "authority" is approached for help. After all, a nuclear physicist is "dependent" in relation to the auto mechanic who repairs his or her car, while the mechanic is "dependent" in relation to the barber who cuts his hair, and on and on. The person in the "authority" role of the hypnotic relationship can be looked upon as lending his or her ability to the patient as a proxy for the patient's own ego functions. With this prosthetic help from the therapist, the patient may take a more effective stance toward his or her infantile complexes and thereby is able to begin maturation. When the treatment helps the patient to feel strong, adequate, and mature, he or she then is able to face the infantile shadow side of his or her own feeling and behavior. Emotional insight often occurs first; intellectual and verbal insight follow.

RANGE AND EFFECT POSSIBLE
BY SYMPTOM ALTERATION

Wolberg (1948) clearly delineates those areas in which direct symptom removal may be beneficial, even though admitting its limitations. "Results are best," says Wolberg, "when the need for symptom-free functioning constitutes a powerful incentive." He also states "that relief from a symptom may improve the patient's self-respect and alter his whole pattern of adjustment."

Symptom suppression as used today is far different from a crude hypnotic suggestion to simply take away whatever is bothering the patient (Hodge, 1959; Schneck, 1959; Slater and Flores, 1963; Yanovski and Curtis, 1968). Spiegel (1967a,b) uses the term "symptom alteration," which he defines as "simply direct guidance which veers the patient's attention away from his symptoms and concomitantly reminds him that more resourceful and effective means are available for his use in coping with problems of adaptation."

Actually, a wide range of hypnotic effect is to be considered in the alteration of symptoms. The suggestion may simply be given for the symptom to diminish or approach a vanishing point. This may be very effective in symptoms that are "empty," that is, have no active psychodynamic meaning. Instead of being suppressed the symptom may be diminished to some degree, not removed entirely, as usually done when dealing with organic pain, since the total alleviation of pain could mask warning signs of further disease processes. If the patient is resistant to giving up the symptom, perhaps a less disturbing activity can be substituted under hypnosis; for example, a facial tic may be suppressed and a finger movement introduced.

Permissive suggestions can be given that the patient will give up the symptom when he or she decides to do so, not necessarily at the time of hypnotherapy. This may be an effective approach with patients whose symptoms seem to involve a dominance-submission conflict.

It is essential not to rupture or blatantly destroy a symptom that may have a serious psychodynamic meaning for the patient. Instead, the symptom may be diminished, substituted with a less pathological symptom, or altered to a form less disturbing to the patient's life. In some cases, the meaning of the symptom should be explored before any attempt is made to modify it with hypnotherapy (Crasilneck, 1978). For example, a woman in her fifties was referred by her dentist with a severe condition of gagging, which prevented much needed dental work, except under general anesthesia. Although the symptom appeared to be "empty" by initial history, a more extensive review of her problem revealed that it apparently began when her husband repeatedly coerced her into performing fellatio on him against her will. She had developed such excessive gagging that she could not even brush her teeth, although the original psychodynamic meaning had been lost to conscious awareness. After uncovering this hidden cause, she responded adequately to hypnotherapy and her neglected dental work was completed satisfactorily.

Frequently it is possible to discover, under hypnosis, the meaning of the symptom, but instead of removing the symptom the choice is made to leave the symptom intact, letting the patient work through the conflict at his or her own speed in psychotherapy or psychoanalysis. For example, a 23-year-old woman had suffered for years from recurrent bouts of tinnitus, which reached a peak at her engagement party, where she fainted in response to a friend's joking remark "I see you've decided to walk the plank!" Hoping to cure the symptom, for which no organic basis could be identified, she entered psychoanalysis. Four months of work made little headway, and the analyst referred her for hypnotherapy in the hope that hypnotic suggestion might uncover memories that her defenses kept hidden.

She was allowed to regress under hypnosis to whatever age she wished, being asked to signal by a finger movement when she was experiencing some past event connected with the tinnitus. She regressed to age six, reliving in a vivified manner her first childish sexual play with a neighborhood boy, which had produced intense guilt feelings. Several days later a group of her playmates approached her to play "pirate." In the game, she learned, to her distress, that they knew of her "badness" and were going to have her "walk the plank" in punishment. They blindfolded her, spun her around on the edge of the swimming pool, and pushed her in. Terrified, she heard the muffled sound of their screaming as she sank under water. A gardener fortunately was at hand and rescued her, but the event had been the most traumatic of her childhood. Although she consciously remembered it, she had not connected the sound of the screaming as she fell into the water with the tinnitus she had experienced. The other times she had experienced severe attacks of tinnitus now made sense—once on a boat trip to Europe while watching bathers diving into the pool and once when she dropped a piece of ice into a cup of hot coffee, feeling nauseated as it was spinning and melting. She also recalled a time later in childhood when she had been reading a book on pirates and suddenly slammed it shut with unexplained fear.

It was felt that having the patient suddenly remember this event might rupture ego defenses that had shown their tenacity over many years. Amnesia was induced for all that she had remembered in hypnotic age regression. After consultation with the analyst, it was decided to help her to remember these buried traumas during waking psychotherapy. This approach was rapidly successful, and she married a few months later, with no indication that the tinnitus would recur.

The importance of a slow assimilation into the waking ego of psychodynamic material obtained under hypnosis is exemplified by the case of an 18-year-old married young woman who had virtually destroyed her nasal septum through excessive picking of her nose (Crasilneck 1983). In spite of the conscious realization that she was injuring herself, she was unable to restrain the habit and would dig at her nose violently to "remove all the drainage." Under hypnotic age-regression she recalled an early childhood memory, about age 4, when an older uncle involved her in sex play. She remembered what must have been his ejaculate on her hand. It had resembled the "drainage" from her nose. Even at age 4, she realized that they had done something "bad" and that she could not tell her parents. Her symptom seemed to be an unconscious enactment meant to undo an original and consciously forgotten event.

It was deemed unwise for her to suddenly face the buried memory, as it might have created an ego-state that was regressive and perhaps flooded with anxiety.

While in trance, during the next several sessions, she was led to remember the events, gradually, at progressively more advanced ages, until the formerly repressed memory was near her present age. At such time it arose spontaneously into her conscious memory and was assimilated without undue trauma. Her nosepicking compulsion then yielded readily to hypnotherapy of a more direct and suggestive manner.

Symptom alteration may sometimes be relatively quick and effective and should not be considered as always second best to extended psychotherapy. Erickson (1953) has reported one hypnotic treatment relieving psychosomatic headache, with relatively good adjustment for a 15-year follow-up period. The woman patient was told that at the onset of her headache she would go to her room, sleep half an hour, wake up, and give vent to anger at whomever she wished, giving rein to her fantasy, and then would sleep for another half hour, awakening refreshed. She followed the instructions explicitly. The headache vanished, although the patient had little if any insight into the anger behind it.

Haley (1961), using Erickson's framework, speaks of a "therapeutic bind," in which the patient can no longer control the behavior of the hypnotist by maintaining his or her symptom but rather finds that to exert his or her own influence it is necessary to relinquish the sumptom as a means of manipulating others. Also utilizing Erickson's technique of revivification, Klemperer (1963) reports results that seem to be achieved by the patient experiencing the past state while being able to converse simultaneously about it on an adult level.

Feeling that the past fears about symptom removal have been excessive, Hartland (1965) states that "few patients will abandon their symptoms . . . until they feel strong enough to do without them." He suggests that the effectiveness of symptom removal is enhanced by antecedent psychotherapy. His "ego-strengthening" technique consists essentially of positive suggestions for self-worth and effectiveness.

Hershman (1981) has found the teaching of self-hypnosis of value in symptom alteration; he cites particular advantages that include the absence of masking physical symptoms of a progressive nature and the absence of the potential abuse that can occur with medications.

SYMPTOM SUBSTITUTION

We have felt that as long as a symptom has deep psychological meaning for the patient, it will not easily yield to hypnosis, making working-through of the symbolic meaning imperative in resistant cases (Crasilneck, 1958). Symptom substitution may be useful when the presenting complaint is debilitating but does not easily respond to direct suggestion.

A successful businessman who presented with aphonia, being able to converse only in a forced whisper, is a good example of the employment of symptom substitution. Under hypnoanalysis we quickly learned that he had immense repressed hostility toward a supervisor who had continually encouraged him to "speak up" during conferences, then ridiculed him for whatever ideas he expressed. Unable to retaliate without endangering his position with the company, he had developed the conversion symptom of a virtual loss of speech. When he did not seem able immediately to abandon the symptom, it was suggested that it would be largely replaced by a soreness in his right great toe. This particular substitute symptom was chosen for a specific reason—he had expressed desire to "kick the hell" out of his supervisor. As he resolved his conflict and in a mature fashion was able directly to tell his employer of his anger, defending himself appropriately, the soreness of the toe was gradually diminished under hypnosis.

A young career military noncommissioned officer was successfully treated by Crasilneck (1979) with hypnotherapy for conversion symptoms of unilateral facial paresthesia concurrent with blurred vision on the same side. These symptoms occurred abruptly after he lost a boxing match and with it the title that he had acquired for his company in the boxing matches the preceding year. The symptoms had been present for 6 months, failing to yield to intensive neurological and psychiatric treatment. A careful history revealed that although he won his previous bouts he had caused permanent brain damage in one of the defeated opponents. He had refused to fight the next year, but was urged and constrained with unofficial disciplinary pressure to defend "the honor of the company." His fear of possibly injuring an opponent caused ambivalence, which may have contributed to his losing the match. Under hypnotic regression, he recalled the first moments after he lost the fight. He was relieved that no one had been injured, but was overcome with two thoughts: (1) "Now I have lost face in front of my men," and (2) "I can't face them to see their reactions." In a classic example of conversion hysteria, he then experienced the physical symbolic form of his thoughts, the paresthesia possibly symbolizing "loss of face" and the blurred vision representing not wishing to see the men's reactions to him. The fact that his symptoms occurred only unilaterally may have expressed the underlying ambivalence of his conflict.

Although this repressed material sufficiently explained the problem, the symptoms were not removed immediately with hypnosis. Instead, he was given a posthypnotic suggestion that as he exercised by squeezing a rubber ball with the hand on his afflicted side, his symptoms would abate, diminish, and finally vanish. The patient was returned to the referring physician, who was an excellent hypnotherapist and who would continue the treatment. Over several weeks following hypnotic suggestion, his physician used hypnoanalysis allowing the patient to gain intellectual and emotional insight into his problem. The paresthesia disappeared shortly thereafter, and his vision returned to normal.

There is no doubt that spontaneous substitute symptom formation does occur in some cases. Also, sometimes a symptom once removed by hypnosis may recur until the underlying conflict is resolved.

Some years ago a woman was referred by her psychiatrist with the diagnosis of acute conversion reaction. She was 38 years of age and married. She had experienced the sudden onset of a persistent clinching of her teeth one evening when she returned home after having a dental extraction and found her husband, with whom she had a good marriage relation, about to strike one of their children. She reported that she had not eaten anything since her dental surgery and had only taken a few sips of water. Hypnosis was rather easily induced, which is frequently the case with hysterical patients, and she responded easily to suggestions to open her mouth to eat and drink. She was instructed to return the next day, at which time the next day the condition of clenched teeth had returned.

She was inducted again into hypnotic trance and given a suggestion that she would again relax her jaws but that another symptom of lesser severity might, if needed, substitute for the clenched teeth. She awoke with complete freedom of movement in her jaw but with a feeling of constriction in her right arm. Inquiry about the substitute sympton revealed that at the time she had seen her husband about to strike the child she had begun to call him "a son-of-a-bitch" and with her right hand had started to pick up a ladle to hit him. At that very moment her teeth had locked tightly shut.

Anamnesis established the original traumatic situation behind her symptom formation. Twenty years earlier she had married against her parents' wishes and, in their opinion, beneath her station in life. She had moved with her husband to a tenement dwelling in a distant city, where she soon fell under the control of her aggressive and domineering mother-in-law. During a particularly heated argument with the mother-in-law she called the older woman "a son-of-a-bitch" and had said in anger "I hope you die!" Within the hour her husband's mother had suffered a near-fatal heart attack, and our patient formed a strong unconscious fantasy about the powerful nature of her death wishes.

It is easy to understand how the impulse to curse her husband would have stirred an unconscious fear that such an angry name might magically cause him, like her mother-in-law, to suffer a coronary occlusion or other severe disease. The wish to protect her husband from her anger, which she fantasized as magically powerful, was suddenly thrust against the angry impulse itself with symptom formation a compromise "way out" for both conflicting impulses.

Six months later, after extensive hypnoanalysis and working through, she was dismissed from therapy, symptom free.

We would never deny the importance of careful attention to conflicts behind symptoms. We feel that symptoms should not be directly removed without attempting to give the patient insight.

It would be enlightening to attempt experimentally direct hypnotic removal of the symptoms of severely neurotic persons in a cloistered setting. If more severe substitute symptoms followed, or if transient psychotic states ensued, it would be a confirmation of the classic psychoanalytic theory. If this did not happen—and neurosis could be effectively treated in this manner—much reconceptualization would be needed.

REFERENCES

Crasilneck HB: The control of pain and symptom management, in Bowers MK (ed): Introductory Lectures in Medical Hypnosis. New York, Institute for Research in Hypnosis, 1958

Crasilneck HB: The psychological aspects of hypnodontia. Presented at a workshop at Baylor University Dental School, Dallas, Texas, 1978

Crasilneck HB: Use of hypnosis in conversion reaction. Presented at grand rounds Lakland Air Force Base, San Antonio, Texas, 1979

Crasilneck HB: (Panelist) The use of hypnosis in symptom alteration. Swedish Society for Clinical and Experimental Hypnosis, Stockholm, Sweden, 1983

Erickson MH: The therapy of a psychosomatic headache. J Clin Exp Hypn 1:2–6, 1953

Haley J: Control in brief psychotherapy. Arch Gen Psychiatry 4:139–153, 1961

Hartland J: The value of "ego-strengthening" procedures prior to direct symptom-removal under hypnosis. Am J Clin Hypn 8:89–93, 1965

Hershman SH: Methods for habit disruption, in Wain, HJ: Theoretical and Clinical Aspects of Hypnosis. Miami, Symposia Specialists, Inc., 1981, pp 135–133

Hodge JR: The management of dissociative reactions with hypnosis. Int J Clin Exp Hypn 7:205–215, 1959

Klemperer E: Symptom removal by revivification. Am J Clin Hypn 5:277–280, 1963

Meldman MJ: Personality decompensation after hypnotic symptom suppression. JAMA 173:359–361, 1960

Schneck JM: Symptom relief, authority, substitution, and suggestibility, with special reference to hypnotherapy. Dis Nerv Syst 20:1–4, 1959

Slater RC, Flores LS: Hypnosis in organic symptom removal: A temporary removal of an organic paralysis by hypnosis. Am J Clin Hypn 5:248–255, 1963

Spiegel H: Is symptom removal dangerous? Am J Psychiatry 123:1279–1283, 1967a

Spiegel H: Hypnosis: An adjunct to psychotherapy, in Freedman AM, Kaplan HI (eds): Comprehensive Textbook of Psychiatry. Baltimore, Williams & Wilkins, 1967b

Wolberg LR: Medical Hypnosis. Practice of Hypnotherapy, vol. 2. New York, Grune & Stratton, 1948, pp 1–2

Yanovski A, Curtis GC: Hypnosis and stress. Am J Clin Hypn 10:149–156, 1968

6
Hypnosis in the Control of Pain

Many theories have been advanced to explain the effectiveness of hypnosis in the control of pain, ranging from cortical inhibition to role-playing. Some researchers have even suggested that reports of effective pain relief by hypnosis are fraudulent or that the supposed hypnotic anesthesia was actually due to surgical shock. Others have suggested that pain is not actually diminished by hypnoanalgesia but that hypnotic subjects either do not fully report the pain they experience or else develop amnesia for the experienced pain (Barber, 1964). Experimental work by Hilgard (1975, 1980) and Hilgard and his colleagues demonstrated the reality of the effectiveness of hypnosis in the control of pain, both in the laboratory and clinically (Hilgard and Hilgard, 1975). His description of a "hidden observer" in the patient's mind; a part that may with appropriate hypnotic suggestions remember the nonexperienced pain, lends support to Hilgard's neodissociation theory of hypnosis.

The utility of hypnotic intervention in acute and chronic pain is now widely appreciated (Barber, 1982; Bassman and Wester, 1983; Chiasson, 1983; Crasilneck 1978a,b, 1979a,b, 1982, 1983; Ewin, 1978; Finer, 1982; Kroger, 1977; Melzack and Perry, 1975; Mutter and Karnilow, 1984; Sachs, 1977; Spiegel and Spiegel, 1978; Sternbach, 1982; Walker, 1980; Wester and Smith, 1983). Ewin (1978) distinguishes between the patient's pain and suffering; the removal of suffering aids in the alleviation of pain. The components of suffering he suggests are (1) nonacceptance, (2) fear of the unknown, (3) pessimism, (4) feeling that suffering has no end, (5) guilt and resentment. When effective, hypnotherapy can provide a treatment that is expeditious, inexpensive, nonaddicting, and safe in comparison to surgical and chemical alleviation of pain (Wain, 1980).

EVIDENCE OF EFFECTIVENESS OF HYPNOSIS

As early as 1932, Sears demonstrated that hypnotized subjects manifested less reaction to painful stimuli than did a nonhypnotized control group (Sears, 1932). Physiological signs such as psychogalvanic responses, facial flinching, and pulse rate were compared between experimental and control groups. A significant difference between the two groups existed, the hypnotized group showing significantly less reaction to the pain than the nonhypnotized controls. However, the hypnoanalgesia produced did not approach the pain-free state that one would have obtained if the patient had been anesthetized with chemical anesthesia.

Hightower (1966), Lettew (1971), Levendula (1961), and Sacercdote (1962, 1968) have given impressive case reports of pain relief with hypnosis. Wolfe (1962) was able to relieve severe pain in a chronic and terminal illness in a 60-year-old man suffering from chondrosarcoma, maintaining pain relief for the last 16 months of the man's life. In a random series of 17 patients with chronic intractable pain, Lea, Ware, and Monroe (1960) administered hypnosis for pain relief. Three improved sufficiently to be taken off all medications, and nine improved significantly in that the character of the pain was changed and less medication was needed. Of the five failures, four had severe complicating psychiatric problems. In this study it was also noted that medium or light hypnosis was as effective as the deeper state of somnambulism in effecting pain relief, a conclusion that does not seem valid in our own experience. Braun (1975) has also discussed failures in the use of hypnosis in the control of pain.

West, Niell, and Hardy (1952) observed that patients under hypnosis seemed unable to discriminate different intensities of experimentally produced pain. Galvanic skin responses also diminished.

Erickson (1966) found it useful to intersperse psychotherapeutic suggestions among those employed to induce and to maintain a hypnotic trance. Horvai (1966) emphasized that increased suggestibility of the patient, following hypnotic pain relief, may facilitate the psychotherapeutic work in other areas that trouble the patient. Cheek (1966) was able to employ hypnosis for effective pain relief in a patient who suffered severe disabling head and neck pain for 5 years, pain that was unrelieved with three surgical attempts and the usual methods of orthopedic treatment. August (1963) relieved disabling pain of 10 years' duration after 13 days of hypnotherapy.

Perhaps the only conclusion on which all authorities agree is that we do not know how or why hypnosis controls organic pain. Marmer wrote (1959):

> The nature of the actual mechanism by means of which chemical anesthetics produce their effect on the central nervous system is still unknown. All answers are hypothetical and theoretical. Many of the mechanisms of normal sleep are not well understood. Fortunately, this has never interfered with the clinical progress of anesthesiology. We all have learned how the drugs we use work clinically, even though we may not understand completely by what mechanism. So it is with hypnosis.

The reality of hypnotic analgesia, however, seems firmly demonstrated by the prize-winning work of Hilgard (1967, 1969, 1971). In his study, those subjects who were highly responsive to hypnosis were able to block ischemic pain for 18 to 45 minutes. They also showed increased tolerance for the pain of immersing an arm in cold water. It was notable that the mere induction of hypnosis alone without suggestions for analgesia (what we have termed "neutral hypnosis") did not significantly increase pain tolerance. Hilgard (1969) demonstrated a clear correlation between subject's verbal reports and the temperature of the water, leading him to state "that there is no physiological measure of pain which is either as discriminating of fine differences in stimulus conditions, as reliable upon repetition, or as lawfully related to changed conditions, as the subject's verbal report."

McGlashan, Evans, and Orne (1969) demonstrated that the pain relief obtained with hypnosis was conceptually distinguishable from a mere placebo response. They considered two components in hypnotic analgesia: the placebo response itself, and "a distortion of perception specifically induced during deep hypnosis."

Evans and Paul (1970) have reported that suggestion without hypnosis would procure a decrease in a subject's report of pain, although neither suggestions nor hypnotic induction procedures decreased certain physiologic responses. Black and Friedman (1968) measured the effects on the plasma cortisol levels of pain and emotion in eight deep trance hypnotic subjects. They concluded, among other things, that hypnotic suggestions of fear and anxiety can produce a rise in the plasma cortisol levels in some subjects and that in these subjects the hypnotic suggestion of anesthesia effectively prevents the full rise of the cortisol levels usually produced by pain.

Hilgard agrees with Evans and Paul that laboratory studies have not as yet produced a sufficient theoretical and experimental framework for the very striking pain relief achieved by clinical hypnosis, as reported, for example, by August (1963), Bartlett (1963), Cheek (1966), Crasilneck (1978b, 1979b, 1982, 1983), Erickson (1966), Meares (1967), Sacerdote (1962), and Wolberg (1948). Hilgard (1969) states, "Clinicians are at present far ahead of our laboratories in the hypnotic reduction of pain . . .," and adds (1971), that unless these experimental studies "are carried out eventually in the hospital, the information gained in the laboratory will tend to be idle and useless."

At least one component in the hypnotic diminution of pain is the decrease in anxiety that can be achieved with trance (Shor, 1962). It seems apparent that the physiological stimulus of pain is embroidered by psychological associations and fears. Conversely, when hypnosis is used to reproduce the experience of pain, respiratory and emotional changes seem easily reproduced while changes in blood pressure, skin temperature, and pulse rate may be only poorly produced (Dudley, Holmes, and Ripley, 1966). Even when clinical pain relief with hypnosis is not achieved, some partial improvement, even marked relief, may possibly result (Kehoe, 1967). Teaching the patient self-hypnosis for pain relief may be useful.

Some have emphasized the possible role of endorphins, which are opiate-like substances produced in the body, in hypnotic relief of pain; such possibilities are intriguing but not clearly established at the present time (Goldstein and Hilgard, 1975; Kroger, 1977; Olness, Wain, and Ng, 1980).

THEORIES ABOUT HYPNOSIS AND PAIN RELIEF

Although numerous theories have been formulated concerning why hypnosis blocks the perception of pain, they generally can be grouped in three categories, paralleling the theories of hypnosis. These emphasize (1) psychological mechanisms, (2) physiological mechanisms, or (3) a combination of the two mechanisms.

Barber (1964) propounds a psychological theory—that of role playing. Those individuals who feel that subjects who respond to pain while in a state of "hypnosis" are seen as simply playing a role, responding as a person is "supposed to" respond when he or she is not perceiving pain. Barber's many carefully designed laboratory studies emphasized antecedent variables that, in his opinion, account for the "hypnotic" phenomena observed. Barber consistently argues against using a hypnotic "state" as an explanatory principle.

It is difficult to accept the psychological approach as being a complete answer. Our empirical observations lead us to strongly consider a combination of physiological and psychological factors at work in the hypnotic control of pain. In individuals who enter deep levels of trance one observes a shift toward slower respiration, pallor of the skin (especially around the lips), slow speech in answering questions, and a certain degree of lethargy upon awakening from trance.

It may well be that hypnosis evokes some as yet unidentified type of neurological involvement that blocks the perception of pain. Guze, who stresses the physiological mechanisms in hypnosis, wrote (1961):

> It seems to me that hypnosis is a phenomenon which involves the reticular system and is manifest in the sensory motor effect which expresses itself in imagery and bodily experience. The activation period extends from deep sleep at the low activation level to cortical bombardment. The greater the bombardment from the ascending reticular activating system, the higher the activation.

Reyher (1968) has considered a phylogenetic model of hypnosis:

> When the induction procedure (which is really sensory restriction or a kind of sensory deprivation) succeeds, the phylogenetically older structures of the brain, which are now in control of overall brain functioning, are able to mediate behavior that is difficult or impossible to produce in the waking state. The compulsive quality of suggestions indicates that the operator has assumed the ego-function of analyzing and integrating sensory input. He has become the subject's eyes and ears, and his suggestions act in the same way as spontaneous impulses in the subject. These older structures (maybe the anterior cingulate gyrus) are known to have connections with many parts of the brain and to have inhibitory and excitatory influence over these areas.

There has been little experimental or clinical observation relevant to possible neurological mechanisms involved in hypnotic relief of pain. A possible neurophysiological basis for hypnosis, rather than purely a role-playing or psychological mechanism, is strongly suggested (1) by an unusual response during brain surgery under hypnosis (see Chapter 9), (2) by the success of hypnosis in naive children, (3) in persons not culturally acquainted with how a hypnotized person is supposed to behave, and (4) by the verbal reports of subjects who are clinically sophisticated. The following case reports are from our own work.

An example follows (Crasilneck and Hall, 1973) of good hypnotic response in a patient seeming unfamiliar with the concept of hypnosis. A 43-year-old housewife of very meager socioeconomic and educational background had been admitted to the hospital because of acute discomfort in both eyes. Examination and review of her history by the ophthalmologist revealed that she had corneal dystrophy. She had previously had two corneal transplants in her right eye, in May 1963 and February 1964. Results were disappointing, and she was discharged as incurable. The left eye developed Fuch's endothelial erosion. Her vision was reduced to noting gross hand movements with the right eye and to 20/40 vision in the left eye. Another corneal transplant was recommended. The patient at this time required heavy doses of narcotics for pain relief. Because of extreme discomfort and the possibility of additional chronic and acute pain associated with further surgery, psychiatric consultation was requested. The psychiatrist saw the patient for two weeks of extensive treatment but felt that he could offer little help. The psychiatric report suggested that any psychological problems were a secondary response to the severe organic pain. In addition, the patient had a very limited intelligence. Hypnosis for pain control was then considered.

At the first interview the patient appeared to be quite weak and in pain. She was crying pitifully and begging for narcotics. She apparently did not comprehend an explanation that an attempt would be made to hypnotize her. She was requested to close her eyes, which she finally did. This woman then responded in an excellent manner, with deep somnabulism evident in about 10 minutes as judged, among other signs, by the ability to open her eyes while remaining in trance. She was given the suggestion that she would "have much less pain in your eyes . . . you will more easily tolerate discomfort in your eyes, . . . you will not require a great amount of medicine, and you will be much more relaxed." Following the first hypnotic suggestion, she did not request narcotics again. She reported "a little hurt in the eyes, but sorta like a headache." Her previously described regression was replaced by a feeling of definite hope and cooperation.

Surgery was performed with excellent results. The patient did not ask nor require postoperative narcotics, but only aspirin on three occasions. The patient was dismissed one month later with good return of visual acuity.

It was our opinion that although this patient was never really cognizant of the meaning of hypnosis nor had any insight into its use, she nevertheless responded in a maximum fashion.

ORGANIC PAIN

There would seem to be marked differences between pain that originates in the laboratory and the severe pain perceived, perhaps over many months, by a patient with an organic disorder. It would seem obvious that the experience of pain that is induced in a laboratory experiment for several minutes cannot realistically be compared with the pain manifested by patients with metastatic tumor or thermal injury covering over one-half of the body surface or severe rheumatoid arthritis. This difference in pain in clinical experimental subjects is well appreciated by Hilgard (1969).

Our own observations suggest that there is some central inhibition of pain perception, perhaps analogous to that obtained when psychosurgery is done for relief of intractable pain and perhaps related to the Melzack-Wall "gate theory," with a central hypnotic change as the "gate-closing" stimulus. In such cases, according to Kalinowsky and Hoch (1961):

> . . . there is no actual loss of sensory perception in any particular area of distribution of sensory pathways. What is impaired is a more complicated and not yet fully understood mental process of attachment or detachment which modifies the primary sensory perception into a secondary awareness of caring or not caring. . . . It may be mentioned that in lobotomized patients the perception of applied pain, for example, in the usual sensitivity test to a needle, is not only preserved but the reaction of the patient to painful stimuli is even accented.

In contrast to this, however, the hypnotized patient seems to be able to block pain reaction to discrete body areas. This can lead to complications if the therapist is not fully aware of the limits of the area in which anesthesia has been induced. Hypnosis has been successful, for example, in decreasing the postoperative pain of defecation following hemorrhoidectomy. In such cases it is important to limit the suggested analgesia to the anal area rather than inducing anesthesia "below the waist." If such a broad analgesia were inappropriately induced, the patient might not be aware, for example, of a need to urinate.

We were among the first to report the clinical observation that patients with organic pain were unusually good subjects, seemingly because of a greater motivation and need for relief. Also, in cases seen for pain relief there seems to be a greater correlation between depth of trance and effectiveness of suggestions than in such motivational uses of hypnosis as reinforcing a desire to diet. Although depth of hypnosis does not generally correlate with the effectiveness of suggestions, in the case of severe organic pain it has seemed to us that the greater the depth of trance, the more likely it is that the suggestions for pain relief will be successful. Veldesy (1967) has taken the opposite view, stating that results are inversely proportional to illness severity.

At times hypnosis may be useful in aiding in the differential diagnosis of organic or functional pain. Although suggestions for relief may be effective in pain of either type, we have usually found that pain of organic origin tends to return more rapidly, usually within several hours after the first successful hypnotic induction. Thus, the hypnotic analgesia seems to fade at about the same rate as such chemical analgesics as morphine or meperidine. In contrast, pain of a functional origin may be relieved for days or weeks, even after the first few inductions. With repeated hypnosis, however, the length of effectiveness may dramatically increase in either organic or functional pain. If this differential response to suggestion for pain relief is to be used to decide between these two types of pain, the distinction must be based on the length of response to the first few successful treatments. Once the patient's pain relief is hypnotically reinforced on several occasions, both organic and functional pain may be relieved for equal periods of time.

In order for hypnosis to succeed, most of the time, in the control of organic pain, reinforcement of the pain control should occur before the pain exacerbates (Crasilneck, 1979b, 1984). It is vital to reinforce the control of pain with hypnosis as soon as the patient is aware of the return of the pain. The patient should be informed of this, so that he or she will be prepared for reinforcement sessions. This may be necessary at 3- to 5-hour intervals in the first 24-hour period. However, the pain may be controlled for 6 to 8 hours on the second day, 14 to 18 hours the third day, and 24 to 28 hours the fourth day. By the end of the first week, the patient may be reinforced every third day; by the end of the second week, every fourth day; and by the end of the third week, once a week and so on. Each patient should be taught self-hypnosis at the second session.

The following case illustrates the fashion in which the patient's response to hypnotic suggestions for pain relief may aid in deciding whether the pain is of organic origin (Crasilneck and Hall, 1973):

A woman hospitalized for diagnosis of an unusual pain in the left upper quadrant of the abdomen was seen in consultation after usual x-ray and laboratory procedures had failed to establish an unambiguous diagnosis. We were simply asked to give an opinion as to whether the pain was likely to be functional in nature. After the first hypnotic induction, she obtained good relief for about 4 hours, after which the pain returned. She was again hypnotized, and once more pain was greatly relieved, the effect again diminishing in a few hours. On the basis of this observation, she was considered to have most probably pain of organic origin, which was confirmed when a later exploration laparotomy revealed an unexpected tumor. Although decisions about surgical exploration should not be made on the basis of such responses alone, the evidence of a differential response to hypnosis can be a useful clinical observation, among others, to aid in difficult and crucial choices.

In most cases of chronic organic pain, we have been careful to phrase suggestions in such a manner that not all perception of pain is blocked. For example, the subject might be told, "The pain will grow much less, but there will be some remnant of pain left, although the majority of the discomfort will reduce itself considerably and you will be aware of only the slightest degree of pain." It is obviously important, from a medical standpoint, to leave sufficient perception of pain so that any change in the course of the organic illness will be detectable in clinical signs and symptoms.

There are only a few conditions in which it is permissible to block all pain perception with hypnosis: during surgery, during medically attended childbirth, in fulminating arthritis attacks, and in terminal illness. Total relief of pain might also be suggested for discomfort such as that of shingles but should not be attempted in any condition in which worsening of the patient's condition might be communicated through changes in pain symptoms (Crasilneck, 1983).

There is case report (Smith and Balaban, 1983) on pain relief of a patient with systemic lupus erythematosus. Phantom limb pain is discussed by Siegel (1979).

A type of chronic pain problem that we have seen several times a year is that of the orthopedic patient who has had repeated surgery for a herniated disk, usually having had one or two unsuccessful attempts at fusion of the lower back to produce stabilization and reduce pain. Hypnosis has usually produced diminution of pain by 80 or 90 percent (based on patient's verbal estimates), lasting in most cases for several weeks but requiring periodic reinforcement.

It is obvious that in such an orthopedic patient, it would be unwise to remove all pain, since a further herniation might occur at an intervertebral space different from those previously treated. If all pain were removed by hypnosis, an important diagnostic clue might be obscured, and there would be greater danger of increased impairment.

There are cases in which such considerations are not important, notably in terminal cancer patients for whom hypnotic analgesia may allow a decreased amount of narcotics and a clearer, more lucid mind during their last days. Even in these cases, however, some residual amount of pain perception may be desirable as an indicator of treatable complications.

All pain can be removed by hypnosis for a controlled period of time, as in surgery, tooth extractions, or delivery. In these cases the patient would otherwise be under chemical anesthesia and, in either case, would be closely monitored for signs of change in physiological functioning. When all pain is removed for such procedures, it is important to implant the suggestion that it will return during the immediate postoperative period, when it will again be important in monitoring the patient's condition.

Case Examples

Hypnosis is of value in a wide range of pain problems. The following are some typical cases we treat with successful results.

CASE 1

A young woman in her early twenties presented a diagnostic problem of continually worsening headaches over a 3-week period. Symptoms of dizziness, confusion, stiff neck, and a low-grade temperature added to the differential of psychological or organic causes. Although initially skeptical about hypnosis, she was a good subject. Initial hypnotic suggestions were given for most of the pain to "come under control." She experienced several hours of relief from her first sessions of hypnotherapy. A few days after her first hypnotic session, she developed dizziness, fever, and disorientation. Although the nursing staff was concerned that this might have been a side effect of hypnosis, they were reassured that it was not. A small bleeding aneurysm was discovered by the radiologist in the frontal area of the patient's brain. It was surgically treated without complication. She was seen daily for hypnotherapy and rapidly continued to improve. She learned self-hypnosis in order to control the pain after she was discharged. She was cautioned to not remove all her pain, even if she felt able to do so, since there might be other physiological changes causing pain that would require further medical investigation.

CASE 2

A 50-year-old man on workman's compensation because of severe leg pain described a burning pain in the left foot with some perception of soft tissue swelling. The admitting impression was of reflex sympathetic pain, possible causalgic in type. A number of diagnostic procedures were performed, but none were definitive about the cause of his pain. He was treated with twice-weekly hypnotherapy sessions, using a direct symptom attenuation approach. He soon described his pain as having diminished to "4" on a 10-point scale of subjective pain. Within 3 months, he felt such improvement that he chose to return to his job. Although the mechanism of hypnotic pain relief is not clear, the subjective improvement in such cases may be dramatic. He had been in various other forms of treatment for approximately a year before the hypnotherapy was considered.

CASE 3

A woman in her mid-forties suffered from a chronic problem of a large arteriovenous fistula, which required repeated surgical intervention and intraoperative embolization. In the process of these treatments she developed a severe sensory neuritis. Many pain-relief techniques had been unsuccessful before hypnosis was tried. She was seen for hypnosis daily during her hospitalization, even more frequently when the pain was more severe. The pain was diminished to "where I barely feel it." After her discharge, the hypnotic suggestions for pain relief were repeated weekly, sometimes by telephone. She now comes for hypnotic reinforcement on an as-needed basis, usually no more than every 3 months.

HEADACHE PAIN

An excellent example of how hypnosis can be used for pain relief is the headache. It should be remembered, however, that headache can mask organic problems, even brain tumor. It is our practice, therefore, to accept for hypnotic treatment only those cases of headache where thorough medical workup has been done by a competent physician. These are often cases of several years' duration. Many treatments have usually been tried with only transient relief.

In the screening interview and initial hypnotic sessions it is not always possible to define a psychological dynamic behind the pain of a headache. In such cases symptom suppression may be tried, but the therapist must continually strive for glimpses of hidden emotional meaning that may not become apparent until the pain has begun to diminish. Almost without exception, we have eventually found some emotional "pain" that seemed to lend a dynamism and impetus to the headache. This has frequently been some hidden feeling of guilt, as in one middle-aged husband who had developed headache after breaking off an extramarital affair that had continued for almost a year. Headaches may function in an interpersonal way as attention-getting devices or as a means of controlling a relationship. At times the roots lie in childhood, perhaps from identification with a parent or other significant adult who also suffered from head pain.

Damsbo (1979) favors a hypnotic technique for relieving tension headaches through having the patient intentionally make a tight fist, and suggests that the tension in the muscles of the head be transferred to the fist. A facsimile of head pain has been produced under hypnosis, implicating psychological factors (Dudley, Holmes, and Ripley, 1968).

BACK PAIN

Hypnosis is proven of value in many cases of chronic low back pain (Cohen, 1979; Crasilneck, 1978a, 1979a), although it is of lessened value in patients who appear masochistic, or have marked secondary gain from their symptoms, or are significantly depressed, or have a low frustration tolerance. Decrease in pain medication is a frequent additional benefit from treatment. It is useful to start with an intensive period of hypnotherapy, daily or more frequently, gradually decreasing the frequency of hypnotherapy as the patient's pain lessens. Self-hypnosis can often be employed to lengthen the effectiveness of the posthypnotic suggestions for pain relief (Crasilneck, 1979b, 1983; Glick 1983).

The back seems to be a particularly troublesome part of the anatomy. Back pain may be of primary organic origin, as after repeated surgical intervention for a herniated nucleus pulposus or for spinal fusion. Some back pain seems to be largely psychogenic, as in hysterical conversion reactions. Back pain may be part of a picture of neurasthenia or psychasthenia fatigue.

Hypnosis can be of aid in back pain of organic or functional origin, provided that proper attention is given to ruling out organic factors that require medical treatment. Organic pain may not be as easily relieved as functional pain, but repeated reinforcement or posthypnotic suggestions may increase their effectiveness. Some patients have been treated for years with hypnosis every 4 to 6 weeks to diminish chronic pain. After a number of repetitions it is possible to determine the approximate time that relief will last before the suggestions begin to decay. Appointments can then be spaced accordingly to allow maintenance without severe pain or overdependence on medications.

With such periodic reinforcement and with development of ability to use self-hypnosis, hypnotherapy is of great value in the *maintenance* of pain relief.

In 1963 a woman was referred to Crasilneck from a nearby medical center. She previously had had four surgical procedures on her lower back, two for herniated disks and two attempts at spinal fusion. Her pain was severe, limiting her activities to a marked degree, and consideration was given to neurosurgical sectioning of some of the pain tracts to try to increase her functioning. Hypnosis was suggested on a trial basis before neurosurgery.

She was seen weekly for the first month, then every second week, every third week, and finally, at present, once every month to 6 weeks for a 30-minute session. She has achieved 90 percent pain relief, although she continues to require reinforcement. She was not pushed for total absence of pain, because it was felt that other problems may be masked and because she was an independent type of woman who would stress herself if all the pain were removed. A remnant of discomfort was always present; the author emphatically proclaims that total pain removal encourages problems. Other writers have concurred in avoiding total symptom removal (Gurgevich, personal communication, 1980). She is again able to work as a babysitter and to care for her home and husband. It is likely that she will continue to need hypnotic treatment, perhaps on a more extended schedule, for the rest of her life.

We consider this to be a justified use of hypnosis for maintenance of function in a woman who would otherwise have undergone irreversible surgical destruction of a portion of her nervous system. Since 1966, this patient has returned for a reinforcement session once every 6 to 8 weeks. She is adept at using self-hypnosis and is free from pain and discomfort most of the time.

CHRONIC PAIN SYNDROME

There are neurophysiological, psychodynamic, and behavioral differences in acute and chronic pain. Acute pain involves increased cardiac rate and stroke volume, elevated blood pressure, pupil dilitation, palmar sweating, increase in blood steroids, hypernatremia, escape behavior, and anxiety states. Chronic pain is a more subtle state with less autonomic arousal but often having more pervasive psychological patterns. Chronic pain is often associated with sleep disturbance, appetite decrease, constipation, psychomotor retardation and social withdrawal, all marks of depression (Goodman and Griffin, 1983; Stewart, 1983). In addition, there may be irritability and lowered pain tolerance, as well as psychodynamic changes, as a sense of victimization. A test for the presence of chronic pain is to ask the patient "Since this pain started has there ever been *any* time when you were completely free of pain?" If the patient answers "no" to this question, there is presumptive evidence of the chronic pain syndrome (Ewin, 1981).

In utilizing hypnotherapy with chronic pain, clear and open communication with the patient is essential. Hypnotherapy is impractical for some patients because of the number of reinforcement sessions that may be needed. As with many psychological treatments, it is more effective in intact personalities (Kepplinger et al., 1983) and in those who are highly motivated. Self-hypnosis may extend the usefulness of hypnotic treatment in chronic and organic pain (Crasilneck, 1982, 1983; Elton, Burrows, and Stanley, 1980; Sachs, 1982).

TECHNIQUES

A variety of hypnotherapeutic procedures may be used in the treatment of acute and chronic pain (J. B. Barber, 1982a,b; T. X. Barber, 1982). One of the most frequently used by Crasilneck (1983) is to induce glove anesthesia in the finger or hand, test it with measured pressure of a blunt nailfile as the patient watches, feeling no pain, and then suggest transfer of the analgesia to the afflicted pain site. It is sometimes possible to substitute another sensation, such as pressure, warmth, or coolness, for all or part of the pain sensation. The pain may be displaced and diminished by suggesting that it is experienced partially or wholly in another part of the body, or even "outside" the body. Also, the ego that is experiencing the pain may at times be dissociated from the central ego, as in Hilgard's experiments that reveal a "hidden observer," which is a subsystem of the personality that experiences the pain while the central ego is relieved of pain.

Sacerdote (1982) suggests additional techniques, including associating the pain to a pleasant memory, induced amnesia, reinterpretation of the meaning of the pain, and focusing on the teleological usefulness of the pain. He also recommends the induction of dreams that influence the meaning of the pain, and such unusual techniques as the elicitation of mystical states and distortion of space and time perception. Erickson (1982) has described an "interspersal technique" in which suggestions are embedded in other conversational material that plays upon the subject's antecedent interest in certain subjects.

The interpersonal meaning of pain should be assessed (Heinrich, Cohen, and Naliboff, 1982). In some subjects the actual perception of pain is not decreased, but the patient is able to tolerate it more easily (Chaves and Barber, 1976). Hypnosis should always be attempted with severe pain problems since many patients who might otherwise by unhypnotizable can, in the appropriate context, be helped to utilize hypnosis (Schafer and Hernandez, 1978).

CHILDREN AND ADOLESCENTS

Hypnotherapy is now well known in the treatment of pain and in other problems of children and adolescents, largely because of the pioneering work of Baumann (1981) and Gardner and Olness (1981). In addition to ordinary uses, hypnotherapy is of particular value in treating the terminally ill child.

PAIN RELIEF IN CHILDREN

The definitive work on hypnosis with children has been published by Gardner and Olness (1981). They pay careful attention to the attitude of the child and tailor hypnotic interventions accordingly. Direct suggestions for pain relief may be used, with such imagery as glove anesthesia or a switchbox that can modify pain. Distancing suggestions—moving the pain away from the body or to a different part of the body—may be more effective in some children. Antithetical suggestions of relaxation or laughter may be helpful, as may distraction techniques. Finally, they suggest that in some instances, focusing attention directly on the pain can be effective; i.e., asking the child to notice the "color" or "size" of the pain in an imaginary scene in which the child is "inside" the pain. This technique is somewhat analogous to the selective misdirection of confusion techniques in hypnotic induction.

SUMMARY

Management of pain problems remains one of the first and most enduring uses of hypnosis. It should be used with care by persons aware of the diagnostic and treatment problems of organic illness. In proper perspective hypnosis can alleviate much otherwise unapproachable pain and can help maintain the functional ability and dignity of many patients otherwise dependent on large quantities of medication.

REFERENCES

August RV: Hypnosis in obstetrics and in gynecology, Schneck JM (ed): Hypnosis in Modern Medicine, Springfield, Ill., Charles C Thomas, 1963

Barber JB: Incorporating hypnosis in the management of chronic pain, in Barber JB, Adrian C (eds): Psychological Approaches to the Management of Pain. New York, Brunner/Mazel, 1982a, pp 49–59

Barber JB: Techniques of pain management, in Barber JB, Adrian C (eds): Psychological Approaches to the Management of Pain. New York, Brunner/Mazel, 1982b, pp 108–185

Barber JB, Adrian C (eds): Psychological Approaches to the Management of Pain. New York, Brunner/Mazel, 1982

Barber TX: The effects of "hypnosis" on pain. A critical review of experimental and clinical findings. Br J Med Hypnot 15:30–37, 1964

Barber TX: Hypnosuggestive procedures in the treatment of clinical pain: Implications for theories of hypnosis and suggestive theories, in Milton T, Green CJ, Meagher RE, Jr (eds.): Handbook of Clinical Health Psychology. New York, Plenum Press, 1982, pp 521–560

Bartlett E: Control of postoperative pain with autohypnosis. Am J Clin Hypn 6:166–168, 1963

Bassman SW, Wester WC: Hypnosis and pain control, in Wester WC, Smith AH (eds): Clinical Hypnosis: A Multidisciplinary Approach, Philadelphia, J.B. Lippincott Co., 1983, pp 236–287

Baumann FW: Hypnosis in the treatment of urinary and fecal incontinence: A twenty-year experience, in Wain HJ (ed): Theoretical and Clinical Aspects of Hypnosis. Miami, Symposia Specialists, Inc., 1981, pp 107–123

Black S, Friedman M: Effects of emotion and pain on adrenocortical function investigated by hypnosis. Br Med J 1:477–481, 1968

Braun BG: Failures with pain control. Presented at the 27th annual meeting of the Society for Clinical and Experimental Hypnosis, Chicago, 1975

Chaves JF, Barber TX: Hypnotic procedures and surgery: A critical analysis with application to "acupuncture analgesia". Am J Clin Hypn 18:217–236, 1976

Cheek DB: Therapy of persistent pain states. I. Neck and shoulder pain of five years duration. Am J Clin Hypn 8:281–286, 1966

Chiasson SW: Hypnosis gains legitimacy, respect in diverse clinical specialties, JAMA 249:319–323, 1983

Cohen SB: My aching back. Am J Clin Hypn 22:69–70, 1979

Crasilneck HB: The use of hypnosis in the treatment of low back pain. Presented at the American Society of Clinical Hypnosis Meeting, St. Louis, 1978a

Crasilneck HB: The use of hypnosis in acute and chronic pain. Presented at the pain workshop, First International Congress on Clinical and Experimental Hypnosis, Malmo, Sweden, 1978b

Crasilneck HB: Hypnosis in the control of chronic low back pain. Am J Clin Hypn 22:71–78, 1979a

Crasilneck HB: Reinforcing the control of pain with hypnosis before it exacerbates. Presented at the Workshop on pain, International Society of Clinical and Experimental Hypnosis, Melbourne, Australia, 1979b

Crasilneck HB: The use of hypnosis in chronic pain. Presented at the Pain Workshop, Society of Clinical and Experimental Hypnosis Annual Meeting, Boston, 1982

Crasilneck HB: (Panelist) Hypnosis in the treatment of chronic and organic pain. Presented at the meeting of the International Congress of the Israel Society of Hypnosis in Psychotherapy and Psychosomatic Medicine in collaboration with the European Society of Hypnosis in Psychotherapy and Psychosomatic Medicine, Haifa, Israel, 1983

Crasilneck HB: The use of hypnosis in pain problems, in Symonds EM, Zuspan FP (eds): Clinical and Diagnostic Procedures in Obstetrics and Gynecology: Part B: Gynecology. New York, Marcel Dekker, Inc., 1984, pp 297–417

Crasilneck HB, Hall JA: Clinical hypnosis in problems of pain. Am J Clin Hypn 15:153–161, 1973

Damsbo AM: Tension headache treated with hypnosis, in Burrows GD, Collison D,

Dennerstein L (eds): Hypnosis. Amsterdam, Elsevier/North-Holland Biomedical Press, 1979, pp 157–164

Dudley DL, Holmes TH, Ripley HS: Hypnotically induced and suggested facsimili of headpain. J Nerv Ment Dis 144:258–265, 1968

Elton D, Burrows GD, Stanley GV: Pain can be controlled by self hypnosis, in Burrows GD, Dennerstein L (eds): Handbook of Hypnosis and Psychosomatic Medicine. Amsterdam, Elsevier/North-Holland Biomedical Press, 1980, pp 269–292

Erickson MH: The interpersonal hypnotic technique for symptom correction and pain control. Am J Clin Hypn 8:198–209, 1966

Erickson MH: The interspersal technique for symptom correction and pain control, in Barber JB, Adrian C: Psychological Approaches to the Management of Pain. New York, Brunner/Mazel, 1982, pp 100–117

Evans MD, Paul G: Effects of hypnotically suggested analgesia on physiological and subjective responses to cold stress. J Consult Clin Psychol 35:362–371, 1970

Ewin DM: Relieving suffering—and pain—with hypnosis. Geriatrics 33:87–89, 1978

Ewin DM: Constant pain syndrome: Its psychological meaning and cure using hypnoanalysis, in Wain HJ (ed): Theoretical and Clinical Aspects of Hypnosis. Miami, Symposia Specialists, Inc., 1981, pp 41–49

Finer B: Treatment in an interdisciplinary pain clinic, in Barber JB, Adrian C: Psychological Approaches to the Management of Pain. New York, Brunner/Mazel, 1982, pp 186–204

Gardner GG, Olness K: Hypnosis and Hypnotherapy with Children. New York, Grune & Stratton, 1981

Glick D: (Panelist) Acute and chronic back pain treatment with hypnotherapy. Presented at the meeting of the International Congress of the Israel Society of Hypnosis in Psychotherapy and Psychosomatic Medicine, Haifa, Israel, 1983

Goldstein A, Hilgard ER: Lack of influence of the morphine antagonist naloxone on hypnotic analgesia. Proc Natl Acad Sci USA 72:2041–2043, 1975

Goodman ED, Griffin AN: Adjunctive hypnotic symptom control in chronic illness. Paper presented the American Society of Clinical Hypnosis Annual Scientific Meeting, Dallas, Texas, 1983

Gurgevich S: Personal communication, 1980

Guze H: Psychological theories of hypnosis, in Kline MV (ed): The Nature of Hypnosis. New York, Institute for Research in Hypnosis, 1961

Heinrich RL, Cohen MJ, Naliboff BD: Rehabilitation of pain patients: Coping in interpersonal contexts, in Barber JB, Adrian C: Psychological Approaches to the Management of Pain. New York, Brunner/Mazel, 1982, pp 118–136

Hightower PR: The control of pain. Am J Clin Hypn 9:67–70, 1966

Hilgard ER: The use of pain-state reports in the study of hypnotic analgesia to the pain of ice water. J Nerv Ment Dis 144:506–513, 1967

Hilgard ER: Pain as a puzzle for psychology and physiology. Am Psychol 24:103–113, 1969

Hilgard ER: Pain: Its reduction and production under hypnosis. Am Philosoph Soc 115:470–476, 1971

Hilgard ER: The alleviation of pain by hypnosis. Pain 1:213–231, 1975

Hilgard ER: Hypnosis in the treatment of pain, in Burrows GD, Dennerstein L (eds): Handbook of Hypnosis and Psychosomatic Medicine. Amersterdam, Elsevier/North Holland Biomedical Press, 1980, pp 233–267

Hilgard ER, Hilgard J: Hypnosis in the relief of pain. Los Altos, Ca., William Kaufman, 1975

Horvai I: Indications for hypnosuggestive pain management in neurology and psychiatry. Psychother Psychosom 14:468–470, 1966

Kalinowsky LB, Hoch PH: Somatic Treatments in Psychiatry. New York, Grune & Stratton, 1961, p 286

Kehoe MJ: Facial pain: Hypnotic suggestion as a method of treatment. Am J Psychiatry 123:1577–1581, 1967

Kepplinger B, Sampson KH, Mauer NL, Linz A: (Panelists) The position of hypnotherapy in the psychiatric assessment of chronic pain patients, 1983. Presented at the International Congress of the Israel Society of Hypnosis in Psychotherapy and Psychosomatic Medicine in collaboration with the European Society of Hypnosis in Psychotherapy and Psychosomatic Medicine, Haifa, Israel, 1983

Kroger WS: Clinical and Experimental Hypnosis (ed 2). Philadelphia, J.B. Lippincott, 1977, p 233

Lea PA, Ware PD, Monroe RR: The hypnotic control of intractable pain. Am J Clin Hypn 3:5–8, 1960

Lettew JL: Use of hypnosis in the treatment of long standing spastic torticollis. Am J Clin Hypn 14:124–126, 1971

Levendula D: Two case presentations: Treatment of central pain with reconstruction of the body-image—hypnoanalysis of a travel phobia. Int J Clin Exp Hypn 9:238–289, 1961

McGlashan TH, Evans FJ, Orne MT: The nature of hypnotic analgesia and placebo response to experimental pain. Psychosom Med 31:227–246, 1969

Marmer MJ: Hypnosis and Anesthesia. Springfield, Ill., Charles C Thomas, 1959

Meares A: Psychological control of organically determined pain. Ann Austral Coll Dent Surg 1, 1967

Melzack R, Perry C: Self-regulation of pain: The use of alpha-feedback and hypnotic training for the control of chronic pain. Exp Neurol 46:452–469, 1975

Mutter CB, Karnilow A: Hypnosis: A viable option in chronic pain management. Am J Clin Hypn, 1984, in press

Olness K, Wain HG, Ng L: A pilot study of blood endorphin levels in children using self-hypnosis to control pain. Dev Behav Pediatr 1:187–188, 1980

Reyher J: Hypnosis, in Vernon J (ed): Introduction to Psychology. Dubuque, Iowa, Brown, 1968

Sacerdote P: The place of hypnosis in the relief of severe protracted pain. Am J Clin Hypn 4:150–157, 1962

Sacerdote P: Psychophysiology of hypnosis as it relates to pain and pain problems. Am J Clin Hypn 10:236–243, 1968

Sacerdote P: Techniques of hypnotic intervention with pain patients, in Barber JB, Adrian C: Psychological Approaches to the Management of Pain. New York, Brunner/Mazel, 1982, pp 60–83

Sachs LB, Feuerstein M, Vitale J: Hypnotic self-regulation of chronic pain. Am J Clin Hypn 20:106–113, 1977

Sachs LB: Teaching hypnosis for the self-control of pain, in Barber JB, Adrian C (eds): Psychological Approaches to the Management of Pain. New York, Brunner/Mazel, 1982, pp 84–89

Schafer DW, Hernandez A: Pain and the context of therapy. Int J Clin Hypn 26:143–153, 1978

Sears R: An experimental study of hypnotic anesthesia. J Exp Psychol 15:1–22, 1932

Shor RE: Physiological effects of painful stimulation during hypnotic analgesia under conditions designed to minimize anxiety. Int J Clin Exp Hypn 10:183–202, 1962

Siegel EF: Control of phantom limb pain by hypnosis. Am J Clin Hypn 21:285–286, 1979

Smith SJ, Balaban AB: A multidimensional approach to pain relief: Case report of a patient with systemic lupus erythematosus. Int J Clin Hypn 31:72–81, 1983

Spiegel H, Speigel D: Trance and Treatment: Clinical Uses of Hypnosis. New York, Basic Books, Inc., 1978, pp 251–262

Sternbach RA: The psychologist's role in the diagnosis and treatment of pain patients, in Barber JB, Adrian C (eds): Psychological Approaches to the Management of Pain. New York, Brunner/Mazel 3–20, 1982

Stewart RM: (Panelist) Pain Workshop. Society of Clinical and Experimental Hypnosis Annual Meeting, Boston, 1983

Veldesy FA: Pain and hypnosis. Am J Clin Hypn 5:153, 1967

Wain HJ: Pain control through the use of hypnosis. Am J Clin Hypn 23:41–46, 1980

Walker, W: Hypnosis as an adjunct in management of pain. South Med J 73:362–364, 1980

West LJ, Niell KC, Hardy JD: Effects of hypnotic suggestion on pain perception and galvanic skin response. AMA Arch Neurol Psychiatry 68:549–560, 1952

Wester WC, Smith AH (eds): Clinical Hypnosis: A Multidisciplinary Approach. Philadelphia, J.P. Lippincott Co., 1983

Wolberg LR: Medical Hypnosis. The Principles of Hypnotherapy, vol. 1. New York, Grune & Stratton, 1948

Wolfe LS: Hypnosis and pain: A clinical instance. Am J Clin Hypn 4:193–194, 1962

7

Hypnosis as a Method of Anesthesia

One of the first attempts to perform surgery under hypnosis took place in France in 1821; 8 years later (also in France) Jules Cloquet removed the breast of a 64-year-old woman while she was mesmerized. Surgery took 12 minutes and was without incident in terms of movement or complaints of pain. In 1842, M. Squire Ward, an English surgeon, performed a mid-thigh amputation while the patient was hypnotized. By 1851, James Esdaile had performed several thousand minor surgical procedures and approximately 300 major surgical procedures in which the only anesthetic used was hypnosis. In 1880, J. Milner Bromwell gave a demonstration of hypnotic anesthesia to a group of physicians at Leeds, England.

In spite of these impressive reports, medical interest turned away from hypnosis in surgery and toward the new, developing field of chemical anesthesia. Prime factors for this rejection of hypnosis were the reliability of chemical agents as well as the frequent lack of psychological skills needed to induce and manage the hypnotic state.

A renaissance in hypnosis for anesthetic purposes has occurred in the United States only since the 1950s. The renewed interest was reviewed by Marmer (1959). In another essay, Marmer (1963) listed eight cogent reasons for the use of hypnosis in anesthesiology:

1. To overcome fear, apprehension, and anxiety in order to reduce the tension associated with the anticipated anesthesia and surgery.

2. For sedation, either in conjunction with or as a substitute for drug medication.
3. To increase patient cooperation and bring about peace of mind.
4. To produce analgesia and anesthesia.
5. To make for a more pleasant and more comfortable recovery from anesthesia and surgery.
6. To permit the use of posthypnotic suggestions to aid in the postoperative recovery of the patient by reducing the incidence of postoperative nausea and vomiting and by permitting deep breathing and necessary coughing, thereby helping to reduce postoperative pulmonary complications. Also, to raise the pain threshold and reduce the need for postoperative narcotics as well as to encourage earlier fluid intake and easier urinary output.
7. To produce operative amnesia.
8. To help establish better postoperative morale and motivate the patient toward getting well.

Marmer's reasons are all valid. It is important to note that he often suggests the possibility of combining hypnosis with other techniques. In his opinion the primary disadvantage of hypnosis as a method of anesthesia was that not all patients could be hypnotized; he estimated that only 10 percent could achieve a level necessary for surgery under hypnoanesthesia alone. Another disadvantage is that hypnosis often requires considerably more time than chemical anesthesia, since several training sessions may be needed. Also, for some surgical procedures the hypnotic trance will not produce the deep degree of muscular relaxation needed to maintain a quiet operative field for the surgeon.

In addition we would stress that there is a possibility that hypnosis may activate emotional conflicts if these are present but unsuspected in a neurotic or borderline subject (Rosen, 1957). As a precaution we have employed psychiatric screening before using hypnosis for anesthesia. Marmer suggests that those patients undergoing intensive psychotherapy or psychoanalysis should not be hypnotized for anesthesia without the express permission of the therapist.

Rodger (1962) suggests that in using hypnosis the anesthesiologist "can escape from the limitations of an impersonal drug orientation and enter into a significant communicative relationship with his patient." This is doubtless the goal of good anesthesiology, even without hypnosis, but may be enhanced with the use of hypnotic procedures, particularly since they allow for more psychological interaction when the patient is in altered states of consciousness during induction for surgery, during surgery, and in the immediate postoperative phase of recovery.

Hypnosis was never intended to replace chemical anesthesia. Rather, it should be seen as a useful modality in making psychological and emotional contact with the patient, who is always apprehensive about surgical procedures. This is equally true with children (Antitch, 1967; Betcher, 1958; Daniels, 1962; Klopp, 1961). Since emotions, no matter what kind, have a definite influence on bodily function, Wallace (1959) feels that the modification of emotion by hypnosis may be a distinct aid in anesthesiology. Many others have attested to the utility of hypnosis as a part of anesthesiology practice (Anderson, 1957; Bartlett, 1975; Bernstein, 1965; Betcher, 1960; Cohen, 1980; Ewin, 1983; Lassner, 1964; Marmer, 1969; Succar, 1963).

The analgesic effect is obtainable in a number of persons and in apparently light stages of hypnosis (Horvai, 1959), though surgical anesthesia by hypnosis alone may require a greater depth. Evans and Paul (1970) conclude experimentally that an adequate clinical evaluation of hypnotic analgesia has not yet been done, though some of their objections seem to have been met by Hilgard's work (1967). There is some evidence (Halliday and Mason, 1964) that the loss of sensation in hypnoanalgesia and hypnoanesthesia is not attributable to attenuation of the sensory messages in the afferent pathways on their way to the cortex; therefore, by implication, it is most likely to be at a cortical level.

Those clinicians who have studied the use of hypnosis in anesthesia seem to have agreed on its utility in facilitating preoperative and postoperative care. Anxiety and pain can be prevented or diminished (Corley, 1965; Finer, 1966; Tinterow, 1960). In some cases postoperative pain seems greatly diminished (Paris, Mosgedis, and Durante, 1960). Autohypnosis has been employed for this purpose also. Vomiting may be controlled (Tyson, 1964), an advantage when fractures are reduced in the emergency room, particularly with children. In reporting 100 cases in which hypnotic suggestions were given in the recovery room for improved posthypnotic recovery, Bensen (1971) reported that 72 percent had little or no postoperative pain, bleeding was 90 percent controlled, and 98 percent had normal thirst and appetite. The series of 100 surgical procedures consisted largely of hemorrhoidectomies, dilettage and curettement, and tonsillectomies, with some removal of growth and tumors.

At present there is wide acceptance of hypnosis as an important adjunct in the practice of anesthesia (Carli, 1982; Cheek, 1981; Crasilneck, 1980; Erickson, 1979; Finer, 1980; Fredericks, 1980; Gherardi, 1982; Guantieri, 1982; Kasasian, 1982; Kroger, 1977; and Scott, 1974). Hypnoanesthesia and hypnoanalgesia now are also utilized with children (Gardner and Olness, 1981).

AWARENESS UNDER CHEMICAL ANESTHESIA

A valuable and surprising area of study has grown out of the use of hypnosis in anesthesia. Cheek (1959), who pioneered the research, found by use of an ideomotor signaling technique (movement of a finger to indicate responses) that many postsurgery patients who had had chemical anesthesia seemed to remember, under hypnosis, the events of the surgery, including at times remarks made in the operating room that had caused anxiety and worry. These disturbing memories are uncovered by Cheek, then "explained and reasoned until they can be understood and, if necessary, pardoned or forgotten."

Even though amnesic during the waking state for the events that happened under anesthesia, when hypnotized, the patient may remember hearing various sounds and remarks. On the basis of these findings Cheek (1960, 1964) urged all members of the surgical team to give "helpful" suggestions to the anesthetized person, avoiding any remarks that might be interpreted to be negative. Erickson (1963) has reported informal studies in 1932 that suggested that a painful procedure can be split under chemical anesthesia into separate items, only one of which remains conscious.

Trustman, Dubovsky, and Titley (1977) and more recently Cheek (1981) have reviewed the clinical and theoretical aspects of awareness under chemical anesthesia. Bowers (1976) concludes that people can register information and be profoundly affected by it although unconscious of it. It is not clear, however, whether hypnosis is a necessary procedure for the retrieval of such information.

Hilgard, Hilgard, and Newman (1961) have reported that various sequelae during and following the induction of hypnosis may have been related to earlier and unpleasant experiences with chemical anesthesia. Some evidence also revealed that childhood experiences had a similar influence. Brunn (1963) in a unique report describes his own ability to experience and remember events while undergoing dental extractions with chemical anesthesia. Hartman (1969) suggests the use of a term "parahypnosis," coined originally by Van Dyke, to describe a state in which "the patient is surgically insensitive to pain and is apparently unconscious, but is able to hear voices and sounds." He concluded that "in the light of these findings, it is extremely important that all conversations in the operating room and delivery room be carried out in the firm belief that the patient can hear and does hear everything that is said and that what he hears is being interpreted by him within the framework of his own perceptual field, including his perceptual distortions."

In a double-bind study, Pearson (1961) played recorded suggestions during anesthesia, suggesting a reduced postoperative stay in the hospital. A control group received a placebo recording. Surgeons were unable to differentiate between patients who had received suggestions and those who had not, nor was there any difference in the use of narcotics between the two groups. Nevertheless, the patients who had received the suggestions while "unconscious" during surgery were discharged an average of 2.42 days sooner than the control group, a difference that was statistically significant. Pearson, writing in 1961, assumed a conservative cost of $35 per day of hospitalization; thus, the reduction in hospital time for the 43 patients in the experimental group represented a cost saving of more than $3500. With the increased costs of hospitalization today, the saving would be much greater, of course.

Levinson (1965) has also contributed to the clinical study of whether patients could remember, under hypnosis, suggestions given while they had been in surgical anesthesia. Four recalled the words, four awakened from trance without recalling, and two did not respond.

In 1958 Crasilneck and Erwin studied the postoperative stage in which patients previously given a posthypnotic suggestion would begin to show response. It was found that they would give the sign suggested in previous hypnotic sessions *before* they would exhibit the ordinary signs associated with awakening from anesthesia, suggesting that hypnosis may function at a rather "deep" level of consciousness. This is consistent with the studies that find the patient has responded while apparently unconscious during surgery.

At the University of Texas Southwestern Medical School in Dallas, lectures on hypnosis are included in the residency program in anesthesiology. M. T. Jenkins, chairman of the department, was involved in some of the pioneer work on the task of adapting hypnosis to the special needs of modern anesthesiology. In the December 1956 issue of the *Journal of the American Medical Association* Crasilneck jointly published, with Jenkins and E. James McCranie, a discussion of special indications for hypnosis as a method of anesthesia (Crasilneck, McCranie, and Jenkins, 1956). In 1959, a revised listing of these indications was reported together with case examples, some of which are given below.

EXAMPLES OF SPECIAL INDICATIONS FOR HYPNOSIS IN ANESTHESIOLOGY

Hypnoanesthesia may be used for selected operations in situations where certain chemical agents are contraindicated because of allergic reaction or hypersensitivity.

A 36-year-old woman was sensitive to procaine. Because of this she objected to the use of any local anesthetic agent. For the previous 3 years she had refused to allow her dentist to perform even minor procedures without administration of a general anesthetic. Injection of procaine, according to her physician, resulted in severe reactions, characterized primarily by edema of the face and body, urticaria, and nausea and vomiting. Since it was impractical to administer an anesthetic each time she required dental procedures, the patient soon refused to return to her dentist. Most of her teeth eventually developed caries. Because of the complexity of the total situation, we were asked to evaluate the patient as a suitable subject for the use of hypnosis as an anesthetic. Personality evaluation indicated an individual relatively free of emotional symptoms other than extreme fear of dental procedures. After a discussion of hypnosis she proved to be an excellent subject and was soon capable of entering a state of somnambulism. Thereafter, on five separate occasions dental procedures lasting approximately 2 hours each were successfully performed with the patient under hypnosis. During these procedures she was free of all pain and apprehensiveness. Eventually her fears of dental work were greatly diminished, and now she is capable of undergoing at least minor procedures without hypnosis.

Hypnoanesthesia may be used for certain surgical procedures during which it is desirable to have the patient able to respond to questions or commands.

During the course of a stereotactic neurosurgical procedure, it was of vital importance to confirm the location of the probe by having the patient voluntarily respond. To facilitate both the analgesia of the scalp and maintain a calm emotional state in the patient during this lengthy procedure, hypnosis was utilized together with local anesthesia.

Hypnoanesthesia may be indicated for those patients where fear and apprehension of general anesthesia are so great as to contribute to anesthetic risks.

A 10-year-old boy required extensive dental work, but he refused to go to the dentist's office because he remembered being hurt painfully several years before by another dentist. General anesthesia was considered, but the child's apprehension was so great that he fought any attempt to induce unconsciousness, either by injection or inhalation. There was some apprehension that his fearful arousal would make him more sensitive to some possible side effects of chemical anesthesia.

In an attempt to avoid hospitalization, hypnosis was employed. The child responded as a good hypnotic subject on the first induction, and he seemed to deepen his trance as the inductions were repeated. Some abreaction of the previous dental trauma was obtained, and he was given posthypnotic suggestions for relaxation and well-being during his visits for dental work.

His first visits to the dentist required only local anesthesia. He was calm, cooperative, and experienced no overt anxiety. On several later visits to the dentist he required no chemical anesthesia whatsoever; he remained helpful and at ease.

Hypnosis is indicated when organic problems interfere with diagnostic or surgical treatment.

A 34-year-old single woman with severe congenital heart disease had repeated x-ray examinations over a period of years that revealed an extension of the pulmonary artery shadows with congenital changes consistent with a diagnosis of Eisenmenger's complex. Approximately 6 months before the time of referral the patient began having extreme difficulty with her menses. Menstrual flow lasted from 15 to 17 days. At the onset of period bleeding was described as excessive and heavy, resulting in spotting during the last few days. A pelvic examination revealed the patient to be a nulligravida with a virginal introitus. Because the hymenal ring was so tight and because the patient was extremely anxious and tense, her gynecologist was unable to perform an adequate pelvic examination. The gynecologist was of the opinion that dilation of the cervix and curettage of the uterus were indicated for purposes of diagnosis. However, both the gynecologist and cardiologist felt that the patient presented a definite anesthetic risk. Although it was agreed that a caudal or a saddle block would be acceptable, it was also agreed that hypnoanesthesia might be preferable if the patient were a suitable subject.

Personality evaluation revealed that the patient was very immature emotionally and highly dependent on her mother. Her social activities were limited and were always approved by the mother beforehand. She seldom dated and was extremely naive and fearful of any kind of sexual activity, preferring not to be alone in the company of men. Because of her emotional immaturity and numerous neurotic conflicts, it was feared that the extensive use of hypnosis might arouse more overt symptoms of psychiatric illness. However, it was decided that this risk was worth taking because of her physical status. After reasonable rapport had been established with the patient and the possible use of hypnosis had been explained to her, she accepted the proposal, although she was obviously anxious about how she would respond to this method.

Actually, she turned out to be a good subject and was hypnotized three times prior to surgery to condition her to enter a state of somnabulism. A pelvic examination was done by the gynecologist during the third session under hypnoanalgesia. It was suggested to the patient that she would be free of pain and completely relaxed during the examination. While the patient was in a state of hypnosis, the gynecologist reported that it was possible to do a very adequate bimanual examination. There was neither subjective nor objective evidence of pain, tension, or anxiety during this procedure.

The patient was operated on a week later. No medicaments were administered preoperatively. After she was hypnotized and hypnoanesthesia established, cervical dilation was accomplished, and endometrical curettage was then performed. The patient remained in a deep state of hypnosis throughout the entire operative procedure and evidenced no perception of pain. She was given a posthypnotic suggestion that there would be no cramping or undue discomfort. After her return to the recovery room the posthypnotic suggestions were in effect, with no pain, cramping, or discomfort reported by the patient. At the end of the hour it was then suggested that normal bodily sensations would return to her. She was awakened from the hypnotic sleep and was amnesic for the entire procedure. Her pulse, blood pressure, and respiration showed no significant deviations before, during, or after the surgery. Her recovery was uneventful and free of complications.

Steinberg (1965) reports the use of hypnoanesthesia for a 90-year-old patient during repair of a hernia. He comments on the complete absence of need for analgesic drugs during her postoperative course and concludes that hypnoanesthesia is a valuable adjunct in the poor anesthesia risk cases.

Hypnosis has been reported of value in the performance of transcutaneous renal biopsy in 8 out of 10 subjects (Gruttad'auria, Tigoli, and Borghi, 1978). Hypnosis is of use in upper gastrointestinal endoscopy (Jackson and Middleton, 1978). Premedication and postoperative pain medication was reduced by the use of hypnosis in 13 patients undergoing pedicle graft surgery (Scott, 1976). Bower (1973) has reported a transuretheral resection of the prostate and Rausch (1980) a cholecystectomy, both done under self-hypnosis. In an impressive audiovisual presentation, Wain (in press) has demonstrated surgery of the nasal septum done entirely under hypnoanesthesia. Cohen (1980) has discussed hypnotic self-anesthesia. Schwartz (1965) has shown the practicality in some urological cases of the surgeon also inducing the hypnoanesthesia.

Hypnosis may be an anesthetic agent of choice when it is important to observe the patient's state of consciousness during surgery (Jones, 1977) as in therapeutic embolizations of carotid and vertebral arteries (Bank and Kerber, 1979) and for monitoring of intraoperative spinal cord function (Crawford et al., 1976). With hypnoanesthesia, even when some chemical anesthesia is used as well, it is possible to awaken the patient, perform tests as needed to determine the effect of procedures already performed and then to re-anesthesize the patient and complete the surgery. L. D. Egbert (1983) of the Department of Anesthesiology at the University of Texas Health Science Center at Dallas has described in detail to us the case of a young medical student who requested hypnosis for anesthesia during therapeutic embolization of an arteriovenous malformation of his scalp. During the radiological procedures the patient complained of difficulty in swallowing in spite of the fact that fluoroscopy demonstrated a normal swallowing reflex response. The following day he was taken to the operating room for the surgical removal of part of the arteriovenous malformation. Although hypnoanesthesia was not necessary during the surgery, he did allow the endotrachial tube to be inserted without any difficulty or complications under hypnoanesthesia, at which time the general anesthesia was started and surgery went well. Pursuant to this case was the fact that a junior surgical staff member, and a relative of the patient exacerbated the patient's anxiety concerning the effects of hypnoanesthesia. Such negative comments exemplify the prejudice that still exists toward this modality by naive and untrained personnel.

HYPNOSIS COMBINED WITH CHEMICAL ANESTHESIA

Although hypnosis can be used as the sole means of anesthesia in surgical cases (Tinterow, 1960)—tonsillectomies (Monteiro and de Oliveira, 1958), hysterectomies, hemorrhoidectomies, and other surgical procedures—this does not mean that its primary use is as the sole anesthetic agent. In some cases the use of hypnosis alone may have been to prove the efficacy of the trance state. It is our impression that most anesthesiologists consider hypnosis as an adjunct to chemical anesthesia, adding flexability and increased psychological care to the induction of anesthesia. Our own experience suggests that hypnosis is best used in this fashion so that should it prove insufficient in a particular surgical case, or for a particular purpose, chemical means also can be employed without loss of confidence by either patient or physician.

Others have confirmed our conclusion. At a 1973 panel on medical uses of hypnosis, Ronald Katz, a professor of anesthesiology, stated that in his experience hypnosis is best combined with other anesthetic methods rather than used alone, except in special situations. Marmer in *Hypnosis in Anesthesiology* (1959) gives numerous case reports in which hypnotic analgesia and anesthesia were reinforced with pharmacological agents. This would seem in most cases to be the recommended procedure.

At an anesthesia grand rounds in 1982 at the University of Texas Health Science Center at Dallas, both the current chairman of anesthesia and his illustrious predecessor agreed that at the present state of the art and science of anesthesia, hypnosis is best utilized as an ancillary to chemical anesthesia rather than as a sole means of anesthesia, even though in responsive subjects some surgical procedures can be performed by hypnoanalgesia alone (Giesecke, 1982; Jenkins, 1982). Similar views were expressed by another chairman of anesthesia at a meeting of the New England Society of Hypnosis, a component section of the American Society of Clinical Hypnosis (St. Amand, 1980). This is a position with which we entirely agree. There are special indications for the inclusion of hypnosis in anesthesia (Crasilneck, McCranie, and Jenkins, 1956; Finer, 1980), but hypnosis may be of use in many other ways in the practice of anesthesia, one of the most important being to reduce preoperative anxiety (Fredericks 1978, 1980; Wester and Smith, 1983).

In our experience we have consistently found that some of the greater values of hypnotherapy are to reduce pre- and postsurgical anxiety; to reduce post-surgical physical and psychological discomfort; to help patients urinate and defecate more easily after surgery; to increase patients' appetites when appropriate; to give positive suggestions on the healing process, and to aid patients through the rehabilitation phase of their illness.

**ADVANTAGES AND DISADVANTAGES
OF HYPNOANESTHESIA**

In summary, while hypnosis possesses many advantages as a means of anesthesia, it suffers from the disadvantage of (1) being time consuming for induction, (2) not being as certain to produce a level of surgical anesthesia in most patients as are the chemical anesthetics, and (3) not producing as profound a state of muscular relaxation as chemical agents.

In selected cases, however, hypnosis may be the technique of choice, either alone or in combination with chemical agents. It has great ease of administration, may be removed immediately when desired, and circumvents undesired postoperative reactions such as nausea, which may occur with standard anesthetic agents. In addition, the hypnotic state allows the use of posthypnotic suggestion for such special purposes as pain relief, inducing required exercise to prevent immobilization, or helping the patient to maintain an awkward position with minimal discomfort.

We have found hypnoanesthesia warranted in situations where

1. Certain chemical agents are contraindicated because of respiratory, cardiac, or other disease.
2. The patient is allergic to the preferred anesthetic agent.
3. The repeated use of anesthetics, has tended to have a debilitating effect on recovery of a patient with an already disturbed physiology, as in cases of severe burns.
4. Fear and apprehension of chemical anesthesia are so severe that they contribute significantly to anesthetic risks.
5. It may be desirable to have the patient in a conscious or semiconscious state and able to respond to questions, such as in chemopallidectomy.

Although not all anesthesiologists are trained in hypnosis or in the psychological theories necessary for its safe applications, they should be exposed to the advantages and disadvantages of its use so that they will recognize those special situations in which hypnotic anesthesia or analgesia may be the preferred technique, either alone or combined with chemical means. It is well to remember Van Dyke's evaluations of hypnosis in anesthesiology: "There is no safer anesthesia than this" (1965).

REFERENCES

Anderson MN: Hypnosis in anesthesia. J Med Assoc Ala 27:121–125, 1957
Antitch JL: The use of hypnosis in pediatric anesthesia. J Am Soc Psychosom Dent Med 14:70–75, 1967
Bank WO, Kerber CW: Medical hypnosis during therapeutic embolization of the carotid and vertebral arteries. Neuroradiology 17:249–252, 1979.
Barlett E: Use of hypnoanesthesia in the control of pain. Symposium, 18th annual meeting The American Society for Clinical Hypnosis, Seattle, 1975
Bensen VB: One hundred cases of post-anesthetic suggestion in the recovery room. Am J Clin Hypn 14:9–15, 1971
Bernstein MR: Significant values of hypnoanesthesia: Three clinical examples. Am J Clin Hyp 7:259–260, 1965
Betcher AM: Hypno-induction techniques in pediatric anesthesia. Anesthesiology 19:279–281, 1958
Betcher AM: Hypnosis as an adjunct in anesthesiology. NY State J Med 60:812–822, 1960
Bower DE: Transurethral resection under self hypnosis. Am J Clin Hypn 16:132–134, 1973
Bowers KS: General anesthesia and unconscious hearing, in Hypnosis For the Seriously Curious. New York, W. W. Norton, 1976, pp 134–137
Brunn JT: The capacity to hear, to understand, to remember experiences during chemoanesthesia: A personal experience. Am J Clin Hypn 6:27–30, 1963

Carli C: (Panelist) Ninth International Congress on Hypnosis and Psychosomatic Medicine, Glasgow, Scotland, 1982

Cheek DB: Unconscious perception of meaningful sounds during surgical anesthesia as revealed under hypnosis. Am J Clin Hypn 1:101–113, 1959

Cheek DB: What does the surgically anesthetized patient hear? Rocky Mt Med J 1960

Cheek DB: Further evidence of persistence of hearing under chemo-anesthesia: Detailed case report. Am J Clin Hypn 7:55–59, 1964

Cheek DB: Awareness of meaningful sounds under general anesthesia: Considerations and a review of the literature 1959–1979, in Wain HJ (ed): Theoretical and Clinical Aspects of Hypnosis. Miami, Symposia Specialists, 1981, pp 87–106

Cohen SB: Being one's own anesthesiologist. Am J Clin Hypn 22:121–123, 1980

Corley JB: Hypnosis and the anesthetist. Am J Clin Hypn 8:34–36, 1965

Crasilneck HB: Hypnoanesthesia: Modern day concepts. Presented at grand rounds, Department of Anesthesiology, University of Texas Health Science Center, Dallas, Texas, 1980

Crasilneck HB, Erwin KW: The effects of general anesthesia on post-hypnotic suggestion. J Clin Exp Hypn 6:45–49, 1958

Crasilneck HB, McCranie EJ, Jenkins MT: Special indications for hypnosis as a method of anesthesia. JAMA 162:1606–1608, 1956

Crawford AH, Jones CW, Perisko JA, Herring JA: Hypnosis for monitoring intraoperative spinal cord function. Anesth Analg (Cleve) 55:42–44, 1976

Daniels E: The hypnotic approach in anesthesia for children. Am J Clin Hypn 4:244–248, 1962

Egbert LD: Personal communication, 1983

Erickson MH: Chemo-anesthesia in relation to hearing and memory. Am J Clin Hypn 6:31, 1963

Erickson JC III: Hypnotic strategies in the daily practice of anesthesia, in Burrows GD, Collison DR, Dennerstein L (eds): Hypnosis. Amsterdam, Elsevier/North-Holland Biomedical Press, 1979, pp 195–199

Evans MB, Paul GL: Effects of hypnotically suggested analgesia on physiological and subjective responses to cold stress. J Consult Clin Psychol 35:362–371, 1970

Ewin DM: Hypnosis in surgery and anesthesia, in Wester WC, Smith AH (eds): Clinical Hypnosis: A Multidisciplinary Approach. Philadelphia, J.B. Lippincott Co., 1983, pp 210–235

Finer B: Experience with hypnosis in clinical anesthesiology. Särtryck Ur Opuscula Medica 4:1–11, 1966

Finer B: Hypnosis and anesthesia, in Burrows GD, Dennerstein L (eds): Handbook of Hypnosis and Psychosomatic Medicine. Amsterdam, Elsevier/North-Holland Biomedical Press, 1980, pp 293–305

Fredericks LE: Teaching of hypnosis in the overall approach to the surgical patient. Am J Clin Hypn 20:175–183, 1978

Fredericks LE: The value of teaching hypnosis in the practice of anesthesiology. Int J Clin Exp Hypn 28:6–15, 1980

Gardner GG, Olness K: Hypnosis and Hypnotherapy with Children. New York, Grune & Stratton, 1981, pp 222–224

Gherardi D: Personal communication, 1982

Giesecke AH, Jr: Personal communication, 1982

Guantieri G: (Panelist) Ninth International Congress on Hypnosis and Psychosomatic Medicine, Glasgow, Scotland, 1982

Gruttad'auria C, Tigoli F, Borghi M: The use of hypnotism in transcutaneous renal biopsy: Preliminary results. Ateneo Parmense (Acta Biomed) 49:421–426, 1978

Halliday AM, Mason AA: The effect of hypnotic anesthesia on cortical responses. J Neurol Neurosurg Psychiatry 27:300–312, 1964

Hartman BJ: Parahypnosis: Unconscious perception under chemoanesthesia. J Natl Med Assoc 61:246–247, 1969

Hilgard ER: A quantitative study of pain and its reduction through hypnotic suggestion. Proc Natl Acad Sci USA 5716:1581–1586, 1967

Hilgard JR, Hilgard ER, Newman DM: Sequelae to hypnotic induction with special reference to earlier chemical anesthesia. J Nerv Ment Dis 133:461–478, 1961

Horvai I: On the question of hypnosuggestive analgesia. Acta Univ Med 7:469–475, 1959

Jackson J, Middleton W: The use of hypnosis for analgesia in upper gastrointestinal endoscopy. Aust J Clin Exp Hypn 6:21–23, 1978

Jenkins MT: Personal communication, 1983

Jones CW: Hypnosis and spinal fusions by Harrington instrumentation. Am J Clin Hypn 19:155–157, 1977

Kasasian AH: (Panelist) Ninth International Congress on Hypnosis and Psychosomatic Medicine, Glasgow, Scotland, 1982

Katz R: Panel discussion on use of hypnosis as a method of anesthesia. Twenty-fifth Annual Meeting. Society of Clinical and Experimental Hypnosis, Irvine, Calif., 1973 (unpublished)

Klopp KK: Production of local anesthesia using waking suggestion with the child patient. Int J Clin Exp Hypn 9:59–62, 1961

Kroger WS: Clinical and Experimental Hypnosis (ed 2). Philadelphia, J.B. Lippincott Co., 1977, pp 212–220

Lassner J: Hypnosis in anesthesiology: An international symposium. Berlin, Springer-Verlag, 1964, p 51

Levinson BW: States of awareness during general anesthesia. Preliminary communication. Br J Anaesth 37:544–546, 1965

Marmer MJ: Hypnosis in Anesthesiology. Springfield, Ill., Charles C Thomas, 1959

Marmer MJ: Hypnosis in anesthesiology and surgery, in Schneck JM (ed): Hypnosis in Modern Medicine (ed 3). Springfield, Ill., Charles C Thomas, 1963

Marmer MJ: Unusual applications of hypnosis in anesthesiology. Int J Clin Exp Hypn 17:199–208, 1969

Monteiro AR de C, de Oliveira DS: Amigdalectomia sob hipnose [Tonsillectomy under hypnosis]. Medicine cirsugia formaria 267:315–320, 1958

Paris RJ, Mosgedis OH, Durante JE: Removal of gunshot under hypnotic anesthesia. Hypnologia (Buenos Aires) 2:5–7, 1960

Pearson RE: Response to suggestions given under general anesthesia. Am J Clin Hypn 4:106–114, 1961

Rausch V: Cholecystectomy with self-hypnosis. Am J Clin Hypn 22:124–129, 1980

Rodger BP: Hypnosis in anesthesia: Some psychological considerations. Am J Clin Hypn 4:237–243, 1962

Rosen N: Hypnosis and self-hypnosis in medical practice. Md State Med J 6:297–299, 1957

St. Amand A: The use of hypnosis in anesthesiology. Presented at the New England Component Section Meeting of the American Society of Clinical Hypnosis, 1980

Schwartz BE: Hypnoanalgesia and hypnoanesthesia in urology. Surg Clin North Am 45:1547–1555, 1965

Scott DL: Modern Hospital Hypnosis: Especially for Anesthetists. London, Lloyd-Luke, 1974

Scott DL: Hypnosis in pedicle graft surgery. Br J Plast Surg 29:8–13, 1976

Steinberg S: Hypnoanesthesia—a case report on a 90-year-old patient. Am J Clin Hypn 7:355–356, 1965

Succar J: Hypnosis y Anestesia. Rev Pera Anestes 1:13–20, 1963

Tinterow MM: The use of hypnotic anesthesia for major surgical procedure. Am Surg 26:732–737, 1960

Trustman R, Dubovsky S, Titley R: Auditory perception during general anesthesia—myth or fact? Int J Clin Exp Hypn 25:88–105, 1977

Tyson DB: The control of vomiting for short anesthetic procedures. Am J Clin Hypn 6:229–231, 1964

Van Dyke PB: Hypnosis in surgery. J Abdomin Surg 7:1–5, 26–29, 1965

Wain HJ: Septoplasty. Am J Clin Hypn, 1984, (in press)

Wallace G: Hypnosis in anesthesiology. Int J Clin Exp Hypn 7:129–137, 1959

Wester WC, Smith AH: Clinical Hypnosis: A Multidisciplinary Approach. Philadelphia, J.B. Lippincott Co., 1983

8
Hypnosis and Surgery

The surgeon can find many useful applications of hypnosis (Crasilneck and Jenkins, 1958; Crasilneck, McCranie, and Jenkins, 1950; Dias, 1963 a,b; Grant, 1974), some similar to the uses of anesthesiology. Emphasizing emotional factors in surgery, Kolouch (1968) pointed out that "the surgeon himself is . . . a most potent and useful ataractic in the treatment of fear in the surgical patient." Wangensteen (1962) describes the effectiveness of hypnosis in making it possible for patients to experience comfortably procedures that would otherwise be long-enduring and disagreeable. The usefulness of hypnosis for the surgeon has been attested by many others, including Bravo (1974), Doberneck et al. (1950), Ewin (1974), Jones (1962), Mun (1966), Teitelbaum (1967), Todorovic (1959), and Van Dyke (1970). Kroger (1977) stresses the importance of preoperative rehearsal with a patient who is to have hypnoanesthesia. The various steps of the operation are rehearsed in sequence, so that surprises for the patient are minimal during the surgical procedure.

One of the primary uses of hypnosis is in improving the postoperative course, during which pain, nausea, and discomfort are frequently a problem. Werbel (1964) suggests posthypnotic suggestion to prevent a violent awakening from anesthesia in patients who have had unpleasant awakening in previous surgical experiences. Kolouch (1964) reviewed the postoperative convalescence of 254 surgical patients during which hypnosis had been used to instill purposeful, optimistic expectations of a simple recovery period. Results were generally encouraging, though three factors seemed to reduce the effectiveness of the hypnotic suggestions: (1) the increasing magnitude of the surgery, (2) "personality defects" in the patients, and (3) postoperative surgical complications (see Kolouch, 1962). Field (1974) was unable to demonstrate differences in hypnotic and control subjects in postoperative course, although depth of hypnosis did correlate with lessened anxiety on the day of surgery and an increased speed of recovery.

In a direct comparison of 11 hemorrhoidectomy patients who had hypnosis with 11 patients who did not have hypnotic treatment, Werbel (1960) noted a striking relief of postoperative pain in the hypnotic group, finding only minimal pain from the first bowel movement after surgery in all of the cases in which posthypnotic suggestion had been used for pain relief. He later (1963) reported 14 consecutive cases, 11 with no pain, 2 with moderate pain, and 1 with severe pain. Day (1965) also discussed the role of hypnosis in anorectal surgery. Wiggins (1968) found that two patients undergoing surgery for pedicle attachments were able to relieve their postoperative pain to the extent that no pain medication was required for over 2 weeks. Their preoperative training period in hypnosis had been 1¹/₂ weeks.

In one case Gruen (1972) taught self-hypnosis for relaxation and other suggestions for 3 weeks prior to heart surgery. Suggestions focused on feeling comfortable and happy after the operation and on the quick return of normal physiological functions. Recovery was considered to be better than average, with no pain medication required from the third postoperative day.

The "dumping syndrome" that occurs in from 6 to 38 percent of all patients following gastrectomy (Bonello et al., 1960) consists of postprandial distress, fullness, nausea, belching, perspiration, dizziness, palpitation, and other vasomotor symptoms. Bonello and his associates (1960) reported symptomatic relief of this syndrome by hypnosis in 56 percent of 36 gastrectomy patients treated over a 3 year period. Dorcus and Goodwin (1955) achieved remission of dumping syndrome in all of four patients treated by hypnosis. Somma Pena (1960) used hypnotherapy to relieve persistent vomiting and toxic confusion in a 63-year-old patient.

Urinary retention, another frequent postoperative complication, can often be alleviated with hypnotherapy. Doberneck and his associates (1961) achieved relief of postoperative urinary retention in 80.9 percent of 21 patients, while the patients requiring catheterization in spite of hypnosis had only two catheterizations each. Day (1964) reported a series of 106 cases, concluding that hypnosis decreased the need for catheterization by 40 percent. Chiasson (1964) reported 7 cases of relief of postoperative urinary retention with hypnosis. There is some evidence that hypnosis may shorten the postoperative rehabilitation period. Bonilla, Quigley, and Bowen (1961) compared the rehabilitation time for 9 consecutive uncomplicated arthrotomies in which hypnosis was used to enhance the postoperative course. There were also 9 control cases. The rehabilitation time for the hypnotic group was 27 days compared with 46 days for the controls. Sacerdote (1963) described how hypnosis may be used to speed rehabilitation when hysterical or conversion symptoms are interfering. He treated a young patrolman who underwent successful knee surgery but failed to move the leg after surgery. Hypnosis was difficult to induce, but when it had been achieved, the patrolman was able to flex and extend the leg and walked from the room with a cane.

There are reports that suggest hypnosis may aid in diminishing edema around a trauma site (Lait, 1961) and may accelerate wound healing (Bowers, 1966; Cheek, 1961). These observations lack firm experimental verification, although the findings of Chapman, Goodell, and Wolff (1959) suggest the possibility that tissues may be made less vulnerable to injury under hypnosis. Pellicone (1960) found hypnosis useful in treating burns, but he did not have the impression that it influenced the rate of healing.

Pain, of course, can often be attenuated with hypnosis (Bryant, 1957–1958; Egbert et al., 1964; Siegal, 1979). Phantom pain—the persistent sense of pain in the area of an amputated extremity—is an extremely disturbing postoperative complication. Cedercreutz (1952, 1961) treated phantom pain with hypnosis in 100 amputees. Both the pain and the phantom limb sensations themselves were relieved in 22 percent of the cases, and in another 13 percent the pain was considerably diminished. Cedercreutz found it particularly useful to suggest sensations of warmth in the stump.

SURGICAL USES OF HYPNOSIS

In addition to indications for hypnosis in anesthesia, the surgeon should be aware of special situations in which he or she might wish to employ hypnosis as part of the operative procedure and hospital care. These indications are not completely distinct, of course, from those for anesthesia, but here they are considered separately for emphasis and clarity, together with illustrative case examples.

Pulmonary Infection

In situations where severe pulmonary infection increases the risk of inhalation anesthesia, hypnosis may offer a ready means of maintaining the patient in a calm, pain-free state during needed surgical procedures.

A 44-year-old married woman was hospitalized with a diagnosis of active and extensive pulmonary tuberculosis. This patient also had a history of being treated for tubercular meningitis. During the course of her present illness she began complaining of abdominal cramping and excessively long menses. Gynecological examination was done, and the results indicated cancer of the cervix. Local radium needle implantation in the cervix was the indicated treatment.

The patient's anxiety concerning her respiratory condition, coupled with her past history, made her very fearful of general anesthesia. Hypnoanesthesia was suggested and fully explained to her. After rapport was established, hypnosis was attempted. The patient was able to enter a somnambulistic depth of hypnosis after two hours of conditioning. During the operative procedure the cervical radium implantation was accomplished without difficulty. She did not complain of any pain or discomfort and was able to sleep approximately three hours postoperatively without any sedation. Her recovery from surgery was uneventful and free of any complications.*

Control of Movement During Surgery

Many procedures can be performed under local anesthesia for the control of pain, but pain is not the only factor. It is important too that the surgeon have a quiet, tranquil patient so that no unexpected movement of the patient occurs.

The patient was a 23-year-old woman who had previously undergone surgery for resection of an acoustic neuroma. Postoperatively she had a persistent residual facial palsy. A second phase of surgery was being done in order to restore the damaged facial nerve. The surgeon wished to operate under local anesthesia so the patient could report changed sensations in the affected areas. The patient had previously demonstrated a low pain threshold, however, and the surgeon anticipated that she might react adversely to any pain produced inadvertently during a local anesthesia procedure.

The patient was obviously quite anxious about the operation and, since her cooperation would be necessary during certain phases of the procedure, the surgeon suggested the possibility of using hypnosis. Initially she was doubtful and apprehensive, but she was willing to cooperate and said she would "try my

*Reprinted from Jenkins MT, Crasilneck HB: Hypnoanesthesia, Am J Nurs 59:12–15, 1959. Copyrighted by American Journal of Nursing Company. With permission.

best." She was conditioned for the operation by being hypnotized twice prior to surgery. During the operation she did not move or complain of any pain or discomfort. She answered the surgeon readily and without doubt or hesitation when questioned about the sensations she perceived. The procedure was completed in five hours and was accomplished without apprehension or fear or any untoward reaction on the part of the patient. She responded to the posthypnotic suggestion that she would sleep for about four hours postoperatively. Her recovery was uneventful and free of complications.*

Need for Patient Response

In some procedures, particularly in neurosurgery, the anatomical landmarks are not always sufficient to allow the surgeon to identify the area of diseased tissue or the target for ablative procedures. During chemopallidectomy for severe Parkinson's disease, for instance, it may be considered important to have the patient conscious and cooperative if the surgeon wishes to judge the patient's changing response before producing the desired lesion.

A 50-year-old man had a 20-year history of tremors due to Parkinson's disease following encephalitis. His palsy was so severe that he could not lift a half-filled glass of water to his lips without spilling it. Because of his severe tremor, he could not eat or do many of the other basic activities of daily life without assistance.

The patient was a candidate for chemopallidectomy, which involves injections, first of procaine and then of ethyl alcohol, into the hypothalamus. In this procedure, the brain is exposed, and the needle is placed with x-ray guidance. The correct location of the needle is verified by the absence of tremors when the patient is asked to move his extremities. Local anesthesia alone would not be adequate for this procedure, as the patient's tremor was so pronounced that he was unable to hold his head still. The persuasive argument for the use of hypnosis was the need for the patient to be awake so he would be able to follow directions when he was told to move his hands and arms.

In preoperative work with the patient it was found that he could be hypnotized, and so hypnoanesthesia was undertaken and was supplemented only by the local agent used for infiltration of the scalp. With the micrometered placement of the long hypodermic needle and the frequent x-ray checks of position, the operative procedure took several hours. The patient, under the influence of hypnosis, was able to cooperate during this entire time and was

*Reprinted from Jenkins MT, Crasilneck HB: Hypnoanesthesia. Am J Nurs 59:12–15, 1979. Copyrighted by the American Journal of Nursing Company. With permission.

able to move his fingers and his hands in a coordinated fashion without palsy or tremors when the needle was in the desired position.*

Monitoring of the Electroencephalogram During Surgery

An epileptogenic focus was to be removed from the cortex of a 14-year-old girl. Technically, the procedure could have been done with only local anesthesia infiltrated into the scalp, but it was anticipated that she might not remain quiet during the long procedure. General anesthesia was considered for this reason, but would have added another factor—that of the anesthetic effect—the interpretation of the continuous electroencephalographic monitoring during surgery.

A 14-year-old girl had developed epileptic convulsions after a head injury four and one-half years prior to her admission to the hospital. The convulsions occurred at the rate of two or three per day and were usually preceded by an aura consisting of a "tingling sensation in the fingers of both hands" and accompanied by a loss of consciousness of from 30 to 60 seconds. Electro-encephalographic studies revealed a focal discharge in the right temporal lobe. Anticonvulsive medication was successful only to the extent of reducing the number of daily seizures.

Since conservative treatment was not considered adequate and since there was a temporal focus, it was decided to perform a temporal lobectomy with electroencephalographic monitoring. It became necessary to consider the effects of anesthetic agents given by inhalation or intravenously upon the electroencephalographic patterns. Since it is well established that there are no alterations in the brain wave patterns in even the deepest state of hypnosis [except from sleep to waking changes in some cases], it was decided to try hypnosis plus local infiltration of the scalp with procaine for the anesthesia. The possibility of using hypnosis was discussed with the patient. She proved to be an excellent hypnotic subject and was hypnotized four times before surgery to condition her to enter the somnambulistic state required for the proposed surgery.

At operation the scalp line of incision was injected with a 2 percent solution of procaine. She was then hypnotized and, after she had entered a state of somnambulism, the surgical procedure was started. During most of the operation the patient was relaxed and comfortable. She did, however, complain of a mild pain while the dura was being separated from the bone. Twice during the nine-hour procedure it was necessary to inject the scalp with additional

*Reprinted from Crasilneck HB, McCranie EJ, Jenkins MT, Special Indications for Hypnosis as a Method of Anesthesia. JAMA, 162:1606–1608, 1956. With permission.

Figure 8-1.   The skull has been opened, using local anesthetic infiltrated into the scalp together with hypnotic suggestioins for relaxation, comfort, and freedom from pain and anxiety. The therapist is seen in the lower right.

local anesthetic because of the patient's perception of pain, especially upon forceful retraction of the scalp margin. The abnormal spiking electrical focus was confirmed by electroencephalographic tracings, and the proposed excision was performed. The patient did not complain of pain during this excision except on one noteworthy occasion when, as a blood vessel in the hippocampal region was being coagulated, the patient suddenly awoke from the hypnotic trance. She was immediately rehypnotized and was able again to enter a deep state of somnambulism. The surgeon then purposefully restimulated the same region of the hippocampus—once again, the patient abruptly awakened from trance but was quickly rehypnotized. (The fact that the patient woke from the hypnotic state when the hippocampus was stimulated has led to considerable interest and speculation on our part as to the neurophysiology of hypnosis and it opens another avenue for investigation.) The final electroencephalograms were completed and the patient was given 100 mg of thiopental sodium intravenously. Upon completion of the operation, she was able to answer questions but was amnesic concerning the surgery because of posthypnotic suggestion given prior to awakening. She had also been given a posthypnotic suggestion that she would experience a prolonged sleep, which she did for six hours without further sedation. The postoperative course was very satisfactory and free of complications.*

*Reprinted from Crasilneck HB, McCranie EJ, and Jenkins MT. Special Indications for Hypnosis as a Method of Anesthesia. JAMA 162:1606–1608, 1956. With permission.

Figure 8-2.   While remaining calm in hypnosis, the patient moves his tongue
at the hypnotherapist's suggestion, allowing the neurosurgeons to evaluate the
effect of probe placement before a surgical lesion is made for treatment of
severe Parkinson's disease.

Another case of hypnotic anesthesia in neurosurgery was reported
by Nayyar and Brady (1963).

A 38-year-old uncooperative man had traumatic epilepsy secondary to a
gunshot wound of his right frontal area. A frontoparietal depressed fracture had
resulted, with transient hemiplegia for 2 months, leaving a residual of right-
sided headache and grand mal seizures. He manifested personality changes of
rage, depression, and suspiciousness.

Hypnosis was chosen because general anesthesia would interfere with
electrocorticographic monitoring of the debridement and topectomy. Likewise,
local anesthesia was considered inadvisable because of the patient's hostile,
suspicious, and uncooperative attitude. He was capable of developing deep
anesthesia by hypnotic training in three sessions. The only pain during surgery
occurred when traction was applied to the dura. In addition to hypnosis there
was little chemical anesthesia—only local chemical anesthesia—only local use
of xylocaine and intravenous Demerol. He was cooperative, complained of
little discomfort, and seemed relaxed and calm.

Postoperative Control

Surgical management does not end when the patient leaves the
operative theater. Human factors in the postoperative behavior of the
patient must also be considered. At times hypnosis may greatly aid the

patient in following the needed postoperative instructions of the surgeon.

For example, an elderly man had undergone eye surgery for cataract, but because of his severe emphysemic cough had ruptured some of the fine stitching. When the procedure was repeated, hypnosis was employed in the postoperative course not only to keep him calm and still but also to inhibit his coughing while the eye tissues began to heal. Wollman (1964) has reported hypnosis as aiding a patient who had to undergo prolonged postoperative positioning in a half-shell body cast. Wiggins and Brown (1968) employed hypnosis to aid two patients who had pedicle attachments of the right ankle above the left knee because of gunshot sounds. Motivational morale was considered excellent.

Kelsey and Barrow (1958) used hypnosis with a 24-year-old man who had lost tissue from the forepart of the right foot, which was to be repaired with a pedicle graft from the abdomen, transported via the left forearm. With hypnosis the patient was able to maintain the required positions for 28 days. Before each graft the efficacy of the suggestions was tested overnight by suggestion of "lock" and later "unlock it."

Leonard, Papermaster, and Wangensteen (1957) controlled trance suggestions by symptoms of the dumping syndrome following gastrectomy. Bensen (1971) contends that suggestions given at a particular time during the phase of recovery from chemical anesthesia will function as posthypnotic suggestions to enhance postoperative recovery.

SURGICAL TREATMENT OF BURN PATIENTS

In the severely burned patient there are a number of complicating factors that often constellate a vicious negative cycle, too frequently leading to death. These factors are (1) the constant pain, (2) loss of appetite, (3) the requirement for repeated painful procedures, such as debridement of dead tissues, (4) contractures resulting from failure to exercise because of pain, and (5) a syndrome of severe psychological regression and negativism, which may greatly slow rehabilitation. Hypnosis has been shown to be of benefit in all of these problem areas.

In the early 1950s our group was the first to report that hypnosis could aid greatly in the treatment of severely burned patients (Crasilneck et al., 1955). A young woman had been burned (second and third degree) over 90 percent of her body surface. She was fearful and in constant severe pain. It was possible with hypnosis to give her relief from most of the pain, produce calmness, and alleviate much of her anxiety. Although she died 3 days later in spite of heroic medical and surgical care, it was clearly established that hypnosis was of great benefit in allowing the woman to die with minimal pain and suffering. One of the problems of the severely burned patient, as already noted, is loss of appetite. In the past this has sometimes led to severe negative nitrogen balance at a time when the need to build new tissues is great. Hypnosis was found to be of marked aid in increasing food intake. A case illustrating how hypnotherapy increased food intake, decreased pain, and calmed the patient follows:

A 24-year-old man was subjected to hypnosis after 18 months of hospitalization for a 45-percent body surface burn. His course in the hospital had been progressively on the downgrade and was characterized by a weight loss of 40 lbs [18.1 kg] from 130 to 90 lbs [59 to 40.8 kg]; a loss of muscle mass; multiple unsuccessful skin-grafting attempts; chronically infected granulating wounds and infected donor skin sites; extreme weakness with refusal to attempt to leave the bed or to move his extremities; the development of decubitus ulcers and severe contractures of hands, ankles, knees, arms, and neck; the persistent complaint of pain and request for narcotics; an increasing dependence and regression to puerile behavior at times; the refusal to eat despite the attentions and compassionate pleas of resident surgeons, dietitians, nurses, and relatives, despite lengthy explanations of the importance of food to his recovery and despite a blunt coercive approach; the failure to improve significantly while being force fed through a small polyethylene nasogastric tube; complaints of fullness and nausea with forced feedings of varied volumes and composition and finally refusing to permit the tube for feedings; and the failure to obtain lasting improvement in appetite with the administration of corticotropin.

Soon after rapport was established between the patient and the therapist and hypnotic and posthypnotic suggestions were started, the patient began to anticipate with eagerness each meal; within a few days he was consuming about 4200 calories each day. Six weeks after hypnosis was started, he gained 30 pounds [13.6 kg]; he became ambulatory, exercised faithfully, gained strength and muscle mass rapidly; skin-grafting procedures were rewarded by 90 percent "takes;" spontaneous epithelialization was rapid, and small granulating areas healed; he began doing things for himself that he had previously demanded that others do; he became cheerful, left his room frequently, and sought the company of nurses and other patients. Narcotics were discontinued, and there were no complaints of pain. Twelve weeks after beginning hypnosis he was discharged from the hospital in an ambulatory state with nearly all wounds healed. In this patient a progressively downward course was arrested and reversed after the application of hypnotic suggestion. The food intake became adequate, his attitude improved, he complained of no pain, he became ambulatory, and recovery ensured.*

*Reprinted from Crasilneck HB, McCranie EJ, Jenkins MT, Special Indications for Hypnosis as a Method of Anesthesia. JAMA, 162:1606–1608, 1956. With permission.

Figure 8-3. A severely burned patient is placed in hypnosis for pain relief using an arm-levitation induction technique. Suggestions were given that the arm would be cold, numb, devoid of pain sensation from the fingers to the shoulder "as if it is enclosed in a thick leather glove."

We have had very good results in increasing food intake with severely burned patients. A typical preparation of a burned patient follows:

"I am going to ask you to stare at this coin that I'm holding and as you do so, pay no attention to any other sounds or noises. You are aware that you are

Figure 8-4.   Hypnotic suggestions for "feelings of pressure but no pain" were
continued throughout the surgical debridement of dead tissue and changing of
bandages. Posthypnotic suggestions were then given for relaxation and for
"only a remnant of discomfort."

breathing more rapidly and also that as you stare intensively at this coin, your
eyelids are beginning to blink and to feel heavy. As you feel them getting heavy
and drowsy, just let them close . . . that's it . . . they are fluttering . . . closing
and closed . . . closing and closed . . . and as I continue talking, you will enter
a very deep level of hypnosis . . . for in so doing you are going to get well . . .
a very deep and sound level. . . . As you are aware of a heavy feeling in your
extremities, your arms and legs . . . as you are aware of this . . . nod your
head . . . Good. . . . a deeper and a sounder state. . . . Now the finger that I
touch will lose all feeling. . . . Now as that finger feels and is numb . . . nod
your head, yes. . . . Good. . . Now open your eyes. . . . You will note that I
am stimulating that finger very hard with the point of my nail file, but you have
absolutely no sensation of pain. Pressure, but no pain. Now normal sensations
return to your finger. As you feel the file just barely stimulating your finger, pull
it away. . . . Good, . . . Relax . . . now you can realize the power of the mind
over the body and if you can block pain . . . real pain . . . then, you can allow
your body to respond to other suggestions equally well. You are now in a very
deep state of relaxtion. . . . You are going to hear some soft music that is
pleasurable to you . . . and as this occurs, nod your head, yes. . . . Good . . .
and now a very deep and relaxed state of mind and body. Because of the power
of your mind over your body . . . you are going to be able to definitely increase

your food intake. This food intake is going to help you to get well . . . it is an integral part of your rehabilitation, and you will eat all the food prescribed by your doctor. The food will taste good. . . . You will enjoy your food . . . realizing that with every mouthful you digest you are improving your physical and mental state. . . . Food intake is going to help you get well. . . . You will be hungry much of the time and you will eat not only the regular meals, but also the supplemental food ordered for you. *You will be hungry and your appetite will definitely increase . . . you will have a craving for each meal* because in your case food intake is an absolute necessity to health and you will eat every meal with enjoyment . . . knowing this food is making you get well very rapidly. As I slowly count from ten to one backwards, you will fully awaken . . . relaxed, at ease, and hungry.''

Skin grafting is usually necessary in severely burned patients. This can be a painful procedure, and the fear and apprehension of the patient may be a complicating factor for the staff and for himself or herself. Pain may also interfere with exercise that is necessary to prevent contractures as the burned and grafted area heals. Both the pain and anxiety associated with the treatment of burns may be decreased with hypnotherapy (Hartley, 1968; Papermaster et al., 1960).

The use of hypnosis for both of these problems is shown in the case that follows:

A 33-year-old man was admitted to the hospital with a burn over 45 percent of the body surface. During the first 30 days he was operated on several times for the removal of devitalized tissue and for skin grafting. Because of pain it became necessary to administer a general anesthesia for dressing changes. The patient complained bitterly of pain in the donor and other operative sites after each procedure under general anesthesia. He refused to exercise his hands and fingers, which had been burned. With these first 30 days serving as a control period, hypnosis was used as the analgesia for subsequent dressing changes and debridement. These procedures were then performed without complaint; with hypnotic sleep used as anesthesia, a split-thickness skin graft was cut. There was no manifestation of discomfort. The patient was given the posthypnotic suggestion that there would be no pain in the donor area, that he would exercise his hands, and that he would be hungry. On awakening he complained of hunger and reported an absence of sensation in the donor area.

Three days later normal sensations were returned to the area by hypnotic suggestion. He exercised his hands as instructed, every 30 minutes, so faithfully tht it was necessary to limit this activity, for he even exercised them during sleep! Subsequent posthypnotic suggestion had to be made so that he would exercise only during waking hours. After the patient had entered a moderate to deep level of trance, he was told the following:

"Exercise is most important to your recovery. . . . You can and will exercise your hand for 15 minutes out of each waking hour, as prescribed by your doctor. . . . There will be only minimal, if any, discomfort. . . . However, you will protect your hand . . . but you will stretch the muscles . . . make a fist as the doctor showed you and will want to do this, because exercise will help you to get well. . . . You will exercise for 15 minutes out of each waking hour . . . because you want to get well. . . . You can reinforce these suggestions yourself, and anytime we are ready to work together you can attain a deep level of trance when I give you the posthypnotic suggestion of tapping on this table five times with this fountain pen . . . you will awaken and you will follow these instructions carefully . . . as I count from ten to one, you will be fully awake.''

The avoidance of repeated general anesthetics and narcotics, in addition to establishing a will to exercise his hands were the therapeutic benefits obtained from hypnotic suggestion in this patient.*

Hypnosis can decrease the use of narcotics that may otherwise be demanded in large quantity by the burn patient who is in severe pain.

A 32-year-old man was admitted to the hospital with a mixed superficial and deep dermal burn over 35 percent of the body surface. He was subjected to hypnosis after arriving at the hospital about 4 hours after the injury. No narcotics were required during the acute phase of injury or at any time during his 18 days of hospitalization. Complete alleviation of pain was obtained with hypnosis in this man throughout his hospital course.

Schafer (1975) described his effective use of tape-recorded hypnotic suggestions that were employed on a burn ward when dressings were to be changed. Bernstein (1963) asserted that hypnosis did not always produce anesthesia, but it did increase pain tolerance. Dehenterova (1967), Finer and Nylen (1961), and Pellicone (1960) have also described the use of hypnosis in the treatment of burns.

Dabney Ewin of Tulane Medical School has produced a prodigious amount of work in the use of hypnosis in the treatment of burns (Ewin 1978, 1980, 1983). Ewin stresses that the more rapidly hypnotherapy can be instituted after injury, the better the results are likely to be. He cites one example (Ewin, 1978) of a young man who stepped into a vat of molten metal that had a temperature of 1750°F. Hypnosis was instituted within 4 hours of the injury and was of great benefit in pain relief as well as possibly decreasing swelling and edema and increasing blood flow to the injured tissues. In a clinical study, Kaplan and Moore (1983) have attemped to measure increased blood flow to one of two bilaterally injured limbs following hypnotic suggestions. The psychological value of hypnotherapy in decreasing anxiety and speeding recovery in burn patients is widely appreciated (Crasilneck, 1978a,b,

*Reprinted from Crasilneck HB, McCranie EJ, and Jenkins MT. Special Indications for Hypnosis as a Method of Anesthesia JAMA 162:1607, 1956.

1979, 1981; Finer, 1980; Hart, 1980; Margolis and De Clement, 1980; Schafer, 1978; Wakeman and Kaplan, 1978).

After the pain of the burned area is under control, and the anxiety of the patient is in a state of quiescence, the rapport with the patient is at its zenith. As the hypnotherapy continues to control food intake, exercise, and ambulation, the therapist at this point must use psychotherapy in order for the patient to vent his anger, resentment, and frustration. Combining hypnotherapy and psychotherapy in conjunction with hypnoanesthesia works well for most burn victims (Crasilneck, 1978a, 1979, 1981).

A research design by Hammond, Keye, and Grant (1983) evaluated the effects of sunburn equally distributed on both thighs with hypnoanalgesia given in treating only one thigh. None of the 6 subjects reported pain in the anesthesized thigh, temperatures were significantly lower, and there was much less redness on the skin.

Bernstein (1963, 1965) has reported on the use of hypnosis on a ward caring for burned children, outlining the reaction and interaction of the staff. He cautions against a magical overexpectation of hypnosis by the staff, as it later may lead to a rejection of the usefulness of hypnotherapy. The tendency to overexpectation apparently is related to an underlying sense of helplessness in a situation that mobilized a great affective desire to be of benefit to the children. The use of hypnosis with children who have been burned is discussed by Gardner and Olness (1981) and by La Baw (1973b).

PRECAUTIONS IN THE USE OF HYPNOSIS

Hypnosis is not always successful for anesthesia, and the surgeon or anesthesiologist should be prepared—and ready—to use chemical agents if necessary. With testing for effectiveness of hypnoanalgesia made in practice hypnotherapy sessions before surgery, there is less likelihood that a switch to chemical anesthesia will be necessary during actual surgery. On neurosurgery patients, for instance, the effectiveness of analgesia can be tested by piercing the scalp with a sterile needle while the patient is under hypnoanesthesia. Werbel (1967), however, describes a case in which it was necessary to switch to chemical anesthesia at the last minute. According to Werbel, hypnosis also is not particularly successful for anesthesia in abdominal surgery. If an abdominal incision is to be made, however, the skin can be clamped with forceps under hypnoanalgesia to test the effectiveness of the patient's trance. In addition to such testing of analgesia we try to rehearse with the hypnotized patient the kinds of experiences (and their purpose) that he or she is likely to experience in surgery. This avoids unexpected surprise and possible interference with hypnosis.

Although we personally know of no similar case, Yanovski and Briklin (1967) have reported a spontaneous, dramatic, and "at the time uncontrollable" abreaction that took place on an operating table while the patient's abdomen was open. In that case, though, hypnosis was the sole anesthetic agent employed, a practice that we feel is seldom indicated. We consider hypnosis an adjunct to chemical anesthesia in major surgery. Furthermore, it is essential to consider the psychological interaction involved in hypnosis (Mahrer 1960).

Whenever possible, too, hypnotic induction should take place in advance of surgery. This permits time to judge in each instance whether the patient is sufficiently responsive for hypnosis to be employed alone or whether it may be advisable to combine it with other techniques. The degree of the patient's insensitivity to pain also should be tested before surgery. Some gynecologists test hypnoanalgesia by applying a tissue clamp to a fold of the vaginal mucosa. Such tests can indicate if the patient needs further conditioning before the surgical procedure.

Nurses, orderlies, and other personnel should be instructed on how to relate to the hypnotized patient when in the operating room. In general, this will be in the same manner as with a patient under chemical anesthesia, but there are important exceptions. The patient may be more aware of chance remarks made in his presence, and nothing should be said that would not be acceptable if the patient were awake. No one should say, for example, "It looks like a hopeless case" or "It's bleeding too much" or any remark that might frighten or upset the patient if he or she were fully conscious.

With hypnoanesthesia the area of anesthesia may be clearly delimited to a particular part of the body. Should the patient be touched in an area for which a suggestion of anesthesia has not been given, he or she may respond abruptly.

Some modifications of hypnotic technique may be found useful during surgery. The patient should be told that he or she will hear *only* the voice of the hypnotherapist and not be distracted by other voices or sounds. It is often helpful to add a suggestion that time is passing rapidly for the patient during the surgery. Although the surgery has been "rehearsed" under hypnosis, there may be changes in procedure in the operating room. If it is possible to anticipate the moves of the surgeon, suggestions can be tailored to forewarn the patient of sensations so that they will not startle him or her. For example, if the obstetrician is about to suture an episiotomy on a woman under hypnoanesthesia, the hypnotherapist might tell her, "In a moment you may feel a slight pressure sensation near your rectum, but there will be no pain.''

Posthypnotic suggestions for minimal pain and discomfort may help the patient. It is again important, though, not to remove all organic pain with the suggestion (see Chapter 6). The patient may be told that he or she will take fluids easily and will be able to defecate and urinate with no difficulty.

With a thermal injury, the surgeon usually does some debridement and cleaning of the area with an antiseptic solution. Good hypnotic subjects in a deep state of hypnoanesthesia usually respond very well to this type of preoperative conditioning. In the event they tend to awaken from trance or complain of pain, further attempts at conditioning can be made; however, if pain persists, during a second conditioning trial, further efforts for hypnoanesthesia should be discontinued.

CONCLUSION

With increasing understanding of the effects of states of consciousness on the body, we feel that hypnosis—or hypnoticlike techniques—will become a standard part of good anesthetic practice. Research is still needed, but we feel that such attention to the mind as well as the body of the surgical patient will eventuate in decreased nausea, decreased postoperative recovery time, improved food intake, attenuated pain, more rapid exercise and ambulation, and enhanced motivation for rapid and complete rehabilitation.

REFERENCES

Bensen VB: One hundred cases of post anesthetic suggestion in the recovery room. Am J Clin Hypn 14:9–15, 1971

Bernstein MR: Management of burned children with the aid of hypnosis. J Child Psychol 7:93–98, 1963

Bernstein MR: Significant values of hypnoanesthesia: Three clinical examples. Am J Clin Hypn 7:259–260, 1965

Bonello FJ, Doberneck RC, Papermaster AA et al: Hypnosis in surgery. I. The postgastrectomy dumping syndrome. Am J Clin Hypn 2:215–219, 1960

Bonilla KB, Quigley WF, Bowen WF: Experiences with hypnosis and surgical service. Milit Med 126:364–370, 1961

Bowers WF: Hypnosis: Useful adjunct in surgery. Surg Bull 46:8–10, 1966

Bravo L: Hypnosis in surgery. Presented at the annual meeting of the Society of Clinical Experimental Hypnosis, Montreal, 1974

Bryant ME: Hypnosis: Its use in control of pain in major injuries. Br J Med Hypn 9:36–37, 1957–1958

Cedercreutz C: Hypnosis in the treatment of phantom limb. Finska Laksalls Handl 95:170–175, 1952

Cedercreutz C: Hypnosis in surgery. Int J Clin Exp Hypn 9:93–95, 1961

Chapman LF, Goodell H, Wolff NG: Changes in tissue vulnerability induced during hypnotic suggestion. J Psychosom Res 4:99–105, 1959

Cheek DB: Unconscious reactions and surgical risk. West J Surg Obstet Gynecol 69:325–328, 1961

Chiasson SW: Hypnosis in postoperative urinary retention. Am J Clin Hypn 6:366–368, 1964

Crasilneck HB: (Panelist) The use of hypnosis in the treatment of thermal injuries. Institute for Study of Human Knowledge, Los Angeles, 1978a

Crasilneck HB: The use of hypnosis in acute and chronic pain. Presented at the Pain Workshop First International Congress on Clinical Hypnosis, Malmo, Sweden, 1978b

Crasilneck HB: The use of hypnosis in the treatment of burns. Presented at the Workshop on Pain, International Society of Clinical and Experimental Hypnosis Meeting, Melbourne, Australia, 1979

Crasilneck HB: The use of hypnosis in the treatment of thermal injuries. Paper presented at American Society of Clinical Hypnosis Annual Meeting, Boston, 1981

Crasilneck HB, Jenkins MT: Further studies in the use of hypnosis as a method of anesthesia. J Clin Exp Hypn 6:152–158, 1958

Crasilneck HB, McCranie EJ, Jenkins MT: Special indications for hypnosis as a method of anesthesia. JAMA 162:1606–1608, 1956

Crasilneck HB: Stirman JA, Wilson BJ, McCranie EJ, Fogelman JM: Use of hypnosis in the management of patients with burns. JAMA 158:103–106, 1955

Day WA: Use of hypnosis in anorectal surgery. Dis Colon Rectum 7:331–335, 1964

Day WA: Use of hypnosis in anorectal surgery. J Am Soc Psychosom Dent Med 12:65–74, 1965

Dehenterova J: Some experiences with the use of hypnosis in the treatment of burns. Int J Clin Exp Hypn 15:49–53, 1967

Dias MM: The first surgical operation under hypnosis. Rev Brasil Cir 46:399–400, 1963a

Dias MM: Hypnosis in surgery. Rev Brasil Med 20:318–325, 1963b

Doberneck RC, Griffen WO Jr, Papermaster AA, et al: Hypnosis as an adjunct to surgical therapy. Surgery 46:229–304, 1950

Doberneck RC, McFee AS, Bonello FJ, Papermaster AA, Wangensteen OH: The prevention of postoperative urinary retention by hypnosis. Am J Clin Hypn 3:235–237, 1961

Dorcus R, Goodwin P: The treatment of patients with the dumping syndrome by hypnosis. J Clin Exp Hypn 3:200–202, 1955

Egbert DL, Battit GE, Welch CE, Bartlett MK: Reduction of post-operative pain by encouragement and instruction of patients. N Engl J Med 270:825–827, 1964

Ewin DM: A case of reflex sympathetic dystrophy of the left hand cured by hypnosis. Presented at the 17th Annual Scientific Meeting of the American Society of Clinical Hypnosis, New Orleans, 1974

Ewin DM: Clinical use of hypnosis for attenuation of burn depth, in Frankel FH, Zamansky HS (eds): Hypnosis at Its Bicentennial. New York, Plenum Press, 1978, pp 155–162

Ewin DM: Hypnosis in burn therapy. In Burrows GD, Dennerstein L (eds): Handbook of Hypnosis and Psychosomatic Medicine. Amsterdam, Elsevier/North-Holland Biomedical Press, 1980, pp 269–275

Ewin DM: Hypnosis in surgery and anesthesia, in Wester WC, Smith AH (eds): Clinical Hypnosis: A Multidisciplinary Approach. Philadelphia, J.B. Lippincott Co., 1983, pp 210–235

Field PB: Effects of tape-recorded hypnotic preparation for surgery. Int J Clin Exp Hypn 22:54–61, 1974

Finer B: Hypnosis and anesthesia, in Burrow GD, Dennerstein L (eds): Handbook of Hypnosis and Psychosomatic Medicine. Amsterdam, Elsevier/North-Holland Biomedical Press, 1980, pp 293–305

Finer BL, Nylen BO: Cardiac arrest in the treatment of burns and report on hypnosis as a substitute for anesthesia. Plast Reconstr Surg 27:49–55, 1961

Gardner GG, Olness K: Hypnosis and Hypnotherapy with Children. New York, Grune & Stratton, 1981, pp 230–235

Grant G: Suggestion and hypnosis in surgery. Aust J Clin Hypn 2:6–12, 1974

Gruen W: A successful application of systematic self-relaxation and self-suggestions about postoperative reactions in a case of cardiac surgery. Int J Clin Exp Hypn 20:143–151, 1972

Hammond DC, Keye WR, Grant CW: Hypnotic analgesia with burns: An initial study. Am J Clin Hypn 1983 (in press)

Hart RR: The influence of a taped hypnotic induction treatment procedure on the recovery of surgical patients. Int J Clin Exp Hypn 28:324–332, 1980

Hartley RB: Hypnosis for alleviation of pain in treatment of burns: Case report. Arch Phys Med 49:39–41, 1968

Jenkins MT, Crasilneck HB: Hypnoanesthesia. Am J Nursing 59:12–15, 1959

Jones CG: Associated uses of hypnosis in surgery. Am J Clin Hypn 4:270–272, 1962

Kaplan JZ, Moore LE: Medical News. JAMA 249:321, 1983

Kelsey D, Barrow JN: Maintenance of posture by hypnotic suggestion in patient undergoing plastic surgery. Br Med J 1:756–757, 1958

Kolouch FT: Role of suggestion in surgical convalescence. Arch Surg 85:304–315, 1962

Kolouch FT: Hypnosis and surgical convalescence: A study of subjective factors in postoperative recovery. Am J Clin Hypn 7:120–129, 1964

Kolouch FT: The frightened surgical patient. Am J Clin Hypn 10:89–98, 1968

Kroger WS: Clinical and Experimental Hypnosis (ed 2). Philadelphia, J.B. Lippincott Co., 1977, p 216

LaBaw WL: Adjunctive trance therapy with severely burned children. Int J Child Psychother 2:80–92, 1973b

Lait VS: Effect of hypnosis on edema: A case report. Am J Clin Hypn 3:200, 1961

Leonard AS, Papermaster AH, Wangensteen OH: Treatment of postgastrectomy dumping syndrome by hypnotic suggestion. JAMA 165:1957–1959, 1957

Mahrer FJ: Hypnosis and the surgical patient. Am J Proctol 11:459–465, 1960

Margolis CG, De Clement F: Hypnosis in the treatment of burns. Burns 6:253–254, 1980

Mun CT: The use of hypnosis as an adjunct in surgery. Am J Clin Hypn 8:178–180, 1966

Nayyar SN, Brady JP: Elevation of depressed skull fracture under hypnosis. JAMA 181:790–792, 1962

Papermaster AA, Doberneck RC, Bonello FJ, Griffen W Jr, Wangensteen OH: Hypnosis in surgery. II. Pain. Am J Clin Hypn 2:200–224, 1960

Pellicone AJ: Hypnosis as adjunct to treatment of burns. Am J Clin Hypn 2:153–156, 1960

Sacerdote P: Hypnosis as an important adjunct in orthopedic surgery: A clinical instance. Am J Clin Hypn 6:75–77, 1963

Schafer DW: Hypnosis use on a burn unit. Int J Clin Exp Hypn 23:1–14, 1975

Schafer DW: Patient's reaction to hypnosis on a burn unit, in Frankel FH, Zamansky HS (eds): Hypnosis at Its Bicentennial. New York, Plenum Press, 1978, pp 229–235

Siegel EF: Control of phantom limb pain by hypnosis. Am J Clin Hypn 21:285–286, 1979

Somma Pena PJ: Hypnoterapia post-operatoria. Rev Lat Am Hypn Clin 1:14–15, 1960

Teitelbaum M: Hypnosis in surgery and anesthesiology. Anesth Analg 47:509–514, 1967

Todorovic DD: Hypnosis in military medical practice. Milit Med 34:121–125, 1959

Van Dyke PB: Some uses of hypnosis in the management of the surgical patient. Am J Clin Hypn 12:227–235, 1970

Wakeman RJ, Kaplan JZ: An experimental study of hypnosis in painful burns. Am J Clin Hypn 21:3–12, 1978

Wangensteen OH: New operative techniques in intestinal obstructions. Wis Med J 62:159–169, 1962

Werbel EW: Experiences with frequent use of hypnosis in a general surgical practice. West J Surg Obstet Gynecol 68:190–191, 1960

Werbel EW: Use of hypnosis in certain surgical problems. Am J Clin Hypn 7:81–83, 1964

Werbel EW: Hypnosis in serious surgical problems. Am J Clin Hypn 10:44–47, 1967

Wiggins SL, Brown CW: Hypnosis with two pedicle graft cases. Int J Clin Exp Hypn 16:215–220, 1968

Wollman L: Hypnosis for the surgical patient. Am J Clin Hypn 7:83–85, 1964

Yanovski A, Briklin B: Spontaneous abreaction during major surgery under hypnosis. Psychiatr Q 41:496–524, 1967

9
Hypnosis:
Its Use with Cancer Patients

Hypnotherapy has increasingly become an important tool in the treatment of cancer patients, both in the relief of the side-effects of chemotherapy and in the management of many types of psychological reactions—family dynamics (Pettitt, 1979), psychotherapy (Shapiro, 1982–1983), and even perhaps adding to longevity of terminal cancer patients (Newton, 1982–1983; Meares, 1982–1983). The American Society of Clinical Hypnosis devoted an entire combined issue (October 1982–January 1983) to the uses of hypnosis and hypnotherapy in the treatment of cancer patients, and there have been many other discussions of the utility of hypnosis (Elitzur, 1983; Kroger, 1977; Sacerdote, 1980).

WITH UNCONSCIOUS PATIENTS

The extent to which the patient responds to the hypnotic procedure is shown in a striking clinical observation that 8 of 10 patients dying of cancer were found, in one of our studies, to continue their response to a hypnotic command to touch the thumb and fourth finger of one hand even though they revealed no other evidence of interaction with the environment and were considered clinically unconscious by their attending physicians (Crasilneck and Hall, 1962). When the response ceased to be elicited, death followed in each case within 48 hours.

Fisher (1954, 1955), however, believed that the only fundamental difference between simple posthypnotic suggestions and "conditioned reflexes" acquired during hypnosis is the degree to which the experimenter explicitly communicates his suggestions. It would be of theoretical interest to have a control series of similar moribund patients who had previously been conditioned to the same response but not hypnotized. Considerations for humane treatment of the dying, however, make it most unlikely that such a control series will ever be studied.

Finally, one must consider the possibility that the hypnotherapist's continued visits, with suggestion of freedom from pain, can be extremely valuable to the dying patient even if he or she is unable to communicate verbally. If this is the case, the patients reported in the above paper (Crasilneck and Hall, 1962) may have responded to the finger-thumb suggestion in order to maintain, however, tenuously, contact with the therapist. The patient's relationship with the therapist was, in effect, his last contact with "reality" in a situation where such contact would ordinarily be discontinued. A response from the patient would not be necessary, of course, to assure the continuance of routine medical care. Alternatively, the terminal patient may not have been as strongly motivated for the continuance of medical care as he was for the continuance of the human relationship inherent in his response to the hypnotherapist.

It must be considered that psychological processes may continue in a patient even after signs of ordinary social responsiveness cease. Jung (1959) has reported such a case in which an elderly woman who had been in analysis discontinued treatment as it became apparent to her that her neurotic conflicts were about to be revealed. She soon, however, developed a terminal illness during which she lapsed into a semicomatose state. She could be heard talking to herself, unaware of her surroundings. From the things that she said in this state, Jung felt that she had resumed, in her terminal condition, examination of the very problems she had avoided in psychoanalysis. She seemed to work through the conflict and soon died, without ever regaining consciousness.

Such an observation, even if rare, re-emphasizes the need to treat the terminal patient with consideration and humaneness, even if he or she appears unconscious. When used with appropriate skill in selected cases, hypnosis may be a powerful technique toward such a goal.

WITH CONSCIOUS PATIENTS

A hypnotherapist might be asked to see a cancer patient, for example, where surgical or radiation treatment has successfully eradicated tumor growth or in cases that are advanced and may become terminal.

In the first instance hypnosis would be utilized in motivating the patient for rehabilitation procedures and dealing with emotional conflicts, whether they preceded the illness or resulted from it.

A 38-year-old mother underwent radical mastectomy for breast cancer, followed by a course of radiation, which was interrupted because of nausea. Hypnosis was introduced to control this nausea, and was successful. Suggestions were then extended to diminish her severe anxiety, and she was taught a self-hypnotic procedure to aid in falling asleep. During the time of her nausea, she had lost considerable weight, but quickly gained weight again when it was suggested in trance that she would be hungry at every meal and would eat everything that was offered to her on the hospital tray. After discharge from the hospital, she was seen on an outpatient basis for several months, and hypnotherapy was used to alleviate some pain she had in an area of scarring, after it had been determined by the surgeon that the pain did not represent a recurrence. Nevertheless, the pain was only diminished, not removed, so that it could still serve as an indicator of organic processes.

The effectiveness of hypnosis was dramatically illustrated 17 years ago in the case that follows:

A married woman in her early forties, the mother of three children, was diagnosed as having inoperable cancer of the stomach. In a very straightforward manner, she inquired of her physician about the probable remaining life span. She was told it was almost certainly a matter of only a few months. She then turned her attention to planning the remaining time, asking if she would be hospitalized and if she would require much sedation and narcotics.

Her physician explained that hospitalization might be necessary and that it was customary to give some medication—narcotics for pain, possibly tranquilizers for any severe anxiety. He did mention, however, that hypnosis might supplement or replace some of the medication if she had an aversion to taking drugs.

The woman outlined her goals as (1) remaining in a normal state of clear consciousness for as long as possible, (2) staying at home with her husband and children if feasible, and (3) being able to die gracefully, not overly sedated, but relatively free from pain. She accepted the offer of hypnotherapy.

At first she was seen weekly, but as her condition approached a terminal stage, she was visited several times a week. She achieved her goals, staying at home until the final week of her life, when she was hospitalized. She remained clear in her thinking until the last few days, when some chemical sedation was used. Although there was no hope for her recovery, she spent her last months in the manner that she wished and died an easy death, with dignity.

Hypnosis is not indicated in all cases of terminal cancer, but certain guidelines can suggest when its use might be of aid. Hypnosis should be considered in a terminal case (1) if the patient is anxious to avoid medication or has a fear of medication clouding consciousness, (2) to control pain without the side effects of narcotic drugs, (3) to aid in maintaining adequate food intake and delay cachexia, and (4) to help the patient psychologically to face the end of his life as normally as possible, with no unnecessary loss of contact with those he loves.

There have been numerous studies reporting the use of hypnosis as an adjunctive treatment in cancer patients, particularly for pain relief. It may also be helpful in decreasing anxiety of certain treatment procedures, such as bone-marrow punctures or radiation treatment involving unfamiliar machinery, often with the patient alone in the treatment room. Other uses are for stimulating appetite and for helping to maintain a relatively hopeful, active emotional state.

In cancer surgery the surgeon has the delicate task of giving his patient "certainty, clarity, and attention without attacking his hope" (Golden, 1965). In reviewing 15 years of clinical experience in the use of hypnosis with cancer patients, Sacerdote (1965, 1966) suggests an experimental study comparing hypnosis to other treatments in terminal patients, a thought echoed by LaBaw (1969) in a paper titled "Terminal hypnosis in lieu of terminal hospitalization."

Hypnosis may be helpful in assisting the patient to accept the diagnosis, facilitating surgery and postoperative recovery, relieving pain without excessive narcotics, and decreasing such side effects of radiation therapy as severe nausea and vomiting (LaBaw et al, 1975; Chong, 1968). It is at times possible to maintain the patient in alert, rational contact until shortly before actual death. In this respect, Caracappa (1963) reported the case of a 37-year-old woman with generalized carcinoma of the ovaries and breasts who remained alert, rational, and interested in her family. On the evening of her death she kissed her baby, said, "Goodnight, darling," and soon expired.

Erickson (1959) suggests the use of time distortion to decrease perception of pain, altering memory to prevent painful recall and anticipation. He stresses that while hypnosis can be used alone as a means of pain control in many patients, it is more often and more properly employed as an adjuvant to chemical means.

Morphis (1952) has done outstanding work with cancer patients. He has developed a somewhat unique hypnotic approach in which the patient's mind is emotionally dissociated from the part of the body in which the tumor is localized. This may be done through spatial suggestions, as "Your arm with the tumor in it feels to you as if it were located across the room.'' This technique may be likened to an intentional production of a state of mind that sometimes occurs spontaneously as a defense against severe anxiety. Outstanding reports on the use of hypnosis with terminal patients have been published by Butler (1954), Cangello (1961), Marmer (1959), and Sacerdote (1968). Clawson (1975) has even raised the theoretical possibility that hypnosis might itself have some effect to fight cancer.

PAIN

The utility of hypnosis in diminishing pain in some patients is clearly established (Margolis, 1982–1983). This may be of particular use in cancer patients where the chronic course of the disease often leads to increasing amounts of pain medications. Toward the terminal days and weeks of such a disease process, there may be a difficult choice between administering medications to relieve the pain or withholding medications to allow the patient to enjoy his or her last days, to whatever extent is possible without loss of consciousness as a result of high levels of pain medication. Hypnosis may provide a personal sense of coping, a feeling that is not facilitated by high doses of medication (Barber and Gitelson, 1980; Dempster, Balson, and Whalen, 1976; Olness, 1981). The following two case histories were recently seen by Crasilneck:

A 71-year-old attorney had several surgical procedures for cancer of the tongue followed by repeated chemotherapy and radiotherapy. He was readmitted by the surgeon because of an increased tumor mass in the side of his neck, together with some chest pain. He had a history of reactions to numerous medications. The limited options for pain relief were discussed with the patient and his wife: chordotomy, nerve block or transcutaneous nerve stimulation, acupuncture, or hypnosis. He chose hypnotherapy and was seen on a weekly outpatient basis for 9 months before his death. Except for the last 3 days, he required little pain medication. His pain management also included instruction in self-hypnosis and the use of a hypnotic induction tape-recording made specifically for him for that purpose.

A 46-year-old woman with cancer of the stomach wished only two things: to be free of pain and to survive through the Christmas season, which had deep religious meaning to her. During the initial session of hypnotherapy, her pain was rapidly brought under control and she was taught self-hypnosis. Through periodic reinforcement she was relatively free of pain without large doses of medication. Her family was devoted to her, and as with most terminal cancer patients, the family endured agonizing, guilt-ridden, self-doubting and angry thoughts, especially in terms of their helpless inadequacy about her dying.

They tried to coerce her into being more positive about survival. Members of the family, at times, unduly pressure the cancer patient to fight harder to get well (Oliver, 1982–1983). However, Crasilneck's patient frequently reiterated that she wished "to live through Christmas day." When it was suggested that she might live until the Fourth of July, she said, "Christmas is enough." She died peacefully, 4 days after enjoying Christmas with her family.

CONTROL OF SIDE-EFFECTS

Improvements in chemotherapy for treatment of cancer have not eliminated undesirable side effects. Many patients stop treatment because of dread of these results of chemotherapy (Wain, 1983). Acute effects include nausea and vomiting, as well as the tremendous psychological stress associated with chemotherapy. Hypnosis is frequently useful in controlling or diminishing these undesirable side-effects of chemotherapy (Rosenberg, 1982–1983; Redd, Rosenberger, and Hendler, 1982–1983). At times there can even be anticipatory emesis in chemotherapy; this, too, can be modified with hypnosis (Hoffman, 1982–1983).

Our suggestions are of the form "time will go by rapidly, your anxiety and fears will be much less . . . you can sleep for long periods of time during and following treatment . . . nausea and vomiting will be minimal, however, *if you have to vomit you can* . . . should you be asleep when you need to vomit you can awaken, vomit, and immediately go back to a deep, restful, peaceful sleep . . . time will pass by quickly . . . hours will seem like minutes . . . there will be little discomfort and vomiting will grow less with each treatment."

**HYPNOTHERAPY COMPARED WITH
PSYCHOTHERAPY OR PSYCHOANALYSIS**

Ordinary psychological treatment, such as psychotherapy or psychoanalysis, is difficult to institute or continue in a patient with terminal illness. We all have some fear of death and disability. This fear may also involve a dislike of again becoming almost completely dependent on the care of others, as in infancy. In classic psychoanalytical language, such anxieties might be called "castration fear." Such fears may be awakened in the mind of the therapist as he or she sees the patient day after day slowly approaching death. These anxieties in the therapist may work against effective help for the patient. In addition, it is difficult to find motivations in the terminal patient for working on the ordinary conflicts of everyday living that are usually dealt with in psychotherapy.

Hypnosis offers distinct advantages in such a situation. It is focused directly on those problems of immediate concern to the patient—pain relief, maintaining appetite and interest, and being reassured that his or her condition will not lead to abandonment. This last goal can be approached, of course, in a psychotherapeutic way without hypnosis, although pain relief and appetite maintenance are not easily influenced by such means.

Hypnosis has the added advantage of being a more structured situation than psychotherapy. Thus it allows the response of the patient to vary from the conversational tone of establishing rapport and making personal contact at each visit to the state of deep trance in which the response asked of the patient may be minimal, perhaps only the movement of a finger. In the hypnotic state the patient may be almost entirely passive without incurring the loss of self-esteem that passivity might elicit were he awake. The feeling of being passively at ease, but still the object of attention from a helpful adult, may characterize both the hypnotic state and the blissful state of the nursing infant.

There are many emotional similarities between the beginning of life and its end, between birth and death. In childhood the conscious mind slowly emerges from the oceanic feeling of immersion in unconsciousness. As death approaches, the conscious personality seems to be reimmersed gradually in the unconscious. Both processes are facilitated by the presence of a caring person. But unlike the usual warm response to young children, those caring for the dying are often faced with great anxiety, as the approaching death of the patient reminds them of their own mortality. It is not infrequent that those caring for the terminal patient begin to withdraw emotionally as an unconscious mechanism to defend against their own fears. This is one of the most distressing experiences of the dying, the feeling of being deserted, perhaps treated in a purely professional way or surrounded with an air of forced cheerfulness.

In using hypnosis with terminal patients, we have always included the suggestion, "you will be free of tension, tightness, stress and strain, you will be relaxed and at ease, and your body will be relatively free of discomfort." Whatever the specific wording of the hypnotic suggestion, these thoughts should be included, we feel, in working with any terminal patient.

Patients are told:

You will have a minimum of discomfort. . . . You will be relaxed . . . at ease. . . . You will have a feeling of well-being . . . sleeping when you desire . . . and reinforcing these suggestions yourself . . . as frequently as you desire. . . . You can eat well and enjoy the food intake the doctor has ordered for you. . . . Discomfort, anxiety, and tension will be minimal and under control most of the time . . . you will be relaxed and at ease. . . . You can rest well, secure in the knowledge that your unconscious mind will allow you to be free of excessive tension and any physical or psychological discomfort.

These suggestions may be reinforced as often as necessary with periodic and frequent self-hypnosis.

CHILDREN WITH CANCER

Children with cancer pose many special problems, both for the treating staff and for the parents (Gardner and Lubner, 1982–1983). Children often do not consciously understand the nature of their disease or the meaning of painful procedures such as bone-marrow aspiration. Gardner and Olness (1981) thoroughly discuss the use of hypnosis with such children, giving a number of case examples. In one of them, the mother's soothing statements to her dying son on Christmas day were noted to resemble in many ways the rhythm and reassurance of his usual hypnotic induction. A measurable decrease in pain can be induced with hypnosis, which makes many necessary medical procedures less disturbing to the child (Hall MD, 1982–1983; Hilgard MD and Le Baron, 1982; Zeltzer and Le Baron, 1982). Hypnotherapy may alleviate the fear of death (Gardner, 1976; Miller, 1980).

SELF-HYPNOSIS

Whenever possible, we teach self-hypnosis to cancer patients, suggesting to them that they can achieve pain relief and subjectively alter their sense of time. In those who are good hypnotic subjects time can often be speeded or retarded in sensed duration, whichever the patient feels is more comforting. We also suggest that self-hypnosis may be used to induce a form of reverie in which pleasant experiences of the patient's past may be reviewed in a vivified form, bringing forth the most pleasant thoughts possible.

The type of suggestion taught in self-hypnosis is as follows:

I will be virtually free of pain. . . . I will eat as much as I can, enjoying my food. . . . I will sleep as often as I wish, going to sleep easily and awakening calm and refreshed. . . . I will be free of fear, calm and unafraid, with little anxiety or tension . . . I can review as I wish the pleasant experiences of my past life, my family's affection, the warmth of my friendships . . . and past problems will fall into place, no longer of any great concern. . . . My body will respond maximally to any medical treatment that will prolong my life or increase my comfort. . . . I am calm and at ease . . . knowing that the immense power of my unconscious mind can help me both mentally and physically.

I have a built-in immune system . . . my immune system can block and destroy the cancer cells in my body. . . . I have a powerful built-in psychological immune system . . . and nothing is beyond the power of my unconscious mind. . . . My powerful build-in immune system can . . . and will destroy these cancer cells that have invaded my body. . . . My immune system can and will contain the tumor . . . arresting the growth . . . and finally destroy this invader of my body. . . . I can and will destroy these cancer cells because of the omnipotent power of my immune system and . . . my unconscious mind. . . . I will recover . . . I will get well. . . . I will get well. . . .

THE QUESTION OF REGRESSION AND LONGEVITY

There is no clear agreement on the possible effects of hypnotherapy in lengthening the life-span of cancer patients or even, in some reported cases, seeming to induce a regression of the cancer. Finkelstein and Howard (1982–1983) conclude that there is enough evidence to support the regression of cancer in some patients. Meares (1982–1983) cites a number of cases of regression of cancer following a form of intensive meditation that is characterized by extreme simplicity and stillness of the mind; communication may be by "unverbalized phonation" and touch to achieve a profound decrease in anxiety. Levitan and Johnson (1983) also discuss the use of touch in increasing response to hypnosis in some situations. In a well-reported series of cases, Newton (1982–1983) also concludes that "our results . . . strongly suggest that this type of intervention can result in lengthening the duration of life and in some instances arrest and reverse the disease process."

There is speculation that hypnotherapy may activate the immune system (Hall HR, 1982–1983). Gardner and Lubner (1982–1983), while not objecting to the use of hypnosis to attempt to improve longevity in cancer patients, caution that "it is important to recognize the problems of evaluating the method and the dangers inherent in holding such patients basically responsible for their own cures . . . many sick children and parents already have a tendency toward irrational self-blame . . . it is encumbent on us not to exacerbate this problem."

FAILURE OF HYPNOSIS IN CANCER CASES

Discussing reasons for the failure of hypnosis in cancer cases, Cangello (1962) mentions a fantasy of some persons that suffering may lead to eternal life, or that relief of pain might cause the patient to be sent home when he or she has unexpressed reasons for wanting to remain in the hospital. Cangello found in his experience that an authoritative or semiauthoritative approach was most effective.

Schom (1960) reported a case in which the patient, who did not consciously know she had advanced cancer, refused hypnosis after the initial induction. She had two hallucinations during this one hypnotic trance—first, of a cow stepping into a clear pool of water and, second, of a dancer unraveling a bale of brown lace, which gradually filled the room. She had awakened with a fear of being smothered by this lace. Schom speculates that this may have been an autosymbolic representation of the neoplasm of which she was consciously unaware.

It seems clear to us that there were also elements in the hallucinations—such as the calmness of the cow and the gracefulness of the dancer—that might well have represented an attempt of the unconscious mind to autonomously produce soothing images to compensate for conscious anxiety. Unfortunately, the patient's abrupt ending of hypnotherapy did not allow this aspect of the hallucinations to be explored for her benefit.

DEATH AND DYING

As described at the beginning of this chapter, patients approaching death often seem to utilize hypnosis, even if it is offered for another purpose, as a means of communication during the terminal phase of their illnesses. It is not only an enhancement of the quality of life that is desired (LaBaw, 1983), but the experience of trance may greatly diminish the fear of death and aid the terminal patient and those ministering to him or her (Grosz, 1979). Levitan (1983) suggests that in some instances it is of benefit to help the patient in hypnosis, to experience fantasies about his or her approaching death—who is there, how they react emotionally, etc. This is essentially a specialized psychotherapy technique in unique circumstances and should be used with caution. In summary, hypnosis often produces unexpected or even unintended additional benefits in the dying patient, most probably by releasing deeper archetypal images that picture death as a natural part of the life process.

CONCLUSION

Hypnosis is a useful technique in rehabilitation of cancer patients as well as in easing the discomfort of advanced cases. The unique aspects of hypnotherapy may make it the psychological treatment choice for some patients.

REFERENCES

Barber J, Gitelson J: Cancer pain: Psychological management using hypnosis. Cancer 30:130–136, 1980

Butler B: The use of hypnosis in the case of the cancer patient. Cancer 7:1–14, 1954

Cangello VW: The use of hypnotic suggestion for pain relief in malignant disease. Int J Clin Exp Hypn 9:17–22, 1961

Cangello VW: Hypnosis for the patient with cancer. Am J Clin Hypn 4:215–226, 1962

Caracappa JM: Hypnosis in terminal cancer. Am J Clin Hypn 5:205–206, 1963

Chong TM: The use of hypnosis in the management of patients with cancer. Singapore Med J 9:211–214, 1968

Clawson TH: The hypnotic control of blood flow and pain and the potential use of hypnosis in the treatment of cancer. Am J Clin Hypn 17:160–169, 1975

Crasilneck HB, Hall JA: The use of hypnosis with unconscious patients. Int J Clin Exp Hypn 10:141–144, 1962

Dempster CR, Balson PM, Whalen B: Supportive hypnotherapy during radical treatment of malignancies. Int J Clin Exp Hypn 24:1–9, 1976

Elitzur B: The use of hypnosis with hemodialysis patients. Presented at the International Congress of the Israel Society of Hypnosis in Psychotherapy and Psychosomatic Medicine in collaboration with the European Society of Hypnosis in Psychotherapy and Psychosomatic Medicine, Haifa, Israel, 1983

Erickson MH: Hypnosis in painful terminal illness. Am J Clin Hypn 1:117–121, 1959

Finkelstein S, Howard M: Cancer prevention—a three year pilot study. Am J Clin Hypn 25:177–183, 1982–1983

Fisher S: The role of expectancy in the performance of posthypnotic behavior. J Abnorm Soc Psychol 49:503–507, 1954

Fisher S: An investigation of alleged conditioning phenomena under hypnosis. J Clin Exp Hypn 3:71–103, 1955

Gardner GG: Childhood death, and human dignity: Hypnotherapy for David. Int J Clin Exp Hypn 24:122–139, 1976

Gardner GG, Lubner A: Hypnotherapy for children with cancer: Some current issues. Am J Clin Hypn 25:135–142, 1982–1983.

Gardner GG, Olness K: Hypnosis and Hypnotherapy with Children. New York, Grune & Stratton, 1981, pp 245–269

Golden JS: Emotional reaction to cancer surgery. Hosp Med 1:34–35, 1965

Grosz HJ: Hypnotherapy in the management of the terminally ill cancer patient. J Indiana State Med Assoc 72:126–129, 1979

Hall HR: Hypnosis and the immune system: A review with implications for cancer and the psychology of healing. Am J Clin Hypn 25:92–103, 1982–1983

Hall MD: Using relaxation imagery with children with malignancies: A developmental perspective. Am J Clin Hypn 25:143–149, 1982–1983

Hilgard J, Le Baron S: Relief of anxiety and pain in children and adolescents with cancer: Quantitative measures and clinical observations. Int J Clin Exp Hypn 30:417–442, 1982

Hoffman ML: Hypnotic desensitization for the management of anticipatory emesis in chemotherapy. Am J Clin Hypn 25:173–176, 1982–1983

Hypnosis and Cancer (Special Issue). Am J Clin Hypn 25:89–199, 1982–1983

Jung CG: The psyche and death, in Feifel H (ed): The Meaning of Death. New York, McGraw-Hill, 1959, pp 3–15

Kroger WS: Clinical and Experimental Hypnosis (ed 2). Philadelphia, J.B. Lippincott Co., 1977, pp 282–285

LaBaw WL: Terminal hypnosis in lieu of terminal hospitalization. An effective alternative in fortunate case. Geront Clin 11:312–320, 1969

LaBaw WL: Helping the dying to live—through hypnosis. Med World News 249:322, 1983

LaBaw WL, Holton C, Tewell K, Eccles D: Use of self-hypnosis by children with cancer. Am J Clin Hypn 17:233–238, 1975

Levitan AA: Hypnotic death rehearsal. Paper presented at the American Society of Clinical Hypnosis Regular Meeting. Houston, Texas, 1983

Levitan AA, Johnson JM: The role of touch in hypnotherapy. Paper presented at the American Society of Clinical Hypnosis Regular Meeting, Houston, Texas, 1983

Margolis CG: Hypnotic imagery with cancer patients. Am J Clin Hypn 25:128–134, 1982–1983

Marmer MJ: Hypnosis in Anesthesiology. Springfield, Ill., Charles C Thomas, 1959, p 109

Meares A: A form of intensive meditation associated with the regression of cancer. Am J Clin Hypn 25:114–121, 1982–1983

Miller JA: Hypnosis in a boy with leukemia. Am J Clin Hypn 22:231–235, 1980

Morphis O: Personal communication, 1952

Newton, BW: The use of hypnosis in the treatment of cancer patients. Am J Clin Hypn 25:104–113, 1982–1983

Oliver GW: A cancer patient and her family: A case study. Am J Clin Hypn 25:156–160, 1982–1983

Olness K: Imagery (self hypnosis) as an adjunct therapy in childhood cancer: Clinical experience with 25 patients. Am J Pediatr Hematol Oncol 3:313–321, 1981

Pettitt GA: Adjunctive trance and family therapy for terminal cancer. NZ Med J 89:18–21, 1979

Redd WH, Rosenberger PH, Hendler CS: Controlling chemotherapy side effects. Am J Clin Hypn 25:161–172, 1982–1983

Rosenberg SW: Hypnosis in cancer care: Imagery to enhance the control of the physiological and psychological "side effects" of cancer therapy. Am J Clin Hypn 25:122–127, 1982–1983

Sacerdote P: Additional contributions to the hypnotherapy of the advanced cancer patient. Am J Clin Hypn 7:308–319, 1965

Sacerdote P: Hypnosis in cancer patients. Am J Clin Hypn 9:100–107, 1966

Sacerdote P: Involvement and communication with the terminally ill patient. Am J Clin Hypn 10:244–248, 1968

Sacerdote P: Theory and practice of pain control in malignancy and other protracted or recurring painful illness. Int J Clin Exp Hypn 18:160–180, 1970

Sacerdote P: Hypnosis in terminal illness, in Burrows GD, Dennerstein L (eds): Handbook of Hypnosis and Psychosomatic Medicine. Amsterdam, Elsevier/North-Holland Biomedical Press, 1980, pp 421–442

Schom RC: Addendum to "hypnosis in painful terminal illness." Am J Clin Hypn 3:61–62, 1960

Shapiro A: Psychotherapy as an adjunct treatment for cancer patients. Am J Clin Hypn 25:150–155, 1982–1983

Wain HJ: Hypnosis in cancer. Paper presented at the American Society of Clinical Hypnosis Annual Meeting. Denver, Colorado, 1983

Zeltzer L, Le Baron S: Hypnosis and nonhypnotic techniques for reduction of pain and anxiety during painful procedures in children and adolescents with cancer. J Pediatr 101:1032–1035, 1982

10
Hypnosis in the Treatment of Psychosomatic Illness

Many illnesses are caused by organic factors, such as pneumonia. These organic diseases are those studied most easily by laboratory techniques. Some other illnesses, such as psychoneurosis, seem to be almost entirely functional, with psychological conflict their predominant etiologic factor. Neither group is exclusive. There are always psychological reactions to organic illness, and the functioning of the body is clearly affected by the emotional state of the patient's mind. Cultural stereotypes, such as aging, may contribute to psychosomatic problems (Sachs, 1982). Stress is conceptualized as the mediating link between environmental, social, and psychological factors and the onset of psychosomatic illnesses (Sachs, 1983).

There has been increasing recognition, particularly since the 1940s, that some diseases seem to fall between the primarily organic and the primarily psychological illnesses. Conditions that fall into this category come readily to mind—peptic ulcer, ulcerative colitis, bronchial asthma, some skin disorders, and some cases of arthritis. Such disorders are generally referred to as "psychosomatic," although the term "psychophysiological" has been more in vogue during recent years.

No clear dividing line exists between psychosomatic disorders and the adjacent categories of physical and emotional illnesses. Franz Alexander introduced a distinction between illnesses manifesting primarily through the voluntary nervous system and those principally affecting the involuntary autonomic system. The latter are termed "psychosomatic," while those expressed through the voluntary musculature are considered more conversion "reactions" and are thought to have a more symbolic meaning.

For example, a man who felt dominated by his aggressive wife, yet felt that to speak to her of his anger would not be gentlemanly, developed a symptom of hoarseness. This change in his voice expressed simultaneously both the desire to speak and the inhibition of speech. The symptom thus had a symbolic meaning as well as being expressed through a voluntary system. It would be considered a conversion reaction. In contrast, a man with strongly repressed anger if he had inherited a high level of pepsinogen might tend to develop peptic ulcer. The ulcer would have little if any symbolic meaning, would be expressed through the nonvoluntary automatic nervous system, which controls gastrointestinal motility and secretion and would be considered a psychosomatic or psychophysiological disease.

In the early years of interest in psychosomatic illnesses Helen Flanders Dunbar (1939) defined a number of personality profiles, based on depth interviews, that she felt were associated with specific types of psychosomatic disorder. Today there is more emphasis on defining a nuclear conflict and relating the emotional effect on the body to the development of structural changes in organ systems. It may be that for an extended time, perhaps years, the physical effects of emotional states may be reversible but may lead over a prolonged period of time to structural changes which are not reversible even if the emotional conflict is alleviated.

Hypnosis has long been used in attempting to influence the nonvoluntary aspect of neural functioning (Erickson, 1943; Wolberg, 1947). Raginsky (1960) was a widely recognized writer in the field of hypnosis and psychosomatic medicine. His section "Hypnosis in internal medicine and general practice" in *Hypnosis in Modern Medicine* (1953), edited by Jerome Schneck, is a classic introduction to this entire subject.

With psychosomatic problems it is vitally important to use hypnosis with due regard to the organic factors that may be involved. The organic factors may include drug addition (Kolouch, 1970). The psychodynamic meaning of any conflict underlying the symptom must be explored—in psychotherapy, in psychoanalysis, or in hypnoanalysis. Pure symptom removal, without concurrent work on the emotional conflict, could possibly lead to an unexpected substitute symptom.

In some cases of psychosomatic illness, when the patient is not motivated or willing for such exploration, we have limited hypnotic suggestion to inducing a sense of profound relaxation with no attempt to suppress directly the presenting symptom. This was effective in producing symptomatic relief in an 80-year-old man with a history of diverticulitis. In this case it was interesting that the patient, a very intelligent and professional man, spontaneously worked on a dream he had remembered from 20 years previously. The interpretation of the dream linked the illness with a traumatic childhood situation involving his mother. In this case it seemed that relief of his general sense of anxiety and tenseness allowed repressed traumatic material to reach consciousness. This is the reverse of the classic analytic approach, in which meaning is first explored and symptomatic relief expected to follow. Such a case is unusual, the ordinary approach being a mixture of hypnosis and psychotherapeutic exploration. It illustrates, however, the push toward health that is active in the unconscious.

Hypnosis has been used experimentally to induce psychosomatic changes. If the hypnotized subject is told to hallucinate a frightening situation, his or her heart rate will rise, as in a fear reaction. In a control study published in the *International Journal of Clinical and Experimental Hypnosis* in 1959, we reported that hypnosis itself, without specific suggestions for change, did not alter the pulse or respiration rate. Blood pressure was also unaffected. We introduced the term "neutral hypnosis" to describe the trance state without specific suggestions having been given (Crasilneck and Hall, 1959).

Chapman, Goodell, and Wolff (1959) published laboratory demonstrations of the effectiveness of hypnosis on nonvoluntary bodily reactions. In this study one arm of the subject served as a control. The hypnotized subject was told, for example, that the right arm was resistant to injury while the left arm was very vulnerable. Equivalent areas of both arms were then subjected to a measured thermal stimulus. The resistant arm showed very little response, measured by the presence and size of a wheal and flare reaction. In contrast, the "vulnerable" arm showed marked response.

If one imagines similar "vulnerability" being induced by unconscious conflict in other involuntary and supposedly automatic processes in the body, it is easy to conceive that psychosomatic stress might lead to structural organic change. Some clinical observations strongly support the possibility that hypnosis might directly affect processes that are otherwise outside of conscious influence. Among these observations are those of removal of warts, discussed in the chapter on dermatology. Warts have been shown to be a viral-induced tumor of the skin. Although it is clearly established that in many cases they may be influenced by hypnotic suggestions, there is as yet no clear conceptualization of what intermediary mechanisms may be involved in actually producing their regression.

Among others, Bernstein (1965), Lassner (1969), Morton (1960), Takaishi (1971), and Wright (1966) have written about the use of hypnosis in psychosomatic medicine. In 1969, an international congress for hypnosis and psychomatic medicine was held in Paris. Spiegel and Spiegel (1978) caution about the necessary differential diagnosis of conversion symptoms and neurological diseases. They also discuss how inadvertent remarks by physicians about a patient's physical condition can, in suggestible persons, predispose the patient to the development of psychosomatic symptoms.

GASTROINTESTINAL DISORDERS

Man's gastrointestinal system seems very responsive to emotional influence (Dias, 1963a,b; Lewis, 1943). This is reflected in such idiomatic expressions as "I can't *stomach* that" and "It's a *gut* feeling." Various parts of the digestive tract are subject to different disorders. Spasm of the cardiac sphincter at the juncture of the esophagus and stomach is a frequent effect of anxiety. This causes a sense of mass in the sternal chest area, the so-called "globus hystericus." Often it feels as if swallowed food "hangs" in the throat. Although frequently a general symptom of anxiety, without any symbolic content, in some instances a clear meaning can be established by investigating the events occurring at the time of the onset.

One woman who came to us for hypnosis for globus hystericus denied any unusual stress in her life. As the history of the symptoms was reconstructed, however, she began to make angry remarks about her husband. Several times she said, "I can't stomach the crap he puts out!" She finally admitted that several months before the globus began her husband began to have difficulty having erections. He persuaded her, against her wishes, to perform fellatio to stimulate him. He soon attempted to make this his preferred mode of sexual contact with her, which she greatly resented, expressing her dislike partially through the "closing up" of her throat by the globus hystericus. A frequent mild form of globus hystericus appears as an exaggerated difficulty in swallowing pills. This often responds well to hypnotherapy. Schneck (1958) reports a case of cardiospasm, apparently without such unconscious meaning, successfully treated with hypnosis. Hypnosis is frequently helpful in diminishing some symptoms of reflex of gastric secretion into the esophagus in cases of hiatal hernia, although the mechanism involved is not clearly understood. Self-hypnosis can often be quickly learned and is of an aid in this condition.

At times, surprisingly psychological meanings may be found behind gastrointestinal disorders. We recently saw an 18-year-old man who had an inability to eat certain foods, becoming nauseated and often vomiting, even if he saw them listed on a menu. It was found that all the foods to which he reacted were "breast" foods—chicken breast, breast of veal, and the like. Although unable to eat chicken breast, he had no difficulty with drumsticks, wings, or backs. He could eat the dark meat of Thanksgiving turkey but not the white meat from the breast of the bird. The usual sort of exploration of his past yielded no clue to explain his strange symptom. Under hypnosis age regression was successful, however, and he suddenly remembered that until age seven he had still nursed his mother's breasts, at her insistence. After his memory became conscious, his therapy rapidly progressed. In several months he was completely free of his nausea and vomiting.

Although the stomach itself is subject to functional disorders, its overactivity and excessive secretion may also contribute to the formation of peptic ulcer. Hypnosis has been used with peptic ulcer patients who have difficulty following their diet. In addition to suggestions that they will "adhere to the diet prescribed by your doctor," they are told, "Your stomach secretions will become normal, you will ingest and digest your food easily, and the unconscious mind, which may have contributed to the ulcer by expressing tension, will now aid in its healing by producing a feeling of calm, peaceful well-being." We do not know, of course, that the hypnotic suggestions for more normal stomach functioning have any direct effect; they may have effect only through the patient's staying with his or her ulcer diet. They are included, however, since there are some studies that intimate direct suggestion may influence autonomic functioning, as in heart rate (Whitehorn, 1939), even though this may occur through the intermediate production of an emotional fantasy. The usual clinical outcome with ulcer patients seems quite satisfactory. Zane (1966) has presented in detail a case of successful hypnotic treatment of an ulcer patient.

Eichorn and Tracktir (1955), using good control procedures, studied 24 male subjects in three states (prehypnotic, hypnotic, and posthypnotic) measuring gastric free hydrochloric acid, total acid, volume of stomach secretions, and pepsin. Although the prehypnotic and posthypnotic conditions showed a difference only in pepsin, which tended to rise after hypnosis, *all* the factors measured decreased *during* the hypnotic state. Such experimental findings add weight to the clinical observation of improvement with hypnotic treatment.

In some postgastrectomy ulcer patients, hypnosis has been used to alleviate the "dumping syndrome," a tendency toward weakness and nausea, perhaps with vomiting, occurring when the resected stomach fails to permit a regulated flow of stomach contents into the small intestine. Leonard, Papermaster, and Wangensteen (1957) first emphasized hypnosis in the successful treatment of this syndrome (see Chapter 8). Lait (1972) successfully treated with hypnoanalysis a woman whose recurrent compulsive vomiting could be traced to a childhood trauma when she was 10 years old.

The general effectiveness of hypnosis in calming the gastrointestinal tract extends to the lower bowel as well (Dias, 1963a,b). Hypnosis has been reported as useful in dietary management in such severe problems as ulcerative colitis. Posthypnotic suggestion for analgesia during the first few painful days following hemorrhoidectomy has been successful in many cases. Silber (1968) has discussed hypnosis in the treatment of encopresis (involuntary psychological fecal soiling).

RESPIRATORY DISORDERS

Asthma

The most common psychosomatic disorder of the respiratory system is asthma, which may vary from a mild state to the life-threatening status asthmaticus. Like all psychophysiological disorders, asthma is probably caused by multiple etiological factors, each contributing to the clinical picture. Among these, emotional factors are generally considered significant. In fact, some clinicians still quote French and Alexander's symbolic definition of asthma (1941) as "a repressed cry for the lost mother."

More generally, the asthmatic seems to experience emotional tension in connection with the onset of his attacks. Obviously, this is a two-way interaction, the disease itself feeding anxiety as well as responding to anxiety originating in other areas of life.

Perhaps one of the most striking responses we have seen in the hypnotic treatment of asthma was in the wife of a young physician. When first seen, she had been in status asthmaticus for 3 days. She was being administered oxygen and many appropriate medications but had apparently responded poorly to treatment. She was an excellent hypnotic subject and readily entered a deep trance, although she had no previous experience with hypnosis and was unacquainted with the therapist. Within 10 minutes she responded to suggestions for the relief of her respiratory distress. She began to breathe more easily and soon recovered from the acute attack. Hypnotherapy was continued, however, for 6 months following her hospital discharge. During this time she worked through her previously unexplored feeling about a dominant but cold mother and her weak, ineffectual father.

In such a situation as status asthmaticus it is necessary to first seek symptomatic relief and only then, in a calmer atmosphere, begin psychotherapeutic exploration of the underlying conflict. During this phase of the treatment various techniques can be used in addition to hypnoanalysis or conventional psychotherapy. For example, one patient seemed to experience marked relief of recurrent minor attacks of asthma soon after he painted a symbolic picture. The picture seemed, on amplification, to show the release of air from an area shown as "beneath the diaphragm." In other instances dream interpretation has been a rapid technique for delineating the area of unconscious conflict.

A number of authors have reported hypnosis as helpful in decreasing the symptoms of asthma (Chong, 1965; Collison, 1968; de la Parra, 1960; Hanley, 1974; Koster, 1955; Kusano et al. 1969; McLean, 1965; Magonet, 1956, 1960; Maher-Loughnan et al. 1962, 1968, 1970; Moorefield, 1971). Sinclair-Gieben (1960) reported the case of a 60-year-old man in status asthmaticus who responded quickly to "simple hypnosis." Rose (1967), using autohypnosis, helped patients to distinguish between wheezing and asthma so that wheezing did not produce fear of asthma. Schneck (1954) successfully treated with hypnosis a chronic case of psychogenic dyspnea.

In 1968 the Research Committee of the British Tuberculosis Association published the results of a 1-year study of the effects of hypnosis on 252 asthma patients followed for 1 year. Hypnosis and autohypnosis were used with 127, while a group of 125 served as controls. Some patients did not complete the experiment, for various reasons. At the end of the study a group of independent clinical assessors considered the asthma to be much better in 59 percent of the hypnosis group and in 43 percent of the control group, a statistically significant difference (British Tuberculosis Association, 1968).

Brown (1965) had advocated a treatment approach in which the asthmatic, under hypnosis, may be taught to induce and stop asthma attacks. Three asthmatic patients were studied by Clarke (1970) who found that hypnotic suggestions of asthma caused a measureable decrease in forced respiratory volume at 1 second, an effect usually reversible by suggestions of relaxation. Edwards (1960) in a study of 6 hospitalized asthmatic patients concluded that they could benefit from hypnosis both physiologically by a lessened resistance of the air passages and psychologically by a greater calm. This finding was echoed by White (1961) in a study of 10 asthma patients over a period of 6 to 11 months. Although most of these patients reported improvement and most became socially more active, there was no predictable effect on the respiratory function. Sutton (1969) was able to teach 3 of 8 asthmatic children to use autohypnosis. All three improved during the next year. Only two of the five remaining children improved.

In a restrospective analysis of 121 asthmatic patients, Collison (1975) found that two factors tended to be associated with successful treatment with hypnosis: youthfulness and the ability to enter a deep trance, particularly when there were significant psychological factors present and the asthma was not severe. Subjective improvement, he found, was independent of age, severity of illness, and levels of trance achieved. Aronoff et al. (1975) measured an average improvement of 50 percent beyond the baseline spirometry in 17 asthmatic children following induction of hypnosis. Neinstein and Dash (1982) report improvement in asthma over a 1-year period in a single case. Hypnotic induction of emotions may produce exacerbation of asthma (Clark, 1979). Hypnotherapy is an excellent approach in many cases of asthma (Bauman, 1983; Collison, 1980). Experimental evidence of improvement of asthma with hypnosis was provided by Smith, Wain, and Evans (1981). Twelve mild asthmatics able to withhold all bronchodilator medications for greater than 24 hours underwent a metacholine bronchial challenge test. On the same day following return to baseline respiratory functioning, hypnotic intervention was performed. A control group underwent two tests on the same day without hypnosis. Clinical studies and comparisons suggest that hypnosis can effect an increase in methacholine tolerance in some subjects with asthma.

TECHNIQUE WITH ASTHMATIC CHILDREN

Asthma is primarily a childhood disease, often with marked emotional components. Many asthmatic children can be benefited by hypnotherapy, and some modifications of adult techniques are useful.

After being introduced, the child is asked to sit in a comfortable chair. Rapport is established as quickly as possible. Then the child's asthmatic problem is discussed. The child is told that hypnosis can be most beneficial in the control of such problems. When it is apparent that the child is willing, and motivated to participate in hypnosis, we have generally asked the child to follow this procedure:

"Look at a spot on the ceiling. As you continue looking at this spot, you will begin to relax as much as possible. You will notice that your eyelids begin to feel heavy . . . yes . . . starting to flutter . . . and so just let them close and relax just as much as you can. Let your arms and hands hang limp at your side . . . your body is so relaxed . . . your legs and feet at ease.''

If the patient is younger than 13 years of age, we usually hold the child's hand to establish the best rapport and sense of security possible. Children are then told the following:

"How cooperative you can be indicates that you are in a state of hypnosis. If you can cooperate with your mind, you can also relax every muscle in your body, but especially the muscles that control the breathing in your chest . . . and you can become much more relaxed and as you feel yourself relaxing still more, squeeze my hand, yes. . . . Good . . . just relax as much as you can. Now I want you to imagine that you are looking at your television set at home . . . can you see it? Good, now you are going to see the set come on and a movie of cowboys riding on horses. As you see this, nod your head. . . . Good. . . . You will notice that the horses are running very fast and they are breathing hard and fast . . . like your breathing . . . can you see this? Can you feel this? . . . Good . . . but now the horses are beginning to run more slowly. . . . Breathing is becoming slower and easier and your breathing is slowing down. [The therapist should talk in tempo to the patient's breathing rhythm.] . . . That's it. . . . The horses are slowing down . . . slower now . . . walking . . . breathing almost normal. . . . The wheezing is much less . . . so relaxed. . . . The television scenes fade out. . . . Just let yourself be as comfortable as possible . . . all over . . . secure, relaxed and at ease. I take your hand again. Now I give you the suggestion that you will smell a nice odor. . . . You can smell this nice odor. . . . You can smell this nice odor and when you do . . . squeeze my hand. . . . Good. . . . Now a very deep and sound state of relaxation . . . and breath deeply and slowly, deeply and slowly . . . enjoying the nice odor and you see that your rapid and hard breathing is slowing down . . . your wheezing is less . . . relaxed, so relaxed and at ease . . . free from tension. . . . Your lungs and chest muscles are so relaxed. Smelling the nice odor and now you see your breathing is deep and relaxed, taking deep relaxed breaths . . . so relaxed and at ease. Now the odor is gone. I release your hand. Anytime you need to relax yourself you can do so . . . by closing your eyes and giving yourself these same suggestions just as I have or anytime you are ready to work with me. . . . If I take out my fountain pen and tap it on my desk five times, you can enter this same depth of trance. Do you understand? . . . Good. . . . Remember that you can enter this deep state and your asthma will become controlled. As I slowly count from ten to one, backward, you will be fully awake and your breathing will be normal and the asthma will be gone.''

Hyperventilation

Although not usually classified as a psychosomatic disease, hyperventilation syndrome is one of the most common psychiatric disorders appearing as physical symptoms. In this condition tension and anxiety lead to chronic overbreathing, which has the effect of producing a severe drop in carbon dioxide tension. The loss of carbon dioxide can lead to alterations in the acid–base balance of the blood, inducing changes in the blood vessels. The patient may first experience a paradoxical sense of breathlessness, as if the air breathed had no oxygen. This sense of breathlessness causes the patient to breathe faster, increasing the underlying problem. Concurrently with these changes in the blood the patient often feels a sense of impending doom. This is described as one of the most terrifying experiences imaginable, the patient often fearing that he or she may die at any minute. At most, the condition leads to transient loss of consciousness, which then produces an automatic correction of the breathing disorder. The only real danger in hyperventilation is that the person may fall during the moments of lightheadedness, perhaps injuring himself or herself.

Hyperventilation does not lead to any structural change in the body, even with repeated episodes. The immediate treatment is to increase the level of carbon dioxide in the blood, either through having the patient breathe a mixture of oxygen and carbon dioxide or through the simpler and very effective technique of rebreathing the same air, as in a paper bag, so that the accumulation of carbon dioxide in the rebreathed air corrects the low blood levels. The psychological treatment of hyperventilation consists of modifying whatever personality factors predispose to anxiety. Hypnotherapy is very useful in this regard, for the relaxation that accompanies hypnotic induction gives the patient an immediate experience of how the body feels when relaxed and free of tension.

Coughing

The cough reflex is one of the innate protective mechanisms of the body and is necessary to clear the bronchial tree of excessive secretions and foreign material. There are cases, however, in which the normally protective reflex becomes exaggerated, either in force or in excessive repetition. Coughing in itself may then constitute a clinical problem.

One particularly striking example was a 12-year-old boy we saw who had previously had an ulcerative mucosal lesion on the tracheal bifurcation. This had been demonstrated by broncoscopy, and a biopsy taken at that time had shown an infective etiology. Although the ulcer itself had healed rapidly after the institution of appropriate antiobiotic therapy, the cough persisted. In many ways it resembled an animal bark. It seemed to occur spontaneously and in an automatic fashion.

During clinical interviews there was no correlation with the type of material being discussed.

At the time that he was first seen the boy had been in treatment with a child psychiatrist, who had defined some of the dynamics of the family. The cough, though, had not improved. The boy had been admitted to the hospital, but his unusual cough disturbed the entire wing. It literally could be heard for the entire length of the hallway, some 100 feet.

During the screening interview there was some suggestion that his symptom might be related to angry interactions in the family. The boy was either unable or unwilling to produce the cough on request, though it continued in the automatic fashion throughout the interview.

This child proved to be an excellent hypnotic subject. From the first hypnotic induction the cough vanished. He was given specific suggestions: "Your throat muscles will be relaxed and at ease. . . . The itchy irritability will decrease. . . . Your breathing will be normal and easy. . . . Your excessive, abnormal cough will stop."

It is important again to emphasize that such direct suggestions for symptom removal would not have been given had the patient not already had a thorough medical workup that demonstrated that the original organic lesion on his trachea had completely healed. He was seen for 5 consecutive days for hypnosis, and he did not again have the abnormal cough. He remained in treatment for 1 month to make certain that some dynamic psychological factor was not overlooked. None was found, and treatment was terminated. He was a normal, healthy boy.

Hiccoughs

Everyone has experienced hiccoughs, caused by a spasmodic contraction of the diaphragm accompanied by sudden closure of the glottis. Most cases respond to simple treatments—holding the breath or breathing into a paper bag to increase the concentration of carbon dioxide in the blood or ocular pressure, which stimulates the vagus nerve. Occasionally, hiccoughs fail to respond to such informal treatments. In some severe cases temporary chemical blocking of the vagus or phrenic neural innervation of the diaphragm is elected. At times this may be by permanent surgical section of the nerve on the affected side of the diaphragm.

A number of years ago when Pope Pius XII suffered from a prolonged case of hiccoughs, attention became focused on this rare complication of a common minor disorder.

In 1950, Kirkner and West reported the use of hypnosis in a case of persistent hiccoughs, and in 1955, Dorcus and Kirkner reviewed the use of hypnosis in the treatment of persistent hiccoughs in 18 cases, most of which had been treated previously without success by other means. Of their patients, 14 were permanently relieved, 1 improved only temporarily, and 3 did not respond to the hypnotic treatment. Theohar and McKegney (1970) reported a case of persistent hiccoughs successfully treated with hypnosis. They also reviewed the psychodynamics involved. Others who have discussed their hypnotic treatment of hiccoughs include Bizzi (1964) and Bendersky and Baren (1959).

A typical case of persistent hiccoughs referred to us occurred after gastrectomy in a young man in his middle twenties. He did not respond to the use of carbon dioxide and other medical treatments. Hypnotic induction was somewhat difficult because of the distraction of the hiccoughs. He was given suggestions that the hiccoughs would gradually cease and that he would be relaxed. During the hour in which hypnotic suggestions were given, the hiccoughs decreased markedly in severity and in frequency, but they were still present. The following morning, however, they had vanished and did not recur. Smedley and Barnes (1966) have detailed the successful hypnotic treatment of hiccoughs in a patient with an aortorenal graft.

Not all cases are so successful, particularly if there seems to be an emotional conflict involved. An engineer in his thirties was seen by us in the hospital because hiccoughs were interfering with his work. He responded rapidly to hypnotic treatment and the hiccoughs vanished. When he returned to the job, which he disliked, they immediately began again. At this time, the patient resigned from his job, was found to be free of the symptom, and declined further treatment.

DISORDERS OF THE CARDIOVASCULAR SYSTEM

The induction of neutral hypnosis itself, without any specific suggestions, does not seem to affect the blood pressure, heart rate, or respiratory rate. We were the first to call this state "neutral hypnosis." It has been well demonstrated, however, that hypnosis can increase the heart rate and blood pressure if it produces a subjective emotional state, often with vivid fantasy, which in turn influences the autonomic nervous system. Thus, hypnosis can be beneficial when the cardiovascular system is involved.

Blushing

Although not generally considered a psychosomatic problem since no pathologic condition arises and there is no permanent organic change, excessive blushing can be so socially embarrassing that it interferes with normal enjoyment of life. Hypnotherapy has been reported of value in a case of blushing (Welsh, 1978). In our experience, it is usually necessary to use more than direct symptom removal. Supportive psychotherapy, ego-strengthening techniques, and in some cases exploration of unconscious psychodynamics are needed. In many cases, the concomitant use of group psychotherapy to increase social and interpersonal skills is of great benefit.

Bleeding

There have been many reports, particularly in the dental literature, that tooth extractions done under hypnosis bleed much less than those done with chemical analgesia (Lucas, 1965; Newman, 1971; Petrov, Traikov, and Kalendgiev, 1964). Some dentists and oral surgeons have found that under hypnosis a bleeding tooth socket can be caused to bleed more or less profusely by the appropriate suggestions. Control of blood flow has also been suggested as the most probable mechanism in the hypnotic removal of warts (Bowers, 1976a; Clawson and Swade, 1975).

In a controlled study on the effect of hypnosis on bleeding there was no effect on clotting factors and bleeding time between the waking control state and hypnosis (Crasilneck and Fogelman, 1957). This does not, however, settle the question since the volunteer subjects in this study did not have the same motivation as a patient undergoing possibly painful tooth extraction nor was it possible to measure the important mechanism of vasoconstriction, which may well account for the striking clinical reports.

Buerger's and Raynaud's Diseases

Hypnosis in cardiovascular cases seems most useful in producing the effects of relaxation and decrease of tension, which may have a secondary beneficial effect on high blood pressure, angina, tachycardia, and other disorders. In helping patients with Buerger's disease to stop smoking, hypnosis is particularly useful. Some cases of Raynaud's disease also seem to improve with suggestions that the patients' fingers will feel less painful and that the blood supply to their extremities will be normal, adequate, and warming (Braun, 1979; Jacobson et al., 1973; Norris and Huston, 1956; Zikmund, 1962).

Between 1950 and 1975, we have induced hypnosis for about four dozen cases of Raynaud's disease, with remission or marked improvement of symptoms in approximately 60 percent. These had been medically diagnosed and had usually been treated medically for some time before hypnosis was suggested.

Typical of those cases responding successfully was a 32-year-old housewife who had to constantly wear surgical gloves when doing housework, since the slightest touch of something cool was likely to produce severe pain and blanching of her fingers. The poor vascular supply to the extremities of her fingers had caused a deep ulcer to form beside the nail of one finger, with a lesser pitting in an adjacent finger. Her hands were cool to the touch because of diminished blood flow. She held them carefully to avoid injury.

We found her to be an exceptionally good subject for hypnosis, and direct suggestions were given for the improvement of blood flow to her hands. Within 3 months her hands were generally warm and the ulcerated area had begun to heal satisfactorily.

Because of variations in the course of Raynaud's disease and its recognized influence by emotional factors, we cannot be certain, in the absence of strict controls, that hypnosis was the active factor in the improvement of these cases. Improvement did seem to occur, however, when hypnosis was introduced into the treatment plans.

Cardiac Neurosis

It is possible to approach cardiac neurosis effectively with a combination of hypnosis and psychotherapy or by hypnotherapy alone. Some patients actually suffered a coronary attack, but many attributed to their hearts pain that arises in other places—in an arthritic involvement of the costochondral junctions of the sternum, in splenic flexure syndrome, in the manifestations of a hiatal hernia. The common denominator was anxiety, perhaps even fear of imminent death.

One successful rancher came to us for treatment because of a fear of heart attack, although his cardiologist had assured him that his cardiac function was normal according to all indicators. The patient would not leave his house without his wife. He bought a sphygmomanometer and constantly took his blood pressure and pulse. He was never without an oxygen tank nearby. Routine psychiatric treatment for several months made no headway against his flood of anxiety. He was then treated for years with a combination of hypnosis for reassur-

Figure 10-1. Chronic poor circulation due to Raynaud's disease had caused recurrent infection and ulceration of the fingers, particularly under the fingernails (note dark areas). This can be seen most easily in the photograph in which her fingers are bent. (under the nail of the second finger).

Figure 10-2.   After weekly hypnotherapy for 6 months, followed by monthly visits for the remainder of the year, the circulation of the hands seemed to improve and there were no ulcerations. The darkness in these photographs on the patient's left first finger was caused by a rope burn and was not symptomatic of Raynaud's disease. Although spontaneous remissions of this disease are possible, there had been no comparable periods of freedom from symptoms.

ance and relaxation and psychotherapy for exploration and treatment of his underlying problem. He gradually responded and resumed a normal life.

Nuland (1968) found hypnosis of benefit in patients whose emotional response to myocardial infarction was disturbing. Kupfer (1954) traced one case of functional heart disorder to a childhood experience in which the patient's seductive mother allowed him to lie "in his father's place." With the recovery of this memory under hypnotherapy the patient seemed to improve. Schneck (1948) emphasized the symbolic nature of some physical symptoms.

Hypertension

Hypnosis has been used in treating essential hypertension or high blood pressure, often in conjunction with diet and medication. Suggestions are given for relaxation, calmness, freedom from feelings of anger, and the promotion of a sense of well-being and health. Suggestion of warmth is helpful at times, possibly by enhancing peripheral vasodilation, and self-hypnosis may be of some aid as well.

It is important to check the blood pressure with some frequency, not just at hypnotherapy sessions, although it should be remembered that any excessive anxiety about blood pressure may, in itself, increase the level at the time of measurement. In refractive cases, we generally institute an exploration of unconscious psychodynamics.

Cardiac Effects

Raginsky (1959) has described marked cardiac effects, including auricular and ventricular standstill up to five seconds, each terminated by a normal sinoauricular beat, in a 65-year-old man under hypnosis who had previously had a bilateral sinucarotid neurectomy for Stokes-Adams syndrome. For Yanovski (1962), hypnosis aided in interrupting, at least temporarily, severe cardiovascular disturbances of psychosomatic origin. In treating a case of extrasystoles, Schneck (1953) found that the symptom related to an identification by the patient with his father, who had pulmonary infections. Collison (1970) has used hypnosis to decrease anxiety and the likelihood of arrhythmias during cardiac catheterization.

Our primary approach with cardiac effects has been to decrease such factors as obesity or smoking. Frequently we have treated the psychological problems of cardiac neurosis. This disorder, characterized by an excessive fear of heart disorder, seems to respond well to hypnotherapy or to a combination of psychotherapy and hypnotic symptom control.

Headache

Vascular headaches, such as migraine, are often accompanied by tension headache of musculoskeletal origin. Both types are discussed together in the section on musculoskeletal disorders in this chapter.

GENITOURINARY DISORDERS

Psychosomatic disorders of the genitourinary system are fairly frequent, possibly because of the inevitable symbolic meaning of bladder training and sexual function. Normal function of the bladder or the sexual organs requires a delicate balancing of voluntary and involuntary responses. While the uretheral sphincter can be brought under volitional control, the actual emptying of the bladder is a reflex action only partially assisted by voluntary contraction of the abdominal muscles and diaphragm.

Sexual arousal and achievement of penile erection in the male are largely involuntary, as is ejaculation. Erection and ejaculation can even occur in a paraplegic with complete transection of the spinal cord so that no sensation at all comes to the conscious awareness during intercourse. But conscious factors, as well as anxiety or unconscious conflict, can certainly interfere with normal sexual functioning. Because of the importance of treating sexual disorders with psychotherapy as well as hypnosis, we have reserved discussion of impotence, frigidity, and premature ejaculation for Chapter 18.

Enuresis

The ability to inhibit urination during the night is normally acquired by all children early in life. At times, there is a delay in acquiring this ability, even to near age 10 or 12. Usually, however, bladder control is complete by the time a child begins to want to spend some time away from home with friends, though it is not rare to find cases of enuresis in draftees in their late teens and early twenties.

In our experience the hypnotic techniques have proven effective in about 65 percent of those enuretics treated. In one technique the hypnotized patient is touched in the bladder area and pressure applied while he or she is told, "When you experience this sensation of pressure in your bladder, your sleep will be immediately interrupted, and you will go to the bathroom in 'light sleep' and urinate." Since it involves touching a hypnotized patient, this technique is used only when proper chaperonage is present. The immediate experience of pressure in the suprapubic area seems to add to the effectiveness of the suggestions. In a second technique the patient is not touched, rather he or she is told, "When you begin to feel a pressure in your bladder, you will immediately awaken, go to the bathroom, and void." Concomitant psychotherapy often delineates hostility as an underlying dynamic in enuresis. Verson (1961) and Aboulker and Chertok (1962) have described hypnotic techniques for treating enuresis and incontinence.

Hypnosis has been used in the short-term treatment of enuresis (Stanton, 1979) and in successful inhibition of a hyperreflexic bladder (Godec, 1980). In a case involving organic factors as well hysterical conversion reaction, hypnotherapy was successful in treating the conversion symptoms (Frentz, Wilcox, and Epstein, 1981). In an elaborate study, Freeman and Baxby (1982) reported in the *British Medical Journal* the treatment of incontinence caused by an unstable detrusor.

Fifty women with proved detrusor instability completed 12 sessions of hypnotherapy, focusing on direct symptom removal. Recorded cassettes were used to provide further reinforcement between sessions of hypnotherapy. Twenty-nine patients were symptom free, 14 improved, and 7 remained unchanged. Three months after treatment, cystometry in 44 of the subjects showed stability in 22 and significant improvement in 16, while 6 were unimproved. The authors concluded that psychological factors were important in "idiopathic" detrusor instability. Nachman and Feldman (1983) report the case of an enuretic young male who responded within 7 sessions of hypnotherapy as part of a multidimensional approach.

Urinary Retention

Some cases involve an inability to urinate rather than difficulty in simply initiating urination. If severe, these problems quickly come to the attention of a urologist. One such patient, a 25-year-old divorcee, had a history of difficulty voiding for the 6 years that had elapsed since the birth of her child (Allen, 1972). There had been severe episodes of urinary tract infection, leading finally to the need for intermittent catheterization. Cystoscopy examination revealed only mild cystitis but no obstruction, and no denervation was found with EMG recordings. At this point she was referred for hypnosis.

During the first hypnotic session her symptoms came under control, and she had little trouble voiding for the period of observation, including four more visits for hypnosis. She was anxious and had complained of being sexually frigid during her marriage. In many ways she was still under the domination of her parents, whom she described as demanding and cold. One of her chronic fears was that her ex-husband would somehow be able to take her child away from her. Although continuation of psychotherapy was strongly recommmended to her, she terminated treatment after the 5 sessions because her urinary symptoms had ceased.

Urinary retention treated by hypnosis has been reported by Werner (1962). Cucinotta (1961) used a very permissive hypnotic technique in a similar case, telling the patient that no one had any charge over her, and that everything that occurred would be the result of her own choice. She voided spontaneously for the first time in 11 days since her catheter had been removed. Van Dyke (1972) utilized training in self-hypnosis and to allow a patient to regress to the traumatic episode that seemed to have initiated the symptom. Brown (1959) reviewed uses of hypnosis in genitourinary diseases.

"Pee-Shy" Problems

There is a type of psychosomatic genitourinary symptom seldom discussed, possibly because few of those suffering from it seek treatment from urologists, psychiatrists, or clinical psychologists. This is the so-called "pee-shy" person, one who is unable to urinate in a public restroom, particularly when others are present. The symptom may be so embarrassing that the sufferer may never spend the night away from home, may avoid trips, and may even decide not to marry. This seemingly minor problem can constitute a very dominating symptom around which the patient's entire life may have to be arranged unless treatment is successful. Many have speculated that there are problems of sexual identity confusion at an unconscious level, but the cases we have seen suggest a variety of causes. One man first developed this symptom as a boy, when he was urinating in a restroom next to an older boy who looked at his penis and said "Yours is so small you're probably not even a boy, you're a girl." Another man became "pee-shy" as an adolescent when someone accused him of masturbating because after urinating he was shaking a residual drop of urine from the tip of his penis. The problem is much more common in men than in women, suggesting that some Oedipal fantasy of castration may be a frequent factor.

Treatment consists of helping the patient separate urination from the associations that have accumulated around it, often from the type of traumatic past experience that we have cited. Hypnosis is used in a reassuring, calming way, with suggestions for ease and relaxation in the usually anxiety-filled situation. Most cases improve moderately or greatly; few fail to respond at least to some degree.

We would estimate that this "pee-shy" problem is more common than is generally realized. There are some persons who probably adapt their lives to this symptom, avoiding any situation that would present it as an urgent disorder needing immediate treatment. One man who had suffered for years in silence came for treatment only when his first grandchild was born. He wished to get over the difficulty before his grandson was big enough to go on fishing trips with him. Hypnotic reconditioning, coupled with psychotherapy for repressed homosexual fantasies, led to virtually complete alleviation of the symptom after a few months of treatment.

MUSCULOSKELETAL DISORDERS

Psychophysiological disorders of the musculoskeletal system can easily blend with actual physical problems or with the symbolic expressions of conversion neurosis. In many cases it is difficult to make a differential diagnosis, particularly when pain is the primary symptom. Hypnosis may at times be useful in deciding whether pain is organic or functional. Organic pain tends to recur more quickly after hypnotic treatment than does pain of functional origin. This rule does not hold where there is strong secondary gain, where the underlying psychodynamic conflict is particularly strong, or where repeated sessions of trance have increased the effectiveness of hypnosis. Used with due respect for other signs and symptoms, however, such observations may help in establishing the diagnosis.

Headache

This widespread disorder may arise from a variety of causes, emotional or physical, sometimes far removed from that place where the pain is felt. The brain itself is free of pain fibers, except around the blood vessels, so that most headache is of extracranial origin. Intracranial causes of headache, such as brain tumors or expanding intracranial masses, act through traction or strain on the coverings of the brain or the blood vessels. Migraine headache is probably caused by a contraction of cerebral blood vessels followed by an overdilation that produces pain. It may respond to medications that cause vasoconstriction, such as ergotamine preparations. Extracranial causes of headache include temporal arteritis, eye strain, pain from the sinus cavities, and pain originating in other structures of the head and neck.

The most frequent cause of headache, however, is "tension," resulting in muscular pain. The pain of tension headache generally occurs in the occipital region and the forehead, though it may present in any part of the head. It most likely arises from prolonged contraction of muscle—the neck muscles, the muscles of the jaws, or the muscles of the forehead and scalp.

Many times the headache can be associated with some definite area of identifiable stress, such as crisis in a marriage, unpleasantness with persons at work, or particular problems with children. One woman had headache of uncertain origin, having had a thorough neurological examination without any organic cause being identified. We asked her to keep a diary that would record for each day the presence or absence of headache, its intensity, its relation to her menstrual cycle, the presence of edema on a one-to-four scale of increasing intensity, and any important emotional interraction that occurred during the day. After keeping the diary 2 weeks, she reported only one headache. Inquiry revealed that she had awakened with the headache the morning that her ex-husband was to come to take their 8-year-old son for a visit. The night before the headache she had dreamed that she was pursued by someone who was going to take her child away, and there was nowhere to escape from him. Only after her feelings about her ex-husband had been explored did she reveal the depth and complication of her difficult relations with her present marriage partner. The use of hypnosis was postponed until she more thoroughly understood the emotional origin of her headache.

Hypnosis may be helpful for headache of either functional or organic origin, but it should be used only when there is relative certainty that there is no serious organic etiology to be treated. If the headaches are on a functional basis, the underlying conflict should be identified, if possible, and treated in addition to seeking symptomatic relief of pain.

Our hypnotic suggestions follow the formula, "Your headaches will become less intense, less in number, less in frequency, and will become less debilitating. They will diminish in intensity until you are ready to give them up." It is important to note the permissive cast of the suggestion that the headaches will diminish "until you are ready to give them up." This permits the patient to retain the headache, perhaps in a diminished form, if it is serving a necessary function in his unconscious conflict.

The suggestion is always given that the patient will be able to have a "normal headache" but that this type of headache will "pass away normally." This is to prevent the hypnotic suggestions from interfering with headache that might arise from other causes. Usually a self-hypnosis procedure also is employed. The patient is told, while in trance, that should a headache begin he or she will be able to stop it by putting his or her right hand on the abdomen, closing the eyes, and giving himself or herself suggestions for pain relief similar to those that have been given during treatment sessions.

In a study of 48 patients, Schlutter, Golden, and Blume (1980) found no significant difference in pain relief in hypnosis compared with fontalis electromyographic feedback, and biofeedback combined with Jacobson progressive relaxation. Hypnosis alone was as effective as biofeedback, and biofeedback combined with relaxation was equally effective. Drummond (1981) has reviewed 10 years of literature of hypnosis in the treatment of headache.

The usual duration for treatment of recurrent headache by hypnosis is about 3 months (weekly visits), and the success rate seems comparable to that for inhibiting the smoking habit.

Migraine Headache

Migraine headache is vascular in origin, but it is often mixed with components of tension headache, hence its discussion here. Harding (1959) has lectured and written extensively about the hypnotic treatment of migraine headache. In a study of 25 migraine sufferers who had been refractory to the usual chemical treatments, 23 were successfully hypnotized and treated with symptom removal techniques. Six were relieved of headache for periods ranging from 6 months to as long as $2^1/_2$ years. Six had a reduction in severity of frequency of attacks, while the rest were considered failures (including 10 who did not respond to the questionnaire). According to Harding, migraine may be a pattern of response learned from a significant figure in the patient's past. Hypnotic treatment is considered safe if the patient is otherwise well adjusted, with migraine an isolated symptom.

Cedercreutz (1972) has discussed, in a complex case history from Finland, the hypnotic treatment of migraine over a period of years. The symptoms did not finally clear until an anamnesis under hypnosis revealed that at the age of 5, during a civil war, the woman had seen her schoolteacher killed by a Russian soldier.

Techniques of behavior therapy desensitization, employing hypnosis for relaxation, have been discussed by Dengrove (1968). Horan (1953) also reports successful use of hypnotherapy in migraine treatment. The need to know the psychodynamics of the patient is emphasized strongly by most authors, notably Blumenthal (1963), Hanley (1964), and Van Pelt (1954). In a study by Anderson, Basker, and Dalton (1975), 10 of 23 hypnosis patients achieved remission of migraine, compared with 3 of 24 treated with medication. Andreychuk and Skriver (1975) have reported treatment of migraine with hypnosis and biofeedback handwarming techniques. This topic has been further elaborated by Ansel (1977), Bowers (1976b), Graham (1975), and McDowell (1975). Daniels (1980) reported excellent results in using hypnosis to increase hand temperature without concomitant biofeedback, while Howard, Reardon, and Tosti (1982) reported hypnosis of use in combination with other techniques in the treatment of migraine.

Torticollis

Torticollis is a unilateral spasm of the neck muscles, particularly the sternocleidomastoid, producing a violent turning of the head to one side. The etiology is uncertain. Some consider it similar to a muscle dystonia; others emphasize psychological factors. Myositis may be involved as well as nerve injury, particularly in children. Whatever its origin, prolonged torticollis can lead to hypertrophy of the neck muscles and marked interference in normal patterns of living.

We have been most impressed with psychogenic factors in the cases that have come to our attention. One woman had been engaged in extramarital intercourse with a man at the office where she worked when the door opened suddenly and they were discovered in flagrant delecti by a coworker. Her torticollis began at that point, her head being pulled in the direction to which it had involuntarily jerked when the door opened. A similar situation had occurred, without abrupt discovery, in a second woman who was in a boat at night with her lover.

Not all psychogenic causes involve questions of sexual morality. One young woman with torticollis frequently described her husband as "a pain in the neck." At other times the torticollis seems to be a symbolic expression of trying to look at things in the "right" way—with the head frequently turning toward the right. The conflict involved may be of any variety.

Torticollis is one of the most difficult problems to treat with hypnosis. Discovery of the underlying meaning does not usually lead to spontaneous cure. Even after insight has been obtained, some take 6 months or longer of regular reinforcement of posthypnotic suggestions for the habit pattern to be broken. Even then, improvement may be gradual and slow. Friedman (1965) has had successful treatment of torticollis by hypnosis as have Ampato (1975) and LeHew (1971).

In some cases it is not possible to establish a likely psychogenic origin. Though such cases may be due to undefined organic causes, they still may respond to prolonged use of hypnosis.

Blepharospasm

Some neurologists content that blepharospasm, a sudden involuntary contraction of the orbicularis oculi muscles, usually in both eyes simultaneously, is primarily a disorder of the aged and does not have a neurotic basis (Adams, 1958). In the cases referred to us, however, an emotional meaning is almost always found during the course of the treatment. The meaning of the symptom is commonly an unconscious desire not to "see" or understand something in an important interpersonal relationship.

In deep trance the subject is told to open his or her eyes easily and without spasm. When the subject accomplishes this, a mirror is held in front of him or her so that he or she can see his or her eyes open in a normal manner, without blepharospasm. The subject is then told, while still in trance, that he or she will be able to accomplish the same relaxation while in the waking state. If an emotional basis is suspected, further exploration of the symptom meaning may be pursued under hypnosis. In cases of probable organic origin or if no psychodynamic basis can be identified, direct suggestion for symptom suppression is continued. In general, the hypnotic treatment of blepharospasm is more rapid than that of torticollis.

Whiplash

Another disease entity where physical and psychological factors may be quite difficult to disentangle is whiplash, which is persistent neck pain following traumatic hyperextension, often in auto accidents. In some cases there is an element of obvious secondary gain that may delay relief of symptoms by influencing the unconscious mechanisms that prolong the pain. Secondary gain may work in reverse, however, and unconscious guilt for the unwilled exaggeration of pain may prolong symptoms long after an insurance claim is settled.

In many cases of prolonged pain it may simply be that the organic causes of pain persist, but their treatment does not produce sufficient relief.

Suggestions given during hypnosis for whiplash are similar to those for other pain relief. It is important, naturally, that a competent orthopedic surgeon or neurologist certify that there is no organic condition that would be masked by hypnotic removal of pain. In any case, suggestions are worded in such a way that not all pain is removed so that pain is still an indicator of organic changes that might need attention.

One young man suffering from whiplash had been treated with hypnosis for relief of pain after his orthopedic situation stabilized. Although free of pain, he was rehypnotized (with his consent) as part of a demonstration of hypnosis to medical students. While in trance, the mere mention of the word "red" was sufficient to cause him visibly to tense his neck, apparently because of the association to the original accident that occurred when he was stopped at a red light and was hit from behind by another car. Remarks such as "Look out, it's going to hit!" would produce the same reaction while he was in the trance state.

Psychogenic Back Pain

Back pain may well represent a secondary gain or conversion response if all physical examinations prove negative; therefore the therapist should explore the psychodynamic meaning of the back pain. Crasilneck presents three case histories of psychogenic back pain:

CASE 1

A 28-year-old man who is a top executive in a large Dallas firm, was referred for hypnotherapy. Rapport was established easily because the patient was motivated and cooperative. He entered a deep level of trance, became relaxed and at ease and, during the course of the first session complained about the tremendous responsibilities of his job. He made such references as "everything is on my back," "there's too much pressure on my back," "that's just another load on my back," and "the load on my back keeps getting heavier and heavier."

During the ensuing weeks of treatment using a combination of psychotherapy and hypnotherapy, the patient began to delegate some of the responsibilities of his job and eased the pressures he had endured substantially, without negating the position of his executive ability. The backaches diminished and eventually disappeared. At one of his last sessions he said, "My new assistant has taken most of the pressure off my back and life is more pleasant."

CASE 2

A 16-year-old boy complained of severe back pain each time he was required to attend physical education class. His family physician referred him for hypnotherapy. It soon became apparent that whenever the boy was requested to perform certain exercises at school, the pain was a means of repressing panic for his homosexual thoughts while performing the exercises.

After several weeks of psychotherapy and hypnotherapy the boy gained insight into his thoughts and worked out his repressed sexual feelings enabling him to accept his homosexuality, thereby alleviating the backaches.

CASE 3

A 35-year-old woman was referred by an orthopedic surgeon who had found no physiological evidence for her intermittent and repeated back problems over a 4-year period. After rapport was established and age regression was agreed upon, the woman was regressed to an incident before the onset of her back problems. Her idiomotor signalling was expressed at a given time 5 years earlier at which time she stated that her back pain was worsening.

She was told to relax and relieve the tension in her back and that she would be able to relate the experience without further pain to her back. As soon as she was free of most of her pain, she described in detail the foreplay during an evening with her husband; that he had asked her to get down on the floor on her hands and knees while he mounted her "dog fashion," quickly inserting his penis into her anus and ejaculating almost immediately after several painful thrusts. She moaned with pain and was progressed to a later date when she felt more comfortable and at ease.

Upon awakening, she had less pain in her back and was able to move more easily. During the course of treatment it became apparent that she developed back problems in order to avoid another traumatic "dog fashion" experience. Her husband accompanied her on two sessions at her request, and her feelings about the incident were discussed. It was disclosed that the husband frequently tried to pressure her into assuming the "dog fashion" position during coitus in the 4-year period. The patient discussed her feelings at great length, and her husband assured her that he would never make the request again. In the course of hypnotherapy she gained intellectual and emotional insight into her back problem and eventually the pain abated.

Arthritis

Some authorities speculate that there may be psychogenic factors operative in certain cases of arthritis, seeming to correlate personality stress with exacerbations of symptoms in rheumatoid arthritis and other conditions. Whatever may be the final scientific opinion on these supposed psychogenic factors, we have not been impressed with the utility of treating acute arthritic problems with prolonged courses of psychotherapy. It may be that psychological factors, if operative, have been overshadowed by organic joint changes long before the patient presents for psychological treatment. One can certainly see the repressed hostility and feelings of hopelessness described with arthritis, but it is difficult to imagine that these are causitive factors rather than emotional reactions to a painful and frustrating disease. The observed correlation of emotional stress to periods of increased arthritic symptoms does not necessarily imply psychogenic etiology.

Whatever the origin of arthritis, the pain of this unfortunate disease often can be alleviated with hypnosis. We have used hypnosis at times to diminish pain and allow increased function in joints that have been operated for various deformities. This is done only when the patient remains under the close supervision of an orthopedic surgeon or rheumatologist who can adequately assess the condition of the joint and institute other methods of treatment as they appear indicated. Such a combination of hypnosis with orthopedic care can at times allow the patient to use the joint to a greater degree, increasing the enjoyment of life, even though the underlying orthopedic problem is not altered.

Maintenance hypnotherapy may be practical in some cases of arthritic pain. A practicing physician who developed rheumatoid arthritis had become addicted to morphine in seeking enough pain relief to permit him to continue to practice medicine. Realizing the dangers of his situation, he was voluntarily hospitalized and withdrawn from narcotics, hypnosis being substituted to decrease his pain. We taught him self-hypnosis quite rapidly and have seen him only at decreasing intervals for reinforcement. He has continued to practice, free of addiction. Although he might be said to have an "addiction" to hypnosis, this is certainly more controlled, more appropriate, and less destructive than the true chemical addition that has been displaced.

Stein (1964) discussed an unusual case of a woman treated with hypnosis for painful calluses on three toes of her left foot and for painful and deformed arthritic feet. Although the initial intention had been for pain relief, a 3 year follow-up revealed marked improvement in the calluses—complete disappearance on two toes and a 90 percent reduction on the third. Arthritic pain had virtually vanished. These improvements seemed to be a side-effect of treatment.

Thakur (1982) has reported a case in which hypnotherapeutic methods were of significant help in controlling pain and increasing mobility in a woman with rheumatoid arthritis.

Tinnitus

The origin of tinnitus, a ringing sound in the ears, may be physical or psychological. In many instances it is not possible to clearly decide the cause. It may involve musculoskeletal origin in the fine muscles of the inner ear, may arise from neural or vascular disorder, or may occur as a psychophysiological symptom.

The most usual presentation is of a subjective sense of a "ringing" or vibration in the ear. This may be of such severity that surgical destruction of the cochlea may be considered, exchanging deafness for relief of the tinnitus. Our experience is that hypnosis, in good subjects, can often achieve 50 percent reduction in the symptom, probably through blocking awareness at a cortical level. There is some evidence, however, that hypnosis can product temporary selective deafness to tones of specific frequency in somnambulistic subjects (Black and Wigan, 1961), which might indicate a mechanism of action in the relief of tinnitus.

Minalyka and Whanger (1959) described an unusual case in which a "clicking" could be heard up to 2 feet from the patient's head, synchronous with the pulse. Examination revealed that the source of the unusual sound, which resembled the snapping of finger nails, was spasm of the muscles of the palate and eustachian tube. Four hypnotic sessions were completed, with some initial difficulty in achieving trance. As the patient gradually learned to relax, the sound stopped for the first time in 9 years, and the patient was free of tinnitus for 48 hours. Subsequently, it was present only during conditions of marked stress, during which he could modify it by using autosuggestion techniques. This unusual type of tinnitus was reported also be Pearson and Barnes (1950). Brattberg (1983) has treated tinnitus through the use of recorded audio cassetes.

CONCLUSION

In conclusion, in this chapter we have attempted to demonstrate that hypnosis is of value in the differential diagnosis of many psychophysiological conditions and may be a useful adjunct to the treatment of those who are resistant to purely insight-oriented psychotherapy. Even in those problems for which no clear psychogenic factor can be defined hypnosis may offer some relief of symptoms. Hypnosis is more than relaxation, suggestibility, and the placebo response, and is of benefit in many cases of psychosomatic disorder (Frankel, 1975).

REFERENCES

Aboulker P, Chertok L: Emotional factors in stress incontinence. Psychosom Med 24:507–510, 1962
Adams RD: Disturbances of the motor system, in Harrison TR (ed): Principles of Internal Medicine. New York, McGraw-Hill, 1958
Allen TA: Psychogenic urinary retention. South Med J 65:302–304, 1972
Ampato JJ: Hypnosis: A cure for torticollis. Am J Clin Hypn 18:60–62, 1975
Anderson JAD, Basker MA, Dalton R: Migraine and hypnotherapy. Int J Clin Exp Hypn 23:48–58, 1975
Andreychuk T, Skriver C: Hypnosis and biofeedback in the treatment of migraine headache. Int J Clin Exp Hypn 23:172–183, 1975
Ansel EL: A simple exercise to enhance response to hypnotherapy for migraine headaches. Int J Clin Exp Hypn 25:68–71, 1977
Aronoff GM, Aronoff S, Peck LW: Hypnotherapy in the treatment of bronchial asthma. Ann Allergy 34:346–362, 1975
Bauman F: Asthma. Quoted in Medical World News. JAMA 249:320, 1983
Bendersky G, Baren M: Hypnosis in the termination of hiccups unresponsive to conventional treatment. Arch Intern Med 104:417–420, 1959
Bernstein AE: The uses and misuses of hypnosis in psychosomatic illness. Med J Aust 52:831–835, 1965
Bizzi B: On two cases of hysteric hiccough and hysterical sneezing treated with hypnosis. Rass Stud Psichiat 53:60–66, 1964
Black S, Wigan ER: An investigation of selective deafness produced by direct suggestion under hypnosis. Br Med J 2:736–741, 1961
Blumenthal LS: Hypnotherapy of headaches. Headache 2:197–202, 1963
Bowers KS: The hypnotic control of blood flow, in Hypnosis for the Seriously Curious. New York, W. W. Norton, 1976a, pp 144–147
Bowers KS: Hypnosis for the Seriously Curious, New York, W. W. Norton, 1976b, pp 147–149
Brattberg G: An alternative method of treating tinnitus: Relation-therapy primarily through the home use of a recorded audio cassette. Int J Clin Exp Hypn 31:90–97, 1983
Braun BG: Hypnotherapy for Raynaud's disease, in Burrows GD, Collison DR, Dennerstein L (eds): Hypnosis. Amsterdam, Elsevier/North-Holland Biomedical Press, 1979, pp 141–156
British Tuberculosis Association: Hypnosis for asthma: A controlled trial. A report of the research committee of the British Tuberculosis Association 4:71–76, 1968
Brown EA: The treatment of bronchial asthma by means of hypnosis as viewed by the allergist. J Astham Res 3:101–119, 1965
Brown TD: Hypnosis in genito-urinary diseases. Am J Clin Hypn 1:165–168, 1959
Cedercreutz C: The big mistakes: A note. Int J Clin Exp Hypn 20:15–16, 1972
Chapman LF, Goodell H, Wolff HG: Changes in tissue vulnerability induced during hypnotic suggestion. J Psychosom Res 4:99–105, 1959

Chong TM: The treatment of asthma by hypnotherapy. Med J Malaya 18:232–234, 1965

Clark P: Experimental exacerbation and relief of asthma under hypnosis, in Burrows GD, Collison DR, Dennerstein L (eds): Hypnosis. Amsterdam, Elsevier/North-Holland Biomedical Press, 1979, pp 95–96

Clarke PS: Effects of emotion and cough on airways obstruction in asthma. Med J Aust 1:535–537, 1970

Clawson TA, Swade RH: The hypnotic control of blood flow and pain: The cure of warts and the potential for the use of hypnosis in the treatment of cancer. Am J Clin Hypn 17:160–169, 1975

Collison DR: Hypnotherapy in the management of asthma. Am J Clin Hypn 11:6–11, 1968

Collison DR: Cardiological applications of the control of the autonomic nervous system by hypnosis. Am J Clin Hypn 12:150–156, 1970

Collison DR: Which asthmatic patients should be treated by hypnotherapy? Med J Aust 1:776–781, 1975

Collison DR: Hypnosis and respiratory disease, in Burrows GD, Dennerstein L (eds): Handbook of Hypnosis and Psychosomatic Medicine. Amsterdam, Elsevier/North-Holland Biomedical Press, 1980, pp 327–339

Crasilneck HB, Fogelman MJ: The effects of hypnosis on blood coagulation. Int J Clin Exp Hypn 5:132–165, 1957

Crasilneck HB, Hall JA: Physiological changes associated with hypnosis: A review of the literature since 1948. Int J Clin Exp Hypn 7:9–50, 1959

Cucinotta S: Acute urinary retention successfully treated with hypnosis. Am J Clin Hypn 3:201–202, 1961

Daniels LK: The effect of automated hypnosis and hand warming on migraine: A pilot study. Am J Clin Hypn 19:91–94, 1980

de la Parra R: Tratamiento del asma bonqual en estado hysontia. Acta Hypnol Lat-Am 1:60–71, 1960

Dengrove E: Behavior therapy of headache. J Am Soc Psychosom Dent Med 15:41–48, 1968

Dias MM: Hypnosis in irritable colon. Rev Brasil Med 20:132–134, 1963a

Dias MM: Hypnosis and prolonged suggested sleep in gastroenterology. Hospital (Rio) 64:983–993, 1963b

Dorcus RM, Kirkner FJ: The control of hiccoughs by hypnotic therapy. J Clin Exp Hypn 3:104–108, 1955

Drummond FE: Hypnosis in the treatment of headache: A review of the last ten years. J Am Soc Psychosom Dent Med 28:87–101, 1981

Dunbar HF: Psychosomatic histories and techniques of examination. Am J Psychiat 95:1277, 1939

Edwards G: Hypnotic treatment of asthma. Br Med J 1:492–497, 1960

Eichorn R, Tracktir J: The effects of hypnotically induced emotions upon gastric secretions. Gastroenterology 29:432–438, 1955

Erickson MH: Hypnotic investigation of psychosomatic phenomena. I. Psychosomatic interrelationships studied by experimental hypnosis. Psychosom Med 5:51–58, 1943

Frankel FH: Hypnosis as a treatment method in psychosomatic medicine. Int J Psychiatry Med 6:75–85, 1975

Freeman RM, Baxby K: Hypnotherapy for incontinence caused by the unstable detrusor. Br Jed J (Clin Res) 284(6332):1831–1834, 1982

French TM, Alexander F: Psychogenic factors in bronchial asthma. Psychosom Med Monograph 4. Washington, National Research Council, 1941

Frentz GD, Wilcox ME, Epstein AW: Reversal of urinary tract diversion after recovery from hysterical conversion reaction. South Med J 74:1158–1159, 1981

Friedman H: Brief clinical reports: Hypnosis in the treatment of a case of torticollis. Am J Clin Hypn 8:139–140, 1965

Godec CJ: Inhibition of hyperreflexive bladder during hypnosis: A case report. Am J Clin Hypn 22:170–172, 1980

Graham GW: Hypnotic treatment for migraine headaches. Int J Clin Exp Hypn 23:165–171, 1975

Hanley FW: Hypnotherapy of migraine. Can Psychiatr Assoc J 9:254–257, 1964

Hanley FW: Individualized hypnotherapy of asthma. Am J Clin Hypn 16:275, 1974

Harding CH: Hypnosis and migraine or vice versa. Paper presented at the 11th Annual Meeting of the Society for Clinical and Experimental Hypnosis, San Francisco, August, 1959

Horan JS: Hypnosis and recorded suggestions in the treatment of migraine: Case report. J Clin Exp Hypn 1:7–10, 1953

Howard L, Reardon J, Tosti D: Modifying migraine headache through rational state directed hypnotherapy—a cognitive-experiential perspective. Int J Clin Exp Hypn 30:257–269, 1982

Jacobson AM, Hackett TP, Surman OS, Silverberg EL: Raynaud phenomenon: Treatment with hypnotic and operant technique. JAMA 225:739–740, 1973

Kirkner FJ, West PM: Hypnotic treatment of persistent hiccup: A case report. Br J Med Hypnot 1:22–24, 1950

Kolouch FT: Hypnosis in living systems theory: A living systems autopsy in a polysurgical, polymedical, polypsychiatric patient addicted to talwyn. Am J Clin Hypn 13:22–34, 1970

Koster S: Serious and dangerous cases of organic and functional diseases cured by hypnosis. Br J Med Hypn 7:2–15, 1955

Kupfer D: Hypnotherapy in a case of functional heart disorder. J Clin Exp Hypn 2:186–190, 1954

Kusano T, Honda T, Ago Y, Kuriyama K: Use and abuse of hypnotherapy for bronchial asthma. Jpn J Hypn 12:33–37, 1969

Lait VS: A case of recurrent compulsive vomiting. Am J Clin Hypn 14:196–198, 1972

Lassner JC (ed): Hypnosis and psychosomatic medicine: Proceedings of the International Congress for Hypnosis and Psychosomatic Medicine. Am J Clin Hypn 2:266, 1969

LeHew JL III: Use of hypnosis in the treatment of long-standing spastic torticollis. Am J Clin Hypn 14:124–126, 1971

Leonard AS, Papermaster AA, Wangensteen OH: Treatment of postgastrectomy dumping syndrome by hypnotic suggestion. JAMA 165:1957–1959, 1957

Lewis JH: Studies in psychosomatics: Influence of hypnotic stimulation on gastric hunger contractions. Psychosom Med 5:125–131, 1943

Lucas ON: Dental extractions in hemophiliac: Control of the emotional factors by hypnosis. Am J Clin Hypn 7:301–307, 1965

McDowell MH: The utilization of biofeedback instrumentation in hypnotherapy. Presented at the 27th annual meeting of the International Society of Clinical and Experimental Hypnosis, Chicago, 1975

McLean AF: Hypnosis in "psychosomatic" illness. Br J Med Psychol 38:211, 1965

Magonet AP: Hypnosis in asthma. J Clin Exp Hypn 4:92, 1956

Magonet AP: Hypnosis in asthma. Int J Clin Exp Hypn 8:121–127, 1960

Maher-Loughnan GP: Hypnosis and autohypnosis for the treatment of asthma. Int J Clin Exp Hypn 18:1–14, 1970

Maher-Loughnan GP, Kinsley BJ: Hypnosis for asthma—a controlling trial. Br Med J 4:71–76, 1968

Maher-Loughnan GP, Macdonald N, Mason AA, Fry L: Controlled trial of hypnosis in the symptomatic treatment of asthma. Br Med J 5301:371–376, 1962

Minalyka EE, Whanger AD: Objective tinnitus aurium hypnotically treated. Am J Clin Hypn 2:85–86, 1959

Moorefield CW: The use of hypnosis and behavior therapy in asthma. Am J Clin Hypn 13:162–168, 1971

Morton JH: Hypnosis and psychosomatic medicine. Am J Clin Hypn 3:67–74, 1960

Nachman A, Feldman B: Integration of hypnosis in couple therapy of primary enuresis: A report, in Wester WC, Smith AH (eds): Clinical Hypnosis: A Multidisciplinary Approach. Philadelphia, J.B. Lippincott Co., 1983, p 45

Neinstein LS, Dash J: Hypnosis as an adjunct therapy for asthma: Case report. J Adolesc Health Care 3:45–48, 1982

Newman M: Hypnotic handling of the chronic bleeder in extraction: A case report. Am J Clin Hypn 14:126–127, 1971

Norris A, Huston P: Raynaud's Disease studied by hypnosis. Dis Nerv Syst 17:163–165, 1956

Nuland W: The use of hypnotherapy in the treatment of the postmyocardial infarction invalid. Int J Clin Exp Hypn 16:139–150, 1968

Pearson MM, Barnes LJ: Objective tinnitus aurium: Report of two cases with good results after hypnosis. J Phila Gen Hosp 1:134, 1950

Petrov, P, Traikov D, Kalendgiev: A contribution to psychoanesthetization through hypnosis in some stomatological manipulations. Br J Med Hypn 15:8–16, 1964

Raginsky BB: Hypnosis in internal medicine and general practice, in Schneck JM (ed): Hypnosis in Modern Medicine, Springfield, Ill., Charles C Thomas 1953, pp 28–60

Raginsky BB: Temporary cardiac arrest induced under hypnosis. Int J Clin Exp Hypn 7:53–68, 1959

Raginsky BB: The use of hypnosis in internal medicine. Int J Clin Exp Hypn 8:181–194, 1960

Rose S: A general practitioner approach to the asthmatic patient. Am J Clin Hypn 10:30–32, 1967

Sachs B: Coping with stress. Unpublished paper, 1983.

Sachs B: Aging well. Presidential address, 29th Annual Meeting of the Academy of Psychosomatic Medicine, 1982

Schlutter LC, Golden CJ, Blume HG: A comparison of treatments for prefrontal muscle contraction headache. Br J Med Psychol 53:47–52, 1980

Schneck JM: Psychogenic cardiovascular reaction interpreted and successfully treated with hypnosis. Psychoanal Rev 35:14–19, 1948

Schneck JM: Hypnoanalytic study of a patient with extrasystole. J Clin Exp Hypn 1:11–17, 1953

Schneck JM: A hypnoanalytic investigation of psychogenic dyspnea with the use of induced auditory hallucinations and special additional hypnotic techniques. J Clin Exp Hypn 2:80–90, 1954

Schneck JM: Hypnotherapy for achalasia of the esophagus (cardiospasm) Am J Psychiatry 114:1042–1043, 1958

Silber S: Encopresis: Rectal rebellion and anal anarchy? J Am Soc Psychosom Dent Med 15:97–106, 1968

Sinclair-Gieben AHC: Treatment of status asthmaticus by hypnosis. Br Med J: 1651–1652, 1960

Smedley WP, Barnes WT: Postoperative use of hypnosis on a cardiovascular service: Termination of persistent hiccups in a patient with an aortorenal graft. JAMA 197:371–372, 1966

Smith LJ, Wain HJ, Evans R III: The effects of hypnosis on bronchial response to methacholine in asthma. J Allergy Clin Immunol 67:44, 1981.

Spiegel H, Speigel D: Trance and Treatment. New York: Basic Books Inc., 1978

Stanton H: Short term treatment of enuresis. Am J Clin Hypn 22:103–107, 1979

Stein C: "Grandma" revisited in her eighty-ninth year. Am J Clin Hypn 6:273–275, 1964

Sutton PH: A trial of group hypnosis and autohypnosis in asthmatic children. Br J Clin Hypn 1:11–14, 1969

Takaishi N: Personal communication, 1971

Thakur KS: Hypnotherapy for rheumatoid arthritis. Presented at the annual meeting of the American Society of Clinical Hypnosis, Denver, 1982

Theohar C, McKegney FP: Hiccups of psychogenic origin: A case report and review of the literature. Compr Psychiatry 11:377–384, 1970

Van Dyke PB: The case of the recalcitrant bladder. Am J Clin Hypn 14:256–259, 1972

Van Pelt SJ: Migraine, emotional and hypnosis. Br J Med Hypnot 6:22–24, 1954

Verson RD: Unatecnica rapida para el tratamiento de la enuresis. Rev Lat-Am Hypn Clin 2:18–21, 1961

Welsh DK: Hypnotic control of blushing: A case study. Am J Clin Hypn 20:213–216, 1978

Werner WEF: Hypnosis in the prevention, control and therapy of urinary retention. Am J Clin Hypn 5:64–66, 1962

White HC: Hypnosis in bronchial asthma. J Psychosom Res 5:272–279, 1961

Whitehorn JC: Physiological changes in emotional states. Res Publ Assoc Res Nerv Ment Dis 19, 1939

Wolberg LR: Hypnotic experiments in psychosomatic medicine. Psychosom Med 9:337–342, 1947

Wright ME: Hypnotherapy and psychosomatic hypotheses. Am J Clin Hypn 8:245–249, 1966

Yanovski AG: The feasibility of alteration of cardiovascular manifestations in hypnosis. Am J Clin Hypn 5:8–16, 1962

Zane MD: The hypnotic situation and changes in ulcer pain. Int J Clin Exp Hypn 14:292–304, 1966

Zikmund V: Vplyo pschickych podnetov na prejavy Raynaudovijchoroby. Bratislavske Likarske Listy 41:259–265, 1962

11
Hypnosis in the Treatment of Nutritional and Dietary Problems

In 1955 our group was the first to report the use of hypnosis to increase appetite in severely burned patients whose inadequate food intake imperiled their recovery. A more definitive report followed in 1956 (Fogelman and Crasilneck), expanding the uses of hypnosis to other problem areas of food intake. Not only was hypnotic suggestion shown to increase total caloric consumption, but it was also able to modify poor food intake associated with gastrointestinal dysfunction, to aid in overcoming specific food dislikes, and to aid in alleviating the effect of pain on food intake.

As one of the basic activities of any organism, food intake and eating acquire deep psychological meanings. Freud emphasized that the oral stage of psychosexual development is centered around the infant's mouth as an erogenous zone. Erikson expanded the meaning of the oral stage, suggesting that the basic task of that early period was the achievement of a basic trust in existence and avoidance of a pervasive sense of distrust and fear. Other psychoanalysts focused on specialized aspects. Melanie Klein spoke of a depressive position occurring at 6 to 8 months of age, during which the infant seemed to realize that his or her good mother image and his or her bad mother image referred to the same person. Jung, although concentrating on the problems of middle life, wrote about infancy in terms of nutritional needs.

Many mothers seem to relate to their children in terms of food and nutrition. The closeness and importance of nursing is obvious, whether it is breast feeding or giving the infant a prepared formula while offering body contact and warmth. In early infancy such "food language" is expected, but some mothers continue it far beyond the stage in which other forms of communication and other needs become paramount. How many of us remember being told as children, "Eat everything on your plate!" How many well-meaning mothers have encouraged their children to eat by reminding them of "all the starving children who need the food," as if leaving food uneaten were somehow equivalent to causing starvation somewhere in the world.

Food is easily equated with love and affection—birthday cakes, special dishes, unusual seasonal foods such as turkey at Thanksgiving, fruit cake at Christmas. Even if the importance of an early oral stage of development were not emphasized, all children go through years of conditioning around food choices and tastes. Certain foods may acquire strong emotional overtones.

Caloric intake, over a period of time, must necessarily influence body weight and proportion, linking appetite changes with changes in body image. Some obese people unconsciously equate body fat with protection, either as a symbolic "wall" behind which they "hide" or in a more interpersonal way as making them less attractive to others and decreasing the likelihood of sexual advances. Surprisingly, in some cases exactly the reverse is true. A woman, for example, may resist losing weight for fear that it will make her less attractive to her husband because he may worry more about her fidelity if she is slimmer. Some persons who have grown up in poverty may even have unconscious psychodynamics in which the husband considers his wife's obesity as symbolic of the fact that he is able to provide her with excess food, a mark of his own masculinity.

Overeating may, of course, be an obsession. At times such an obsession with food can be traced to eating habits of childhood. We have seen a number of cases in which the patient has "won" a battle over diet with the parents at an age before 5 years. In one instance a child was underweight until age 4, when the family physician advised the parents to "let her eat whatever she wants to." The child then ate *only* peanut butter sandwiches for a year, establishing her "control" of her diet, but this "victory" led to her overeating in teenage and adult years, causing problems in self-esteem and relationship. When the anger underlying overeating was explored, she was able to manage her appetite on a more realistic basis.

Some of the smokers whom we have treated with hypnosis have had weight gain, but only to an average of 4 pounds (Crasilneck and Hall, 1968). In contrast, people who discontinue a long-standing habit of compulsive smoking without the aid of hypnosis seem to have more excessive weight gain. It appears at times if hypnosis exerts an "authority" that is more compelling and less conflictual than mere "resolve" of "making up one's mind" to lose weight.

In many patients the psychodynamic mechanism behind obesity seems to be "loving oneself." Often childhood experience has included a family situation in which the parents either desired the child to eat more or complained because the child was overweight. In either case food intake can become an emotionally charged area in which the obese neurotic continues to struggle with the parents in fantasy. If the patient has had a "feeding mother," who expressed affection by offering varieties or quantities of food, this activity of the parent may be internalized by the patient, who assuages unhappiness, loneliness, or guilt by symbolically feeding himself as the parent would have done in a similar circumstance.

An unconscious fantasy of pregnancy is sometimes seen in women who are overweight. The wife of a general practitioner of medicine was jealous that her husband seemed always to be away at night with women patients who were at term. Her obesity represented unconsciously both fantasied pregnancy, which would cause her husband to pay similar attention to her, and simultaneously was a compensation through feeding for what she felt deprived of in an emotional way.

Some obese men, particularly, have an unconscious equation between strength and size. Their excessive body weight is equated unconsciously with an ability to defend themselves against attack, often against a fantasied "castrating" father image.

DECREASING FOOD INTAKE

Jean Mayer (1973), who organized the 1969 White House Conference on Food, Nutrition and Health, has called obesity our "national problem, if not, indeed national obsession."

Hypnotherapy can often help in treating obesity, an observation that is one of the most clinically confirmed in all the literature on hypnosis (Cohen, 1979; Crasilneck and Hall, 1976; Goldstein, 1981; Kroger, 1977; Mann, 1981; Nuland, 1974; Spiegel and Spiegel, 1978; Stanton, 1975). Ringrose (1979) found that more than 85 percent of 159 obese patients lost notable amounts of weight with hypnosis. It is important to also be concerned with body image changes, not simply with weight loss (Halpern, 1983). Obese patients who are good hypnotic subjects are more likely to be successful with weight loss (Deyoub and Wilkie, 1980). Effectiveness of hypnotherapy for weight loss may be enhanced by demonstrating to the subject, through a challenge test such as hand-levitation, that he or she is experiencing an actual hypnotic state. Mott and Roberts (1979), in reviewing the literature of hypnotherapy for obesity, criticize the anecdotal nature of many reports and the lack, in many cases, of long-term follow-up results.

Before hypnotherapy is attempted, each obese patient should be cleared by a physician to rule out such medical conditions as hypothyroidism. In our practice, after a patient has been given medical clearance, each is then screened. At this time we attempt to note any emotional factors of significance and to define any overdetermined meanings of the obesity. The general emotional stability of the patient is assessed. Those for whom hypnosis seems contraindicated are recommended for psychotherapy.

Each patient treated for obesity is requested to keep a daily diary of all food ingested; from this record the caloric intake is calculated. Unless there are medical reasons to the contrary, each is asked to maintain a total daily caloric intake of no more than 900 calories. It is suggested that daily weights be recorded, and weight is checked independently at each office visit. A full-length photograph is requested at the beginning of treatment so that there will be some objective standard of appearance to which the changing body image can be compared.

Patients are instructed, during the nonhypnotic portion of the session, to walk at least a mile daily to decrease any anxiety associated with dieting. Other forms of daily exercise are substituted if more convenient.

During the hypnotic state a typical patient is told:

"You simply will not be hungry. . . . The limited food intake can and will satisfy your hunger needs. . . . You will eat slowly and enjoy the food you are eating . . . you will eat slowly, masticate your food slowly . . . you will enjoy every mouthful . . . You will have a full feeling in your stomach much sooner than usual . . . and as you are aware of this full feeling in your stomach much sooner than usual . . . You will be relaxed and at ease, free from tension, tightness, stress, and strain, free from excessive hunger. . . . Because of the power of your unconscious mind you will want to lose this weight. . . . You can and you will tolerate this diet with minimal desire for food. . . . You will be proud of every pound you lose and you will perceive yourself as becoming thinner, less obese, and more like you've wanted to be. . . . You will not continue a habit pattern of overeating in which you have been taking certain risks concerning your physical and psychological health . . . you will want to lose weight and you can lose weight. . . . Regardless of circumstances you will maintain your diet without fanfare or resentment . . . you simply will be relaxed and at ease, free from hunger and tension, and tightness. . . . The weight loss will be consistent and permanent."

Women still undergoing menstrual cycles are allowed diuretics for any temporary increase of body weight as a result of fluid retention during the premenstrual portion of their cycle. Weight gain connected with the cycle is defined as acceptable and temporary.

During weight loss all patients reach periodic "plateaus" of weight. The importance of these is minimized by discussing in advance the possibility of such plateaus. When such a hiatus in weight loss is reached, some additional psychotherapeutic intervention may be necessary, since some patients tend to become discouraged and mildly depressed at such times.

In our practice we have seen fewer complications through the hypnotic treatment of obesity than we have noted in the use of hypnosis to increase food intake. This may perhaps be attributable to the more severe medical condition of many patients who require hypnosis to stimulate food ingestion.

The association of overeating and feelings of boredom or neglect is a recurrent case history. The woman who is married to a businessman who travels may console herself with food in his absence. Women married to men whose work is seasonal may overeat at seasons when their husbands are too busy to spend time with the family. For instance, a young woman married to a successful accountant gained weight rapidly during each income tax season when her husband worked long hours day after day. She had not realized the correlation of her weight problem with his work until discussion in hypnotherapy made it obvious. As she gained insight in therapy, she was able to achieve marked weight loss on an apparently permanent basis.

Glover (1961) reported an average weight loss of 30 pounds in 4 months in 27 obese patients treated with a hypnotic technique. In treating this problem, Brodie (1964) suggested that the obese person would become a gourmet, "who eats with good taste in every sense of the word." A similar approach was employed with groups of patients by Mann (1953), whose hypnotic instructions were designed "to convert the craving for large quantities of fattening food to an appreciation of the delight in learning to enjoy subtle flavors of small portions of nonfattening foods."

A more aversive approach was employed by Tilker and Meyer (1972) for a 20-year-old female student. When the paired aversive stimulus (nausea) began to work, she considered quitting treatment but was persuaded to continue when hypnosis was added. She finally lost 18 pounds. It seemed to the therapists that hypnosis added to the

Figure 11-1.   An overweight woman, previously unable to lose weight permanently, is shown at 190 pounds, before hypnotherapy, and at 136 pounds
after 6 months of dieting with hypnosis for appetite suppression.

compulsive nature of the task motivation. The patient herself felt that
she could accept the negative suggestions of nausea if "they would
happen and I did not have to make myself do it."

Hershman (1955) reported good results in three cases of obesity
treated with hypnosis. Wollman (1962) had "noteworthy success" with
450 obese cases. Winkelstein (1959) outlined hypnotic approaches to
weight reduction.

Hanley (1967) reported an average weight loss of 2 to 3 pounds per
week using group hypnosis. Flood (1960) has applied hypnotherapy
successfully in treating unhappy, obese adolescents. Major contributions to the use of clinical hypnotherapy in the treatment of obesity
have been made by Cheek and LeCron (1968), Erickson (1961), Raginsky (1963), Schneck (1963), and Wolberg (1948).

The following five cases, from our own files, are typical of the
many obesity problems we have treated:

A teenage girl who came for obesity told how she was left at home each day between the time her mother went to work and her father, often intoxicated, returned from his work. She felt lonely and insecure. Her mother always said, when leaving, "Be sure and fix some supper for yourself and your father." Fearing that he would come home drunk, she would eat to reduce her anxiety. Soon her problem of obesity became a center of family concern, and she felt interest from her parents where she had previously felt neglected. An additional factor seemed to be her anxiety about beginning to date, her overeating acting as both a reducer of anxiety and as a barrier toward recognition of her attractiveness. When these emotional factors were defined and understood, she responded well to hypnosis and lost weight easily.

A woman in her early fifties had lost her husband to a younger, slimmer woman. At first, in her anger and depression, her weight simply increased. Then, when she learned that her ex-husband had not entirely lost romantic interest in her, she became motivated to diet and came for treatment. Much of the work of therapy was in clarifying the causes that led to the breakup of the marriage and to understanding a hostile dependency game among members of her own family. She was not certain that she was hypnotized, or that treatment would be successful, until one day when she started to go into a doughnut shop and "My hand just didn't want to open the door." With this slight reminder she recalled her resolve to lose weight and turned away from the tempting pastries. She subsequently lost a significant amount of weight, but she did not maintain her lower weight after ending treatment.

Fortunately, negative results such as found in this case do not occur very often. Most patients are proud of and pleased with their weight loss and maintain the new body image, in spite of the frustrations and conflicts of daily living.

A woman in her forties recalled that when she was six years old she had to wear the cast-off clothes of her older sister. Embarrassed, she secretly decided to get fat so that she could not wear the old clothes that embarrassed her. This strategy worked, but overeating became a conditioned habit that she could not break without treatment. As she was able to work out previously unconscious anger toward her parents, her compulsive eating diminished and she was able to achieve her desired weight.

A successful professional man had battled unsuccessfully with an overweight condition for years, although advised by his own physician that his health would be benefited by dieting. He weighed approximately 250 pounds and was 5½ feet in height. He understood many of the causes of his weight problem. As a child, he had been quite poor, sometimes hungry. He had been of small stature and felt inferior in size, as well as being from a minority ethnic group. He had successfully overcome his feelings of inferiority by outstanding success in his professional work, which brought him financial and social success. It was as if he had unconsciously promised himself, "I will never be hungry again." In spite of these understandings, he was unable to lose weight until hypnotherapy seemed to interrupt the compulsive aspects of his behavior. He lost 85 pounds and maintained the lowered weight.

A 32-year-old mother of two teen-age children was referred for a problem of chronic obestiy. She was 5 feet, 3 inches tall and weighed 225 pounds. No medical problem was found by the referring internist. Screening interviews revealed a pleasant, at times comical, person who had "been fat all my life and I have been on every diet ever thought of." She had no signs or symptoms of clinical depression and seemed very sincere and highly motivated for hypno-analysis in the treatment of her obesity.

She was seen once a week, receiving a combination of hypnosis and analytic psychotherapy. This allowed her to ventilate her feelings as well as maintain a chosen diet of 900 calories a day. She lost an average of 10 pounds per month.

Some of her comments concerning her problem were as follows: "As a child whenever I was upset and would cry and run to my mother she would always say for me to dry my tears, that everything would be fine, that I was a good girl. Then she would send me to the ice box for milk and cookies. I remember crying my eyes out the night of the big high school formal. As usual I was without a date, and there I was in my room eating candy and ice cream and consoling myself. Sweets and food were to me like alcohol to a drunk. I used to hide candy bars in the house, vowing I would never eat one of them but knowing that I would." She continued, "Now, whenever my husband and I argue or the kids upset me, I often head straight for the refrigerator just like when I was a kid. Food was my pacifier, my substitute love, my solace."

As treatment continued, she achieved further insight into her eating habit and enjoyed increasing mastery of it. By one year she had lost her goal of 75 pounds and had maintained her new weight 8 months later, at the time of this writing. She was very proud of her new body image, pleased with herself for achieving a goal she had long desired, and was beginning to move more freely in social and family relationships.

One of the most common pleasurable associations of childhood is with food. In adult years, when the stresses of life fall more directly on one's shoulders, often without the comfort of a secure family, it is not surprising that food is frequently a means of reassurance. One adult patient always had grilled pimento cheese sandwiches and chocolate malts when he felt depressed and unloved. These were the daily food his mother had given him as a child to "build up strength" after pneumonia.

Tragically, the adult does not often realize the roots of the craving for food and adds further to his or her self-rejection by critizing his or her inability to control eating. Frequently a slight amount of psycho-

Figure 11-2. An overweight woman, previously unsuccessful at dieting, is shown at 200 pounds, before hypnotherapy, and at 127 pounds after 7 months of dieting assisted by hypnosis for appetite suppression.

therapeutic probing will make the pattern known, and the compulsive aspect of eating may then yield to hypnotic reconditioning of the habit patterns.

The typical case of mild to moderate obesity seems largely a habit disturbance that is amenable to a relatively brief period of treatment. In a series of 350 obese patients treated with hypnotherapy, we have found the average weight loss is 10 pounds per month in good subjects. Eighty percent of the patients treated with hypnotherapy lose their weight permanently. By the time the weight-loss goal has been achieved, our patients have insight into coping with the compulsive eating habit. They are advised and encouraged to use self-hypnosis to reinforce the suggestions. It has been our experience that, in the 20 percent group, those who terminated treatment before weight goals were achieved also failed to attain both emotional and intellectual insight concerning the etiology of their obesity.

INCREASING FOOD INTAKE

Fogelman and Crasilneck (1956) detailed the case of an 8-year-old-boy who had severe spinal poliomyelitis causing quadriplegia. Following more than a year of hospitalization, the youngster weighed 34 pounds and showed severe emaciation and depletion. All efforts to encourage additional food intake had been unsuccessful, whether by family physicians, nurses, or other ward personnel. He might promise to eat certain of his favorite foods, only to refuse when they were actually at hand. He sipped water and ate only bits of hamburgers. Daily caloric intake was only slightly over 300 calories. Gradually his condition became critical.

Hypnotherapy was begun when it became apparent that his course was progressing to an extreme state. Although he was originally negativistic, sullen, shy, and withdrawn, rapport was established. It was suggested that he would not only relish all his regular meals, but would also desire additional feedings. The next day he ate all the food on his regular diet and the following day began to request supplemental feedings to satisfy his hunger. The day after that he consumed over 1200 calories. After his eating pattern had been reconditioned, he was able to consume food without hypnotic reinforcement. He became cooperative and friendly and was eventually discharged from the hospital for extended rehabilitation procedures for the residual limitations of his poliomyelitis.

Induction suggestions for increased food intake are the same as in other patients treated with hypnosis. Specific suggestions include:

Because of the power of the unconscious mind, you can and will accomplish any goal necessary. . . . I give you the strongest of strong suggestions that you will be hungry . . . you will be hungry for meals and if, on the advice of your doctor, supplementary feedings are necessary for your health and recovery. . . . you will also tolerate these well. . . . You will be hungry, you will ingest and digest your food easily . . . food will taste good . . . you will enjoy eating, for you will do all in your power to sustain life . . . you will feel hungry and you will eat to satisfy your hunger. . . . You will be able to tolerate more and more food as prescribed by your physicians . . . food will be a source of comfort in the fact that in eating the food you are getting well . . . you will tolerate the increase in food easily, consistently, until you have reached the desired goal advised by your physicians.''

In increasing food intake with hypnosis it is important to recognize and guard against complications which may occur. Acute overfeeding can lead to sudden gastric dilitation and "food shock." There may be other complications, such as the possibility of irritating an eroded esophageal mucosa in severely burned patients. All treatment with hypnosis should be under the close supervision of the primary physician, who can most correctly assess the relation of increased food intake to other factors in the treatment program.

The results of increasing food intake by hypnosis in 12 patients are presented in Table 11-1.

CHANGING FOOD PATTERNS

With hypnosis it is possible not only to increase or decrease the total daily caloric intake, but also to modify the desire for food in specific therapeutic ways.

It is sometimes medically indicated for a person to restrict their dietary intake in some special way, even though the total caloric measure of food does not require changing. A diabetic diet, for example, may be very important in achieving and maintaining a balanced daily dose of insulin. Persons with reactive hypoglycemia may have to rely almost entirely on dieting to achieve a sense of stability, since any sugar in the diet may trigger an episode of weakness and anxiety; other special dietary needs include salt-restricted diets in congestive heart problems and the avoidance of certain foods to which they have severe allergic reactions.

The usual form of hypnotic suggestion is

You will not crave for food that you should not wish to eat (for example sugar and sweets for diabetics). . . . You will easily remember to avoid these items, and you will find your ability to remain on this diet becoming stronger and more automatic each day . . . you simply will not crave these items of food.''

Specific suggestions have been used to change the food patterns of children who have become fixated on an originally fad diet. One girl, age 3, had eaten only junior foods, refusing all table food, and deigning to take only potato chips in addition to canned foods, but even then only licking the salt from the chips. Examination of the family situation quickly revealed that the problem was a struggle for control between the girl and her mother. The mother demanded that the child eat more appropriate foods, while the girl seemed to enjoy frustrating her mother's wishes, skillfully changing the subject of conversation whenever food was mentioned. Within five hypnotic sessions the child was eating ice cream, tomato soup, and malted milks, and slowly beginning to accept solid table foods. Shibata (1967) has reported five similar cases. Erickson (1943) used hypnosis to remove a conditioned aversion to orange juice.

Table 11-1
Hypnosis and Food Intake in Surgical Diseases

Patient Age Sex (years)	Food Intake	Weight Gain	Dietary Restrictions	Progression of Disease	Pain	Specific Symptons
A.A. 30 M	* Adequate	Adequate	Low residue diet	Acute ulcerative colitis	Abdominal cramps	Diarrhea with colitis
	† Adequate	None	Continued (no change attempted)	Converted to remission, normal bowel movement	Relief of cramps	Relief of diarrhea, normal bowel
C.H.	* 1200 calories per day	No control period	None		Severe pain in burned areas	Severe mental depression and personality changes
C.H. 30 M	† 7600 calories per day	Maintained preinjury weight	None	Burn debridement and graft under hypnosis, repeated change of dressings under hypnosis	Relief of pain	Hypnotherapy alleviated symptoms
F.P. 29 M	* 2400 calories per day	86 lbs	Violent dislike of liver and green salads	Hospital for 5 months with malnutrition, rheumatoid arthritis, and multiple cutaneous abscesses	Pain in cutaneous ulcers	Malnutrition with sequelae
	† 4000 calories per day	104 lbs: gain of 18 lbs in 30 days	Ate liver and green salads with relish	Discharged after 30 days, wounds healed	Relief of pain	Relief of recurrent infection

Patient	Caloric intake	Weight	Diet	Condition	Pain status	Appetite
D.J. 8 M	* 318 calories per day	Malnurished, underweight: weight 34 lbs	Refused all food except hamburgers	Severe spinal polio with quadriplegia	Muscle contractions with pain	Anorexia
	† 1255 calories per day	Gaining weight, true weight not known	Unrestricted diet	No change	Hypnosis not applied	Good appetite
F.V. 31 F	* Inadequate: less than 1400 calories per day	80 lbs	None	Chronic alcoholic, anorexia, and severe pain	Severe abdominal pain and addiction	Pain and anorexia
	Ate well: 3 meals and supplements	130 lbs 1 year later	None	Living and well today, still a chronic alcoholic	Relief of pain, required no drugs	Pain free, excellent appetite
B.W. 25 M	* Food refused: intake poor despite tube feedings, etc.	Progressive decrease to 90 lbs	Refused to eat most foods, even those of his own selection	Apathy, indifference, refusal to cooperate: Failure of skin grafts—poor healing, 19 months morbidity	Constant pain, narcotics required continually	Skin grafts refused to take due to malnutrition
	† Ate with gusto and without discrimination	Progressive gain to 130 lbs in 6 weeks	Nonrestrictive	Cooperative: 3 months after hypnosis wounds healed, "take" of skin grafts—discharged	Free of pain, no nacrotics	"Take" of skin grafts after nutritional defects corrected

* Before hypnosis
† After hypnosis

Table 11-1 (continued)

M.K. 41 F	* Irregular for 20 years, never enjoyed foods	No weight gain in 20 years	On restricted diet for 20 years: no greens, roughage, spices	15–20 watery bowel movements per day for 20 years	Abdominal cramps at irregular intervals	No insight into emotional aspects of chronic diseases
	† Adequate intake with enjoyment of meals	Gained 15 lbs in 8 weeks	No dietary restrictions and no ill effects of ad lib diet	2–4 bowel movements per day for 6 months	Absence of cramps, feeling of well-being	Improved understanding of emotional factors, acceptance of illness
H.T. 28 M	* 1900 calories per day	No control period, too ill to be weighed	No absolute restrictions but no specific cravings		Severe pain due to burns and scar	Fear of death, severe heart disease
	† Peak of 8250	Adequate nutrition: maintained in spite of illness	No restrictions: specific compulsion to eat tuna fish	Burn debridements and grafting under hypnosis: satisfactory and rapid course of convalescence	Relief of all pain, surgery performed without anesthesia	Operation under hypnosis, confidence and will to get well

J.T. 36 M	* Inadequate food intake	20 lbs weight loss	None	Chronic ulcerative colitis in acute exacerbation with hemorrhage, 6 bowel movements per day	Abdominal cramps	Colonic bleeding and diarrhea
	† Overate: had to be restricted in dietary intake	Gained 20 lbs in 3 months	None	Hypnosis as a supplementary form of therapy, converted to remission, 2 bowel movements per day	Relief of abdominal cramps with hypnosis	Relief of symptoms
G.H. 14 F	* Postoperative colectomy, refusal to eat	Weight: 75 lbs	None	Weakness and malnutrition: poor convalescence	None	Severe anorexia
	† Ate everything following hypnosis	Gained 30 lbs, to 115 lbs in 6 months	None	Returned to school and doing well	None	Ate well and regained strength
L.H.	* 1850 calories per day	No control period, too ill to be weighed	None		Severe pain due to burns	None
	† 8200 calories per day	Maintained preinjury weight	None	Burn debridement and graft under hypnosis: satisfactory and rapid course of convalescence	Relief of pain, surgery under hypnosis	None

Modified from Fogelman M., Crasilneck H. "Hypnosis and food intake" *Am Diet Assoc* 32:520, 1956.
* Before hypnosis
† After hypnosis

Table 11-1 (continued)

P.B. 74 M	* Adequate	Adequate	None: large intake of cathartics	Diverticulosis and diverticulitis in exacerbation: bowel fixation, drug dependent, life revolved around bowel movements, constipated 27 years	Persistant abdominal cramps, "belly butterflies"	Constipation
	† Adequate	Adequate	No cathartics	In remission 1 year: no cathartics, regular bowel movements each day, bowel fixation resolved	Relief of symptoms	Normal bowel movements

Modified from Fogelman M., Crasilneck H. "Hypnosis and food intake" *Am Diet Assoc* 32:520, 1956.
* Before hypnosis
† After hypnosis

PAIN AS A FACTOR IN DIET

When pain is associated with eating, inadequate nutrition is frequently seen. When it does occur, persistent pain saps the will of the patient, may predispose him or her to addiction to narcotic drugs, and may exasperate attempts to treat inadequate nutrition.

A woman in her early thirties previously hospitalized for narcotic addiction was rehospitalized within a few years for alcoholism and a history of abdominal pain and frequent bloody stools. She was found to have acute ulcerative colitis, which required colectomy. After surgery she made frequent demands for narcotics, and her body weight fell to below 100 pounds. Her surgeon deemed it of utmost importance that her regressive physical and psychological status be altered and requested us to attempt hypnosis. Under hypnosis she was told that she would feel little pain and that she would comfortably consume whatever meals or supplementary feedings were suggested by her physicians. In the posthypnotic state her pain markedly diminished and no further analgesic drugs were given during hospitalization. Hypnosis was periodically reinstated to enhance the suggestions for food intake. She was discharged free from pain and gaining weight.

Hypnosis for relief of pain in nutritional deficiency must be undertaken judiciously, with full concurrence of the primary physician, for fear of masking signs and symptoms of serious organic dysfunction. When used with such caution, however, it is a powerful and relatively safe treatment modality in many cases of severe pain.

HYPEREMESIS

The excessive and prolonged vomiting sometimes associated with pregnancy (hyperemesis gravidarum) may have either organic or psychological causes. If persisting past the first trimester of pregnancy, the possibility of its representing a psychophysiological disorder is increased. Although sometimes responding poorly to pharmacological treatment, hyperemesis can reach such proportions that it can upset the acid–base balance of the mother's body and threaten the viability of the fetus.

Such cases often present an emergency situation. Rapid hypnotic induction is indicated. The patient is placed in a moderately deep trance. To dramatically demonstrate how the mind can influence the body, anesthesia is induced in one finger. Then, with the patient's eyes open, the fingertip is stimulated with a dull nail file to prove anesthesia to the patient. The anesthesia is then removed and the finger again pricked, the patient feeling pain. Suggestions are then given that the mind can also control the body so as to limit or remove the excessive vomiting.

The nausea and the vomiting will simply discontinue . . . You can and will digest foods easily without fear or excessive tensions or anxieties . . . You simply will be relaxed and at ease; your mind and your body relaxed . . . You can and will ingest and digest foods easily, with little or no nausea or discomfort.

Such suggestions need to be reinforced two or even three times a day for the first several days until symptoms are under control. Hypnosis may then be spaced at two times a week or less, gradually decreasing in frequency as the symptoms are brought under post-hypnotic control. The patient is taught self-hypnosis as rapidly as possible to enhance reinforcement.

As in other emergency cases, the hypnotic treatment of hyperemesis may have to be undertaken before a complete exploration of psychodynamics is possible. After the symptom is controlled, unconscious meanings can be more thoroughly investigated. In some cases, of course, no psychodynamic meaning for the vomiting can be found. In our experience there is no higher incidence of complications, such as anxiety, in these cases treated hypnotically with symptom suppression than in those for which a dynamic meaning can be delineated. Most likely, there are both organic and psychological causes for hyperemesis, each case representing an admixture of both etiologies.

ANOREXIA AND BULIMIA

The clinical syndrome "anorexia nervosa" usually occurs in young women and is one of the strangest and most life threatening of psychiatric problems. Apparently in good physical health, the patient refuses to eat or eats only token amounts, gradually wasting in strength as weight is lost. In severe cases the patient may actually die of this disorder.

Bulimia is a compulsive habit of inducing vomiting after food intake. Although it may occur as an attempt at weight loss, or as a fad among young persons, it may also constitute a serious complication of the anorexic syndrome. Bulimia may also occur as a clinical syndrome in its own right. While hypnotherapy is a useful treatment choice with bulimia or anorexia, in our experience these persons require careful and often extended hypnotherapy. Thakur (1982, 1983) reports an improvement rate of 75 percent in these disorders, using hypnotherapy together with gestalt principles and paradoxical interventions. Gross

(1984) has used hypnosis successfully in treating 50 patients suffering from anorexia nervosa.

We seldom recommend direct symptom removal as the initial approach in bulimics because marked psychodynamic factors are often evident, including repressed anger, hostile or dependent manipulation of the family members, and unconscious avoidance of sexuality or pregnancy. At a deeper level the meaning of both anorexia and bulimia may be to symbolically remove from the body (as an image of the personality) a feared internal introject of a hostile parental image. We have found our best results occur when the hypnoanalytic approach is fatherly and supportive. Even with ordinary pressure for insight and understanding, the patient may leave treatment or intensify the symptoms of anorexia or bulimia. However, the recognition of life-threatening factors that may lead to death is occasionally the turning point in this disease.

Psychoanalytic speculation about the causes of anorexia nervosa has centered on a sexualized meaning that became associated with food intake. One rather mild case began in a high school girl after a girl friend became pregnant. She noticed people watching the girl friend's abdomen as the pregnancy became more and more apparent. The patient became concerned that she, too, would mistakenly be thought pregnant since she was slightly overweight. To counter this fear, she began to eat less and less, losing to a point that caused anemia and fatigue.

In spite of advice from her family physician that she must increase her food intake, the patient continued to lose weight. When it was obvious that her weight was dangerously low, we were called to see the patient with the hope that hypnotherapy might counter the negative attitude towards food intake.

After we established rapport, hypnosis was accepted by the patient and she was able to enter a deep trance. She was then told, "You will be hungry. Food will taste good, and your body weight will be necessary for your own good health and welfare." The patient began increasing her caloric intake, starting with her next meal. Her body weight, although on the slim side, came into the normal range for her height. She was encouraged continually to verbalize her many feelings of shame, sorrow, and hostility concerning her girl friend's pregnancy. She was also quite aware of strong libidinous drives within herself, which had caused much guilt. When she was able to express the affect concerning her conflicts, the obsessive thoughts concerning food intake resolved themselves. One year later, although no longer in treatment, she was a slim attractive young lady who could accept the actions of others without introjecting their feelings. She understood that libidinous drives are normal in adults and that they should not lead to feelings of guilt, shame, and masochistic acts.

More esoteric theorists have suggested that severe cases of anorexia nervosa may reflect an imbalance of the force of the "life instinct" and "death instinct." The so-called "death instinct" was a late conceptualization by Freud, and not all psychoanalysts followed him in this direction of thought. Among those who accepted and elaborated Freud's thinking were the famous American psychiatrist Karl Menninger and the British analyst Melanie Klein, who influenced not only the English school of Freudian psychoanalysis, but also the British Jungians, of whom Michael Fordham, a child analyst, is perhaps the best-known writer.

Without wishing to take a definitive position on the concept of death instinct, we have seen some cases that strongly suggest such an idea. Such a situation occurred with a young woman in her early twenties who had progressively lost weight for a period of several months. No organic cause had been found despite thorough searching by competent internists. She was not maintaining even her diminished body weight, and tube feedings had not reversed the negative nitrogen balance. As nearly as could be determined, her anorexia began at a time when she took a job as the only woman in an office with more than a dozen men. Although there had been no overt sexual approaches, she had felt conspicuous in this situation. Otherwise, her past life had been uneventful, anamnesis revealing only some suggestion of overdependence on her mother and some possible fantasies concerning her father. She had dated a normal amount but had remained a virgin.

Hypnosis was requested in an effort to reverse her weight loss since her condition became critical. She was a good hypnotic subject, entering a deep trance on the first induction. The next day there was marked response. She ate virtually all of the food offered in her first two meals. When she was seen in the evening, however, her attitude had changed. She seemed to have sensed that she was giving up her symptom and resisted. Further attempts at induction were unsuccessful. Despite continued medical care, she continued to lose weight and, in a few days, was found dead in her bed. No clear cause for her death was found on autopsy.

This fatal case of anorexia nervosa, though rare in our experience, is one of those that suggests that the concept of death instinct may be applicable. While obviously deteriorating throughout her hospitalization, the patient showed no sign of anxiety about her condition. Perhaps extended psychoanalytic or hypnoanalytic therapy might have reversed events, but there was insufficient time for this to be instituted, for hypnosis was requested only when the patient was already in physical difficulty.

Most cases of anorexia nervosa have a more favorable outcome. Somewhat more than half of those 70 cases we have treated with hypnosis have shown marked improvement. Because of the debilitated state of most patients referred for treatment, direct suggestion for increased food intake is given. Once the patient has begun to eat and the medical situation is stabilized, exploration of psychodynamics is begun, using either hypoanalytic techniques or more conventional treatments. It is important that such treatment always be included. It is not enough to simply remove the symptom without making some attempt at diminishing the unconscious psychodynamics that precipitated the condition.

Not all cases of anorexia nervosa follow the general pattern of an unconscious connection between food intake and sexual impulses "forbidden" by the patient's conscience, usually based on an over rigid and primitive superego structure. At times anorexia seems to be the expression of a "giving up." Perhaps in rare cases it represents an activated death instinct.

A man in his early fifties had undergone four surgical procedures in five months for recurrent gastric bleeding. A few weeks after the last operation, he was readmitted with a history of becoming withdrawn and gradually lapsing into a stuporous state, with marked nausea and vomiting. He was examined by both an internist and a neurologist, and a tentative diagnosis of diffuse encephalopathy was suggested. Intravenous fluids gradually improved that state of consciousness, but the patient was unable to retain food, became increasingly antagonistic and belligerent, and absolutely refused to eat. A psychiatric consultant saw the patient daily for 2 weeks without notable effect. The man's weight had dropped to 75 pounds, and his state was considered critical. At this point hypnosis was considered as an emergency measure.

When first offered hypnotherapy, the patient shook his head in a negative fashion and whispered "I just want to die." He was asked to close his eyes and hypnotic induction was begun. In approximately 10 minutes the patient was in a deep state of somnambulism and was given the posthypnotic suggestion that he could ingest and digest the foods prescribed by his physician, that he would be relaxed and at ease most of the time and experience a strong desire to live.

He was seen twice the first day and on the second day successfully ate and retained all three meals. On the third day, though still weak, he smiled and said, "By golly, I'm not very hungry, but I must eat the food when they bring it in and it's beginning to taste better." By the fourth day he was sitting up in bed and spontaneously remarked, "I think I'm going to make it—all of a sudden I want to live." On the fifth day the patient was not only eating three meals a day, but also requested supplementary feedings during the afternoon. Hypnotherapy continued daily during the second week. It was discontinued at the end of the third week. Even though hypnosis was discontinued, the only change noted in the fourth week was a decrease in food intake to normal amounts. At that time the patient was discharged to continue in outpatient psychotherapy, and he was taught to use self-hypnosis.

He was seen weekly for 1 year for intensive treatment, at no time manifesting a recurrence of the anorexia. In discussing the hospitalization he said, "I just wanted to die." After hypnosis had been begun in the hospital, he said he "just made up my mind to live." The hypnotic suggestions had apparently quickly been taken over by his ego in a syntonic manner, being given the same status as his own conscious desires. This did not seem to result, as far as we were aware, in any unusual transference problem during the ensuing psychotherapy, in which he worked through a number of neurotic conflicts, including his severe depression.

Daves (1961) in treating a 12-year-old girl who had anorexia nervosa started by using hypnosis, but in this case electroconvulsive therapy was finally employed. One of the best scientific reviews of food-intake psychology is *Eating Disorders* by Bruch (1973).

DANGERS IN MODIFICATION OF FOOD INTAKE WITH HYPNOSIS

When used under the supervision of a competent physician as part of an overall treatment plan, hypnosis is as safe, in our opinion, as any other potent medical treatment for modification of food intake. It is important that adequate consideration be given to possible side effects. A psychologist or psychiatrist can best evaluate emotional complications that might arise from hypnosis and can assess the possible benefits of treatment as compared to any potential dangers. However, the questions of physical side effects of treatment are best evaluated by the physician in charge. This is particularly crucial when severely ill patients are treated. For example, although increased food intake can be induced with hypnosis in a severely burned patient, care might be necessary if the esophagus were also burned, since the food intake could irritate the burned mucosa and could induce bleeding. Forced food intake also might be contraindicated, for instance, if there is any suspicion of perforation of the stomach or gastrointestinal tract.

SUMMARY

The modification of food intake by hypnotherapy is a dramatic therapeutic tool in many cases. When increasing food intake enhances the survival chances of a critical patient, hypnosis may be a treatment of choice. When excessive weight burdens the cardiac, circulatory, or other vital systems, hypnosis should be considered. Modification of body image and appetite by hypnotherapy can be physically and psychologically beneficial.

REFERENCES

Brodie EI: A hypnotherapeutic approach to obesity. Am J Clin Hypn 6:211–215, 1964

Bruch H: Obesity, Anorexia Nervosa, and the Person Within. New York, Basic Books, 1973

Cheek DB, LeCron LM: Clinical Hypnotherapy. New York, Grune & Stratton, 1968

Cohen SB: Hypnosis for obesity. Am J Clin Hypn 22:1–2, 1979

Crasilneck HB, Hall JA: The use of hypnosis in controlling cigarette smoking. South Med J 61:999–1002, 1968

Crasilneck HB, Hall JA: Clinical hypnosis: Applications in smoking and obesity problems. Dallas Med J 62:296–302, 1976

Daves HK: Anorexia nervosa. Dis Nerv Syst 22:627–631, 196!

Deyoub PL, Wilkie R: Suggestion with and without hypnotic induction in a weight reduction program. Int J Clin Exp Hypn 28:333–340, 1980

Erickson MH: Hypnotic investigation of psychosomatic phenomena. III. A controlled experimental use of hypnotic regression in the therapy of an acquired food intolerance. Psychosom Med 5:67–70, 1943

Erickson MH: The Practical Application of Medical and Dental Hypnosis. New York, Julian, 1961, p 470

Flood AO: Slimming under hypnotism: The obese adolescent. Med World (London) 93:310–312, 1960

Fogelman MJ, Crasilneck HB: Food intake and hypnosis. J Am Diet Assoc 32:519–523, 1956

Glover FS: Use of hypnosis for weight reduction in a group of nurses. Am J Clin Hypn 3:250–251, 1961

Goldstein Y: The effect of demonstrating to a subject that she is in a hypnotic trance as a variable in hypnotic interventions with obese women. Int J Clin Exp Hypn 29:15–23, 1981

Gross M: Hypnosis in the therapy of anorexia nervosa. Am J Clin Hypn 26:175–181, 1984

Halpern S: (Panelist) Body image phenomena during hypnointrospection: An illustrated case history. Presented at the International Congress of the Israel Society of Hypnosis in Psychotherapy and Psychosomatic Medicine in collaboration with the European Society of Hypnosis in Psychotherapy and Psychosomatic Medicine, Haifa, Israel, 1983

Hanley FW: The treatment of obesity by individual and group hypnosis. Can Psychiatr Assoc J 12:549–551, 1967

Hershman S: Hypnosis in the treatment of obesity. J Clin Exp Hypn 3:136–139, 1955

Kroger WS: Clinical and Experimental Hypnosis (ed 2) Philadelphia, J.B. Lippincott, 1977, pp 202, 206

Mann H: Group hypnosis in the treatment of obesity. Am J Clin Hypn 1:114–116, 1953

Mann H: Hypnosis in weight control, in Wain HJ (ed): Theoretical and Clinical Aspects of Hypnosis. Miami, Symposia Specialists, Inc., 1981, pp 135–140

Mayer J: Empty calories don't count. Mod Med 41:44–46, 1973

Mott T Jr, Roberts J: Obesity and hypnosis: A review of the literature. Am J Clin Hypn 22:3–7, 1979

Nuland W: Hypnosis and weight control. Presentation at annual meeting of the Society of Clinical Experimental Hypnosis, Montreal, 1974

Raginsky BB: Hypnosis in internal medicine and general practice, in Schneck JM (ed): Hypnosis in Modern Medicine. Springfield, Ill., Charles C Thomas, 1963

Ringrose CAD: The use of hypnology as an adjunct in curbing smoking, obesity and hypertention, in Burrows GD, Dennerstein L (eds): Handbook of Hypnosis and Psychosomatic Medicine. Amsterdam, Elsevier/North-Holland Biomedical Press, 1979, pp 223–238

Schneck JM: (ed): Hypnosis in Modern Medicine (ed 3). Springfield, Ill., Charles C Thomas, 1963

Shibata JI: Hypnotherapy of patients taking unbalanced diets. Am J Clin Hypn 10:81–83, 1967

Spiegel H, Spiegel DR: Trance and Treatment: Clinical Uses of Hypnosis. New York, Basic Books, 1978, pp 220–228

Stanton HE: Weight loss through hypnosis. Am J Clin Hypn 18:94–97, 1975

Thakur KS: Hypnotherapy for bulimia. Unpublished paper, 1982

Thakur KS: Hypnotherapy for anorexia nervosa and accompanying somatic disorder, in Wester C, Smith AH: Clinical Hypnosis: A Multidisciplinary Approach. Philadelphia, J.B. Lippincott, 1983, pp 476–493

Tilker HA, Meyer RG: The use of covert sensitization and hypnotic procedures in the treatment of an overweight person: A case report. Am J Clin Hypn 15:15–19, 1972

Winkelstein LB: Hypnosis, diet, and weight reduction. NY State J Med 59:1751–1756, 1959

Wolberg L: Medical Hypnosis, vol. I, The Principles of Hypnotherapy. New York, Grune & Stratton, 1948

Wollman L: Hypnosis and weight control. Am J Clin Hypn 4:177–180, 1962

12

Hypnosis in the
Control of Smoking

Although tobacco smoking has a long cultural history, the drug nicotine was isolated only in 1828. It is an extremely toxic drug that acts virtually as fast as cyanide. One ordinary cigar may contain two lethal doses (Goodman and Gilman, 1956).

In recent years a vast change has occurred in public attitudes toward smoking. In a series of governmental publications the hazards of the smoking habit have been outlined, and various laws have been enacted to discourage consumption of cigarettes. In 1966 the Public Health Service published statistics on mortality from various diseases associated with smoking. Cigarette packages must now carry the mandatory warning *The Surgeon General Has Determined That Cigarette Smoking Is Dangerous to Your Health.*

In spite of this revolution in public opinion and official governmental policy, it has proven extremely difficult for many persons to stop smoking, even when they are found to be suffering from severe medical illness, such as emphysema, which is directly aggravated by cigarette smoke. There have been many more warnings about the dangers of smoking than there have been ways to stop the habit. In fact when Ford and Ederer (1965) reviewed the techniques for breaking the cigarette habit, they were extremely pessimistic about results of treatment. Their review did not include hypnosis, however, in spite of several reports previously having been published about the utility of hypnosis with problem smokers, notably by Athanasou (1974), Bernstein (1969), Kroger (1963), Miller (1965), Moses (1964), Stein (1964),

Templer (1969), von Dedenroth (1964, 1968), and Wollman (1969). Cohen (1969) also reviewed the literature on hypnosis and smoking for JAMA, once more with a pessimistic air. Even the Department of Health, Education, and Welfare in its *1972 Directory of On-going Research in Smoking and Health* mentioned only one study using hypnosis, though many others had been published, notably the one by Johnston and Donoghue (1971).

HYPNOSIS AS AN EFFECTIVE TREATMENT

The most comprehensive collection of articles on the use of hypnosis in the treatment of the cigarette habit was published in Volume 18 of the *International Journal of Clinical and Experimental Hypnosis* (October 1970). The eight articles and discussions published in that issue won the society's award for the best clinical contributions of the year.

Holroyd (1980) has published a prize-winning evaluative review of hypnosis for the treatment of smoking. In addition to participation in the October 1970 issue of the SCEH Journal, we have reported elsewhere on the effectiveness of hypnosis in the control of smoking addiction (Crasilneck and Hall, 1976). Many others have testified to the usefulness of hypnotherapy in the problem of psychological addiction to tobacco, which causes and aggravates so many medical problems (Bowers, 1976; Chiasson, 1982; Jeffrey, Gentry and Greuling, 1982; Klauber, 1982; Moore, 1982; Ringrose, 1980).

Spiegel, (1970) reported on his single-treatment method to stop smoking. The single session was 45 minutes. It was found that at least one of every five smokers could be helped. Dengrove (1970), in discussing Spiegel's paper, emphasized how behavioral modification techniques might be applied to the smoking problem. Nuland (1970), also discussing the Spiegel paper, stressed that most of those who resumed smoking did so soon after the treatment, 90 of 121 in the first month.

In the same discussion Wright (1970) presented an interesting analysis of the "mythology" that supports the smoking habit:

1. The tension-release function.
2. The social facilitation function (especially when meeting strangers).
3. Pleasure-association functions (including the visual pleasure of watching smoke curling upward).
4. The synthetically enhanced social role (which may rely partially on

"additives that improve taste and combustibility and contribute to the intoxicant effect").

Wright points out the paradoxical way in which a strongly health-oriented society seemed to repress so much of what it knew about the health problems associated with smoking.

It is important to understand a patient's specific psychodynamic reasons for smoking. Although many patients have what we have called an "empty habit, " that is, one which had an original psychodynamic meaning but has now become a mere habit or deeply ingrained pattern, no longer serving the original purpose. Ewin (1977) offers a particularly useful grouping of explanations about why people are motivated to smoke in spite of conscious knowledge that it is undermining their health and statistically decreasing their lifespan. Ewin cites iatrogenic reasons, self-destructive tendencies, sexual sublimation, peer pressure, defiance, and visualization of the "breath of life" as unconscious motives for smoking. The iatrogenic "physician-induced" causes are of this form: the patient may have had coronary or other serious disease and had considered to stop smoking, only to be told by his or her physician that "stopping might be too hard," coupled with a suggestion that he or she merely "cut down on smoking." This well-meaning suggestion, Ewin notes, may be unconsciously interpreted as "if you stop smoking you will have too much stress and might die," an unconscious linkage of smoking to life. A similar unconscious linkage occurs when the smoker has had a past experience, perhaps of near-drowning, in which there was great relief when he or she was finally able to draw breath. Such a traumatic event places a strong premium on reassurance that one can breathe; reassurance is unconsciously provided (by smoking) because the breath is visualized with cigarette smoke. Other unconscious motives according to Ewin are hidden self-destructive wishes, peer pressure to smoke, and continuing unconscious defiance of a parental injunction not to smoke cigarettes. There may also be hidden sexual gratification connected with the original oral stage (nursing) of psychosexual development.

Prior to the induction of hypnosis, Watkins (1976) discusses with patients their "excuses" for smoking. Among these he lists smoking as an excuse for a break from work tasks, socialization, a pacifier for troublesome emotions, and keeping the hands and mouth busy. To replace these unconscious excuses, he suggests positive substitutions of the right to take a break without smoking, learning to socialize and listen to someone without a cigarette, having conscious emotional control, and finding substitute habits (such as gentle rubbing of the fingers) to substitute for the motor habits of smoking. Watkins also suggests concentration on some aversive images, such as panting when exercising, or a physician saying essentially "I told you so" when finding serious medical problems associated with smoking. In general, our own approach minimizes such aversive images.

Nuland and Field (1970) found an improvement rate of 60 percent in treating smokers with hypnosis. The increased effectiveness was achieved by a more personalized approach, including feedback, under hypnosis, of the patient's own personal reasons for quitting. These researchers also employed a technique of having the patient maintain contact by telephone between treatments and utilized self-hypnosis in addition.

TECHNIQUE

Our own contribution to this symposium (Hall and Crasilneck, 1970) reviewed our work originally published in the *Southern Medical Journal* (Crasilneck and Hall, 1968). Our particular technique had developed over a number of years. We had worked toward finding a way in which hypnosis could be used as a means of controlling the habit of cigarette smoking without excessive frustration or craving for tobacco, without substituting some other severe habits, and with an efficiency of treatment such that cost would not be excessive and time would not be a limiting factor in the number of people who could be treated.

Our results were based on a series of 75 consecutively treated adult male cigarette smokers, most of whom had been referred by physicians because their cigarette smoking was complicating some medical problem. Diagnosis included coronary artery disease, chronic bronchitis, asthma, and Buerger's disease, although the most frequent medical problem was emphysema.

Our technique, based on trials of various formats over a period of years, consisted of a screening interview for each patient, during which the personality structure is investigated. A determination was made over whether the use of tobacco was serving a major neurotic need. Those persons who were found to have extremely severe depression and those who had psychotic problems, especially if they were of a paranoid nature, were usually excluded. During the screening we answered any questions that the patient had about the nature of hypnosis. An attempt was made to minimize any unrealistic anxieties concerning trance induction. All patients were told that they could later be seen for psychotherapy should there be other problems besides smoking. Every attempt was made to encourage the patient to feel free to communicate any discomfort or disturbance,either during the time of treatment or afterward. We feel that this greatly decreased the danger of significant substitute symptoms. An interesting finding from an additional series of 75 smokers was that 93 percent of those interviewed for hypnotherapy of the smoking habit had a parent or parents who smoked.

Following the screening interview, patients were then seen for four hypnotic sessions. Generally, the depth of hypnosis gradually increased with the repeated inductions, even though depth of trance does not necessarily correlate with effectiveness of treatment, as we previously stressed.

Before specific suggestions are given for smoking cessation, the patient is given two tests that show convincingly that a hypnotic state has been achieved. We routinely use glove anesthesia and the testing of fingers (thumped with a blunt nail file) and arm catalepsy. The importance of these two exacting tests is: "If you have the unconscious power to block pain, you can reduce your craving for cigarettes. If you have super strength in your arm, you can exert the same strength in giving up a habit that is threatening life." The specific suggestions that are then given are of the general form:

"You will not crave excessively for a habit negatively affecting your health. . . . Your mind can block the perception of discomfort, as when your finger felt insensitive to the pressure of the sharp nail file. . . . Your mind will function in such a manner that you will no longer crave for a habit that has negatively affected your life with every drag of cigarette smoke you have taken into your lungs. . . . You will block the craving for tobacco . . . a habit that is causing your heart and your lungs to work much harder than necessary, forcing your lungs to labor beyond all necessity, stressing and straining these vital organs . . . like a car constantly driven in low gear . . . constantly laboring uphill . . . stressing and straining the motor. . . . But because of the great control of your unconscious mind, the craving for this vicious and lethal habit will grow steadily and markedly less until it rapidly reaches a permanent zero level. . . . You simply will not crave for cigarettes again. . . . You will be relaxed and at ease, pleased that you are giving up a habit which has such a negative effect upon your life and well-being. . . . You are improving your life by giving up cigarettes and you will continue to do so. . . . You will not smoke cigarettes again. . . . You will not be hungry or eat excessively . . . your craving will reach a permanent zero level . . . through the virtually omnipotent and godlike power of your unconscious mind, you can and you will be able to resist a craving that is harmful to your body . . . you will treat your body with kindness and consideration . . . your body that serves you so unselfishly . . . you will no longer consciously or unconsciously choose to impose this undeserved burden of smoking on your heart, your lungs, your circulation, and the vital organs of your body . . . you will treat your body with kindness, as if it were your closest friend . . . you will find that through the immense power of your unconscious mind you will be able to overcome this old, outgrown, outworn addiction, which we now know, statistically, robs you of 4 minutes of life with every cigarette you smoke. . . . You will be able to give up this dirty and unhealthy habit. . . . As you permit your body to rid itself of this undeserved burden of smoking, your lungs will again become efficient, your red blood cells will carry more oxygen to all your vital organs, you will feel more alert and alive . . . and you will have a justifiable sense of pride for having worked toward and accomplished this important, healthy, worthwhile goal. . . . You are no longer a smoker, you are using your own free will, you are treating yourself in a healthy, proper manner. . . . You will not be excessively nervous or tense . . . you will not gain excessive weight . . . you will exercise, you will walk a mile a day, if your physician approves . . . you will sleep well . . . your craving for tobacco will be minimal and will rapidly decline to a zero level at a rapid pace. . . ."

The statements about absence of craving or declining of craving may appear contradictory; the important point is to recognize and acknowledge that *some* subjects may have a sense of continual "craving," which does not necessarily mean that the hypnotic suggestion is ineffective. It is important that the subject realize the impact of hypnosis in spite of some continued desire for tobacco. Careful attention to subtle meanings of the suggestions increases the impact on many patients. As they move toward abstinence from tobacco, the suggestions may be worded more forcefully toward absence of craving.

After each use of hypnosis the patient is encouraged to discuss unusual dreams, thoughts, or feelings that he or she might have experienced.

The first three hypnotic sessions are given on consecutive days. Between the third session and the fourth, which is scheduled 1 month later, the patient is instructed to call the office daily for the first week, twice the second week, and then once a week until the fourth induction of hypnosis. In some cases, where reinforcement is deemed very important, the patient is asked to call daily for the entire month. The patient is told that each call reinforces the posthypnotic suggestion and increases his or her resistance to smoking. This telephone report is customarily given to the secretary, though we at times talk to the patient directly when there is some unusual difficulty. We request that each patient walk at least 1 mile each day as a means of decreasing tension and improving pulmonary ventilation. If the patient wishes, other forms of exercise might be substituted. We routinely suggest holding a cinnamon stick as they would a cigarette for those patients who need a substitute, and the patient occasionally will put the cinnamon stick in their mouth. This need usually diminishes by the fourth session. Each patient returns 1 month from the third induction for his or her last hypnotic session.

Other Techniques

Many variations of hypnotherapy techniques have been suggested to help in the treatment of habitual smoking (Shewchuk et al., 1977). Collison (1980) administers a questionnaire with several paper-and-pencil tests to patients before treatment, producing a self-review of the smoking habit and its meaning and cost. Flooding techniques are used by some (Powell, 1980). Group hypnotic sessions produced an 84 percent success rate by the fourth session, with 68 percent remaining free of the smoking habit 10 months later, according to Sanders (1977). A technique of having patients rapidly smoke many cigarettes has been reported by some (Barkley, Hastings, and Jackson, 1977), who also found a group approach less effective than individual treatments, although only marginally less effective than the group rapid smoking procedure.

There is continuing interest in techniques that involve a single hypnotic session in the treatment of smoking, although we continue to prefer a multisession approach, which we find produces a higher rate of success. Grosz (1983) reported an 18-month follow-up on 506 smokers treated with a single session of hypnosis; 27.2 percent were free of smoking 18 months after the treatment concluded. The relapse rate seemed higher in smokers who initially reported more pleasure in smoking. A 25 percent abstinence rate after 6 months was reported after a one-session hypnotic treatment by Berkowitz, Ross-Townsend, and Kohlberger (1979). In a similar follow-up at 6 months, Stanton (1978) found that 45 percent remained non-smokers.

Gaston and Hutzell (1976) report hypnosis to reduce smoking in a deaf patient; induction was achieved through lip-reading. MacHovec and Man (1978) compared hypnosis and acupuncture, finding hypnosis more effective. Spiegel and Spiegel (1978) strongly suggest self-hypnosis as an aid to the treatment of smoking with hypnosis.

Results

Although results initially seemed good by clinical impression, we sent a questionnaire to the 75 patients to determine if improvement endured. All persons receiving the questionnaire had gone at least 1 year beyond their last visit, although the range between the last hypnotic session and the time of sampling varied between 1 and 4 years, with a mean of 26 months. In addition to the structured questionnaire, spontaneous comments were solicited; anonymity was suggested if it would permit the respondent to be more frank.

Of the 75 questionnaires sent, 67 were returned, an 89-percent response rate. Of those responding, 82 percent had not smoked cigarettes at all since the fourth reinforcement session. Of these, 78 percent had not substituted any other "oral" habit. Of those who had substituted, however, no substitute habit seemed as serious as the previous habit of cigarettes. Several who substituted indicated that they now smoked cigars or a pipe or had begun to chew gum regularly. The cigar smokers uniformly claimed not to inhale smoke.

Of the total group, 64 percent were no longer smoking nor substituting any other oral habit. Some 18 percent, however, had continued smoking at the pretreatment rate. The remaining 18 percent were not smoking cigarettes; they had substituted another oral habit, usually as innocuous as those mentioned.

Before treatment these men had smoked cigarettes for a mean period of 27 years, with an average consumption of two packs per day. Over 90 percent had made major previous efforts to stop smoking, but their average length of abstinence before treatment was only 1 week. Of those who successfully discontinued smoking, only 3 percent felt that they still had a definite craving for tobacco, although 14 percent had an occasional desire; 83 percent felt that they had no further desire for tobacco.

Since many patients had feared that giving up smoking would lead to overeating and weight gain, it was encouraging to find that the average weight gain had been only 4 pounds. This may have been the result of including an explanation in the waking state that when smoking was stopped, food would begin to taste better. The patients were cautioned that this improved taste might tempt them to eat more. Instead, it was proposed that in both the hypnotic and the waking states they eat the same amount of food as before but enjoy more thoroughly the improved taste.

Those who had resumed smoking and were considered treatment failures had usually gone back to cigarettes following some traumatic incident involving frustration or anger. None reported that they later had quit smoking once they had spontaneously resumed the habit.

None of the questionnaires indicated any psychological disturbance, in either the structured questions or the free-response comments. Most comments were of appreciation, were void of hostility, and seemed to emphasize a sense of pride and self-esteem at having accomplished a worthwhile goal.

Cigarette smoking usually begins as a seemingly innocuous habit, often as a way of attempting to look more adult or to conform to peer models of behavior. It may soon become a strongly fixed habit, so fixed that some smokers may even have anxiety—the so-called "nicotine fit"—when they desire to smoke but are without cigarettes. The habituation may progress to the point that the person seems unable to refrain from smoking even when it constitutes a clear and obvious threat to health.

This strong habituation seen in some cases has added fuel to the fears of those who anticipate that hypnotic removal of smoking may lead to other, more serious substitutions. The occurrence of substitute symptoms of greater severity, however, seems rare. Most reports of such cases in the literature are isolated, though sometimes dramatic, examples; they most often occur in distinctly neurotic individuals. Also, there has been no distinction in most instances between an old-style authoritarian symptom removal and the techniques just detailed in which the symptom is gently suppressed by persuasive, permissive suggestions that are designed to be ego-syntonic. Numerous writers have reviewed and questioned the occurrence and severity of substitute symptoms. Among them have been Crasilneck (1958, 1982), and Crasilneck and Hall (1968), Erickson et al. (1961), Raginsky (1963), and Wolberg (1948).

Pederson, Scrimgeour, and Lefcoe (1979) found that counseling, in addition to hypnotherapy, added to their successes. Perry and Mullen (1975) documented that highly susceptible hypnotic subjects did better than less susceptible ones by at least 50 percent more improvement. Shewchuk et al. (1977) noted that younger, more educated smokers were more likely to choose hypnosis as a preferred method of treatment. Berlin (1980) noted that the Harvard Group Scale of Hypnotic Susceptibility could predict, with some accuracy, who would stop smoking, whether or not suggestions for smoking abstinence were given in a hypnotic or waking state; they suggest that the scale measures a factor of willingness to accept positive and useful suggestions.

Typical Case History

Typical of many of the patients whom we have seen for smoking was a man in his early forties. He came for hypnotherapy only at the suggestion of his internist. He had been smoking about two packs a day since his late teens and had no history of abstinence, except on rare occasions when he was in bed with flu or immediately after a minor surgical procedure. He had experienced no severe health problems, though he had begun to notice a morning cough and some shortness of breath on those occasions when he exercised strenuously. He did not seriously worry about his smoking, feeling that he could quit any time it became necessary. His father had smoked until the age of 72 and had died of unrelated causes. His mother had never used tobacco.

He had visited his internist only at his wife's repeated requests and was somewhat surprised that his examination revealed that his vitalometry showed a decreased vital capacity, although he did not clearly know the meaning of this finding. He knew that emphysema might be worsened by smoking but did not realize the serious and progressive implications of the disease, having never known anyone personally who had a severe form of the illness.

At his initial screening he was found to be emotionally stable, well motivated in his work, with a good family and social adjustment. His smoking seemed habitual, not the expression of a neurotic conflict. He had no fears of hypnosis, although he doubted that he would be hypnotizable.

On the first induction he reached light trance, which deepened considerably on the second induction the next day. He still felt some slight craving for tobacco, but he did not smoke. He wondered if he had been "really" hypnotized, since he had always mistakenly thought of hypnosis as being "put to sleep" like anesthesia instead of a cooperative learning experience.

He conscientiously exercised by walking a mile each day as suggested and increased his fluid intake and chewed sugar-free gum when he felt the need for some activity to replace the smoking. On the third visit he no longer craved for cigarettes, reported sleeping much better at night, and felt quite confident that he was through smoking. He already had pride in his accomplishment. He was asked to call the office daily to give the secretary a progress report, thereby reinforcing the posthypnotic suggestion that he would not smoke and strengthening his resistance to cigarettes with each call.

He did not smoke at all for the 30 days before the last visit. He seemed very pleased with himself and felt that he had been able to overcome a habit to which he had been enslaved for several decades of his life. He entered a state of somnambulism during the last reinforcement session and had not resumed smoking to the time of the writing, some 6 months later.

SUMMARY

Most excuses for smoking during the treatment period are some form of stress—"an argument with my wife," "an important business deal." At times we have been unable to avoid the impression that the stress may have been deliberately provoked by the patient to provide an excuse to smoke. On the other hand, we have seen many patients who tolerate great stresses during the treatment period without even thinking of resuming smoking. Car wrecks, illnesses in the family, difficulties at work—none seem particularly troublesome for the patient who is responding well to hypnosis. Even one man who felt that giving up smoking was "like betraying an old friend, one who has stood by me in all the tough spots of my life" gave up cigarettes easily after the first visit.

At times those who "lapse" during the treatment time report an immediate sense of guilt, which often helps strengthen their resolve to stop. It is rare, in our experience, for anyone to drop out of the program during the four hypnotic sessions.

During the 30 years that we have been developing our treatment plan (Crasilneck, 1982), and teaching it to others, we have noted that our students' results, too, have been comparable in effectiveness. Our method of treatment today is essentially the same that we described in our treatment of the 75 adult male smokers. The suggestions we use are generally the same in all cases, with no prolonged effort to induce deeper states of hypnosis in subjects who seem to only enter light trance. Results are relatively independent of depth of trance.

As public recognition of the dangers of smoking increase, it is possible that the success rate we have found with medically referred patients may be obtained by those with no present medical problem but with concern for their future health.

REFERENCES

Athanasou TA: Smoking behavior and its modification through hypnosis: A review and evaluation. Aust J Med Sophrology Hypnotherapy 2:4–15, 1974

Barkley RA, Hastings HE, Jackson TL Jr: The effects of rapid smoking and hypnosis in the treatment of smoking behavior. Int J Clin Exp Hypn 25:7–17, 1977

Berkowitz B, Ross-Townsend A, Kohlberger R: Hypnotic treatment of smoking: The single-treatment method revisited. Am J Psychiatry 136:83–85, 1979

Berlin FS: Smoking decreased after hypnosis. Arch Gen Psychiat 37:1200–1201, 1980

Bernstein DA: Modification of smoking behavior: An evaluative review. Psychol Bull 71:418–440, 1969

Bowers KS: Hypnosis, asthma and smoking, in Hypnosis for the Seriously Curious. New York, W. W. Norton, 1976, pp 149–152

Chiasson SW: Methods for weight and smoking. Presented at the American Society of Clinical Hypnosis 25th Annual Meeting, Denver, Colorado, 1982

Cohen SB: Hypnosis and smoking. JAMA 208:335–337, 1969

Collison DR: Hypnosis in respiratory disease, in Burrows GD, Dennerstein 1 (eds): Handbook of Hypnosis and Psychosomatic Medicine. Amsterdam, Elsevier/North-Holland Biomedical Press, 1980, pp 333–338

Crasilneck HB: The control of pain and symptom management, in Bowers MD (ed): Introductory Lectures in Medical Hypnosis. New York, Institute for Research in Hypnosis, 1958

Crasilneck HB: Smoking habituation: A 27-year study of the use of hypnosis in the control of cigarette smoking. Presented at the American Clinical Hypnosis Annual Meeting, Denver, Colorado, 1982

Crasilneck HB, Hall JA: The use of hypnosis in controlling cigarette smoking. J South Med Assoc 61:99–1002, 1968

Crasilneck HB, Hall JA: Clinical hypnosis: Applications in smoking and obesity problems. Dallas Med J 62:296–302, 1976

Dengrove E: A single-treatment method to stop smoking using ancillary self-hypnosis-Discussion. Int J Clin Exp Hypn 18:251–256, 1970

Erickson MH, et al: The Practical Application of Medical and Dental Hypnosis. New York, Julian, 1961, p 1319

Ewin DM: (Panelist) Hypnosis to control the smoking habit. American Occupational Health Conference, Boston, 1977

Ford S, Ederer F: Breaking the cigarette habit. JAMA 194:139–142, 1965

Gaston CD, Hutzell RR: Hypnosis to reduce smoking in a deaf patient. Am J Clin Hypn 19:125–127, 1976

Goodman LS, Gilman A: The Pharmacological Basis of Therapeutics (ed 2). New York, Macmillan, 1956, pp 620–627

Grosz HJ, Grosz Z: Single hypnosis treatment of 506 cigarette smokers: An eighteen month follow-up. Presented at the International Congress of the Israel Society of Hypnosis in Psychotherapy and Psychosomatic Medicine in collaboration with the European Society of Hypnosis in Psychotherapy and Psychosomatic Medicine, Haifa, Israel, 1983

Hall JA, Crasilneck HB: Development of a hypnotic technique for treating chronic cigarette smoking. Int J Clin Exp Hypn 18:283–289, 1970

Holroyd J: Hypnosis treatment for smoking: An evaluative review. Int J Clin Exp Hypn 28:341–357, 1980

Jeffrey TB, Gentry WR, Greuling JW: Evaluation of a dual induction hypnotic approach to modifying smoking behavior. Presented at the American Society of Clinical Hypnosis 25th Annual Meeting, Denver, Colorado, 1982

Johnston E, Donoghue JR: Hypnosis and smoking: A review of the literature. Am J Clin Hypn 13:265–272, 1971

Klauber RW: Hypnosis: smoking and weight control. Presented at the American Society of Clinical Hypnosis 25th Annual Meeting, Denver, Colorado, 1982

Kroger WS: Clinical and Experimental Hypnosis in Medicine, Dentistry and Psychology. Philadelphia, J.B. Lippincott, 1963

MacHovec FJ, Man SC: Acupuncture and hypnosis compared: Fifty-eight cases. Am J Clin Hypn 21:45–47, 1978

Miller MM: Hypno-aversion treatment of nicotinism. J Nat Med Assoc 56:480–482,, 1965

Moore MM: The cessation of smoking by hypnosis. Presented at the American Society of Clinical Hypnosis 25th Annual Meeting, Denver, Colorado, 1982

Moses FM: Treating smoking habit by discussion and hypnosis. Dis Nerv Syst 25:185–188, 1964

Nuland W: Discussion of Spiegel H: A single-treatment to stop smoking using ancillary self-hypnosis. Int J Clin Exp Hypn 18:235–250, 1970

Nuland W, Field PB: Smoking and hypnosis: A systematic clinical approach. Int J Clin Exp Hypn 18:290–306, 1970

Pederson LL, Scrimgeour WG, Lefcoe NM: Variables of hypnosis which are related to success in a smoking withdrawal program. Int J Clin Exp Hypn 27:14–20, 1979

Perry C, Mullen G: The effects of hypnotic susceptibility on reducing smoking behavior treated by a hypnotic technique. J Clin Psychol 32:498–505, 1975

Powell DH: Helping habitual smokers using flooding and hypnotic desensitization technique: A brief communication. Int J Clin Exp Hypn 28:192–196, 1980

Raginsky BB: Hypnosis in internal medicine and general practice, in Schneck JM (ed): Hypnosis in Modern Medicine (ed 3). Springfield, Ill., Charles C Thomas, 1963, p 47

Ringrose CAD: The use of hypnology as an adjunct in curbing smoking, obesity and hypertension, in Burrow GD, Dennerstein L (eds): Handbook of Hypnosis and Psychosomatic Medicine. Amsterdam, Elsevier/North-Holland Biomedical Press, 1980, pp 223–238

Sanders S: Mutual group hypnosis in smoking. Am J Clin Hypn 20:131–135, 1977

Shewchuk LA, Dubran R, Burton D, Forman M, Clark RR, Jaffin AR: Preliminary observations on an intervention program for heavy smokers. Int J Addict 12:323–336, 1977

Spiegel H: A single-treatment method to stop smoking using ancillary self-hypnosis. Int J Clin Exp Hypn 18:235–250, 1970

Spiegel H, Spiegel DS: Trance and Treatment: Clinical Uses of Hypnosis. New York, Basic Books, 1978, pp 210–219

Stanton HE: A one-session hypnotic approach to modifying smoking behavior. Int J Clin Exp Hypn 26:22–29, 1978

Stein C: Displacement and reconditioning technique for compulsive smokers. Int J Clin Exp Hypn 12:230–238, 1964

Templer DI: Aversive conditioning through hypnosis to reduce smoking. Association for Advancement of Behavior Therapy Newsletter 4:9, 1969

US Department of Health, Education and Welfare: 1972 Directory of On-going Research in Smoking and Health. Washington, DC, US Government Printing Office, 1974

von Dedenroth TEA: The use of hypnosis with "tobaccomaniacs." Am J Clin Hypn 6:326–331, 1964

von Dedenroth TEA: The use of hypnosis in 1000 cases of "tobaccomaniacs." Am J Clin Hypn 10:194–197, 1968

Watkins HH: Hypnosis in smoking: A five-session approach. Int J Clin Exp Hypn 24:381–390, 1976

Wolberg LR: Medical Hypnosis, vol. I, Principles of Hypnotherapy. New York, Grune & Stratton, 1948

Wollman L: Hypnotherapy for cigarette smoking. J Am Soc Psychsom Dent Med 16:55–57, 1969

Wright ME: A single-treatment method to stop smoking using ancillary self-hypnosis: Discussion. Int J Clin Exp Hypn 18:261–267, 1970

13

Applications of Hypnosis
in Pediatric Problems

The trance state can be a great aid in treating many pediatric problems, including dental procedures (Shaw, 1959), for children are almost universally good hypnotic subjects (Collison, 1974; Cooper, 1975; La Scola, 1968; London 1962, 1966; O'Grady, Hoffman, 1984). At the same time the natural suggestibility of children makes it even more important for the therapist to be aware of the psychodynamics and possible unconscious meanings of the hypnotic situation. The inability of a child to enter trance might suggest possible brain damage according to Jacobs and Jacobs (1966), but we do not agree with this position.

Hypnosis has been used with a 10-year old boy with eczema, complicated by behavioral problems (Mirvish, 1978) and seemed to help the course of rheumatoid arthritis in a 10-year old girl (Cioppa and Thal, 1975).

Franz Baumann is considered one of the outstanding authorities in the use of hypnotherapy in pediatrics. Gardner (1976, 1977), Gardner and Hinton (1980), and Olness (Gardner and Olness, 1981; Olness and Gardner, 1978) have done pioneering work, also, in the application of hypnotherapy to children and adolescents. They have established hypnotherapy with children as a standard component of insightful practice in pediatrics and child psychiatry. Andolsek and Novik (1980) consider that hypnotherapy is still underused in children. There is increasing recognition of the usefulness of this modality in pediatrics and child psychiatry (Eddie, 1975; Wester and Smith, 1983; Williams and Singh, 1976). Olness (1977) has suggested in-service education in the use of hypnosis in a children's hospital.

Children are most frequently brought for consultation because of behavior problems. Often the "sick" child is merely the identifiable patient in a situation where the real "sickness" is a disorganized family structure, with tensions between the parents becoming evident in the problems of the child. Some psychoanalysts have even suggested that dreams of disturbed children are more appropriately seen at times as relating to the family situation than to the inner psychological state of the child.

These considerations make it imperative that the child's problem be seen in the context of the entire family situation. Enuresis, for example, which is a frequent problem, may be indicative of an organic urinary dysfunction, of a simple habit pattern, or of severe anxiety or may reflect the child's unconscious expression of anger at some family tension. It may also be a bid for special consideration and attention. At times, in fact, it is the family itself that should be treated, with the expectation that the child will improve as family stresses are decreased.

Once it has been determined that the child's problem can be most easily treated by seeing the child himself or herself as the patient, certain special considerations in hypnotic technique should be observed.

SPECIAL HYPNOTIC TECHNIQUES FOR CHILDREN

Wright (1960) has concisely outlined modifications in hypnotic technique that are particularly applicable to children, and we agree with his approach.

1. The shorter attention span of the child requires a more interesting induction procedure. While the usual adult patient will respond well to the monotonous repetition of relaxation suggestions, the child may become bored and restless. If eye-fixation techniques are used, it may be more effective with the pediatric patient if a moving stimulus is employed, such as a pendulum or rotating light. Another method on induction is a suggested fantasy of watching a movie or television screen, the action taking place on the "screen" while the ego assumes a more and more passive observer's role. The therapist, of course, may alter the dramatic action that is to be seen on the "screen" as a means of deepening the trance. The suggestive input of the therapist should be continuous with chil-

dren, with no long pauses or instructions to "indicate when you experience" the suggested image.

2. The child should have some form of immediate reward and praise for his or her achievement and effort. The less time that elapses between action and reward, the more rapidly the response can be conditioned.

3. The therapist should represent the authority and strength of the adult world in a nonthreatening way—not attempting to overwhelm the child or frighten him or her into submission but reassuring and leading the child in a friendly manner.

4. Suggestions must be phrased in the language and imagery that the child understands, thus facilitating the child's internalizing the suggestions as part of his or her ego-syntonic psychic world. Examples and images that find a recognized place in the child's experience and memory are more effective than abstract and generalized statements.

5. There should be no sudden and unexpected changes in tone or content of the suggestions given, for these might arouse anxiety and interfere with rapport. More than with the adult patient, transitions from one suggestion to another should be smooth. If possible, suggestions should be foreshadowed, as "In a moment I am going to ask you to imagine a blank television screen, just like the one watch at home, then when you see the blank screen clearly in your imagination a picture will begin to form on the screen. Do you begin to see the blank screen?"

Utilizing these principles, the therapist might proceed with a typical induction in which he does not try to specify the minute details of the scene, leaving this to the child's own very alive imagination. In fact, the participation of the child's imaginative ability is a principal factor in his or her entering hypnosis.

"Please look at this coin I am holding in my fingers slightly above your eyelids . . . just keep looking at the coin, and you will notice that very soon your eyes will begin to feel tired and they will start to blink and want to close, and as you feel them getting heavy, just let them close . . . heavy eyelids . . . closing, closing, and closed . . . good . . . so relaxed and at ease. Now, notice your one hand that is resting on your stomach. It comes up and down with every breath you take . . . can you feel this happening?. . . . Good . . . up and down, and a deeper sleep . . . a much deeper sleep. Now you won't pay any attention to your hand . . . but think about your leg . . . the right one. It begins to feel just sort of heavy like it feels like concrete . . . heavy . . . so heavy. . . . You can't raise it . . . try . . . try again . . . but it won't move . . . good. . . . Now, normal feeling returns to your leg and a much deeper and sounder and

relaxed state. . . . So relaxed . . . so drowsy . . . your right arm and fingers. As
I count to three, slowly . . . your right arm and fingers will become so straight
and strong and hard. You won't be able to budge or bend your arm or fingers.
. . . 1 . . . 2 . . . 3, good. It feels like a steel bridge . . . your arm so strong and
rigid . . . try to bend it . . . you can't. . . . Regular feeling now returns to your
arm and hand . . . good . . . and still a deeper state of relaxation . . . so sleepy.
. . .

    Do you have a television at home? If you do, nod your head . . . yes . . .
good. . . . You will now see the set come on and a funny picture is on the screen
. . . a cowboy clown . . you see it . . . he is doing something real funny . . .
you're smiling. . . . O.K. . . . the television picture fades out and you are so
drowsy and relaxed . . . lying there like a rag doll . . . so relaxed and at ease.
. . . Every muscle in your body is very relaxed as you watch the T.V. screen
in your imagination . . . completely and totally relaxed . . . so comfortable . . .
so completely at ease . . . simply watching this funny picture . . . and now as
this picture fades out, you will go into a deeper, a sounder state . . . so
comfortable and so secure . . . free from tension and tightness and stress and
strain. . . . You are now going to hear some very beautiful music, your favorite
kind of music . . . and as you hear your favorite music you will think of other
pleasant thoughts . . . things you like to do . . . things you really like . . . and
as this is occurring you will nod your head slightly "yes" [the child responds].
. . . You are tremendously relaxed, as much as you have ever been relaxed.
. . . You are secure. . . . You have a really strong desire to overcome your
problem . . . your unconscious mind is strong and powerful . . . and is going to
work hard for you and get you well. . . . I now give you the suggestion that . . .
[here the specific therapeutic suggestions are included]."

The trance is terminated very, very slowly with children so that
they experience their transition to the waking state in a gentle manner.
Before terminating the hypnotic state, the child is told,

    "When we do this again, you will be able to relax even more than you did
today . . . and you can enter a deeper level if you want to do so . . . and as your
problem [complaint being treated] improves, you will be so proud of yourself
for doing better, for learning to do [or not do] something that is important to
yourself . . . your mother and father will be so proud of you . . . I will be proud
. . . and most of all you will be proud . . . and pleased that you are able to do
more [specific suggestion], free of tension and tightness and stress and strain.
. . . Now as I slowly count from ten to one backward, you begin to feel wide
awake again, feeling your normal self, and rested and relaxed just like you had
experienced a restful nap or a drowsy time after you had been playing hard and
doing things you really like to do."

Notice that such phrasing as "restful nap" and "drowsy time"
tends to avoid emphasis on sleep, which may be a source of conflict

with some children, particularly if they have been in recent confrontations with a parent over bedtimes.

Gardner (1974) has published a review of hypnosis with children, outlining variables in therapist, patient, setting, and—the important but often neglected variable—parent's attitudes. In adapting hypnotic techniques to children, Gardner focuses on several techniques that have wide applicability: (1) concrete suggestions, using specific and not general images, such as "eating lots of good, tasty roast beef" instead of "good food"; (2) imaginative techniques, such as the television techniques that we have described; (3) regressive techniques to both detoxify past traumatic experiences and to revivify past successes as a motivational technique; (4) ego-strengthening techniques emphasizing a sense of ability to master the problems at hand, with resultant good feelings of achievement; (5) self-hypnosis to extend the hypnotic influence by repetition.

There is no clear answer to this important question of the earliest age at which hypnosis may be used with children, since what is meant by *hypnosis* determines the response. Is the soothing rhythmical rocking of a disturbed 6-month-old baby, resulting in his or her falling asleep, to be assimilated to the concept of adult hypnosis? Some authors have felt hypnosis can be induced in infants (Cullen, 1958; Krojanker, 1969). If the induction of hypnosis is thought of as a verbal technique, then clearly the earliest age at which it can be seen is one requiring some verbal understanding from the child, often about age 5 (Hilgard, 1971; London, 1963; London and Cooper, 1969).

We have used hypnosis with children as early as age 3 agreeing with Antitch (1967). Our case was a boy who was so overactive that he would completely dominate the attention of his parents, throwing food, beating other children, soiling himself repeatedly. The referring pediatrician had tried placing the child on massive doses of tranquilizers and amphetamines, but short of producing a sedated state these had not been particularly effective. Conventional psychotherapy in a playroom had produced little or no results. Even the possibility of childhood psychosis was considered. The child was initially so active in the hypnotherapy setting that he deliberately poured a cup of hot coffee on the therapist.

It was possible to use a TV screen technique with him only with the modification of holding his hand, which seemed to bring some calmness and reassurance. His responses to suggestions were indicated by squeezing the therapist's hand rather than by verbal response. In hypnosis he was told that he would be helped with his problem so that he would be able to learn to have people like him for being a good boy, that it would not be necessary to get attention by upsetting people. After ten sessions of hypnotherapy he began to respond. Counseling with the parents produced a different expectation for him in the home, rewarding each positive change that he made and reinforcing the image of a "good boy" whenever appropriate. He soon became a normal, adjusted child, still full of life and energy but not disruptive.

Andolsek and Novik (1980) suggest the utility of involving parents in the process of treating children with hypnotherapy. Younger children may respond better to induction techniques that do not involve eye closure (Laguaite, 1976). Use of imagery that has special appeal to some children can be useful, such as imagery of science fiction (Elkins and Carter, 1981) and personalized fairy tales (Levine, 1980) tailored to the child's own needs. A dissociation model, highlighting social roles and ego states, is useful in some conceptualizations of hypnotherapy with children and adolescents. The psychodynamics of hypnosis may be particulary evident in children. Call (1976) suggests that hypnosis allows the child to share reality testing with the hypnotherapist as the infant did earlier with the all-powerful parent.

ANXIETY SYMPTOMS

Anxiety is a frequent presenting problem with children, although it rarely—in our experience—takes the more fixed forms that are seen in adult neurotics. Hypnotherapy may well be the method of choice in the anxiety problems of childhood, according to Ambrose (1968). Much anxiety seems to be situational and may be easily related to recent changes in the family structure or relationships. It is often sufficient, in light trance, to reassure the child of the love of his or her parents and bolster his or her feelings of self-esteem (Jacobs, 1962).

It is understandable, for instance, that the child may feel insecure when there has been a recent separation or divorce of the parents, or when a near relative has died (often a grandparent), or when the family has moved from one location to another. Moving from one house to another, even in the same town, may seem like a relatively minor change to adults, whose work and social relationships can remain unchanged, but to the child it can constitute a complete change of environment. Often old friendships cannot be continued since the child lacks the mobility of his parents; a beloved teacher may have been abandoned abruptly in a move from one school to another, not to mention the need for adapting to a different set of school and neighborhood friends.

School Phobia

One of the most frequent forms of anxiety that we have seen in children has been school phobia. Classically, this occurs in a child who is leaving the home for the first time to enter school, either kindergarten or first grade. The child often refuses to attend school, pleading fear for the mother's health while he or she is away, saying he or she is afraid of being lost in the unfamiliar school, or simply showing overwhelming symptoms of anxiety when he or she attempts to leave the home.

An unexpected fantasy may lie behind the child's anxiety. One 7-year-old boy who steadfastly refused to go to school revealed under hypnosis the source of his fears. His mother, meaning well, had impressed upon him that when he went to school, it was important that he get along with both the teachers and the students and that he should do what he was told. Since the mother had failed to make a distinction between teachers and pupils in "doing what you're told," he had developed strong fantasies around a piece of misinformation—the older neighborhood children had told him that on the playground at school the older boys would pull his pants down and he would be exposed. Thus far the fantasy was near consciousness, but there were undoubtedly deeper levels of fantasy in which Oedipal themes were involved, perhaps even that of fantasied homosexual rape. The child received a great deal of relief from the discussion of this fantasy in the waking state. He was asked if the persons who told him this always told the truth, whether he actually knew of such events happening (which he did not), and whether he really felt, when he considered it, that his mother had intended to tell him to obey the children in the same manner as the teacher. Perhaps the supportive, nonthreatening relationship with the male therapist also helped him to overcome his fears. In any case, his school phobia rapidly abated, and he began attending classes without anxiety.

In treating school phobia we usually attempt a rapid relief of the symptom, giving suggestions for this as soon as the underlying psychodynamics are clear. This is to prevent the fears increasing, in fantasy, the longer the child is away from the actual school situation. Parents frequently need counseling as to how to respond to the child's symptoms so that they are neither too supportive nor overly critical of his fear.

In another child it was discovered that his fear of school was actually fear of the station-wagon bus that came for him each morning. In his mind he had associated the station wagon with an ambulance that had taken a sick child in the neighborhood to the hospital. With clarification of the distinction of these two vehicles and a discussion of his own fear of sickness, the school phobia dramatically lessened. Lawlor (1976) felt that hypnosis aided school phobia more rapidly than did traditional psychotherapeutic techniques.

Childhood Fears

There are, of course, many anxieties of childhood that do not manifest themselves as school phobia. Other forms of phobia may involve fear of certain objects or situations. Although these fears may have an origin in actual traumatic events, they often express a symbolic meaning as well.

A grade-school girl was brought to treatment because of a persistent fear of cats and other furry animals, for which no conscious explanation could be found in her past experiences. Under hypnosis, using an age-regression technique, we found that the fear had begun at a time when she had been in the outhouse privy on the farm where she was living as a child. She had been masturbating, feeling mixed excitement and guilt, when the door began to slowly open. Frightened and fearing discovery, she had run from the outhouse, only to trip over the family cat that had apparently pushed the door open. She was bruised in the fall, skinning her knees, and had gone crying to the house, ashamed to tell what had happened. At first her aversion had been to cats, though later it had generalized to other small animals. As time passed, she remembered only the fear of animals, seeming to forget the onset.

Under hypnosis, after the original traumatic situation had been uncovered, she was asked to imagine that she was the only spectator in a darkened theater. A red light came on, a buzzer sounded, and she saw a large red curtain rise, revealing a stage. It was suggested that on the stage she would see the original situation—the outhouse, herself, the cat. She was told, "Now you will see what really went on, and you will compare and contrast it to what you remember." From the point of view of her present, older ego, she watched the childhood scene unfold with a detached, more objective eye. After hypnosis was terminated, the events were discussed with her in the waking state, emphasis being placed on the way that her guilt and fear at the forbidden masturbation had been transferred to the cat, then to other similar animals. Her "phobic" symptoms rapidly improved.

Hypnosis has been used successfully for other phobias. Schneck (1966), for example, treated germ phobia in a child by hypnoanalysis.

Dash (1981) found hypnosis valuable in the rapid treatment of a needle phobia in a 5-year-old cardiac patient.

Sleep Disturbance

Anxiety in children may appear during sleep, the so-called "pavor nocturnus," in which the child feels very afraid but is not fully awake. In these cases it is well to inquire thoroughly into any bedtime fantasies of the child. Such inquiry should be pursued sufficiently before a hypnoanalytic approach is instituted.

Frequent nocturnal fantasies involve fear of injury to the child himself or herself or to one of the parents. Sometimes other members of the family are involved, usually a sibling who is unconsciously perceived as a rival for the attention of the parents.

Such fantasies may arise from an Oedipus complex, a particular configuration of intrapsychic object representations in which the child most often feels a desire to take an adult role with the parent of the opposite sex and, therefore, feels in competition with the parent of the same sex. In male children, usually between ages 5 and 7, such fantasies may involve a fear of "castration" by the father. "Castration" may be perceived as any curtailment. In girls the Oedipus complex is thought to eventuate in anger at the mother for having "stolen" a fantasied penis that the girl imagines she had once had. Although our experience frequently confirms the castration anxiety in boys, the corresponding formulation for girls seem less focused and more uncertain.

Although early psychoanalytic literature tended to emphasize the literal sexual fantasies of children, the Oedipus complex can be taken in a more psychosocial way as the fantasy of becoming suddenly an adult, overcoming childish limitations without having to go through the difficult and prolonged process of growth. Seen in such a way, the Oedipal conflict becomes less a sexual conflict than a universal experience of anticipating adulthood. Clinically both forms of Oedipus complex are seen frequently.

A number of years ago we had the opportunity to follow the dreams of a 3 1/2-year-old boy who was not in therapy. For several weeks he had suffered from fears when going to sleep. One night the fears awakened him. He was crying. Tearfully, he told his parents of a dream in which "bad animals" had broken into the house and were threatening to kill his father, while he and his mother hid under his (the child's) bed. One week later his night terror had begun to subside. When asked to retell his dream, he said, "There were bad animals outside the house, but we had the doors locked and they couldn't get in." After a further week his memory of the dream had become, "There were some bad animals in the woods and daddy and I are taking guns and going out to kill them." After another week he completely denied having had the dream at all.

In this progressive change in the memory of what seems to be a clearly Oedipal dream, one can see, as if in outline, the progressive change of the fantasy as defenses against the original dream are brought gradually into play. What seemed at first to be a representation of primitive aggression against the father, the parent of the same sex, was gradually transformed into a healthy identification with the father ("going out hunting together") and then finally was repressed completely.

Sometimes the child is witness to a so-called "primal scene," seeing the parents engaged in sexual intercourse. Not understanding adult sexuality, he or she may assimilate such a scene to fighting and anger and develop a fear of the stronger parent—the father—injuring the weaker parent—the mother. As this thought is too anxiety-producing, the child may unconsciously elaborate a "screen memory," a less frightening memory that carries the feeling and affect of the more traumatic one. It is frequently not possible to establish clearly the "primal-scene" experience, even when it would seem by inference to have been probable. Such secondary elaborations occurred in the memory of the "bad-animal" dream.

The child with night terrors is told in the waking state that the situation at night is safe, that his or her fears are associated with fantasies that are different from reality. The fantasies are frightening; the reality is not. The child is told that we will talk about his or her fantasies whenever they disturb him or her, but in the meantime hypnosis will help him or her to sleep more easily and comfortably (Taboada, 1975).

Hypnotic suggestions are given for calmness and a feeling of security and safety when going to sleep (Jacobs, 1964). Parents have frequently noted, in successful subjects, that the child appears more calm while asleep, with less muscle tightness, bruxism, and other signs of anxiety.

Psychological Management

Hypnotherapy is of value in a number of psychotherapuetic situations that may arise with children. Lazar and Jedlieczka (1979) decreased manipulative behavior and helped to relieve asthma in only one session of hypnosis with a retarded child. Gardner and Tarnow (1980) used hypnosis as an adjunctive treatment in an autistic boy. Incorporated with other techniques, Kellerman (1981) helped a 12-year-old boy with obsessional matriarchical thoughts in three sessions of hypnosis; a 2-year follow-up showed no recurrence of the symptoms.

HABIT PATTERNS

There are three common habit pattern disturbances of childhood—enuresis, thumb sucking, and nail biting. We refer to these as "habit patterns" since it is not at all clear that these symptoms invariably represent deeper psychopathology.

Although a hidden meaning may be discovered, it often appears that the symptom may have begun as a motivated, dynamic response to conflict. Over the course of time, however, it has become what we term a mere "empty habit" that no longer is driven by the original conflict.

Enuresis

We have discussed fully the frequent problem of enuresis in childhood in Chapter 10 on psychosomatic symptoms. Bed wetting not only is a source of conflict between the child and the parents, but in later years of childhood it causes social isolation and a sense of inferiority in relation to peers. Organic causes of urinary dysfunction must always be ruled out by thorough medical examination before psychological treatment is undertaken (Collison, 1970). It is then important to assess the degree, if any, to which the symptom is used as a hidden expression of hostility, fear, or anxiety. Practical changes should be suggested in the way that the problem is handled by the family—such as having the child launder his or her own bed linen, emptying the bladder before retiring, not drinking fluids after the dinner meal, and using different settings of an alarm clock to try to identify a time during the night when enuresis is more likely to occur (Solovey and Milechnin, 1959). It has been our experience that hypnosis, in good subjects, is successful in improving or eliminating enuresis in 80 percent of such cases.

Hinman and Baumann (1976) caution that psychologically conditioned incoordination of voiding may produce damage to the mid and upper urinary tracts. Suggestion and hypnotherapy are of marked utility in helping some patients establish coordinated micturition. Hypnotherapy is also of aid in fecal incontinence (Baumann, 1981).

Braun (in press) has described hypnotherapy in the conjoint treatment of an enuretic child and a polyphobic mother.

Thumb Sucking

Although normal in early childhood, where it perhaps represents a need for oral gratification, thumb sucking often continues into a later age, causing social embarrassment and shame (Morban-Laucer, 1961). In general, a compulsive thumb sucking that persists beyond the first year of school would warrant professional attention, particularly if it is a source of conflict between child and parent or if it is causing notable embarrassment for the child with his or her friends.

We use both an intellectual and an emotional approach in explaining to the child how prolonged thumb sucking may destroy the curvature of the teeth, requiring later orthodontic correction. The child's feelings about his or her appearance are elicited, and an appeal is made to the child's desire to be more mature and attractive.

If there is an underlying traumatic or symbolic basis for the thumb sucking, it can usually be clarified by an interview under hypnosis, utilizing either the fantasied theater technique (as described with phobias) or using age regression to the time when thumb sucking would ordinarily have been given up as an outworn habit. If such dynamics are uncovered, their working through must become a primary goal of treatment.

Under hypnosis the child is told that his or her thumb will begin to taste bitter and that this will act as a reminder that he or she no longer wishes nor desires to suck his or her thumb. The child is told that should he or she put the thumb in his or her mouth, the bitter taste will motivate him or her to remove it. Any improvement is given immediate and ample praise, both to the child and the parents, as the symptom has usually become a focus of hostile interaction between parents and child. Self-hypnosis is quite often taught in the control of this problem.

Nail Biting

By the time nail biters are referred for professional help, most ordinary lay remedies have been tried without success. Those cases that have come to our attention have been impressive in the almost masochistic appearance of the symptoms. Not only nails are bitten, but cuticles are torn and lacerated, frequently leading to infections and paronychia.

The customary exploration for psychodynamic meaning is made, together with a clarification of the family structure and interaction that may contribute to symptoms in the child. Any conflict situations that are uncovered are handled in usual psychotherapeutic ways. If there is a hidden guilt—masturbation, stealing, or having done something "dirty" with the hands—this is worked through in psychotherapy or hypnotherapy.

Under hypnosis the patient is told:

"When you begin to put your hands toward your mouth, there will simply be an automatic and opposite withdrawal movement. You will no longer wish, nor desire, to continue this outgrown, unwanted habit that injures your hands and embarrasses you before your family and friends."

This negative suggestion is carefully balanced with a positive suggestion:

"As you begin to discontinue the habit of biting your nails, you will feel a sense of well-being and self-approval. You will begin to respect your fingernails and hands and be proud of them. Each time that you successfully avoid nail biting, you will feel proud of yourself for accomplishing a worthwhile and desirable goal."

As an accompaniment to hypnotherapy, both boys and girls are asked to learn appropriate techniques to care for their fingernails—buffing, manicuring with or without clear nail polish, and care of their cuticles.

Gardner (1978) discusses the application of hypnotherapy to the management of childhood habit disorders. Kohen, Olness, and Colwells (1980) reviewed 500 pediatric behavioral problems treated with hypnotherapy. Reaney (1984) also reviewed the utility of hypnotherapy in treating habit disorders.

SPEECH DISORDERS

Although speech disorders of a psychogenic nature may affect any age group, the most common form—stuttering—seems characteristically to have an onset in childhood. Orton (1937) emphasizes two characteristic times of onset: at the time speech is being learned, about age 2 to 3, and at the time that writing is learned in the first years of school. Barbara (1959) distinguishes between "stuttering," which is repetitious speech, and "stammering," which is hesitant speech, although both terms are used interchangeably in ordinary discussions.

The theories of stuttering are varied, according to Barbara, ranging from purely neurological to psychological and even sociological. In his noted review of hypnotherapy for children Ambrose (1963) has considered the stammerer "first and foremost suffering from an inhibition of aggressive drives.'' Falck (1964) states that ''the person who stutters is a person who has become confused about speech and his own relationship to the process.''

It is not always possible to understand the actual situation out of which the stuttering or stammering arose, but in some cases it is not deeply repressed and requires simply a careful anamnesis. For example, one teenage girl who was a stutterer had begun when she was 8 years old. She had been riding with her father in the car when, unexpectedly, the father stopped and picked up a woman other than her mother, with whom he seemed very friendly. Although nothing overtly sexual occurred, her father had cautioned her, after he had driven the woman home again, not to tell her mother. The stuttering began that night when she returned home and had continued with varying severity for several years. Such a discrete onset is rare, but more general situations of stress, based on the same dynamics, are frequent. Stuttering may unconsciously represent a desire to speak and a simultaneous desire not to speak—for a fear of the consequences of speaking.

In some instances stuttering has seemed to begin with a single traumatic situation. A child who had been treated very affectionately by his parents was left for the first time with a babysitter when he was 3 years old. The parents habitually rocked him to sleep each night and gave clear instructions to the babysitter to do the same. The sitter, however, let him cry for over 3 hours before he fell asleep in his crib. As the parents recalled, his hesitant speech had begun the next morning.

Another child began to stutter on his first day in kindergarten, but careful exploration of his feelings revealed that the symptom was related to a fear that his mother had died. The night before his first day in kindergarten, when he had begun to have some anxiety about this new adventure, his mother developed acute appendicitis and was rushed to the hospital for surgery. When the school bus came for him the next morning, he felt that it was to take him away because his mother was not coming home, that she had died. His stuttering had begun that very day and continued even after his mother returned to the home. The patient remained in treatment for several months. His fears were slowly reduced. He gained good insight into his original anxiety. When this was coupled with extensive hypnotherapy, his normal speech returned.

While it is beyond question that many stutterers are vastly improved with speech therapy and with conventional psychotherapy, we feel that hypnosis offers some unique aids to treatment of speech disorders. First, hypnosis itself has a calming and tranquilizing influence, and it can diminish anxiety that is sometimes heightened by uncovering inquiry in psychotherapy. Second, under hypnosis the patient is not challenged to immediately give up the speech disorder, but instead he is told that it will greatly improve. Specific suggestions may include "sliding" through the word at the first indication of stuttering so that he tends to stutter only on the initial syllable while "sliding" through the rest of the word. This tends to focus the anxiety about stuttering in a specific place rather than having it recur throughout a word. Third, more general suggestions are given for feeling confident and calm in speaking, and a posthypnotic cue may be added—that when the patient begins to speak he or she will feel some of the same relaxation and well-being that he or she has experienced in the hypnotic state. A useful technique is to record the patient's improved speech while he or she is under hypnosis. The recording is played back in the waking state, giving the patient an improved image of his or her own capabilities for more effective speech. Finally, the stutterer is taught techniques of self-hypnosis and told to utilize them daily. At times it is suggested that he or she will practice speaking in front of a mirror so that visual feedback may be used to counteract partially the habit pattern of stuttering.

Moderate to marked improvement is the usual outcome of hypnotherapy for stuttering (Granone, 1966; Rousey, 1961). If the patient is sufficiently motivated, improvement can usually be seen after 3 to 4 months or less of weekly hypnotherapy sessions (Madison, 1954); the usual length of treatment, however, seems to be about 1 year before it can be assumed that maximum benefit has been obtained.

McCord (1955) has published an excellent review of hypnosis as a treatment of stuttering. Other significant case histories have been presented by Grable (1968) and Hubbard (1963). Moore (1946) employed hypnosis as adjunct therapy in 40 cases, resulting in increased fluency and relaxation.

After hypnosis has been induced to the deepest level, the following suggestions are given:

"Your speech will be very soft-spoken, relaxed and at ease. . . . Your previous fears and tensions and staccato and jerking type of talking will be replaced by a smooth and flowing manner of speaking. . . . Your fears of talking to strangers, to groups of people, on the telephone, reciting in class will be greatly reduced because of the great power of your unconscious mind. . . . Your speech will be soft, secure, and you will be much more relaxed and at ease, pleased that you can speak without stammering or stuttering. . . . Now speak in a whisper without stammering or stuttering and hear how your voice sounds."

We have found that if a stutterer is asked to speak in a whisper, either in or out of hypnosis, his speech usually improves. Such speech acts as a repatterning and an experience of improved speech, a process that seems to be greatly accelerated by the use of hypnosis. A similar demonstration of improvement can often be seen if the stutterer is asked to sing or speak in unison with the therapist during a therapy session.

SUPPRESSION AMBLYOPIA

The movement of each eye is controlled by six different muscles, which must act in a coordinated fashion for smooth visual ability. When there is marked imbalance in the coordination of the two eyes, it may not be possible for the visual images to be fused. As a compensatory response, the vision in the less dominant eye may be suppressed. This prevents the visual impression of the dominant eye from being distracted by a second or double image from the nondominant eye. This inhibition of vision in the nondominant eye is "suppression amblyopia." It is extremely difficult to reverse when it has become a fixed pattern. Thus, the child with such a condition becomes essentially sightless in the suppressed eye, although the retinal function and the optic nerves and tracts presumably remain intact.

The muscular imbalance that led to suppression can be corrected surgically in most cases, but the vision in the suppressed eye does not automatically return. In attempting to reawaken the suppressed vision, the "good" eye is often covered with a patch so that the child is encouraged to rely on the "bad" eye again. The time during which the dominant eye is covered or patched is very disturbing to the child, and it may in fact involve some risks. The child is not able to see as well and, therefore, is undertaking more risk in such ordinary daily situations as crossing busy streets, playing games,and simply functioning in household situations. In addition, there is the embarrassment and possible ridicule from playmates and children at school.

In 1957 Browning and Crasilneck reported a pilot study of treating suppression amblyopia with hypnosis. This was the first attempt at hypnosis for treatment of this condition. Of the 9 children studied, all showed some degree of improvement in near vision, and 6 showed improvement in distant vision. Three years later a follow-up study was done with the same children; 1 of the 9 was not available at the time of retesting.

Over the 3-year period after this study all those children who had improved with hypnosis showed some regression, though not always to the level of severity they had before hypnosis was originally tried. The most striking finding was that although the hypnotically stimulated visual improvement had regressed over the 3-year period, the degree of previous improvement that had been obtained with hypnosis was restored in only one session of hypnosis. These findings, though based on a small sample, suggest that hypnosis has marked value in treating this visual disorder of childhood, which is by no means rare.

In one of the cases the original use of hypnosis was followed by surgical correction of the strabismus and intense orthoptic training. Both the near and distant vision results were 20/20 following the rehypnosis 3 years after the initial sessions. Although these 8 cases are too few to generalize, they are strongly suggestive.

As mentioned in the Smith, Crasilneck and Browning report (1961), waking suggestion had been attempted to induce improvement in visual functioning without hypnosis, but had failed to alter the baseline readings. This may again suggest a neurological effect of hypnosis that is not obtainable with nonhypnotic waking encouragement, although the nature of this difference is unclear.

Preceding the initial child study by 1 year, an attempt had been made to alleviate suppression amblyopia in 9 adults, but the results had been disappointing (Browning and Crasilneck, 1957). Age-regression techniques had been attempted in two of these patients without adding to the visual ability. We have more recently undertaken the treatment of one case of suppression amblyopia in an adult because vision was failing in the "good" nonsupressed eye as a result of disease. After more than a year of weekly hypnotic sessions some improvement seemed evident, the patient being able to distinguish figures on television, whereas initially only light, shadow, and movement were seen. It is still uncertain if improvement will be to a degree that makes the suppressed eye practically useful. At present the use of hypnosis in treating suppression amblyopia in adults remains uncertain, but with children results appear to be favorable and encouraging.

DYSLEXIA

The inability to recognize and read words normally causes much stress in children affected by dyslexia. While this disorder has provoked increasing concern of educators and while numerous training techniques have been used, there has been little exploration of the possible use of hypnosis in alleviating reading disability. In our own experience approximately three-fourths of the children presenting to us with dyslexia show moderate to marked improvement following hypno-therapy.

Suggestions given in the hypnotic trance follow this general pattern:

"Your vision is simply going to improve. . . . You can recognize words with much more ease. . . . Once you have learned the word, it will make an impression upon your unconscious brain and mind, and recall of this word in the future will be much easier. . . . Your memory for words that you learn will become implanted in your mental processes and will be recalled in a smooth, coordinated fashion. There will be an excellent coordination between your eyes, your brain, and your memory . . . and your reading capabilities will continuously improve until they return to normal. . . . You will be much less anxious and much less afraid in your reading and learning habits. . . . Your reading is going to improve consistently."

During the initial sessions it often seems that a child pronounces new words very carefully, with attention to each syllable. When the same word is subsequently used, pronunciation and recognition seem to become much more rapid and automatic.

One young woman, now in her twenties, came for treatment at age fourteen, her parents and the teachers in the special school she attended being convinced she was retarded. Psychiatric consultation had shown no overt area of neurotic conflict. We questioned the presence of mental retardation because her spoken vocabulary seemed too advanced for her supposed mental age. Although able to speak well, with a range of vocabulary, she could read only the simplest words. "I," "but," and "and" were the only words that she consistently read aloud. After extensive hypnotherapy lasting a few years, she graduated from high school, passed both the written and practical part of her driver's license test, and has become more functional.

LEARNING PROBLEMS

Perhaps the greatest problem preventing children from learning at their optimal rate is anxiety. Pressure for performance may create such anxiety, particularly in test situations, that the child may be unable to report information that he otherwise knows quite well. In such cases the relief of tension that can be obtained with hypnosis may result in improved classroom learning. In rare cases there is too little anxiety for best performance—the child is not motivated to success. Hypnother-apy, by altering self-concepts, may be a motivational aid in such problems as well. McCord (1956, 1962) has furnished two case reports of improved performance after hypnosis.

Johnson et al. (1981) found that group administration of hypnosis, even by persons only moderately trained in hypnosis, could have a significant effect on improving self-esteem in children with learning disorders.

Exam Anxiety

Lodato (1968) used hypnosis to help people with examination anxiety in such situations as driver tests, stenographic tests, and tests for a course in statistics. Hammer (1954) compared normal and post-hypnotic performances in 9 subjects in the areas of motor capacity, attention and perception, association, learning and memory, speed of reading comprehension, and application of abstract ability. Hypnosis improved the performance of his subjects. Suggestions of sleep were not used in order to minimize drowsiness. Presentation or recorded material during sleep as a means to facilitate learning has been found by Kulikov (1964) to be more effective in hypnosis than in nocturnal sleep.

Goldburgh (1968) tested 130 undergraduate students with examination anxiety. Hypnosis was found more beneficial than a tranquilizer, while the medication was more effective than expressive-directive treatment. In contrast, Eagan and Eagan (1968) did not find hypnosis helpful in a series of 28 experimental subjects.

We have been quite pleased, over the years, with the relief achieved by most of our hypnotherapy patients whose anxiety during examinations has diminished, leading to improvement in test scores.

Reading

In a summer reading clinic Krippner (1966) employed hypnosis to improve reading skills. Of the 9 pupils who were hypnotized, 8 fell above the class median improvement (5 months better than at the beginning of the 5-week improvement program). A majority of the nonhypnotic group fell below the median, the difference between the two groups being significant at the 0.05 level.

Many clinicians have noted a prolonged benefit from hypnotherapy that may persist even after the immediate examination or learning situation has passed. Fowler (1961) states that "even after the lapse of many weeks . . . he is able to concentrate much more deeply when he studies . . . the members of the controlled groups that were not hypnotized do not indicate that such experimental benefits have come to them."

NEUROLOGICAL DISORDERS

Hypnosis is of value in both the diagnosis and treatment of a wide range of neurological disorders in children. Abnormal movements can be reduced (Lazar, 1977). Psychogenic disorders may be more clearly differentiated from organic problems (Glenn and Simonds, 1977).

Minimal Brain Injury

In an organ as complicated and intricate as the human brain, injuries that do not produce gross abnormalities, such as paralysis, may still underlie subtle changes in the functioning of the child. Such injury, often attributed to the difficulties of birth, may be correlated at times with a problem of hyperactivity. The hyperactive child seems to have a shortened attention span, a decreased ability to control impulses, and exhibits some emotional lability. These symptoms may secondarily cause difficulties between the parents and the child; such children may simply be harder to control. Disruption of their school classes may impair learning and thereby produce further complications.

Hypnosis is not a primary treatment for minimal brain damage, but it may be of great value when adequate neurological evaluation has been completed and appropriate medications are being tried. Perhaps the primary benefits of hypnosis lie in producing a prolonged decrease in anxiety in the child, in reinforcing the child's capacity to recognize his or her lability, and in having the child apply increased conscious control toward the more marked outbursts of emotion. We know of no direct evidence that hypnotherapy produces any measurable changes in such variables as the electroencephalogram. In fact, the evidence seems to suggest that hypnosis does not alter EEG patterns. This does not, however, completely rule out the possibility that some balance of excitation or inhibition in the nervous system could be shifted.

Typical of minimal brain damage is an 8-year-old girl, in the third grade at school, who had difficulties in adjusting in school. She had been seen attempting to cheat on exams, and at home she had a strained relationship with her mother, stemming largely from the mother's feeling of frustration at her inability to control the child's erratic behavior. She was not well accepted by children of similar age in her neighborhood, having frequent quarrels when playing with peers.

Neurological evaluation suggested hyperactivity on the basis of minimal brain disorder; an abnormal electroencephalogram further supported this impression. She was tried on diphenylhydantoin with some slight improvement.

We were asked to evaluate the child to ascertain if psychological factors might be of importance in the total picture. On psychiatric examination the child seemed to realize that something was wrong with her and had some grasp of how she felt "different" at various times. The usual motivational conflicts seen in neurotic behavior were not prominent. Also, she seemed to be functioning at an average level of intelligence, though her vocabulary and her intellectual grasp of some questions suggested a higher potential.

Hypnosis was instituted on a trial basis to decrease anxiety and instill a sense of confidence in the child. She was told that she would find herself wanting to study more and would find pleasure and gratification in doing the very best job possible. She was told in the trance that some of the energy that was causing her trouble would be redirected into more useful work. She would find herself capable of making better grades in school. Such a suggestion for improved grades would not have been made had it not seemed, on balance, that the reality of her situation was such that she had not been using her full capabilities. She was next told that she would be able to concentrate much better and would begin to enjoy getting along in school and with her parents.

Following each hypnotic session, the child was encouraged to discuss her fears, her fantasies, her feelings about past failures, and any unusual problems or successes that she had experienced since the last visit.

At the end of 9 weeks her report card had come up one letter grade, on average. Her attention span seemed improved, and her ability to concentrate seemed more stable. She was enjoying school more and showed marked improvement on her examinations. Her interpersonal relations with her parents, her schoolmates, and her teachers indicated good adjustment. Six months later her grades were above average, and she had become more happy. Her anxiety was rarely sufficient to cause any of her past difficulties.

Throughout her treatment great care was taken not to set goals that were unrealistically high for her apparent abilities, as this would have induced a further conflict of perhaps greater severity than her presenting complaints. This precaution makes accurate clinical assessment of great importance in using hypnosis for such cases.

Parker (1979) reported hypnosis to treat a child's impaired writing performance resulting from neurological damage.

Epilepsy

Raginsky (1963) reported that hypnosis could decrease the frequency of psychomotor epileptic seizures. In several cases it has seemed to us that the frequency of grand mal seizures decreased after a suggestion for such a decrease was repeated over a period of time in hypnotherapy. The mechanism for such an effect is unknown, and more observation is necessary to clearly establish that hypnosis is of clear benefit in such cases. Epilepsy is discussed in Chapter 14 on neurology.

Cerebral Palsy

Disorders of movement, caused by brain damage, may produce severe psychological problems, which, in turn, make it difficult for the child to use his or her affected musculature to full capacity. As with adult patients recovering use of limbs after strokes, hypnosis may be an important tool for increasing motivation for improvement in cerebral palsy. Under hypnosis the child is told that it is important for him or her to use his or her brain to full capacity, that the affected extremities will improve in function as they are exercised, and that the child will find himself or herself having an increasing desire to use his or her body to its full available capacity. Care is taken not to phrase the suggestions in such a manner that the child feels compelled to exceed his or her realistic capacity, but an attempt is made to strongly motivate the child for the maximum function that is physically possible. When improvement occurs, the patient's self-image seems to be enhanced. This is encouraged by verbal praise. Results have seemed beneficial in most cases.

TRAUMA

Hypnosis should be considered in certain special situations of trauma in children. These situations are, in general, the same as those where it could be used in adults—in treatment of severe burns, in special indications for hypnosis as a method of anesthesia, in the food-intake problems, and in increasing motivation for rehabilitation procedures.

In addition to the physical distress of a traumatic injury or burn, the child may suffer the burden of separation from the parents on whom he or she feels so dependent. Self-conscious use of the intensified transference feelings that are possible under hypnosis may be used to reassure the burned child, or the child in the orthopedic case, that a significant and caring adult is concerned for his or her welfare. This benefit may occur in addition to the specific effect suggested—as decreased pain, ability to tolerate well an uncomfortable position necessary for healing, and the need to increase food intake. When a child is injured and requires surgical treatment, hypnosis may be at times quite useful as a sole anesthetic or as an aid to chemical anesthesia. Should the child have eaten just before the trauma, hypnosis may induce sufficient pain relief for minor procedures, and it may help the patient avoid the vomiting that inhalation anesthesia may entail. At times hypnosis has been used to aid the pain relief and increase the cooperation of children whose fractures were reduced in the emergency room, avoiding the need for general anesthesia.

Rehabilitation procedures after trauma may be extended, painful, and frustrating. As with adults, hypnosis may act as a motivating factor in such cases.

CHARACTER DISORDERS

Unlike neurotic conflicts, which involve anxiety, character disorders are fixed ways of behaving and thinking that are relatively conflict-free for the person affected, causing him or her little anxiety, although disrupting greatly his or her adaptation to society. Examples of characterological problems are the passive-aggressive personality, in which the subject uses unresponsiveness and passivity—"helplessness"—to express underlying hostile feelings; the immature personality, who relates in a manner more primitive than his or her age; the sociopathic personality, who manipulates the environment with no real depth of feeling and concern for those involved. Whereas the occurrence of anxiety or depression causes the neurotic to modify his behavior—or attempt to do so—the person with a characterological problem only experiences it as a difficulty when he or she is "caught" in his or her unsocial behavior.

In children and adolescents the diagnosis of character disorders is very difficult, since in these age groups the personality is still in the process of formation, and behavior that would be clearly characterological in an adult, with a more fixed personality, may simply be part of the child or adolescent's testing behavior. Until the ego identity is clearly formed, it is difficult to say that it has been fixed in a pathological structure. Despite this real limitation on the use of the concept before adulthood, one can often see in disturbed children what appears to be the forerunners of future character problems.

The handicap in diagnosis is balanced by the chance to influence, through therapy, the formation of character structure that has not yet "jelled" into an undesirable form. Adult character disorders are difficult to treat outside of institutions, and the adult ability to feign normal behavior makes institutionalization difficult to maintain for a sufficient time for treatment to be effective. Cleckley (1955), writing the classic monograph on character disorders, referred to them as the "mask of sanity," and speculated that character disorders may actually be more disruptive to society than psychosis, although more difficult to diagnose and treat. Sociopaths have been described as having "lacunae" or "holes in the super-ego," the part of the personality that involves feelings of conscience, so that situations that would ordinarily arouse guilt or anxiety are simply not responded to in the conventional way. The person thus lacks the normal amount of inner control.

While the adult with a fixed character disorder is difficult to treat, since he or she is not really motivated for change except in situations where he or she is "caught," it is more possible to treat the precursors of character disorders in children, largely because it is still possible for the parents to control most of the child's environment (his rewards and punishments) and the child can, therefore, be made more motivated to examine his or her behavior. This is particularly true of the child in preteen or early teen years while there is still a naturally occurring positive identification with the parents. Treatment is enhanced, of course, if the parents are themselves stable and mature.

What signs does one look for in diagnosing an incipient character disorder? Frequent indicators include lying, cheating, stealing, lack of respect for the property of others, minimal guilt feelings in situations where guilt is evident, lack of response to reasonable punishment and rule setting, and an excessive disrespect for parents and authority figures. These symptoms reflect both a lack of adequate ego structure and insufficient internalization of early authority relationships.

Under hypnosis the child with an incipient character problem is allowed to vent his or her true feelings, true fears, and hostilities. In the controlled situation of hypnosis, with the child in an induced passive state, the therapist acts the role of an appropriate, mature, and reasonable superego. The child is told that he or she will not want to respond in a childish, passive, immature way simply because he or she is frightened and thinks that he or she cannot "make it" in an adult and responsible way. With hypnosis the transference is intensified and acts as a balance to the lack of control in the outside world. With the patient in trance the therapist may represent deeply introjected parent figures, or even the control inherent in unconscious processes themselves. Thus, the suggestions carry not only the interpersonal authority of the professional and the patient relationship, but also the implied authority of the unconscious in relation to the ego.

As would perhaps be anticipated, hypnosis for character problems has proven much more reliably effective in children than in adults. The most effective treatment involves some counseling with parents as well so that improvements in the child are reinforced in the home environment. The effectiveness decreases some after approximately age 18.

Mellor (1961), Goncalves-Gonzaga (1961), and others have used hypnosis effectively in the treatment of delinquency.

DRUG ABUSE

The increasing problem of drug abuse among teenagers appears more often as a symptom than a primary diagnosis. Not infrequently the child or the parents attribute to the use of drugs problems that actually arise in a conflict situation. In the case of psychedelic drugs, such as LSD and psylocybin, there may be "flashbacks," transient recurrences of the drug experience without having ingested further drugs. These recurrent manifestations seem to be triggered at times by anxiety and may in some cases represent hysterical symptoms.

With markedly addicting drugs, such as heroin, cocaine, and morphine, treatment in an inpatient setting, under medical supervision, is necessary for safe and controlled withdrawal. Such drugs as marijuana, amphetamines, and tranquilizers, which are more psychologically habituating than physically addicting, can be successfully treated on an outpatient basis, though hospitalization often may be needed simply to control access to drugs.

The use of hypnosis in addiction problems is not widespread. In our experience it has proven useful in selected cases where the addicted person is deeply motivated to change. It is not a substitute for medical management, where that is indicated, but may make the psychological effects of withdrawal less disrupting. Two uses of hypnosis seem important in this respect: (1) substituting the sense of relaxation and well-being that can be induced in the trance state for the narcoticizing effect of the drug and (2) the use of hypnosis to build motivation and resolve to follow through on the decision to withdraw from the use of drugs. Both of these uses of hypnosis are combined, in all cases, with explorative and supportive psychotherapy. Success has been most marked when it was possible to identify and treat the underlying stresses that drugs had been used in a vain attempt to control. Success may also be anticipated when the drug use has not represented an inappropriate attempt to solve conflicts but has been simply a pattern that the child has fallen into because of peer pressure and environment. In the latter situation ego-strengthening therapy, allowing the child to use more autonomy and self-choice, is a key to eliminating the dependence on drugs.

Baumann (1970) found that hypnosis for controlling drug abuse was most helpful in adolescents who feared possible harm to their physical health, though less effective in those who maintained that their drug use was harmless. His findings thus confirm our own impression of the effectiveness of hypnosis increasing with the patient's motivation for change.

O'Conner (1982) reported the utility of hypnosis in adolescents addicted to glue sniffing and solvent abuse.

NUTRITIONAL PROBLEMS

Childhood is a time of rapid growth, requiring nutrition adequate to support the high metabolic rate needed for growth. Realizing this, mothers frequently become greatly concerned when there is alteration in the eating pattern of a child. Most concerns center over the quantity of food ingested—either too little, leading to malnutrition, or too much, causing obesity. At times the child develops food preference of abnormal nature, restricting himself or herself to one type of food to the dismay of the parents. At other times it is important for the child to maintain a particular diet, as in treatment of severe diabetes, and the parents experience difficulty in persuading the child to adhere to the prescribed dietary limitations.

In children who are either underweight or obese, often an underlying hostility toward a parent or authority figure is unconsciously involved. This may occur at a very early age, during the phase of negativism that is characteristic of children of about age 3, but it may persist even into adulthood. When such a mechanism of hostility is involved, it seems more important for the child to prove that he or she is in control of the situation than for the child to achieve what he or she states is the conscious goal—either to gain or to lose weight. Children have even admitted in the course of therapy that they enjoy food more when it is "stolen," sneaked without the parent's knowledge. This is not to say that in such cases the child is consciously aware of his or her motivation, which may have become automatized and unconscious through repetition or repression. In such situations it is necessary to first understand the meaning of the eating pattern, exploring and abreacting the affects involved, before hypnosis can be successful in obliterating the habit pattern itself.

Other unconscious patterns that are found, though more rarely, are desires to have a child, the obese abdomen being equated with pregnancy. When pregnancy fantasy is involved, exactly the reverse effect may be found—the girl losing weight, even to a life-threatening degree, to reassure herself that she is not pregnant. In severe cases this may eventuate in anorexia nervosa, which we have discussed more fully in Chapter 11.

A teenage girl who swore convincingly that she had adhered to her prescribed diet was found to be sneaking candy and other food at school. When the mother questioned the school dietician, she was told that the girl always came through the line taking only the food that had been prescribed on her special diet. Some of her teachers, however, had noticed that she was frequently eating on the playground during the lunch recess, and friends of the girl confirmed that they had slipped her extra food, candy, and other "forbidden" items. Much of the girl's pleasure in overeating seemed to come from her ability to "fool" her parents, which neurotically far outweighed the pleasure that she experienced from losing weight and improving her appearance. Some discussion of her motives in therapy led to clarification and to her ability to choose her goals more consciously and more appropriately.

In addition to hypnosis, children and teenagers being treated for obesity are asked to "weigh in" at each visit. Any loss of weight is praised, though failure to lose or some slight weight gain since the last visit is not criticized but is fully discussed. For a patient with severe obesity, photographs are taken before treatment begins and then at regular intervals of weight loss (perhaps every 20–25 pounds) to give the patient a visual impression of the changes in his or her body image as the desired weight is approached. As part of the treatment regime, each patient records the daily food intake, computing the total calories eaten. Also, at least a mile of walking is suggested daily, both for the exercise and for the sense of vigor that regular use of the body includes.

Food fads—if not outright phobias of certain foods—may occasionally present problems, particularly in the early teens. These food habits may have begun in childhood, with the family and the patient simply adjusting to the unusual food choice. Like children suffering from enuresis, these food faddists often seek psychological help when they enter teenage years and begin visiting friends overnight. More activity with peers causes them to find their previously tolerated symptom to be embarrassing and ostracizing.

Such food restrictions have included a girl who would only eat potato chips, a child who avoided all meats, and several patients who had inordinate fondness for certain brands of canned food. When motivation for change is high, which is usually the case when a patient with a long-standing problem comes for treatment, the success of hypnosis in eradicating such food problems is impressive. Usually by the time treatment is sought, the secondary gain of the food abnormality has begun to wane, and the discomfort and embarrassment of the symptom have increased with increasing age.

Hypnosis is useful in treating children who seem well motivated and nonneurotic but who have difficulty adhering to medically prescribed diets. The most frequent example of this situation is the juvenile diabetic, who finds difficulty in maintaining his or her dietary restrictions. Hypnotic suggestions for adhering to the diet may help initiate the formation of a habit pattern that requires little reinforcement.

PAIN

Quite recently we were asked to see an eight-year-old child with the diagnosis of leukemia. In addition to routine office visits, therapy, and laboratory workup, he had been hospitalized seven times for treatment since the diagnosis was made at age 6.

Although there were periods of remission and exacerbation, the current hospitalization of 3 weeks had been extremely difficult, and the patient was described as quite ill physically. Psychologically he was antagonistic, negativistic, frightened, petulant, and he began refusing required therapeutic procedures. The child had perceived a great deal of pain from many diagnostic tests required (for example, bone marrow biopsies). The frequent injections were becoming intolerable for him. Also, he was aware that two of his best friends had recently died from leukemia in the hospital. He could not sleep well, ate very little, and was becoming quite depressed. Acupuncture was attempted for relief of pain but gave only 26 hours of relief.

After establishing rapport, the child entered a very deep state of hypnosis. He was given the suggestions that (1) he would have much less pain, (2) he would tolerate all procedures with much less discomfort, (3) he would be hungry for all meals prescribed, (4) he would realize that his "powerful, big, strong, unconscious mind" could help him to get well, (5) he would be hungry and would eat all of his meals which would make him strong, and (6) he could use self-hypnosis to reinforce all of the above.

There was an immediate improvement noticed by the entire staff. He tolerated all therapeutic procedures without complaining and used self-hypnosis with excellent results. He ate all of his meals. The fear of dying diminished. This negative, sullen, depressed, seriously ill child had manifested an abrupt change to a cooperative child who is responding well to treatment.

He was discharged from the hospital 1 week later in a state of remission. We will see him on an out-patient basis when necessary.

A 4-year-old child with inoperable brain cancer was referred for hypnosis to help control his discomfort. The child was in continual pain, refused to eat, cried constantly, and demanded that the mother remain with him most of the time. It was necessary that he be given narcotics several times daily for his pain. He had a special nurse during the day, and the pediatrician saw him at least five times a week. Frequently he would cry out in agonizing pain. The mother and father could scarcely bear to see their son's continued suffering. At this time the pediatrician requested that the child be seen for possible hypnotherapy.

The mother and father were specifically asked if the child had ever heard of hypnosis. To their knowledge he had no idea of the concept. When first seen he was lying in bed crying and holding his head. When he learned another doctor was to see him he literally became hysterical with fright. But when left alone with the therapist for about 10 minutes his crying stopped. He then tearfully asked if he were going to get "medicine or a shot." The therapist assured him that he would not get a shot and asked if he knew what hypnosis meant. The child was completely puzzled and knew nothing of the concept. He was then asked to stare at a cigarette lighter and within 15 minutes was in a state of somnambulism. Then he was given the suggestion that he would have much less pain, would eat better, would sleep well, and would enjoy television and magazines. Soon it was possible to reduce narcotic injections from five or six daily to only a minimal amount of Demerol. He ate considerably better, was able to take naps mornings and afternoons, enjoyed watching certain television programs, would look at pictures with interest, and was much more cooperative. He was seen daily the first month, three times a week the second month.

His last appointment for hypnosis came at 7:00 A.M. during the first week of the third month after hypnotic treatment began. He smiled when the therapist entered the room. When asked how he felt, he replied "pretty good, but I have a headache." Under hypnotic suggestion most of the pain was removed and the patient responded well. After his lunch that day, he took a nap and sometime during this period he expired. He died peacefully, not addicted, not in constant pain.

This naive child had never heard of hypnosis, yet responded with almost total relief of pain in spite of the fact that he did not know how a hypnotized person was supposed to respond.*

CANCER

Cancer that occurs in children produces many complications, including pain. Acute and chronic pain were alleviated with hypnotic suggestions in an adolescent girl during the last few months of her life (Ellenberg et al., 1980). Olness (1981) found that 19 of 21 patients with childhood cancer obtained some relief of pain and other benefits from the use of hypnotic exercises.

Zeltzer, Dash, and Holland (1979) reported that two adolescents with sickle cell disease were able to exert some control over both the frequency and intensity of recurrent painful vaso-occlusive crises.

Other workers noted for the application of hypnosis to children with cancer are Gardner, Hilgard, and LeBaron (Gardner, 1981).

BLEEDING

There are reports that hypnotherapy may aid some hemophilic children in actually controlling bleeding (Fung and Lazar, 1983). Sanders (1981) describes hypnotic self-control strategies in hemophilic children.

SUMMARY

Children constitute perhaps the best group of hypnotic subjects. Hypnotherapy can benefit many acute and chronic problems of both emotional and physical origin encountered in pediatric practice.

REFERENCES

Ambrose G: Hypnotherapy for children, in Schneck JM (ed)): Hypnosis in Modern Medicine (ed 3), Springfield, Ill., Charles C Thomas, 1963, p 217
Ambrose G: Hypnosis in the treatment of children. Am J Clin Hypn 11:1–5, 1968
Andolsek K, Novik B: Use of hypnosis with children. J Fam Pract 10:503–507, 1980
Antitch JLS: The use of hypnosis in pediatric anesthesia. J Am Soc Psychosom Dent Med 14:70–75, 1967
Barbara D: Stuttering, in Arieti S (ed): American Handbook of Psychiatry. New York, Basic Books, 1959

*Reprinted with permission from Crasilneck HB, Hall JA: Clinical Hypnosis in Problems of Pain. Am J Clin Exp Hyp 15:153–161, 1973.

Baumann FW: Hypnosis and the adolescent drug abuser. Am J Clin Hypn 13:17–21, 1970

Baumann FW: Hypnosis in the treatment of urinary and fecal incontinence, in Wain HJ (ed): Theoretical and Clinical Aspects of Hypnosis. Miami, Symposia Specialists, Inc., 1981, pp 107–123

Braun BG: Conjoint hypnotherapy of an enuretic child and a polyphobic mother, in David ET, Healy JM (eds): Case Studies in Hypnotherapy. New York, Guilford Press, in press

Browning CW, Crasilneck HB: The experimental use of hypnosis in suppression amblyopia: A preliminary report. Am J Ophthalmol 44:1468–1478, 1957

Call JD: Children, parents, and hypnosis: A discussion. Int J Clin Exp Hypn 24:149–155, 1976

Cioppa FJ, Thal AD: Hypnotherapy in a case of juvenile rheumatoid arthritis. Am J Clin Hypn 18:105–110, 1975

Cleckley H: The Mask of Sanity. St. Louis, C. V. Mosby, 1955

Collison DR: Hypnotherapy in the management of nocturnal enuresis. Med J Aust 1:52–54, 1970

Collison DR: Hypnotherapy with children. Aust J Clin Hypn 2:106–114, 1974

Cooper L: Symposium—hypnotherapy with children. Annual meeting of the Society for Clinical and Experimental Hypnosis, Chicago, 1975

Cullen SC: Current comment and case reports: Hypnoinduction techniques in pediatric anesthesia. Anesthesiology 19:279–281, 1958

Dash J: Rapid hypno-behavioral treatment of a needle phobia in a five year old cardiac patient. J Petiatr Psychol 6:37–42, 1981

Eagan RM, Eagan WP: The effect of hypnosis on academic performance. Am J Clin Hypn 2:30–34, 1968

Eddie C: Hypnotherapy in pediatrics. Australia Nurses J 3:25–30, 1975

Elkins GR, Carter BD: Use of science-fiction based imagery techniques in child hypnosis. Am J Clin Hypn 23:274–277, 1981

Ellenberg L, Kellerman J, Dash J, Higgins G, Zeltzer L: Use of hypnosis for multiple symptoms in an adolescent girl with leukemia. J Adolesc Health Care 1:132–136, 1980

Falck FJ: Stuttering and hypnosis. Int J Clin Exp Hypn 12:67–74, 1964

Fowler WL: Hypnosis and learning. Int J Clin Exp Hypn 9:223–232, 1961

Fung E, Lazar BS: Hypnosis as an adjunct in the treatment of von Willebrand's disease. Int J Clin Exp Hypn 31:256–265, 1983

Gardner GG: Hypnosis with children. Int J Clin Exp Hypn 22:20–38, 1974

Gardner GG: Attitude of child health professionals toward hypnosis: Implications for training. Int J Clin Exp Hypn 24:63–73, 1976

Gardner GG: Hypnosis with infants and preschool children. Am J Clin Hypn 19:158–162, 1977

Gardner GG: Hypnotherapy in the management of childhood habit disorders. J Pediatr 92:838–840, 1978

Gardner GG, Hinton RM: Hypnosis with children, in Burrows GD, Dennerstein L (eds): Handbook of Hypnosis and Psychosomatic Medicine. Amsterdam, Elsevier/North-Holland Biomedical Press, 1980, pp 205–231

Gardner GG, Olness K: Hypnosis and Hypnotherapy With Children. New York, Grune & Stratton, 1981

Gardner GG, Tarnow JD: Adjunctive hypnotherapy with an autistic boy. Am J Clin Hypn 22:173–179, 1980

Glenn TJ, Simonds JF: Hypnotherapy of a psychogenic seizure disorder in an adolescent. Am J Clin Hypn 19:245–249, 1977

Goldburgh SJ: Hypnotherapy, chemotherapy, and expressive-directive therapy in the treatment of examination anxiety. Am J Clin Hypn 11:42–44, 1968

Goncalves-Gonzaga J: Beneficios de la hypnoterapia en los trastornos de conducta juveniles. Rev. Lat-Am Hypn Clin 1:57–60, 1960

Grable RH: A refractory speech problem successfully treated with hypnosis. Am J Clin Hypn 11, 1968

Granone F: Hypnotherapy in stuttering. Minerva Medica [Suppl. 3]:2158–2159, 1966

Hammer EF: Post-hypnotic suggestion and test performance. J Clin Exp Hypn 2:178–185, 1954

Hilgard ER: Hypnotic phenomena: The struggle for scientific acceptance. Am Sci 59:567–577, 1971

Hinman F Jr, Baumann FW: Complications of vesicoureteral operations from incoordination of micturition. J Urol 116:638–643, 1976

Hubbard OE: Hypnotherapy of a patient complaining of a speech defect. Am J Clin Hypn 5:281–294, 1963

Jacobs L: Hypnosis in clinical pediatrics. NY State J Med 62:3781–3787, 1962

Jacobs L: Sleep problems of children: Treatment by hypnosis. NY State J Med 65:629–634, 1964

Jacobs L, Jacobs H: Hypnotizability of children as related to hemispheric reference and neurological organization. Am J Clin Hypn 8:269–274, 1966

Johnson LS, Johnson DL, Olson MR, Newman JP: The uses of hypnotherapy with learning disabled children. J Clin Psychol 37:291–299, 1981

Kellerman J: Hypnosis as an adjunct to thought-stopping and covert reinforcement in the treatment of homicidal obsessions in a twelve year old boy. Int J Clin Exp Hypn 29:128–135, 1981

Kohen D, Olness K, Colwells HA: 500 Pediatric behavioral problems treated with hypnotherapy. Presented at the annual meeting of the American Society of Clinical Hypnosis, Minneapolis, November, 1980

Krippner S: The use of hypnosis with elementary and secondary children in a summer reading clinic. Am J Clin Hypn 8:261–266, 1966

Krojanker RJ: Human hypnosis, animal hypnotic states, and the induction of sleep in infants. Am J Clin Hypn 11:178–179, 1969

Kulikov VN: Obuchenie vo sne [sleep learning]. Sov Ped 28:51–58, 1964

Laguaite J: The use of hypnosis with children with deviate voices. Int J Clin Exp Hypn 24:98–104, 1976

Lawlor ED: Hypnotic intervention with "school phobic" children. Int J Clin Exp Hypn 24:74–86, 1976

LaScola RL: Hypnosis with children, in Cheek DB, LeCron LM (eds): Clinical Hypnotherapy. New York, Grune & Stratton, 1968

Lazar BS: Hypnotic imagery as a tool in working with a cerebral palsied child. Int J Clin Exp Hypn 25:78–87, 1977

Lazar BS, Jedlieczka ZT: Utilization of manipulative behavior in a retarded asthmatic child. Am J Clin Hypn 21:287–292, 1979

Levine ES: Indirect suggestions through personalized fairy tales for treatment of childhood insomnia. Am J Clin Hypn 23:57–63, 1980

Lodato FJ: Hypnosis: An adjunct to test performance. Am J Clin Hypn 2:129–130, 1968

London P: Hypnosis in children: An experimental approach. Int J Clin Exp Hypn 10:79–91, 1962

London P: The Children's Hypnotic Susceptibility Scale. Palo Alto, Calif., Consulting Psychologists Press, 1963

London P: Child hypnosis and personality. Am J Clin Hypn 8:161–168, 1966

London P, Cooper LM: Norms of hypnotic susceptibility in children. Dev Psychol 1:113–124, 1969

Madison L: The use of hypnosis in the differential diagnosis of a speech disorder. J Clin Exp Hypn 2:140, 1954

McCord H:Hypnotherapy and stuttering. J Clin Exp Hypn 3:210–214, 1955

McCord H: Hypnosis as an aid to the teaching of a severely mentally retarded teenage boy. J Clin Exp Hypn 2:21–23, 1956

McCord H, Sherrell CI: A note on increased ability to do calculus post-hypnotically. Am J Clin Hypn 4:124, 1962

Mellor NH: Hypnosis in juvenile delinquency. Am J Clin Hypn 4:133, 1961

Mirvish I: Hypnotherapy for the child with chronic eczema: A case report. S Afr Med J 54:410–412, 1978

Moore WE: Hypnosis in a system of therapy for stutterers. J Speech Disord 11:117–122, 1946

Morban-Laucer FA: Sucking habits in the child and their origins in psychological traumas. Am J Clin Hypn 4:128, 1961

O'Conner D: The use of suggestion techniques with adolescents in the treatment of glue-sniffing and solvent abuse. Hum Toxicol 1:313–320, 1982

O'Grady DJ, Hoffman C: Hypnosis with children and adolescents in the medical settings. In Wester WC, Smith AH (eds): Clinical Hypnosis: A multidisciplinary approach. Philadelphia, JP Lippincott, 1984, pp 181–209

Olness K: In service hypnosis education in a children's hospital. Am J Clin Hypn 20:80–83, 1977

Olness K: The terminally ill child, in Gardner GG, Olness K (eds): Hypnosis and Hypnotherapy with Children. New York: Grune & Stratton, 1981, pp 247–248

Olness D, Gardner GG: Some guidelines for uses of hypnotherapy in pediatrics. Pediatrics 62:228–233, 1978

Orton S: Reading, Writing, and Speech Problems. New York, W. W. Norton, 1937

Parker J: The use of hypnosis to restore a child's impaired writing performance resulting from neurological damage. Aust J Clin Exp Hypn 7:225–230, 1979

Raginsky BB: Hypnosis in internal medicine and general practice, in Schneck JM (ed): Hypnosis in Modern Medicine (ed 3), Springfield, Ill., Charles C Thomas, 1963

Reaney JB: Hypnosis in the treatment of habit disorders, in Wester WC, Smith AH (eds): Clinical Hypnosis: a multidisciplinary approach. Philadelphia: J.B. Lippincott, 1984, pp 305–324

Rousey CL: Hypnosis in speech pathology and audiology. J Speech Hear Disord 26:258–267, 1961

Sanders S: Hypnotic self-control strategies in hemophilic children. J Am Soc Psychosom Dent Med 28:11–21, 1981

Schneck JM: Hypnoanalytic elucidation of childhood germ phobia. Int J Clin Exp Hypn 14:305–307, 1966

Shaw SI: A survey of the management of children in hypnodontia. Am J Clin Hypn 1:155–162, 1959

Smith GC, Crasilneck HB, Browning CW: A follow-up study of suppression amblyopia in children previously subjected to hypnotherapy. Am J Ophthalmol 52:690–695, 1961

Solovey G, Milechnin A: Concerning the treatment of enuresis. Am J Clin Hypn 2:22–30, 1959

Taboada E: Night terrors in a child treated with hypnosis. Am J Clin Hypn 17:270–271, 1975

Wester, WC, Smith AH (eds): Clinical Hypnosis: A Multidisciplinary Approach. Philadelphia, J.B. Lippincott Co., 1983

Williams DT, Singh M: Hypnosis as a facilitating therapeutic adjunct in child psychiatry. J Am Acad Child Psychiatry 15:326–342, 1976

Wright ME: Hypnosis and child therapy. Am J Clin Hypn 2:197–205, 1960

Zeltzer L, Dash J, Holland JP: Hypnotically induced pain control in sickle cell anemia. Pediatrics 64:533–536, 1979

14

Hypnosis in Neurological Problems and Rehabilitation

Hypnosis lends itself to use in neurology (1) in differential diagnosis of functional and organic problems, (2) in maximizing functional ability even in cases when full recovery is not possible, (3) in diminishing pain and improving the patient's ability to tolerate the discomforts of his or her illness, (4) in increasing motivation for rehabilitation, and (5) in special neurological problems.

DIFFERENTIAL DIAGNOSIS

Hypnosis often can assist in the differential diagnosis of functional and organic neurological problems (Rudlova and Rudlova, 1961). Most hysterical phenomena can resemble organic paralysis or other lesions, a similarity that had led Charcot to consider hysteria as having a physiological basis. An arm may appear equally paralyzed because of a nerve lesion or severe neurotic conflict. Specialized tests, such as nerve conduction studies, may be necessary to help make the etiology clear. Careful observation of a person during a period of natural sleep may reveal bodily movement that gives insight into the actual range of motor functioning. In many instances hypnosis also can aid in distinguishing between these types of disability.

A woman in her late twenties was seen by us in consultation because of an inability to walk that had lasted for several months. The neurologist had suspected a psychogenic basis, and under hypnosis she was indeed able to walk easily without the apparent weakness that she had exhibited when awake.

Inquiry under hypnosis revealed that she had severe guilt feelings about an extramarital affair in which she had been involved just prior to her husband's accidental death in an automobile wreck. Her need for a conversion symptom was accepted, and the hysterical symptom was restored to her before she was awakened from trance. It was recommended that she enter long-term intensive psychotherapy, which she did, with eventual cure of her "paralysis."

In the use of hypnosis for differential diagnosis in neurological cases it is not always possible to establish a meaning of the symptom without intensive and prolonged anamnesis in psychotherapy or psychoanalysis. Nevertheless, hypnosis can often suggest the origin of the symptom, although the understanding of underlying psychodynamics may have to be gradually formulated as information is slowly acquired.

A young male was in a severe automobile accident on his way to college. After regaining consciousness, he was found to have a foot-drop on the right, which failed to improve as he recovered from the accident. Under hypnosis he was able to walk freely, with no evidence of the difficulty. He entered psychotherapy, and only later was it learned that at the time of the accident he had been driving to a college that was the choice of his mother but not of himself. His anger at being "forced" to go to this undesired college had apparently been expressed in his unconscious "unwillingness" to give up the foot-drop.

Dorcus (1956) employed hypnosis to demonstrate the psychological origin of feigned paraplegia. The patient had been hospitalized for 7 years, confined to a wheelchair and could not move his legs. Under hypnosis, however, he was easily able to move his lower extremities and was later, under close observation, found to be actually walking about his room when he thought no one was watching. Magonet and Philip (1961) used hypnosis not only in the differential diagnosis of functional and organic dysphagia but in treatment as well. Miller (1983) has reported 3 cases of psychogenic seizures in which hypnosis was useful in both diagnosis and treatment.

A useful differential point in deciding about organic or functional tremor is the length of time that hypnosis will improve the symptom. As the result of our work with hundreds of cases over the years, we have come to the conclusion that hypnosis may actually relieve tremor of organic origin—but only for short periods of time, usually 1 to 4 hours. Functional tremor, on the other hand, may be relieved for days following a single successful hypnotic induction.

A 28-year-old woman who had suffered a tremor of her hands all her life when under emotional pressure came for treatment because the symptom interfered with her work as a manicurist. Hypnosis was able to completely abolish the tremor, but for only half an hour. On the basis of this observation she was thought to have an organic problem and was referred to a neurologist. His impression was that she suffered from a familial tremor that was increased by voluntary movement.

Neurological examinations under hypnosis may allow the better assessment of the degree to which the patient is actually attempting to carry out the suggested movements. In cases difficult to test conventionally hypnosis may help in audiologic examinations (Hallewell et al., 1961). These techniques of examination under hypnosis make use of the very strong motivation that can be engendered in the trance state.

A woman in her early fifties was hospitalized with weakness in her right arm. In addition she had a great deal of obvious psychological difficulty and depression. We found that under hypnosis the weakness could be significantly diminished, the effect lasting about 1 hour before the weakness resumed. This observation was repeated on three separate occasions with the same result. The weakness was considered on this basis to be most likely organic. The condition gradually worsened, localizing signs appeared, and she died of a rapidly expanding brain tumor without ever being discharged from the hospital.

A 45-year-old woman was referred for pain in the right chest and axilla for which neurological examination and subsequent examination by an orthopedic surgeon found no organic explanation. A psychogenic basis was suspected. Psychiatric consultation failed to illuminate any clear emotional conflict that might be expressed by the pain, if on a conversion basis, nor was there any example of a similar symptom in the patient's past associations with emotionally significant persons—parents, sibling, close friends, husband, etc. She was hypnotized on three separate occasions; in each instance the pain was almost completely relieved, but only for a period of 3 to 4 hours. This strongly suggested that it was generated by an unsuspected organic lesion since psychogenic pain tends to longer relief with hypnosis. Even the expected effect of increasing relief with repetition of hypnosis, whether the pain was organic or functional, was not observed. On the strength of this observation, her neurologist asked for a further consultation by a chest surgeon, who found some abnormality in the shape of one rib and, on thoracotomy, identified a nonmalignant bony growth that had displaced one intercostal nerve. When this was surgically corrected, her pain was completely relieved. Five years later there had been no return of symptoms.

Buell and Biehl (1949) studied the effect of hypnosis on parkinsonian tremor. In one case posthypnotic suggestion was able to abolish the tremor for 6 to 9 minutes. In the other case abolition of the tremor was achieved only during hypnosis itself. In another patient it was improved but not abolished under hypnosis. Becker (1960) has used hypnosis to decrease the tension and blocking effects sometimes seen in parkinsonism. Bird (1948) was able to decrease parkinsonian tremor in hypnotic trance of only moderate depth.

Stambaugh (1977) used hypnotherapy to aid in depression associated with parkinsonian disease. Stewart (1983), a neurologist, is presently studying the effects of hypnosis in the control of parkinsonian disease.

Weil (1983) used hypnosis to aid in the control of seizures in a woman with an inoperable cerebral neoplasm; the seizures were completely controlled only when hypnotherapy (with some exploration of psychodynamics) was added to the antiepileptic medications. When psychological factors are significant in epileptic behavior, hypnotherapy is often of value (Gravitz, 1979). Stein (1980) used hypnosis successfully in diminishing intention tremor in an 82-year-old patient. With appropriate modification, such as optical fixation, vibratory stimulation, air currents, etc., hypnosis can be successfully employed even with deaf patients, the important factor being a clear communication of the suggestion to enter an altered state of consciousness (Gravitz, 1981). Hypnosis can be used diagnostically as an aid in differentiating between true epilepsy and pseudoepilepsy (Gross, 1980).

Backus (1962) abolished optokinetic nystagmus, which was apparently an organic basis, by giving a negative hypnotic hallucination for the normal appearance of the room. He concluded that the optokinetic-reflex response was not a definitive means of differentiating hysterical and true blindness.

MAXIMIZING FUNCTION

Even in proven cases of neurological deficit where recovery is not possible, hypnosis may be helpful in assisting the patient to use his or her remaining abilities to their maximum (Baer, 1960; Becker, 1963; Wright, 1960; Yensen, 1963). Although the mechanism for such effect is not always clear, it may often be usefully conceptualized as a change in the balance of facilitating or inhibiting neural impulses. The reported improvement of epilepsy after hypnotic treatment (Abe, 1971; Knowles, 1964) may involve some change in the excitability of the cortex around the epileptogenic focus, although experimental validation of this hypothesis is lacking. It may be that the disabled are more readily hypnotized because of their need for therapy (Becker, 1963).

A 55-year-old man was referred to us for hypnotic motivation treatment in his rehabilitation from a complete occlusion of the left internal carotid artery, which left him with right hemiparesis and dysphasia. The target symptom was improvement of his speech function. He was seen for weekly hypnotherapy sessions, utilizing direct suggestions for improvement, for a period of 6 months. He regained approximately 40 percent of the lost function of his speech and gait, but the most important improvement was the development of high motivation for rehabilitation in all areas of his functioning, both physical and psychological.

Owen-Flood (1952) reported treating epilepsy with hypnosis, limiting attacks to nighttime and decreasing their severity. He did not, however, publish detailed case reports as to his method. Pasquarelli and Bellak (1947) have published a case report of a man suffering from both hysterical convulsions and idiopathic grand mal epilepsy. The hysterical convulsions were entirely abolished by hypnosis, while the genuine epileptic seizures could be relegated to the time when the patient was asleep.

Dorcus (1956) found that hypnosis, though not foolproof, was useful in many instances in separating organic epilepsy from hysterical seizures. In a total series of 142 patients Peterson, Sumner, and Jones (1950) and Sumner, Cameron, and Peterson (1952) found that suppressed epileptics who could remember, under hypnosis, what had happened during their seizures might be suffering from psychogenic seizures. There was a high correlation between such recall and normal EEG patterns. Knowles (1964) suggests hypnotherapy in some cases where drug therapy is not sufficiently effective. We once attempted hypnotic age regression of an epileptic to an age prior to the onset of his seizures to determine if the EEG would improve, but (as expected) no change in the EEG pattern was seen (McCranie and Crasilneck, 1953). Higley (1958), however, found that such age regression of aid in treating paralysis following poliomyelitis.

LeHew (1971) noted great improvement in a case of torticollis ("wryneck") of 48 years' duration. Shires, Peters, and Krout (1954) reported the use of hypnosis in a subject with hemiplegia, claiming that recovery was both more rapid and more complete than when routine physical therapy measures were used alone. Chappell (1961, 1964) was able to reduce spasticity by means of hypnotic relaxation in four patients with transverse myelitis involving complete paralysis and anesthesia below the level of the lesion. Vann (1971) has employed hypnosis for the anxiety associated with Huntington's chorea.

In 20 cases of severe head injury in which, after recovery, there existed both anterograde and retrograde amnesias, a marked recovery of memory was achieved in 7 cases through the use of deep hypnosis (Milos, 1975). We have often used hypnosis in differentiating post-traumatic amnesia of an organic nature from that of psychogenic origin.

In many instances, the residual amnesia has both components. In an experimental study of intentionally induced posthypnotic amnesia, Howard and Coe (1980) found that subjects who felt their suggested amnesia as "voluntary" were able to more readily remove the amnesia than were those subjects who experienced the amnesia as happening involuntarily.

Very often simple suggestions for relaxation, given in trance, will produce improvement in function in a wide range of neurological disorders. In cases of multiple sclerosis the beneficial effects of hypnosis have been reported by Ambrose (1955), Brunn (1966), McCord (1966). Improvement may be produced by a combination of relaxation and increased motivation for normal functioning. Although palliative, such treatment may add to the psychological well-being of the patient and to his or her functional ability. Hypnotherapy has also been used to help multiple sclerosis patients achieve bowel and bladder control (Baer, 1961).

Some transient improvement in function may be produced in mild cases of myasthenia gravis, apparently through increased motivation. However, the primary benefit of hypnosis to such patients seems to be the relief of anxiety about their worsening physical state. Improved body image, induced hypnotically, has been suggested by Fogel (1971) as an aid in treating spasm.

Patients with peripheral nerve lesions should achieve reactivation as rapidly as possible to prevent permanent damage; hypnosis may be of help even with muscles that have only weak reinnervation (Pajnter et al., 1980)

Although hypnosis may transiently improve the symptoms of cerebral palsy (Secter and Gilberd, 1964; Spankus and Freeman, 1962), the chief benefit consists of decreasing anxiety. Improvement may also be expected in anxiety symptoms of patients with psychosis secondary to organic brain syndrome caused by cancer (Eliseo, 1974).

Approximately 50 percent of patients referred to us with Ménière's disease seem to improve when given hypnotic suggestion for less dizziness. Relief is not as remarkable as in diminishing pain with hypnosis, however. In many cases of narcolepsy, direct suggestions for being more alert and wakeful during daylight hours can lead to improvements. Neither published reports nor our own cases have been numerous enough to form a clear impression of whether the different parts of the syndrome—sleep paralysis, cataplexy, and hypnogogic hallucinations—are differentially affected by hypnosis.

We have seen many cases of Gilles de la Tourette's disease, an exotic neurological syndrome consisting of violent ticlike movements together with explosive use of foul language. Some have thought this syndrome to be psychogenic, but we believe that there is probably a predisposing neurological basis. Approximately half of our patients improved markedly with prolonged hypnotherapy, a few improved slightly, while others seemed unresponsive, though they were good hypnotic subjects. Similar results have been reported by Erickson (1965) and Lindner (1967).

Hypnosis has been used in specialized neurosurgical situations, several of which have been discussed in Chapter 7. There are two primary indications for considering hypnosis in a neurosurgical procedure: (1) to lessen the amount of anesthesia so that neurological observations requiring the patient's cooperation of verbal reporting can be accomplished during the surgical procedure and (2) to decrease anxiety and movement in patients who are undergoing neurosurgical procedures under local anesthesia.

PAIN RELIEF

Hypnosis for pain relief has been discussed in Chapter 6. However, it also needs to be considered in this chapter where pain is a significant problem in a neurological case. At times the direct suggestions for pain relief seem to produce unexpected benefits of decreased spasm, although the mechanism of such change is not clear.

A 60-year-old woman was referred for hypnotic pain relief for severe nocturnal cramping in her legs. She had taken large quantities of medication for sedation and pain relief, but with no lasting improvement. Over a number of years she had undergone repeated surgery on one knee, and had to walk with the aid of crutches. Her course was one of progressive deterioration of the knee joint, constant pain, and habituation to medications for pain relief. She was a good hypnotic subject, achieved pain relief of 75 percent (her estimate), decreased her medication, and was functionally improved. She incidentally reported that she seemed to have lost most of the cramping that had often bothered her at night.

Dorcus (1956) reported the use of hypnosis and autohypnosis in a young war veteran who suffered severe pain from a spinal injury. The most frequent spinal pain problem we have seen is that occurring after repeated attempts at spinal fusion following laminectomy for herniated disk. These are discussed more fully in the surgery chapter in the section relating to orthopedic problems.

The pain of trigeminal neuralgia can sometimes be alleviated with hypnosis (Shafer, 1962), which should be attempted before destruction of the stellate ganglion is considered. Other severe pain may yield to hypnosis, including migraine headache (Blumenthal, 1961), which is discussed in Chapter 6. In our practice severe facial pain has yielded to hypnosis:

A man in his mid-thirties had severe facial pain that began with an infection in his jaw but had persisted after the infection had been cleared with antibiotics. Diphenylhydantoin sodium was administered without relief, and he found himself increasingly unable to maintain his work schedule because of the constant discomfort. Several injections of local anesthetic had produced only transient relief, and destructive section of the nerve was to be considered if no relief could be found with hypnosis. After repeated hypnotic inductions, with direct suggestion for pain relief, his discomfort diminished by 80 percent, according to his own estimate. At the time of writing he has been treated for over a year, with periodic reinforcement of suggestions for pain relief being given at monthly intervals.

A particularly interesting type of neurological pain syndrome is that of the painful "phantom limb." Phantom limb refers to the subjective sensation of an amputated extremity still being present, often felt to be in the same position in which it was at the time of the amputation, particularly if the amputation had been traumatic. Many times pain seems to be localized in the phantom. Although not all phantom limbs are painful, those that are can be a complicated problem in management. In some instances attempts have been made to section the nerves from the stump, for the pain is thought to arise from continued stimulation of the nerves, probably by developing scar tissue. At times sections have been made in the pain pathways in the spinal cord itself without diminishing the phantom pain. Such observations suggest that the pain and the sensation of the phantom limb may arise in the cortex rather than in the severed peripheral nerves. Hypnotic suggestion is given that the pain will gradually diminish and the phantom limb becomes smaller and smaller until it finally vanishes into the stump. Successful relief of phantom pain by hypnosis is often remarkable (Bachet, 1969; Papermaster et al., 1960).

Sacerdote (1983) has pioneered understanding of the psychodynamics of hypnotic relief of pain. Significant relief of cervical headache was achieved with nine hypnotic sessions combined with group therapy and self-administered relaxation exercises (Carasso et al., 1983). Of the 23 patients who completed the program more that 95 percent achieved significant improvement.

Direct hypnotic suggestions for relief of headache and vertigo led to improvement in more than half of 155 skull injured patients, the improvement lasting more than 1 year (Cedercreutz, Lahteenmaki, and Tulikoura, 1976). Therapeutic outcome was absent in patients who could not achieve even a light hypnotic trance, but those in light trance were as clinically responsive as those achieving deep trance.

INCREASING MOTIVATION
IN NEUROLOGICAL PROBLEMS

Hypnotherapy has been of value in the rehabilitation of patients who have suffered cerebrovascular or traumatic brain injury (Alexander, 1966; LaScola, 1975). We (Crasilneck and Hall, 1970) reported three such cases, which were representative of 25 similar cases seen over a 9-year period. Four of the 25 cases were unresponsive to hypnosis and, therefore, could not be treated with hypnotherapy. Such therapy had been of benefit in retraining speech (Kirkner, Dorcus, and Seacot, 1953) and in treating aphasia following strokes (Erickson, 1963).

Of all problems seen in clinical practice, one of the most difficult in our experience is working with rehabilitation cases after traumatic or vascular injury to the central nervous system. Neurosurgeons, neurologists, orthopedic surgeons, psychiatrists, psychologists, physical therapists, speech therapists, occupational therapists—and others are involved, often in a team effort. Despite the involvement of many branches of the healing professions, too frequently the patient achieves only a slow or inadequate return to normal levels of functioning.

It is difficult, with statistics, to convey the emotional tone of this problem. In the area of so-called "cerebrovascular accidents," the New York Life Insurance Company statistics show 2 million patients a year, and "strokes" have been listed as third among fatal diseases in this country. The Institute of Life Insurance states that there are now some 1.2 million Americans alive after having experienced a "stroke." Months of hospitalization and specialized care are often required by patients who survive cerebrovascular lesions, as is also true for those subjected to traumatic cerebral lesions in highway accidents and elsewhere. Many recover with minimal difficulty, but there remain a large number who, for apparently psychological reasons, do not achieve the full extent of recovery that their physical status would allow.

We have been interested in the problems of recovery and rehabilitation of these patients for a number of years and have at times observed the effectiveness of hypnosis in aiding rehabilitation, as outlined by Wright (1960). Such cases have been complicated particularly by a difficulty in communication between the injured person and those able to speed his recovery (Mason, 1961). Another factor may be the understandable difficulty that physical therapists, physicians, and others have in working over an extended period of time with a patient who seems incapable of giving normal human responses to their prolonged efforts to aid him.

For years we felt that hypnotic induction is difficult, if not impossible, in patients with severe cerebral physiological insult, presumably because of their decreased ability to comprehend suggestions and maintain a normal attention span. Encouraged, however, by our experience with hypnotic response in clinically unconscious patients in terminal condition (Crasilneck and Hall, 1962), we have made efforts to utilize hypnosis, when requested, in patients who because of cerebral injury are considered poor hypnotic subjects by ordinary criteria. We now realize that hypnosis can be successful in some patients with cerebral insult. We have found that a usual induction technique utilizing progressive relaxation, eye closure, and heaviness can be employed with the following modifications: (1) the therapist must speak very slowly; (2) he or she must use a simple vocabulary; (3) he or she should increase the repetitions given for each suggestion; and (4) he or she must persevere in continuing to visit the patient in spite of minimal response or any negative countertransference. It is also necessary to use a more intuitive evaluation of the patients' response to suggestion. Initially, for example, a decrease in eye or body motility might be taken as a sign of response. Of course, one may at times infer the presence and estimate the depth of hypnosis from such nonverbal signs as eye closure, arm catalepsy, and glove anesthesia. Virtually all patients, during the course of hypnotherapy, become capable of giving unequivocal responses of verbal or nonverbal nature.

Hypnosis has been gratifying particularly in the following types of patients:

1. Patients with poor motivation toward their rehabilitation.
2. Patients who have manifested extreme anxiety, negativism, and depression in response to efforts at rehabilitation.
3. Patients who gave the impression, to trained observers, of showing a "death instinct," by which we mean a nonverbalized but apparent desire not to survive.
4. Patients unable to communicate adequately with physicians and ancillary personnel, whether for neurological or motivational reasons.

In most cases hypnosis was not planned as a routine part of the treatment program; it was introduced only when it became obvious that the patient was not responding adequately to conventional rehabilitation procedures. In some instances the patient was beginning to regress from gains already made.

In the 3 cases that are reported here (Crasilneck and Hall, 1970), hypnosis was followed by a marked reversal of psychological attitude and, subsequently, of physiological functioning. This was also true, though sometimes less dramatic, in 18 similar cases. Four of the 25 patients did not respond to the induction procedure and were not continued beyond three sessions. All four of the nonhypnotizable patients died within a month of being seen in consultation.

Case 1

A 31-year-old woman was having dinner with her family when she suddenly fell to the floor unconscious. No prodromal signs or symptoms preceded this event. Within 30 minutes she was seen in the emergency room of a local hospital where it was noted that she made spontaneous movements of both her arms and her right leg but no voluntary movements of her left leg. Her pupils were round, regular, and equally reactive to light, but her right eye was deviated laterally. The left corner of her mouth was thought to be drooping. An atraumatic spinal tap was performed, yielding grossly bloody spinal fluid with a pressure of 235 mm of fluid.

Her past history was unremarkable. The patient's husband stated that the patient had not been suffering from any chronic disease processes. In retrospect, he recalled that she had frequently complained of a right-sided supraorbital headache, but she had otherwise been in good health.

The initial impression was that the patient had experienced an acute subarachnoid hemorrhage from an intracranial aneurysm on the right carotid artery. Bilateral biplane carotid angiograms performed 4 days after admission confirmed the presence of an aneurysm, and 2 days later a trial ligation of the right internal carotid artery was attempted. The artery was occluded for 30 minutes without progression of localizing neurologic signs, and ligation was considered successful. A Crutchfield clamp was loosely applied around the artery, and the skin was sutured about its handle.

On the day following surgery the clamp was closed because of the sudden onset or retro-orbital pain, nuchal rigidity, and bilateral extensor responses to plantar stimulation. After 4 days, however, further symptoms appeared and transfrontal craniotomy was performed, revealing an aneurysm involving the right internal carotid and two of its branches. The aneurysm was thin-walled, and evidence of both old and recent hemorrhage was found. The aneurysm was completely isolated through ligation of the right carotid artery, the right posterior communicating artery, and the ophthalmic artery.

The patient recovered well from the surgical procedure and was discharged to a nursing home, approximately 1 month postoperatively. At the time of discharge she was disoriented, suffered a left hemiplegia, and was essentially unable to communicate. In spite of encouragement from her physician and nurses to eat and drink, she refused, and frequent intravenous fluids were needed. She was negativistic, hostile, and did not speak. When not sleeping, she simply stared into space. It was at this point that hypnosis was considered, as it had been successful in burn patients refusing to take adequate nourishment.

During the first session the patient did not respond verbally to any questions and showed no movements of her body. During the visit an eye-fixation method was used. The actual induction technique was approximately as follows:

"As you notice, I am holding this half dollar slightly above the level of your vision. I want you to stare intently and intensely at this half-dollar. As you do so you will start to breathe deeply . . . and slowly . . . and you will begin to loosen the muscles in your body . . . your head . . . your forehead . . . your eyelids . . . your face . . . your neck . . . your shoulders . . . your entire body . . . to your legs and feet. . . . Your eyelids are becoming very heavy. . . . Your eyelids are blinking, and they are closing."

After 1 or 2 minutes the patient's eyes closed, and it was evident she could not easily open her eyes when the challenge request was made. Suggestions were then given for arm catalepsy.

"You are going to sleep. . . . You are going into a deep state of trance. . . . Your right arm is becoming very tense and tight, like steel, like a board soaked in water for days . . . so tense, so rigid, that nothing can budge it or bend it."

After arm catalepsy was achieved, suggestions were given for return of normal sensation and function to the arm. Then skin anesthesia was induced in one finger, followed by vigorous stimulation with the tip of a nail file. As expected, the patient failed to show normal pain response. Eventually she achieved a deep state of hypnosis. She had the ability to open the eyes without affecting trance and could experience hallucinations of bitter medicine on the tip of the tongue and of hearing church bells. Both hallucinations were accompanied by suggested body movements. We do not mean to imply, however, that results were necessarily proportional to "depth," as we have observed excellent responses in some patients in "light" trance, particularly in controlling cigarette smoking.

The patient was given the suggestion that she would be hungry, would eat three meals a day, would generally become more cooperative, and would feel less depressed. She was also given the post-hypnotic suggestion to go again into deep hypnosis when the therapist tapped three times on the table but to respond to no one in a non-professional setting. The suggestions were accepted, for upon awakening from trance she ate the food that was offered. She spontaneously smiled and attempted to speak but appeared to be aphasic.

The patient was seen daily for the next 30 days. She responded well to posthypnotic suggestion for food intake, exercise, and cooperation with the nursing home staff. In addition, she was told that her speech could and would return and that she would "consciously and unconsciously" want to "get well."

The patient was moved to her home, where she continued to be seen three times a week for a period of 30 days. She was now eating normally, exercising well, and her aphasia slowly improved. She was encouraged to read primers, which she did, and her speech, concentration, and reading abilities showed steady improvement. Ninety days after her accident her physical rehabilitation showed marked gains. It was reported by the physical therapist that she responded much better than the average patient. After being seen twice a week during the next 60 days, her aphasia became minimal, she walked with some assistance, and she again became interested in herself and her family. The patient was seen once a week for the balance of the year, hypnotherapy continuing until it was judged that maximal recovery had occurred. Suggestions for improved physical functioning were carefully titrated to stay within her actual capabilities as they increased.

The patient developed a strong positive transference, more rapidly than patients in nonhypnotic therapy. This seemed to have more of a dependency than an erotic meaning to her, since she would worry when the therapist was out of town or otherwise unavailable.

Suggestions were continued that she would want to get well "for herself," and gradually she began to show pleasure in exhibiting her improving skills, as in walking, for her husband as well as for the therapist. She next began to have interest in putting on make-up and getting out of bed "to show the children I care." Gradually her range of concern included the physical therapist, an ill neighborhood child, and more distant family. Concurrently, the intensity of her transference on the therapist diminished. During the last month she was given no hypnosis, and supportive psychotherapy was substituted.

At the time that hypnotherapy was discontinued she walked with a cane, spoke with little difficulty, and manifested her preaccident personality. Now she still shows physiological impairment on her left side, but her speech is normal and she has returned to her previous social life.

In an interview concerning her initial perceptions of her illness, the patient reported that she had felt confused most of the time, could not express her thoughts verbally, felt depressed, and wanted to die. Immediately following the use of hypnosis she stated that she would automatically become hungry before meals, that she felt compelled to exercise, and had a strong desire to get well.

Case 2

A 21-year-old young woman was seen in the hospital 4 weeks after being involved in a motor vehicle accident. Immediately after the accident she was reported to have been comatose with decerebrate posturing and bilateral dilation of her pupils. She was said to have made no voluntary movements. Although numerous bruises were described, x-ray films had revealed no fractures. She was treated with tracheostomy to maintain an adequate airway. With treatment for cerebral edema the degree of decerebrate posturing decreased.

A neurological examiner found spastic quadraparesis, more severe on the right, and a "masklike" facial appearance. He also noted that she did not respond to verbal commands. Restlessness was decreased with Thorazine, and a brain scan was reported as within normal limits. The EEG revealed only minimal desynchronization of the entire cortex with a focus of slowing in the left temporal region.

Approximately 4 months after the accident she was discharged, having had extensive physical therapy. At this time she had great difficulty in following verbal commands, although her spastic quadraparesis had improved, mostly on the left. Babinski's sign, however, was elicitable bilaterally.

Physical therapy efforts had been impeded by her refusal to exercise adequately either during or following her scheduled treatment hours. She was negativistic and uncooperative when approached. During the visits of special tutors from the school system she stared into space, giving the impression of being confused and unable to comprehend. It was after her discharge from the hospital that hypnotic intervention was first considered.

During the first two sessions no trance induction was attempted, but an effort was made to establish rapport. She seemed to have a marked degree of depression, together with confusion of thought, rigidity of responses, and stereotypy. She was sullen, withdrawn, and hostile, rejecting all efforts to help her with the words "I can't do it" often accompanied by tears. During the third session she was told that she was going to be hypnotized and that this method would allow her to use her full capabilities, both psychological and physiological, in making a recovery.

As she entered even a minimal hypnotic state, she was told that her unconscious mind was "so strong that it can overcome this temporary physiological impairment." Soon after this suggestion was given, she suddenly and dramatically seemed to enter a much deeper state of trance, which was confirmed by production of positive and negative hallucinations.

The patient entered a state of somnambulism, and she was given suggestions to exercise her hand and arm for 15 minutes out of every waking hour and to learn and study the materials presented by her tutors. Moreover, she was given a direct suggestion that she would find herself wanting to "get well."

After this third session the patient's parents reported a dramatic change. She began exercising her hand and arm in a compulsive fashion. When asked if she wanted her tutor to return, she immediately agreed. From the time lessons were resumed, she seemed to make a concerted effort at studying.

Four weeks after hypnotherapy began, this patient spontaneously arose from her wheel chair and asked her father and mother to help her try to walk. She was successful and began walking daily. Eight weeks later, however, there was concern as her improving mood gave way to a type of hostility and depression that had not been noted by her parents before the accident. One week later, though, she began menstruating for the first time since her accident, and the mood improved. She began talking about her fears of the future, but she expressed a desire for maximum recovery. She was discharged from hypnotherapy after 4 months.

At a follow-up appointment 1 year later she walked with the use of a cane, she smiled appropriately, and her frustration tolerance seemed excellent. Her thought content was good, with little evidence of sterotypy or rigidity. She joked about some of her experiences in walking and going back to school. Her plans for the future seemed realistic, and she expressed hopes that some orthopedic procedures might improve her functioning.

Subsequent reports from her parents revealed that she had redeveloped an active social life, with many friends, and had begun to consider marriage at some time in the future.

Case 3

A 10-year-old boy in good health accidently fell from a tree in his backyard, striking his head on a concrete patio some 15 feet below. In the ambulance taking him to the hospital he vomited, aspirated vomitus, and became cyanotic and dyspeneic in spite of oxygen administration. On his arrival at the emergency room an adequate airway was established by tracheostomy, and his dilated pupils returned to a normal size, although the right was larger than the left. His right eye deviated laterally. An ecchymosis was noted behind the right ear and over the right occipitoparietal area. An x-ray revealed that there was some separation of the right lambdoidal suture. A right retrobrachial carotid angiogram revealed no shift of midline structures or evidence of subdural hematoma. The boy was put on antibiotics and steroids and was given an injection to reduce cerebral edema.

Several days later the patient was transferred to a nearby hospital with a diagnosis of cerebral edema secondary to cerebral contusion and concussion. Over the next 3 months his condition remained essentially unchanged. At the time of his hospital discharge, about 3 1/2 months after the fall, he was maintaining a constant fetal posture. His eyes were open in a fixed stare, but he made no sign of recognition and did not talk with anyone. The mother's fear was obvious, and comments about his poor condition were made openly by the family.

For 2 months after returning home he was visited weekly by his pediatrician, who considered hypnosis only at the mother's request, although he was doubtful that it could be of benefit.

An interview with the mother established that the child, who spent most of his time staring into space, had regressed to a state of almost complete dependence. Until the accident his school, social, and family adjustments had been considered normal by the parents and physician. School records were unremarkable. After the accident he required spoon feeding. Because of incontinence of urine and feces he was clothed in diapers and needed frequent bathing. Occasionally he cried out, seemingly in pain. He had not spoken a word, the mother said, since his accident.

Our initial session with the child verified the mother's description. His only response was to cry out when a mild pain stimulus was applied through pressure on the supraorbital ridges. He made no response to verbal requests. When his mother, father, sisters, or dog were brought into the room, he gave no sign of recognition. Because of his lack of response, his mother thought he might have become deaf from injury, although this had not been tested. It was not a hopeful picture, but we made an effort, speaking extremely slowly with clear enunciation and many repetitions.

He was first told that he could be helped if he could cooperate. Then he was instructed to close his eyes, which he did not do. Then the lids were gently closed manually by the therapist, and the boy was given a repeated suggestion that he could enter deep hypnosis. When it was thought he had entered trance, he was told that he could get well and upon awakening could communicate through eye movements, blinking once for no and twice for yes.

He was given instructions for awakening and was asked, "Can you hear me?" He blinked two times. Asked if he could say any words, he blinked only once for no. Following a series of such questions and answers a sense of basic communication was established. For the first time we felt optimism about the possible benefit of hypnotherapy.

His mother was instructed to communicate with him, allowing him to respond with eye blinks, which she did successfully. Thus it was determined that the child had expressive aphasia but understood conversation and could respond, encouraging us to undertake a sustained course of treatment.

The patient was seen usually once a week for the next year. During the third visit, while the therapist was talking to the mother in the presence of the child, it was observed that each time that the word diaper was mentioned the boy, after a delay of a few seconds, would utter a primitive cry, apparently an emotional response to his regressive manner of dress. To test the observation, diaper was again deliberately mentioned and the delayed response from the child again elicited. This was the first indication that he was aware of his environment and had emotional responses to events.

At each visit the patient was given repetitive suggestions that speech would return, that he would begin to exercise his limbs, that his thinking would clear, that he would begin to eat more, and that he would recover from his illness. Three months after therapy began he seemed to be attempting to utter words. During one of the sessions at this stage he was instructed to open his eyes, at which time a piece of candy was held in front of him. He was told that he could have the candy if he would name it out loud. Slowly he pronounced the word candy, speaking for the first time in 9 months. Thereafter, his speech began to return slowly but consistently. Although the process seemed painful, he began to exercise and was soon able to feed himself, quickly gaining proficiency after his first awkward attempts. He seemed to enjoy being with his family. Eleven months after therapy began he was working simple math problems, rote memory was almost normal, and retentive memory was within normal range. He exhibited some originality of thought with good intellectual control over his emotions.

In a conference with his pediatrician, neurosurgeon, and neurologist the decision was reached that he should be hospitalized for intensive rehabilitation treatment. He was given the posthypnotic suggestion that he could and would respond to his maximum capacity. He was hospitalized for 3 months, followed by weekly visits at his home by physical, occupational, and speech therapists. Reinforcement of posthypnotic suggestion was reduced to monthly sessions and was discontinued one year after the initial monthly visit.

The patient now speaks normally and walks with braces and a cane. He is a pleasant, happy boy, seldom incontinent, and has started going to a school for crippled children, where he receives excellent progress reports. He is learning to type, prints well, and reads at a normal rate. The prognosis for full educational rehabilitation is excellent.

Summary

Damage to the central nervous system is often assumed to be directly proportional to the clinically observed deficit in function, but the relation of these factors is actually quite problematical. The defects that a brain-injured patient may show in attempting to adapt to one situation, for instance, to efforts in rehabilitation, may change drastically when he attempts to adapt to another situation, such as that of hypnotic induction. Certain "behavior of a patient" may indeed be communication response from the patient to those whom he or she feels are demanding "well" behavior, a demand that he or she feels inadequate to fulfill.

The cases reported here, as well as a great deal of our work with hypnosis over the years, can be cast in a motivational framework, leading to improvement in such serious conditions as negative nitrogen balance in severe burn injuries and to an ability to cease smoking cigarettes in patients with emphysema and other vascular or pulmonary conditions. We have repeatedly demonstrated the usefulness of hypnosis in altering motivation and behavioral patterns that were adversely affecting physical health. Of particular interest, though its meaning is not certain, is the observation of the response to hypnotic induction in unconscious, terminally ill cancer patients who have been previously hypnotized for relief of pain. In rehabilitation cases of this kind the motivation and persistence of the therapist may be equally crucial. Careful observation is required since such patients may be aphasic and unable to respond rapidly to hypnosis. Delayed posthypnotic responses may occur initially, and only consistent efforts over an extended period of time are likely to yield positive results. The difficulty that these patients have in communicating necessitates reliance more on the nonverbal signs of trance induction and requires careful discernment by the therapist.

It is well known, of course, that the conscious motivation of a person may be at great variance with his unconscious wishes, the overt behavior being a result of the complicated interaction of these two topographical "areas" of the "mind." Is it possible that hypnosis can directly influence the unconscious set of a person's motivational framework, tipping the balance in favor of recovery even when the conscious mind acts in a defensive and negativistic way?

We agree with Goldstein (1939) that "the basic motivation of the living being is to realize its own nature; that is, to realize all its capacities to the highest degree possible in a given situation." It is this innate tendency that we hope was stimulated in the case histories by the repeated suggestions toward health and achievement.

Looking at these reports in an interpersonal way, one might speculate that the particular framework of the hypnotherapist-subject relationship may have allowed the therapist to approach the injured patient in a way that was not possible for the other rehabilitation personnel, perhaps because of their own feelings of anxiety and helplessness or to the negativistic "catastrophic response" that such patients may show when faced with frustrating demands. The responses that are required of the subject by the hypnotherapist are clear and simple, compared with usual demands of the environment. The induction technique may offer the injured patient a chance to begin meaningful communication at a level that he or she feels is not overly demanding, thus decreasing his or her need to respond with behavior designed to establish a role as in "ill person." The control that the hypnotherapist may use in structuring the situation of trance induction also allows him or her to avoid those areas of response in which the patient, if he or she complied, would be forced to demonstrate behavior that would confirm his or her illness. For example, while the patient is aphasic, verbal responses are not requested by the hypnotherapist.

In such patients we found greater negativism and resistance to treatment, as well as marked positive transference when improvement began. These reactions are handled, of course, with the usual psychotherapeutic techniques. The therapist attempting to work with such cases should also be aware of the danger of his or her own discouragement and countertransference (Fromm, 1968).

In Case 3, the response of the boy to the structured hypnotherapy situation certainly encouraged the therapist and led to a changed expectation for recovery by the family and others. This changed expectation may be an important aspect of the success of hypnosis in working with these problems; it is becoming evident that the expectations of those in the patient's environment, either positive or negative, have a strong influence on the level of rehabilitation achieved by a recovering person (Hall, 1966).

The hypnotherapeutic relationship is structured largely by the therapist and may be tailored so as to require a minimal response from the subject, perhaps for this reason being less frustrating than demands for "normal" motivation of which the injured person may be incapable. Thus the "catastrophic response" of which Goldstein (1939) speaks was not elicited in the cases detailed. Instead, the motivation pattern seemed to change, leading rapidly to improvement in more measurable areas. It is entirely possible, of course, that the improvement observed following hypnosis may have been partially coincidental, since in each case hypnosis was one of the last treatment modalities employed. Perhaps natural healing processes had already progressed markedly, without the patient or others being aware of it, at the time hypnosis was first employed. This view is not entirely convincing, however, because of the close coincidence in time between hypnotic suggestion and improvement. Still, we are reporting clinical results, not experimental findings, and must be cautious in extrapolating too far beyond what can be replicated.

Some experimental reports, however, suggest that hypnosis can induce either increased resistance or vulnerability to thermal injury under laboratory conditions. Whether it can also have a positive effect on healing rate in other areas remains an open question, although in the cases presented here we would not wish to suggest any effect other than increased motivation for recovery. It is possible that direct hypnotic suggestion may produce physiological changes that are not mediated through motivational change. This is an interesting and valid experimental question which we raised, in passing, some time ago, but such discriminations are not possible in the clinical situations reported in this text.

It does not seem plausible to explain the responses described in these cases as the result of so-called "role-playing;" this concept seemed equally inadequate in describing our experience with terminal patients. The whole thrust of our research has been to aid in clinically difficult situations where more conventional forms of psychotherapeutic intervention have not seemed promising. Any question about the existence or nature of a hypnotic "state" has seemed secondary to helping suffering people. Thus, we have not hesitated, at any time, to use psychotherapeutic intervention, together with direct suggestion, when it seemed indicated.

Neurophysiology and Hypnosis

There is increasing interest again in identifying possible neurophysiological correlates of hypnosis. This is an area in which the interweaving of clinical observation and experimental investigation may prove fruitful in increasing our theoretical models for understanding hypnosis (Sarbin and Slagle, 1980). Barolin (1982) considers hypnosis as a basal status of the human organism in a state of partial deprivation of external stimuli; in this condition suggestions seem to have an enhanced effect, even though (in activated hypnosis) there is no differentiation in the EEG from the awake state. Hernandez (1977) suggests that hypnosis has particular effect in the midbrain, pons, and medulla. There have been studies of slow oscillations of brain potentials in hypnosis, but with no clear conclusion (Aladzhalova, Rozhnov, and Kamenetski, 1976). Bauer and McCanne (1980) found no significant difference between control and hypnotized subjects on heart rate, electrodermal recording, frontalis muscle tension, and occipital EEG. In a study of pain perception in hypnotized subjects, Sternbach (1982) found that atropine interfered with hypnotic analgesia in low-hypnotizable subjects, but only insignificantly in highly hypnotizable subjects.

A group of Hungarian researchers have produced a number of valuable studies of the psychophysiology of hypnosis. Using decrements in evoked potential as a measure of general activation, Meszaros, Banyai, and Greguss (1980), measured the level of general activation to be higher in the awake state than in hypnosis. There were also observations that suggested that hypnosis alters information processing, perhaps accentuating the processing of stimulus patterns. In another study (Banyai, Meszaros, and Greguss, 1982), it was found that selective attention is the most important aspect of inducing the altered state of consciousness associated with hypnotic induction. This was true in induction techniques that were widely variant: activity-decreasing, traditional trance induction procedures, and active-increasing suggestions. This suggests that alteration of activity level is likely to be a by-product of the type of induction chosen rather than an essential component of hypnosis (Banyai, Meszaros, and Greguss, 1980).

Hemispheric Lateralization

A number of studies tend to support the hypothesis that hypnosis involves a greater activation of the holistic and gestalt processing of the right hemisphere (in right-handed persons). Meszaros, Banyai, and Greguss (1982) found greater right hemispheric dominance in highly hypnotizable subjects, measuring conjugate lateral eye movements as the indicator. Using the autokinetic effect, Graham and Pernicano (1979) found a relationship between hypnotizability and the nondominant hemisphere. Wall (1983) states that hypnosis involves a shift from left brain to right brain cognitive processing. Frumkin, Ripley, and Cox (1978) found a similar shift toward right hemisphere functioning, using a dichotic listening task with 20 subjects. In a study of 86 subjects, Sackeim (1982) found that right-handers were more responsive on the left than on the right side of the body during hypnosis. Roberts et al. (1975), however, found that auditory feedback could be used to train subjects to produce a difference in skin temperature in one hand relative to the other, a result unrelated to hypnotic susceptibility. Carter, Elkins, and Kraft (1982) have reviewed the literature on hemispheric asymmetry as a model for hypnotic phenomena.

Animal Hypnosis

Tonic immobility in animals has often been considered to be related to the hypnotic response in humans. Animal hypnosis studies may suggest hypotheses to be considered in the conceptualization of hypnosis and are a valuable source of neurophysiological models. An opioid mechanism in animal hypnosis is suggested by Carli, Farabollini, and Fontani (1981), who found that high doses (15 mg/kg) of naloxone abolished the potentiation of the duration of hypnosis induced in rabbits by morphine (in the presence of painful stimuli). Whishaw, Flannigan, and Schallert (1982) showed that hypnotized rabbits have the same atropine-sensitive EEG found in spontaneously immobile rabbits; they suggest that the maintenance of normal EEG during animal hypnosis allows normal escape movements once the immobility has served its defensive function. Higher values of corticosterone were found in rabbits susceptible to animal hypnosis, suggesting a correlation with a more active adrenocortical system (Carli, Farabollini, and di Prisco, 1979). That animal hypnosis decreases electrocorticographic and behavioral manifestations of pain seems established, but the mechanism or level of brain function involved is not certain (Carli et al., 1976). Carli (1982) defines animal hypnosis as a prolonged immobility response with various physiological variables altered.

CONCLUSION

In the years to come hypnosis will become part of the standardized diagnostic procedure in neurology, especially in cases of difficult diagnosis between functional and organic problems, to aid in the control of severe pain, and to reduce drug dependence. In pain problems self-hypnosis will become important. In rehabilitation of neurological patients, hypnosis will be found of aid, although it will be crucial to keep suggestions for improvement within a realistic level of aspiration.

REFERENCES

Abe T: The combined method of brief psychotherapy and autogenic training for epileptic patients. Japan J Hypn 15:43–45, 1971

Aladzhalova NA, Rozhnov VE, Kamenetski SL: Human hypnosis and super-slow electrical activity of the brain. Zh Nevropatol Psikhiatr 76:704–709, 1976

Alexander L: Hypnosis in primarily organic illness. Am J Clin Hypn 8:250–253, 1966

Ambrose G: Multiple sclerosis and treatment by hypnotherapy. J Clin Exp Hypn 3:203–209, 1955

Bachet: Donneés nouvells sur l'hypnose. Ann Med Psychol (Paris) 2:440, 1969

Backus PS: An experimental note on hypnotic ablation of optokinetic nystagmus. Am J Clin Hypn 4:184, 1962

Baehr RF: Hypnosis, an adjunct in the treatment of neuromuscular disease. Arch Phys Med 41:514–515, 1960

Baehr RF: Hypnosis applied to bowel and bladder control in multiple sclerosis, syringomyelia and traumatic transverse myelitis. Am J Clin Hypn 4:22–23, 1961

Banyai EI, Meszaros I, Greguss AC: Alteration of activity level: The essence of hypnosis or a by-product of the type of induction? in Proceedings of the 28th International Congress of the Physiological Society, Budapest. London, Pergamon Press, 1980

Banyai EI, Meszaros I, Greguss AC: Psychophysiological comparison of active-alert and traditional relaxational hypnosis, in Sinz R, Rosenzweig, MR (eds): Psychophysiology. Amsterdam, Elsevier/North-Holland Biomedical Press, 1982, pp 225–230

Barolin GS: Experimental basis for a neurophysiological understanding of hypnoid states. Eur Neurol 21:59–64, 1982

Bauer KE, McCanne TR: Autonomic and central nervous system responding during hypnosis and simulation of hypnosis. Int J Clin Exp Hypn 28:148–163, 1980

Becker F: Medical hypnosis in physical medicine and rehabilitation. J Med Assoc Ga 49:233–235, 1960

Becker F: Modifications of anxiety through the use of hypnosis in physical medicine. J Am Geriatr Soc 11:235–237, 1963

Bird HW: Varying hypnotizability in a case of Parkinsonism. Bull Menninger Clin 12:210–217, 1948

Blumenthal LS: Hypnotherapy of migraine and other types of chronic headache. Am J Clin Hypn 3:174–178, 1961

Brunn JT: Hypnosis and neurological disease: A case report. Am J Clin Hypn 8:312–313, 1966

Buell FA, Biehl JP: The influence of hypnosis on the tremor of Parkinson's disease. Dis Nerv Syst 10:20–23, 1949

Carasso RL, Peled O, Kleinhauz M, Yehunda S: Treatment of cervical headache with hypnosis suggestive therapy and relaxation techniques. Presented at the International Congress of the Israel Society of Hypnosis in Psychotherapy and Psychosomatic Medicine in collaboration with the European Society of Hypnosis in Psychotherapy and Psychosomatic Medicine, Haifa, Israel, 1983

Carli G: Animal hypnosis: An attempt to reach a definition. Arch Ital Biol 120:138–159, 1982

Carli G, Lefebvre L, Silvano G, Vierucci S: Suppression of accompanying reactions to prolonged noxious stimulation during animal hypnosis in the rabbit. Exp Neurol 53:1–11, 1976

Carli G, Farabollini F, di Prisco CL: Plasma corticosterone and its relation to susceptibility to animal hypnosis in rabbits. Neurosci Lett 11:271–274, 1979

Carli G, Farabollini F, Fontani G: Effects of pain, morphine and naloxone on the duration of animal hypnosis. Behav Brain Res 2:373–385, 1981

Carter BD, Elkins GR, Kraft SP: Hemispheric asymmetry as a model for hypnotic phenomena: A review and analysis. Am J Clin Hypn 24:204–210, 1982

Cedercreutz C, Lahteenmaki R, Tulikoura J: Hypnotic treatment of headache and vertigo in skull injured patients. Int J Clin Exp Hypn 24:195–201, 1976

Chappell DT: The reduction of spasticity in paraplegia with hypnosis. Am J Clin Hypn 3:213–225, 1961

Chappell DT: Hypnosis and spasticity in paraplegia. Am J Clin Hypn 7:33–36, 1964

Crasilneck HB, Hall JA: The use of hypnosis with unconscious patients. Int J Clin Exp Hypn 10:141–144, 1962

Crasilneck HB, Hall JA: The use of hypnosis in the rehabilitation of complicated vascular and post-traumatic neurological patients. Int J Clin Exp Hypn 18:149–159, 1970

Dorcus RM: The use of hypnosis as a diagnostic tool, in Hypnosis and Its Therapeutic Application. New York, McGraw-Hill, 1956

Eliseo TS: Three examples of hypnosis in the treatment of organic brain syndrome with psychosis. Int J Clin Exp Hypn 22:9–19, 1974

Erickson MH: Hypnotically oriented psychotherapy in organic brain damage. Am J Clin Hypn 6:92–112, 1963

Erickson MH: Experimental hypnotherapy in Tourette's disease. Am J Clin Hypn 7:325–331, 1965

Fogel S: Muscular spasm disease and body image distortions. Am J Clin Hypn 14:16–23, 1971

Fromm E: Transference and counter-transference in hypnoanalysis. Int J Clin Exp Hypn 16:77–84, 1968

Frumkin L, Ripley H, Cox G: Changes in cerebral hemispheric lateralization with hypnosis. Biol Psychiatry 13:741–750, 1978

Goldstein K: The organism: A holistic approach to biology derived from pathological data on man. New York, American, 1939

Graham KR, Pernicano KM: Laterality, hypnosis and the autokinetic effect. Am J Clin Hypn 22:79–84, 1979

Gravitz MA: Hypnotherapeutic management of epileptic behavior. Am J Clin Hypn 21:282–284, 1979

Gravitz MA: Non-verbal hypnotic techniques in a centrally deaf brain-damaged patient. Int J Clin Exp Hypn 29:110–116, 1981

Gross H: Hypnosis as a diagnostic tool. Am J Clin Hypn 23:47–52, 1980

Hall JA: Rehabilitation of mental patients; employers' problems. Tex State J Med 62:50–53, 1966

Hallewell JD, Goetzinger CP, Allen ML, Proud GO: The use of hypnosis in audiologic assessment. Acta Otolaryngol 61:205–208, 1966

Hernandez PR: Neurophysiological bases of hypnosis. Neurol Neurocir Psiquiatr 18:7–26, 1977

Higley HE: The treatment of paralysis with hypnosis. Am Ostrop Assoc J 57:389–390, 1958

Howard ML, Coe WC: The effects of context and subjects' perceived control in breaching posthypnotic amnesia. J Pers 48:342–359, 1980

Kirkner FJ, Dorcus RH, Seacot G: Hypnotic motivation of vocalization in an organic motor aphasic case. J Clin Exp Hypn 1:47–49, 1953

Knowles FW: Hysterical fits and epilepsy: Problems of diagnosis and treatment. NY State J Med 63:598–600, 1964

LaScola R: Hypnosis in stroke rehabilitation. Presented at the annual meeting of the American Society of Clinical Hypnosis, Seattle, 1975

LeHew JL III: Use of hypnosis in the treatment of long-standing spastic torticollis. Am J Clin Hypn 14:124–126, 1971

Lindner H, Stevens H: Hypnotherapy and psychodynamics in the syndrome of Gilles de la Tourette. Int J Clin Exp Hypn 15:151–155, 1967

McCord H: Hypnotically hallucinated physical therapy with a multiple sclerosis patient. Am J Clin Hypn 8:313–314, 1966

McCranie EJ, Crasilneck HB: The electroencephalogram in age regression. Psychiatr Q 29:85–88, 1953

Magonet A, Philip MD: Hypnosis in dysphagia. Int J Clin Exp Hypn 4:291–295, 1961

Mason CF: Hypnotic motivation of aphasics. Int J Clin Exp Hypn 4:297–301, 1961

Meszaros I, Banyai EI, Greguss AC: Psychophysiological correlates of hypnosis. Karl Marx Univ Leipzig, Math-Naturwiss R 29:235–240, 1980

Meszaros I, Banyai EI, Greguss AC: Evoked potential correlates of verbal versus imagery coding in hypnosis. Presented at the 8th International Congress of Hypnosis in Psychosomatic Medicine, Glasgow, Scotland, 1982

Miller HR: Psychogenic seizures treated by hypnosis. Am J Clin Hypn 25:248–252, 1983

Milos R: Hypnotic exploration of amnesia after cerebral injuries. Int J Clin Exp Hypn 23:103–110, 1975

Owen-Flood A: Hypnotism in epilepsy. Br J Med Hypnot 3:49, 1952

Pajntar M, Jeglic A, Stefancic M, Vodovnik L: Improvements of motor response by means of hypnosis in patients with peripheral nerve lesions. Int J Clin Exp Hypn 28:16–26, 1980

Papermaster AA, Doberneck RC, Bonello FJ, Griffin WO Jr, Wangensteen OH: Hypnosis in surgery. II. Pain. Am J Clin Hypn 2:220–224, 1960

Pasquarelli B, Bellak L: A case of co-existence of ideopathic, epileptic, and psychogenic convulsions. Psychosom Med 9:137, 1947

Peterson DB, Sumner JW, Jones GA: Role of hypnosis in differentiation of epileptic from convulsive-like seizures. Am J Psychiatry 107:428–433, 1950

Roberts AH, Schuler J, Bacon JG, Zimmerman RL, Patterson R: Individual differences and autonomic control: Absorption, hypnotic susceptibility and the unilateral control of skin temperature. J Abnorm Psychol 84:272–279, 1975

Rudlova B, Rudlova L: Hypnosa v neurologii (hypnosis and neurology). Ceskisl Psychol 5:251–254, 1961

Sacerdote P: Hypnotic pain control, neurophysiology, psychodynamics, philosophy. Presented at the International Congress of the Israel Society of Hypnosis in Psychotherapy and Psychosomatic Medicine, Haifa, Israel, 1983

Sackeim HA: Lateral asymmetry in bodily response to hypnotic suggestions. Biol Psychiatry 17:437–447, 1982

Sarbin TR, Slagle R: Psychophysiological outcomes of hypnosis, in Burrows GD, Dennerstein L (eds): Handbook of Hypnosis and Psychosomatic Medicine. Amsterdam, Elsevier/North-Holland Biomedical Press, 1980, pp 53–83

Secter II, Gilberd MB: Hypnosis as a relaxant for the cerebral palsied patient. Am J Clin Hypn 6:363–364, 1964

Shafer TA: Hypnosis in the management and control of trigeminal neuralgia: Two case reports. Am J Clin hypn 5:138–140, 1962

Shires EB, Peters RM, Krout H: Hypnosis in neuro-muscular re-education. US Armed Forces Med J 5:1519–1523, 1954

Spankus WH, Freeman LG: Hypnosis in cerebral palsy. Int J Clin Exp Hypn 10:135–139, 1962

Stambaugh EE: Hypnotic treatment of depression in the parkinsonian patient: A case study. Am J Clin Hypn 19:185–186, 1977

Stein VT: Hypnotherapy of involuntary movements in an 82-year-old male. Am J Clin Hypn 23:128–131, 1980

Sternback RA: On strategies for identifying neurochemical correlates of hypnotic analgesia: A brief communication. Int J Clin Exp Hypn 30:251–256, 1982

Stewart MR: (Panelist) Society of Clinical and Experimental Hypnosis Annual Meeting, Boston, 1983

Sumner JW, Cameron RR, Peterson DB: Hypnosis in differentiation of epileptic from convulsive-like seizures. Neurology 2:395–402, 1952

Vann D: Successful hypnotherapy for anxiety neurosis in Huntington's chorea. Med J Aust 2:166, 1971

Wall TW Jr: Hypnotic phenomena, in Wester WC, Smith AN (eds): Clinical Hypnosis: A Multidisciplinary Approach. Philadelphia, J.B. Lippincott Co., 1983, pp 57–72

Weil A: (Panelist) Use of hypnotherapy in convulsive disorder with parietotemporal angioblastoma. Presented at the International Congress of the Israel Society of Hypnosis in Psychotherapy and Psychosomatic Medicine in collaboration with the European Society of Hypnosis in Psychotherapy and Psychosomatic Medicine, Haifa, Israel, 1983

Whishaw IQ, Flannigan KP, Schallert T: An assessment of the state hypothesis of animal "hypothesis" through an analysis of neocortical and hippocampal EEG in spontaneously immobile and hypnotized rabbits. Electroencephalogr Clin Neurophysiol 54:365–374, 1982

Wright ME: Hypnosis and rehabilitation. Rehabil Lit 21:2–12, 1960

Yensen R: Hypnosis and movement re-education in partially paralyzed subjects. Percept Mot Skills 17:211–222, 1963

15

Hypnosis and Emotional Problems: Psychiatry, Clinical Psychology, and Psychotherapy

Psychiatrists and psychologists are deeply involved in hypnosis—in experimental work on its nature and in its clinical application in the realm of emotional disorders. Many who are primarily experimental investigators of hypnosis have in addition made noted clinical contributions, while many clinicians have advanced the theories of hypnosis, both directly and indirectly, by stimulating research through detailed clinical reports of unusual phenomena (Crasilneck, 1975; Naruse and Fujimara, 1975).

In a book devoted to clinical applications of hypnosis it would be an inappropriate detour to attempt an overview of the immense amount of experimental work done by psychologists and others in the study of hypnosis. Though not always directly applicable to the treatment of emotional disorders, such studies are the foundation upon which clinical hypnosis rests, much as the practice of medicine rests upon such laboratory disciplines as biochemistry, anatomy, physiology, embryology, and pharmacology. The fact that a review of experimental work is omitted does not detract in the least from our appreciation of its importance. We are unwilling to treat such a complex and important area in a merely cursory fashion, as would be necessary in a volume devoted to clinical applications.

Those interested in examining the recent literature on experimental hypnosis would find useful the volumes of the *International Journal of Clinical and Experimental Hypnosis*. Many experimental articles also have appeared in the *American Journal of Clinical Hypnosis* and the volume *Hypnosis: Research Developments and Perspectives* edited by Fromm and Shor (1972). Of value also is the extensive clinical research project, *Personality and Hypnosis*, relating hypnotizability to other imaginative experiences, by Hilgard (1971).

When hypnosis was initially employed there was little appreciation of the difference between physical and emotional disorders. Many of the early "cures," such as some by Mesmer, were probably of a hysterical or conversion neurosis origin. Today this distinction of physical and psychological is more clearly recognized though many problems fall on the border.

Hypnotherapy has increasingly recognized basic applications in the treatment of emotional disorders. It should always, however, be used by practitioners who have a thorough understanding of the psychodynamics of the emotional problems and would be able to treat the same disorders by more conventional, non-hypnotic means.

Hypnotherapy is increasingly recognized as useful in psychiatry and psychosomatic medicine (King, 1980; Sachs, 1982; Torem, 1984; Wain et al., 1981; Werner, 1983). Additionally, there are clinical modifications combining hypnotherapy with other techniques, such as behavioral modification (Kroger, 1980). Hypnotherapy is so adaptable to the facilitation of other treatment interventions that Mott (1982) has suggested that hypnosis be considered primarily in that way—as an enhancement of other techniques rather than a free-standing method of psychotherapy. There are some experimental studies, such as that of Smyth (1982) that encourage the experimental study of hypnotically induced conflict in a laboratory setting.

HYPNOSIS AND THE TREATMENT
OF EMOTIONAL DISORDERS

Hypnosis has a long and impressive history in the treatment of neurotic disorders. In 1895 Breuer and Freud published *Studien über Hysterie*, in which hypnosis was the primary treatment employed. Freud later abandoned hypnosis in favor of his developing techniques of psychoanalysis. In the beginning chapters we reviewed the decline of hypnosis after Freud's rejection of it as a treatment for neurotic disorders and its re-emergence as a recognized part of treatment by the onset of World War II.

Kubie and Margolin (1944) did much to bridge the gap between orthodox psychoanalytic thinking and hypnosis, their efforts tending to make hypnosis again acceptable as a part of the treatment techniques available for neurotic problems. Schneck (1954a,b) has discussed in detail the uses of hypnosis in psychiatry, and Wolberg's two volumes on *Medical Hypnosis* (1948) are a classic presentation of the ways in which hypnotic techniques may be of aid in various psychiatric problems. Other writers and commentators have enhanced hypnosis' reception in psychotherapy circles (Dinges, 1984; Karlin, 1984; London, 1984). Conn (1971) has described ways of inducing what appears to be a hypnotic state without suggestions of sleep; he views hypnosis as an aid in ego integration by "hypnosynthesis." English (1962) describes the use of hypnosis in exploring personality conflicts. At a professional meeting of hypnotherapists Schafer (1971) presented an excellent integrative view of hypnosis in terms of ego boundaries, utilizing Fairbairn's concept of ego-object relationships.

As Freud himself remarked, hypnosis has proved most valuable in the treatment of war neuroses, cases in which the combat soldier is overwhelmed by his feelings in battle, often having severe and recurrent nightmares of the battle situation. Hypnosis may be used to abreact this overwhelming affect, relieving the symptoms and preventing their being elaborated into more complicated neurotic patterns. Watkins (1949) wrote in depth of such problems during World War II. In combat situations hypnosis is particularly useful in emergency psychiatric treatment where the prime objective must be to return as many soldiers to their station as possible in the least amount of time (Arluck, 1965). Hypnosis is often the treatment of choice.

Modification of Anxiety

Anxiety, one of the most common human emotions, can be a normal part of life if it does not exceed a manageable range. In the clinical treatment of emotional disorders, however, anxiety is usually found to be a presenting symptom, either directly or as the basis for symptoms that arise from it through various mechanisms of defense. Many authors have emphasized that anxiety is the chief characteristic of neurotic illness (Ambrose, 1958). It is useful to think of anxiety as the reverse of ego strength. That is, the more ego strength, the better a person is able to cope with the demands of life; and the better one can cope, the less the anxiety. Conversely, a sense of inadequacy in dealing with those life situations that are normal and unavoidable—such as interpersonal situations, sexuality, work, and so on—is expressed as anxiety. Anxiety has been compared with fear whose stimulus is unknown because it is unconscious. If a person has rapid pulse, sweating, and a subjective sense of anxiety or terror in the presence of actual danger, the emotional reaction is designated as "fear" and is considered normal to the situation. If the same physical symptoms are present but no external threat can be seen, the emotional state is called "anxiety," although there may be a threat in the unconscious mind that is even more fear-provoking than any actual danger.

Thus, anxiety may be thought of as fear of an internal object. Such fears are usually based on earlier and forgotten memories or fantasies to which the present realistic situation is inappropriately assimilated.

It should be remembered that anxiety is not always a negative sign and that its absence is not always healthy. A person who does not feel ordinary amounts of anxiety in a situation that is objectively threatening may not meet outer challenges in a realistic and effective manner. The absence of anxiety may in some cases mean that the person has given up and is no longer struggling to cope. A person going into a psychotic episode often has marked anxiety, but when the psychotic delusion becomes fixed, anxiety may diminish, even though the illness actually is more severe.

Although anxiety is present in psychotic states, it seems more characteristic of neurotic disorders, those in which a sense of reality is maintained even though the neurotic feels a troubling inner schism—part of his or her personality working against his or her conscious purposes. This is not the "split-mind" that is popularly considered to be the meaning of schizophrenia. It is more a sense of the mind existing in unintegrated parts.

For effective psychotherapy of neurotic problems it is necessary that the patient be within a certain optimal range of anxiety. Most frequently, the neurotic patient is overwhelmed by too much anxiety. In such situations anxiety may be displaced from an unconscious conflict and attached to a specific situation or stimulus as in phobia or it may be "free-floating"—pervading all aspects of the patient's life. This excessive anxiety may be so disrupting that the patient is unable to deal effectively with his or her conflicts. For such a patient it may be necessary to lower the anxiety level with hypnotic suggestions for relaxation or with tranquilizers before effective therapy can begin.

In rarer cases, particularly with characterological disorders, the patient may have too little anxiety to be motivated for painful psychodynamic exploration of underlying conflicts. Then hypnotherapy may be used to uncover the deeper conflict-laden thoughts. Often free or directed associations under hypnosis will suffice, although resistant patients may require a more elaborate process of age regression under hypnosis to revivify traumatic conflictual situations from the past.

Isham (1962) found hypnorelaxation and psychotherapy equally effective in the relief of anxiety, and in his opinion both were superior to drug therapy. Mordey (1965) used hypnosis to treat stage fright, while Perin (1968) noted that relief of anxiety in the trance state made the patient able to face the real-life situation with greater equanimity. Kalinowsky and Lerner (1960) concluded that hypnosis may act as a specific relaxant. Moss (1958) has successfully employed hypnosis in treating chronic anxiety. Meares (1956a,b) has found hypnotic symptom removal effective in cases where the initiating conflict is no longer active and in which there was no secondary gain. The role of hypnosis in situations requiring crisis intervention should be remembered (Frankel, 1974), for some of these situations may seem to involve spontaneous trance phenomena. Prehypnotic suggestions may also be useful in anxiety states (Schneck, 1975). As a matter of fact, hypnosis may be the treatment of choice in anxiety states (Armstrong, 1974).

An absolute must for the practitioner using hypnosis for emotional disorders is that he or she be well-trained not only in hypnotic techniques but in the diagnosis and treatment of emotional disorders as well.

Control of Distressing Symptomatology

Even if a patient is consciously motivated for effective psychotherapy, his or her unconscious resistances may interfere with the progress of therapy through the production of distressing physical symptoms. These may be not only the symptoms of anxiety itself, but they also take the form of hyperventilation syndrome, symptoms of cardiospasm and peptic ulcer, abdominal cramping, the weakness of psychasthenia, and myriad other somatic equivalents of anxiety.

As in the case of severe anxiety, these symptoms may themselves prevent effective psychotherapy. In many cases such symptoms can be abolished or attenuated with hypnosis, permitting psychotherapy to proceed in a more normal manner (Bornstein et al., 1980; Haley, 1967; Schneck, 1958). Spiegel and Linn (1969) have termed the improvement in psychotherapy following the hypnotic removal of a single persisting symptom the "ripple effect." An example from our case-history files follows:

An unmarried man in his late thirties came for treatment because of a general dissatisfaction with life. He experienced recurrent difficulties in his work, frequently changing jobs after having developed a severe conflict with someone in charge of the work he was doing. With such authority figures he seemed to have a "love–hate" relationship, ambivalently desiring their praise and attempting to prove their untrustworthiness. He had made many previous attempts at psychotherapy, which were interrupted by his moving away— ostensibly because of changes in his employment situation. During the first few visits it was found that any attempt to discuss his emotional difficulties led to severe abdominal cramping that caused him several times to leave the treatment room to go to the bathroom for an urgent bowel movement. Attempts to interpret his reaction elicited intellectual assent but no change in the symptoms.

Hypnosis was useful in alleviating the cramping. Although initially not a good subject, he reported that after the first induction of hypnosis he had slept peacefully through the night, a rare occurrence. Repeated inductions gave increasing relief, which permitted psychotherapy to proceed.

Recovery of Repressed Material

One of the most unique contributions of hypnosis to the treatment of neurotic problems is its facility in rapidly uncovering repressed material. Several specialized techniques have been employed for this purpose, all directed toward the same goal. Often a controlled dissociation of the usual ego state is a technique of value (Fromm, 1968). Unlike narcosynthesis, hypnotic techniques entail none of the risk of untoward laryngospasm or sensitivity reactions to intravenous drugs, and many feel that the level of consciousness is more easily titrated by hypnosis (Simon, 1967). Also, the patient's necessary defenses are not as likely to be forcibly overcome, thus avoiding a sense of psychological "rape" if deeply repressed material is elicited and then presented to the patient without adequate appreciation of defense mechanisms.

It cannot be too strongly emphasized that the uncovering of repressed material and its presentation and utilization in psychotherapy are distinct processes. Producing the buried memories by hypnosis or any other technique does not achieve in itself the integration of the recovered material (Lopez-Ibor, 1975). The patient must be led to explore the previously unconscious thoughts, integrating them with his or her conscious ego structure so that a re-repression is not necessary to preserve psychic equilibrium. It may be necessary to understand the way in which each patient may use his or her own particular symbols (Meares, 1956a).

An example of a hypnotic session to uncover repressed material is presented below.

After reaching a state of somnabulism, our patient is told, "Nothing is beyond the recall of one's unconscious mind . . . you can remember material, events, facts, experiences, even if they are distasteful, or very shocking, and so you are going back in terms of time and space . . . going back to every space of time where you can remember. . . . You can remember quite clearly what happened [here indicate the past time to be remembered, as "two weeks ago"] when you were [specify the experience]. You are reliving the exact experience. You are again feeling the emotion. . . . You are having the same thoughts, the same anxiety, the same fears. . . . It is happening to you again. . . . Now you can recall every detail . . . [stress] every detail. You can feel the tension and tightness in your body. . . . You can remember and feel exactly what is happening. Now tell me everything that is happening.

Occasionally the "repressed" material obtained under hypnosis is later found to have been conscious before hypnotherapy. In such cases, it is the willingness to communicate the material that is facilitated by hypnosis. An associative process under hypnosis also may often enhance the willingness to communicate.

Age regression can be employed in the search for repressed memory or affect (Crasilneck, 1977; Raikov, 1980). Schneck (1977a) describes hypnotherapy in the recovery of repressed memories of sexual assault 10 years after the traumatic event. The exploration was suggested by difficulty encountered in weight loss, illustrating a common occurrence, the displacement of affect from the disturbing memories. Age progression is also useful in some cases (Sexton and Maddock, 1979), the hypnotized patient being asked to "experience" what they will be like at some time in the future, perhaps after the target symptom has been improved. Age regression has also been employed to facilitate needed exercise of traumatically injured bodily parts, such as finger flexors (Finkelstein, 1982), and in the diagnosis of hysterical hemiplegia (Kampman, Hirvenoja and Ihalainen, 1979).

Hypnotherapy is a most useful technique for the recovery of some repressed and dissociated memories (Crasilneck, 1980c). The trance state allows freedom from the usual dominant ego-image and lessens the need for usual persona social interaction. This permits the ego to reidentify safely with past situations, often permitting recall that is state-specific to the ego-image of the past.

A young nun (Crasilneck, 1980a) was unable to participate in communal singing. She had no sense of conflict and could converse easily but found singing alone or with others very difficult. It was as if she could not open her mouth. Hypnotic age-regression evoked vivid memories of her strict father telling her to "Keep your mouth shut!" After affective recall of that recurrent childhood experience, she found herself again able to sing freely.

A young man had a complaint of not being able to eat in the presence of others, a symptom that caused distress in his family and social life. A thorough conscious anamnesis of his history was essentially unrevealing. In hypnotic trance, with suggestions of age regression to memories associated with the symptom, he revealed a traumatic incident not reported in the waking state: at age 16 an older boy had forced him to perform fellatio, an experience that was so traumatic to him that he had never discussed it with anyone. Although further therapy was necessary in the waking state, the return of this strongly repressed affective memory was the turning point in his therapy.

In the above two instances, the common symptom of embarrassment in situations where the mouth was open had actually quite different unconscious meaning, illustrating the importance of finding discrete psychodynamic meanings rather than using hypnotherapy for blanket removal of symptoms.

A young married man whose wife was pregnant with their first child found that he had increasing anxiety as the time of delivery approached. Rational discussions had little effect on his symptom. When hypnotically regressed to age 3, however, he remembered attending his first funeral, that of an aunt who had died in childbirth. He remembered his childhood confusion on hearing several people whisper, "The baby killed her." With this buried memory uncovered, he took a more realistic attitude toward the approaching birth of his own child.

At times, the symptom is related to a repressed memory through a surprising word association. Such associations of meaning are rare but do occur and may represent an unconscious displacement of the affect of the memory from the original traumatic event to a less-threatening substitute meaning. For example:

A woman was referred to Crasilneck with a troublesome tremor of her hands, for which no convincing neurological explanation could be found. As she said, "Every time I play cards, which is twice a week, my hands tremble uncontrollably." She had not responded to medications. She was a good hypnotic subject and entered a deep trance readily. In that relaxed state, she was told to go back in time with part of her mind, until she felt an experience related to her hand tremor. She was silent for some time and then began to cry. Asked to speak about what she was experiencing, she recalled her anguish at her mother's death. When visiting her dying mother in the hospital, her mother had reached out to her and asked to hold her hand. Although the patient was phobic of the dripping intravenous fluids and the needles, and though the dying woman "didn't look like my mother," she held her mother's hand momentarily and then released it, repulsed by the cancer-ridden body lying in bed. The affective release of this memory led to complete cessation of the tremor within several more weeks of hypnoanalysis. There was an apparent unconscious connection between her *hand* tremor, her mother's request to hold her *hand*, and her initial statement of not being able to *hold a hand* of cards.

In the final stage of her treatment, a small movement of clicking two fingernails together substituted for the tremor, a voluntary movement replacing an involuntary one. Later, the substitute symptom, too, diminished in frequency.

Although most of the significant memories recovered in hypnotic age regression seem to be real memories, there is no absolute way to be certain that they are not imaginal constructions rather than memories. When the purpose is therapeutic improvement, the distinction is not crucial, for the therapist can judge whether the supposed memory aids or retards therapeutic gain. In forensic situations, however, the actual truth or falsity of the recovered memory may be quite important and may require ancillary confirmation from nonhypnotic sources.

At times, what is recovered in hypnotherapy is not a memory but a new connection between events that were already conscious.

A middle-aged woman was referred to Crasilneck for hypnosis with what was thought to be somewhat psychotic behavior: whenever she discovered skin blemishes anywhere on her body, she would remove them with a razor blade, cutting out the blemished area entirely, particularly when they occurred on her face. Some months before the onset of this dangerous activity, she had been raped by an unknown man, who had stuffed his dirty handkerchief in her mouth to prevent her screams. Although she was conscious of the events of the rape, she had not consciously related the blemish behavior to that event. It became clear that she had unconsciously equated the rape with a blemish and was symbolically attempting to "cut out" the results of the rape. It required extensive psychotherapy, with both hypnosis and waking discussion, to thoroughly free her from this sadomasochistic compulsion.

The most controversial area of memories recovered under hypnosis is the question of alleged memories of past lives. There is absolutely no doubt that such memories can be elicited, but there is immense doubt that they refer to actual past lives, a question that would necessitate a great amount of independent verification, which, to our knowledge, has never been convincingly presented. Nevertheless, there are some patients in whom memories of "past lives" seem to bring a therapeutic improvement, although such improvement should be considered a result of the psychodynamic meaning of the "memories" rather than as proof of reincarnation.

A woman in her forties had been divorced from her only husband for several years and had been separated for some time before the divorce. She consciously had no desire for her former husband but did not feel free to consider marriage with any other man, although she did establish several successive and close relationships with men. She requested hypnotic age regression because she felt she had a "karmic link" with her former husband.

Hypnosis had not been a part of her previous psychotherapy, which had lasted for several years, both before and after her divorce. Within several sessions of hypnotic age regression, she began to experience a vivid "memory" of being a prisoner of war in a camp with her former husband in a "past life," in which they were both men. In the memory, she had arranged an escape from the camp, but he refused to accompany her. She had always felt responsible for him and wanted to go back for him. This "memory," even if it was merely a vivid imaginal construction, served to free her from her sense of fixation on her former husband. She was then able to see more clearly other conflicts that inhibited her in new close relationships.

Hypnotic Age Regression

One of the most important therapeutic advantages in the use of hypnosis is in the process of hypnotic age regression—allowing the subject to experience an earlier period of life while in trance. Age regression may be classified as "biological" age regression or "psychological" age regression, (the latter sometimes referred to as "partial" age regression). In "biological" age regression there appears to be an actual return to an earlier stage of development in the patient's orientation and often is accompanied by the re-establishment of earlier biological patterning. For example, if the subject is regressed to age 6, he or she will respond exactly as he or she did at the 6-year-old level. It is often possible to verify these facts of past history with a member of the family. The patient will speak as a 6-year-old, manifest psychomotor behavior, reason and respond emotionally as a 6-year-old. In the partial type of age regression there is a more simulated response, the subject usually remembers as they think they should have remembered at that age.

During age regression, memories are often accompanied by emotional abreactions that may be minor in nature or may be quite volatile. Crasilneck (1980c) was asked to present a videotaped grand rounds at a hospital in Dallas where a patient had been amnestic for approximately 3 weeks.

Following the patient's initial admission to the hospital numerous neurological examinations, in addition to a sodium amytal interview were administered with negative results. In the final analysis, the diagnosis was that of retroactive amnesia, and hypnotherapy was suggested.

After establishing rapport with the patient, he entered a very deep level of trance and was systemically regressed to a period of 18 months before the onset of the amnestic state. He recalled his name and the names and ages of his wife and children. He was brought forward in time at a slow pace until he was able to relate his experiences and feelings to the incidents that occurred in his life. The following was elicited:

The patient had been a soldier in Vietnam, under extreme pressure most of the time, when his closest friend became a psychiatric casualty and was returned to the States. He remembered feeling a poignant "loss" after his friend left him behind. About 2 months later he was discharged from Service; shortly thereafter his mother became critically ill and was "close to death" for several weeks, but recovered about the same time that his home of 10 years burned to the ground. All these reiterated as feelings of "great loss" that completely enveloped him most of the time. As the progression ensued we were approaching the present year. "While driving home from work about 3 weeks ago," the brakes of his car ceased to function and as he pumped them frantically, he realized that he was going to "lose my life" and as he collided with another car at the intersection, he slipped into an amnestic state. Since he no longer could tolerate these great losses and near-losses in his life, this was the only way to escape his own existence.

The patient was brought out of trance, but was allowed to remain amnestic. He remained hospitalized during hypnotherapeutic treatment, and was seen every other day for 2 weeks until his memory returned. He was given reinforcement of a positive nature: "Your fears will lessen as you go deeper into a somnambulistic state . . . with each breath you take you will feel more confident about facing the realities of living. . . . You want to remember . . you want your memory to return . . . you can and you will remember who you are. . . . I will help you to find the way back. . . . Because of the omnipotency of your unconscious mind you can and will not be afraid of remembering."

The patient was confident that even though his life was filled with fearful events, he would overcome his losses and near-losses and move on in a positive and optimistic manner. The patient was told the following on the second session: "Even though your memory is enveloped in a cloud, the cloud will break up and separate . . . the cloud will no longer engulf your memory . . . they will part and thin and float away clearing your mind of the cloudiness and with the sudden clearing, normal perception and memory will return to you."

He soon became sufficiently well to be discharged from the hospital, but continued hypnotherapy for the next 3 months.

Another case of videotaped grand rounds involved a hospitalized man who had paralysis of the right arm and leg of 8 months duration. The diagnosis was unclear despite numerous investigative psychological and neurological examinations by the referring psychiatrist before Crasilneck (1980b) was asked to see the patient for psychotherapeutic examination.

After establishing rapport the patient stated his willingness to be hypnotized and to get well. He was told that age regression may uncover valuable information, and if it were agreeable, it was worth trying. Within 5 minutes the patient entered a very deep level of trance; demonstrated excellent glove anesthesia in the left hand, and rigid catalepsy in the left arm, "showing the strength your mind has over your body." He was given the suggestion while in a state of somnambulism that he could and would lift his right arm, which he did slowly and laboriously. He did the same with his right foot. He was given the suggestion that he would rise from his wheelchair and extend his hands to Dr. Crasilneck to hold, as he walked a few steps. This was done also, and he returned to his wheelchair with help.

The patient was told that he would be going back in terms of time and space to a point in his life when he felt the problem began. In his somnambulistic state he was told: "Once you have seen something . . . heard something . . . emotionally felt something or have been exposed to an ecstatic or traumatic experience, you can and will remember it in detail. Nothing is beyond the power of your unconscious mind . . . because it is of such an omnipotent force, you can and will recall everything . . . and you will relate every detail to me." The patient by this time had regressed to his youth.

"I am now 16 years old. I am in love with Barbara. I got her pregnant, but can't marry her because I can't support her. I must get away." Then a long pause. Crasilneck asked, "What is happening? What are you thinking?" These questions were repeated several times. The patient after an interminably long pause answered, "I joined the Service. I left her to have the baby alone."

"How did you feel?"

"I felt like a rat."

The patient related that after being discharged from the Service he returned home and eventually married Barbara and legitimatized their child. Four years later, Barbara became ill with cancer and within a year became terminal. As the patient began to relive the memory of her death, he had only a mild abreaction obviously suppressing much affect. He shed one tear; his lips quivered slightly and there was only a minute tremor in his voice. Continuing to speak in the first person, present tense, he said, "Barbara is dying . . . she is whispering to me that she wants me to be brave . . . she is holding my hand . . . but has very little strength in her hand. She is telling me to always take care of the baby. The doctor is asking me to leave the room because she is having a bad convulsion. A few minutes later the doctor comes out to tell me that Barbara is dead." Approximately 3 months after his wife's death, the patient began to feel a weakness throughout the right side of his body that eventually became fulminant resulting in complete paralysis.

Continuing with the regressed state as it was at the point of the paralysis, Crasilneck asked the patient about the meaning of his paralysis in relation to his emotional feeling concerning his wife's death. His reply was, "When Barbara died, a part of me died, also."

Posthypnotic suggestions were made concerning his desire to recover, his responsibility to his daughter and to work out his guilt feelings with greater understanding. The hypnotherapeutic age regression ended; the patient seemed to feel much better in terms of his future, and he was returned to his psychiatrist to complete treatment.

Association under Hypnosis

The hypnotic state seems to facilitate a more easy evocation of Freudian free associations or of the more controlled amplifications that were utilized by Jung.

The classic technique of free association under hypnosis is begun by putting the patient into a trance, light or deep, then suggesting that he or she will be able to converse easily with the therapist without awakening. The patient is next told to report verbally whatever comes into his or her mind—without censoring anything. If free associations are being elicited to the components of a dream, the patient is given each motif in turn and then instructed to give his or her associations as they occur, again without censorship.

Various fantasy techniques have been suggested to facilitate a free flow of imagery. Wolberg (1948) may suggest to a patient that he or she is sitting alone in a theater in front of an unopened curtain, asking the patient to indicate by lifting a particular finger when he or she can clearly visualize the scene (see Chapter 4). The patient is then told that the house lights are dimming, that a spotlight centers on the curtains, the curtains open, and the action begins. The patient is then asked to report what he or she sees, no further instructions being given. Many variations of this technique are possible. They may be tailored to the interests and needs of the individual. Schneck (1955) has proposed that conversations during hypnotic scene visualization may be helpful for patients who have difficulty with visual imagery. This is similar to the blending of hypnotic and gestalt techniques proposed by Levendula (1963).

Jung approached dream symbols in a different manner than Freud, considering them to be symbolic expressions of psychic reality rather than disguised signs for repressed conscious thoughts (Hall, 1975). Rather than "free associations," in which the associative stream of thought moves from association to association (and therefore farther from the original image), Jung preferred "amplification," in which associations were continually started anew from the original dream image.

Hypnosis may be used to facilitate the amplification type of imagery. The subject is told that as he or she holds a particular image from a dream in his or her mind, other images will appear about it. If this process becomes activated into a dramatic flow, the state of *active imagination* may be induced. Although too involved for a short presentation here, this technique consists of treating the fantasy as if it were a real situation (during the time of trance) and refraining from doing anything in the fantasy that would not be done if it were actually occurring. This rule for treating the imaginative sequence as if it were real differentiates active imagination from fantasy and daydreaming.

At times buried memories are uncovered using associative techniques under hypnosis. Such memories are then utilized in the psychotherapy process.

A man in psychotherapy with us found that he was continually preoccupied with the thought of witnessing an execution. Under hypnosis he was asked to picture himself observing an execution. When he indicated, by finger movement, that an image had formed, he was asked to describe the scene. It was a hanging in a prison courtyard. The scene spontaneously changed, and he was witnessing a time from his early childhood when his father, angered at the family dog, had punished the animal by putting its leash, attached to the dog's collar, over a railing. He had then hoisted the dog into the air by its neck. The patient had been terrified at the sight of the struggling dog. The scene, of course, was symbolic of many other interactions with the father, and the dog symbolized a part of the patient himself. The affect released with this memory was of great help in motivating him to explore further his neurotic problems concerning his father. As those old conflicts were eliminated in therapy, he lost his preoccupation with execution fantasies.

Stimulation of Dreams

At times when amnesia cannot be directly lessened with hypnosis, the trance state can be employed to suggest that the patient have dreams that will indirectly disclose the lost memories (Brady and Rosner, 1966; Sacerdote, 1967, 1972, 1983). Such dreams may be symbolic, but they often give a literal clue.

A distressed middle-aged housewife was referred for consultation to help her remember where she had misplaced a certain locket that was a valued memento of her mother. She remembered having it within the last month, but a thorough search of her home had failed to disclose it. She feared that it might have been lost on the street. Under hypnosis she had no better memory than when awake, although she seemed to go into an adequate depth of trance. When direct questioning was unproductive, she was told that during the night she would dream of the whereabouts of the locket.

She had the following dream: Among rows of differently colored books she was looking for a particular book that she could not remember. Her associations to the dream were unproductive and did not yield the symbolic statements that are often found in dreams. Instead, she remembered that she had last been in her library about the time that the locket was lost. When asked what she had been reading, she did not recall.

She was instructed under hypnosis that upon awakening to go again to her library and to try to remember which books she had been examining. In the presence of the books she soon remembered that she had been looking at a book on Vietnam. She found the book and opened it. Inside it, as a bookmark, was the missing locket!

The dynamic meaning was then immediately clear. Her only son was in military service in Vietnam, and she had an almost constant fear for his safety. The locket may have been used as a bookmark in an unconscious gesture to link the sense of security that she had felt with her mother (represented by the mother's locket) with her son, for whose safety she felt such constant anxiety. But the need to avoid the anxiety about the son was sufficient also to repress the memory of the locket.

Hall (1977) has extensively discussed the clinical use of dreams from a Jungian point of view. Hypnotic dreams are considered a form of imaginal material that may range from fantasy, through guided imagination, to the Jungian technique of active imagination, a method of utilizing the imaginal ability of the psyche to deal with internal object representations as if they were "objective," although they have objectivity only as psychic contents. Hall views nocturnal dreams as "deeper" and more reliable in revealing unconscious psychodynamics than hypnotic dreams or other imaginal material, since nocturnal dreams have the least amount of conscious ego distortions. In the Jungian view, nocturnal dreams not only reveal which complexes are constellated (a revelation available through other imaginal techniques as well), but they also indicate what the Self or Central Archetype is doing with the activated complexes in the service of individuation and the resolution of neurotic conflicts.

Baker (1983a) and Scagnelli (1977) independently suggest self-hypnotic production of dreams as a treatment method of borderline patients.

NEUROSES

Anxiety Neurosis

A frequent form of neurosis is the anxiety that occurs in many situations and is not in response to fearful stimulus. Anxiety neurosis is distinguished from phobias by being diffuse in nature, not limited to a particular phobic situation. Hypnosis is of benefit, both in calming the excessive anxiety through relaxation techniques and in using the methods of hypnoanalysis to uncover underlying fears and fantasies.

A 45-year-old bachelor came to us for hypnotherapy with a story of an anxiety-permeated life. No area of his activity was free of anxiety, which diffused his business, family, and social relationships. After initial screening and anamnesis, he was found to be a good hypnotic subject. Hypnoanalytic sessions led quickly to a marked decrease in anxiety, while exploration of his past history under trance conditions began to reveal the story of a boy dominated by a seemingly unfeeling and perfectionist father. At an early age the patient had been showing one of his father's pedigreed dogs when the animal acted disorderly. Ignoring the dog, the father shouted, "You idiot!" at the boy, in front of all the family friends. This was typical of many repeated, though less dramatic, interactions with his father.

Later, when he went into the family business, the dog-show experience was repeated in numerous ways. Full of feelings of inadequacy and inferiority, the patient had been unable to establish an intimate relationship of any duration, though he dated and was active sexually.

As he assimilated in his conscious life the material mined during hypnosis, his confidence grew and he began to function more on the higher level of his natural abilities. His business greatly expanded, and he courted and married a woman he admired. His impetuous, adolescent thinking was replaced by controlled, mature judgment.

Hypnotherapy in the relief of anxiety can be applied in three primary ways: (1) direct suggestion for mobilization of coping abilities, (2) self-hypnosis for decreased symptomatology and increased coping, and (3) the various techniques of hypnoanalysis, to uncover and master repressed unconscious conflicts (Barnett, 1983) as in the treatment of chronic nailbiting (Bornstein, 1980). Such unconscious factors as a traumatic experience of fellatio, for example, may be found behind complaints of fear of choking (Epstein and Deyoub, 1981). Although some studies found little difference between hypnosis and meditation in the relief of anxiety (Benson et al., 1978), hypnotherapy seems to allow a more active intervention in correcting disturbed unconscious patterning.

Hysterical Neurosis

Historically, hypnosis has been of special benefit in hysterical neurosis, which is often characterized by a psychogenic loss of function. Often there are flamboyant emotions. There are two major types of hysterical neurosis, the conversion type and the dissociative type.

Formally these are called "conversion reaction" and "dissociative reaction."

CONVERSION TYPE OF HYSTERICAL NEUROSIS

Hypnosis may be used in the differential diagnosis and treatment of conversion symptoms (Abraham, 1968). Conversion in this concept refers to the manner in which an unconscious conflict may lead to a somatic expression that reveals both (1) the unconscious wish and (2) the defense against it. Often the wishes involved in the conflict are of a sexual or aggressive nature. A woman with a strong desire to strike her husband, but who had deeply ingrained inhibitions about being aggressive, suffered a hysterical paralysis of her right arm on a conversion basis. Another woman who engaged in sexual intercourse at the insistence of her boyfriend, despite severe guilt feelings, developed a loss of sensation in her pelvic area—expressing both the desire for sexual gratification (through the marked attention to the genital region) and the defense against this desire (through the anesthesia that denied her any sensation).

Unlike psychophysiological disorders, conversion symptoms tend to occur in the voluntary musculature or in the special senses, such as sight. They usually have a symbolic meaning, which can often be demonstrated in subsequent psychotherapeutic exploration. Also of diagnostic importance is the manner in which the conversion reaction binds anxiety so that the patient may appear quite calm in spite of what would seem to be a severe loss of function in the affected part of his body—the so-called *la belle indifference.*

Our two examples of conversion symptoms show how guilt played a prominent role. In each case evaluation of the symptom under hypnosis was important in making the diagnosis and initiating the process of working through.

A young woman who had been embezzling funds from her employer, a distant relative of her mother's, had a symptom of shortness of breath, chest pain radiating to the left arm, sweating, and a sense of overwhelming fear whenever she attempted to board an airplane for necessary business trips. On several occasions, she had so alarmed the crew of the plane that the takeoff had been delayed so that she could be returned to the terminal for medical attention. Repeated medical examinations failed to reveal any pathological cause of the symptoms. Under hypnosis the symptoms were easily reproduced and relieved, demonstrating that it was of functional rather than organic cause. Faced with this fact, the woman tearfully revealed that she had severe anxiety about her theft. Whenever the doors of the airplane were shut, she had terrifying thoughts of being discovered, tried, and sent to prison. The doors of the plane symbolized to her the shutting of prison doors behind her. Later she

was able to repay the stolen funds without her employer's knowledge. Hypnotherapy was effective in allaying the feelings of insecurity and resentment that
had led to the theft. She now flies without fear.

A farm woman was referred from opthalmology with a case of hysterical
blindness that had occurred suddenly after a visit from her son who worked as
a bank teller. Funduscopic examination was normal, and her pupils were
reactive to light. She would not attempt convergence, and her eyelid reflexes
were present inconsistently when a hand was abruptly moved toward her face.
Under hypnosis she moved her eyes easily and saw normally. Regressed
hypnotically to the time at which the blindness occurred, she was able to reveal
that her son had told her on that day that he had been stealing from the bank
where he worked and feared that he would soon be discovered. Her wish not
to "see" the guilt of her son had been so strong that she symbolized it by the
psychogenic blindness. She was not psychologically minded and subsequent
attempts at psychotherapy added little to the initial relief obtained with hypnosis. The son requested counseling for his own difficulties. With increased
insight into his motives, he sought legal advice and repaid the money. Though
he was discharged from his job, he was not prosecuted by his former employer.

Conversion symptoms may take many forms. Most frequently
they involve an apparent loss of physical abilities. Kodman (1958)
studied a small sample of children who showed nonorganic hearing
losses, presumably on an emotional basis. Although their hearing
seemed essentially normal, they complained of an inability to hear
adequately in certain situations in the home and classroom. Laboratory
tests were made of their hearing before and after hypnotherapy sessions, the results indicating that quantitative improvement was brought
about by hypnotherapy in each case except one. No symptom substitution was noted.

Wilkins and Field (1968) used hypnotic abreaction in treating
hysterical loss of vision in two patients. The abreacted emotions were
of helpless dependency, expressed under hypnotic age regression.
They interpreted the hysterical blindness as self-castration motivated
by guilt as well as a symbolic exhibition of dependent helplessness.
Successful treatment is also reported by Gruenewald (1971) in a man
suffering for 2 years from hysterical blindness in his only eye. Patterson
(1980) presented a case report on hysterical monoclular blindness.

Moskowitz (1964) helped a 32-year-old ranch worker give up a
symptom of loss of strength in the left arm. The strength of the arm was
measured repeatedly, both in and out of hypnosis, until the symptom
completely remitted. Bryan (1961) has suggested that brief hypnotic
treatment of conversion hysteria is possible. Stein (1975) briefly treated
by hypnosis a clear case of conversion cephalalgia.

Hypnosis can also add to the tools available in some crisis situations involving legal investigations (Heaver, 1975; Johnston, 1975). We have at times been asked to help in the examination of individuals as an adjunct to such techniques as polygraph testing and amytal interviews. Hypnosis has been used in these situations only with the informed consent of the subject and with the understanding that the information elicited in this altered state of consciousness did not, in itself, have more reliability than the conscious statements of the subject. Most often, hypnosis was used as an added way for the subject to reassure those who doubted his truthfulness.

During the police investigation of a notorious multiple murder case, a man turned himself in to the local authorities, claiming to be the killer. Thorough interrogation showed that he was familiar with all relevant published material in the case. He even claimed some information that the police could not evaluate as true or false. Suspecting the possibility that he was mentally deranged the police requested a psychiatric evaluation, and the psychiatrist then suggested including an examination under hypnosis.

The man at first gave much the same information as he had in the awake state. There were no overt signs of anxiety, although polygraph testing was not done during the interview. When closely questioned, however, regarding the internal consistency of his story, he seemed at first attempt to come out of trance. He then relaxed and, while remaining in hypnosis, admitted that he had claimed to be the killer for a sense of importance and to be "taken care of" for a while in jail.

Subsequent information collaborated his admission. He had not been in the vicinity of the murders at the time that they were committed nor did his information agree with that later uncovered in the investigation.

Hypnosis was useful in disclosing his malingering, though it was not, by itself, conclusive.

Quite recently we were requested by the court to use age regression on a 16-year-old boy whose testimony was "blurred" by trauma. The results obtained under hypnosis were legally substantiated; they exonerated the boy and changed his entire future.

Pelletier (1977) used hypnotic age regression in the successful treatment (in seven sessions) of a case of hysterical aphonia. Age regression was also utilized by Zannoni (1979) to cure a case of hysterical blindness. Patterson (1980) reports a similar case of monocular hysterical blindness treated with hypnotherapy. Spiegel and Spiegel (1978) advocate hypnotherapy as often the treatment of choice in psychosomatic and conversion symptoms.

Cohen and Suter (1982) studied 57 patients with poorly controlled or atypical seizures. Suggestion that a saline solution would provoke a seizure proved 48 to have psychogenic seizures. In a case with unusually clear psychodynamics, Caldwell and Stewart (1981) described the masterful use of hypnosis to alleviate a hysterical seizure disorder in a 15-year-old boy following his testifying in a case of attempted homosexual rape.

In the use of hypnotherapy in conversion disorders, it is important to structure the therapy in such a manner that the patient has a face-saving way of giving up the symptom (Carasso, Peled, and Yehuda, 1983).

DISSOCIATIVE TYPE OF HYSTERICAL NEUROSIS

In dissociative hysterical neurosis (formerly called dissociative reaction) there are alterations in the state of consciousness or in the sense of identity, producing at times dramatic symptoms such as amnesia, somnambulism, fugue, and multiple personality (Eliseo, 1975).

Fugue states involve loss of memory on a psychogenic basis, resembling clinically the loss of memory that may occur on a neurophysiological basis after severe trauma to the head. In contrast to the traumatic loss of memory, however, it is often possible to piece together a story that explains, in terms of unconscious motivation, why the loss of memory occurred at a particular time and in a specific manner. Although the lost memory frequently may be recovered with hypnosis, care should be taken in attempting to remove the amnesia too abruptly. Should the amnesia be serving an important psychodynamic defensive function, its sudden removal might precipitate a severe anxiety attack of even more undesirable symptoms. We have found it best to couch suggestions for return of memory in a somewhat permissive way, allowing the patient to maintain at least a partial memory loss should it be necessary for his or her immediate stability. Regardless, information usually is obtained that gives the therapist needed orientation in planning for further treatment.

For Schneck (1954a) hypnosis is perhaps the most advantageous of several techniques used to dispel amnesia. Several authors have discussed some differences between amnesia that spontaneously appears under hypnosis and that induced by intentional posthypnotic suggestions (Evans, 1966; Orne, 1966). Spontaneous amnesia may include mere primary process thinking and may appear to involve more dissociation. In a clinical setting it is important only to note the occurrence of spontaneous amnesia and to consider its meaning as an indication of fluctuating depth of trance or as a sign of possible increased repression of certain material.

The case that follows is typical of a type of psychogenic amnesia that may frequently be seen in the emergency rooms of metropolitan hospitals.

A 17-year-old girl, angry after an argument with her mother and step-father, had walked away from her home at night, intending to walk to the house of an aunt some miles away. While crossing a long bridge, she was offered a ride by an older man whom she did not know. The man drove to a secluded area, where he repeatedly raped her. Hours after leaving home she was found by a policeman wandering aimlessly in a deserted area. Brought to the emergency room, she denied any memory after the man had picked her up. She was vague and obviously disturbed.

Following an arm-levitation induction, the patient entered a state of somnambulism. She was told the following: "Recall of feeling and emotions often helps us get well even if such events are frightening. Your recent experience was so frightening that you have forgotten many facts about yourself, but under a state of hypnosis you can recall . . . everything that you have forgotten . . . every fact . . . every emotion . . . every detail . . . and so you are going to go back in terms of time and space . . . back in terms of space and time . . . to that experience that caused you to lose your memory . . . you are going back to the exact time and you can recall, relive . . . revive . . . feel . . . and experience everything that happened."

As the patient began to talk, cry, and abreact the traumatic scene that led to her amnesia, her memory abruptly returned and she dramatically abreacted the rape scene, struggling frantically against an imagined attacker and crying out in fear and pain. As the re-enactment subsided, she regained her composure, had an intact memory for the entire event, and was reunited with her family.

She was followed in the psychiatric clinic afterward and given an opportunity to understand not only her repressed feelings about the assault, but also the difficulties with her family that had led to the situation. This use of hypnosis is almost directly parallel to its utility in traumatic battle situations.

There are many instances of minor amnesias, not approaching the dramatic amnesias and fugue states, that are, nevertheless, extremely important to the persons involved. Often, the amnesia is for an important but misplaced object. Several years ago we were consulted by a woman who remembered that her grandfather had owned an unusual stock certificate that might have been, she thought, the missing certificate for land granted to the Texas and Pacific Railroad in the early days of Texas. The certificate, if presented, would have been worth millions. A diligent search had been made of the grandfather's house and papers without success. In this instance hypnosis did not uncover any additional information, perhaps because the woman had no real past knowledge of the whereabouts of the certificate. In any case, it was never found.

Kaplan and Deabler (1975) report the successful treatment of a man with severe dissociative hysterical disorder of 5 years duration, treatment requiring only eight sessions utilizing age regression techniques. Spiegel and Fink (1979) hypothesize that patients with hysterical psychosis are highly hypnotizable, compared with patients with schizophrenic and psychotic diagnosis (Ham, Spanos, and Barber, 1976).

Multiple Personality

A somewhat rare but dramatic psychiatric disorder, multiple personality, is perhaps best known to the public through the famous book *The Three Faces of Eve*, by Thigpen and Cleckley (1957). Prince's earlier case (1908) of "Miss Beauchamp" was similar, and the literary story of Dr. Jekyl and Mr. Hyde expressed in a dramatized form the fashion in which two or more personalities may inhabit the same mind.

Reference to multiple personality as "split personality" has led to the erroneous conclusion by some laymen that it is a form of schizophrenia, which literally means "split mind." Multiple personality, based on a dissociation of the personality, however, is more often thought of as a severe form of hysterical neurosis.

It is sometimes difficult to tell which personality is primary, as the apparently invading personality may represent quite clearly the split-off and repressed portions of the patient's mind. This is similiar to Jung's view (1957) of mediumistic "controls" as prefigurations of future personality growth in the medium herself.

A unique demonstration of hypnosis in the ongoing treatment of a patient with multiple personality has been presented by Newton (1968). Hypnosis was also used in the case of Eve, reported by Thigpen and Cleckley.

In spite of these well-known cases, Gruenewald (1971) has contended that hypnosis is contraindicated in treatment of multiple personality. According to her, there is a danger that the patient may interpret hypnosis as a sanction for the dissociative process. She points out that the secondary personality may, like the hypnotized subject, have access to material not available to ordinary consciousness.

Bowers and Brecher (1955) have noted the emergence of multiple personality in the course of hypnotic investigation. They felt that an obsessive compulsive defense countered the hysterical dissociative tendency of the personality to break into several part personalities.

Verson (1961) reported hypnotic treatment of obsessive ideas without evoking dissociation, however. Morton and Thoma (1964) have also reported minor states of multiple personality associated with hypnosis. Gruenewald (1978) conceptualizes multiple personality as a category sue generis on a continuum from neurosis to psychosis. Hypnosis is widely recognized as useful in treating multiple personalities (Kloft, 1982; Howland, 1975). One of the most prolific writers about hypnosis and multiple personality is Bennett Braun (1979a, 1980a, 1980b, 1983), who reports diagnosing 51 cases over a period of 4 years (although he did not treat all of the cases diagnosed). Braun (1979b) feels that hypnosis does not create multiple personality, as some critics have suggested, but rather rapidly uncovers dissociations that already exist in the patient; he therefore is increasingly of the opinion that hypnosis can legitimately be used in the diagnostic procedures in cases of multiple personality. Kampman (1976) has offered experimental evidence that the production of secondary personalities is not a rare ability. He tried to create multiple personality behavior, limited to the experimental situation, in 78 volunteers able to enter deep hypnosis. Thirty-two were able to achieve multiple personalities in hypnosis, and he judged that these were clinically healthier and more adaptive than those who were unable to do so, a finding of variance with the observations of some others. Mirow (1983) used videotape and audiotape as therapeutic tools in treating a patient with multiple personality. Abrams (1983) highlights the complications of differential diagnosis in the legal use of multiple personality as a defense implying lessened responsibility. These include frank malingering and the modification of the trance state by histrionic individuals.

While overt cases of multiple personality are rare in most practices, there are milder dissociative states that are commonplace in the various forms of neurosis. The psychic structure that Jung called the *shadow* is a normal part of all personalities and consists of a repressed alter-ego that is unacceptable to the present ego-image. The shadow may, at times, take over the executive ability of the normal ego, leading to mild dissociated states that resemble a pale form of multiple personality; there is not, of course, the dissociation of memory that is characteristic of classical multiple personality (Hall, 1984b).

Phobic Neurosis

Unlike anxiety neurosis, in which anxiety is diffuse, in phobic neurosis it is bound more to a specific object or situation, which is often symbolic of some hidden, unconscious thought or buried memory.

There are many types of phobic reactions with exotic names such as claustrophobia (fear of closed spaces), agoraphobia (fear of open spaces), acrophobia (fear of heights), thanatophobia (fear of death), and many others, limited only by available combinations of Greek roots.

One reason that phobias are difficult to treat is the problem of persuading the phobic patient to face the object of his or her fear thereby to learn of its harmlessness. Fear of riding in elevators is a common phobia, and in its milder forms may be something that many persons experience.

A 32-year-old married woman came for treatment because she feared riding in elevators, in airplanes, or getting caught in traffic. Her chief fear was of driving over bridges, at which times she felt panic as if she were exposed and vulnerable. Her fears were so great that she was unable to work and was even unable to pick up her children from school on many occasions when her fears were particularly marked.

She had seen a number of therapists and had unsuccessfully undergone behavioral modification treatment. It was decided to use hypnotic age regression to investigate her history. Through ideomotor signals with her fingers she indicated when she felt that she had regressed "to an age commensurate with the onset of the fears."

This proved to be age 5. She was told to remember, in the hypnotically revivified role of her 5-year-old ego, what had happened at the beginning of her fears.

She recalled that she had been spending the summer with her grandparents, who owned a truck stop with a gas station and a cafe. She had become acquainted with some of the truckers and considered them her friends. They frequently gave her candy and other gifts.

One day while sitting in the open end of a parked trailer, dangling her legs back and forth, she was suddenly aware that a young boy, whom she did not know, had crawled under the trailer and was attempting to insert a finger into her vagina. She was both frightened by and interested in the unusual sensation. Knowing that "something was wrong," she had not told her grandparents of the event. She had disturbing dreams thereafter, and within a few months, as the dreams became less frequent, she developed the fear of bridges. Asked under hypnosis if she felt any similarity between bridges and the experience when she was 5-years-old, she said "I'm up high, I'm unprotected and can't get away. People can see me!"

Her symptoms did not disappear with this memory, though it was possible to trace many other events in her life that seemed to follow a similar pattern of guilt and fear. After many months of treatment, using age regression and more conventional psychotherapeutic means, she gradually gave up the phobic symptoms. Later she relinquished much of her anxiety.

Another common mild phobic neurosis is excessive fear of speaking in public, a symptom that causes many men and women to avoid promotions in their work, since the advancement might lead to the necessity of making presentations before an audience. In milder forms this is simply what is commonly called "stage fright." It is not uncommon for students with this problem to say "I don't know" when asked to answer a question that they actually know quite well but would rather appear stupid than face the anxiety of speaking before the class.

Perhaps in its deepest roots this fear of speaking in public has some aspect of what is theoretically called "castration anxiety," a fear that if one becomes prominent or seen, he or she is likely to be injured. In terms of Jungian analysis it also includes the fear that the *shadow* (the unacceptable, hidden part of oneself) will be seen and that the *persona* (the "good front" we wish to present to others) will not give adequate protection.

A 30-year-old business executive was considering resigning from a key post in a major corporation because in presenting verbal reports he almost invariably experienced rapid breathing, increased sweating, a sense of his heart "jumping," and frequently felt that he was blushing. He would be unable to sleep the night before a presentation. At meals he would become nauseated and unable to eat. The height of his anxiety would come when he entered the meeting room and saw the table lined with company officers waiting to hear his report. On one occasion he feigned a "virus," stating that he would be unable to make the meeting as scheduled. After this subterfuge his symptoms became even more frequent and troubling.

When his internist found no organic basis for his symptoms, he was referred to us for exploration of possible emotional causes. In the anamnesis it was learned that he had forced himself to join several social clubs, in which he had held offices, in an attempt to "wear out" his neurotic response, but without benefit. He had also taken two courses in public speaking, which diminished his anxiety somewhat during the time of the classes, possibly because everyone was in much the same state as himself and a spirit of helpful camaraderie prevailed. Soon after the courses were finished, however, he found that the improvement had not generalized to his work situation.

His personal history revealed one interesting point. He had been valedictorian of his high school class and had given the traditional address without anxiety or disturbance. He had grown up in a strict religious home in which his father repeatedly admonished him, while pointing his finger at the boy, to "walk the straight and narrow path." He remembered that his father had always said, "You can tell when someone is doing something wrong—you can see it in their eyes."

In hypnoanalytic probing it was learned that when he was out of town with other associates, he frequently was involved with women he met at business functions. He had no real desire for such infidelities, but he did not want to be thought different from his peers. He had on several occasions great guilt feelings for his sexual activities, with revivification in his imagination of "What would my father say if he were alive and knew?"

A correlation was made in time of occurrence between his sexual guilt feelings and exacerbations of his fear of speaking. A particular meaning seemed to attach to occasions when men in the audience pointed their fingers at him when asking questions. This unconsciously recalled his father's characteristic gesture when admonishing him to "be good." On one occasion he spontaneously broke into anxiety and tears during hypnoanalysis. He had been experiencing, in trance, the feeling of being before a company meeting and exclaimed "I'm not worthy of speaking before all these good men!"

He responded very well to a combination of hypnotic reconditioning of his self-concept and working through his fears and conflicts centered on parental father figures. Working through his transference feelings was also crucial, and he came to see the therapist as a nonjudgmental, kindly figure. He decided that having affairs was not necessary to his sense of masculinity, lost his phobia of speaking to groups, and continued to be productive and successful in his career. He was taught to use self-hypnosis prior to making any presentations. This gave marked relief of anxiety, and he was soon able to speak effectively without this aid, though it remained available to him.

Fear of Flying

Fear of flying is a common and widespread phobia that interferes with many persons leading a normal social and business life. Bakal (1981) reports successful treatment of flight phobia with hypnosis, as does Burrows (1975). Psychodynamically, the fear of flying is closely rated to a fear of dependency. We have seen a number of pilots and cabin attendants who had a fear of flying as passengers but no fear of flying when they were working. Clearly, the difference is the sense of mastery involved in being part of the flight process rather than a passive passenger. In some instances, it has been necessary to work through the dependency/independency conflict in the process of alleviating the fear of flying.

In treating phobias, it is important to carefully differentiate the symptoms for those of a primary origin in anxiety or depression (Waxman, 1983). Frankel and Orne (1976) found that phobic patients were more hypnotizable than a control group of persons seeking hypnotherapy for smoking. Hypnotherapy is often of particular usefulness with phobic problems, which are related to hysteria in psychodynamics (Cohen, 1981; Frankel, 1980). There may be any number of particular phobic situations, depending on the individual patient: hospital phobia (Waxman, 1978), phobia of slugs (Gustavson and Weight, 1981), phobia connected with hand-washing compulsions (Scrignar, 1981), fear of injections (Daniels, 1976), and even unusual fears, such as fear of mayonnaise (Van Dyke and Harris, 1982). One of the most common phobic situations in which hypnosis is utilized is agoraphobia, fear of being in open public places (Daubner, 1980; Schmidt, 1983a).

Obsessive Compulsive Neurosis

The patient is bothered by the constant intrusion of seemingly meaningless thoughts or actions in the obsessive compulsive neurotic state. He or she seems powerless to stop these thoughts or actions without creating marked anxiety. Lady Macbeth's famous hand-washing compulsion—symbolic of her guilt at the murder of the king—exemplifies this type. Other manifestations of this state may be rituals of putting things in a certain order or performing certain actions. Some writers, for example, must go through a pencil-sharpening ritual before composing. There seems to be an attempt to control outer events, and the anxiety associated with them, by controlling inner thought or the small, repetitive actions of everyday life. In a sense, obsessive compulsive neurosis is an introverted way of handling anxiety, while hysterical neurosis is more extraverted and is more manipulative of the environment and other persons.

Obsessive compulsive neurotics have usually been, in our experience, good hypnotic subjects, probably because of their disabling and obvious disturbances. They have much to gain from an improvement, however slight, in their compulsive behavior. Studying various types of hypnotic intervention in patients with obsessional thoughts, Barone, Blum, and Porter (1975) found that their best results were obtained in suggesting that the patient's mind become blank.

A Jewish merchant had great difficulty in his business, since after he closed for the day he was unable to put aside compulsive thoughts that he had forgotten to lock the doors of his store. Even when witnesses saw him lock the doors, and he had tested the lock, he might awaken in the night and feel compelled to dress and drive to the business location to check them once again. He had some fear about his business success in a more realistic way and was particularly concerned that he would not be able to do as well financially as his father. The symptoms had begun about a year after his father's death. In hypnotic exploration no clear cause could be found, although there were several possibilities. First, he had once lost a mezuza, a religious object, and his father had been very angry, saying that God might be displeased for such inefficient caretaking. Second, he had promised his father, shortly before his father's death, that he would attend Saturday Sabbath services regularly. When he failed to maintain that observance after his father's death, he had feelings that he was robbing his father of something the father valued. Through a reversal mechanism this may have become a fear that he himself would be robbed. There were also many implications of classical Oedipal psychodynamics in his situation.

Even though a clear etiology was not established, he gradually gave up his symptoms and did not seem to replace them with substitutes. It is important to mention that direct symptom removal was not used and that all hypnotic suggestions for improvement were couched in a permissive, nonauthoritarian way.

Depressive Neurosis

Depression is a common clinical disorder. In its milder forms it may simply be the "blue" or "off days" that everyone has at some time. When depression deepens, however, and passes from a mere mood to a fixed state, it can constitute a severe emotional disorder, usually spoken of as depressive syndrome or depressive neurosis.

Depression of severe depth and fixity may constitute a life-threatening emotional disorder, for the depressed person may begin to have involuntary thoughts of suicide. At times the person may feel that he or she has commited the "unforgivable sin," or some other delusion of unworthiness. Or he or she may feel that "everyone would be better off without me." It is only a short step from such thoughts of unworthiness to thoughts of actual suicide. In clinical practice it is well always to distinguish the patient who has thoughts that "life is not worth living" from the patient who has actual thoughts of suicide, including plans about how to do away with himself. The former state ("life isn't worth it") is not as dangerous in suicide potential as the latter, though one must always be alert for a worsening of depressive symptoms.

Other symptoms that often accompany the picture of depression are loss of interest, poor memory, decreased appetite and weight loss, decreased sexual interest (including at times impotence), constipation, and poor sleep. These are not invariable concomitants of depression; their opposites may even occur—for example, an increase in appetite rather than a loss of hunger.

It is the risk of suicide, however, that makes depression dangerous, something to be treated carefully and with understanding. The presence of frank suicidal thinking is a relative contraindication, in our opinion, to the use of hypnosis in an outpatient setting, except in very special and rare circumstances.

Why is this so? Because the psychodynamics of depression often involve anger of an intense degree. In reactive depression, that which follows some disappointment in life, the anger may be easily traced to outer circumstances. In more complex cases, however, it may refer to a deeply repressed infantile anger, going even as far as the oral stage of psychosexual development. The techniques of hypnosis move much more rapidly than ordinary psychotherapy into the situations involving "transference" distortions by the patient in which the therapist may be seen as an important figure from the past, often a parent or spouse. Such distortion may make the patient overreactive to real or imagined slights from the therapist, or he or she may wish to "punish" the therapist for his or her imagined lack of care for the patient.

If depression is severe enough, it is not possible to work in an ordinary psychotherapeutic way, as the patient's withdrawal and lack of affective response interfere with his developing an observing and reflecting ego function to deal with the neurotic parts of his personality. In such regressed patients hypnosis may be seen as a motherly caring function, which may be soothing to the patient. However, more active hypnoanalytic techniques may not be advisable.

Paradoxically, the most dangerous time in the treatment of depression is when the patient seems to begin improving. Surprisingly, it is at this stage that suicide is most likely. Many have speculated that the explanation for this chain of events is that the severely depressed patient does not have the energy to consider suicide. As he or she begins to improve and energy levels rise, action may become possible before the mood of depression is thoroughly lifted. This seems to be the most crucial time no matter what method of treatment is being used—psychotherapy, hypnoanalysis, antidepressant medication, electroconvulsive therapy, or other approaches.

Depression without active suicide thoughts is not a contraindication to the use of hypnosis. We would not hesitate to use hypnosis to decrease smoking in a man dying of emphysema, for example, even though he might have some depression secondary to his physical condition. In fact, if hypnotherapy can relieve conditions contributing to a reactive depression, it may be instrumental in improvement of the depression itself (Matheson, 1979).

When hypnotherapy is employed for treatment of a condition presenting primarily as depression, we are careful to avoid a symptom-removal approach. Suggestions are, "your mind and your body will be free from tension, tightness, stress, and strain . . . You will be able to cope with your problems more realistically. . . . You'll be less tense and afraid." We do not give direct suggestions for the removal of the depression itself, rather we handle any anger or other affect that may be uncovered in a psychotherapeutic way, perhaps with hypnosis. In other words, our approach is to increase the patient's ego strength and to enhance his ability to deal with the problems leading to depression. Hypnoanalytic exploration of the past may be utilized, and we often employ concomitant medication with antidepressant drugs.

Chambers (1968) reports the hypnotic treatment of a woman who refused to undergo usual antidepressant treatments. Part of her symptomatology was a compulsion to eat raw potatoes. He studied this compulsion while the patient was deeply hypnotized, interpreting his findings in psychoanalytic terms. Rosen (1955) discussed hypnotically induced regression as an emergency measure in a suicidally depressed patient. He felt that the obliteration and then the reconstitution of "more mature ego boundaries" was therapeutic. Abrams (1964a) described hypnosis as a valuable adjunctive measure in the development of a relationship with the patient, in uncovering repressed material, and in the creation of artificial situations in which the individual can learn to express the unacceptable angry feelings. Miller (1983b) has outlined a number of hypnotic techniques that may be used in treating depression. These include in addition to such usual techniques as relaxation, such psychodynamic factors as modeling, focusing on reality, emphasis on facts and the mode of their expression rather than on affect, and reforming of circular and self-reinforcing depressive thoughts. Gruber (1983) reports the use of hypnotherapy to decrease affective instability, utilizing such techniques as teaching the patient to evoke two opposite states of mind and alternate them, perhaps allowing a sense of freedom from the compulsive identification with either state.

While hypnosis can be used in treating depression, we strongly advise that such use be only by therapists adequately grounded in psychodynamics; even then it should be used with caution and care.

Neurasthenic Neurosis (Neurasthenia)

The chief symptom of neurasthenic neurosis is a feeling of lack of energy, with chronic complaints of weakness and fatigue—all in the absence of any physical explanation. Sometimes the sufferer feels a sense of exhaustion, as if the slightest effort is too complicated, too strenuous.

In some ways neurasthenic neurosis resembles depression, for in depression a sense of loss of normal energy can also be encountered. There is in neurasthenic neurosis, however, none of the severe depressive affect, even leading to thoughts of self-destruction. Instead, the sense of loss of energy exists somewhat in isolation. There is also no clear picture of the symptoms being used to manipulate others.

The hypnotic approach to this condition consists of (1) symptom amelioration, and (2) hypnoanalysis for the understanding and correction of underlying dynamics. The approach is often in this order since the feeling of fatigue interferes with therapy itself. Once the symptom begins to improve, the treatment is not terminated but is shifted toward an exploration of psychodynamic conflicts. These often seem to be of a depressive nature in our experience, though it is not always possible to lead the patient to an experience of the depressed emotion. At times unfulfilled longings for a return to childhood dependence are found, which may involve in treatment an alteration of the dependence-independence relationships in the family structure.

In rare instances it has been impossible to identify an underlying conflict, and treatment has consisted of decreasing the symptom itself.

Depersonalization Neurosis

Symptoms of depersonalization may occur in transient stress situations without warranting the diagnosis of a neurotic disorder. Many persons in severe situations—such as auto accidents, the death of a relative, or sudden and unexpected disaster—may experience a sense of "this isn't really happening." Alternately it may seem "this really isn't happening to *me*." Such experiences represent a massive and acute defense against overwhelming anxiety.

If such feelings of depersonlization or de-realization ("The world isn't real") persist over a significant period of time, they may indicate a depersonalization neurosis. In a sense this neurosis may represent a partial stage of multiple personality, stopping at the point where the ego perceives the sense of psychic dissociation but falling short of the reorganization into "separate" personality structures.

The psychodynamics of this disorder are quite similar to the dissociative aspects of hysteria, and they can be treated in much the same manner. It is important to be cautious in employing hypnosis with any disorder in which dissociation is a prominent feature, though it has been our impression that such use is possible by therapists well-schooled in psychodynamics. The reassurance of the therapist taking a clear, firm approach is perhaps more important when the symptoms involve a tendency toward dissociation. This clarity and firmness must be based on a secure understanding of the psychological defense mechanisms involved.

Hypochondriacal Neurosis

Presumed disease of bodily organs is not infrequent in neurosis, and when it predominates the clinical picture may be considered hypochondriacal neurosis. These fears do not reach a delusional quality and may respond to reality testing. There are no actual losses of function, as in some hysterical conversion symptoms. In men a frequent fear is of heart disease, while in women a dread of suspected breast tumors is often seen. The organ chosen for the focus of anxiety may be symbolically important—the heart representing emotional warmth or courage, the breast an ability to nourish and give, the brain a problem in thinking and understanding.

The treatment of hypochondriacal symptoms is discussed at length in Chapter 10.

PSYCHOTIC STATES

There has been little exploration of the possible use of hypnosis in treating psychotic states, either acute or fixed. Perhaps this is because of the fear so often expressed that removal of symptoms with hypnosis may provoke severe reactions. There is also some danger of the psychotic seeing the hypnotic relationship as domination, loss of control, or dependency (Conn, 1960).

Perhaps such caution is unwarranted. Hypnosis, after all, can be looked upon as a unique type of interpersonal situation and, as such, need be no more frightening than the intense relationships that are formed when conventional psychotherapy is attempted with schizophrenics. Needless to say, the therapist should not undertake the hypnotic treatment of any case that he or she would not feel competent to treat by conventional means (Abrams, 1964b; Alexander, 1967) and he or she should be prepared to offer whatever environmental changes might be necessary should the patient be disturbed. These would most usually be hospitalization and alteration of the patient's internal environment through drug therapy. Schneck (1954a) has highlighted the manner in which some hypnotherapy patients experience fantasies of omnipotence and masochistic submission, the satisfaction of dependency needs, and sexual strivings that may be both heterosexual and homosexual. He also mentions that hypnosis is seen by some as symbolic death and rebirth. Such fantasies may be complex and involved, just as material elicited in intense nonhypnotic transference neurosis.

A number of years ago, we attempted, in collaboration with Carmen Miller Michael, Ph.D., the hypnotic treatment of a woman in her twenties who had been brought to an emergency room and hospitalized. The young woman had been found walking completely naked in the middle of the day on one of the main streets of Dallas. When questioned about the strange behavior, she had said, "I'm not naked. I'm Lady Godiva, and I was wrapped in my hair and riding my horse." The horse had not been seen by the arresting officer, and it was obvious that her hair was insufficient to cover the more private areas of her anatomy.

Hypnosis was induced, and in the trance state she ceased to treat her delusional ideas as if they were real, conversing in a very normal and polite manner. The entire session of some 45 minutes was recorded on a wire recorder, with plans to compare her responses over several hypnotic sessions. Unfortunately, however, the wire slipped the spool and became unusable. The following day, when an attempt was made to repeat hypnosis, the patient turned her back and refused to look or speak to her examiners. She improved with hospitalization, medication, and milieu therapy.

Bowers (1961) and Bowers, Brecher-Marer, and Polatin (1961) have reported some success in the hypnotic treatment of schizophrenics. They attempted to use hypnotic age regression to take a paranoid patient back to the "time" before his thinking became bizarre. Erickson (1970) reported the utility of hypnotic training in three cases of manic-depressive psychosis and one case of schizophrenia. Abrams (1963, 1965) who also found schizophrenics hypnotizable—as did Green (1969)—had success in fostering insight and attitudinal changes. Moore (1975) and Volgyesi (1959) have also reported benefit from hypnosuggestive methods.

Scagnelli (1975) and Wolberg (1948) recommended hypnosis as an adjunct in the treatment of schizophrenia in some cases, advising that it be used primarily as a means of inducing a relaxed pleasurable state, thus strengthening the relations of the therapist to the patient. Analytic probing is to be avoided, he feels, nor should the schizophrenic be given direct suggestions for symptom removal. Wolberg cites the case of a hebephrenic schizophrenic who improved when hypnosis was used to induce memories of music, which had been his chief source of pleasure prior to his illness.

Scagnelli (1976, 1980, 1982) and Scagnelli-Jobsis (1982) have reviewed literature on the use of hypnosis with psychotic and borderline patients, concluding that psychotics can be hypnotized and in many instances may benefit from the skilled use of hypnotherapy. Spiegel (1983) has disagreed with some of Scagnelli's conclusions of the use of hypnotherapy with psychotic patients, considering them premature conclusions. Scagnelli-Jobsis (1983) has responded to his critique, suggesting some inconsistency in his previous attitude toward this complicated and unsettled question in the field of hypnotherapy. In our own view, hypnotherapy with psychotic patients should be undertaken only in a hospital setting and then with caution and clinical reserve. With psychotic patients, of course, a major focus must be upon ego-strength and the ability to integrate uncovered dynamic material, which can easily be elicited with hypnosis in psychotic and borderline patients. It is well to remember that in dealing with these patients with hypnotherapy or other techniques, there should always be more structure (ego-strength, medication, hospital milieu, positive transference) than pressure from the unconscious of the patient, evidenced by delusions, delusional transference reactions, and acting-out of unconscious impulses, etc.

Reporting on his experience with hypnosis in more than 100 schizophrenic patients, Saadia (1983) essentially agrees with Scagnelli. Murray-Jobsis (1983) describes in detail the use of hypnotherapy with severely disturbed patients. Ham, Spanos, and Barber (1976) discuss suggestibility in hospitalized schizophrenics.

In a comparison of music therapy and hypnosis with hospitalized schizophrenics, Ihalainen and Rosberg (1976) found that hypnosis appeared to have a real influence only when suggestions of relaxation were given.

In chronic psychotic patients, hypnotizability may be an adaptive regression (Lavoie et al., 1976). In a study of suggestibility in hospitalized schizophrenics, 19 variables accounted for up to 48 percent of the variance; these included age, marital status, education, duration of hospitalization, psychopathological behavior, and cooperativeness. Lavoie and Sabourin (1980) have reviewed clinical and experimental studies of hypnosis and schizophrenia. Baker (1983b,c) has published an excellent recent review of hypnotic techniques with psychotics.

The use of hypnosis with psychotic patients, at best, is a very unsettled area where the dangers may be marked. However, there are enough suggestions of possible benefit that carefully conducted experimental use by qualified clinicians should be encouraged in appropriate hospital settings. A critical review of the use of hypnotic techniques with psychotics has been published by Abrams (1964b).

CHARACTER DISORDERS

The sociopathic or character disorders include the type of personality disorder that was formerly referred to as psychopathic. Unlike psychotics, sociopaths are clearly able to differentiate reality from their fantasies. Unlike neurotics, they seldom suffer severe anxiety or guilt feelings, except in transient situations where they come into severe conflict with authority figures who enforce more acceptable rules of behavior. The conflict of the sociopath is not internalized, as in neurosis, but exists between the individual and the surrounding society so that the "symptoms" are often deviant or unacceptable behavior rather than intrapsychic discomfort.

Treatment of these disorders is extremely difficult since the patient is poorly motivated to change except during times of particular stress. Often successful treatment requires hospitalization, where rewards and punishments of the patient's behavior can be easily administered, affording essentially an opportunity to relearn a sense of responsibility that had not been adequately developed in childhood.

We have not found hypnotic techniques to be of any marked additional help to the standard psychotherapy approaches in the treatment of sociopathic disorders. If the degree of disorder is limited to a particular area of life, or otherwise circumscribed as in habit of gambling, hypnosis may be tried to bolster the patient's desire to change. Such treatment should be undertaken only as an adjunct to intensive psychotherapy. Lewis (1979) reports a case of schizoid personality improved with hypnotherapy.

SEXUAL DISORDERS

Most sexual dysfunctions have an emotional origin, and hypnotherapy can be of help in many instances. We have devoted a separate chapter (Chapter 18) to the treatment of impotence and frigidity (or orgasmic dysfunction, the more modern and preferred term) since these are the most frequent sexual problems encountered in clinical referrals.

Hypnotherapy should be considered, however, in other problem areas of sexual functioning. Knowles (1965) used hypnotherapy beneficially in treating exhibitionism and peeping-Tom activity. Roper (1965) treated 3 patients whose exhibitionism had been present for more than 5 years. He found no recurrence of the undesirable activity at follow-up, which ranged from 1 to 5 years in the three instances.

Transvestism (dressing in the clothes of the opposite sex) does not necessarily indicate homosexual functioning. Biegel (1967) and Wollman (1968) have reported hypnotic and hypnoanalytic applications in its treatment.

Homosexuality can be treated with hypnotherapy according to a number of case reports (Abarbanst-Brandt, 1966; Magonet, 1959; Schneck, 1950). Although no longer in itself a diagnostic classification, homosexuality can cause much unhappiness in patients and their families. Extremely high motivation for change is needed, but when that is present, hypnoanalytic exploration of underlying fantasies may be of great benefit. At least one-third of well-motivated patients we have seen seem able to attain a preference for heterosexual adaptation.

Conn (1968) and Canty (1958) have shown the effectiveness of hypnotherapy in the treatment of sex offenders. Conn has stressed that the necessary factor for recovery seems to be an effective working relationship rather than depth of trance or success in regressive techniques to revivify past experience.

A number of authors report success in using hypnotherapy in the treatment of exhibitionism (Epstein and Deyoub, 1983; Polk, 1983; and Mutter, 1981). Mutter emphasizes giving strong ego-dystonic suggestions about avoiding the unacceptable urges, suggestions that the patient will be able to resist the impulses, and then using hypnoanalytic procedures to explore the underlying meaning of the symptom.

ALCOHOLISM

If a patient has strong unconscious motivation to relinquish a symptom of alcoholism, hypnosis may be of significant aid (Bjorkheim, 1956). If deeper motivation for change is lacking, hypnosis is of little help. If, as is sometimes the case, the patient has little motivation for improvement but presents himself or herself for consultations only to satisfy a family member, treatment success is not usually seen. In general, however, alcoholics are good hypnotic subjects (Hartman, 1966).

Hypnotherapy, especially direct symptom removal, is never used alone with alcoholics. Rather, it is combined with counseling, psychotherapy, group therapy, or marital counseling. Some use of tranquilizers or antidepressant medication may be made, and if the referring physician has already begun the alcoholic on disulfram (Antabuse) therapy, it may be continued.

After reasons for excessive use of alcohol are sufficiently explored in the waking or hypnotic state, suggestions are given under hypnosis that are very similar to those we use for persons who cannot stop smoking.

"You will be relaxed and at ease. . . . Your body will not be extremely tense and nervous . . . but you will be extremely relaxed. . . . The craving for alcohol will diminish very, very rapidly. . . . You will not be thinking about alcohol, nor craving for alcohol. . . . You will note that the intake of other kinds of fluids will satisfy your oral needs. . . . You will sleep very well . . . deep, sound, relaxed, restful sleep, secure in the knowledge that you will no longer crave for this habit that has had such a negative effect upon your life. . . . You will have the strength, the desire to permanently give up this habit of drinking alcohol. . . . You will give up this habit with minimal discomfort, relaxed and at ease, secure in the knowledge that you are changing this habit.''

Additional reinforcement with self-hypnosis several times a day is recommended.

Many reports of successful use of hypnosis in the treatment of alcoholism are found in both older and more recent literature (Cotlier, 1938; DeJong, 1896; Fox, 1965; Granone, 1971; Meyers, 1944). Feamster and Brown (1963) report a 3 year follow-up of a patient successfully treated for alcoholism with hypnotherapy. His attempts to drink, after therapy, resulted in a strong aversion to alcohol and a willingness to use brief hospitalization as a safety-valve. Miller (1959) had some alcoholics re-experience unpleasant hangover effects under hypnosis. Paley (1952) describes hypnotherapy as furthering a relaxation of defenses, making the alcoholic patient more approachable in psychotherapy. Scott (1968) presents an unusual case of apparent hypnosis in an alcoholic, without an intent to induce hypnosis.

Abrams (1964c) found mixed response in treating alcoholics with hypnosis, while Edwards (1966) found hypnosis to be of no additional value when added to conventional treatments for alcoholism.

In a comparison of alcoholics and college students Field and Scott (1969) found the alcoholics to be more alert and conscious during hypnosis and to show more impulsive enthusiasm for hypnosis, possible because of the alcoholic personality or slight organicity.

When subjects have responded well and any underlying neurotic causes of alcoholism have been removed, we at times use hypnotic suggestion to give them permission to drink very moderately in a social setting, switching after one or two alcoholic drinks to nonalcoholic substitutes. In general, the results have been gratifying, although some feel complete abstinence to be preferred (Langen, 1967).

Alcoholics are not significantly less hypnotizable than controls (Lenox and Bonny, 1976), and hypnotherapy can be used in many ways in the treatment of alcoholism, including ego-strengthening techniques (Mastronardi, 1980; Gabrynowicz, 1977). In our experience, it is vitally important to correctly assess the motivation for treatment of the alcoholic and to employ sufficient supportive measures, including group processes and conjoint therapy if indicated.

ADDICTION

Hypnotherapy is of value in treating addictions other than alcohol in conjunction with medical withdrawal from the abused drugs (Hartman, 1972; Koster, 1957). Although an authoritative approach has been reported as successful with drug addicts (Ludwig, Lyle, and Miller, 1964), we ourselves invariably prefer to approach addiction problems in a psychodynamic fashion, seeking to understand the meaning of the addiction in the patient's psychic economy. Symptom removal may then be undertaken, we feel, with more safety.

Results with marijuana have been generally satisfactory when the patient presents himself or herself for treatment, unrewarding when he or she is brought by parents or other authorities. In our experience court-referred cases are least likely to result in permanent change.

Whenever the withdrawal is from truly addicting drugs, such as heroin, hypnosis is best used as an adjunctive treatment in a hospital setting. The same precaution is suggested for hallucinogenic drugs such as LSD. Levine and Ludwig (1966) found hypnosis and psychotherapy to aid in modifying the LSD experience and to structure it in ways that can be potentially therapeutic.

MILITARY APPLICATIONS

Hypnosis achieved widespread use in treating combat neurosis during World War II. Abreaction of combat neurosis rapidly returned many soldiers to duty. Similar utility is reported in treating veterans of the Vietnam conflict, who have additional problems caused by the social conflict about the acceptability of the war itself. Spiegel (1981) has used hypnosis in facilitating grief work in Vietnam veterans. Brenda and Benedict (1980) found hypnosis helpful in treating dissociative symptoms of delayed stress syndrome in Vietnam veterans. Dempsey and Granich (1978) treated stuttering as a result of Korean war trauma, a symptom that had persisted for 19 years, using hypnotherapy. There are recent reports from the war in Lebanon (Levy and Neumann, 1983).

Many of the problems that occur in civilian practice are also found in military populations, enhanced at times by the stresses of the military situation. Garver, Fuselier, and Booth (1981) report hypnotic treatment of amnesia in an Air Force basic trainee. Reid (1975) used hypnosis in the treatment of a number of military trainees suffering from somnambulism.

ALTERED STATES

Schafer (1981) has described an area too little studied in the hypnosis literature—unrecognized, unintended altered states of consciousness. When such states are examined, they often are found to arise in situations that have some of the same characteristics as hypnotic induction—passivity of the ego, non-ego suggestions from outside, and the elicitation of strongly toned affective imagery. Present states may be contaminated by old repressed ego states. The affect-bridge technique is often helpful. Fromm (1983) emphasizes that ego passivity is pathological, while ego *receptivity* and ego activity are healthy, the latter being equivalent to the conscious experience of free will. Fromm (1977) also has discussed a psychodynamic model of spontaneous imagery compared with induced imagery in altered states of consciousness.

Altered states of consciousness, utilizing hypnosis, have been used to enhance sports performance (Unesthal, 1983) through the imaginal creation of an image of good performance. This is an excellent nontreatment example of how hypnotherapy can alter ego-images that affect actual performance in the everyday world. Neuromuscular facilitation and controls of arousal levels are mediating factors (Garver, 1977).

Ericksonian Treatments

The complex and inspiring hypnotic treatment techniques of Milton Erickson have been documented in a large number of publications and with explicit examples in *Hypnotic Realities* (Erickson, Rossi, and Rossi, 1976). Erickson's techniques have become an area of special study for many interested in hypnosis. Erickson strongly emphasized indirect suggestions, often blurring the distinction between ordinary conversational interaction and hypnotic suggestion, and utilized special emphasis of language to carry indirect messages together with the official communication. Erickson was a master at linking together various suggestions, such as telling a patient that when she had subjectively completed the review he had suggested, she would awaken. The awakening, then, is tacit admission that she has completed the previous suggestion. Zeig (1980) discusses Erickson's technique of prescribing some symptoms. Erickson has been an inspiration for the development of neurolinguistic programming (Kasdan and Lifshutz, 1983). Tilton (1983) has reported the use of Ericksonian techniques, such as pseudo-orientation in time and the melding of hypnotic and real "memories" in the treatment of agoraphobia.

Transference and Countertransference (T/CT)

Much of the hypnosis literature pays little attention to a problem that is central to much of the psychoanalytical and psychotherapy literature—the issue of transference (distortions of the analyst in the mind of the patient) and countertransference (similar distortions of the patient in the mind of the analyst). This lack of emphasis is unfortunate, since hynotherapy involves a rapid intensification of the T/CT aspects of therapy. The patient must have great implicit trust in the therapist to allow the rapid changes in consciousness that can take place in the hypnotic state. Many case reports, for example, emphasize positive results from ego-strengthening and symptom-removal suggestions, with little discussion of the role that transference/countertransference plays in such results (Diamond, 1980). Lazar and Dempster (1984) caution that operator variables (T/CT) are deeply important in successful hypnotherapy. Lindner (1984) carefully documents patient reactions to questions of the therapist's health.

Hall (1984a) has discussed T/CT from a Jungian perspective. Jung emphasized the field quality of T/CT and the inevitability of some distortion in the mind of both the therapist and the patient, although that is not necessarily antitherapeutic, since the best therapy results when the patient's problem has some (but not excessive) resonance in the mind of the therapist. Transference and countertransference are specific formulations of what is really a transformative field of therapist–patient interaction, where the intent is therapeutic transformation of the patient, although the therapist may also be positively (or negatively) affected in the treatment process (Hall, 1983a). There is no more evident example of this than hypnotherapy, where the therapist may also experience a light trance state while working with the patient. Some attempts to utilize dual trance, however, seem to us to go too far, producing confusion and lack of focus. The therapist must always be in charge of the boundaries of the situation, inducing and terminating the trance state in the patient. Such control by the therapist is not authoritarian, but is necessary for the patient to experience the sense of safety necessary to enter deep trance states. It is now commonly recognized, also, that patients who do not enter hypnosis in a party or stage hypnosis setting may be very good hypnotic subjects in the more serious environment in the clinical use of hypnosis, where there are proper safeguards, professional responsibility, and clear therapeutic goals.

The transformative field characteristic of the hypnotic T/CT interaction are sometimes strikingly demonstrated. We know of a therapist who suffered from pronounced anxiety about flying until he successfully treated a colleague for the same symptom in several hypnotherapy sessions. Apparently as a by-product, the therapist simultaneously lost his own fear of flying.

The essential experience of the hypnotized person is the ability to experience altered or distorted perception that is suggested by the therapist (Frankel, 1978). This ability also permits unconscious conflicts to more easily arise, some of which may distort the T/CT field in a negative manner. Hall (1984b) has discussed how one patient emerged from a light trance state having identified the therapist with a negative figure in a dream and himself with the victim in the dream, a paranoid state that persisted for about 48 hours before the normal therapeutic alliance reappeared. Dream images are a potent source for understanding the state of the patient's unconscious mind, and can usefully be integrated into hypnotherapy (Hall, 1977).

The Ego in Hypnoanalysis

Our ordinary clinical language is based largely upon the waking experience of psychoanalysis. Many dream and hypnotic states are difficult to describe without modifications of terminology (Hall, 1983b). *Ego* has both a deep structure (in Jungian terms, an archetypal core) and a more superficial and changeable identity structure. It is useful to think of the ego itself as the inherent sense of I-ness, the sense of being a center of subjectivity, receiving impressions and initiating actions. Ego-image refers to a particular image of oneself, and there may be many, although there is always a *dominant-ego-image*, a preferred or characteristic self-image. In both ordinary nocturnal dreams and in hypnosis, the ego itself is able to dissociate from the accustomed dominant-ego-image and experience other ego-images that have been less focal in the personality structure. Awareness of these changes, permits the therapist to intervene more rationally in the unconscious material of the patient. There is apparently an innate tendency toward health in the psyche, so that deficient or excessively skewed ego-images are always under pressure to participate in a more healthy way in the total personality. Although this tendency to healthy growth is present, it should not be relied upon to replace good conscious therapeutic judgment, for there are also ego-images that are unacceptable (many of these cluster in an alter-ego image that Jung called the shadow).

Schmidt (1983b) finds that discussing the nature of the ego aids some patients in entering hypnosis, which they are able to understand as a diversion of attention rather than a loss of control.

Amnesia

Amnesia can be induced in some hypnotic states, and may arise spontaneously in some patients. Induced posthypnotic amnesia is often a convincing demonstration of the reality of hypnosis. The reality of this effect is often shown by noting the number of remembered events that can be recalled before and after a posthypnotic suggestion that "now you can remember everything." Wagstaff (1977), however, has suggested that there is a strong compliance effect in this demonstration, a suggestion that seems to slight the obvious presence of compliance in virtually all hypnotic phenomena. The surprising fact is that subjects are often able to comply with suggestions (as the removal of warts) that it would be impossible for them to comply with in an ordinary waking state, showing that hypnosis is a way of influencing unconscious processes at the psychophysiological level (Chertok, 1982). Hypnosis is widely recognized as a useful technique in treating psychogenic amnesia and fugue states (MacHovec, 1981).

Resistance

Resistance to hypnosis occurs in some patients but should be differentiated from the inability to enter a trance state, which seems to have a different basis. If a patient is unable to enter a significant depth of hypnosis, this *may* be a resistance, but it also may simply indicate that the patient falls into that part of the population that cannot respond to hypnosis (roughly 20 percent of an unselected population). When resistance does occur, it may be due to misconceptions about hypnosis, for instance the widespread belief that hypnosis is always unconsciousness and that the hypnotist can "control the mind of the patient." Popular TV and movie presentations of hypnosis continue to perpetuate this misunderstanding. Resistances may reflect more specific fantasies as well, often a fear of passivity or an imagined sexual meaning to the hypnotic state. There are normal fluctuations in trance depth, even in good hypnotic patients, and these can at times be related to questions of resistance—the patient may spontaneously lighten the trance to avoid uncovering unconscious material that is approaching consciousness, or may be lightening trance in response to an ambiguity in the language of the therapist.

Self-Psychology and Hypnosis

At the growing edge of current psychoanalytic thinking are reconceptualizations of the language of self. Kohut (1971) has been the major figure in this movement, which echoes an earlier emphasis of Jung, couched in different language. The concern with *self* has connection, too, to the object-relations emphasis of Guntrip (1968). Wester and Smith (1983) discuss the patient's self-organization as a factor in the efficacy of hypnotherapy.

In a metaphorical sense, the self is a field of potential ego-states that lies outside but accessible to the dominant ego-image. The ego itself is capable of experiencing many of these states and moving toward their integration. From a Jungian viewpoint, the archetypal self (the central archetype) is the actual center of the psyche and regulates, to some extent through dream images, the contents of the self-field surrounding the current ego state.

AFFECT-BRIDGE

There is still much confusion in the use of self-language, but the field of hypnotherapy has much to contribute, including many unique observations that throw light upon the phenomena that must be considered in discussions of self. One of the most striking of these is the *affect-bridge technique* introduced by Watkins (1978). The affect-bridge, simply stated, consists of using the experience of a common affect to discover and experience, in hypnosis, various object-relational patterns (or structures of complexes) that underlie the same affective patterning. The subject in hypnosis is told to visualize a particular scene that is associated with the affect under treatment. He or she is then told to retain the affective feeling but to allow the scene itself to fade away. The subject is then instructed to let himself or herself go "backward in time" until he or she finds another scene that has the same affect; this, too, is experienced and the regression repeated.

In addition to discovering the nature of complexes linked together by a particular affective state, the affect-bridge technique can be used to help the ego dis-identify from a particular complex upon which it had based its tacit identity. This is done by setting up two distinct imaginal experiences, one associated with the affective state under treatment and the other with a neutral pleasant state. By appropriate suggestions, the patient is helped to rapidly alternate his or her ego-identity, in trance, between the two states. This often has the effect of giving the patient an experience of the optional quality of the affect-producing state, so that it can be experienced as one option among others rather than as a fixed and unavoidable identity. Watkins (1980) has also highlighted the value of permitting the patient to silently abreact some emotional neurosis, using perceptive and experiential modes, but not verbal expression.

Techniques

Hypnotic techniques in psychiatry, clinical psychology, and psychoanalysis utilize all techniques that are applied in other areas of hypnotherapy plus some specialized techniques such as the affect-bridge. The question of techniques in hypnoanalysis is different for one major reason—new techniques can be multiplied almost at will, and technique alone will not substitute for a thorough grounding in good psychotherapy training. The serious student of hypnotherapy should stay continuously open to the creation of unique therapeutic suggestions tailored to the individual needs of particular patients. The techniques we review here should be considered examples of particular forms that have been useful to others.

Walch's (1976) red-balloon technique has the patient imaginatively experience a helium-filled red balloon to which feeling of guilt (or other undesirable emotions) are attached and "floated away." Erickson (1982) used an interspersal technique, placing the important suggestion among other remarks. Kroger (1983) favors mixing hypnotic suggestions with imagery conditioning in what he calls a "hypno-behavioral model." Psychodrama can easily be melded with hypnotic techniques (Finer, 1983). There is a long history and tradition in Europe of autogenic training, using particular images to affect physiological functioning; autogenic training is quite close to hypnotherapy (Wallnoefer, 1983). Levine (1983) shows the compatibility of hypnotherapy with many of the techniques of gestalt therapy. Hypnosis has been combined with systematic desensitization (Surman, 1979). Some hypnotic treatment sessions have been conducted by telephone (Stanton, 1978). Hancock and Hackett (1979), among others, have explored "mutually induced trance" as a therapeutic modality, although we generally feel this to be an experimental rather than a therapeutic modality.

Applicability

As a collection of techniques to influence and explore the unconscious, hypnosis has wide applicability in many therapeutic fields, such as with hospitalized and ambulatory patients (Sampson, Schmidbauer, and Klingler, 1980) with geriatric patients (Granone, 1982), and in the growing field of consultation-liasion psychiatry (Sandor, 1980; Wain, 1979).

Group therapy is a new frontier of applicability for hypnosis. Braun (1980b) has reviewed the history of hypnotic-like techniques in group psychotherapy and has suggested guidelines for the utilization of group hypnotherapy. Crasilneck and Hall (1984) have discussed the utility of hypnotic techniques in groups at an annual meeting of the American Group Psychotherapy Association.

Hypnosis has usefulness with muscular dystonia, which affects such varied activities as musicians, telegraphists, golfers, etc. (Ambrose, 1983). Tremor may be improved with hypnotherapy (Fogel, 1976). Dysphonia (Giacalone, 1981) and stuttering (Crasilneck 1970; Miller, 1983a) may respond. Various sleep disorders have been improved with hypnotherapy in some patients; these include insomnia (Bauer and McCanne, 1980; Baskar, 1979; Barabasz, 1976), sleepwalking (Reid, Ahmed, and Levie, 1981), and sleep paralysis (Nardi, 1981; Schneck, 1977a). Hypnosis is used in a wide variety of psychosomatic problems (Spiegel, 1980) that influence the outcome of psychotherapy as well as in habit disorders that may have defensive meaning (Reaney, 1983).

Outcome

Studies of outcome are crucial in evaluating various treatment modalities, although it is difficult to interpret some results. In psychotherapeutic treatment in depth, for example, the patient often quickly overcomes the initial complaint, but stays in treatment much longer to understand and influence more subtle aspects of his or her functioning. Sampson et al. (1983) report that 80 percent of patients were relieved of "general" problems with one to three sessions of hypnotherapy per week for 2 to 6 weeks, sometimes using group hypnosis. Nace et al. (1982), however, did not find that hypnotic techniques led to greater improvement over a brief 10-session model of therapeutic intervention.

In our own experience, hypnotherapy can often be a rapid method of treatment in selected cases; in those where psychodynamic considerations are less important, such as habit patterns (smoking, some eating patterns) and generalized problems without deep psychodynamic meaning (some traumatic reactions, general uneasiness about situation matters, as flying) we find, however, that the maximal therapeutic outcome is enhanced when hypnotherapy is combined with whatever amount of conventional psychotherapy or psychoanalysis is needed to reach the desired goal: a mature, stable, self-correcting individual who expresses deep self-esteem and self-acceptance.

SUMMARY

A physician in the latter phases of treatment recently described his perceptions of hypnotherapy. He stated that at first he felt that his fears were akin to that of walking through a mine field, an experience he had when he was in service.

"In walking through a mine field you can place your foot gently on a twig and be blown to bits. My mind was a mine field of psychic trauma and during the course of hypnotherapy, Dr. Crasilneck, you taught me to use a psychological map to avoid the psychic mine fields and the destruction that went with it. As time went on there were fewer and fewer mistakes and I repeated errors less and less. Whenever I stepped on a psychological mine, the shocks were softer because I learned how to handle them. Now, at the end of treatment, I have good insight and understand that there will be traumas, shocks, and psychic mine fields in my life, but I have learned to adjust to them."

This seems to us one of the best descriptions of what hypnotherapy can accomplish in the patient with extreme psychiatric problems.

Hypnotherapy has great adjunctive value in the treatment of emotional disorders, both acute and chronic. As we acquire greater understanding of unusual states of consciousness, hypnotherapy will acquire a recognized and secure place in the armamentarium of psychotherapy.

REFERENCES

Abarbanst-Brandt A: Homosexuals in hypnotherapy. J Sex Res 2:127–132, 1966
Abraham A: Hypnosis used in the treatment of somatic manifestations of a psychiatric disorder. Am J Clin Hypn 10:304–309, 1968
Abrams S: Short-term hypnotherapy of a schizophrenic patient. Am J Clin Hypn 5:237–247, 1963
Abrams S: Implications of learning theory in treatment of depression by employing hypnosis as an adjunctive technique. Am J Clin Hypn 6:313–334, 1964a
Abrams S: The use of hypnotic techniques with psychotics, a critical review. Am J Psychother 18:79–94, 1964b
Abrams S: An evaluation of hypnosis in the treatment of alcoholics. Am J Psychiatry 120:1160–1165, 1964c
Abrams S: The effects of motivation upon the intellectual performance of schizophrenic patients. Am J Clin Hypn 8:37–43, 1965
Abrams S: The multiple personality: A legal defense. Am J Clin Hypn 25:225–234, 1983
Alexander L: Clinical experience with hypnosis in psychiatric treatment. Int J Neuropsychiatry 3:118–124, 1967
Ambrose G: Hypnosis in the treatment of nervous debility. Excerpta Medica 11:1208, 1958
Ambrose G: (Panelist) Dystaxia and allied muscular dystonia-treatment by hypnoanalysis. Presented at the International Congress of the Israel Society of Hypnosis in Psychotherapy and Psychosomatic Medicine in collaboration with the European Society of Hypnosis in Psychotherapy and Psychosomatic Medicine. Haifa, Israel, 1983
Arluck EW: Hypnoanalysis: A case study. Excerpta Medica 18:1187, 1965
Armstrong ML: The treatment of anxiety states by hypnotherapy. Aust J Med Sophrology Hypnotherapy 2:21–25, 1974

Bakal PA: Hypnotherapy for flight phobia. Am J Clin Hypn 23:248–251, 1981

Baker EL: The use of hypnotic dreaming in the treatment of the borderline patient: Some thoughts on resistance and transitional phenomena. Int J Clin Exp Hypn 31:19–27, 1983a

Baker EL: Resistance in hypnotherapy of primitive states: Its meaning and management. Int J Clin Exp Hypn. 31:82–89, 1983b

Baker EL: The use of hypnotic techniques with psychotics. Am J Clin Hypn 25:283–288, 1983c

Barabasz AF: Treatment of insomnia in depressed patients by hypnosis and cerebral electrotherapy. Am J Clin Hypn 19:120–122, 1976

Barnett EA: Hypnosis in the treatment of anxiety and chronic stress, in Wester WC, Smith AH (eds): Clinical Hypnosis: A Multidisciplinary Approach. Philadelphia, J.B. Lippincott Co., 1983, pp 458–475

Barone DF, Blum GS, Porter MV: Experimental analysis of techniques for eliminating obsessions. Int J Clin Exp Hypn 23:236–248, 1975

Baskar MA: Insomnia and hypnotherapy, in Burrows GD, Collison DR, Dennerstein L (eds): Hypnosis. Amsterdam, Elsevier/North-Holland Biomedical Press, 1979, pp 173–188

Bauer KE, McCanne TR: An hypnotic technique for treating insomnia. Int J Clin Exp Hypn 28:1–5, 1980

Benson H, Frankel FH, Daniels M, Sahniewind H, Nemiah J, Sifneos P, Crassweller K, Greenwood M, Kotch J, Arns P, Rosner B: Treatment of anxiety: A comparison of the usefulness of self-hypnosis and a meditational relaxation technique. An overview. Psychother Psychosom 30:229–242, 1978

Biegel HG: Three transvestites under hypnosis. J Sex Res 3:149–162, 1967

Bjorkeim J: Alcoholism and hypnotic therapy. Br J Med Hypnot 7:23–32, 1956

Bloom PB: Integrating hypnosis into psychotherapy. Presented at the meeting of the Society for Clinical and Experimental Hypnosis, San Antonio, TX, 1984

Bornstein PH, Rychtarik R, McFall M, Winegardner J, Winnett R, Paris D: Hypnobehavioral treatment of chronic nailbiting: A multiple baseline analysis. Int J Clin Exp Hypn 28:208–217, 1980

Bowers MK: Theoretical considerations in the use of hypnosis in the treatment of schizophrenia. Int J Clin Exp Hypn 9:39–46, 1961

Bowers MK, Brecher S: The emergence of multiple personalities in the cover of hypnotic investigation. J Clin Exp Hypn 3:188–199, 1955

Bowers MK, Brecher-Marer S, Polatin, AH: Hypnosis in the study and treatment of schizophrenia—a case report. Int J Clin Exp Hypn 9:119–138, 1961

Brady JP, Rosner BS: Rapid eye movements in hypnotically induced dreams. J Nerv Ment Dis 143:28–35, 1966

Braun BG: Clinical aspects of multiple personality. Presented at the 22nd Annual Scientific Meeting of the American Society of Clinical Hypnosis, San Francisco, 1979a

Braun BG: Hypnosis creates multiple personality: Myth or reality? Presented at the Society of Clinical and Experimental Hypnosis National Meeting, Denver, 1979b

Braun BG: Hypnosis for multiple personalities, in Wain HJ (ed): Clinical Hypnosis in Medicine. Miami, Symposia Specialists, Inc., 1980a, pp 209–217

Braun BG: Hypnosis in groups and group therapy, in Burrows GD, Dennerstein L (eds): Handbook of Hypnosis and Psychosomatic Medicine. Amsterdam, Elsevier/North-Holland Biomedical Press, 1980b, pp 481–495

Braun BG: Neurophysiologic changes in multiple personality due to integration: A preliminary report. Am J Clin Hypn 26:84–92, 1983

Brenda JO, Benedict BD: The Vietnam combat delayed stress response syndrome: Hypnotherapy of "dissociative symptoms". Am J Clin Hypn 23:34–40, 1980

Breuer J, Freud S: Studies in Hysteria (Studien über Hysterie). New York, Basic Books, 1957

Bryan LL: Hypnotherapy of conversion hysteria. Am J Clin Hypn 3:226–230, 1961

Burrows G: Personal communication. Annual meeting, Australian Society of Clinical and Experimental Hypnosis and the West Australian Society of Medical Hypnosis, Melbourne, 1975

Caldwell TA, Stewart RS: Hysterical seizures and hypnotherapy. Am J Clin Hypn 23:294–297, 1981

Canty A: Use of hypnosis in uncovering etiology of sexual psychopathology. J Soc Ther 4, 1958

Carasso RL, Peled, O Yehuda O: (Panelists) Contradicting suggestion in wakefulness for differential diagnosis and brief therapy in acute (hysterical) conversion reaction. Presented at the International Congress of the Israel Society of Hypnosis in Psychotherapy and Psychosomatic Medicine in collaboration with the European Society of Hypnosis in Psychotherapy and Psychosomatic Medicine, Haifa, Israel, 1983

Chambers HH: Oral erotism revealed by hypnosis. Int J Clin Exp Hypn 16:151–157, 1968.

Chertok L: The unconscious and hypnosis. Int J Clin Exp Hypn 30:95–107, 1982

Cohen RJ, Suter C: Hysterical seizures: Suggestion as a provocative EEG test. Ann Neurol 11:391–395, 1982

Cohen SB: Phobias. Am J Clin Hypn 23:227–230, 1981

Conn JH: The psychodynamics of recovery under hypnosis. Int J Clin Exp Hypn 8:3–16, 1960

Conn JH: Hypnosynthesis: Dynamic psychotherapy of the sex offender utilizing hypnotic technique. J Am Soc Psychosom Dent Med 15:18–27, 1968

Conn JH: Hypnosynthesis. Am J Clin Hypn 13:208–221, 1971

Cotlier L: Chronic alcoholism treated by hypnotic suggestion and psychic re-education of personality. Rev Argent Neurol Psiquial 3:102–109, 1938

Crasilneck HB: (Panelist) The use of hypnosis in stuttering. Presented at the American Society of Clinical Hypnosis, Chicago, 1970

Crasilneck HB: Hypnosis and clinical pain problems. Presented at the annual meeting of the American Society of Clinical and Experimental Hypnosis, Seattle, 1975

Crasilneck HB: The use of hypnosis in age regression. Presentation: A case of Dora. Distinguished Faculty Psychology Staff, U.S. Army, Ft. Ord, 1977

Crasilneck HB: The use of hypnosis in age regression. Presentation at the American Society for Clinical Hypnosis, Nova Scotia Component Section Meeting, Halifax, 1980a

Crasilneck HB: A case requiring age regression. Presented at Grand Rounds, University of Georgia, Augusta, 1980b

Crasilneck HB: A case of psychogenic amnesia. Presentation American Society for Clinical Hypnosis, Component Section Meeting, Boston, 1980c

Crasilneck HB, Hall JA: The utility of hypnotic techniques in group therapy. Presented Ann Amer Group Psychoth Assoc. Dallas, 1984

Daniels LK: Rapid in-office and in-vivo desensitization of an injection phobia utilizing hypnosis. Am J Clin Hypn 18:200–203, 1976

Daubner B: Hypnotherapy of pathological anxiety, in Pajntar M, Roskar E, Lavric M (eds): Hypnosis in Psychiatry and Psychosomatic Medicine. Yugoslavia, Soc Clin Exp Hypn 15–22, 1980

DeJong A: Inebriety and its treatment by hypnotism. Med Res 49:479–481, 1896

Dempsey GL, Granich M: Hypno-behavioral therapy in the case of a traumatic stutterer: A case study. Int J Clin Exp Hypn 26:125–133, 1978

Diamond MJ: The client as hypnotist: Furthering hypnotic change. Int J Clin Exp Hypn 28:197–207, 1980

Dinges DF: Integrating hypnosis into psychotherapy. Presented at the annual meeting of the Society for Clinical and Experimental Hypnosis, San Antonio, TX, 1984

Edwards G: Hypnosis in treatment of alcohol addiction: Controlled trial, with an analysis of factors affecting outcome. Q J Stud Alcohol 27:221–241, 1966

Eliseo T: The hypnotic treatment of sleepwalking in an adult. Am J Clin Hypn 17:272–276, 1975

English OS: Some dynamic concepts of human emotions in relation to hypnosis. Am J Clin Hypn 4:135–140, 1962

Epstein SJ, Deyoub PL: Hypnotherapy for fear of choking: Treatment implications of a case report. Int J Clin Exp Hypn 29:117–127, 1981

Epstein SJ, Deyoub PL: Hypnotherapeutic control of exhibitionism. A brief communication. Int J Clin Exp Hypn 31:63–66, 1983

Erickson MH: Hypnosis: its renascence as a treatment modality. Am J Clin Hypn 13:71–89, 1970

Erickson MH: Pain: interspersal technique, in Barber J, Adrian C (eds): Psychological Approaches to the Management of Pain. New York, Bruner/Mazel, 1982

Erickson MH, Rossi EL, Rossi SI: Hypnotic Realities. New York, Irvington Publishers Inc., 1976

Evans FJ: Two types of posthypnotic amnesia: Recall amnesia and source amnesia. Int J Clin Exp Hypn 14:162–179, 1966

Feamster JH, Brown JE: Hypnotic aversion to alcohol: Three-year follow-up of one patient. Am J Clin Hypn 6:164–166, 1963

Field PB, Scott EM: Experience of alcoholics during hypnosis: Am J Clin Hypn 12:86–90, 1960

Finer B: (Panelist) Hypnosis and psychodrama. Presented at the International Congress of the Israel Society of Hypnosis in Psychotherapy and Psychosomatic Medicine in collaboration with the European Society of Hypnosis in Psychotherapy and Psychosomatic Medicine, Haifa, Israel, 1983

Finkelstein S: Re-establishment of traumatically disrupted finger flexor function: A brief communication. Int J Clin Hypn 30:1–3, 1982

Fogel S: Psychogenic tremor and asomatognosia. Am J Clin Hypn 19:57–62, 1976

Fox R: Psychiatric aspects of alcoholism, Am J Psychother 19:408–416, 1965

Frankel FH: The use of hypnosis in crisis intervention, Int J Clin Exp Hyp 22:188–200, 1974

Frankel FH: Hypnosis and related clinical behavior. Am J Psychiatry 135:664–668, 1978

Frankel FH: Phobic disorders in hypnosis, in Burrows GD, Dennerstein L (eds): Handbook of Hypnosis and Psychosomatic Medicine. Amsterdam, Elsevier/North-Holland Biomedical Press, 1980, pp 171–183

Frankel FH, Orne MT: Hypnotizability and phobic behavior. Arch Gen Psychiatry 33:1259–1261, 1976

Fromm E: Dissociative and integrative processes in hypnoanalysis. Am J Clin Hypn 10:174–177, 1968

Fromm E: An ego-psychological theory of altered states of consciousness. Int J Clin Exp Hypn 25:372–387, 1977

Fromm E: The theory and practice of hypnoanalysis, in Wester WC, Smith AH (eds): Clinical Hypnosis: A Multidisciplinary Approach. Philadelphia, J.B. Lippincott Co., 1983, pp 142–154

Fromm E, Shor R (eds): Hypnosis: Research Developments and Perspectives. Chicago, Aldine-Atherton, 1972

Garynowicz J: Hypnosis in a treatment programme for alcoholism. Med J Aust 1:653–656, 1977

Garver RB: The enhancement of human performance with hypnosis through neuromotor facilitation and control of arousal level. Am J Clin Hyp 19:177–181, 1977

Garver RB, Fuselier GD, Booth TB: The hypnotic treatment of amnesia in an Air Force basic trainee. Am J Clin Hypn 24:3–6, 1981

Giacalone AV: Hysterical dysphonia: Hypnotic treatment of a ten-year-old female. Am J Clin Hyp 23:289–293, 1981

Granone F: Hypnotism in the treatment of chronic alcoholism. J Am Inst Hypn 12:32–40, 1971

Granone F: Therapeutic hypnosis in geriatrics, medical, psychological and sociological considerations of aging. Minerva Med 73:3201–3206, 1982

Green JT: Hypnotizability of hospitalized psychotics. Int J Clin Exp Hypn 17:103–108, 1969

Gruber LN: Hypnotherapeutic techniques in patients with affective instability. Am J Clin Hypn 25:263–267, 1983

Gruenewald D: Hypnotic techniques without hypnosis in the treatment of dual personality. J Nerv Ment Dis 1:153, 1971

Gruenewald D: Analogues of multiple personality in psychosis. Int J Clin Exp Hypn 26:1–8, 1978

Guntrip H: Schizoid Phenomena, Object Relations, and the Self. London, Hogarth, 1968

Gustavson JL, Weight DG: Hypnotherapy for a phobia of slugs: A case report. Am J Clin Hypn 23:258–262, 1981

Haley J (ed): Advanced techniques of Hypnosis and Therapy. Selected Papers of Milton H Erickson. New York, Grune & Stratton, 1967

Hall JA: Hypnosis in jungian analysis. Presented at the annual meeting of the American Society of Clinical and Experimental Hypnosis, Seattle, 1975

Hall JA: Clinical Uses of Dreams: Jungian Interpretations and Enactments. New York, Grune & Stratton, 1977

Hall JA: Transference and counter-transference. Presented at the National Jungian Ghost Ranch Conference, Albuquerque, 1983a

Hall JA: Pseudo-objectivity as a defense mechanism: Polanyi's concept of dynamo-objective coupling. J Am Acad Psychoanal 12:199–209, 1983b

Hall JA: Dreams and transference/countertransference: The transformative field. Chiron: A Review of Jungian Analysis 1:31–51, 1984a

Hall JA: Toward a psycho-structural theory: Hypnosis and the structure of dreams, Am J Clin Hypn 26(3):159–165, 1984b

Ham MW, Spanos NP, Barber TX: Suggestibility in hospitalized schizophrenics. J Abnorm Psychol 85:550–557, 1976

Hancock JC, Hackett E: Mutually induced trance as a therapeutic mode, in Burrows GD, Collison DR, Dennerstein L (eds): Hypnosis. Amsterdam, Elsevier/North-Holland Biomedical Press, 1979, pp 165–171

Hartman BJ: Hypnotic susceptibility in chronic alcoholics. J Natl Med Assoc 58:197–198, 1966

Hartman BJ: The use of hypnosis in the treatment of drug addiction. J Natl Med Assoc 64:35–38, 1972

Heaver L: Hypnosis in the investigation of crime. Presented at the American Society of Clinical Hypnosis 18th Annual Meeting, Seattle, 1975

Hilgard J: Personality and hypnosis. Am J Clin Hypn 14:63–64, 1971

Howland JS: The use of hypnosis in the treatment of a case of multiple personality. J Nerv Ment Dis 161:138–142, 1975

Ihalainen O, Rosberg G: Relaxing and encouraging suggestions given to hospitalized chronic schizophrenics. Int J Clin Exp Hypn 24:228–237, 1976

Isham AC: Hypnorelaxation: Therapy for tension state. Am J Clin Hypn 5:152, 1962

Johnston DC: Experience with the courts in Southern California. Symposium "Hypnosis and the Legal Process." Society of Clinical and Experimental Hypnosis 27th Annual Meeting, Chicago, 1975

Jung C: On the psychology and pathology of so-called occult phenomena. Collected Works, vol I, Psychiatric Studies. London, Routledge and Kegan Paul, 1957, pp 3–88

Kalinowsky I, Lerner M: Medicina psicosomatica e hipnosis en a enfermedades carderiovasculares. Acta Hipn Lat-Am 1:69–77, 1960

Kampman R: Hypnotically induced multiple personality: An experimental study. Int J Clin Exp Hypn 24:215–227, 1976

Kampman R, Hirvenoja R, Ihalainen O: Hypno-analytic therapy of hysteric hemiplegia by means of secondary personalities, in Burrows GD, Collison DR, Dennerstein L (eds): Hypnosis. Amsterdam, Elsevier/North-Holland Biomedical Press, 1979, pp 121–126

Kaplan JM, Deabler HL: Hypnotherapy with a severe dissociative hysterical disorder. Am J Clin Hypn 18:83–89, 1975

Karlin RA: Intermediate psychiatry workshop at the annual meeting of the Society for Clinical and Experimental Hypnosis, San Antonio, TX, 1984

Kasdan MS, Lifshutz H: (Panelists) The unconscious frame: A hypnotic technique developed in neuro-linguistic programming. Presented at the International Congress of the Israel Society of Hypnosis in Psychotherapy and Psychosomatic Medicine in collaboration with the European Society of Hypnosis in Psychotherapy and Psychosomatic Medicine, Haifa, Israel, 1983

King B: Hypnosis as a treatment modality in psychiatric practice. Aust J Clin Exp Hypn 8:37–40, 1980

Kloft RP: Varieties of hypnotic interventions in the treatment of multiple personality. Am J Clin Hypn 24:230–240, 1982

Knowles FW: A note on hypnotherapy in sexual deviation: Report of two cases. Am J Clin Hypn 7:353–354, 1965

Kodman F Jr, Patti FA: Hypnotherapy of psychogenic hearing loss in children. Am J Clin Hypn 1:9–13, 1958

Kohut H: The Analysis of the Self. New York, International Press, 1971

Koster S: Pain, insomnia, drug addiction and hypnosis. Br J Med Hypnot 8:17–24, 1957

Kroger WS: Hypnotherapy and behaviour modification, in Burrows GD, Dennerstein L (eds): Handbook of Hypnosis and Psychosomatic Medicine. Amsterdam, Elsevier/North-Holland Biomedical Press, 1980, pp 509–516

Kroger WS: Hypnotherapy and behavior modification, in Wester WC, Smith AH (eds): Clinical Hypnosis: A Multidisciplinary Approach. Philadelphia: Lippincott 1983, pp 115–122

Kubie LS, Margolin S: The process of hypnotism and the nature of the hypnotic state. Am J Psychiatry 100:611–622, 1944

Langen D: Modern hypnotic treatment of various forms of addiction, in particular, alcoholism Br J Addict 62:77–81, 1967

Lavoie G, Sabourin M: Hypnosis and schizophrenia: A review of experimental and clinical studies, in Burrows GD, Dennerstein L (eds): Handbook of Hypnosis and Psychosomatic Medicine. Amsterdam, Elsevier/North-Holland Biomedical Press, 1980, pp 377–419

Lavoie G, Sabourin M, Ally G, Langlois J: Hypnotizability as a function of adaptive regression among chronic psychotic patients. Int J Clin Exp Hypn 24:238–257, 1976

Lazar BS, Dempster CR: Operator variables in successful hypnotherapy. Int J Clin Exp Hypn 32:28–40, 1984

Lenox JR, Bonny H: The hypnotizability of chronic alcoholics. Int J Clin Exp Hypn 76:419–425, 1976

Levendula D: Principles of gestalt therapy in relation to hypnotherapy. Am J Clin Hypn 6:22–26, 1963

Levine J, Ludwig AM: The hypnodelic treatment technique. Int J Clin Exp Hypn 14:207–215, 1966

Levine BT: (Panelist) Hypnosis in gestalt therapy. International Congress of the Israel Society of Hypnosis in Psychotherapy and Psychosomatic Medicine in collaboration with the European Society of Hypnosis in Psychotherapy and Psychosomatic Medicine, Haifa, Israel 1983

Levy A, Neumann M: (Panelists) The role of suggestion in the treatment of combat reactions within a specific military installation during the war in Lebanon. Int Cong Israel Soc Hypn in Psychoth and Psychosom Med in collabor with Eur Soc Hypn in Psychoth and Psychosom Med. Haifa, Israel 1983

Lewis BJ: Treatment of a schizoid personality using hypno-operant therapy. Am J Clin Hypn 22:42–46, 1979

Lindner H: Therapist and patient reactions to life-threatening crisis in the therapist's life. Int J Clin Exp Hypn 32:12–27, 1984

London RW: Intermediate psychiatry workshop at the annual meeting of the Society for Clinical and Experimental Hypnosis, San Antonio, TX, 1984

Lopez-Ibor J: Personal communication, 1975

Ludwig AM, Lyle WH, Miller JS: Group hypnotherapy techniques with drug addicts. Int J Clin Exp Hypn 12:53–66, 1964

MacHovec F: Hypnosis to facilitate recall in psychogenic amnesia and fugue states: Treatment variables. Am J Clin Hypn 24:7–13, 1981

Magonet AP: The healing voice. Int J Clin Exp Hypn 7:229, 1959

Mastronardi V: Breaking the drinking habits of alcoholics with hypnosis: Psychological and technical dynamisms. Minerva Med 71:1265–1267, 1980

Matheson G: Modification of depressive symptoms through Posthypnotic Suggestion. Am J Clin Hypn 22:61–64, 1979

Meares A: A note on hypnosis and the mono-symptomatic psychoneurotic. Br J Med Hypnot 8:26–28, 1956–1957a

Meares A: Recent work in hypnosis and its relation to general psychiatry. Med J Aust 43:1–5, 1956b

Meyers TJ: Hypnosis in the treatment of chronic alcoholism by hypnotic aversion. J Am Osteopath Assoc 14:172–174, 1944

Miller HR: Presentation of 11 stutterers over the past three years. Presented Ann Mtg Am Soc Clin Hypn. Dallas, Texas 1983a

Miller HR: Depression and hypnotherapy of depression, in Wester WC, Smith AH (eds): Clinical Hypnosis: A Multidisciplinary Approach. Philadelphia, J.B. Lippincott Co., 1983b, pp 421–457

Miller, MM: Treatment of chronic alcoholism by hypnotic aversion. JAMA 171:1492–1495, 1959

Mirow S: (Panelist) The use of videotape and audiotape as therapeutic tools for rapid personality integration during hypnotherapy in a patient with multiple personalities. International Congress of the Israel Society of Hypnosis in Psychotherapy and Psychsomatic Medicine in collabor with European Society for Hypnosis in Psychotherapy and Psychosomatic Medicine. Haifa, Israel, 1983

Moore MR: Treatment of psychosis with hypnosis: Report of a case. Presented at the annual meeting of the American Society of Clinical and Experimental Hypnosis, Seattle, 1975

Mordey T: Conditioning of appropriate behavior to anxiety producing stimuli: Hypnotherapy of a stage-fright case. Am J Clin Hypn 8:117–121, 1965

Morton JH, Thoma E: A case of multiple personality. Am J Clin Hypn 6:216–225, 1964

Moskowitz AE: A clinical and experimental approach to the evaluation and treatment of a conversion reaction with hypnosis. Int J Clin Exp Hypn 12:218–227, 1964

Moss CS: Therapeutic suggestion and autosuggestion. J Clin Exp Hypn 6:109–115, 1958

Mott T Jr: The role of hypnosis in psychotherapy. Am J Clin Hypn 24:241–248, 1982

Murray-Jobsis J: Hypnosis with severely disturbed patients, in Wester WC, Smith AH: Clinical Hypnosis: A Multidisciplinary Approach. Philadelphia, J.B. Lippincott Co., 1983, pp 368–404

Mutter CB: A hypnotherapeutic approach to exhibitionism: Outpatient therapeutic strategy. J Forensic Sci 26:129–133, 1981

Nace EP, Warwick AM, Kelley RL, Evans FJ: Hypnotizability and outcome in brief psychotherapy. J Clin Psychiatry 43:129–133, 1982

Nardi TJ: Treating sleep paralysis with hypnosis. Int J Clin Exp Hypn 29:356–365, 1981

Naruse G, Fujimara K: Hypnosis in Japan. Presented at the annual meeting of the American Society of Clinical and Experimental Hypnosis, Seattle, 1975

Newton BW: Multiple personality. Presentation at the annual meeting of the Society of Clinical and Experimental Hypnosis, Palo Alto, Calif., 1968

Orne MT: On the mechanisms of posthypnotic amnesia. Int J Clin Exp Hypn 14:121–134, 1966

Paley A: Hypnotherapy in the treatment of alcoholism. Bull Menninger Clin 16:14–19, 1952

Patterson RB: Hypnotherapy of hysterical monocular blindness. A case report. Am J Clin Hypn 23:119–121, 1980

Pelletier AM: Hysterical aphonia: A case report. Am J Clin Hypn 20:149–153, 1977

Perin CT: The use of substitute response signals in anxiety situations. Am J Clin Hypn 10:207–208, 1968

Polk WM: Treatment of exhibitionism in a 38-year-old male by hypnotically assisted covert investigation. Int J Clin Exp Hypn 31:132–138, 1983

Raikov VL: Age regression to infancy by adult subjects in deep hypnosis. Am J Clin Hypn 22:156–163, 1980

Reaney J: Hypnosis in the treatment of habit disorders, in Wester WC, Smith AH: Clinical Hypnosis: A Multidisciplinary Approach. Philadelphia, J.B. Lippincott Co., pp 1983, 305–324

Reid WH: Treatment of somnambulism in military trainees. Am J Psychother 29:101–106, 1975

Reid WH, Ahmed I, Levie CA: Treatment of sleep-walking: A controlled study. Am J Psychother 35:27–37, 1981

Roper P: The use of hypnosis in the treatment of exhibitionism. Can Med Assoc J 94:72, 1965

Rosen H: Regression hypnotherapeutically induced as an emergency measure in a suicidially depressed patient. J Clin Exp Hypn 3:58–70, 1955

Saadia M: (Panelist) Hypnotherapy and schizophrenia: a fallacy or a therapeutic tool? International Congress of the Israel Society of Hypnosis in Psychotherapy and Psychosomatic Medicine in collaboration with European Society for Hypnosis in Psychotherapy and Psychosomatic Medicine. Haifa, Israel, 1983

Sacerdote P: Therapeutic use of induced dreams. Am J Clin Hypn 10:1–9, 1967

Sacerdote P: Some individualized hypnotherapeutic techniques. Int J Clin Exp Hypn 20:1–14, 1972

Sacerdote P: (Panelist) Induced dreams, hypnography and hallucinated hypnoplasty in medicine and psychiatry. International Congress of the Israel Society of Hypnosis in Psychotherapy and Psychosomatic Medicine in collaboration with European Society for Hypnosis in Psychotherapy and Psychosomatic Medicine. Haifa, Israel, 1983

Sachs BC: Hypnosis in psychiatry and psychosomatic medicine. Psychosomatics 23:523–525, 1982

Sampson KH, Schmidbauer H, Klingler D: Hypnosis and modified hypnotherapeutic methods: Indications and results in hospitalized and ambulatory patients. Wein Med Wochenschr 130:379–381, 1980

Sampson KH, Bengesser G, Kepplinger P, Purgyi P: (Panelists) International Congress of the Israel Society of Hypnosis in Psychotherapy and Psychosomatic Medicine in collaboration with European Society for Hypnosis in Psychotherapy and Psychosomatic Medicine. Haifa, Israel, 1983

Sandors RS: Hypnosis as an "entree" for consultation-liaison psychiatry. Gen Hosp Psychiatr 2:65–68, 1980

Scagnelli J: Hypnotherapy with schizophrenic and borderline patients. Presented at the annual meeting of the American Society of Clinical and Experimental Hypnosis, Seattle, 1975

Scagnelli J: Hypnotherapy with schizophrenic and borderline patients: Summary of therapy with eight patients. Am J Clin Hypn 19:33–38, 1976

Scagnelli J: Hypnotic dream therapy with a borderline schizophrenic: A case study. Am J Clin Hypn 20:136–145, 1977

Scagnelli J: Hypnotherapy with psychotic and borderline patients: The use of trance by patient and therapist. Am J Clin Hypn 22:164–169, 1980

Scagnelli-Jobsis J: Hypnosis with psychotic patients: A review of the literature and presentation of a theoretical framework. Am J Clin Hypn 25:33–45, 1982

Scagnelli-Jobsis J: Hypnosis with psychotic patients: Response to Spiegel. Am J Clin Hypn 25:295–298, 1983

Schafer DW: On the conceptualization of hypnosis. Presented at a meeting of the Society for Clinical and Experimental Hypnosis, Chicago, 1971

Schafer DW: The recognition and hypnotherapy of patients with unrecognized altered states. Am J Clin Hypn 23:176–183, 1981

Schmidt FK: (Panelist) A case of agoraphobia treated through hypnosis and audio tapes. Int Cong Israel Soc Hypn in Psychoth and Psychosom Med in collabor with Eur Soc Hypn in Psychoth and Psychosom Med. Haifa, Israel 1983a

Schmidt FK: (Panelist) Graphic depiction of the ego under hypnosis to aid in briefing patients. International Congress of the Israel Society of Hypnosis in Psychotherapy and Psychosomatic Medicine in collaboration with European Society for Hypnosis in Psychotherapy and Psychsomatic Medicine. Haifa, Israel, 1983b

Schneck JM: Some aspects of homosexuality in relation to hypnosis. Psychoanal Rev 37:351–357, 1950

Schneck JM: Studies in Scientific Hypnosis. Baltimore, Williams & Wilkins, 1954a

Schneck JM: The divided personality: A case study aided by hypnosis. J Clin Exp Hypn 2:220–232, 1954b

Schneck JM: Hypnotic interviews with the therapist in fantasy. J Clin Exp Hypn 3:109–116, 1955

Schneck JM: Hypnotherapy for achalasia of the esophagus. Am J Psychiatry 114:1042–1043, 1958

Schneck JM: Prehypnotic suggestion in psychotherapy. Am J Clin Hypn 17:158–159, 1975

Schneck JM: Sleep paralysis and microsomatognosia with reference to hypnotherapy. Int J Clin Exp Hypn 25:72–77, 1977a

Schneck JM: Hypnotic elucidation of isolation and displacement following a sexual assault. Dis Nerv Syst 38:934–935, 1977b

Scott EM: Hypnosis without conscious intent in an alcoholic. Q J Studies Alcohol 29:709–711, 1968

Scrignar CB: Rapid treatment of contamination phobia with hand-washing compulsion by flooding with hypnosis. Am J Clin Hyp 23:252–257, 1981

Sexton RO, Maddock RC: Age regression and age regression in psychotic and neurotic depression. Am J Clin Hyp 22:37–41, 1979

Simon B: Hypnosis in the treatment of military neurosis. Psychiatric Opinion 4:24–29, 1967

Smyth LD: Psychopathology as a function of neuroticism and hypnotically implanted aggressive conflict. J Pers Soc Psychol 43:555–564, 1982

Spiegel D: Hypnotizability and psychoactive medication. Am J Clin Hypn 22:217–222, 1980

Spiegel D: Vietnam grief work using hypnosis. Am J Clin Hypn 24:33–40, 1981

Spiegel D: Hypnosis with psychotic patients: Comment on Scagnelli-Jobsis. Am J Clin Hypn 25:289–294, 1983

Spiegel D, Fink R: Hysterical psychosis and hypnotizability. Am J Psychiatry 136:777–781, 1979.

Spiegel H, Linn L: The "ripple effect" following adjunct hypnosis in analytic psychotherapy. Am J Psychiatry 126:53–58, 1969

Spiegel H, Spiegel D: Trance and Treatment: Clinical Uses of Hypnosis. New York, Basic Books, 1978, pp 263–285

Stanton HE: Hypnotherapy at a distance through the telephone. Am J Clin Hypn 20:278–281, 1978

Stein C: Brief hypnotherapy for conversion cephalalgia. Am J Clin Hypn 17:198–201, 1975

Surman OS: Postnoxious desensitization: Some clinical notes on the combined use of hypnosis and systemic desensitization. Am J Clin Hypn 22:54–60, 1979

Thigpen CH, Cleckley HM: The Three Faces of Eve. New York, McGraw-Hill, 1957

Tilton P: Pseudo-orientation in time in the treatment of agoraphobia. Am J Clin Hypn 25:267–269, 1983

Torem M: Use of hypnosis in psychiatry. Presented at Am Society of Clinical Hypnosis Workshop, Cincinnati, June, 1984

Unestal LE: (Panelist) Inner mental preparation for sport and life. International Congress of the Israel Society of Hypnosis in Psychotherapy and Psychosomatic Medicine in collaboration with European Society for Hypnosis in Psychotherapy and Psychosomatic Medicine. Haifa, Israel, 1983.

Van Dyke PB, Harris R: Phobia: A case report. Am J Clin Hypn 24:284–287, 1982

Verson RD: A technique to control hallucinatory obsessive ideas. Am J Clin Hypn 4:115–116, 1961

Volgyesi von FA: Schezophrenie, schezoide psychopathien und derun hypnosetherapie. Acta Psychother Psychosom Orthopaedag 7:37–52, 1959

Wagstaff GF: An experimental study of compliance and post-hypnotic amnesia. Br J Soc Clin Psychol 16:225–228, 1977

Wain HG: Hypnosis on a consultation-liaison service. Psychosomatics 20:678–689, 1979

Wain HG, Smith LJ, Evans R: Hypnotic intervention in the asthmatic response to methacholine: An analysis of the importance of hypnotic capacity and individualized strategies in hypnosis. J Allergy Clin Immunol 67:44, 1981

Walch SL: The red balloon technique of hypnotherapy: A clinical note. Int J Clin Exp Hyp 24:10–12, 1976

Wallnoefer H: (Panelist) The analytic advanced autogenic training. International Congress of the Israel Society of Hypnosis in Psychotherapy and Psychosomatic Medicine in collaboration with European Society for Hypnosis in Psychotherapy and Psychosomatic Medicine. Haifa, Israel, 1983.

Watkins JG: Hypnotherapy of War Neurosis. New York, Ronald, 1949

Watkins JG: The Therapeutic Self. New York, Human Sciences Press, 1978

Watkins JG: The silent abreaction. Int J Clin Exp Hypn 28:101–113, 1980

Waxman D: Hospital phobia: A rapid disensitation technique. Postgrad Med J 54:328–330, 1978

Waxman D: (Panelist) The treatment of phobic illness: an overview. International Congress of the Israel Society of Hypnosis in Psychotherapy and Psychosomatic Medicine in collaboration with European Society for Hypnosis in Psychotherapy and Psychosomatic Medicine. Haifa, Israel, 1983

Werner TR: Hypnosis in psychiatry, in Wester WC, Smith AH (eds): Clinical Hypnosis: A Multidisciplinary Approach. Philadelphia, J.B. Lippincott Co., 1983, pp 353–367

Wester WC, Smith AH: Sources of efficacy in the hypnotic relationship—an object relations approach, in Wester WC, Smith AH (eds): Clinical Hypnosis: A Multidisciplinary Approach. Philadelphia, J.B. Lippincott Co., 1983, pp 85–114

Wilkins LG, Field PB: Helpless under attack: Hypnotic abreaction in hysterical loss of vision. Am J Clin Hypn 10:271–275, 1968

Wolberg LR: Medical Hypnosis, vols I, II. New York, Grune & Stratton, 1948

Wollman L: Cross-gender identity (transexualism). J Am Soc Psychosom Dent Med 15, 1968

Zannoni MD: A case of hysterical blindness with symptom removal in one session, in Burrows GD, Collison DR, Dennerstein L (eds): Hypnosis. Amsterdam, Elsevier/North-Holland Biomedical Press, 1979, pp 247–251

Zeig JK: Symptom prescription and Ericksonian principles of hypnosis and psychotherapy. Am J Clin Hypn 23:16, 1980

16
Hypnosis in Obstetrics and Gynecology

Pregnancy is one of the most archetypal human conditions, manifesting profound influence not only on the altered physiology of the gravid woman but also in the mind and imagination of mankind. In his book *The Great Mother: The Study of an Archetype* Neumann (1963), a noted Jungian psychoanalyst, discusses the various stages and levels of the experience of motherhood and how they manifest in individual psychology. The experience of the archetypal situation of pregnancy and giving birth is one of the most profound experiences available to a woman. Some primitive cultures practice *couvade,* a ritual participation of the father during the pregnancy and confinement of the mother giving evidence of the emotional meaning of pregnancy even in male psychology.

The pregnant woman undergoes profound psychological changes that are as important and crucial as the physical alterations in her body. At the most conscious and social level she begins to adapt to the culturally defined role of the expectant mother. At a more intimate interpersonal level she experiences changes in her relationship with the child's father, both because of the physical changes in her body and because of the changed interpersonal situation. The father may feel closer to her because of her pregnancy, participating in the growth of the child with positive emotions. In other instances (or perhaps to a slight degree in all cases) the father may feel some jealousy and

351

estrangement from the mother as the insistent demands of the pregnancy draw more of her time and concern away from him.

At a still deeper level the expectant mother must integrate her accustomed self-image with all of those ideas and feelings that she has associated with motherhood, based partly on remembered experience of her own mother and partially on the culturally defined role of being a mother. It is not uncommon for the woman expecting her first child to become more demanding of both herself and her mate, refusing to tolerate, as a mother-to-be, the feelings and attitudes that she previously permitted. Pregnancy may be a time of deep change in her self-image. At the deepest psychological level the woman undergoing pregnancy touches on the archetype of the mother, with its fascinating and sometimes terrible affects and images.

Special situations may be intensified by pregnancy. Examples are unwed mothers, women whose previous experiences of childbirth have been unpleasant, or women who have built their primary self-esteem on a life model that is threatened by their approaching motherhood. There may be a tendency to sink into passivity, only partly explainable by the altered metabolic state and body image.

Although physically childbirth is the same experience throughout the world, the emotional experience varies greatly from culture to culture, from individual to individual, and even in the same individual in subsequent pregnancies. In Western culture childbirth is often anticipated as a painful and disagreeable experience. Unresolved sexual conflicts or the lack of privacy or modesty during childbirth may produce tensions that impede the birth process and intensify anxiety and pain.

Hypnosis has been found by many to significantly increase the ease and speed of labor and to decrease anxiety and discomfort (Baer, 1957; Carter, 1963; Cheek and LeCron, 1968; Chiasson, 1983; Corley, 1963; Hartman and Rawlins, 1960; Hoffman and Kopenhauer, 1961; Kohl, 1962; Kroger, 1963a; Symonds and Zuspan, 1983; Werner, 1965; Zuspan, 1973). Many other psychological techniques used in facilitating ease of childbirth are derived from hypnosis (Vellay, 1964), even in Russia (Nikolayev, 1954). Evaluation under hypnosis has also been suggested for women who want abortions (Rosen, 1953).

Crasilneck (1984) has reviewed all the major indications and uses of hypnotherapy in obstetrics and gynecology. Reports on the subject matter have also been made by August (1961), Ferraris (1982), and Jensen (1979).

One of the common and most difficult problems in the first trimester of pregnancy is hyperemesis, excessive vomiting that may occur early in pregnancy and may progress to the point of dehydration, hospitalization, and even loss of the fetus (Crasilneck, 1984). Successful hypnotic treatment of 28 women with this problem, all of whom had not responded well to other methods, was reported by Fuchs, Brandes, and Peretz (1967).

Fuchs (1983) studied 138 women with severe first trimester vomiting; all improved. An unexpected finding was that those treated in group hypnotherapy sessions did better than those treated with individual hypnotherapy sessions. Fuchs et al. (1980) regard hypnotherapy as the treatment of choice in hyperemesis gravidarum. Henker (1976) used adjunctive psychotherapeutic measures in treating 10 consecutive pregnant women for severe intractable vomiting.

Typical of our experience with hypnosis for hyperemesis is the case that follows:

The wife of a young attorney did not realize at first that she was pregnant, attributing her increasingly severe nausea and vomiting to flu. Her symptoms persisted for over a week, during which time pregnancy was confirmed. It was not possible for her to smell food without immediate emesis. She was hospitalized, given intravenous fluids, but failed to improve, and psychological consultation was requested. She was given the hypnotic suggestions that she was "relaxed. . . . The thought and the taste of food will not be discomforting. . . . You will ingest and digest your food easily . . . realizing that food intake will give you the strength necessary to adjust well to your pregnancy and to give you and your baby the strength you both need."

She was seen daily for three days, with rapid control of the hyperemesis, then seen weekly for about a month, with no return of symptoms. The remainder of her pregnancy, confinement, and delivery was uneventful.

Another patient, a 29-year-old nurse (gravida 3, para 2), had severe hyperemesis. She had experienced similar difficulty with her first pregnancy, a daughter, who subsequently had seizures attributed to possible poor nutrition of her mother during pregnancy. The mother had been hospitalized with hyperemesis during her second pregnancy; her third pregnancy had begun in a similar manner with marked nausea and vomiting but during the third month she learned about hypnosis and contacted us.

The patient was treated with hypnosis on a daily basis for two weeks. By the fourth day, vomiting had stopped and nausea became minimal. Her motivation was high and she was optimistic about the outcome. After her sixth session, she began to show a marked increase in weight gain, and gained steadily thereafter. It was the first time in three pregnancies that she had demonstrated weight gain.

The patient was taught to use self-hypnosis on the second session. She was seen three times per week from the third to the sixth week; twice each week from the seventh to the tenth week, and then once a week thereafter until term. She was delivered of a healthy son without complications.

Not all cases respond so readily. It has at times been necessary to see a severe case of hyperemesis gravidarum daily for as long as a month. At times it is possible to control the vomiting, allowing food and fluid intake while part of the nauseas persists. In severe cases when there is no response to fluids and medication, hypnosis should be considered as a treatment modality.

The noted obstetrician DeLee (1939, 1955), once wrote that "the only anesthetic that is without danger is hypnotism," chiding his colleagues who neglected "to avail themselves of this harmless and potent remedy." Discussing varying approaches to the use of hypnosis in obstetrics, August (1965) suggests that "whatever combination of chemical and psychological therapy, either, both, or none, must be decided in each specific situation by the physician for the patient." He adds, "The primary and only purpose of therapy must be ever in mind, a normal healthy mother and normal healthy baby."

Pascatto and Mead (1967) in a series of 25 patients showed that those in the experimental group (10) who received hypnosis had a significant reduction of sedation during delivery and less postpartum insomnia, headache, and breast discomfort compared with the control group. The hypnotherapist was a different person than the physician who performed the delivery so that the effect of transference motivation was decreased.

The lessening of chemical anesthesia may be of benefit to the infant as well as to the mother. Moya and James (1960) found the Apgar test (a measurement of the well-being of the infant 1 minute after birth) to be better in a group of infants delivered under hypnosis than in a group whose mothers received cyclopropane anesthesia. The scores of the infants delivered under hypnosis were similar to those whose mothers had regional anesthesia, such as spinal or caudal blocks.

Some obstetricians use group classes in hypnosis before delivery (Malyska and Christensen, 1967), while others feel that individual training is preferable (Mosconi, 1966). We agree with the latter.

August (1960a) attempted hypnoanesthesia in 351 of 442 expectant mothers, finding it successful as the sole analgesic agent for 328 (93.5 percent); in another study (1961) 58 percent of those who underwent hypnosis required no chemical analgesic. Mody (1960) reported 20 patients with an average success rate of 75 percent. In his study "there appeared to be no relationship between the extent of relief of pain and the number of sittings or the depth of hypnosis." Mosconi and Starcich (1961) reported 100 obstetrical cases using hypnotic analgesia. They secured excellent results in 79 percent. Tom (1960) and Werner (1963) have noted the usefulness of hypnosis in decreasing the pain associated with labor and delivery.

Abramson and Heron (1950) have reported a statistically significant difference in length of labor between a group of 88 women who had no hypnosis and 100 women who were trained with hypnosis before delivery. During the first stage of labor, the longest of three stages, the cervix is slowly effaced and dilated so that the baby may pass through. This is usually the most exhausting stage of delivery, particularly in women who are delivering their first baby. Abramson and Heron found that this stage of labor was shortened by an average of 3.23 hours in those women trained with hypnosis, a difference that would occur by chance only three times in a hundred. In women delivering their second or later baby, the time of the first stage was 1.79 hours shorter for the hypnotic group, again statistically significant at the level of $P = 0.04$. Callan (1961) found that hypnosis reduced the average duration of labor in primiparas by 3.7 hours and by 5 hours in multigravidas. Mellgren (1966) found an overall reduction of labor by 2 to 3 hours. Autohypnosis has also been reported to shorten the first stage of labor (Davidson, 1962).

Davenport-Slack (1975) found that both hypnosis and antenatal training resulted in less medication, calmer behavior, and a more positive childbirth experience; but they found little data to support that either hypnosis or antenatal training produced a decrease in length of labor or in reported experiences of pain during childbirth. In a study of 600 women, half primagravidaras and half multigravidaras, Fuchs et al. (1983) found that self-hypnosis was more effective than the Read-Lamaze method in shortening this stage of labor. The self-hypnosis group also had fewer complications, less forceps or vacuum delivery, and the lowest level of infant mortality (0.25 percent compared with 1.0 percent for the Read-Lamaze group and 2.2 percent for the unprepared control group). Complete hypnoanesthesia was achieved in 60 percent of the hypnosis group, and hypnoanalgesia in 35 percent. Samko and Schoenfeld (1975) found that hypnotic susceptibility was not significantly related to Lamaze training nor to the type of childbirth that a Lamaze-trained woman experiences.

Others who have verified the usefulness of hypnosis in delivery include Chertok (1959, 1963), Clark (1956), Collison (1974), Crasilneck (1984), Hoffman and Kopenhauer (1961), Kroger (1962), Oystragh

(1970), and Zuspan (1960, 1973). Coulton (1966) has discussed its use in postpartum problems.

Tiba et al. (1980) found hypnosis highly effective in decreasing fear of labor and delivery, as did Stone and Burrows (1980) and Werner and Schauble (1982). Chiasson (1983) cites the particular value of hypnosis in D & Cs and in cesarean section deliveries.

A very dramatic demonstration of the effect of hypnosis on labor was reported by Rodriguez and his colleagues (1954). They attached a device called an "external tokodynamometer" to the abdominal wall of a young woman in her first labor. While the machine recorded the frequency and strength of contractions, hypnosis was alternately induced and removed. Their tracings show the striking way in which the induction of hypnosis caused an immediate change in the contractions, which became much more regular and forceful, the kind of contractions that are effective in facilitating labor. When the hypnotic trance was terminated, the contractions once more became irregular, but they would resume the regular pattern when hypnosis was again induced. Hartland and Mills (1964) have emphasized that hypnosis may be so facilitating that labor may progress faster than seems evident from the patient's reactions.

There are only two reasons why hypnosis is not the ideal anesthetic agent in all uncomplicated deliveries. First, it can require a number of conditioning visits, ana such a large investment of the therapist's time may be expensive or impossible (Fening, 1961). However, this expenditure of time is not always so marked (Schibly and Aaronsen, 1966), and in one study only 20 minutes was necessary to induce hypnosis for patients in active labor (Rock, Shipley, and Camplule, 1969). Second, not all women are good hypnotic subjects, even with repeated training, and chemical anesthesia may be required at the last minute, particularly if unexpected complications are encountered.

Although hypnosis must be used with caution in all patients with a recognized or suspected potential for psychotic decomposition, Beaudet (1963) has reported the safe use of hypnosis for analgesia during the third delivery of a woman who had experienced two previous episodes of postpartum psychosis. Furthermore, a 2-year follow-up not only showed no recurrence of psychotic symptoms but seemed to suggest that the successful third delivery had added to her mental and emotional stability. Clearly, each case must be individually assessed, but a past history of emotional upset following childbirth is not an absolute contraindication to the use of hypnosis. In fact, several authors have pointedly emphasized the emotional support that the pregnant woman may receive from hypnosis (Newbold, 1950; Spiegel, 1963).

Techniques of Hypnosis for Childbirth

We prefer to begin hypnosis during the first trimester of pregnancy. Women are seen weekly for hypnosis during the first month, then every 3 weeks until 1 month before the estimated date of delivery, when weekly hypnosis is resumed. The therapist should be called immediately after the obstetrician has instructed the patient to report to the hospital delivery room. Once it is established that the patient is in true labor, hypnosis is induced.

In our hypnotic conditioning technique the pregnant woman is shown in the waking state the area in which analgesia is to be induced, then in hypnosis she is told,

"You will be aware of pressure building, but you will feel secure, relaxed, and at ease . . . free from tension, tightness, stress, and strain. . . . The indicated area of your body will simply be anesthetized. . . . You will have no discomfort . . and because you are so relaxed and comfortable, your baby will be delivered with ease."

Kroger (1962, 1963b) includes the induction of glove anesthesia during his hypnotic training for delivery. We use a similar method of inducing hypnoanesthesia in one finger, demonstrating its reality to the patient by vigorously stimulating the tip of the anesthetized finger with the point of a nail file. Kroger also gives suggestions that the glove anesthesia can be transferred to the face and then to the abdomen. He has reported a cesarean section done entirely under hypnotic anesthesia. Gianelli (1968) uses an analogy between defecation and the expulsion of the baby to stress the possibility of childbirth without pain.

August (1960a) has reported more than 1000 deliveries using hypnosis alone. He often finds that as few as six inductions, often with small groups of women who are hypnotized simultaneously, may be sufficient before the onset of delivery. While we agree that it may be possible to induce a satisfactory hypnotic trance in group work, or even when the patient is seen for the first time at the onset of labor, we believe that the preferable technique is as we have outlined. Seeing the patient at regular intervals beginning in the first 3 months of the pregnancy gives her time to become acquainted both with the hypnotherapist and with the state of hypnosis itself. Also, the therapist has an opportunity to learn of the patient's own unique personality pattern and is alerted to any psychodynamics that might cause difficulty during the delivery under hypnosis or in the postpartum period. As a general rule, the depth of trance is increased by repeated hypnosis, and it is always possible that unforeseen complications in the delivery may demand more from hypnosis than was anticipated.

When there are special reasons for inducing hypnosis for delivery, it may be employed even if there has not been an opportunity for prior conditioning. The situation is not ideal from a psychological standpoint, but emergency situations require decisive action. One such case involved a pregnant woman who developed poliomyelitis.

A 32-year-old pregnant woman developed poliomyelitis about six weeks before term. Previously she had experienced three normal pregnancies and deliveries, and her fourth pregnancy had been completely normal prior to the on ,et of the poliomyelitis. Twenty-four hours after the patient's admission to th: hospital, extensive paralysis occurred. Involvement of muscles of respir.tion limited her tidal volume to 200 ml of air as determined by pneumotacho-graphic studies. Her vital capacity at this time was not significantly greater than her tidal volume, and control of pharnygeal secretions was accomplished with difficulty. A tracheotomy was performed, and her breathing was assisted by the use of an intermittent positive-pressure type of respirator. She needed continuous respiratory assistance, and it was elected to continue use of intermittent positive pressure and nebulization with the patient in a comfortable low Fowler position.

On the fourth day the internist felt that delivery was more urgently indicated than ever in order to facilitate respiratory exchange. Consequently, an oxytocin infusion was started. This resulted in excellent uterine contractions. The membranes were ruptured, and labor progressed in a satisfactory way. During this prolonged period of labor the patient had become increasingly anxious and apprehensive. Original plans to utilize a pudendal block to provide anesthesia for delivery were changed. Although use of an inhalation technique of anesthesia was not fundamentally ruled out, hypnosis was given consideration, and one of us (HBC) was consulted by the obstetrician concerning this method of anesthesia.

The idea of using hypnosis was presented to the patient. Although she at first appeared resistant toward the method, rapport was soon established. She was able to enter a somnambulistic state in spite of the fact that labor contractions were already occurring every 3 minutes. She was given the suggestion that her pain would completely cease and that she would become relaxed, unafraid, and cooperative. The suggestions were effective almost immediately. She appeared relaxed and did not show evidence of pain, tension, or apprehension.

She was delivered of a 2664.9-gm (5 lb 14 oz) boy by low forceps without premedication or any anesthesia other than hypnosis. She made no complaint of pain throughout the delivery. The muscles of the perineum were relaxed, and no laceration was sustained. Assisted respiration was continued during the delivery. Following delivery the patient was awakened after being given the posthypnotic suggestion that she would be relaxed and comfortable. The mother made slow but continuous progress, although paralysis of muscles and weakness persisted (Crasilneck, McCranie, and Jenkins, 1956).*

A 32-year-old physician who had had two previous pregnancies asked if we would use hypnosis during her third pregnancy. Her obstetrician was in agreement, since her first two pregnancies were marked by prolonged labor of about 18 hours accompanied by much distress and pain. She responded well to hypnosis and was seen once a week during her pregnancy. Her labor started at 9:00 A.M. and hypnosis was induced immediately. Three hours later she delivered a normal 7 1/2 pound male child. Some of her recorded comments were "I feel relaxed—no tensions, no fears, no anxieties . . . I know the pain perception should be pretty rough at this point . . . but I am comfortable . . . very comfortable . . . just a dull pain . . . like having a period and yet I normally have a low pain tolerance . . . I should be perceiving pain, but I'm not . . . I almost feel like the 3+ drunk, relaxed, lethargic, but my brain is functioning so clearly, only a tight band around my abdomen occasionally . . . I just don't give a damn!"

She did not require nor was she given any anesthetic other than hypnosis during labor and the repair of the episiotomy. Her final comment was "No one could ask for an experience in which the pain was so intense during my first two deliveries and yet completely blocked this time. From the way I felt it must be some kind of psychophysiological cortical lobotomy."**

Since inhalation anesthesia is so safe and effective and since most deliveries are uncomplicated, we feel that hypnosis for delivery is best reserved for cases in which there is an unusual risk attached to chemical anesthesia. A further indication would be cases in which there is a past history of prolonged or difficult labor. Of course, if a physician has a special interest in using hypnosis for deliveries, it is certainly applicable in most cases, provided that he feels that the time required is not excessive. A sympathetic, emotionally sensitive obstetrician who reassures and calms the woman in labor may actually be using hypnoidal influence, even if hypnosis is not employed.

GYNECOLOGY

Many gynecological problems lend themselves to hypnotherapy (August, 1965; Cheek and LeCron, 1968; Chertok, 1959; Glover, 1961; Schwartz, 1963; Zuspan, 1960). Women frequently present the gyne-

---

* Reprinted from Crasilneck H, McCranie E, Jenkens MT. Special indications for hypnosis as a method of anesthesia. JAMA 162:1606–1608, 1956. With permission.
** Reprinted from Crasilneck H, Hall J. Clinical Hypnosis in Problems of Pain. Am J Clin Hypn 15:153–161, 1973. With permission.

cologist with problems that may be only partially physical or may arise from a mixture of organic and functional causes. Those that contain a significant psychological component may be particularly suited to treatment with hypnosis since many persons are not good candidates for prolonged conventional psychotherapy for symptoms that seem (to them) to be physical in origin. In other cases the physical complaint is only a thin disguise for emotional problems that the patient has been hesitant to mention directly, although she may have hinted to her gynecologist over a considerable period of time that something is troubling her. Coulton (1960a), for example, reported the case of a 22-year-old woman whose onset of bleeding immediately followed a humiliating experience of being again dependent on her parents after an unsuccessful reconciliation with her separated husband. In addition to dilatation and curretage, hypnosis was used for emotional ventilation support.

Menstrual Irregularities

Frequent problems are the disorders of the menstrual cycle: amenorrhea (absence of periods), dysmenorrhea (painful menstruation), and menometrorrhagia (bleeding at abnormal times during the cycle). Some women also complain of mittelschmerz, sense of pain or discomfort associated with the time between menstrual cycles when the ovum is released.

It is well known that emotional upset may interfere with the hormonal regulation of the normal menstrual cycle. Worry may cause a woman to miss completely an expected period, or the onset of menstruation may be delayed significantly. When such emotional upset occurs at an unconscious level, it may appear that such changes occur without psychologic cause. Interestingly, Erickson (1960) has reported that many of the same effects may be inducted by hypnosis in certain patients.

When organic factors have been ruled out or when hormonal treatment fails to correct the irregularity, hypnosis may be of value. The suggestions given, after induction, usually proceed in this manner:

"As psychic fears and tensions can bring on alterations in body chemistry and hormonal activity, so can the powerful dynamic unconscious forces reverse or alter such activity. . . . Therefore, I give you the suggestion that you will be extremely relaxed. . . . There will be a return of normal physiological and psychological menstrual activity. . . . The anxieties . . . the tensions . . . will simply become much less . . . and your body will return to normal function."

Such direct suggestions must only be employed, of course, after adequate consideration has been given to elucidating the psychodynamics underlying the disorder. A careful investigation of these factors would include a review of the patient's childhood training about sex and menstrual functioning, a survey of dating and sexual relations, an inquiry into the current state of her marriage or significant emotional relationships, and possibly an inquiry into dream and fantasy life.

In 25 cases of dysmenorrhea treated by hypnosis Leckie (1964) found 80 percent were freed of the symptom, while 20 percent were unimproved. He used direct suggestion in 17 cases, and more complex methods in 3.

We have on occasion found causes of stress that the patient had been unwilling to mention to the referring physician, often because of positive transference feelings for the gynecologist. Guilt over an extramarital affair may be involved as well as persisting guilt for premarital sexual involvements. Early attitudes of the parents and other significant adults may have molded an unnecessarily rigid superego structure which does not allow adequate flexibility or enjoyment in life.

An 18-year-old girl, with no history of pregnancy, was referred for dysmenorrhea that had persisted since her menarche at age twelve. She invariably spent several days of her period each month in the college infirmary, where analgesics, including meperidine, were required, together with bed rest, hot packs, and frequent telephone calls to her mother. The usual hormonal treatments had failed to give her significant relief, and hypnosis was undertaken.

She was a good hypnotic subject. While in trance she was told to remember whatever she could concerning the onset of her menses. She recalled that her mother had also experienced severe pain and cramping during menses and had referred to it as the "curse of the woman." The mother had told the patient that "women smell bad during their periods and their husbands won't have anything to do with them." She had been given the impression that this normal bodily function was quite "dirty."

During 15 hypnotic treatments, including some abreaction of her repressed feelings, she obtained almost complete relief of the dysmenorrhea. The remission of symptoms persisted during a 6-month follow-up period after hypnosis was discontinued.

If thorough evaluation does not reveal a psychodynamic cause, we do not hesitate to employ hypnosis to influence directly the menstrual disorder. Its effectiveness, as in facilitating labor (Rice, 1961), may lie in calming the patient and allowing more normal functioning of the usual hypothalamic regulation of the menstrual cycle.

Sexual Dysfunction

Though many sexual difficulties of women are on psychological basis, they are more likely initially to be brought to the attention of the obstetrician or gynecologist rather than to a psychotherapist. Lack of sexual enjoyment may vary from disappointment at a failure to experience climax during intercourse to such severe vaginal spasm that the male is unable to achieve penetration. Intercourse may be uncomfortable (dyspareunia) or undesired by the women.

Because of the frequency of complaints of sexual dysfunction, we have devoted Chapter 18 to discussion of its causes and its treatment by hypnotic means. Hypnotherapy is helpful in treating some cases of vaginismus (Gottesfeld, 1978), in which there are often marked psychodynamic factors.

Menopause

The symptoms of menopause are varied, but most often emphasized are those of vasomotor instability—hot and cold "flashes," profuse sweating, and faintness. The emotional component of the menopause may be more significant than the physical changes in hormonal levels. Many women see menopause as "the change of life" and may have fantasies that it signals the beginning decline into old age and senility. They may feel their sexual attractiveness will diminish markedly or that they will become useless to their families and children. Involutional depression may begin with menopausal symptoms; often it responds dramatically to psychotherapy combined with hypnosis, provided it has not progressed to the depth at which suicidal thoughts indicate that antidepressant medication or electroconvulsive therapy (ECT) is to be considered. Although hypnosis may be usefully combined with medication for depression, we do not feel that it is employed with much effectiveness during the time in which ECT is being administered, although the induction of hypnotic trance is certainly possible except perhaps during the acute recovery phase from ECT.

With menopausal problems the psychodynamic exploration that accompanies hypnosis should focus adequately on the changing feelings of femininity experienced by the patient. Menopause is presented as the beginning of a new phase of life, with its own tasks and rewards, rather than the termination of the childbearing years.

Pseudocyesis

The strange syndrome of pseudocyesis ("false pregnancy") presents an instructive example in the power of unconscious psychodynamics to alter the patient's physical appearance and mental functioning. Pseudocyesis is a delusion of pregnancy that may cause the woman to protrude her abdomen in such a way as to appear several months pregnant. Menses may cease. It is crucial, of course, to define the mental conflict that led to this particular delusion, which may be treated with a combination of psychotherapy and hypnotic suggestion.

Pain Relief

Hypnosis offers one of the most dramatic tools for pain relief in cases where operative procedures are of little or no avail or where narcotics are failing to give adequate respite from severe organic pain. In the gynecological field such pain may vary from dyspareunia during intercourse to the severe pain of metastatic tumors. A detailed discussion is presented in Chapter 6 on the problems of pain.

The same techniques outlined for pain relief in general apply to the treatment of pain associated with sexual functions, although it is crucial in dealing with sexual areas that any special or symbolic meanings be taken into consideration.

Infertility

An inhibition in completing the sexual act or psychophysiologic disorders such as some anovulatory cycles (Wollman, 1960) can result in infertility. August (1960b) pointed out four ways that hypnosis can help with these problems: (1) helping to understand the psychological background, (2) helping to remove psychological blocks to the consummation of coitus, (3) reducing female tension, and (4) aiding in the normalization of ovarian cycles.

In a number of our cases hypnosis has seemed to facilitate conception in women who have been unable to become pregnant with hormonal treatment, injection of the husband's sperm directly into the uterus, and other techniques following adequate work-up for infertility. In such cases the mechanism by which hypnosis may work is obscure, and there is as yet no statistical assessment of its degree of effectiveness, although Leckie (1965) reported that in 7 of 8 cases, conception followed within a period of approximately 1 year after hypnotherapy. Some endocrinologists have suggested that there may be a neural pathway involved in ovum release, as in lower animals. At least one hypnotic investigator has visualized spasm of the fallopian tubes in a woman with chronic infertility, although it is not clear that this was the origin of her inability to conceive.

Our suggestions given with infertility are,

"You will be relaxed and at ease. . . . The tensions and stresses that have kept you from conceiving will come under control. . . . Because of the power of your unconscious mind, your body can . . . and will . . . conceive . . . allowing you to become pregnant and carrying your baby successfully."

Muehleman (1978) used hypnotic age regression to re-evaluate earlier identifications. The patient achieved pregnancy.

Fetal Movements

Eyal et al. (1983) studied 12 pregnant women and found a significant increase in fetal body movements (as a sign of fetal well-being) during maternal hypnosis, together with an improvement in maternal self-detection of fetal body activity during the posthypnotic period of observation. Zimmer et al. (1983) found similar results.

Breast Growth

Hypnotic enhancement of breast growth is a somewhat controversial use of hypnotherapy. Engorgement of the breasts with blood may be a significant factor in reported increases in breast measurements. In a study of 22 women, Willard (1977) found greater increases in breast size in those women who were good at visual imagery. In a 3-month follow-up of three women treated with hypnotherapy to increase breast size, some regression was noted (Stalb and Logan, 1977), although 81 percent of the gain was retained.

"Birth Trauma"

Hypnosis has been reported of value in the exploration of repressed memories of "birth trauma" (Cheek, 1975), but such studies need careful and serious validation by a number of independent observers.

SUMMARY

In summary, hypnosis can be of help in gynecology in minor surgical procedures, menstrual irregularities, sexual dysfunctions, pain problems, and such psychiatric syndromes as pseudocyesis. Evaluation of emotional meanings, both conscious and unconscious, is particularly important in any symptom that might have hidden sexual meanings.

REFERENCES

Abramson M, Heron WT: An objective evaluation of hypnosis in obstetrics: Preliminary report. Am J Obstet Gynecol 59:1069–1074, 1950

August RV: Obstetric hypnoanesthesia. Am J Obstet Gynecol 79:1131–1138, 1960a

August RV: Hypnosis: An additional tool in the study of infertility. Fertil Steril 11:118–123, 1960b

August RV: Hypnosis in Obstetrics, New York, McGraw-Hill, 1961

August RV: Hypnosis in obstetrics: Varying approaches. Am J Clin Hypn 8:47–51, 1965

Baer W: Hypnosis in obstetrics. Minn Med 40:235–237, 1957

Beaudet SC: Hypnosis in a schizophrenic obstetrical patient. Am J clin Hypn 6:11–14, 1963

Callan TD: Can hypnosis be used routinely in obstetrics? Rocky Mt Med J 58:28–30, 1961

Carter JE: Hypnotic induction of labor: A review and report of cases. Am J Clin Hypn 5:322–325, 1963

Cheek DB: Maladjustment pattern apparently related to imprinting at birth. Am J Clin Hypn 18:75–82, 1975

Cheek DB, LeCron LM: Clinical Hypnotherapy. New York, Grune & Stratton, 1968

Chertok L: Psychosomatic Methods in Painless Childbirth: History, Theory and Practice. London, Pergamon, 1959

Chertok L: Psychoprophylaxis or obstetrical psychotherapy. Fortschr Psychom Med 3:134–148, 1963

Chiasson SW: Hypnosis gains legitimacy, respect, in diverse clinical specialties. MEDICAL NEWS. JAMA 249:319–323, 1983

Clark RN: Training method for childbirth utilizing hypnosis. Am J Obstet Gynecol 72:1302–1304, 1956

Collison DR: Hypnosis in obstetrics. Aust J Clin Hypn 2:20–25, 1974

Corley JB: What is the value of hypnosis in general practice? Am J Clin Hypn 6:6–10, 1963

Coulton D: Hypnotherapy in gynecological problems. Am J Clin Hypn 8:95–100, 1960a

Coulton D: Hypnosis in obstetrical delivery. Am J Clin Hypn 2:144–148, 1960b

Coulton D: Prenatal and post-partum uses of hypnosis. Am J Clin Hypn 8:192–197, 1966

Crasilneck HB: The use of hypnosis in pain problems, in Symonds EM, Zuspan FP (eds): Clinical and Diagnostic Procedures in Obstetrics and Gynecology. New York, Marcel Dekker, 1984, pp 397–417

Crasilneck HB, McCranie MJ, Jenkins MT: Special indications for hypnosis as a method of anesthesia JAMA: 162:1606–1608, 1956

Crasilneck HB, Hall JA: Clinical hypnosis in problems of pain. Am J Clin Hypn 15:153–161, 1973

Davenport-Slack B: A competitive evaluation of obstetrical hypnosis and antenatal childbirth training. Int J Clin Exp Hypn 23:266–281, 1975

Davidson JA: An assessment of the value of hypnosis in pregnancy and labour. Br Med J 5310:951–953, 1962

DeLee ST: Hypnotism in pregnancy and labor. JAMA 159:750–754, 1955

DeLee ST, Greenhill JP: Year book of obstetrics and gynecology. Chicago, Year Book, 1939, p 164

Erickson MH: Psychogenic alteration of menstrual functioning: Three instances. Am J Clin Hypn 2:227–231, 1960

Eyal A, Zimmer E, Fuchs K, Peretz BA: The influence of maternal hypnosis on fetal heart rate, fetal body movements, and maternal fetal movement perception. International Congress of the Israel Society for Hypnosis in Psychotherapy and Psychsomatic Medicine in collaboration with European Society for Hypnosis in Psychotherapy and Psychosomatic Medicine. Haifa, Israel, 1983

Fening W: What is the value of hypnosis in childbirth? Am J Clin Hypn 3:203–205, 1961

Ferraris G: Hypnosis in obstetrics and gynecology. Minerva Med 73:523–529, 1982

Fuchs K: Treatment of hyperemesis gravidarum by hypnosis. Int Cong Israel Soc Hypn in Psychoth and Psychsom Med in collabor with Eur Soc Hyp in Psychoth and Psychosom Med. Haifa, Israel 1983

Fuchs K, Brandes J, Peretz A: Treatment of hyperemesis gravidarum by hypnosis. Hanfuah 72:375–378, 1967

Fuchs K, Paldi E, Abramovici H, Peretz BA: Treatment of hyperemesis gravidarum. Int J Clin Exp Hypn 28:313–323, 1980

Fuchs K, Marcovici R, Peretz BA, Paldi E: (Panelists) The use of hypnosis in obstetrics. Int Cong Israel Soc Hyp in Psychoth and Psychosom Med in collabor with Eur Soc Hypn in Psychoth and Psychsom Med. Haifa, Israel, 1983.

Gianelli A: Il metodo ipnoteco per la preparazione della gestante al porto (An hypnotherapeutic methodology for the preparation of the pregnant woman for childbirth). Rassegna Ipnosi Med Psicosom 8:1566–1570, 1968

Glover FS: Use of hypnosis for weight reduction in a group of nurses. Am J Clin Hypn 3:250–251, 1961

Gottesfeld ML: Treatment of vaginismus by psychotherapy with adjunctive hypnosis. Am J Clin Hypn 20:272–277, 1978

Hartland JH, Mills W: The effects of hypnosis on a complicated obstetric case. Am H Clin Hypn 6:348–350, 1964

Hartman W, Rawlins CM: Hypnosis in the management of a case of placenta abruptio. Int J Exp Clin Hypn 8:103–107, 1960

Henker FO: Psychotherapy as adjunct in treatment of vomiting during pregnancy. South Med J 69:1585–1587, 1976

Hoffman GL Jr, Kopenhauer DB: Medical hypnosis and its use in obstetrics. Am J Med Sci 241:788–810, 1961

Jensen JA: Clinical medical hypnotic treatment of physiological disease—a holistic approach, in Burrow GD, Collison DR, Dennerstein L (eds): Hypnosis. Amsterdam, Elsevier/North-Holland Biomedical Press, 1979, pp 231–239

Kohl GC: Anesthesia in obstetrics. Med Times 90:368–378, 1962

Kroger WS: Psychosomatic Obstetrics, Gynecology and Endocrinology. Springfield, Ill., Charles C Thomas, 1962

Kroger WS: Clinical and experimental hypnosis. Philadelphia, J.B. Lippincott, 1963a, pp 197–198

Kroger WS: Hypnosis for relief of pelvic pain. J Obstet Gynecol 6:763–775, 1963b

Leckie FH: Hypnotherapy in gynecological disorders. Int J Clin Exp Hypn 12:121–146, 1964

Leckie FH: Further gynecological conditions treated by hypnotherapy. Int J Clin Hypn 13:11–25, 1965

Malyska W, Christensen J: Autohypnosis and the prenatal class. Am J Clin Hypn 9:188–192, 1967

Mellgren A: Practical experiences with a modified hypnosis-delivery. Psychother Psychosom 14:425–428, 1966

Mody NV: Report on twenty cases delivered under hypnotism. J Obstet Gynecol India 10:3–8, 1960

Mosconi G: Il metodo ipnotico per la preparazione al parto (Hypnotic preparation for parturition). Minerva Med, [Suppl 3]:2156–2158, 1966

Mosconi G, Starcich B: Preparacion del parto con hipnosis (Preparation for childbirth with hypnosis). Rev Lat-Am Hypn Clin 2:29–34, 1961

Moya F, James S: Medical hypnosis for obstetrics. JAMA 174:80–86, 1960

Muehleman T: Age regression as a possible enhancement to conception: A case report. Am J Clin Hypn 20:282–283, 1978

Neumann E: The Great Mother: An Analysis of the Archetype. New York, Pantheon, 1963

Newbold G: The importance of hypnotism in midwifery. Br J Med Hypnot 2:2–6, 1950

Nikolayev A: Psychoprophylactic preparation of pregnant women for childbirth and painless parturition in the Soviet Union. J Int Fed Gynecol Obstet 2:3–15, 1954

Oystragh P: The use of hypnosis in general and obstetric practice. Med J Aust 2:731–733, 1970

Pascatto RD, Mead BT: The use of posthypnotic suggestion in obstetrics. Am J Clin Hypn 9:267–268, 1967

Rice FG: The hypnotic induction of labor: Six cases. Am J Clin Hypn 4:119–122, 1961

Rock NL, Shipley TE, Camplule C: Hypnosis with untrained non-volunteer patients in labor. Int J Clin Exp Hypn 17-25–36, 1969

Rodriguez L, Reynolds SR, Caldeyro R: Arch Ginc Montevideo 9:16, 1950, as cited by Reynolds SR, Harris JS, Kaiser IH: Clinical Measurement of Uterine Forces in Pregnancy and Labor. Springfield, Ill., Charles C Thomas, 1954, pp 245–247

Rosen H: The emotionally sick pregnant patient: Hypnodiagnosis and hypnoevaluation— psychiatric indication and contra-indications to the interruption of pregnancy. J Clin Exp Hypn 1:8–27, 1953

Samko MR, Schoenfeld LS: Hypnotic susceptibility in the Lamaze childbirth experience. Am J Obstet Gynecol 121:631–636, 1975

Schibly WJ, Aaronsen GA: Hypnosis—practical in obstetrics? Med Times 94:340–343, 1966

Schwartz M: The cessation of labor using hypnotic techniques. Am J Clin Hypn 5:211–213, 1963

Spiegel H: Current perspectives on hypnosis in obstetrics. Acta Psychother 11:412–429, 1963

Stalb AR, Logan DR: Hypnotic stimulation of breast growth. Am J Clin Hypn 19:201–208, 1977

Stone P, Burrows GD: Hypnosis in obstetrics, in Burrows GD, Dennerstein L (eds): Handbook of Hypnosis and Psychosomatic Medicine. Amsterdam, Elsevier/North-Holland Biomedical Press, 1980, pp 307–325

Symonds EM, Zuspan FP: Clinical and Diagnostic Procedures in Obstetrics and Gynecology. New York and Basel, Marcell Dekker, 1983

Tiba J, Baloughi I, Meszaros I, Banyai E, Gregusi A, Jakubecz, E: Hypnos. Svenska foreningen fur klinica och experimentell hypnos, Budapest, Hungary, 1980, pp 109–113

Tom KS: Hypnosis in obstetrics and geynecology. Obstet Gynecol 16:222–226, 1960

Vellay P: Psychology of a pregnant woman and painless childbirth. J Int Fed Gynecol Obstet 2:16–30, 1964

Werner WE: The use of the hypnoreflexogenous technique in obstetrical delivery. Am J Clin Hypn 6:15–21, 1963

Werner WE: Hypnosis and acute uterine inversion. Am J Clin Hypn 7:229–233, 1965

Werner WE, Schauble P, Knudson M: An argument for the revival of hypnosis in obstetrics. Am J Clin Hypn 24:149–171, 1982

Willard RD: Breast enlargement through visual imagery and hypnosis. Am J Clin Hypn 19:195–200, 1977

Wollman L: The role of hypnosis in the treatment on infertility. Br J Med Hypnot 2:3, 1960

Zimmer EZ, Eyal A, Divon MY, Sarna Z, Peretz BA, Vilensky A: The influence of maternal hypnosis on fetal movements. International Congress of the Israel Society of Hypnosis in Psychotherapy and Psychosomatic Medicine in collaboration with European Society for Hypnosis in Psychotherapy and Psycosomatic Medicine. Haifa, Israel, 1983

Zuspan FP: Hypnosis and the obstetrician-gynecologist. Obstet Gynecol 16:740–742, 1960

Zuspan FP: (Panelist) Hypnosis in obstetrics. Presented at the annual meeting of the Society of Clinical and Experimental Hypnosis, Irvine, Calif., 1973

17

The Use of Hypnosis
in Dermatological Problems

A strong connection exists between emotional factors and changes in the skin (Eller and Silver, 1970; Gardner and Olness, 1981; Kroger, 1977; Tobia, 1982). This has been most strikingly demonstrated in a controlled experiment by Chapman, Goodell, and Wolff (1959, 1960) in which 13 subjects were told under hypnosis that one arm would be vulnerable while the other arm would be resistant to injury. Measured amounts of radiant heat were then applied equally to the equivalent areas of each forearm, one hypnotically conditioned as "vulnerable" the other as "resistant" to injury. There were marked differences in response in the two areas, the "vulnerable" arm showing much more apparent injury as evidenced by reddening and local edema. Finger pulse amplitude measurements indicated local minute-vessel dilitation during the phase of increased vulnerability.

In an experimental study of 57 male subjects, Ikemi and Nakagowa (1962) found that skin pathology produced by a conditioning suggestion appeared histologically much the same as that produced by actual contact with noxious lacquer trees. Muftic (1961) had similar observations.

There have been other studies that suggest that hypnosis clearly can decrease apparent harmful reactions of the skin. Dennis and Philippus (1965) tested 5 hospitalized asthmatic subjects and found that suggestion for coldness in the area to which allergens and histamine were applied effectively blocked reactivity. In an experimental series with 47 subjects, Fry, Mason, and Pearson (1964) noted a moderate reduction in skin sensitivity following posthypnotic suggestion. They observed that the mere act of hypnosis alone, without any specific suggestion (what we have termed "neutral hypnosis"), produced a reduction in skin reactivity.

Eight of 12 subjects tested by Black (1963a) were able to inhibit the immediate type of hypersensitivity response when given, under hypnosis, direct suggestions to do so. He concluded that "deep trance" subjects inhibited the response to a greater degree. Black (1963b) also reported a similar effect on the Prausnitz-Küstner reaction. This was shown not to be attributable, apparently, to stimulation of adrenal function. In another study (1963) Black, Humphrey, and Niven gave 4 subjects direct hypnotic suggestion to inhibit a reaction to the Mantoux tuberculin test. Full-thickness skin biopsies were taken for histological examination. The results showed that the tuberculin reaction, as clinically observed, was inhibited by the hypnotic suggestions, but histologically there seemed no observable change in the degree of cellular infiltration. The exudation of fluid, however, seemed to have been inhibited, again suggesting a change in vascular reactivity.

At times the response of the skin to hypnosis seems to be partially a function of whether there has been a previous experience of similar reaction (Ullman, 1946). An early example of this dating back to 1905 was quoted by Vasiliev (1965). An attempt to induce reddening of the skin with a mock mustard plaster was unsuccessful until the subject had experienced a real mustard plaster. It is not clear that hypnosis was actually used in the early test.

These experimental findings are quite suggestive and lend credence to the many clinical accounts of hypnotherapy in dermatological disorders (Biondo, 1975; Cheek, 1961; Fernandez, 1957; Hartland, 1970; Scott, 1964). Together, the experimental and clinical reports suggest that hypnosis could possibly exert a major influence on dermatological problems, at least in those who are ready hypnotic subjects. A negative result, however, was recorded by Beahrs, Harris, and Hilgard (1970). Using well-trained hypnotic subjects, these researchers were unable to alter normal skin reactivity to mumps antigen, trypsin, or histamine by direct hypnotic suggestion.

TREATMENTS OF WARTS BY HYPNOTHERAPY

An attractive 18-year-old girl came in tears to our office for her first appointment. She had severe subungual warts on the fingers of both hands, as well as on the skin of her hands. On dates the boy would reach for her hand, then involuntarily draw back at the strange and unexpected sensation of touching her warts. She had become shy, refused to date, and was beginning to isolate herself from normal friendships. She had had dermatological treatment, including attempts to remove the warts with topical chemotherapy, but the warts had always recurred.

After evaluation of her psychiatric status, she was given direct suggestions under hypnosis that the warts would decrease by 50 percent between her first and second visits, then by 75 percent by the time of her third visit, then would be completely gone. She was an excellent hypnotic subject, and the warts were completely gone within the suggested span of the three weekly visits.

A second patient with warts, a young secretary, felt that she had lost her job because of the unsightly warts as well as hyperhidrosis of the hands. Her excessive sweating called attention to her hands, emphasizing the warts. Although she was married and a mother of several children, she felt that her life was being constricted by her skin condition. Numerous dermatological treatments had failed to eradicate the warts, and some months of psychotherapy had not alleviated her feelings of distress. As with most wart patients, she did not seem to us to have any significant psychopathology, although the warts and hyperhidrosis were in themselves sources of anxiety. She responded well to direct hypnotic suggestion and was free of both the warts and the hyperhidrosis within five visits.

Such experiences as these are impressive to the clinician, and the experience with warts is repeated in other dermatological areas. Perhaps some connection exists between the brain and the skin, both of which are derived from the same layer of embryonic tissue, the ectoderm. In dermatology many treatments are empirical, and the psychosomatic factor may at times be crucial.

In folklore, the ways of "witching" away warts are many, and the success of these may indicate that there are other forms of hypnosis— or that hypnosis evokes some of the same mechanisms in the unconscious mind. In recent years there have been controlled demonstrations of this effect of suggestion of warts. One clinician who reported success in treating warts with hypnosis only took cases that had failed to respond to other treatments, since, as he said, "I did not want to be persuaded into witchcraft except where other witches had failed." Surman, Gottlieb, and Hackett (1972) also reported success in a case where multiple common warts had proven refractory to routine dermatological treatment. Ewin (1974) has presented striking evidence of hypnotic removal of penile condyloma acuminatum, remarkably well demonstrated in Figure 17-1.

Figure 17-1. Dabney Ewin has reported marked success in treating condyloma acuminatum—as shown in these three cases before (left) and after
(right) hypnotherapy. (photographs kindly furnished through the courtesy of
Dr. Ewin.)

Critics of hypnosis have often discounted the effectiveness of this
treatment as a cure for warts by pointing out that warts spontaneously
regress in most cases with or without any treatment at all, hypnotic or
otherwise. This objection was effectively answered by Sinclair-Gieben
and Chalmers (1959), who reported in the *Lancet* a very unique study
in which 14 patients with bilateral warts were treated by hypnosis for
the warts on the most infested side, while warts on the opposite side of
the body in each subject were used for control. In the 10 subjects who

were felt to reach an adequate depth of hypnosis, the warts regressed on the treated side in 5 to 15 weeks but remained on the control side. No effect was found in the 4 subjects judged not to have entered clinical states of hypnosis.

A more recent survey by Barber (1972) reviews the reports of nonhypnotic suggestive treatment of warts (Bloch, 1927; Dudek, 1967; Sulzberger, 1934; Vollmer, 1946). In these studies it was found that warts treated with the suggestion of painting with a supposed therapeutic solution, actually an "innocuous" dye regressed much faster than those not treated with the dye. Again, the question is raised as to what factor is mobilized by hypnosis, and by some other suggestive methods, that is not mobilized necessarily in other treatments. It would be difficult to know if the dye were actually innocuous. It should be noted, however, that Tenzel and Taylor (1969) found neither hypnosis nor nonhypnotic suggestion effective in removing warts in their studies.

Plantar warts may be a particular problem, since they may be excessively painful and may interfere with normal mobility. Here, the cosmetic factor is not paramount so that secondary complications from the sufferer feeling socially acceptable are not so pronounced. A typical case history from our files follows:

A young telephone lineman suffered from plantar warts that made it quite painful for him to climb poles in his work. Usual dermatological treatments had been of no effect, and he had become so discouraged and angry that he had at one time attempted to cut the warts out of his foot with a knife, which only added infection and soreness to the problem of the warts. He had a hostile interaction with a domineering father-in-law, around whom he said he had to "walk softly." At the time he was referred for hypnosis, he had become discouraged and felt that he would have to resign from his job.

After about a month of weekly hypnotic suggestion, the plantar warts began to regress and soon completely vanished. After the warts had vanished, he was continued in psychotherapy for his repressed hostility. When last seen, 10 years after treatment, the plantar warts had not recurred.

Tasini and Hackett (1977) used hypnosis to treat warts in immunodeficient children. Cohen (1978) discusses hypnotherapy of warts. Both Sheehan (1978) and Barber (1978) question whether hypnosis has any special benefit in removal of warts, although their arguments appear somewhat tautological. Warts may be brought under control by autosuggestion (Gravitz, 1981). If the patient has the expectation that hypnosis will cure warts, then in all probability it will work (Johnson and Barber, 1978).

Techniques of Hypnosis

In treating warts, we have used a modification of the suggestions given for substituting one symptom for another. After the patient is in trance, the area around the wart is lightly touched with a pencil, and the patient is told that he or she will simultaneously feel a sense of coolness, of even coldness, about this area. The patient is given the suggestion that the coldness will persist for a day or so and that as it fades, the warts will begin also to fade. This suggestion of coldness is reinforced at each subsequent visit.

For warts and other dermatological problems the hypnotic technique that we have found to be by far most successful involves the induction of cutaneous hallucinations. Following the establishment of rapport, the patient is asked to sit in the most comfortable position possible. He or she is then told,

"Please cup your right hand on your right knee. . . . That's it. . . . Now look at the knuckles of your hand and as you are doing so, your entire body will begin to relax thoroughly. . . . Pay no attention to other sounds . . . just concentrate on your right hand and my voice, realizing that nothing is beyond the power of the mind . . . and of the body. As I continue talking to you and as you continue staring at the back of your cupped hand, you will begin to notice things like the heat in the palm of your hand . . . and perhaps movement in one of the fingers. . . . As this occurs, slightly nod your head . . . yes . . . very good . . . and now you will notice that your hand is becoming very, very light . . . like a feather coming up toward your forehead. . . . Good. . . . Your hand starts to move upward . . . and as your hand continues to rise, keep looking at the back of your hand . . . but notice your eyelids are getting very heavy, very drowsy, and very relaxed. . . . Now when your hand touches your forehead, . . . your eyes will be closed . . . you will be tremendously relaxed and capable of entering a deep level of trance. Your hand and arm comes up, up, up towards your forehead. . . . Now, your hand touches your forehead. . . . Your eyes are closed. . . . You can let your hand rest comfortably in your lap and normal sensation is returning to your right hand and arm. . . . Notice that your eyelids feel heavy . . . so heavy that even though you try to open your eyes for the moment . . . you can't. . . . Go ahead and try . . . but you cannot. . . . Try again . . . but the eyelids are shut tight. . . . Normal sensations return to the eyelids. . . . Now you will enter a much more sound and relaxed state. . . . Now I want you to raise your right arm. . . . That's it. . . . Extend it in front of you, and as I count to three, your arm will become rigid . . . hard . . . like a board soaked in water . . . like steel . . . so tight . . . so rigid . . . those muscles become steel. . . . One . . . tight . . . two . . . very rigid, and three, the whole arm, each finger . . . yes . . . become steel. . . . There . . . nothing can bend that arm or the fingers . . . showing you the power of your mind and body. . . . Now relax the arm and hand. . . . Normal sensation returns and still a much deeper and sounder state of relaxation.

"I now give you the hypnotic suggestion that your right hand will develop the feeling that a heavy thick glove is on your right hand . . . as your hand has developed this sensation, move the forefinger of the right hand. . . . Good. . . . Now you will note some pressure in the forefinger . . . a dull sensation of pressure. . . . Open your eyes. . . . Now you see that in reality I'm sticking your finger severely with my nail file . . . but you are feeling nothing . . . correct? . . . Fine. . . . Normal sensation is returning to your hand. . . . I am now going to stimulate the middle finger. . . . As you feel this . . . nod your head, yes. . . . You see you pulled your hand back, which is an immediate and normal response. You are now aware of the tremendous control that your unconscious mind has over your body. . . . Now close your eyes again. . . . The pleasant odor leaves and still a more relaxed and deeper state of trance. . . . Nothing is beyond the power of the unconscious mind and these warts are going to leave completely and your skin will be void of them. . . . The area that I touch with this pencil . . . this area of warts now begins to feel very cool . . . cool . . . slightly cold. . . . As you feel this, nod your head. . . . Good. . . . Think the thought as I continue talking. . . . The area is cool. . . . The warts are going to leave. . . . The area is cool, and the warts will leave my body because of the power of my mind over my body. . . . Now just relax your thoughts . . . just pleasant, relaxed, serene thoughts. . . . Listen to me . . . my every word. . . *These warts are going to leave. . . . We have demonstrated the control of your mind over your body, and these warts will be gone very shortly.* . . . Your skin will feel slightly cool around the area of the warts for a day or so, and as the coolness fades, the warts will also begin to fade. And so, as I slowly count from ten to one, you will be fully awake . . . free from tension, tightness, stress and strain. These warts are going to fade out."

These hypnotic suggestions are repeated during subsequent visits until the desired results are obtained. If indicated, the patient is told to use self-hypnosis daily; reinforcing the fact that the warts, or other dermatological problem, will regress and completely abate.

In describing their treatment of a patient with resistant warts of the scalp, face, and neck of 2 years' duration, Obermayer and Greenson (1949) also used suggestions of coldness, having the patient imagine that her face was covered with cold compresses that caused it to tingle and itch. Later, this suggestion was changed to the warts beginning to tingle and fall off while her face felt cool. It is possible that suggestions of coldness have some effect on the vasomotor activity in the region of the warts, although this had not been studied, to our knowledge.

Ullman (1959) and Ullman and Dudek (1960) conducted an extensive study on removal of warts by hypnotic suggestion. Over half of the good hypnotic subjects showed complete remission of warts within 4 weeks after the therapeutic suggestions were given. McDowell (1949) found that a woman "of neurotic make-up" was free of moderately severe juvenile warts 18 days after direct hypnotic suggestion that her skin would clear.

OTHER DERMATOLOGICAL PROBLEMS
RESPONDING TO HYPNOTHERAPY

Hypnotic treatment has been successful for numerous dermatological problems. The most extensive review of the uses of hypnosis in dermatology is that of Scott (1960), who cites improvement in a wide range of dermatological conditions treated with hypnotic suggestion. These include atopic eczema, discoid eczema, varicose and contact dermatitis, pruritus, neurodermatitis, psoriasis, urticaria, alopecia areata, and acne rosacea. His reviews may be consulted for a more thorough review of dermatological reports. Vartikovski et al. (1983) use a computer-integrated approach in treating psoriasis.

Ichthyosis

One of the most dramatic reports of the usefulness of hypnosis in dermatology is that of Mason (1952) published in the *British Medical Journal*. The patient was a 16-year-old boy suffering from a severe case of congenital ichthyosis erythroderma of broc, a condition resembling hereditary ichthyosis. His skin was severely cornified and would crack easily at the joints, oozing a bloody fluid. This condition had greatly impaired the patient's social adaptation. Under hypnosis he first was given the suggestion that the skin would begin to clear on his left arm. Within a few days, less than a week, the horny layer began to flake off, revealing reddened skin, which within a few more days began to appear normal. The suggestions were extended in subsequent sessions to other areas of the body. In each instance the improvement immediately followed the hypnotic suggestion, but it did not occur until the suggestions were actually given for the improvement in a particular area. The degree of improvement in various areas varied from 50 to 95 percent after treatment.

As in the wart study of Sinclair-Gieben and Chalmers, this interesting report seems to suggest a discrete effect of hypnosis on skin disorders, one that is localized to the area to which the hypnotic suggestion is directed. Schneck (1954) also reported improvement with a case of ichthyosis. Similarly, Wink (1961) treated two young sisters for congenital ichthyosiform erythroderma. Direct suggestions for improvement were used. Within 2 weeks there were subjective changes followed by objective improvement. Total correction of the condition was not achieved. There are other reports of ichthyosis being improved by hypnosis, the degree of improvement varying from 30 percent to 90 percent (Kidd, 1966).

Pruritus

We have been impressed with the degree of repressed anger that seems apparent in many patients suffering from pruritus. It often seems as if the patient were identifying some area of his body with a fantasied internal object, then punishing the body area by vigorous scratching that could produce inflammation and infection of the skin.

We saw a 21-year-old single man in consultation in the hospital where he had been placed with a severe generalized skin eruption that was weeping and inflamed. He was being treated with steroids and was kept wrapped in moistened towels. Since attempts at elucidating psychodynamics were unsuccessful, he was treated with direct hypnotic suggestion for relief of the symptoms of itching and discomfort. Improvement began rapidly, and within a few days he was able to be discharged for follow-up on an outpatient basis.

During his outpatient visits it became possible to understand the probable psychodynamics behind the skin condition. Several years before his mother had suddenly died, and his father had married a woman who had a son about the same age as the patient. Soon after his father's second marriage he had begun to have the unconscious fear that the step-brother would steal the attention of his father and that he would be again deserted; he unconsciously felt he had been deserted by his mother through her death. As a result, he had developed unconscious death wishes toward the step-brother, wishes against which he was poorly defended. His fantasies had included scratching out the step-brother's eyes. At this point the step-brother was killed in an automobile accident.

To the unconscious mind of the patient, he was guilty of his step-brother's death because of his unconscious wish to scratch out his eyes. This murderous impulse, turned onto himself in expiation and punishment, seemed to be the origin of the severe generalized dermatitis that had been so resistant to medical treatment.

This case illustrates that sometimes it is necessary to bring the symptom under control with direct hypnotic suggestion before psychodynamics can be explored in a period of relative calm.

Alopecia Areata and Trichotillomania

Many dermatological conditions seem to have a mixture of organic and psychological factors. Among those that often seem to have a predominantly psychological etiology is alopecia areata, an area of hair loss of the scalp, bearded portion of the face, or eyelids, frequently caused by trichotillomania, a compulsive habit of pulling hairs from the affected area. We have found that this seems to be an expression of repressed anger and may at times have a symbolic meaning to "pulling one's hair out." A typical origin is in childhood frustration at not being able to "talk back" to parents. Hair-twisting or hair pulling seems to at times originate in such repressed events. It has usually been very amenable to direct hypnotic suggestion combined with a concurrent exploration of sources of stress in the life situation. Others who have reported on the problems of trichotillomania are Galski (1981) and Rowen (1981).

Herpes

One of the most severe dermatological conditions is the pain of herpes zoster or shingles. Women with this disorder often feel unable to bear the pain of wearing a brassiere, and men may find even the touch of a light undershirt produces severe painful sensations. Many of our patients referred for hypnosis have already been through neurological procedures, such as section of nerve roots, without significant relief. Some cases seem to have established pain that persists after evidence of the viral infection wanes, somewhat like the phantom-limb pain that may occur in the "phantom" after amputations. Perhaps this pain is of central origin and is only felt to originate in the previously affected tissues.

In cases of herpes zoster we have not seemed to find any underlying psychopathological meaning of the symptom and have usually begun direct suggestions for symptom suppression after completing a brief personality survey. Suggestions typically take the following form:

"Your discomfort will become much less intense. . . . The burning and the stinging will begin to fade. . . . You'll be much more relaxed and at ease. You will sleep well at night. . . . Because of the power of the unconscious mind the discomfort will become less . . . and less . . . until it fades completely."

Patients with herpes pain are taught from the beginning to use self-hypnosis twice daily for reinforcement of the suggestions. This is done by simply giving the patients a hypnotic suggestion that they can recall the suggestions that have been given them and that they can apply these suggestions to themselves but that they will not employ self-hypnotic suggestions for any other reason that has not been specifically suggested by the therapist.

In herpes simplex ("fever blister") infections of the mouth Cheek (1974) has found that induction of hypnotic suggestions of cold and numbness are particularly effective in promoting healing. Patients are instructed under hypnosis to maintain the anesthesia for 24 hours. Genital herpes infections do not respond as well.

Genital herpes can often be improved with hypnotherapy, although there appear to be marked psychodynamic factors in most cases. One man, for example, responded well to hypnotic suggestions that his herpes would become inactive, although each time his girl friend was to come to town to visit he had a recurrence. A marked ambivalence about his relationship with her was not difficult to infer. A married woman had attacks of genital herpes only when she was out of town without her husband, perhaps as an unconscious defense against extramarital sexual involvements.

Neurodermatitis and Other Skin Problems

Sacerdote (1965) has discussed the treatment of neurodermatitis, with attention to questions of techniques. The use of hypnosis in many other dermatological problems could be found in reports in the medical literature. Hollander (1959) was able to inhibit picking of the face in two women with excoriated acne. Motoda (1971) similarly inhibited scratching to enhance the effect of medication in an eczema case. Eczema treatment by hypnosis has also been described by Goodman (1962) and Portnoy (1961).

Jabush (1969) has published a case of hypnotherapy of a patient with recurring multiple boils, lasting over a 3-year period. Wink (1966) used hypnotic age regression in treating keratosis follicularis. Although improvement was obtained initially with direct suggestions, it seemed that age regression enhanced the persistence of improvement. Successful treatment of angular cheilosis and psoriasis has been described by Secter and Barthelemy (1964).

Vartikovski, Levin and Morozinsky (1983) point out that many alternative medicine systems, such as naturopathy, use imagery of "cleansing" of and suggests similar hypnotic suggestions for psoriasis and other skin conditions.

CONCLUSION

Like Gordon (1955), we have found hypnosis to be quite useful in those cases of severe dermatological problems in which the patient is able to enter deeper states of trance, although it is possible sometimes to attain marked improvement in those only able to achieve lighter stages of hypnosis. In view of the many reports of improvement with nonhypnotic methods of suggestion, particularly with warts, the close connection between the skin and the emotions should be explored more thoroughly in controlled settings.

Finally, during nonhypnotic psychotherapy we have often observed an irregular reddening of the neck (cholinergic urticaria) when embarrassing emotions are being experienced by the patient but not consciously acknowledged. Perhaps this represents a modified or suppressed form of blushing, but it is so common, in our experience, as to constitute a clinical sign of emotional arousal. Surprisingly, we have never observed this sign during hypnosis, and it may in fact clear rapidly with the induction of trance.

In summary, hypnosis is worth a trial in the treatment of resistant dermatological conditions. In some instances where conventional treatments carry risk of cosmetic impairment, as in warts near the eyes, hypnosis may reasonably be tried as an initial treatment, with other means being added if necessary.

REFERENCES

Barber TX: Suggested ("hypnotic") behavior: The trance paradigm versus an alternative paradigm, in Fromm E, Shor R (eds): Hypnosis: Research Developments and Perspectives. Chicago, Aldine-Atherton, 1972

Barber TX: Hypnosis, suggestions, and psychosomatic phenomena: A new look from the standpoint of recent experimental studies. Am J Clin Hypn 21:13–17, 1978

Beahrs JO, Harris DR, Hilgard ER: Failure to alter skin inflammation by hypnotic suggestion in five subjects with normal skin reactivity. Psychosom Med 32:627–631, 1970

Biondo R: Hypnosis and dermatology. American Society for Clinical Hypnosis, 18 annual meeting, Seattle, 1975

Black S: Inhibition of immediate-type hypersensitivity response by direct suggestion under hypnosis. Br Med J 5346:925–929, 1963a

Black S: Shift in dose-response curve of Prausnitz-Küstner reaction by direct suggestion under hypnosis. Br Med J 5346:990–992, 1963b

Black S, Humphrey JH, Niven JSF: Inhibition of Mantoux reaction by direct suggestion under hypnosis. Br Med J 5346:1649–1652, 1963

Bloch B: Uber die kheibung der warzen durch suggestion. Klin Wochensch 2:2271–2275; 2320–2325, 1927

Chapman LF, Goodell H, Wolff NG: Changes in tissue vulnerability induced during hypnotic suggestion. J Psychosom Res 4:99–105, 1959

Chapman LF, Goodell H, Wolff NG: Changes in tissue vulnerability induced by hypnotic suggestion. Am J Clin Hypn 2:172, 1960

Cheek DB: Possible uses of hypnosis in dermatology. Med Times, January 1961

Cheek DB: Personal communication, December 1974

Cohen SB: Warts (editorial). Am J Clin Hypn 20:157–159, 1978

Dennis M, Philippus MJ: Hypnotic and non-hypnotic suggestion and skin response in atopic patients. Am J Clin Hypn 7:342–345, 1965

Dudek SZ: Suggestion and play therapy in the cure of warts in children. A pilot study. J Nerv Ment Dis 145:37–42, 1967

Eller J, Silver S: Psychosomatic diseases of the skin. Behav Neuropsychiatry 1:25–36, 1970

Ewin DM: Condyloma acuminatum: Successful treatment of four cases by hypnosis. Am J Clin Hypn 17:73–78, 1974

Fernandez GR: Hypnotherapy in dermatology. Br J Med Hypnot 9:38–44, 1957

Fry L, Mason AA, Pearson RSB: Effect of hypnosis on allergic skin responses in asthma and hay fever. Br Med J 1:1145–1148, 1964

Galski TJ: The adjunctive use of hypnosis in the treatment of trichotillomania: A case report. Am J Clin Hypn 23:198–201, 1981

Gardner GG, Olness K: Hypnosis and Hypnotherapy with Children. New York, Grune & Stratton, 1981, pp 194–196

Goodman HP: Hypnosis in prolonged resistant eczema: A case report. Am J Clin Hypn 5:144–145, 1962

Gordon H: Hypnosis in dermatology. Br Med J 1:1214, 1955

Gravitz MA: The production of warts by suggestion as a cultural phenomenon. Am J Clin Hypn 23:281–283, 1981

Hartland J: Hypnosis in dermatology. Br J Clin Hypn 1:2–7, 1970

Hollander MB: Excoriated acne controlled by post-hypnotic suggestion. Am J Clin Hypn 1:122–123, 1959

Ikemi Y, Nakagowa SA: Psychosomatic study of contagious dermatitis. J Med Sci 13:335–350, 1962

Jabush M: A case of chronic recurring multiple boils treated with hypnotherapy. Psychiatr Q 43:448–455, 1969

Johnson RF; Barber TX: Hypnosis, suggestions and warts: An experimental investigation implicating the importance of "believed-in efficacy." Am J Clin Hypn 20:165–174, 1978

Kidd CB: Congenital ichthyosiform erythroderma treated by hypnosis. Br J Derm 78:101–105, 1966

Kroger WS: Clinical and Experimental Hypnosis (ed 2). Philadelphia, J.B. Lippincott Co., 1977, pp 253–256

McDowell MH: Juvenile warts removed with the use of hypnotic suggestion. Bull Menninger Clin 13:124–126, 1949

Mason AA: A case of congenital ichthyosiform erythroderma of broc treated by hypnosis. Br Med J 2:422–423, 1952

Motoda K: A case report of the counter conditioning treatment of an eczema patient by hypnosis. Jpn J Hypn 15:46–49, 1971

Muftic MK: Fenomeno vesicatorio por hipnosis (Vesicular phenomenon produced by hypnosis). Rev Lat-Am Hypn Clin 2:29–34, 1961

Obermayer ME, Greenson RR: Treatment by suggestion of cerrucae planae of the face. Psychosom Med 11:163–164, 1949

Portnoy ME: Un caso de asma y eczema tratado con hipnoses (A case of asthma and eczema treated by hypnosis) Acta-hysnol Lat-Am 1:71–76, 1961

Rowen RJ: Hypnotic age regression in the treatment of a self-destructive habit: Trichotillomania. Am J Clin Hypn 23:195–197, 1981

Sacerdote P: Hypnotherapy in neurodermatitis: A case report. Am J Clin Hypn 7:249–253, 1965

Schneck JM: Ichthyosis treated with hypnosis. Dis Nerv Syst 15:211–214, 1954

Scott MJ: Hypnosis in Skin and Allergic Diseases. Springfield, Ill., Charles C Thomas, 1960

Scott MJ: Hypnosis in dermatologic therapy. Psychosomatics 5:365–368, 1964

Secter II, Barthelemy CG: Angular cheilosis and psoriasis as psychosomatic manifestations. Am J Clin Hypn 7:79–81, 1964

Sheehan DV: Influence of psychosocial factors on wart remission. Am J Clin Hypn 20:160–164, 1978

Sinclair-Gieben AHC, Chalmers D: Treatment of warts by hypnosis. Lancet 2:480–482, 1959

Sulzberger MB, Wolf J: The teatment of warts by suggestion. Med Rec 140:552–556, 1934

Surman OS, Gottlieb SK, Hackett TP: Hypnotic treatment of a child with warts. Am J Clin Hypn 15:12–14, 1972

Tasini MF, Hackett TP: Hypnosis in the treatment of warts in immunodeficient children. Am J Clin Hypn 19:152–154, 1977

Tenzel JH, Taylor RL: An evaluation of hypnosis and suggestion as treatment of warts. Psychosomatics 10:252–257, 1969

Tobia L: Hypnosis in dermatology. Minerva Med 73:531–537, 1982

Ullman M: Herpes simplex and second degree burns induced under hypnosis. Am J Psychiatry 103:830, 1946

Ullman M: On the psyche and warts. I. Suggestions and warts: A review. Psychosom Med 21:473–488, 1959

Ullman M, Dudek SZ: On the psyche and warts. II. Hypnotic suggestions and warts. Psychosom Med 22:68–76, 1960

Vartikovski R, Levin G, Morozinsky G: The possible suggestive effect of cleansing in the treatment of psoriasis and other skin conditions. International Congress of the Israel Society of Hypnosis in Psychotherapy and Psychosomatic Medicine in collaboration with European Society for Hypnosis in Psychotherapy and Psychosomatic Medicine. Haifa, Israel, 1983

Vartikovski R, Stav M, Vartikovski A, Zwirn M, Shai Y: Computer-integrated approach in psoriasis using Eriksonian hypnotherapy, biofeedback, and alternative medicine methods. International Congress of the Israel Society for Hypnosis in Psychotherapy and Psychosomatic Medicine in collaboration with European Society for Hypnosis in Psychotherapy and Psychosomatic Medicine. Haifa, Israel, 1983

Vasiliev L: Mysterious Phenomena of the Human Psyche. (Transl by Volochava S). New York, University Books, 1965

Vollmer H: Treatment of warts by suggestion. Psychosom Med 8:138–142, 1946

Wink CAS: Congenital ichthyosiform erythroderma treated by hypnosis. Br Med J 2:741–743, 1961

Wink CAS: A case of Darier's disease treated by hypnotic age regression. Am J Clin Hypn 9:146, 1966

18

The Use of Hypnosis
in Impotence, Frigidity,
and Other Sexual Problems

Even with the current permissiveness in discussion of sexual questions, many persons with basic sexual maladjustment hesitate to seek professional help. We have been consulted frequently about cases of impotence or frigidity that had been present for months or years, adding the burden of continual failure to an initially traumatic situation.

Sexual failure is so closely linked to feelings of self-esteem and adequacy, particularly in the male, that it must invariably be approached with an understanding of the psychodynamics involved. Simple symptom removal without exploration of possible unconscious meanings may lead to panic, depression, conversion reactions, or other symbolic equivalents. Treatment of impotence and frigidity by hypnosis should always involve concurrent psychotherapy, psychoanalysis, or hypnoanalysis.

Though rare as a cause of impotence or frigidity, organic factors first must be ruled out. Such diseases as multiple sclerosis or diabetic neuropathy, which interfere with normal innervation of the penis, must be considered. Conditions producing pain should be considered as possible etiological factors. These may include verrucae acuminata (venereal warts). Severe phimosis, which is a constriction of the foreskin, can be painful. Peyronie's disease, in which the penis bends downward when erect, may also produce pain. It should be standard procedure for a urological or a gynecological consultation to precede treatment of impotence or frigidity to eliminate treatable organic causes.

The use of hypnosis in the diagnosis and treatment of the sexual dysfunctions is receiving increasing attention (Alexander, 1967, 1974; Ambrose and Newbold, 1959; August, 1959; Cheek and LeCron, 1968; Crasilneck, 1979a,b, 1982a; Deabler, 1975; Fabbri, 1975; Hoffman and Kopenhauer, 1961; Jacks, 1975; Kroger and Freed, 1956; Wollman, 1960). It is also a topic of frequent discussion at hypnotherapy workshops (Zuspan, 1973).

Araoz (1982, 1983), Brown and Chaves (1980) emphasize the usefulness of positive ego-strengthening suggestions in hypnotic treatment of sexual problems. Dennerstein (1980) and Dennerstein and Burrows (1979) stress the need for a good history of the sexual dysfunction. The use of hypnosis in sexual dysfunction was extensively reviewed by Hall (1978). Hammond (1983b) describes various approaches utilizing hypnotherapy in both sexual and marital therapy. Fabbri (1976) suggests combining hypnotic treatment of sexual dysfunctions with behavioral modification procedures.

IMPOTENCE IN THE MALE

In most life activities a man in modern culture can rely on any number of props for his sense of adequacy—his clothing, his income, his identification with a business, social, or sports group. Well wishing and social approval from peers can compensate for many fears of inadequacy.

In the sexual act, though, a man functions entirely alone in most intimate contact with a woman who may approve or disapprove of his adequacy in the situation. It is not surprising, then, that failure in the sexual act may cause severe anxiety in a man who is functioning well in his other roles.

Not all cases that present as impotency are actually that problem. At times the husband comes for consultation at the request of his wife because of deficient sexual interest or performance. Some of these men in private consultation confess to being involved in extramarital affairs of which the wife is unaware. Others may be hiding excessive masturbation or even unsuspected homosexual relations. These are not true cases of impotence; rather they are instances of unconventional sexual behavior apparently manifesting as impotence or decreased libido. In many cases the extramarital involvement produces guilt in the man, inhibiting his sexual expression with his wife.

It is generally safe to assume that if an erection can be obtained under any condition, the penis and the innervation and vascular supply needed for potency are intact. This may require careful history taking, for some men report being impotent with their wives while obtaining erections easily with extramarital partners or the reverse may be true. Erections may occur easily with masturbation but not with attempts at intercourse, in which case it is often revealing to inquire into what type of sexual activity or partner is fantasied during masturbation. A man who is unable to achieve erection in a heterosexual situation, but can during masturbation, may have unconscious fantasies of the vagina being dangerous, perhaps even an archaic image of the so-called vagina dentata, the teeth of which might castrate him.

Some men awaken with erections, which most probably accompany the last dream of the night, not necessarily itself sexual in content. If erection is possible in any circumstance, the physical capabilities of the man most probably are intact and attention should be directed to psychogenic causes, which seem to account for most cases of impotence.

Impotence refers to an inability to obtain full erection. It may be complete (no erection) or partial (insufficient erection to achieve penetration of the vagina). In addition, premature ejaculation is a common accompanying symptom, or it may be the primary complaint. Premature ejaculation simply means that the man reaches ejaculation very quickly after penetration, or even before the act of penetration, depriving his partner of the stimulation needed for her enjoyment of the sexual encounter.

Crasilneck (1977, 1979b) discusses the application of hypnotherapy in the treatment of psychogenic impotency in a follow-up study involving 100 consecutive males. In 1982, Crasilneck (1982a) reported another follow-up study of 100 cases; 87 reported freedom from the problem 1 year after the termination of treatment. This work reveals the psychodynamic factors involved in the problem of impotency. Crasilneck (1979a) considers hypnotherapy as the treatment of choice for psychogenic impotency, utilizing uncovering techniques as well as ego-strengthening and new self-image techniques; Deabler (1976) and Ward (1977) are in agreement. Stricherz (1981) discusses various exercises for stimulating erections. Fuchs et al. (1983) discuss various stresses involved in impotency and report good results with hypnotherapy in 9 cases.

Environmental Factors

After ruling out serious organic causes for impotence and before investigating unconscious dynamics, some attention should be given to frequent but often overlooked factors in the environment. This is particularly important with men, since any initial experience of impotence may produce a threat to the sense of male sexual adequacy. That fear itself may provoke further impotence, resulting in an unfortunate chain reaction of increasing sexual dysfunction.

Crasilneck (1982a) lists 22 of the most frequently reported causes for psychogenic impotency: (1) Fear of losing penile erection; (2) Fear of partner's anger for failure during intercourse; (3) Depression and self condemnation of failure; (4) Guilt for extra-marital relations; (5) Anxiety because of failure in extra-marital relations; (6) Fear of getting "caught," which results in failure in heterosexual and homosexual relations; (7) Anxiety over children disturbing the act; (8) Fear of impregnating the partner; (9) Anxiety over venereal diseases; (10) Exposure to such diseases as cancer and herpes; (11) Anxiety and guilt that sex is dirty and sinful; (12) Conflict over Oedipal situation; (13) Anxiety due to change of body image of partner; (14) Fear of penis being excessively small; (15) Depression as result of memories of dead wife; (16) Anxiety over occasional failure with spouse but not lover or vice versa; (17) Guilt over flirtations; (18) Anxiety over inability to ejaculate; (19) Anxiety over premature ejaculation; (20) Fear of failure due to physical and psychological exhaustion; (21) Fear of condition known as vagina dentata "castration by vaginal teeth"; and (22) Anxiety due to not being cognizant of the fact that excessive drinking may cause impotency most of the time.

Traumatic Events

Some cases of sexual dysfunction in men seem best conceptualized as conditioned reflexes initiated by an emotionally traumatic experience, often a repeated trauma occurring in childhood. Many of the men were discovered in childish sex play and severely scolded and threatened. At times, memories of such events arise only after the physical symptoms have begun to improve, as if what might be called "physiological insight" leads to emotional and then intellectual insight into the problem.

After beginning to get erections for the first time in several years, a graduate student was able to remember his older brother scolding him, at about age 10, for sexual explorations with a girl playmate, telling him that his other brother, who was "nice," did not do such things. A memory also followed of a respected high school teacher lecturing sternly against masturbation, an activity he previously had never questioned.

Not all traumatic conditioning events are in childhood, however.

An older man had experienced, in his early twenties, two instances in which intercourse near water was interrupted by strangers. The first occurred when he was with a sweetheart in a canoe, the other, about 3 years later, with another woman on a beach. After these two episodes he had difficulty with erections whenever any reminder of water occurred when he was about to have intercourse. At times the sound of water running was sufficient to cause him to lose his erection. In one specific instance it was simply the sound of one of his children taking a shower just as he was about to achieve penetration.

If organic causes, environmental factors, and conditioning situations have been adequately ruled out, it is necessary to formulate at least a tentative picture of unconscious conflict behind the impotence or premature ejaculation. Only when the therapist feels that he or she has an understanding of such dynamics should he or she attempt hypnoanalysis for alleviation of the symptom.

Oedipal Conflict

Freud's classical understanding of the Oedipal conflict is still the most useful model for the unconscious conflicts underlying sexual dysfunction in the male. Briefly, this is a frequent fantasy in males, being first experienced about age 5 or 6 and normally being revived again at the beginning of adolescence—about age 12 or 13. In fantasy the boy begins to feel he might very soon be as adult as his father and able to win from his father the love of his mother, his father's wife, who is physically the only adult woman with whom he has had sufficient contact to feel love. In Freud's theoretical view the boy gives up such a fantasy because of fear of his father's anger, often taking the fantasied form of physical castration. The boy may fear that if he continues the rivalry with his father, the father will punish him for it by cutting off his penis. This is a deeply unconscious fantasy, of course, and can be demonstrated only indirectly in the adult male, through dreams and fantasy material or through reconstructing a great mass of past experiences.

A middle-aged married man, the father of two children, was referred for treatment of impotence, which had occurred abruptly since the death of his father. It was learned that from age 8 until 12, he had not only slept in the same room with his mother but had shared her bed. The father, who slept in the same room, but in another bed, would at times ask the boy to trade beds, which the child resisted. His father would sometimes angrily remove him.

He remembered erections in early puberty, and thinking of his mother as he masturbated, though he felt in retrospect that she had been more naive than seductive, more babying him than trying to arouse him.

There was also a serious sibling rivalry with an older sister, who was the father's favorite. The patient had each night practiced his drums loudly, partly to irritate the father and sister. The father would angrily threaten to break the drumsticks (symbolic of castration?), but the mother would always intervene on the side of the patient. "Someday you'll kill me with that racket," the father would repeat.

With understanding, his potency was restored, though he remained in therapy for an extended period of time, at his own request, to explore thoroughly his personality.

Therapy was finally successfully terminated after an investigation of the transference relationship showed that he was seeing the therapist as a powerful but benign father image who would protect the patient as long as he was "good" from the fantasied dangers of the image of the castrating father.

The Oedipal dynamics in this case are much clearer than is usual. The reconstruction of the childhood events preceding his marriage, his father's sudden death, and his increasing impotence were accompanied by the abreaction of a great deal of affect under hypnotherapy.

The normal resolution of the Oedipal conflict is for the boy to give up his rivalry with his father and instead identify with the father, planning to grow up to be like the father and therefore able to win a woman like the mother. In pathological cases, where the childhood has been either too threatening or too gratifying, the Oedipal complex may persist like a foreign body in the adult mind, drawing into its influence all close relationships.

For example, one man with such an Oedipal complex progressed steadily in his work for a large corporation, climbing up the ladder of responsibility as long as he was working for some direct supervisor to whom he seemed to relate emotionally as a small boy trying to please his potentially destructive father. Finally, however, the patient was so successful that he was put in charge of a large project with no direct supervisor. He immediately began to have anxiety (theoretically, "castration anxiety") and occasional inability to achieve an erection. He consulted a noted psychiatrist about his condition. After only one interview with the psychiatrist, a man of imposing and stern appearance, the patient became completely impotent. Apparently he had assimilated his relation with the doctor to his unconscious Oedipal fantasy, identifying the psychiatrist with the feared image of a castrating father. He entered psychotherapy with another therapist and was ultimately successful in working through most of his neurotic conflict.

Some unconscious conflicts may arise from a level of development preceding the Oedipal phase. Neumann (1963), for example, mentions a fear of "uroboric incest" in which the male fears being completely overwhelmed by the female, analogous to a fear of being reabsorbed into the maternal womb. This may excite unconscious identification of sexual release with death. In the face of such overwhelming fear, the man may employ unconscious defense mechanisms, frequently producing hypochondriacal symptoms. These are often the unconscious acceptance of a "partial death" (the symptoms) to avoid fear of intercourse, which is connected in fantasy with annihilation or "total death."

Concept of Women

Impotence or premature ejaculation may express an unconscious anger or fear of women. Frequently a feeling of inferiority in the man may cause him to have difficulty with a woman whom he imagines to be somehow superior to himself. One man experienced his first episode of impotence only when he began a liaison with a woman who had been associated with his father in a business relationship. He seemed to have not only Oedipal fears of fantasied retaliation from his father but also a feeling of inferiority to the woman, who was somewhat older. Some men feel sexually insecure with women whom they believe to have had greater sexual experience, often fearing that the woman will compare them unfavorably with other men.

Anger at women may be expressed unconsciously by a man arousing his partner sexually and then, at the point of intercourse, losing his erection through no "fault" of his own. Such behavior may not reflect the man's true feelings about the particular woman involved, whom he may sincerely love. He unconsciously may identify all women with an image originating in an Oedipal fantasy.

Interpersonal Relations

In the investigation of the psychodynamics of impotence and premature ejaculation it is often necessary to formulate some idea of the interpersonal transactions occurring in the sexual life of the patient. In many cases the wife may be expressing disinterest or hostility in oblique and covert ways while officially claiming to act in an adult sexual manner with her husband. One man with impotence reported that his wife invariably asked him to get her a glass of water just as their foreplay was about to culminate in intercourse. Invariably he lost his erection, at which point she taunted him with "You're not much of a man, are you?" Such a transaction is shattering to the male ego, although the man's own neurotic needs may lead him to fall into such a transaction instead of commenting upon the double-bind communication.

Latent Homosexuality

Sexual dysfunction in the male may also be caused by latent or hidden homosexuality. It is immensely important, when dealing with such fantasies, that a distinction be made between homosexuality (a fixed preference for sexual partners of the same sex) and pseudohomosexuality (homosexual fantasies, or even overt behavior, that is actually expressing in sexual language a conflict arising in other areas of the personality). A frequent fantasy of the pseudohomosexual is that of magical repair of his own damaged masculinity through incorporation of the masculinity of a more potent male, which may be symbolized by the other man's penis. Such a fantasy is not far removed from the savage attempting to acquire the courage of a lion by eating the lion's heart or a modern youth attempting to feel "like a man" through joining a masculine organization. When such a psychodynamic picture is found, it must be thoroughly investigated as part of the treatment program. One college student with a fear of becoming homosexual was expressing in these fears the same conflict that his father had manifested in a conversion symptom, both arising from the young man's domineering and "castrating" mother.

Conversion Symptoms

Some sexual dysfunctions seem to be conversion symptoms. Conversion implies that a conflict in one area is expressed in the language of another, usually a psychological conflict showing itself not in words and feelings but in bodily symptoms, often in the voluntary musculature. A man with an unconscious conflict about anger may experience it, for example, as a paralyzed arm, the paralysis symbolizing both the desire to strike and the inhibition of that aggressive action. In a wider sense, sexual conversion symptoms may express, in the language of penile erections, feelings of adequacy or inadequacy that have their true origins in other nonsexual fields of experience. For example, in rapid succession a successful man lost a part of his body through an accidental amputation, a child through an unexpected and fatal illness, and then—perhaps symbolizing his feelings of diminished selfhood—he became sexually impotent. A repetitive problem of similar meaning is that of the healthy man who is partially disabled through an accident that prevents him returning to his usual work. Such men may become withdrawn, experiencing a loss of self-esteem that was previously based on their work productivity or earning ability. Not infrequently they also become sexually impotent on a conversion basis, the impotence reflecting feelings of diminished potency in other areas. Typical of such cases is that of a gambler who became impotent after he began to lose at cards. Impotence also occurred in a graduate student after he failed several crucial examinations.

It is not uncommon for recently divorced men to have transient difficulty with erections. This is not always due to guilt. It may express mourning for the lost home or children. Anxiety over dating may be a factor as well. Widowed men may have a similar response. We know of several cases in which a widower had difficulty discarding momentos of his deceased wife, including clothing. In such instances of continued mourning impotence is often on a clearly psychological bases.

HYPNOTIC TREATMENT OF IMPOTENCE

After thorough medical study of impotence, to rule out organic etiology and treatable environmental and interpersonal causes, the psychodynamics are assessed and clearly formulated. It is then possible to undertake hypnotic treatment of the symptom with relative safety.

Direct hypnotic approach to removal of impotency must be done in a slow, cautious, and realistic manner, more so than in the hypnotherapy of most other symptoms. This is necessary because of the extremely deep and charged meanings associated with sexual function. Hypnosis is preceded by a realistic discussion of possible outcomes. The patient is told before hypnotherapy that there may be a need for a number of inductions because the treatment (1) may be only partially successful, (2) may be markedly successful, or (3) possibly will not be successful at all in diminishing the impotence, even if the patient proves to be a good subject. Far from inducing a fear of failure, we have found that the frank discussion increases the patient's acceptance of hypnosis as a treatment modality, different from mere positive reinforcement.

In each hypnotic session the subject is put into a moderate to deep trance. He is told that he will have "firm erections . . . hard erections . . . rigid erections" and that during intercourse he "will be able to enjoy this pleasurable act."

A 25 year old male who had been married 6 years had a problem of achieving and maintaining erections sufficient for intercourse in about 40 percent of his attempts at coitus with his wife. He had no extramarital or homosexual involvement. He often awakened with erections in the morning confirming the impression of the referring urologist that there was no anatomical interference with the blood or neural supply of the penis.

His sexual difficulty had begun about 3 years before he was first seen, soon after his wife delivered their second child and decided that she "would rather work than be a mother." She became more demanding of him, insisting that he assume more of the household upkeep. He was told when to be home, which, he said, "made me feel like a child under curfew." When he was attempting to get and maintain an erection, she would sometimes shake her finger at him, saying "You'd better make it this time, I won't be frustrated again!" Under hypnosis he suddenly realized that her harsh voice reminded him of a drill sergeant in the army.

These realizations permitted him to choose a more assertive attitude in relation to his wife who became more affectionate. Direct hypnotic suggestions for improved sexual functioning were also given, and he soon had only rare instances of difficulty.

A modification of this technique has proven unusually effective in our sessions for impotence. During the course of hypnotic trance catalepsy is induced in one of the subject's arms. He is told that his arm will become rigid, firm, and hard, "as hard as steel," and "as hard as a board that has been soaked in water." When the arm is cataleptic, he is asked to feel of the rigid arm with the opposite hand, and is told:

"Your penis will become just as hard, just as firm and full, just as rigid as the arm. . . . If you can produce this hardness in one part of your body, you can produce it in your penis. . . . Through the power of the psyche over the soma, the power of the unconscious mind over the body, you will begin to have firm, full, hard erections whenever you are sexually aroused. . . . You do not want to discontinue abruptly or prematurely an act that feels good."

These suggestions, together with interspersed suggestions of relaxation, are repeated for the remainder of the trance time. During each session the patient is being allowed to ventilate his feelings concerning his problem as well as gaining intellectual and emotional insight into the total situation.

Results

With a combination of psychotherapy and hypnosis, from 1968 to 1973, we have found in a series of more than 400 patients, improvement occurs in approximately 80 percent. Treatment is usually continued weekly for 3 to 4 months, then tapered in frequency for a longer period of time. If the symptom is extremely fixed or based on strong unconscious conflicts, a longer period of treatment is warranted before the technique is abandoned. Subsequent follow-up studies (Crasilneck,

1977, 1979a, 1982a) reveal an increase in freedom from impotency without symptom substitution in 87 percent of the patients.

Thus far we have found no severe side effects of treatment of impotence in this manner. We know of no instance, in our experience, of symptom substitution.

The suggestions given for premature ejaculation are virtually the same, but with an emphasis that "anxiety and tension associated with sexual intercourse will be greatly reduced . . . previously experienced feelings of anxiousness and tension will be replaced by enjoying this enjoyable act." Patients are told,

"You will not necessarily attempt to speed up your activities in intercourse, but you will allow your body to respond without excessive tension and fear, and you will not ejaculate prematurely. . . . You will simply be relaxed and at ease, free of tension and tightness and stress and strain . . . and you will NOT ejaculate prematurely."

Hypnotic treatment of impotency also has been reported by Biegel (1971), Dittborn (1958), Gonzaga (1972a), Levit (1971), and Schneck (1970). Doane (1971) described one case of anesthesia of the head of the penis, improved by hypnotherapy. Underlying homosexual problems, which may affect potency, have been hypnotically treated by Alexander (1967) and by Gonzaga (1972b) with improvement.

FRIGIDITY IN THE FEMALE

Orgasmic dysfunction ("frigidity") in the female does not seem to have the devastating psychological impact that accompanies impotence in the male. Perhaps this is part biological, since the woman, even if not aroused, is still able to physically engage in coitus. She may adequately satisfy her male partner even if she received only minimal gratification herself. The male, in contrast, is physically unable to engage in intercourse at all unless he is sufficiently aroused to obtain and maintain penile erection. Thus, it is possible for a woman to "fake it" about her sexual enjoyment, but impossible for the man.

As with men, there are very few organic causes for inadequate sexual response in the woman. A gynecological examination should eliminate organic causes of pain, as vaginitis or, in later years, atrophy of the vaginal mucosa. Libido may vary somewhat with the ovarian cycle, with menopausal changes, or with endocrine therapy, but in the vast majority of cases frigidity is found to be psychological in origin. At times there may be vaginismus, a total spasm of the female pelvic musculature when intercourse is attempted. This, too, has been treated by hypnosis (Schneck, 1965). Milder forms of involuntary spasm or lack of lubrication may induce dyspareunia (painful intercourse), which may secondarily produce avoidance of coitus.

Frigidity should not be considered an all-or-none phenomenon. Some women seem quite able to have enjoyable sexual experiences without achieving orgasm. Women who achieve orgasm may vary from time to time in their responsiveness, at times failing to reach climax. Their enjoyment of the sexual act is usually more dependent on the total emotional gestalt of the sexual situation. Perhaps the most sensible approach is to consider a woman to have sexual inadequacy only if she herself is dissatisfied with her enjoyment.

Some women present themselves for treatment of what they call "frigidity" although inquiry may reveal that they seem to describe having orgasm. Since orgasm has no clearly definable sign, such as ejaculation of semen in the male, some women imagine it to be some extremely exaggerated response, projecting into their fantasy unsatisfied wishes from other nonsexual areas. Other women are disturbed because they or their husbands have taken "mutual orgasm" as the most desirable goal of sexual life. Both may be having entirely adequate orgasm, often only a few moments apart, but feel obliged to strive for "mutuality." In these cases brief counseling of husband and wife may be sufficient to remove the primary causes of dissatisfaction.

Simple educative sessions may remove some fears of free expression during the sexual encounter. Some couples seem to simply need reassurance that pregenital sex play—fellatio or cunnilingus—is permissible within the basic framework of adult sexuality without either partner being considered deviant or "queer."

Wijesinghe (1977) reported dramatic recovery in a case of frigidity treated by short-term hypnotherapy. Cheek (1976) used ideomotor questioning methods in light hypnosis to treat secondary frigidity after radical surgery for gynecological cancer. Ward (1975) reports successful treatment of frigidity with hypnotherapy. Hammond (1983a) used hypnotherapy in treatment of inhibited sexual desire. Fuchs (1980) found hypnotic desensitization valuable in a majority of women treated for vaginismus.

Environmental Factors

When physical factors have been eliminated and counseling has defined clearly the nature of the problem, consideration is given to environmental factors. As with the male, these may be lack of privacy, inadequate time, excessive tiredness, or distractions. Fear of pregnancy or disgreement about the desirability of having children may be involved. It has been amazing to note how many couples who come for sexual counseling have failed to take the primary and obvious step of putting a lock inside their bedroom door so that privacy from their children is assured.

Interpersonal Relations

Before exploring unconscious factors in orgasmic dysfunction, some investigation of transactional roles should be undertaken. Sex may be used as a commodity, a reward. Conversely, withholding of intercourse may express hostility or disapproval. At times this may be in reaction to impotence or premature ejaculation in the male partner. When such an interaction is found, it must be unraveled and faced in a conscious manner by both partners. In severe cases, extended counseling of the couple may be undertaken, or ancillary techniques such as group therapy employed to delineate the neurotic interaction and offer a chance for the establishment of more mature patterns.

"Penis Envy"

Varied unconscious psychodynamics may underlie frigidity. In classical psychoanalysis it is frequently considered to be a result of "penis envy," the supposed unconscious feeling of a woman that she is incomplete because she lacks a penis. There also may be fantasies that the penis is a dangerous and destructive aggressive weapon. A woman with penis envy may secretly long to be a man or, since that is impossible, may desire to control a man (equal to a fantasy of "having" a penis). At times the fantasy takes the form of desire to give birth to a male child, which in the unconscious may be seen as bringing a penis out of her woman's body. The child may then be expected by the mother to fulfill all the wishes that she imagines she would have accomplished had she been born a man.

One woman in her early twenties had been raised in early years as her father's "son," even being called by a diminuitive form of his name by the family friends. In childhood she accompanied him on some brief business trips. She was the father's child, while in the family mythology her younger brother was the mother's child. After graduating from college with honors, she began working. In her work she was meticulous, reliable, and successful. At this time she became involved in her first sexual affair, choosing a man who was quite self-centered and exploitative. During the course of the affair she became depressed and sought psychiatric treatment.

During her sexual experiences with the man she often began to feel genuine sexual pleasure. At these times, however, the feeling of pleasure abruptly vanished and she became completely anesthetic in the vaginal area even being unaware whether his penis was still present or not. Discussion of her feelings revealed a strange ambition, which seemed to make sense only when viewed in the light of an unconscious penis envy. She did not allow him to use contraceptives, nor did she take any steps to prevent pregnancy. Her plan was to eventually become pregnant, at which time she would leave him without explanation, finding a situation in which she could be alone during her pregnancy and confinement. If the child were a boy, she would take her son to a distant city and raise him alone. However, if the child proved to be a girl, she would place it for adoption, return to the affair, and again attempt to become pregnant with a male child.

Clearly, her behavior was not directed at true adult sexual relations but was in the service of a deeply unconscious fantasy of fulfilling the original role as the "son" in her family myth by symbolically achieving a penis, represented by giving birth to a male child who would be masculine in her stead.

Following some months of treatment, she improved in both her sexual responsiveness and her general approach to life. She terminated the affair, began dating a more mature man, and seemed to be moving toward a genuinely feminine identification.

Fear of Parent Reaction

Fear of disapproval by a parent or by a parent image in the superego is also a frequent unconscious dynamic mechanism in frigidity. Such women frequently have had strict, punitive mothers who have defined sexual experience as intrinsically "bad" or have suggested that it is a marital "duty" but not to be enjoyed. Such unfortunate impressions may exist together with conscious values of having a good marriage and experience of motherhood. This creates a conflict between two levels of the woman's self-identity. After such conditioning any enjoyment of sexual life, even within marriage, may be perceived as tarnishing the "good girl" self-image based on fantasied approval from an internalized parent image. Such a superego inhibition may express itself overtly in various ways: an irrational sense of guilt, an inability to relax, a fear of loss of self-control during orgasm, and other emotional complications of the sexual act.

One woman with sexual inhibitions based on a puritanical mother's training presented a most revealing initial dream. In the dream she found herself in bed with her husband, in the bed in which they actually slept and where her sexual inhibitions had caused such conflict that the marriage was in danger. She lay on her left side, facing her husband. Sexual intercourse seemed imminent. Then she gradually became aware of someone else in the bed with them. Turning, she saw that her mother, fully dressed, was lying in the bed behind her, scowling disapproval! This initial dream presented the entire conflict in dramatic form.

Oedipal Conflict

Other unconscious factors may be uncovered. At times an Oedipal conflict may be involved. Rarely a latent or overt lesbianism may be present, though such desires, even when confessed, may be reducible to a more basic dependency conflict or some variation of penis envy.

A 31-year-old married woman without children came for treatment with a severe sexual problem. Although she would sexually submit to her husband, it was with the plea to "please get it over with quickly." At times she became so upset that she would actually beat him off with her fists.

After several sessions of ordinary history and anamnesis hypnosis was used for age regression. She was told, "You will slowly be able to recall all the circumstances involved in your problem and over the next sessions we will be able to explore your hostilities toward men." She spontaneously regressed to an incident that had occurred when she was 6 years old. A neighborhood boy of the same age had asked her to play in his garage, suggesting that they show each other how they looked naked. She had removed her clothes when he suggested that she turn her back to him. Unexpectely, he poured a can of red paint on her hair and skin.

She was frightened and ran quickly to her own home, expecting that her parents would do something to punish the boy. Instead, her father and mother scolded her for being "bad." In fact, the mother made a point of having her parade in front of her brothers and sisters each night, giving her a spanking until the paint had worn away.

Abreaction under hypnosis led to a discussion, in the waking state, of how she had overgeneralized, and in her despair equated all sexual contact, even that with her husband, with the emotional image of the original trauma. This led gradually to a change of attitude and the establishment of a normal sexual response in the marriage.

Hypnotic Treatment

Of course, hypnotic treatment must be integrated with a process of making conscious any deeply unconscious factors that have been discovered and working them through. This is done through a mixture of hypnosis and psychotherapy or through the more specialized approaches of hypnoanalysis, in which some of the actual work of uncovering and facing unconscious material is done with the patient in a trance state.

While adequately dealing with dynamic meanings as they arise, at least part of the force of hypnosis should be directed against the inhibition itself. After induction the woman is told that she will be able to relax completely in her vagina. She is told that the vagina is becoming very sensitive, the clitoris is becoming sensitive, and that when engaging in sexual relations with her husband she will experience a crescendo of increasing sensation and pleasure.

"You can and will experience complete and enjoyable orgasm. . . . You will find the sexual act pleasurable, without guilt, without fear. . . . You will rule out all other thoughts . . . concentrating your body and your mind on this enjoyable act."

We have found it particularly useful in treating sexual problems to have the marital partner present, whenever possible, during the hypnotic induction, though not, of course, during history taking or therapy when privacy of the patient must be preserved. The presence of the husband assures him and the patient that suggestions are directed toward their mutual benefit, with no danger of provoking extramarital involvements. Also, it has seemed of benefit to have the husband aware of the actual suggestions given to his wife, enhancing his expectation and interest.

Whenever possible, we have had the wife present during her husband's treatment for impotence or premature ejaculation, for the same considerations.

Power (1961) and Abraham (1972) have used hypnosis to uncover obscure psychogenic factors in orgasmic dysfunction. Chernenkoff (1969) has a technique of having the woman imagine intercourse with a white square (representing censorship) over the genitals of the male. Richardson (1963, 1968) increased the percentage of climaxes from 24 percent (pretreatment) to an average of 84 percent. Biegel (1972) has used hypnosis to treat female sexual anesthesia. Dolezal (1971) has employed hypnotic techniques to alleviate vaginismus. Amenorrhea after anorexia was treated successfully with waking suggestions that did not involve formal hypnosis (Shalit, 1983). Exhibitionism of 14 years duration was treated by Polk (1983) by a multifactoral approach, including hypnosis. O'Brien and Rabuck (1977) failed to produce nocturnal emissions through hypnotic suggestion. Francuch (1982) believes that infertility may be helped through hypnotherapy, but does not offer clinical data for evaluation.

SUMMARY

Impotence and frigidity may have strong psychological components. Hypnotherapy is often a brief, effective treatment for these disorders, while prolonged hypnoanalytic treatment can benefit many resistant cases.

REFERENCES

Abraham G: Possibilities of hypnosis in the treatment of frigidity. Minerva Med 63:962–963, 1972

Alexander L: Psychotherapy of sexual deviation with the aid of hypnosis. Am J Clin Hypn 9:181–183, 1967

Alexander L: Treatment of impotency and anorgasmia by psychotherapy aided by hypnosis. Am J Clin Hypn 17:33–43, 1974

Ambrose G, Newbold G: A Handbook of Medical Hypnosis. Baltimore, Williams & Wilkins, 1959

Araoz DL: Hypnosis and Sex Therapy. New York, Brunner/Mazel, 1982

Araoz DL: Erotic uses of hypnosis. Contemporary Psychology 28:607–608, 1983

August RV: Libido altered with the aid of hypnosis: A case report. Am J Clin Hypn 2:88, 1959

Biegel HG: Therapeutic approaches of impotence in the male. II. The hypnotherapeutic approach to male impotence. J Sex Res 7:168–176, 1971

Biegel HG: The use of hypnosis in female sexual anesthesia. J Am Soc Psychosom Dent Med 19:4–14, 1972

Brown JM, Chaves J: Hypnosis in the treatment of sexual dysfunction. J Sex Marital Ther 6:63–74, 1980

Cheek DB, LeCron LM: Clinical Hypnotherapy. New York, Grune & Stratton, 1968

Cheek DB: Hypnotherapy for secondary frigidity after radical surgery for gynecological cancer: Two case reports. Am J Clin Hypn 19:13–19, 1976

Chernenkoff W: A case of frigidity. Am J Clin Hypn 11:195–198, 1969

Crasilneck HB: The use of hypnosis in psychogenic impotency: The first follow-up study of 100 consecutive males. Glasgow Society of Clinical and Experimental Hypnosis Glasgow, Scotland, 1977

Crasilneck HB: The use of hypnosis in the control of psychogenic impotency: The second follow-up study of 100 consecutive males. Aust J Clin Hypn 7:147–153, 1979a

Crasilneck HB: The use of hypnosis in the treatment of psychogenic impotency, in Burrows GD, Collison DR, Dennerstein L (eds): Hypnosis. Amsterdam, Elsevier/North-Holland Biomedical Press, 1979b, pp 1–8

Crasilneck HB: The use of hypnotherapy in the treatment of psychogenic impotency: The third follow-up study of 100 consecutive males. Am J Clin Hypn 25:52–61, 1982a

Crasilneck HB: (Panelist) The use of hypnosis in psychogenic impotency. International Society of Hypnosis, Glasgow, Scotland, 1982b

Deabler H: Hypnotherapy of impotence. American Society of Clinical Hypnosis, 18th annual meeting, Seattle, 1975

Deabler H: Hypnotherapy of impotence. Am J Clin Hypn 19:9–12, 1976

Dennerstein L: Hypnosis and psychosexual dysfunction, in Burrows GD, Dennerstein L (eds): Handbook of Hypnosis and Psychosomatic Medicine. Amsterdam, Elsevier/North-Holland Biomedical Press, 1980, pp 341–358

Dennerstein L, Burrows GD: The role of hypnosis in the management of psychosexual dysfunction. Aust J Clin Exp Hypn 7:247–252, 1979

Dittborn J: Hypnotherapy of sexual impotence. J Clin Exp Hypn 4:181–192, 1958

Doane WL: Report of a case of anesthesia of the penis cured by hypnotherapy. J Am Inst Hypn 12:165, 1971

Dolezal A: The role of hypnosis in the treatment of vaginismus. Ile Clin Gynecol, Univ Charles, Prague, In Excerpta Medica 25:222, 1972

Fabbri R Jr: Hypnosis and the treatment of sexual disorders. American Society of Clinical Hypnosis, 18th annual meeting. Seattle, 1975

Fabbri R Jr: Hypnosis and behavior therapy: A coordinated approach to the treatment of sexual disorders. Am J Clin Hypn 19:4–8, 1976

Francuch PD: Messages from Within. Santa Barbara, Calif., Spiritual Advisory Press, 1982

Fuchs K: Therapy of vaginismus by hypnotic desensitization. Am J Obstet Gynecol 137:1–7, 1980

Fuchs K, Zaidise I, Peretz BA, Paldi E: Hypnotherapy in male impotence. International Congress of the Israel Society of Hypnosis in Psychotherapy and Psychosomatic Medicine in collaboration with European Society for Hypnosis in Psychotherapy and Psychosomatic Medicine, Haifa, Israel, 1983

Gonzaga JG: Treatment of male homosexuality by means of hypnosis. Am J Clin Hypn 14:206, 1972a

Gonzaga JG: Sophrological treatment of psychic impotence. Am J Clin Hypn 14:206, 1972b

Hall JA: Hypnotherapy in the treatment of sexual dysfunction. Tex Med 74:45–51, 1978

Hammond DC: Treatment of inhibited sexual desire. Second International Congress of Ericksonian Approaches to Hypnosis and Psychotherapy. Phoenix, Arizona, 1983a

Hammond DC: Hypnosis in marital and sexual therapy, in Stahmann R, Hiebert W (eds): Counseling with Marital and Sexual Problems (ed 3). Lexington, Mass., Lexington Press, 1983b

Hoffman GL, Kopenhauer DB: Medical hypnosis and its use in obstetrics. Am J Med Sci 241:788–810, 1961

Jacks F: Hypnosis and the treatment of sexual dysfunction. Am Soc Clin Hyp, 18th annual meeting, Seattle, 1975

Kroger WS, Freed SC: Psychosomatic Gynecology, New York, Free Press, 1956

Levit HI: Marital crisis intervention: Hypnosis in impotence/frigidity cases. Am J Clin Hypn 14:56–60, 1971

Neumann E: The Great Mother: An Analysis of the Archetype. (transl. Ralph Manheim). New York: Pantheon, 1963

O'Brien RM, Rabuck SJ: A failure to hypnotically produce nocturnal emissions. Am J Clin Hypn 19:182–184, 1977

Polk WM: Treatment of exhibitionism in a 38-year-old male by hypnotically assisted covert sensitization. Int J Clin Exp Hypn 31:132–138, 1983

Power E: Hypnosis as a diagnostic auxiliary medium in internal medicine, gynecology, and obstetrics. Am J Clin Hypn 4:127, 1961

Richardson TA: Hypnotherapy in frigidity. Am J Clin Hypn 5:194–199, 1963

Richardson TA: Hypnotherapy in frigidity and para-frigidity problems. J Am Soc Psychosom Dent Med 15:88–96, 1968

Schneck JM: Hypnotherapy for vaginismus. Int J Clin Exp Hypn 13:92–95, 1965

Schneck JM: Psychogenic impotence with a hypnotherapy case illustration. Psychosomatics 11:352–354, 1970

Shalit E: (Panelist) Brief treatment of a case of post anorectic amenorrhea. International Congress of the Israel Society of Hypnosis in Psychotherapy and Psychosomatic Medicine in collaboration with European Society for Hypnosis in Psychotherapy and Psychosomatic Medicine. Haifa, Israel, 1983

Stricherz M: (Panelist) Hypnosis in sexual problems. Presented at the American Society for Clinical Hypnosis Component Meeting. San Antonio, Texas, 1984

Ward WO: Successful treatment of frigidity through hypnosis. Va Med 102:223–228, 1975

Ward WO: The hypnotherapeutic treatment of impotence. Va Med 104:389–392, 1977

Wijesinghe B: A case of frigidity treated by short-term hypnotherapy. Int J Clin Exp Hypn 25:63–67, 1977

Wollman L: The role of hypnosis in the treatment of fertility. Br J Med Hypnot 2:3, 1960

Zuspan FP: Hypnosis in obstetrical practice. Annual workshop of the Society of Clinical and Experimental Hypnosis, Irvine, Calif., 1973

19
Dental Hypnosis

Hypnodontia, the use of hypnosis in dentistry, has a long history. Facing both acute and chronic pain problems as part of their daily practice, dentists have always as a group had a lively interest in hypnotic techniques (Kehoe, 1967). The interest in hypnodontia is reflected in the many articles about it in dental literature (Badra, 1961; Bernick, 1972; Bodecker, 1956; Cheek and LeCron, 1968; Crowder, 1965; Damseaux, 1959; Di Capua, 1983; Drewer, 1961; Golan, 1975; Hartland, 1966; Klopp, 1975; Kornfield, 1958; McAmmond, 1971; Mason, 1960; Owens, 1970; Roston, 1975; Scott, 1968; Secter, 1965; Shaw, 1958; Thompson, 1963).

Some of the earlier work on the psychology of dentistry as related to hypnosis was done by Burgess (1952). The term "hypnodontics" was introduced by Moss (1956), who defined it as "that branch of dental science which deals with the use and application of hypnosis or any other form of controlled suggestion in the practice of dentistry." Two books of note were published in the 1950s: *Psychosomatics and Suggestion Therapy in Dentistry* by Stolzenberg (1950), and *Clinical Applications of Hypnosis in Dentistry* by Shaw (1958). Shaw stressed that it is often possible to use suggestion techniques in dentistry without formal induction of hypnosis, the more standard hypnotic techniques then being reserved for more troublesome cases. Ament (1955) has published an interesting technique of using hypnotic time distortion to facilitate the wearing of dental prosthetics, the patient being told under hypnosis that the new prosthetic has already been worn for some time.

Bruxism is an unconscious grinding of the teeth that often occurs during sleep. It can destroy dentures and erode normal, healthy teeth. In our case experience, bruxism seems most often related to unconscious, unexpressed anger. Ventilation of affect under hypnosis, as well as exploration of emotional history, is often enough to bring some relief. At times direct symptoms suppression can be useful, even if a precipitating event or unconscious anger is not identified. In such cases, a posthypnotic substitution of a flicking of the fingernails to replace the bruxism may be of benefit. During hypnosis, the patient is given the suggestion that should bruxism begin during sleep, to clench his or her teeth, immediately waken, discontinue the bruxism, and rapidly return to normal, restful sleep. In some instances a bedtime use of self-hypnosis can help inhibit the grinding of teeth through the hours of sleep.

Kuhner (1959) and Singer (1960) have discussed the psychological meanings of the dentist–patient relationship, with Singer emphasizing some of the techniques developed by Adler.

Secter (1960) has written extensively on the use of hypnosis in dentistry, particularly in removal of symptoms such as gagging. Hypnosis has been a valuable aid in control of gagging and has been so used frequently (Ament, 1971; Chastain, 1965; Madamba, 1980; Stolzenberg, 1959, 1961; Weyandt, 1972). Bartlett (1971) has found that gagging responds better to direct suggestion when it is "passively caused"—that is, when it is a conditional reflex whose previous causes are no longer functional. Perhaps a milder form of gagging is seen in a hypersensitivity of the teeth that has no demonstrable organic cause but interferes with good oral hygiene.

A 30-year-old married woman who was the mother of two children was referred to us by her dentist for evaluation for hypnodontia. Her chief complaint was that her teeth were hypersensitive to all types of stimulation and had been for most of her adult life. It was most difficult for her to brush her teeth. She could not tolerate either hot or cold foods or fluids without extreme discomfort. She could not use a dental waterpik or toothpick under any conditions. Despite the fact that she needed extensive dental surgery, the thought of the preoperative examination and postoperative pain had caused her to become intensely anxious and increasingly depressed. Screening revealed that the patient had no major emotional problems, other than the anxiety and reactive depression concerning her mouth. She stated that she easily cried at the thought of dentistry. "It was easier to deliver a baby than go to the dentist." After talking with us she agreed to try hypnodontia.

Good rapport was obtained, and hypnosis was induced by the hand-levitation method. Glove anesthesia was introduced, and the patient, eyes open, viewed her finger being extremely stimulated by a sharp nail file while she felt no pain. When an adjoining finger, which was not anesthetized, was stimulated in a like manner, she immediately withdrew her finger. It thus was obvious to her that hypnoanesthesia could control severe pain. She was then told that each day for a week her mouth would become progressively less sensitive to all types of previously described discomfort. Each day she could tolerate hot and cold liquid with much less pain. She would begin to feel much more secure physically and psychologically concerning any dental procedures.

She was to call the office daily to give progress reports, and she was to use self-hypnosis two times a day to reinforce all suggestions given her concerning her mouth and dentistry. Upon awakening from the trance she felt that she had been "in a deep state of sleep, but I remember most everything that went on—I think." She was assured that recall of events in trance was quite common with many patients. She was then asked to do something orally that she had never been able to tolerate before. She said, "It is impossible for me to suck in air between my teeth—it's so painful I can't tolerate it for one second." She was asked to try and to her amazement she accomplished this with only the slightest discomfort. She was pleased and highly motivated to see how she responded.

The patient called in daily with excellent reports: The sensitivity, pain, fear, and apprehension were virtually at zero 1 week later. Two weeks later, under extensive local anesthesia combined with hypnoanalgesia, her dental surgery was completed without complaint. The patient was discharged 1 week later. Appropriate posthypnotic suggestion for decreased pain, discomfort and for a feeling of ease in her mouth were carried out without difficulty. She now uses self-hypnosis appropriately whenever further dental work is needed. She has been discharged from our care.

Dental procedures are often anxiety-producing, even in persons who are emotionally well-adjusted. Why should this be so? Freud's emphasis on the oral stage of psychological development offers some explanation. This theoretical concept in psychoanalysis refers to psychological experiences that the infant is thought to feel between birth and approximately 18 months of age. Indicative of the importance of oral experience in early infancy is the representation of the mouth and tongue on the cerebral cortex. The amount of cortical area devoted to the hand, the thumb, the mouth, and the tongue are disproportionate to the area that represents the sensory input for the remainder of the body. At this earliest stage of life the oral cavity—or perhaps, more correctly, nutritional activity—is of uppermost concern to the infant. Objects in the field of vision, even fingers and toes, are brought to the mouth and explored. Later, with the eruption of teeth, the oral activity takes on a more aggressive and biting character. Karl Abraham, noting this change, divided the oral stage into two parts—first, the oral retentive, then the oral sadistic stage. The psychoanalyst Erik Erikson has been more impressed with the social aspects of these development stages.

Many later habits may reflect oral character traits. Overeating and such oral activities as smoking and drinking may be unconsciously associated with conflicts or experiences of the oral stage of infant development. Oral fixations may be involved in some homosexual fantasies, and they also may underlie some severe forms of depression.

With this emotional importance of the mouth cavity in normal psychological growth, as well as in some neurotic problems, it is not surprising that dental work may cause anxiety (Pavesi, 1963; Raginsky, 1958; Sandor, 1961). The patient may fantasy that he is helpless and passive, or painful emotional situations may be unconsciously converted into physical pain (Castillo, 1960). Some of the patient's own deeply repressed fantasies or oral aggression may be projected upon the dental situation, producing anxiety and tenseness and interfering with the smooth performance of the dental procedure.

Personality traits of the dentist as well may be involved (Borland and Epstein, 1961), making it advisable that the practitioner employing hypnosis have a stable personality and possess an understanding of the usual psychodynamics involved in dental practice. It is important, for example, to avoid jokes that would be perfectly acceptable in ordinary conversation during a dental session but may be misunderstood if told in the presence of a patient in hypnotic trance (Jacoby, 1967).

Jacoby (1960) has reported on more than 300 patients treated with hypnosis for dental procedures and has suggested the use of tape-recorded instructions to facilitate trance. Staples (1958) has suggested that hypnosis has some characteristics of a learning process and has suggested that understanding of the hypnotic procedure may favorably influence the skills of the dentist, even though used with patients only in the waking state. Smith (1965) has outlined the application of hypnosis to children's dentistry. In an unusual case Cochran and Secter (1965) were able to help restore, with hypnosis, an hysterical loss of taste of four and one-half years' duration. Stolzenberg (1961) used hypnotic age regression to learn that two patients with "dental phobia" had actually not experienced any earlier dental treatment, but had developed their fears through association and hearsay. Penzer (1972) reported an emergency case in which a man who had always passed out when given injections was able to have a tooth filled under hypnosis when it was suggested that the sound of the dental drill would seem like his wife vacuuming in a room adjacent to where he imagined himself to be asleep.

WHEN TO USE HYPNOSIS IN DENTISTRY

The indications for use of hypnosis in dentistry have been aptly summarized by Marcus (1963):

1. To reach patients who do not submit to dental treatment readily.
2. To overcome fear and tension, perhaps based on previous unpleasant experiences in the dental situation.
3. For premedication, either in addition to or instead of chemical medication.
4. To allow for reduction of chemical anesthetic agents and to reduce the unpleasant after effects of chemical anesthesia.
5. To replace chemical anesthesia where the administration of such anesthesia is contraindicated for medical reasons, such as allergies, heart disease, and others.
6. To overcome handicaps such as gagging and such infantile habit patterns as tongue-thrust "swallowing" and thumb sucking.
7. To overcome lack of proper cooperation during such procedures as bite registration or in the wearing of appliances—provided, of course, that this lack of cooperations is not due to faulty construction of the appliance.
8. For the control of flow of saliva and capillary bleeding (although the latter effect has been questioned).
9. To minimize objections to noise and vibration from the dental drill.
10. In the form of posthypnotic suggestion for the control of postoperative sequelae such as pain and bleeding.
11. To aid in the correction of habits with negative effect on the teeth, soft tissues of the mouth, or on dental appliances.

The control of bleeding is widely mentioned in the literature of dentistry (Newman, 1971) but as yet lacks clear experimental verification in regard to hypnosis. One study of clotting factors before and during hypnosis failed to demonstrate any marked change in the trance state, although the factor that might be most likely involved—constriction of small arterioles—would not have been measured by the variables chosen (Crasilneck and Fogleman, 1957). Nevertheless, there are impressive reports that bleeding during dental procedures is lessened under hypnosis—even in hemophiliacs (Dufour, 1968; Lucas, 1965; Newman, 1974). Because of the seriousness of bleeding in hemophiliacs, hypnosis might be considered in any such case.

Much of the use of hypnosis in dentistry is for hypnoanesthesia or hypnoanalgesia (Bartlett, 1970; Kroll, 1962). The case that follows is a good example of such application. Our patient, a 32 year-old-woman, was conditioned for about 30 minutes before her first procedure in the office of her dentist. She was told,

> Close your eyes and begin to allow your body to relax. . . . Just concentrate on feeling like a rag doll . . . limp as a dish rag . . . just void of tightness. . . . Very good . . . Now you will note that your eyelids feel glued together and even though you try hard you cannot open them. . . . All right . . . you tried and could not open them and now just a very deep level, your right arm is going to extend itself in front of you. . . . Good . . . it is becoming very rigid . . . like steel. . . . Nothing can bend it . . . it is tight and rigid . . . Excellent. . . Now relax it, and you will experience a much deeper state of relaxation. . . . Hypnosis is working very well. . . . Now the right forefinger. . . . Concentrate on this finger. . . . I give you the suggestion . . . that it will feel like a thick leather glove is on it. . . . As you are aware of this, nod your head. . . . Good. . . . Now you have no feeling in the finger . . . only pressure. . . . Now open your eyes and notice that I am stimulating your finger with this nail file severely but with no discomfort. . . . Good . . . excellent . . . absolutely no discomfort. Now close your eyes. Please open your mouth and place your anesthetized finger in this part of your mouth. We are going to transfer this anesthesia to your mouth . . . to the teeth, to the gums. These parts will be numb and insensitive to any dental work being done in your mouth. As you feel this anesthesia in your mouth, nod your head, yes . . . Good. Now remove your finger. . . . Now you are going to have a very pleasant thought . . . one or more of your choosing, and as this occurs . . . nod your head, yes. . . . While the doctor is examining you and correcting your mouth . . . you will have no discomfort, and these pleasant thoughts will be uppermost in your mind. You will be secure and unafraid . . . hearing my voice consistently while the doctor is working with you.

The suggestions were reinforced throughout the procedure.
At the end of surgery the patient was told,

> "Your fears and tensions concerning dental procedures will be replaced by a secure feeling that your mouth is being restored without discomfort. You can, in the future, use self-hypnosis during dental procedures, giving yourself the suggestion that 'I will be free of all discomfort in my mouth while the doctor is working with me. . . . My teeth and gums will be numb in the areas being treated and time will go by quickly and I'll have pleasant and secure thoughts throughout the procedures. I can awaken by counting from ten to one.'"

Upon completion of her dental work, the following hypnotic suggestions were given:

> "The surgery went very well and normal sensation will return to your finger and mouth. You will sleep well tonight. . . . You will care for your mouth as the doctor will instruct, and you can use self-hypnosis during sessions with your dentist. As I count from ten to one, you will be fully awake."

Self-hypnosis has also been used by some (Smith, 1970). One psychiatrist, Meares, has recorded his subjective experience while one of his molars was extracted under self-hypnosis as the sole analgesia (McCay, 1963). Petrov, Traikov, and Kalendgiev (1964) reported the successful use of hypnotic analgesia in 49 patients.

As in any surgical procedure, hypnosis may be effective when there are special indications for its use. Chief among these indications are those cases in which the patient is allergic to available chemical anesthetics. One such case (Crasilneck, McCranie, and Jenkins, 1956) was of a woman sensitive to procaine who objected to the use of any local procedures. Since it was impractical to administer general anesthesia as frequently as she needed dental procedures, difficulty arose, and she refused to return to her dentist for needed treatment. Most of her teeth developed caries. Her personality evaluation indicated an individual relative free of emotional symptoms other than extreme fear of dental procedures. After a trial of hypnosis she became an excellent somnambulistic subject. Five separate dental procedures were successfully performed with the patient under hypnosis. During these procedures she was free of pain and apprehensiveness. As her fears diminished, she gradually became capable of allowing minor dental procedures to be done even without the induction of hypnosis.

Another patient has a problem with gagging. Each time the patient, who was a woman in her forties, tried to eat wearing her new complete dentures she gagged.

This woman had for several years refused to wear her partial dentures as she almost invariably experienced gagging several minutes after eating with them in place. Psychological interviews had failed to reveal any deep underlying fantasy or remembered trauma that might explain her symptom. When her last teeth were extracted, and full dentures prepared, her situation became critical, since she was then in a position of either overcoming her gagging or feeling embarrassed at her condition. She responded quite well to the initial hypnotic induction, responded readily to suggestions, and was able to begin wearing the dentures without gagging after six hypnotic sessions. No further inductions of underlying psychodynamics were elicited, and the symptom had not returned at the time of writing.

An exaggerated gag reflex may interfere with performance of dental work. Although this may be a symptom of anxiety and may reflect a deeply repressed conflict from the oral state of psychosexual development, it can often be handled by the dentist in his office by simple reassurance. It is well to remember that persons with psychogenic symptoms have not only conflicts but also strengths, and a change in the emotional climate of the situation, as can be sometimes effected by reassurance, may bring into play defenses that overcome the symptoms of the conflict (Marcus, 1966). When this is not successful, hypnosis may be indicated.

Bruxism is a common reason for dental referrals for hypnotic treatment. It may occur at any time but frequently happens only during sleep.

A young man in his early twenties was referred to us for severe bruxism that was causing malocclusion and excessive wearing of the enamel surfaces of his teeth. Careful anamnesis revealed (1) that the patient's father, who had been a strong, authoritarian *paterfamilias*, had frequently told the children to "keep your mouth shut" when they talked excessively, and (2) that the severe symptoms of bruxism did not begin until after the patient's father was accidentally killed in a motor accident. Some abreaction of emotion followed this clarification of the history of his symptom.

The patient was hypnotized and entered a medium level of trance. He was told the following: "Because you want your mouth to function normally, you can respond to the hypnotic suggestion. . . . Your mouth will be much more relaxed during sleep. . . . You are not going to grind down on your teeth any longer. . . . Should you attempt to do so . . . your sleep will be momentarily disturbed. . . . You will awaken and go right back to sleep. . . . You do not want to damage your mouth and because of the power of the unconscious mind, your mouth will be relaxed during your sleep . . . free from tension, tightness, and grinding of your teeth. . . . Starting tonight, if you attempt to grind your teeth, you will immediately awaken and then go right back to sleep. . . . In this way your mouth is going to get well. . . . Do you understand these instructions? . . . Good . . . as I slowly count from ten to one, you will be fully awake."

Following three more reinforcement sessions his symptoms abated and have not returned 1 year following this treatment.

Many problem dental patients may respond well to hypnosis (Moss, 1963) with modifications of induction techniques (such as written suggestions); even deaf mute patients have been able to benefit from hypnosis for dental work. If a simple induction of hypnosis, using relaxation technique, does not suffice to remove the presenting dental problem when the direct suggestion for such improvement is given, there may be a more major unconscious conflict than is apparent on the surface of the situation. More specialized help may then be indicated, and further hypnotic exploration would be best done by a clinical psychologist or a psychiatrist, who are trained to delve into the unconscious meaning of symptoms and to adequately deal with any upset occasioned by such exploration. Ptyalism or excessive salivation may respond to hypnotic suggestion (Koster, 1957). Although dental procedures under hypnosis have been successfully accomplished in schizophrenics (Marcus and Bowers, 1961) and paranoid patients (Secter, 1964) work with such complicated patients should only be considered in close cooperation with a psychiatrist or clinical psychologist.

Louis Dubin (1983) of Temple University School of Dentistry has reviewed uses of hypnotherapy in dentistry. The ASCH national meeting (Di Capua, 1983; Dubin, 1983; Steingart, 1983) and regional specialty workshops (Golan, 1979b; Staples, 1979) have extensively presented didactic material in the training and the uses of hypnosis in dentistry. Also, Finkelstein (1983) reviews many of the dental uses of hypnosis, and Strosberg (1980) cites uses of hypnosis to promote comfort. Biederman (1984) and Wikstrom (1982) use hypnotherapy to control anxiety as well as pain.

Although the actual techniques of hypnosis are easily learned, (Crasilneck, 1978), Kleinhauz and Eli (1983) caution about the need for a thorough understanding of psychodynamics by those employing hypnotherapy clinically. Vartikovski and Zwirm (1983) suggest that Ericksonian "indirect" techniques, such as weaving the hypnotic suggestions into apparently conversational interactions, may be more effective in some patients than the classical "formal hypnosis."

Dental phobia can be a notable factor in preventing good dental care; such phobia can be modified with hypnosis in many instances (Baker and Boaz, 1983; Crasilneck, 1982; Golan, 1979a; Kelly, 1980; Yamauchi, 1981). Thompson (1979) suggests that better hypnotic trance can be obtained, at least in some subjects, if the traditional emphasis on relaxation is modified.

Pain in the temporomandibular joint can be alleviated with hypnosis (Cohen and Hillis 1979). Barber (1977) claims increased success for a rapid induction technique of hypnosis. Hypnosis is recommended for the noncooperative dental patient (Zwirn and Vartikovski (1983), for patients allergic to anesthesia (Dubin, 1976), or those with multiple allergies (Gheorghiu and Orleanu, 1982; Morse and Wilcko, 1979). Tongue-thrusting has also been treated with hypnotherapy (Gerschman, Reade, and Burrows, 1980; Golan, 1983).

Hypnosis is often more effective with children than is generally recognized (Gardner, 1981). Relaxation and clear suggestions are important. Hypnotherapy with children can be combined with other modes of analgesia if the family is willing to be involved in the treatment process; for example, it may be wise to see the family for a period of time (Bernick, 1974). Sometimes a combination of a chemical agent with hypnosis can be a powerful way of controlling disruptive behavior in children (Rosen, 1983). DiCapua (1980, 1981) describes the advantages of combining hypnosis with nitrous oxide as an analgesia.

CONCLUSION

The dental practitioner familiar with the principles of psychodynamics will find hypnosis useful and effective in making many patients more at ease, less apprehensive, and free of excessive pain.

REFERENCES

Ament, P: Time distortion with hypnodontics. J Am Soc Psychosom Dent Med 2:11–12, 1955

Ament, P: Removal of gagging: A response to variable behavior patterns. Int J Clin Exp Hypn 39:1–9, 1971

Badra A: Hipnose em odontologia. Revista Associacao Paulista Cirurgioes Dentistas 15:238–252, 1961

Baker RS, Boaz D: The partial reformulation of a traumatic memory of a dental phobia during trance: A case study. Int J Clin Exp Hypn 31:14–18, 1983

Barber J: Rapid induction analgesia: A clinical report. Am J Clin Hypn 19:138–147, 1977

Bartlett KA: Hypnotic treatment of Novacain allergy. Am J Clin Hypn 12:222–226, 1970

Bartlett KA: Gagging: A case report. Am J Clin Hypn 14:54–56, 1971

Bernick SM: Relaxation, suggestion and hypnosis in dentistry. Clin Pediatr 11:72–75, 1972

Bernick SM: Relaxation and suggestion in children's dentistry. US Navy Med 63:14–15, 1974

Biederman PD: (Panelist) The use of hypnosis in controlling pain and anxiety. American Society for Clinical Hypnosis Workshop. Baltimore, 1984

Bodecker CF: Hypnosis in dentistry. NY State Dent J 22:226–227, 1956

Borland LR, Epstien S: Psychological evaluation of hypnosis in dentistry. J Am Dent Assoc 62:54–65, 1961

Burgess TO: Hypnosis in dentistry, in LeCron (ed): Experimental Hypnosis. New York, Macmillan, 1952

Castillo CR: Hypnosis as an end and as a means in dentistry and medicine. Hypnologia 2:2–4, 1960

Chastain FR: A case of excessive gagging. Am J Clin Hypn 7:257–258, 1965

Cheek DB, LeCron LM: Clinical Hypnotherapy. New York, Grune & Stratton, 1968

Cochran JL, Sector II: Restoration by hypnotherapy of a loss of the sense of taste of $4^1/2$ years' duration. J Nerv Ment Dis 123:296–298, 1956

Cohen E, Hillis R: The use of hypnosis in treating the temporo mandibular joint pain dynfunction syndrome. Oral Surg 48:193–197, 1979

Crasilneck HB, Fogelman JM: The effects of hypnosis on blood coagulation. Int J Clin Exp Hypn 5:132–137, 1957

Crasilneck HB, McCranie EJ, Jenkins MT: Special indications for hypnosis as a method of anesthesia. JAMA 162:1606–1608, 1956

Crasilneck HB: Psychological aspects of hypnodontia. North Texas State Dental Group, Dallas, 1978.

Crasilneck HB: Hypnodontia. Presented at a workship at Baylor Dental College, Dallas, 1982

Crowder HM: Hypnosis in the control of tongue thrust swallowing habit patterns. Am J Clin Hypn 8:10–13, 1965

Damseaux S: Hypnosis in dentistry. Rev Belge Stomat 56:283–290, 1959

Di Capua NJ: Hypnotic modalities with nitrous oxide analgesia. Symposium on Pain. Univ Calif at Los Angeles, 1980

Di Capua NJ: Nitrous oxide and hypnosis. Presented International Congress on Dentistry. Athens, Greece, 1981

Di Capua NJ: (Panelist) The use of hypnosis in dentistry. American Society for Clinical Hypnosis Annual Meeting. Dallas, Texas, 1983

Drewer CJ, Viljoen PT: Abnormal swallowing habits. J Dent Assoc S Afr 16:38–44, 1961

Dubin LL: Subjective apperception and use of color during dental procedures under hypnosis: Report of a case. Am J Clin Hypn 18:282–284, 1976

Dubin LL: Personal communication, 1983

Dufour J: Tooth extraction under hypnosis in a hemophiliac. Rev Fr Odo-tostomat 15:955–960, 1968

Finkelstein S: Principles of hypnosis in a dental office, in Wester WC; Smith AH: Clinical Hypnosis: A Multidisciplinary Approach. Philadelphia, J. B. Lippincott Co., 1983, pp 337–350

Gardner GG: Hypnosis and Hypnotherapy with Children. New York, Grune & Stratton, 1981, pp 235–237

Gerschman JA, Reade PC, Burrows GD: Hypnosis and dentistry, in Burrows GD, Dennerstein L (eds): Handbook of Hypnosis and Psychosomatic Medicine. Amsterdam, Elsevier/North-Holland Biomedical Press, 1980, pp 443–447

Gheorghiu VA, Orleanu MD: Dental implant under hypnosis. Am J Clin Hypn 25:68–70, 1982

Golan HP: Further case reports from the Boston City Hospital. Am J Clin Hypn 18:55–59, 1975

Golan HP: Control of fear reaction in dental patients by hypnosis. Am J Clin Hypn 13:279, 1979a

Golan HP: (Panelist) American Society for Clinical Hypnosis, New England Component Section. Boston, Mass, 1979b

Golan HP: Use of hypnosis in the control of habits. American Society for Clinical Hypnosis Annual Meeting. Dallas, Texas, 1983

Hartland J: Medical and Dental Hypnosis. Baltimore, Williams & Wilkins, 1966. p 846

Jacoby JD: Statistical report on general practice hypnodontics: Tape-recorder conditioning. Int J Clin Exp Hypn 8:115–119, 1960

Jacoby JD: Practical suggestions for dentists working with the patient in a trance. Am J Clin Hypn 10:39–43, 1967

Kehoe MJ: Facial pain: Hypnotic suggestion as a method of treatment. Am J Psychiatry 123:1577–1581, 1967

Kelly SF: Hypnotizability and the inadvertent experience of pain. Int J Clin Exp Hypn 28:188–191, 1980

Kleinhauz M, Eli I: Hypnosis and hypno-relaxation in dentistry—ways of treatment, indications, and contraindictions. International Congress of the Israel Society for Hypnosis in Psychotherapy and Psychosomatic Medicine in collaboration with European Society of Hypnosis in Psychotherapy and Psychosomatic Medicine. Haifa, Israel, 1983

Klopp KK: Workshiop presentation, Society for Clinical and Experimental Hypnosis, 27th annual meeting. Chicago, 1975

Kornfeld B: Hypnosis as applied in modern dental practice, in Lippincott's Handbook of Dental Practice (ed 3). Philadelphia, J. B. Lippincott, 1958

Koster S: Two cases of monosymptomatic ptyalism cured with hypnosis. Geneesk Gids 35:305–308, 1957

Kroll RG: Hypnosis for the poor risk dental patient. Am J Clin Hypn 5:142–144, 1962

Kuhner A: Evaluation of hypnosis in dental therapeutics from the dentist's veiwpoint. J Am Soc Psychosom Dent Med 6:9–19, 1959

Lucas ON: Dental extractions in the hemophiliac: Control of the emotional factors by hypnosis. Am J Clin Hypn 7:301–306, 1965

McAmmond DM: A comparison of the effects of hypnosis and relaxation training on stress reactions in a dental situation. Am J Clin Hypn 13:233–242, 1971

McCay AR: Dental extraction under self-hypnosis. Med J Aust 1:820, 1963

Madamba J: The use of hypnosis in dentistry. Personal communication, 1980

Marcus HW: Hypnosis in dentistry, in Schneck JM (ed): Hypnosis in Modern Medicine (ed 3). Springfield, Ill., Charles C Thomas, 1963, pp 229–279

Marcus HW: Psychophysiological considerations in dentistry. NY State Dent J 32:301–304, 1966

Marcus HW, Bowers MK: Hypnosis and schizophrenia in the dental situation: A case report. Int J Clin Exp Hpyn 9:47–52, 1961

Mason AA: Hypnotism for Medical and Dental Practiners. London, Secker and Warburg, 1960

Morse, DR, Wilcko JM: Nonsurgical endodontic therapy for a vital tooth with meditation-hypnosis as the sole anesthetic: A case report. Am J Clin Hypn 21:258–262, 1979

Moss AA: Hypnodontics, in LeCron LM (ed): Experimental Hypnosis. New York, Macmillan, 1956, pp 303–319

Moss AA: Hypnosis for pain management in dentistry. J Dent Med 18:110–112, 1963

Newman M: Hypnotic handling of the chronic bleeder in extraction: A case report. Am J Clin Hypn 14:126–127, 1971

Newman M: Hypnosis and hemophiliacs. J Am Dent Assoc 88:273, 1974

Owens HE: Hypnosis and psychotherapy in dentistry: Five case histories. Int J Clin Exp Hypn 18:181–193, 1970

Pavesi PMA: Ipnosi y psicodoncia (Hypnosis and psychoodonology) Anales Espaneoles Odonto-Estomatologia 22:531–541, 1963

Penzer V: Applied hypnodontics: A case report. Am J Clin Hypn 15:46–48, 1972

Petrov P, Traikov D, Kalendgiev: A contribution to psychoanesthetization through hypnosis in some stomatological manipulations. Br J Med Hypnot 15:8–16, 1964

Raginsky BB: Psychosomatics, pharmacology, premedication, and hypnosis in dentistry. Ann Dent 17:6–19, 1958

Rosen, M: Hypnotic induction and nitrous oxide sedation in children. International Congress of the Israel Society for Hypnosis in Psychotherapy and Psychosomatic Medicine in collaboration with European Society for Hypnosis in Psychotherapy and Psychosomatic Medicine. Haifa, Israel, 1983

Roston GD: Workship presentation, Society for Clinical and Experimental Hypnosis, 27th annual meeting. Chicago, 1975

Sandor L: Hypnotic suggestion: Its dynamics, indication and limitation. Ann Den 20:72–73, 1961

Scott RH: Self-described reactions of a phobic dental patient during treatment. Am J Clin Hypn 10:276–281, 1968

Secter II: Some notes on controlling the exaggerated gag reflex. Am J Clin Hypn 2:149–153, 1960

Secter II: Dental surgery in a psychiatric patient. Am J Clin Hypn 6:363–364, 1964

Secter II: Applied psychology in dentistry. Am J Clin Hypn 8:122–127, 1965

Shaw SI: Clinical Applications of Hypnosis in Dentistry. Philadelphia, Saunders, 1958

Singer RM: Dental psychotherapy. J Can Dent Assoc 26:203–209, 1960

Smith SR: The uses and limitations of hypnosis in children's dentistry. Br Dent J 119:499–501, 1965

Smith SR: The significance of autohypnosis in dentistry. Br J Clin Hypn 1:8–13, 1970

Staples LM: Relaxation through hypnosis, a valuable adjunct to change anesthesia. J Am Dent Soc Anesth, October 1958

Staples L: (Panelist) American Society for Clinical Hypnosis New England Component Section. Boston, Mass., 1979

Steingart G: (Panelist) American Society for Clinical Hypnosis, Dallas, Texas, 1983

Stolzenberg J: Psychosomatics and Suggestion Therapy in Dentistry, New York, Philosophical Library, 1950

Stolzenberg J: Hypnosis in orthodontics. Am J Orthod 45:508–511, 1959

Stolzenberg J: Age regression in the treatment of two instances of dental phobia. Am J Clin Hypn 4:122–123, 1961

Strosberg IM: Hypnosis—living—comfort. J Am Soc Psychosom Dent Med 27:29–32, 1980

Thompson KF: A rationale for suggestion in dentistry. Am J Clin Hypn 5:181–186, 1963

Thompson KF: The case against relaxation, in Burrows GD, Collison DR, Dennerstein L (eds): Hypnosis. Amsterdam Elsevier/North-Holland Biomedical Press, 1979, pp 41–45

Vartikovski R, Zwirn M: (Panelist) Application of the Ericksonian hypnotic approach in dentistry and in hypnodentological training programs. International Congress of the Israel Society of Hypnosis in Psychotherapy and Psychosomatic Medicine in collaboration with European Society of Hypnosis in Psychotherapy and Psychosomatic Medicine. Haifa, Israel, 1983

Weyandt JA: Three case reports in dental hypnotherapy. Am J Clin Hypn 15:49–55, 1972

Wikstrom PO: (Panelist) The use of hypnosis in dentistry. Int Soc Clin Exp Hypn Mtg. Glasgow, Scotland, 1982

Yamauchi KT: Dental fear in a chronic schizophrenic: A case report. Am J Clin Hypn 24:128–131, 1981

Zwirn M, Vartikovski R: Integration of densensitization and indirect hypnotic techniques for the non-cooperative dental patient. International Congress of the Israel Society of Hypnosis in Psychotherapy and Psychosomatic Medicine in collaboration with European Society Hypnosis in Psychotherapy and Psychosomatic Medicine. Haifa, Israel, 1983

20
Precautions in the Use of Hypnosis

Hypnosis is fortunately a powerful tool; but unfortunately it can be learned by virtually anyone who takes the trouble to read enough books and practice induction on unsuspecting friends. Some persons try self-hypnosis, which can also be used inappropriately as a "crutch" (Oetting, 1964). Managing the complications that can arise from hypnosis, however, requires sophisticated understanding of the workings of the mind. A good basic rule to follow if deciding to use hypnosis or not is this—if a person cannot treat a problem with nonhypnotic techniques, he or she should not treat it with hypnosis.

For example, a 15-year-old student hypnotized his 6-year-old sister to remove the pain of her toothache. The pain was absent for several days, but when it returned, she was taken to the family dentist who discovered a worsening abscess. Another patient gave himself the self-hypnotic suggestion that he would be nauseated and would vomit at the smell of cigarette smoke. Although he had only intended to stop himself from smoking, the suggestion generalized so that he vomited also in the presence of anyone else who was smoking. He came for treatment to remove the undesirable effects of his poorly worded self-hypnotic suggestion. A young man seen by us had used self-hypnosis to try to increase his long-distance driving beyond any reasonable level of endurance, causing extreme physical stress. Even the best intentions do not guarantee harmlessness for the untrained person employing hypnosis.

POSSIBLE DANGERS OF HYPNOSIS

It is important to recognize the potential dangers of hypnosis as well as its useful applications (Cheek and LeCron, 1968; Scott, 1969). West and Deckert (1965) divide the dangers into four categories— dangers to the subject (patient), dangers to the operator, dangers to medicine, and dangers to hypnosis itself. Dangers to the patient include:

1. The possibility of precipitating a psychiatric illness, such as dissociative neurosis, schizophrenia, paranoid states, and homosexual panics.
2. The danger of making an existing disorder worse, particularly by indiscriminate removal of symptoms that may then recur.
3. The danger of causing regression.
4. The danger of prolonging treatment in patients with passive-dependent and hysterical character disorder.
5. The danger of masking illness.
6. The danger of superficial relief.
7. The danger of excessive dependence.
8. The danger of fantasied seduction.
9. The danger of criminal activity.

All of these dangers can be eliminated or modified by proper screening and the use of hypnosis only by trained persons aware of the complexity of psychological symptoms.

In speaking of dangers to the operator, West and Deckert (1965) cite grandiosity, narrowing one's practice to hypnosis alone, and the danger of psychopathological disturbances in the operator, citing one amateur hypnotist who became obsessed with supposed telepathy experiences. As dangers to medicine they report the dangers of failures when hypnosis is used inappropriately, which may lead to failure to use it when it is indicated; the danger of success leading to hypnosis being oversold, with disappointments as to its realistic limitations; and the danger of untrained "hypnotists" being given the status of de facto psychotherapists to the discredit of psychiatry and psychology as specialities and to medicine as a profession. The dangers to hypnosis itself are the lingering aura of criticism that may be attributed by some to anyone using hypnosis, and the danger of cultism.

McCartney (1961) in discussing his half-century of personal experience with hypnosis concluded, "I have become increasingly convinced of its [hypnosis'] therapeutic value, when properly used, and of its potential destructiveness when misused. It should be put under legal restrictions and scientific control, and only qualified persons should be allowed to apply the technique." Nesbitt (1964) considered the general physician to be competent to use hypnosis, though he stressed that physicians should carefully evaluate their own motives for choosing hypnosis as a treatment method. Tyson (1962) called hypnosis a "calculated risk;" however, he proposed its use in spite of some dangers. Shaw (1961) referred to hypnosis metaphorically as "the mental hypodermic" and considered it to be a valuable dental instrument when properly used. Rosen (1961), however, has expressed the opinion that hypnosis "must be considered a specialized psychiatric procedure regardless of the purpose for which it is used."

Many authorities, among them Conn (1959, 1972) and Friedman (1961), find that there is no danger specifically unique to hypnosis. Instead, the dangers of hypnosis are the dangers that accompany every psychotherapeutic relationship, notably the dangers of transference and countertransference, which are discussed later in this chapter. Among the causes of difficulties with hypnosis are ignorance, overzealousness, lack of understanding of the basis of interpersonal relationships, and irresponsible use of hypnosis for entertainment (Kost, 1965).

Much of the past criticism of hypnosis has come as a result of those rare and unqualified "hypnotists" who indiscriminately remove neurotic symptoms that have strong psychodynamic meanings (Gherardi, 1967). For example, if a nondrinking alcoholic is treated with hypnosis for a smoking addiction without simultaneously handling in a psychotherapeutic manner his or her desire to drink, it is possible that a recurrence of a serious drinking problem may be an undesirable result. Similarly, if pain of organic origin is suppressed with hypnosis, the diagnostic picture may be obscured, a situation that could well lead to the physician being unaware of signs or symptoms that could cause early detection and cure of an otherwise serious condition. If the therapist is well trained, however, even resistances may be put to psychotherapeutic use to benefit lives (Schneck, 1953).

Another inherent safeguard is the ability of the patient to leave treatment or to refuse to enter hypnotic state even though undergoing the induction procedure. The patient with excessive defenses will usually prove to be unhypnotizable.

Some dangers may arise in the treatment of organic conditions by hypnosis if the hypnotherapist is unaware of the complexities of the patients' condition or if there is inadequate communication with other physicians who are in charge of specialized areas of treatment. An example of this difficulty, discussed more fully in the chapter on surgery, is the induction of hypnoanesthesia in a burned extremity for purposes of skin debridement. If the anesthesia is not clearly limited to the time of removal of burned tissue, it may allow the patient to use the arm in an abrasive way, adding to the injury.

A female medical student developed marked anxiety around her study schedule. She had previously, in high school, been treated briefly with hypnosis. No cause for her anxiety appeared in the ordinary clinical history, but under hypnotic age regression she vividly recalled her previous treatment, when a school psychologist had given her a strong posthypnotic suggestion that if she did not study immediately after school she would feel nauseated and ill. With the release of this memory, she was able to recall having seen the school psychologist at a recent social event, which seems to have reawakened, at an unconscious level, his previous suggestion to her.

Untoward reactions to stage hypnosis have been noted (Kleinhauz et al., 1979, 1983), apparently through the resurrection of unsuspected traumatic feelings from the past. Adverse reactions to hypnosis in a usually benign situation of weight loss in adolescents included dissociated state, depersonalization, anxiety and fear, disappointment, and a sense of failure for not entering a deep state of hypnosis (Haber, Nitkin, and Shenker, 1979).

SCREENING TO DETERMINE ACCEPTABILITY FOR HYPNOSIS

As early as 1958 we advocated a distinction between dynamically important symptoms and what we termed *empty habits*—that is, habits that are relatively free of overdetermined unconscious meanings. If smoking is found to be an empty habit, it may be hypnotically suppressed with relative safety from substitute symptoms (Kroger, 1963; Mann, 1961a; Sacerdote, 1962). If, however smoking has a psychodynamic meaning—as with a smoker who has an acknowledged death wish—it must be treated as part of a larger personality problem. Hypnosis or hypnoanalysis might still be used to attack the smoking compulsion, particularly if there were a life-threatening organic condition aggravated by continued smoking. But it would be used as part of an overall treatment approach, including adequate exploration of the conflicts involved. It is important that the therapist not expect (and therefore tacitly suggest) the occurrence of substitute symptoms (Spiegel, 1967). We have consistently adhered to a policy of having at least one screening interview, whether by the hypnotherapist or by a colleague, before a patient is accepted for hypnotherapy. Patients with active suicidal tendencies are not hypnotized until the suicide tendency has been explored and eliminated. Psychotics are screened out, though a rare exception to this rule would be for investigative purposes. In an unpublished study one schizophrenic was regressed in age with hypnosis to a time before the psychotic symptoms first appeared. She showed marked improvement under the regressed condition. Bowers (1960) has presented a similar case and has films of the patient during the procedure.

Also eliminated in the screening procedure are those patients who are inappropriately asking for hypnosis when their difficulties are so pervasive that a wide-ranging psychotherapeutic exploration is indicated. Such patients are usually accepted only when they agree to a wider treatment by psychotherapy, perhaps with hypnoanalysis. Occasionally, they may refuse treatment on such realistic terms. In some cases, however, the patient can be cautiously treated for the presenting symptom by a hypnotic suppression technique, leaving the wider personality problem untouched. Sometimes this success in controlling a limited conflict, as in giving up cigarette smoking, builds confidence and ego strength, which may then encourage the patient to undertake a deeper reconstructive therapy.

QUALIFIED HYPNOTHERAPISTS

A very clear danger of hypnosis is its use by unqualified practitioners for trivial purposes. Several years ago we had an emergency call in the middle of the night from a local hospital. A young college student was continually scratching himself without being able to stop. Hypnotic age regression revealed that he had indeed been hypnotized that very night by a performer at a fraternity stag party, who had told him to imagine that red ants were crawling all over his body. The suggestion had not been removed. When we removed the suggestion under hypnosis in the emergency room, and he was made conscious of the memory, he quickly lost the pruritic symptoms but developed homicidal anger at the amateur hypnotist. He was given the additional suggestion that he would remain calm and that we would be able to help him understand his angry impulses. It was necessary for him to remain in therapy for an extended time to overcome the stresses released by this irresponsible use of hypnosis.

Dangers may arise in clinical use of hypnosis if it is employed by a therapist untrained in the complexities of psychological response. Although the basic techniques of induction may be acquired by anyone, its skillful use requires supervised training usually acquired in a formal program taught by dentists, psychologists, or physicians. It is essential for the therapist to be aware of the many forms of resistance, of transference, and of countertransference.

In psychological terms "resistance" refers to forces in the patient's unconscious mind that interfere with the patient seeing himself or herself, his or her relations, and his or her symptoms in a realistic way. Resistance may lead to maintaining symptoms or feelings that interfere with the patient leading a creative and open life. Severe resistance may be a contraindication to hypnotherapy (Meldman, 1961). In the therapeutic situation resistances often cause the patient to see the therapist in a distorted "transference" way. If positive, transference will enhance the therapist in a patient's mind, even elevating him or her to almost godlike status. If negative, the opposite may occur, the therapist being seen as the source of all the patient's difficulties. Both extremes of transference distortion deny the uniquely human, real person of the therapist.

While some degree of positive feeling for the therapist is essential in hypnotherapy (Crasilneck, 1980), as it is in any professional relationship, the untrained or inadequately trained therapist may be overwhelmed by the patient's positive feeling or excessively bothered by negative transference. Such excessive responses on the part of the therapist to the patient's transference are technically called "countertransference."

Transference and countertransference which are the classical problems of psychotherapy, may be heightened in hypnotherapy (Orne, 1965). Much of the formal training in the therapeutic disciplines of psychiatry and psychology is directed toward making the future therapist aware of their pitfalls (Crasilneck, 1980). The positive aspects are less frequently emphasized, but they are equally important, accounting for much of the traditional "art" of medicine or the subtle effects of a "good bedside manner." Such effects are of some importance, even in organic illness. It has been shown, for example, that the hypnotically induced attitude of resistance or of vulnerability to injury can create a measurable difference in the actual response to real injury.

Frequent indicators of resistance, or of transference phenomena, are encountered during hypnosis. The patient may smile or laugh or make movements of the body in clear contrast to the suggestions to relax and "sleep." An insecure hypnotherapist may take such resistances as an affront to his or her ability, creating immediate countertransference problems. Such resistance should simply be investigated. They often indicate anxiety in the patient. At times they may follow an unrecognized ambiguity in the hypnotic suggestions given.

Much of the discussion about the possibility of inducing, with hypnosis, antisocial acts that the subject would not perform in his or her ordinary waking state derive from a myth of the hypnotized person being dependent on the therapist. This danger is exaggerated (Mann, 1961b). Hypnosis is actually more a cooperative interaction between two persons, one of whom (the subject) allows himself or herself to experience the situation in terms chosen with the subject's own permission by the therapist. Any attempt of the hypnotherapist to misuse the situation usually breaks the implied contract, allowing the subject to terminate trance spontaneously.

Many writers have discussed the possibility of the hypnotic production of antisocial acts (Levendula, 1962). Milgram (1963) arranged an experimental situation in which subjects were asked, in hypnosis, to administer electrical shocks to another subject, who in actuality was a confederate of the experimenter. While 26 subjects obeyed the experimental demands, 14 others broke off the experiment. Barber (1961) reviewing this question of antisocial acts concluded that the concept of trance and hypnosis had a limited role in the production of antisocial acts, citing attitudinal set and social pressures as also important.

While admitting some possibility of influencing antisocial behavior, Watkins, in an insightful essay (1972), felt that the widespread belief in the impossibility of inducing antisocial behavior under hypnosis actually was of protective value since operators are seldom successful in inducing phenomena in which they themselves do not believe.

ANTISOCIAL ASPECTS OF HYPNOSIS

According to Orne (1972), the antisocial aspects of hypnosis are difficult to address experimentally. Both the affirmative and negative positions, as the question is usually asked, are not open to empirical refutation. If the subject does not carry out the suggested antisocial actions, this can be seen as insufficient depth of hypnosis. If the subject does carry out the acts considered antisocial, it is possible to argue that he or she would have done so in any case, with or without hypnosis.

Erickson (1962) has suggested that it is possible that subjects in some of the experiments on antisocial behavior may be responding to cues that are not taken into account by the experimenters. Citing a previous experiment by Rowland (1939), in which hypnotized subjects would be willing to reach for a live rattlesnake, Erickson hypothesized that the subjects may have been aware of the presence of a protective glass that was supposed to be invisible.

The one clear example of hypnosis being considered in a court of law as the cause of antisocial acts is discussed by Reiter (1958). It was a case tried in 1954 in Copenhagen Central Criminal Court, the accused being charged with several bank robberies and with manslaughter. It was alleged in defense that the crimes were really planned by another person who had used hypnosis to induce the defendant to commit them. It is important to note, however, that the supposed hypnotic influence (which was never admitted by the person alleged to have used hypnosis) took place repeatedly over a period of 18 months, and during this time there were many other nonhypnotic influences exerted by the hypnotist over the defendant. Reiter cites only three documented cases in which actual criminal behavior was found to involve hypnotic suggestion, but in all of these Orne (1960) felt that there may have been alternative explanations other than hypnosis. In discussing complications of hypnosis Orne (1965) makes a clear distinction between laboratory uses and those of a clinical nature, where the attempt is to induce more permanent personality change, a distinction that we ourselves have stressed. Blatt, Goodman, and Wallington (1969) emphasized that differences in the effectiveness of hypnosis in clinical and research settings may have some correlation with the therapist's ability to participate subjectively in some of the experiences of the subject.

The ability of a hypnotized subject to control his or her response to polygraph testing was investigated by Weinstein, Abrams, and Gibbons (1970). They hypnotically suppressed information in 6 experimental subjects who were then tested for truthfulness by the "lie detector." They concluded that an individual who has committed a crime may repress the experience sufficiently to pass a polygraph test, while someone who is nervous for other reasons may appear guilty in his or her responses to the machine. Therefore, the polygraph is not foolproof in determining if a person is giving true or false answers.

The frequently quoted arguments about the possibility or impossibility of inducing antisocial behavior in a hypnotic subject are of little force when hypnosis is used by ethical and trained persons. It is our opinion that hypnosis could be used to induce behavior that would be considered antisocial by the subject in his or her ordinary waking state, but only if such antisocial tendencies existed in the patient's unconscious mind and were made compatible with his or her usual conscience; as, for example, having the subject hallucinate in a compulsive somnambulistic state that an ordinary person was actually an evil and dangerous enemy. The schools of psychoanalysis differ greatly in the weight that they assign to such unconscious tendencies, and there is by no means a consensus that all persons have a basic antisocial preponderance in the deeper layers of their unconscious minds. In

Medical Hypnosis, Wolberg (1948) cautions the therapist to be alert for any sign of countertransference feelings in himself or herself, since these feelings may be unconsciously perceived by the subject and may inappropriately influence his or her behavior.

Failures with Hypnosis

There are failures with hypnosis, of course, and the reaction of the individual patient cannot be predicted with accuracy before a therapeutic trial of hypnotherapy. These are the same problems that befall the practice of psychotherapy, however (Altshuler, 1983). Regardless of the therapist's capabilities or the patient's conscious motivation, failures are inevitably encountered. Most of the time the causes are: (1) therapist failure, which may be due to poor hypnotic technique, to inappropriate therapeutic strategies (Hall, 1984), inadequate therapeutic judgment, improper screening of the patient (Crasilneck, 1980), or negative transference; (2) patient failure, which may be due to lack of unconscious motivation, an inability to relinquish neurotic symptoms, unconscious aggression towards the therapeutic milieu, or extreme masochism that interferes with therapy.

At times failures may be caused by a negative interaction between patient and therapist (Lazar and Dempster, 1981). Gruenewald (1981) cautions that failures in hypnotherapy must be considered in the context of failure in psychotherapeutic treatment in general. Hypnotherapy must be structured with regard for the patient's own priorities and needs, both conscious and unconscious.

CONCLUSION

When discussing the dangers of hypnosis, it is only appropriate to mention certain safeguards inherent in the clinical situation.

With adequate screening procedures and when used by trained therapists, the dangers of hypnosis seem rather less than some suggest from reports of isolated cases.

The fear that a hypnotized neurotic might find himself or herself experiencing a psychotic break seems applicable only to "psedoneurotic" schizophrenics. If an ordinarily neurotic person could be made psychotic, with hypnosis, by a direct suggestion that he or she would relinquish his or her neurotic symptoms, the finding would be of immense theoretical importance. It would support the position that neurosis and psychosis are different points on a common continuum rather than relatively discrete processes. To our knowledge, such an experiment has never been undertaken.

In summary we can state that hypnosis is a relatively safe procedure when used in a clinical setting by competently trained therapists, working with the subject's full conscious consent, for an agreed purpose, in order to aid the patient.

REFERENCES

Altshuler KZ: Hypnotherapy and the field of psychotherapy. American Society for Clinical Hypnosis, Annual Meeting. Dallas, Texas 1983

Barber TX: Antisocial and criminal acts induced by hypnosis. Arch Gen Psychiatry 5:301–302, 1961

Blatt SJ, Goodman JT, Wallington SA: Is the hypnotist also being hypnotized?. Int J Clin Exp Hypn 17:160–166, 1969

Bowers M: Discussion, annual meeting of the Society for Clinical and Experimental Hypnosis, 1960

Cheek, DB, LeCron LM: Clinical Hypnotherapy. New York, Grune & Stratton, 1968

Conn JH: Cultural and clinical aspects of hypnosis, placebos and suggestability. Int J Clin Exp Hypn 7:175–185, 1959

Conn JH: Is hypnosis really dangerous? Int J Clin Exp Hypn 20:61–76, 1971

Crasilneck HB: Clinical assessment and preparation of the patient, in Burrows GD, Dennerstein L (eds): Handbook of Hypnosis and Psychosomatic Medicine. Amsterdam, Elsevier/North Holland Biomedical Press, 1980, pp 105–118

Erickson MH: Observations concerning alterations in hypnosis of visual perceptions. Am J Clin Hypn 5:131–134, 1962

Friedman JJ: Psychodynamics in hypnosis failures. Psychosomatics 2:1–3, 1961

Gherardi D: Un caso di dislalia brevemente risoltosi con ipnosi (A case of dyslalia rapidly cured by hypnosis). Riv Psichiatria 2:550–556, 1967

Gruenewald D: Failures in hypnotherapy: A brief communication. Int J Clin Exp Hypn 29:345–350, 1981

Haber CH, Nitkin R, Shenker IR: Adverse reactions to hypnotherapy in obese adolescents: A developmental viewpoint. Psychiatr Q. 51:55–63, 1979

Hall JA: (Panelist) Clinical hypnosis. American Group Psychotherapy Association, Dallas, Texas 1984

Kleinhauz M, Dreyfuss DA, Beran B, Goldberg T, Azikri D: Some after-effects of stage hypnosis: A case study of psychopathological manifestations. Int J Clin Exp Hypn 27:219–226, 1979

Kleinhauz M, Beran B: (Panelists) Potential complications following the misuse of hypnosis. International Congress of the Israel Society Hypnosis in Psychotherapy and Psychosomatic Medicine in collaboration with European Society for Hypnosis in Psychotherapy and Psychosomatic Medicine. Haifa, Israel, 1983

Kost, PF: Dangers of hypnosis. Int J Clin Exp Hypn 13:220–225, 1965

Kroger WS: An analysis of valid and invalid objections to hypnotherapy. Am J Clin Hypn 6:120–131, 1963

Lazar BS, Dempster CR: Failures in hypnosis and hypnotherapy: A review. Am J Clin Hypn 24:48–54, 1981

Levendula D: Hypnosis in criminal investigation. Forensic Med 31:24–30, 1962

McCartney JL: A half century of personal experience with hypnosis. Int J Clin Exp Hypn 9:23–33, 1961

Mann H: Hypnotherapy in habit disorders. Am J Clin Hypn 3:123–126, 1961a

Mann H: Hypnosis: An analysis of unfounded criticisms. Am J Clin Hypn 4:98–101, 1961b

Meldman MJ: Hypnosis is not entirely innocuous. Anesth Analg 40:75–76, 1961

Milgram S: Behavioral study of obedience. J Abnorm Soc Psychol 4:371–378, 1963

Nesbitt WR: The dangers of hypnotherapy. Med Times 7:597–602, 1964

Oetting ER: Hypnosis and concentration in study. Am J Clin Hypnosis 7:148–151, 1964

Orne MT: Antisocial or criminal acts and hypnosis: A case study. Int J Clin Exp Hypn 8:131–134, 1960

Orne MT: Undesirable effects of hypnosis: The determinants and management. Int J Clin Exp Hypn 13:226–237, 1965

Orne MT: Can a hypnotized subject be compelled to carry out otherwise unacceptable behavior? Int J Clin Exp Hypn 20:101–117, 1972

Reiter PJ: Antisocial or Criminal Acts and Hypnosis: A Case Study. Springfield, Ill., Charles C Thomas, 1958

Rosen H: The present status of hypnosis in office medical practice. Med Clin North Am 45:1685–1691, 1961

Rowland LW: Will hypnotized persons try to harm themselves or others? J Abnorm Soc Psychol 34:114–117, 1939

Sacerdote P: The place of hypnosis in the relief of severe protracted pain. Am J Clin Hypn 4:150–157, 1962

Schneck JM: Psychogenic gastrointestinal disorder and cephalalgia with paradoxical reactions to hypnosis. J Nerv Ment Dis 117:130–134, 1953

Scott DL: The complications and dangers of hypnotherapy. Br J Clin Hypn 1:3–10, 1969

Shaw SI: The dangers of hypnosis (the mental hypodermic) as applied to dentistry. Int J Clin Exp Hypn 9:53–57, 1961

Spiegel H: Is symptom removal dangerous? Am J Psychiatry 123:10, 1967

Tyson DB: The calculated risk. Am J Clin Hypn 5:47–51, 1962

Watkins JG: Antisocial behavior under hypnosis: Possible or impossible? Int J Clin Exp Hypn 20:95–100, 1972

Weinstein E, Abrams S, Gibbons D: The validity of the polygraph with hypnotically induced repression and guilt. Am J Psychiatry 126:143–146, 1970

West LJ, Deckert G: Dangers of hypnosis. JAMA 192:9–12, 1965

Wolberg LR: Medical Hypnosis, vol 1, Principles of Hypnotherapy. New York, Grune & Stratton, 1948

21
Self-Hypnosis

"Essentially all hypnosis is self-hypnosis" according to Cheek and LeCron (1968). Self-hypnosis is an ability to enter voluntarily (at one's own suggestion) a state of hypnotic trance. Its aim, according to Wolberg (1948), is "to convince the patient that there is nothing magical about hypnosis" and "to reinforce indefinitely the chosen hypnotic suggestion." Wolberg refers to self-hypnosis as "an actual trance induced by the patient as a result of posthypnotic suggestions given him by the physician." The depth of self-hypnosis may vary from hypnoidal to somnambulistic; however, the majority of people seem unable to achieve as great a degree of depth of self-hypnosis as in heterohypnosis. Unless the self-induction contains specific suggestions not to enter a state of sleep or to return to the hypnosis state should one fall asleep, the person employing self-hypnosis is likely to pass easily into a state of natural sleep. This, of course, presents no danger, but it may interfere with the purposes intended.

There are frequent spontaneous episodes of self-hypnosis, but they are not usually recognized as hypnotic. "Highway hypnosis," for example, is a state of trance induced by the repeated monotony of long hours in driving an automobile. Monotonous scenery may contribute to that state, while activities—chewing gum, changing radio stations, changing seating position, periodic rest stops—tend to prevent this dangerous state. Others have reported similar states of trance when in the presence of a continuously blinking signal light on a moving vehicle of any kind. A number of years ago, this observation led us to suggest to a safety engineer that other, more varied signal devices be employed.

In addition to the drowsy trance states of highway hypnosis, there are other relaxed, lethargic but not sleepy states that are similar to the feeling induced by self-hypnosis. Most people who drive automobiles have, at one time or another, had the remarkable experience of having driven to a destination but not having been aware in memory of any of the aspects of the trip. It is as if the mind were put on "automatic pilot," carrying out its assignment without creating any memorable ripples in consciousness.

In any chronic condition, such as obesity, pain, or cigarette addiction, in our practice we routinely teach self-hypnosis and suggest that the patient practice it daily between office visits. Others also use it for particular situations. For example, Kroger and Freed (1956) and Schneck (1952) have used self-hypnosis extensively in preparing obstetrical patients for delivery under hypnoanalgesia.

In a typical obesity case, the instructions in self-hypnosis may be given after the first several inductions of hetero-hypnosis. Self-hypnosis instructions initially are given while the patient is in hypnosis induced by the therapist. As the instructions for self-hypnosis are given, the patient is instructed to think them through as the therapist says them out loud. Later, the patient repeats the words of the induction in the presence of the therapist before initiating self-hypnosis alone. Sentences are phrased as if the patient himself were saying them. For example,

> I am lying here with my eyes closed, ruling out all other thoughts and feelings. I am now concentrating on my right hand, which is resting comfortably on my abdomen. . . . I am concentrating on the breathing of my abdomen, on the sensitivity of the fingers in my right hand . . . to the texture of the material in my clothing . . . my hand rises and falls with every breath I take . . . and I am beginning to enter a much deeper state. . . I am relaxed, free from tension, free from psychological stress and strain . . . every muscle, every fiber in my body is relaxing . . . from my head, shoulders, arms, torso, legs, feet, toes. . . . My breathing is comfortable and with every breath I take I am entering a much deeper, a much more relaxed state. . . . Now my right leg feels heavy . . . as I feel it, normal sensation returns to my right leg . . . a deeper and sounder state . . . my right arm becomes tense and rigid like steel . . . one, two, three . . . steel . . . this passes. . . . As I slowly count from 1 to 10, which I now start doing, I will progressively enter into the deepest state possible so that I can accept into my unconscious mind and put into effect with my unconscious mind these suggestions—food intake is no longer of great importance to me. . . . I will no longer overeat as I once did, in a hurried, forceful fashion. . . . I will eat extremely slowly, frequently pausing while I eat, respecting my body

rather than gorging it with food . . . the loss of weight will have much more meaning to me than being grossly obese . . . and I am never going to be fat again! . . . I am going to respect my body, and I will not be excessively hungry. . . . I will enjoy eating, but I will not exceed the caloric count prescribed for me. . . . I am so very relaxed, and I am going to know a peace of mind in achieving this weight loss. . . . This weight loss will be permanent. . . . I will maintain my diet in my home and social situations under any conditions because I want to. . . . Now as I slowly count from ten to one I am slowly going to be awakened. . . . I am going to be refreshed, my thoughts will not be obsessed with food or food intake . . . but instead, I will be pleased with every pound that I lose. . . . I am now counting slowly, I am awakening, and I am fully awake at the count of one.

Some persons worry that they may not be able to awaken from a self-induced state of hypnosis. This thought should cause no concern. Discussion with the therapist in such instances often reveals an unexpressed desire for longer periods of relaxation, or may uncover fantasies of passivity that have psychodynamic meaning.

Reinforcement with self-hypnosis is routinely taught in pain problems and other organic difficulties. This allows the patient to reinforce the hypnotic suggestions whenever necessary.

A 53-year-old man was referred for pain associated with cancer of the prostate. After he had shown an ability to obtain significant pain relief with hypnotherapy, self-hypnosis was discussed with him. The procedure followed in teaching him to induce hypnosis in himself was as follows: (1) first a hypnotic state was induced in the usual fashion, the therapist speaking and the patient responding; (2) the patient than was instructed to repeat silently in his own mind each phrase or sentence that was said to him, and (3) to signal by a small movement of a designated finger when he had completed saying the words to himself. He was then told to use the following phrases—or similar ones of his own wording—on inducing self-hypnosis, raising the finger in precisely the same manner as if he were signaling the therapist. The suggestions were of this form:

As I lie in my bed I am going to do all in my power to help myself recover from this illness. . . . I can control most of my discomfort, and I can be very relaxed . . . and now I will begin to concentrate my thinking on the breathing of my abdomen and the texture of the material that my right hand is touching . . . and as I am concentrating my thoughts on the fingertips of my right hand, I slowly raise the forefinger. . . . The increased awareness of the right hand now passes and the forefinger returns to normal position as I enter a deeper and much sounder stage of relaxation. . . . I am becoming free from muscular tension and free from stress and strain. . . . my right leg now begins to feel a little heavy. . . . I am becoming aware of some heaviness in my right leg . . .

some muscular heaviness . . . and as I am aware of this I raise the forefinger of my right hand. . . . I now feel the heaviness and raise and lower my finger. . . . This heaviness now passes, with normal sensation returning to my right hand, and I enter a deeper state, with every muscle in my body beginning to relax. . . . I am becoming extremely relaxed . . . my body, my mind . . . I am relaxed . . . I am becoming free from tension and discomfort. . . . I am having much less discomfort. . . . Now my right hand and fingertips will become rigid . . . very rigid for the moment only . . . extended and rigid, like steel . . . my hand from the wrist to the fingers feels like a board that has been soaked in water for days, very rigid, very tense. . . . This now passes and my fingers become very relaxed . . . and the relaxation spreads throughout my whole body . . . and I enter a deeper state. . . . I am becoming free from tension and strain . . . the discomfort is less and I signal this by moving the forefinger of my right hand.

Now I am aware of a slight itching sensation on the right side of my face, like perhaps a feather lightly touching my cheek . . . as I am aware of this I move the right side of my face. . . . I move the forefinger of my right hand to signify that I am feeling this and the sensation now leaves and I enter one of the deepest states possible . . . my pain is now greatly reduced and I am extremely relaxed. . . . I now am becoming aware of a nice pleasant aroma of perfume that smells good. . . . I breathe in the aroma, and as I am aware of this I so signify by moving the forefinger of the right hand . . . my finger moves because I can smell the fragrance. . . . Now the aroma vanishes and my smell returns to normal and I enter the deepest level of hypnosis possible . . . my pain and my discomfort are virtually gone. . . . I am so relaxed . . . every muscle fiber just extremely and totally relaxed.

And I know that I can consume all the foods given me, which will give me strength. . . . I will follow the treatment prescribed, knowing that I can improve and benefit maximally from the treatments. . . . I will sleep well, and because of the power of my unconscious mind the majority of discomfort will be controlled and I will gain in strength, free from tension, free from tightness, free from the majority of the discomfort. . . .

As I slowly count from ten to one I will gradually awaken from self-hypnosis, relaxed and refreshed, with the knowledge that I am doing all in my power to get well.

A vast and important use of self-hypnosis is in treating cigarette addicts. The person wishing to stop smoking is instructed to sit in a comfortable chair and to think the following suggestions:

With my body relaxed and my mind at ease I can enter a state of deep relaxation where I will be free of tension, tightness, stress, and strain, and as I slowly take ten breaths, I will progressively go into a very deep level of trance, where I will recall the suggestions I have been given about my new and deep desire to avoid the use of cigarettes, which I have decided are against the helpful functioning of my body. . . . Now I am in this depth, and I give myself the suggestions that I will never smoke cigarettes again. . . . no longer insulting my body through interfering with the functioning of my heart, my lungs, and I will no longer systematically destroy my body with this unnecessary habit of smoking. . . . In giving up this habit, my breathing will return to normal. . . . The functioning of my vital organs will be healthy and I am going to be free from excessive craving for this vicious and dangerous habit. . . . If I should see others smoke, it will not disturb me . . . nor will I gain an undue amount of weight. . . . I will not be excessively hungry. . . . I simply will stop smoking, free from tension and tightness and stress and strain, relaxed and at ease . . . my mind relaxed and my body relaxed. . . . I will not be excessively nervous or tense. . . . As I slowly count from ten to one I will fully awake, feeling refreshed and relaxed.

One of the greatest advantages of self-hypnosis is its strengthening the patient's sense of self-reliance and self-control, countering any fears and fantasies about the supposed control by the therapist. This may be of great aid, for example, in childbirth.

Many have considered self-hypnosis to be closely related to *autogenic training* (Geissman, 1962), a series of exercises (such as producing heaviness or warmth in parts of the body) developed at the Berlin Institute by the brain physiologist Oskar Vogt between 1890 and 1900. Autogenic therapy has been popularized in the English-speaking world through the writings of Luthe and Schultz (1969a,b,c) and of Luthe (1970a,b; 1973).

Self-hypnosis is best taught by a therapist, for he or she can assess the subject's stability and caution against potentially harmful overuse of the techniques. Weitzenhoffer (1957) suggests to the patient "While you are in this state, I am going to turn over to you the control of yourself so that you may experience that it is possible for you to control this state of hypnosis by giving yourself the same suggestions that I have been giving you." A definite time for this experience is mentioned (usually a few mintues), and a clear cue is given to the therapist reassuming his or her role in giving hypnotic suggestions.

After this initial experience the patient is told that upon awakening from hypnosis he or she will be able to induce much the same state of mind by giving himself or herself the same or similar suggestions, both for relaxation and hypnotic induction and for improvement of the condition to be treated. Usually, the patient is told that he or she can use self-hypnosis as often as needed for the symptom to be treated. However, it should be clearly specified that certain precautions must be observed. Thus, if it is a pain problem, not all pain is to be removed, even if possible, since some pain should be preserved as a warning sign of any change in the organic condition. In our practice the person is also instructed to follow the pattern of suggestion demonstrated in the training sessions and not to employ self-hypnosis for other purposes that have not been agreed upon.

We have encountered no age restrictions for self-hypnosis, finding it of use in children as well as adults and the elderly. Although a quiet room is helpful for the self-hypnotic induction, it is by no means a requirement, and some persons can induce self-hypnosis amid the excitement of a sports event if they wish.

If reasonably employed, there are few dangers to self-hypnosis. Some unstable persons should not be taught this technique, for they may become psychologically addicted to the relaxed trance state, using it too frequently or in such inappropriate situations that it interferes with daily life. This rarely happens, however. Some neurotic individuals also may be tempted to manipulate their motivation through self-hypnosis rather than face and overcome problems that can be realistically solved. Usually the self-correcting forces of the mind prevent such an overuse, but if self-hypnosis is pushed to an extreme, the corrections may be equally extreme—as marked anxiety or depression.

Some people also see self-hypnosis as a panacea, and this is not proper. It should be employed only for a specific purpose previously agreed only by the therapist and the patient. For example, a woman coming for obesity who uses self-hypnosis should not give herself such suggestions as "I will never argue with my husband." Such attempts to basically alter the personality or the interaction with significant other people requires a psychotherapeutic approach.

We have seen many examples of inappropriate requests for the use of self-hypnosis and have declined to teach the technique in each instance. An attorney once asked for instruction in self-hypnosis so that he could train himself to sleep only 3 hours a night. This was not done. A student of mediocre intellectual ability wished self-hypnosis to help him make straight As; this also was declined. A professional athlete, bent on a successful career, wished to learn self-hypnosis to avoid feeling any pain during the games. This was explained to him as a dangerous procedure since serious permanent injury could result, and he agreed not to use self-hypnosis for that purpose. One obese patient wished her self-hypnosis instructions to specify no more than 300 calories daily, but we felt this was too stringent and unnecessary. Some persons attempt to manipulate their own consciousness with self-hypnosis, a goal that is not only unlikely to succeed but potentially dangerous psychologically. Such an instance was the man who requested self-hypnosis training so that he "could have an affair without guilt." He was treated instead by psychotherapy, not employing hypnosis, until he could more easily understand and accept his complicated and mixed motives.

An entire issue of the *International Journal of Clinical and Experimental Hypnosis* volume 29, number 3, July 1981 was devoted to the subject of self-hypnosis. Alman (1983) has published a handbook of self-hypnosis for individual use as well as a guide for therapists.

Self-hypnosis has been used to diminish pain, in treating psychogenic dysphonia (Horsley, 1982), in treating severe posttraumatic contractures of the hand (Spiegel and Chase, 1980), as an aid in facilitating mourning (Fromm and Eisen, 1982), for anxiety reduction (Davidson, Farnbach, and Richardson, 1978; Ringrose, 1983), hypertension (Case, Fogel, and Pollack, 1980), tinnitus (Brattberg, 1983), and as an aid in the management of hemophilia (LaBaw, 1980).

Unestahl (1983) in a study in the Swedish schools, found that self-hypnosis was an important aid in training athletes and artists, as well as in aiding cancer patients. Soskis (1983) found self-hypnosis of help in a wide range of problems, including management and symptoms of anxiety, tension, and pain. Penzer (1983) describes how autohypnosis may appear spontaneously under stressful conditions; it appears to be an innate coping mechanism in some persons. In a study of self-hypnosis and biofeedback, Dikel and Olness (1980) suggested a synergestic effect between hypnosis and biofeedback.

Self-hypnosis and Hetero-hypnosis

It is interesting to speculate about what is the primary phenomenon: self-hypnosis (autohypnosis) or the ordinary image of hypnosis—hetero-hypnosis—in which there is a relatively active "hypnotherapist" and a relatively inactive patient. Ruch (1975) found that "untrained self-hypnosis was as effective as hetero-hypnosis." He suggests a reconceptualization in which active self-hypnosis is the primary phenomenon; hetero-hypnosis is really guided self-hypnosis, and a hypnotherapist may be either helpful or inhibitory in achieving hypnotic trance. Ruch also suggests that conventional hetero-hypnosis seemed to inhibit later self-hypnosis, while an initial experience of self-hypnosis appeared to enhance subsequent hetero-hypnosis. Johnson (1979) in an exploratory study found no difference in the effectiveness of hetero-hypnosis and autohypnosis.

Garver (in press) had divided self-hypnosis into eight stages: (1) plan the suggestion before trance is induced (it should be positive); (2) an entry cue, (3) neutral imagery, (4) a shift into suggestive imagery, (5) a shift back to neutral imagery, (6) re-orient, (7) posthypnotic sugges-

tion, and (8) exit cue. He clearly appreciates the role of the hypnotherapist in providing clear indications to the subject of when to enter
and when to leave the trance state.

SUMMARY

Self-hypnosis is most properly taught during a trance induced by
the therapist. The motives for using self-hypnosis must be thoroughly
examined to reassure the therapist that the patient does not entertain
unrealistic expectations. With these safeguards, self-hypnosis is an
important adjunct to hypnotherapy, particularly in such recurrent clinical problems as smoking, obesity, pain, asthma, and in the problems of
impotency and frigidity.

REFERENCES

Alman BM: Self-Hypnosis. San Diego, Calif., International Health Publications, 1983
Brattberg G: An alternative method of treating tinnitus: Relaxation-hypnotherapy pri-
    marily through the home use of recorded audio-cassette. Int J Clin Exp Hypn
    31:90–97, 1983
Case DB, Fogel DH, Pollack AA: Intrahypnotic and long term effects of self-hypnosis on
    blood pressure in mild hypertension. Int J Clin Exp Hypn 28:27–38, 1980
Cheek DB, LeCron LM: Clinical Hypnotherapy. New York, Grune & Stratton, 1968
Davidson GP, Farnbach RW, Richardson BA: Self-hypnosis training in anxiety reduc-
    tion. Aust Farm Physician 7:905–910, 1978
Dikel W, Olness K: Self-hypnosis, biofeedback, and voluntary peripheral temperature
    control in children. Pediatrics 66:333–340, 1980
Fromm E, Eisen M: Self-hypnosis as a therapeutic aid in the mourning process. Am J
    Clin Hypn 25:3–14, 1982
Garver RB: The eight steps in autohypnosis. Am J Clin Hypn (in press)
Geissman P: La relaxation recherches ilectroenciphalographiqes (Relaxation, EEG re-
    search). Rev. Med Psychosom 4:75–84, 1962
Horsley IA: Hypnosis and self-hypnosis in the treatment of psychogenic dysphonia: A
    case report. Am J Clin Hypn 24:227–283, 1982
Johnson LS: Self-hypnosis: Behavioral and phenomenological comparisons with het-
    erohypnosis. Int J Clin Exp Hypn 27:240–264, 1979
Kroger WS, Freed SC: Psychosomatic Gynecology. New York, Free Press, 1956
LaBaw WL: Self-hypnosis and hemophilia: The Colorado experience (1968–1980). Hemo-
    philia 2:1–2, 1980
Luthe W: Research and Theory. New York, Grune & Stratton, 1970a
Luthe W: Dynamics of Autogenic Neutralization. New York, Grune & Stratton, 1970b
Luthe W: Treatment with Autogenic Neutralization. New York, Grune & Stratton, 1973
Luthe W, Schultz JH: Autogenic Methods. New York, Grune & Stratton, 1969a
Luthe W, Schultz JF: Medical Applications. New York, Grune & Stratton, 1969b
Luthe W, Schultz JH: Applications in Psychotherapy. New York, Grune & Stratton,
    1969c
Penzer V: Spontaneous autohypnosis under duress. International Congress of the Israel

Society of Hypnosis in Psychotherapy and Psychosomatic Medicine in collaboration with European Society for Hypnosis in Psychotherapy and Psychosomatic Medicine. Haifa, Israel, 1983

Ringrose CAD: (Panelist) Self Hypnosis and behavior therapy: For separation anxiety and/or depression-in a six point program. International Congress of the Israel Society of Hypnosis in Psychotherapy and Psychosomatic Medicine in collaboration with European Society for Hypnosis in Psychotherapy and Psychosomatic Medicine. Haifa, Israel, 1983

Ruch JC: Self-hypnosis: The result of heterohypnosis or vice versa. Int J Clin Exp Hypn 23:282–304, 1975

Schneck JM: Self-hypnosis in obstetrics: Case report and comment. Br J Med Hypnot 3:53–55, 1952

Self-Hypnosis. Int J Clin Exp Hypn 29:189–323, 1981

Soskis DA: Clinical and non-clinical use of a brief-hypnosis exercise. International Congress of the Israel Society of Hypnosis in Psychotherapy and Psychosomatic Medicine in collaboration with European Society Hypnosis in Psychotherapy and Psychosomatic Medicine. Haifa, Israel, 1983

Spiegel D, Chase RA: The treatment of contractures of the hand using self-hypnosis. J Hand Surg 5:428–432, 1980

Unestahl LE: (panelist) The use of systematic self-hypnosis in a school, clinical and athletic setting. International Congress of the Israel Society of Hypnosis in Psychotherapy and Psychosomatic Medicine in collaboration with European Society for Hypnosis in Psychotherapy and Psychosomatic Medicine. Haifa, Israel, 1983

Weitzenhoffer AM: General techniques of hypnotism. New York, Grune & Stratton, 1957

Wolberg LR: Medical Hypnosis, vol 1. The Principles of Hypnotherapy. New York, Grune & Stratton, 1948

22
Forensic Hypnotherapy

In the last several decades, interest in forensic applications of hypnosis has increased dramatically (Crasilneck, 1973, 1979a, 1980b; Holden, 1980; Kluft, 1984; Mutter, 1982; Salzberg, 1977; Scott, 1977; Worthington, 1979). Hypnosis was found valuable in increasing the recall of witnesses as well as in finding unremembered or extenuating circumstances in some persons accused of or convicted of crime (Crasilneck, 1980a; Garver, 1981). As interest in the forensic uses of hypnosis spread, some law-enforcement officers were given instruction in its use, as for example, the Texas Rangers, as described in the Dallas *Morning News* (December 11, 1983). This led to a controversy in the field of hypnosis over whether persons trained only in hypnosis, without the background of professional training in psychiatry, psychology, or other clinical disciplines, should be taught hypnotic techniques to be used in forensic situations (Crasilneck, 1973).

This controversy is far from settled, but a more conservative approach (in favor of hypnosis being in the hands of trained clinicians) can be discerned since the State of New York Court of Appeals (1983) ruled (in *People* v. *Hughes*) that a witness may not testify in a criminal trial to events recalled after undergoing hypnosis. The opinion also raised the issue of hypnotically enhanced memory possibly inducing distortions in the witness' prehypnotic memory, since a person often acquires increased confidence in memories re-experienced under hypnosis (Karlin, 1983).

The acceptability of hypnosis in legal proceedings was widely reported and discussed, both before (*Newsweek*, October 1981) and after the New York decision (Orne, 1983a; Watkins, 1984).

Forensic applications of hypnosis actually have a long history, which is carefully reviewed and documented by Kroger (1977). In the latter nineteenth century, especially in France, similar issues confronted jurists and hypnotherapists (Laurence and Perry, 1983). Gravitz (1983) cites an article in the short-lived *St. Louis Magnet* in 1885 on "A Curious Case of Mesmeric Detection of Crime."

While some advocate the use of hypnosis by police officers in the investigation of crime (Reiser, 1980), the weight of professional opinion seems to be shifting toward a more conservative position (Gravitz, 1980; Orne, 1979; Spiegel, 1980; and Wagstaff, 1982). Both the Society for Clinical and Experimental Hypnosis and the International Society of Hypnosis have cautioned against the improper use of hyperamnesic material, particularly in legal controversies (Marcuse, 1983). Hooks (1982) suggests that carefully developed hypnotic recall may be useful in court. Orne (1983b) expresses concern that hypnotists who are not clinically trained may lead a witness during the interrogation and thereby contaminate the testimony.

Guidelines for the use of hypnosis in forensic situations are gradually developing, although by no means are universally accepted. Ault (1979) discusses the Federal Bureau of Investigation guidelines for the use of hypnosis. Kroger, who has done extensive work with the FBI, emphasizes the use of hypnosis to obtain investigative leads (Kroger and Douce, 1980). Warner (1979) discusses the ways hypnosis can be used in the American judicial system.

Schafer and Rubio (1978) discuss the ideal case for hypnosis in interrogation: where the victim or a witness can give additional information when in hypnotic trance, this information leading to the discovery of further evidence that can stand up in court without the need for the hypnotic interrogation to be presented on its own merit alone. Garver and Kenny (1984) in more than 100 hypnotic interviews for the FBI have developed suggested procedures for the use of hypnosis in interrogation. Their suggestions include (1) withholding the hypnotic interview until conventional methods of questioning have been completed; (2) obtaining voluntary participation in the proposed hypnotic interrogation; (3) finding an appropriate and congenial setting; (4) employing a trained professional as the hypnotherapist (a clinical psychologist or a psychiatrist with special training in hypnosis); (5) establishing that the professional has no prior detailed information about the matter under investigation; (6) videotaping and recording all hypnotic sessions; and (7) the use of proper consent forms. Hibler (1983) also offers guidelines and a sample consent form.

HYPNOSIS AND OBJECTIONABLE ACTS

A question related to hypnosis and the law is whether or not antisocial or objectionable acts can be induced by hypnosis. We have discussed this question also in the chapter on precautions in the use of hypnosis. In reviewing a legal case involving this question, Perry (1979) concluded that there were so many types of influence involved that it was not possible to logically conclude that the hypnotic influence was sufficient to cause the commission of the criminal act. Evans and Gravitz (1983) carefully review the question of coercion through hypnosis and caution moderation in taking either extreme position; hypnosis, like seduction, may influence a person, but is often used as an excuse for what could have occurred without hypnosis. It must also be remembered that there is no "Svengali-like power" wielded by the hypnotist over the hypnotic subject. Levitt et al. (1975) used an experimental design of asking hypnotized subjects to perform two objectional acts (cutting up the American flag and mutilating a Bible). One-fourth of the subjects declined to perform the acts, the authors concluding only that objectionable behavior may be used to gain some experimental information about the possibility of hypnosis being involved in dangerous, criminal, or antisocial acts.

NONADVERSARIAL USES OF HYPNOSIS

At the present time, testimony obtained under hypnosis may not be directly admissible in court. Nevertheless, there are many forensic uses of hypnosis that aid in the legal process. Hypnotic enhancement of the memory of witnesses may aid either the prosecution or the defense provided that the memories lead to the development of evidence that can be substantiated in ways other than the hypnotic recall itself. Hypnotherapy can aid the emotional trauma of rape victims (Mutter, 1983) and may help to circumvent alleged loss of memory of those who commit crime (Scott, 1978). Moss (1983) has used hypnosis to do useful psychotherapeutic work with imprisoned men convicted of serious crimes, including physical assault.

Case One

A 19-year-old man was accused of killing a teenager on a motorbike while driving his car one evening. The defense attorney referred him to Crasilneck for hypnotherapy because the accused had no recall of the alleged event, claiming to have blacked out before the impact. He had said to the police, "I have killed him," because the younger boy's body was on the top of his car, but he remembered no details of the accident. Under hypnotic regression in a somnambulistic stage of trance, he became extremely disturbed, shaking violently, screaming "I can hear him but I can't see him! I can hear him but I can't see him!" He then cried, "My God, I must have killed him!" He became so agitated that it was thought advisable to render him amnestic of that phase of his experience before continuing with the investigation. After the remark "I can hear him but I can't see him," ancillary memories were elicited before the time of the accident. The accused described the type of music playing on the car radio at the time, and named the station from which it originated, the models of the cars parked in front of certain homes on the dimly lit street, and people who were seen. Through these memories it was possible to establish that he had been driving down the darkened street in the direction of where the accident occurred.

The defendant's attorney checked all the evidence carefully, and further contacted the dead boy's parents inquiring about the condition of the motor bike. The parents recalled that the headlight on the motorbike had been broken the night before the accident and was not functioning the night their son was killed, thereby establishing the full meaning of the defendant's statement: "I can hear him but I can't see him".

This amazing piece of evidence established that the light on the dead boy's motorbike was out before the accident, so that the defendant had apparently heard but not seen his approach in the dark. Not only did this aid in resolution of the legal situation, but it more importantly emotionally absolved the accused young man from a sense of guilty frustration at not knowing in what manner he had been involved in the accident.

Case Two

Dora was a 45-year-old woman accused of shooting her husband to death 1 year previously when they were both in a drunken argument (Crasilneck,1979b, 1980a). In hypnotic regression, she entered a deep trance and suddenly exhibited severe emotional abreactions. She showed fear, anxiety, remorse, guilt, and ambivalence, all in great degree. As she hypnotically recalled the events immediately before the shooting, she remembered that her husband had beaten her and was choking her. As she recalled the choking, her voice became suddenly hoarse and saliva drooled from the corner of her mouth. Then the lawyer recalled that when he had first seen her soon after the shooting, she had been inexplicably hoarse, apparently (in retrospect) a result of the choking and red markings were visible on her throat. At another point she repeated feeling nauseated, just as she had on the drunken night of the shooting, and expressed the desire to vomit (which she did on that fateful night). Time distortion moved the time to when her nausea had passed. She remembered that he had threatened her with a gun, and she pleaded with him to put the gun down and "behave." She told him she would take the gun away from him if he did not "put it down," and when he refused to do so, she "wrestled" with him in order to get the gun. She had the gun for a moment, and in his anger he grabbed the barrel of the gun and jerked it towards him, which accidently brought her finger sharply on the trigger—and the gun fired.

A videotape of the entire interview and of her strong emotional reaction during this interrogation under hypnosis has been shown for teaching purposes to a number of groups of medical students who seem to empathatically experience the true nature of her emotional abreaction. The defense attorney persuaded the district attorney to allow the judge (but not the jury) to view the video recording of her hypnoanalytic session. Moved by her apparent sincerity in the description of the events, the judge imposed a suspended 1-year sentence. Without the information of the hypnotic regression, a much more severe sentence would have been likely. This case had first been reported by Crasilneck (1979b) and discussed by Mutter (1979).

Case Three

A man was accused of accidentally killing two young girls on bicycles while he was driving while intoxicated. It was alleged that he had driven from the scene without attempting to offer aid or go for help, a hit-and-run driver. His defense attorney called Crasilneck to use hypnosis in order to develop, if possible, further evidence to aid his client. Under hypnosis, the man admitted his drinking and drunken state, remembered hitting the children accidently, but recalled a new piece of information—that he had tried to enlist the help of several bystanders at the scene of the accident. Perhaps, because of his drunken state, the by-standers had not offered to help him. He recalled then driving to his sister's house to ask her to phone for help for the children. With this added information, the witnesses were re-questioned and admitted that he had asked them to call for aid for the victims before he had driven away. Although he still was prosecuted, this additional evidence of his intent to help considerably diminished the resulting sentence he had to serve.

In all three of these cases, the severe emotional abreaction under hypnosis had to be handled in a psychotherapeutic manner and that is, in our opinion, beyond the capability of persons untrained in psychotherapeutic techniques in addition to being skilled in hypnosis. Therefore, our own position is that such forensic uses of hypnosis, preferably, should be done by trained clinicians who are able to be cognizant of the patient's welfare, as well as elicit information under hypnosis.

REFERENCES

Ault RL Jr: FBI guidelines for the use of hypnosis. Int J Clin Exp Hypn 27:449–451, 1979
Crasilneck HB: The use of forensic hypnotherapy in the practice of law. National College of Criminal Defense Lawyers and Public Defenders. Houston, Texas, 1973
Crasilneck HB: (Panelist) Applications of forensic hypnosis. Univ of Tex Dept of Psychol Austin, Texas, 1979a
Crasilneck HB: The case of Dora. 8th International Congress on Hypnosis and Psychosomatic Medicine in collaboration with 9th Annual Congress of the Australian Society for Clinical and Experimental Hypnosis, Melbourne, Australia, 1979b
Crasilneck HB: The case of Dora. Am J Clin Hypn 23:94–97, 1980a
Crasilneck HB: (Panelist) Psychogenic amnesia and forensic hypnotherapy. East Tex State Univ Commerce, Texas, 1980b
Evans B, Gravitz MA: Is coercion in hypnosis really a myth? A new consideration of an old concern. American Society for Clinical Hypnosis Annual Meeting, Dallas, Texas, 1983
Garver RB: Forensic hypnosis. Paper presented at Nat Coll of Distr Attys at Univ of Houston, 1981
Garver RB, Kenney JW: The collection and preparation of hypnotically enhanced testimony. Am J Clin Hypn 1984 (in press)
Gravitz MA: Forensic uses of hypnosis: Discussion. Am J Clin Hypn 23:103–111, 1980
Gravitz MA: An early case of investigative hypnosis: A brief communication. Int J Clin Exp Hypn 31:224–226, 1983
Hibler NS: Investigative aspects of forensic hypnosis, in Wester WC, Smith AH (eds): Clinical Hypnosis: A Multidisciplinary Approach. Philadelphia, J.B. Lippincott Co., 1983, pp 525–557
Holden C: Forensic use of hypnosis on the increase. Science 208:1443–1444, 1980
Hooks AM: Hypnotically aided testimony: The abandonment of Frye. Rev Litigation 2:231–254, 1982
Karlin RA: Forensic hypnosis—two case reports: A brief communication. Int J Clin Exp Hypn 31:227–234, 1983
Kluft RP: Presentation at Society for Clinical and Experimental Hypnosis, 36th Annual Meeting, San Antonio, TX 1984
Kroger WS: Hypnosis in criminology, in Kroger WS: Clinical and Experimental Hypnosis (ed 2). Philadelphia, J.B. Lippincott Co., 1977, p 434
Kroger WS, Douce R: Forensic use of hypnosis. Am J Clin Hypn 23:86–93, 1980

Laurence JR, Perry C: Forensic hypnosis in the late nineteenth century. Int J Clin Exp Hypn 31:266–283, 1983

Levitt EE, Aronoff G, Duane C, Toner M, Overley M, Parrish MJ: Testing the coercive power of hypnosis: Committing objectionable acts. Int J Clin Exp Hypn 23:59–67, 1975

Marcuse FL: The role of hypnotic hypermnesia in forensic psychology. International Congress of the Israel Society of Hypnosis in Psychotherapy and Psychosomatic Medicine in collaboration with European Society for Clinical Hypnosis in Psychotherapy and Psychosomatic Medicine. Haifa, Israel, 1983

Moss CS: (Panelist) Forensic: the use of hypnosis with imprisoned individuals. International Congress of the Israel Society of Hypnosis in Psychotherapy and Psychosomatic Medicine in collaboration with European Society for Clinical Hypnosis in Psychotherapy and Psychosomatic Medicine, Haifa, Israel, 1983.

Mutter CB: Critique of videotape presentation on forensic hypnotic regression by Crasilneck: The case of Dora. Am J Clin Hypn 23:99–101, 1979

Mutter CB: Forensic hypnosis and admissibility. American Society of Clinical Hypnosis, Denver, Colorado, 1982

Mutter CB: Rape: The offender and the victim. American Journal of Clinical Hypnosis 1983 (in press)

Orne MT: The use and misuse of hypnosis in court. Int J Clin Exp Hypn 27:311–341, 1979

Orne MT: Hypnosis "useful in medicine, dangerous in court". US News and World Report, December 12, 1983a, 86–87

Orne MT: Forensic hypnosis, in Wester WC, Smith AH (eds): Clinical Hypnosis: A Multidisciplinary Approach. Philadelphia, J.B. Lippincott Co., 1983b, pp 497–525

People v Hughes: Opinion. State of NY Court of Appeals 232:1–26, 1983

Perry C: Hypnotic coercion and compliance to it: A review of evidence presented in a legal case. Int J Clin Exp Hypn 27:187–218, 1979

Rangers approach to hypnosis. Dallas Morning News, December 11, 1983

Reiser M, Nielson J: Investigative hypnosis: A developing specialty. Am J Clin 23:45–47, 1980

Salzberg HC: The hypnotic interview in crime detection. Am J Clin Hypn 19:225–258, 1977

Schafer GW, Rubio R: Hypnosis to aid the recall of witnesses. Int J Clin Exp Hypn 26:81–91, 1978

Scott EM: Hypnosis in the courtroom. Am J Clin Hypn 19:163–165, 1977

Scott EM: Hypnosis with an alleged blackout. Am J Clin Hypn 20:209–212, 1978

Spiegel H: Hypnosis and evidence: Help or hindrance? Ann NY Acad Sci 347:73–85, 1980

The trials of hypnosis. Newsweek, October 17, 1981, p 96

Wagstaff GF: Hypnosis and witness recall: Discussion paper. J Roy Soc Med 75:793–798, 1982

Warner KE: The use of hypnosis in the defense of criminal cases. Int J Clin Exp Hypn 27:417–436, 1979

Watkins J: The Bianchi (L.A. Hillside Strangler) case: sociopath or multiple personality? Int J Clin Exp Hypnosis, 32(2):67–101, 1984

Worthington TS: The use in court of hypnotically enhanced testimony. Int J Clin Exp Hypn 27:402–416, 1979

23

The Use of Hypnosis
in the Hospital

Hypnotherapy may offer many benefits to selected hospitalized patients. These various indications will be reviewed here although many of these topics are discussed in greater detail elsewhere in this volume.

The rigid notions of the mind–body duality developed in the last century have persisted surprisingly far into this century. However, even those disorders with an apparently purely physiological etiology are accompanied by psychological impact in every instance. Hypnosis may help in understanding the meaning of this impact and in easing the patient's adjustment to it. Poor adjustment may otherwise result in noncompliance or other behavior exacerbating the disease process.

The current extensive use of double-blind trials is tacit recognition of the remarkable power of the health care professional in influencing the course of disease by suggestion of nonverbal behavior. It may well be that over the millenia the convictions and reassurancies of the doctor were unwittingly suggesting the subsequent recovery, at times even in spite of possible adverse effects of the treatment. The doctor may be a powerful force suggesting recovery and diminishing suffering. It may be time for health care professionals to recognize their potential for suggesting good or ill (as in the operation room) and use this power more carefully. Although the physician is likely to underestimate the importance of the patient's freedom from excessive pain and anxiety, the patient never will. In addition, the use of self-hypnosis for relief of symptoms may give the patient a feeling of mastery in an otherwise extremely dependent hospital milieu.

Hypnosis may prove of benefit in the management of a wide range of general hospital ward problems. Anorexia, insomnia, pruritis, anxiety, hiccoughs, urinary retention, diarrhea, coughing or lack of it, constipation, and acute or chronic pain may all respond in instances where chemotherapy has proven ineffective or contraindicated. Selected symptoms may be alleviated or substituted when appropriate. Crucial points of history such as details of the onset of disease or prior therapy may be elicited when not otherwise obtainable. Insight may be gained into the dynamics of the hostile, uncooperative, or noncompliant patient and the therapeutic alliance restored. The terminal cancer patient may particularly benefit from the hypnotic control of pain and anxiety without the obtunding effect of drugs.

The remarkable technological advances in medicine in the last 2 decades have been accompanied by the extensive proliferation of procedures that are tedious or painful or both. Furthermore, these procedures must often be repeated. Hypnosis, which can offer patients relief from anxiety, pain, and tedium (through amnesia), is employed surprisingly seldom in these settings. The benefits to the physician of a cooperative, conscious, pain-free patient as well as a smoother, more drug-free postoperative course seem evident. Endoscopy, biopsy, radiologic procedures (especially catheterization), hemodialysis, deep pelvic examination and procedures, cardiac catheterization, burn dressing changes, and painful invasive procedures would seem to offer ample opportunities for hypnosis to lessen suffering. The patient requiring surgery or invasive procedures may benefit from prehospitalization hypnotic suggestions for the cessation of smoking, control of obesity, or alleviation of anxiety, or for training in preparation for hypnoanesthesia if it is to be used.

In psychosomatic disorders, psychologic factors may be important in the etiology or exacerbation of disease. The psychosomatic disorders have been set apart from others on the basis of three lines of evidence: (1) a large set of observations, which have revealed that the malfunctioning organ is susceptible to change in function by influence mediated via the autonomic nervous system; (2) the discovery in the biographies of some patients of an inordinately high incidence of resentment, hostility, and suppressed emotionality; and (3) a demonstrable relationship between onset and successive exacerbation of disease and the presence of disturbing and frustrating incidents in the patient's life (Petersdorf and Randolf, 1983).

The disorders listed below are believed to benefit from alleviation of their psychologic component and may be helped by hypnotherapy:

1. *Cardiovascular*: hypertension, angina pectoris, myocardial infarction, congestive heart failure, and arrhythmias, particularly paroxysmal auricular tachycardia and extrasystoles (Wain, Amen, and Oetgen, 1983).
2. *Pulmonary*: asthma, hyperventilation.
3. *Gastrointestinal*: peptic ulcer disease and ulcerative colitis; dumping syndrome.
4. *Hematologic*: rheumatoid arthritis, Raynaud's disease.
5. *Endocrine/metabolic*: diabetes, obesity, hyperthyroidism.
6. *Neuropsychiatric*: migraine or tension headaches, conversion reactions.
7. *Dermatologic*: atopic dermatitis, neurodermatitis, verruca vulgaris (warts).
8. *Obstetric*: vaginal or cesarian deliveries and episiotomy.

In the past 25 years, hypnosis has become more and more a part of the armamentarium of the physicians, dentists, and clinical psychologists in general hospitals. Traditionally, consultation usually came from the department of psychiatry when aid was needed by other divisions. This is no longer the case. With the teaching of hypnosis to medical students at the undergraduate level and resident training in various specialties, it is no longer uncommon to see individuals within their own fields using hypnosis as a part of the total treatment program.

It is virtually impossible to conceive of a specialty in which hypnosis is now not used as a part of treatment, ranging from anesthesiology to allergies, obstetrics, psychiatry, internal medicine, surgery, oncology, oral surgery, orthopedic surgery, neurosurgery, and emergency medicine. Patients are normally seen by their physician with routine physical and psychological examinations done before the use of hypnotherapy. At one time the attitude was quite common that when everything else had been tried hypnosis might be used as a last resort. This is no longer the case. If, for example, the patient enters the emergency room and has functional amnesia, hypnosis may be the method of choice. Hypnosis is frequently the method of choice in problems involving hyperemesis gravidarum, acute and chronic pain problems, and in assisting in diagnostic problems that pose unanswered questions. Quite recently we were asked to see a young man who was unable to walk following a minor car accident. After being admitted to the hospital via the emergency room, and following several days of testing in an attempt to understand his rather bizarre problem, we were asked to see him with the idea of using hypnosis. After establishing rapport, he was hypnotized and given the suggestion that he could move off the bed while holding the therapist's hand and that he could stand and walk. After he walked, it was obvious to the physicians present that the diagnosis was conversion reaction. The patient was requested to return to his bed, resume a supine position, and to freely associate to his problem. Shortly thereafter he abreacted his severe hostility towards his family, stating that he greatly resented having to support them. As a part of the dialogue during the abreaction he said "they are just going to have to learn to stand on their own two feet. I can't do it for them any longer." Following this information he was referred to the department of psychiatry for their further evaluation and treatment.

We have been asked to see patients with massive obesity using hypnosis to help reduce weight and to help in the reduction of weight-related problems such as back pain and hypertension. We have been asked to see individuals with severe pulmonary obstructive disease, obstetrical and gynecological problems, and complicated orthopedic problems as well as problems routinely seen in psychiatry. Hypnoanalytic methods are used with virtually all such patients before, during, and after surgery.

Perhaps one of the greatest values of hypnosis in the hospital situation is that the students may learn from observing their senior physicians and psychologists using this modality with patients. This is especially true in pain clinics and other types of clinical situations. It is not only that they are observing symptom reduction or alteration but they are gaining insight into the many ramifications involved in both physical and psychological aspects of disease.

CONSULTATION-LIAISON

Increasingly, hypnotherapy consultation is available in the departments of psychiatry and psychology in major teaching centers (Parrish, 1975). In many instances, instruction in hypnotherapy techniques is part of specialty training (Haberman, 1984), not only in psychiatry and psychology but in pediatrics and child psychology (Gardner, 1976; Olness, 1977), anesthesiology (Fredericks, 1978, 1980), family practice training (Alon, 1983; Phelps, 1982; Phillips, 1980), dentistry, (Dubin, 1983), and other professions and subspecialities (Pulver and Pulver, 1975; Safer, 1976; Slavick, 1982).

It is no longer uncommon to observe that hypnosis is being presented as the subject matter of grand rounds. Audiovisual tapes describing hypnotic techniques are part of the training of the resident staff in learning treatment methods of hypnotherapy. Lectures and didactic training are coordinated with audiovisual tapes. Psychologists' attitude toward hypnosis are favorable, according to a survey by Kraft and Rodolfa (1982). Hypnosis is growing as a part of available training in schools of psychology (Rodolfa et al., 1983) and is becoming more formalized, and research in hypnosis is growing.

Crasilneck (1984, in press) has reviewed the utilization of hypnotherapy on medical wards in a general hospital, including hypnosis as an aid in differential diagnosis, in alleviating pain, in habit patterns such as smoking (a most important aspect of treating emphysema), and in the various clinical problems associated with psychiatric problems.

When hypnotic skills are not in the usual clinical armamentarium of the individual practitioner, they are often available through liaison services with psychiatry or psychology (Wain, 1979). The frequent availability of introductory courses in hypnosis for professionals increasingly makes learning of hypnosis possible throughout the country, particularly in workshops sponsored by the American Society of Clinical Hypnosis and by regional component groups of the Society for Clinical and Experimental Hypnosis.

As the public becomes more aware of the potential benefits of hypnotherapy, practitioners of various specialities will respond, we believe, with an increasingly available and skilled knowledge of the principles and applications of hypnotherapy. In a random sample of 10 percent of the total patient population of a large medical center (McIntosh and Hawney, 1983), 80 percent had previously heard of the use of hypnosis, more than 36 percent indicated a willingness to accept hypnotherapy if recommended by their doctor, and only 5.5 percent indicated that they would refuse treatment by hypnosis if it was recommended. However, 41 percent were unaware of any medical indications for hypnosis.

SUMMARY

Suggestion has always been an important element of the doctor–patient relationship, but only recently has this been so clearly recognized and begun to be consciously utilized in hypnotherapy. A remarkable range of common ward complaints will respond to traditional or self hypnosis. It is especially of benefit in alleviating anxiety and pain or when the usual chemotherapy is ineffective or contraindicated.

Hypnosis presents excellent opportunities for control of the anxiety, pain, and tedium of procedures but is probably underutilized in the hospital setting. By contrast, use of hypnotherapy to assist in the treatment of disorders with a significant psychological component is well known. The list of such disorders may be expected to expand, and with increasing recognition of the importance of psychologic factors in physiologic disease, the usefulness of hypnosis to the hospitalized patient can only grow.

Perhaps the greatest advantage of utilizing hypnosis in the hospital setting is that it can be used with a variety of patients who have diseases with organic and functional etiologies, and also with cases ranging from the normal uncomplicated delivery to attending those dying patients who choose this method as an aid in approaching the terminal stages of life.

REFERENCES

Alon N: Hypnosis in family therapy. Int Cong Israel Soc Hypn in Psychoth and Psychosom Med in collabor with Eur Soc Clin Hypn in Psychoth and Psychosom Med Haifa, Israel, 1983

Crasilneck HB: Hypnosis on the medical ward, in Weiner FM, Guggenheim FG (eds): A Manual of Psychiatric Consultation and Emergency Care. (in press) 1984

Dubin LL: Personal communications, 1983

Fredericks LE: Teaching of hypnosis in the overall approach to the surgical patient. Am J Clin Hypn 20:175–183, 1978

Fredericks LE: The value of teaching hypnosis in the practice of anesthesiology. Int J Clin Exp Hypn 28:6–15, 1980

Gardner GG: Attitudes of child health professionals towards hypnosis: Implications for training. Int J Clin Exp Hypn 24:63–73, 1976

Haberman MA: Training in hypnosis. A Symposium. San Francisco, 1984

Kraft WA, Rodolfa ER: The use of hypnosis among psychologists. Am J Clin Hypn 24:249–257, 1982

McIntosh IB, Hawney M: Patient attitude to hypnotherapy in a general medical practice: A brief communication. Int J Clin Exp Hypn 31:219–223, 1983

Olness, K: In-service hypnosis education in a children's hospital. Am J Clin Hypn 20:80–83, 1977

Parrish MJ: Predoctoral training in clinical hypnosis: A national survey of availability and educator attitudes in schools of medicine, dentistry, and graduate clinical psychology. Int J Clin Exp Hypn 23:249–265, 1975

Petersdorf RG, Randolf T, (eds): Harrison's Principles of Internal Medicine 10th edition. New York, McGraw-Hill, 1983, p 66

Phelps LA: An analysis of hypnotic training and potential teachers of hypnosis in family practice residency programs. American Society for Clinical Hypnosis Annual Meeting, Denver, 1982

Phillips HR: Personal communication, 1980

Pulver SE, Pulver MP: Hypnosis in medical and dental practice: A survey. Int J Clin Exp Hypn 23:28–47, 1975

Rodolfa ER, Kraft EA, Reilly RR, Blackmore S: The status of research and training in hypnosis in APA accredited clinical/counseling psychology internship sites: a national survey. Int J Clin Exp Hypn 31:284–292, 1983

Safer BA: The role of hypnosis in today's medicine. Ohio State Med J 72:587, 1976

Slavick FH: The use of hypnosis with patients undergoing dialysis treatment. Personal communication, 1982

Wain HG: Hypnosis on a consultation-liaison service. Psychosomatics 20:678–698, 1979

Wain HG, Amen DG, Oetgen WJ: Cardia arrhythmias and hypnotic intervention: Advantages, disadvantages, precautions, and theoretical considerations. Am J Clin Hypn 1983 (in press)

Summary and Conclusions

This book was written to give practical, instructive answers to the questions most often asked about the usefulness of hypnosis in medicine, clinical psychology, and dentistry. It can serve both as text for the study of hypnotherapy in professional training and as a reference source for the clinical applications of hypnosis. We have touched upon technical and theoretical aspects but have maintained the central focus clearly on practical applications, as in our review of the field published in 1978 (Hall and Crasilneck, 1978).

What is hypnosis? Hypnosis is an altered state of consciousness, usually induced through a structured interpersonal situation, in which the therapist works primarily with the patient's unconscious processes in an attempt to evoke a healthy psychological state and a decrease in symptoms.

What conditions can be treated with hypnotherapy? When applied with care by adequately trained personnel, hypnotherapy can be effective in the treatment of a wide range of psychological and physical disorders. In purely psychological disorders hypnosis can be a powerful tool for exploration of causes, modification of attitudes, and dimunition of symptoms. In physical problems, hypnotherapy can aid greatly in the psychological management of pain and other symptoms. In the broad field of psychosomatic disorders hypnotherapy can at times be beneficial when more orthodox therapies have reached an impasse. In some psychophysiological disorders it may be the treatment of choice.

Where does one refer patients for acceptable hypnotherapy? There is no accepted professional group of hypnotherapists as such, just as there are no surgeons who are not physicians. Hypnosis is a tool that should be used within a more comprehensive professional framework of medicine, psychology, dentistry, and perhaps in some other accepted professional fields when their training standards become sufficiently similar to the more traditional specialties.

One of the most reliable ways to find a reputable hypnotherapist is through consultation with one's family physician, the local county medical, psychological, or dental society or through state or national organizations of physicians, psychologists, or dentists. Two of the most respected societies of professionals using hypnosis—the Society for Clinical and Experimental Hypnosis and the American Society of Clinical Hypnosis—do not condone advertising by their members.

What are the dangers of hypnosis? When used by professionals with adequate screening and safeguards, hypnotherapy is remarkably free of serious side effects. Like any powerful treatment tool, however, it can be harmful if misused. Many widespread fears of hypnosis—such as "not waking up"—are unfounded. One does not "lose" control to the therapist; rather one cooperates with him or her in the treatment goals. In our experience the occurrence of substitute symptoms is rare. Unnecessarily authoritarian and coercive suggestions, though, may precipitate psychological defense mechanisms that can usually be avoided by a more permissive and psychodynamic approach.

What is the future of hypnotherapy? We feel that there is a widening awareness and application of hypnotherapy to a complex range of problems. Increasing interest in biofeedback, in altered states of consciousness, and in innovative psychological treatment techniques will make a knowledge of the phenomena and methods of hypnotherapy more important for understanding the true range and ability of the patient's participation in his own treatment.

We hope that the professionals who read this book will have been helped to take a judicious approach to hypnotherapy and will experience the same satisfaction that we have found in extending this important technique to aid a wide range of human suffering.

The future of hypnotherapy depends upon its becoming increasingly incorporated into the basic clinical training of medicine, psychiatry, psychology, dentistry, and related fields. Supervision of clinical hypnotherapy during the years of professional formation will integrate the principles of hypnotherapy into the full range of clinical skills.

Together with enhanced clinical training, it is vital that careful research on the phenomena of hypnosis continue, particularly in greater understanding of the neurophysiology underlying the hypnotic state. Research is on-going at several major medical centers in the United States; such research centers should be supported and expanded.

The role of the professional societies devoted to hypnosis will continue as a major force in the field. Their influence hopefully will not be diluted by the training of persons lacking the requisite clinical training, background, and supervision; hypnosis must remain a tool of application rather than a free-standing field. Factionalism and fads will always occur, of course, but should not be allowed to disrupt the steady, on-going movement of scientific investigation and clinical application.

REFERENCES

Hall JA, Crasilneck HB: Hypnosis. JAMA 239:760–761, 1978

Index